THE BIRDS OF *Illinois*

H. David Bohlen

THE BIRDS OF *Illinois*

ORIGINAL PAINTINGS BY

William Zimmerman

INDIANA UNIVERSITY PRESS • *Bloomington and Indianapolis*

MANUFACTURED IN JAPAN

Library of Congress Cataloging-in-Publication Data

Bohlen, H. David.
    The birds of Illinois/by H. David Bohlen; original paintings by William Zimmerman.
       p.   cm.
    Bibliography: p.
    Includes index.
    ISBN 0-253-31560-3
    1. Zimmerman, William—Criticism and interpretation.
2. Birds—Illinois.   I. Zimmerman, William.   II. Title.
QL684.I3B64 1989
598.29773—dc20   89-45203
                                                              CIP

    1 2 3 4 5 93 92 91 90 89

*This book is dedicated to Illinois birders
who search for remnants of natural beauty
in a fragmented and impoverished landscape.*

CONTENTS

*Birds are listed in taxonomic order
according to the 1983 American
Ornithologists' Union Check-list. In the
Index they are listed alphabetically by
common name.*

Illustrations

Original Paintings by William Zimmerman

Common Loon; Pied-billed Grebe; Double-crested Cormorant; American Bittern; Little Blue Heron; Green-backed Heron and Black-crowned Night-Heron; Tundra Swan; Canada Goose; Wood Duck

Common Goldeneye; Red-breasted Merganser; Ruddy Duck; Turkey Vulture; Osprey; Northern Harrier; Rough-legged Hawk; American Kestrel; Ruffed Grouse

Wild Turkey; Northern Bobwhite; Black Rail and Virginia Rail; Sandhill Crane; Lesser Golden-Plover, Killdeer, Ruddy Turnstone, and Dunlin; Bonaparte's Gull and Forster's Tern; Mourning Dove; Black-billed Cuckoo and Yellow-billed Cuckoo; Common Barn-Owl

Great Horned Owl; Whip-poor-will; Chimney Swift; Ruby-throated Hummingbird; Belted Kingfisher; Downy Woodpecker and Pileated Woodpecker; Acadian Flycatcher and Great Crested Flycatcher; Horned Lark and Water Pipit; Cliff Swallow and Barn Swallow

Blue Jay; Eastern Screech-Owl, Carolina Chickadee, Tufted Titmouse, Red-breasted Nuthatch, and White-breasted Nuthatch; Brown Creeper and Carolina Wren; Golden-crowned Kinglet, Ruby-crowned Kinglet, and Blue-gray Gnatcatcher; Eastern Bluebird and Hermit Thrush

Brown Thrasher; Bohemian Waxwing and Cedar Waxwing; Loggerhead Shrike; Solitary Vireo and Yellow-throated Vireo; Magnolia Warbler, Black-throated Green Warbler, Blackburnian Warbler, Yellow-throated Warbler, Bay-breasted Warbler, and Blackpoll Warbler; Summer Tanager, Scarlet Tanager, and Northern Oriole; Northern Cardinal, Rufous-sided Towhee, American Tree Sparrow, Fox Sparrow, Song Sparrow, Swamp Sparrow, White-throated Sparrow, Dark-eyed Junco, and Evening Grosbeak; Red-winged Blackbird, Rusty Blackbird, and Common Grackle

Acknowledgments

This book could not have been accomplished without the expert help of two volunteers who gave many needed suggestions of both content and grammar. Ron Goetz and Ida Domazlicky accepted this work while they had many other professional and personal commitments, and I thank them sincerely for the time they gave to this volume. Others who helped with records, sharing their notes and photographs for documentation, are Jim Landing, Vernon Kleen, and Dennis Oehmke. Members of the Illinois Ornithological Records Committee also gave advice on records: Joe Milosevich, Richard Palmer, Leroy Harrison, Denny Jones, Richard Biss, John Robinson, Sue Stroyls, Joel Greenberg, and Dave Johnson. For obtaining library materials I would like to thank Orvetta Robinson and Ronald Sauberli at the Illinois State Museum. Typing the manuscript from my hieroglyphics has been no easy task; Lisa Bilello started the work and it was admirably carried on and finished very meticulously by Jo Ann Morris. Many others at the Illinois State Museum gave their support to this project: Director Bruce McMillan, Assistant Director Ed Munyer, and fellow zoologists Tim Cashatt and Rick Purdue. For proposing the project and seeing it through some tough spots, the Director of Indiana University Press, John Gallman, receives my sincere thanks. I also thank editors Kenneth Goodall and Roberta L. Diehl of the Press for their understanding and professionalism. William Zimmerman's plates add greatly to this book; I only wish that all 439 Illinois species could have been rendered in his splendid style. To all Illinois birders and ornithologists who contributed records, thank you (see the list of observers following the Literature Cited section). I also thank personnel of City, Water, Light and Power of Springfield for allowing me onto certain properties so that I could carry on my studies of the birds of Sangamon County.

On a personal note, much has happened since I started writing this book, but through all the turmoil several friends never let me down, including David Hood, Randy Brest, Dennis Oehmke, Ned Riseman, and Patrick Ward. I would like to thank Jacqueline for her sincerity and Laura for her friendship during this time. Continued support of my work by my two daughters, Nicole and Shannon, is appreciated, and I hope they continue to be as individualistic as they have been so far. To Judy I can only say thank you for all you have done for me, which is considerable. For indulging my obsession with birds, thanks go to my mother and father, who always encouraged me, and to my brothers and sisters, who continue to show interest in this book.

Any errors in the text of either omission or commission belong to the author.

H. David Bohlen
Zoologist, Illinois State Museum
January 2, 1989

It would be impossible to list everyone who has assisted in the preparation of this book. I am particularly grateful, however, to the following individuals and companies who have purchased many of the paintings and without whom my part of this publication would have been impossible to complete: Mr. and Mrs. Jeffery Auer, Borden Incorporated, Mr. and Mrs. George Byers, Jr., Mr. and Mrs. Donald H. Clark, Mr. and Mrs. Steven L. Clark, Mr. and Mrs. Ralph Cobey, Mr. and Mrs. Thomas E. Donnelley II, Mrs. Elaine Ewing Fess, Dr. Stephen W. Fess, David and Libby Frey, Mr. Lawrence W. Friel, Jr., Mr. Daniel M. Galbreath, and Dr. and Mrs. G. E. Gustafson. Thanks also to Jay Shuler, for his constant support and advice; DeVere Burt, Director, and Robert S. Kennedy, Deputy Director, Collection and Research Division, for allowing me unlimited access to the bird collection at the Cincinnati Museum of Natural History; Jenny and Art Wiseman, for their assistance in selecting bird skins used; Willard L. Boyd, President, Scott M. Lanyon, Division Head and Assistant Curator of Birds, and David E. Willard, Collection Manager, for their ongoing willingness to loan me specimens from Chicago's Field Museum of Natural History; and the employees of Indiana University Press for their assistance while this work was in progress and especially John Gallman, Director of the Press, for his untiring support and dedication from the project's conception. To my wife, Judy, and children, Martha and Matthew, for their sacrifices and assistance in the many tasks involved in the completion of this book, I dedicate the paintings.

William Zimmerman

Introduction

The purpose of this volume is to make the reader aware, through both prose and art, of the birds of Illinois. It is essentially a plea for the survival of these beautiful forms of life. This is what Illinois once had, the book is saying, and this is what we have now; let us do whatever needs to be done to ensure this diversity of birdlife for the future. I am aware, of course, that all people are not equally interested in birds; nor is everyone interested in the same facets of birdlife. This book was written primarily for birders wishing to know the past and present status of birds in Illinois and to provide them with a quick reference to other aspects of Illinois birds. I hope that others interested in nature will also find answers to their questions about birds in these pages.

A hundred years ago, in 1889, Robert Ridgway completed the first volume of his *Ornithology of Illinois*. The present book is an updated version of that work, but including colored plates. It also supersedes my previous work, *An Annotated Check-list of the Birds of Illinois* (1978); but this book is an expanded version, written for a wider audience. The main emphasis of the data is from 1978 to 1987, although when possible a historical perspective is given. Records and quotations are used from many earlier ornithologists and observers, including Ridgway, Nelson, Eifrig, Coale, Gault, Kennicott, Widmann, Hess, and Musselman. Most of the text is based on sight records, written anecdotally. Any work of this type is merely a recapitulation of past observations contributed by a handful of dedicated people ranging over a relatively large area. Although the Illinois habitat has been ravaged, enough remains that the few active observers can obtain only small views of the total picture of birdlife in the state. As one tries to go back in time through the literature and specimens, there are usually fewer and fewer data until the status of birds in early Illinois is difficult to determine. Old records and specimens become extremely valuable to the researcher trying to reconstruct species population fluctuations. The whereabouts of past data and specimens should be made known so that they can be integrated into the total picture. Thus, the better records we leave today, the better will future workers be able to understand the avifauna of Illinois.

Incomplete though the record is, there is still a plethora of material written about the birds of Illinois, and I have three suggestions concerning any future updating of this work. First, computerize the spring and Christmas bird counts and other records so that they may be retrieved by species and need not be pulled out laboriously by hand. Second, make a complete examination and listing of the available specimens from Illinois for specific and subspecific verification. And finally, allow at least five years—better yet, ten—to do a thorough job.

DESCRIPTION OF THE STATE

It is odd to think of the piece of real estate that is now the state of Illinois as part of one big supercontinent called Pangaea, formed when two land masses, Laurasia and Gondwana, collided. Pangaea then slowly broke up into the continents we know today. When the Laurasia mass was forced apart and the Atlantic Ocean began to form, Illinois, as part of North America, drifted westward. Even before the breakup of Pangaea, volcanic action (a billion years ago), inundation by tropical seas (600 million years ago), and the forests of the coal age (300 million years ago) helped form the underlying layers of Illinois. More recently (500,000 to 10,000 years ago) two glacial ages formed much of the geomorphology that makes Illinois look the way it does today. Schuberth (1986) gives detailed information on the geology of Illinois.

Bounded on the west by the Mississippi River system, on the east by Lake Michigan and the Wabash River, and on the south by the Ohio River, Illinois has numerous avenues of approach and departure for migrating birds. The state is fairly easily divided into three zones (north, central, and south), each with its characteristic birdlife. For simplicity's sake I deemphasize these zones somewhat in describing the status of each species, but they are real phenomena and can be envisioned as one reads the Species Accounts. Illinois is 378 miles long, with extremes of latitude from 36 degrees 59 minutes to 42 degrees 30 minutes. The topography of Illinois is simple, with a total relief of only 967 feet. The highest point (1235 feet) is Charles Mound in Jo Daviess County near the Wisconsin border and the lowest (268 feet) is the junction of the Ohio and Mississippi Rivers at the southern tip of the state. The surface area of Illinois is 56,345 square miles.

Although much of the land is given up to agriculture and urban areas today, Illinois was a mosaic of woodland and prairie before the arrival of the Europeans. Most of the prairie, over 90 percent of the original woodland, and 95 percent of the natural wetlands are gone. But some unique areas remain. Lake Michigan, with almost oceanic qualities, is probably the most dramatic, although it too has been degraded and some of its nesting species, such as the Piping Plover, have been extirpated. Illinois Beach State Park is the only relatively intact portion of the lake shore. During migration the Harlequin Duck, the Purple Sandpiper, the

Whimbrel, and many other species move along the lake but are found very rarely in the remainder of the state, if at all. Lake Michigan parks attract hordes of migrants, for the lake acts as a barrier which many species will not fly over. Many rare western birds occur there, stopped at the edge of the lake as they move east. Nearby, Lake Calumet was a wonderful area for birds before it was swallowed up by Chicago. Its remnants still produce a remarkable variety of birds; it is unfortunate that the remnants cannot be preserved. Farther west in northern Illinois the birdlife is more like that in the rest of the state, but a few summer residents of more northerly distribution are found, including the Least Flycatcher, the Chestnut-sided Warbler, and the Veery. The driftless area in the northwestern corner of the state has white birch thickets and a sharper topography because it escaped glaciation. Winters are harsher in northern Illinois and there are more possibilities of encountering winter finches, Bohemian Waxwings, and Northern Shrikes. Central Illinois was once known for its prairie marshes, but they have been drained. Only Goose Lake Prairie in northern Illinois remains to show how these areas must have looked. Most of the central section, with its rich soil, is now farming country, especially the prairie peninsula. The original prairie is mostly a memory, and the little that remains along railroad rights-of-way supports few birds. Some forest can still be found in the Illinois and Mississippi River valleys. Several large shallow lakes along the Illinois River provide excellent habitat for waterfowl and shorebirds: Rice Lake, Chautauqua Lake, Quiver Lake, Big Lake, and others. Isolated woods in central Illinois—mostly oak and hickory—include Funk's Grove, or Carpenter Park, and Allerton Park along the Sangamon River. Locks and dams built along the Mississippi provide areas for waterfowl, including great concentrations of Canvasback and other ducks near Keokuk and Alton. Most of the marshy areas around East St. Louis have been destroyed, but a few with heron colonies are still there. In southern Illinois the Shawnee Hills offer some extensive woods where southern warblers, Summer Tanagers, Black Vultures, and other southern species are found. A few southern pine forests offer habitat for such birds as Pine Warblers, but these areas are not extensive. Bottomlands and cypress swamps support good populations of birds: La Rue Swamp, Heron Pond, Horseshoe Lake, Mermet Lake, and areas along the Big Muddy and Cache Rivers. Mohlenbrock (1986) describes the natural divisions of Illinois.

The Illinois climate is typically interior continental, with harsh, variable winters and hot, humid summers. Mean average temperatures for Aurora in northern Illinois are 23.3 degrees Fahrenheit in January and 73.5 in July. The highest rainfall average there is 4.23 inches in June, the average annual rainfall 33.9 inches. For Bloomington in central Illinois, average temperatures are 26.7 in January and 76.6 in July, the highest rainfall average 4.31 inches in June, and the average annual rainfall 36.72 inches. At Carbondale in southern Illinois, the average temperatures are 35.0 in January and 79.4 in July, with the highest rainfall average 4.68 inches in May and the average annual rainfall 44.8 inches.

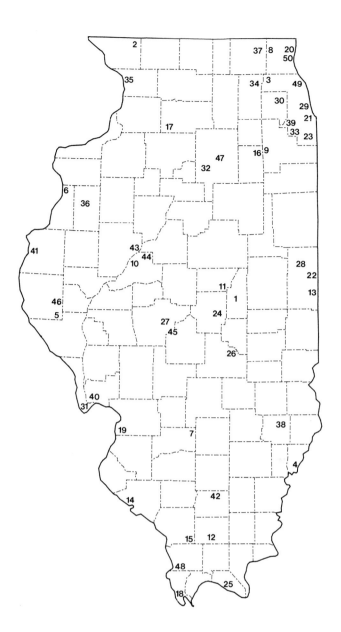

DISCUSSION OF THE BOOK

Species accounts, at the minimum, should explain the status and distribution of birds in Illinois. Other information may be included, such as migration dates, breeding times and places, notes on subspecies, maximum counts, changes in populations and reasons for the changes, migrational movements, behavior, how to identify certain closely related species (or references to helpful sources), and other special features about specific birds. On some very rare sightings, accounts may suggest why a record is accepted or rejected. Current practice in Illinois is that a species that is a prospect for inclusion on the state list must be backed by a specimen, a recognizable photograph, or the written documentation of two reliable observers. The documentation must also be accepted by the Illinois Ornithological Records Committee (IORC). This committee was formed recently to review all pertinent records for birds seen in

Illinois before publication. The IORC publishes its findings periodically in *Illinois Birds and Birding.*

The status of Illinois birds is described in this book in the following terms:

Permanent resident. Present all year in approximately the same locality. (An example is the Black-capped Chickadee.)

Migrant. Pass through the state en route to wintering grounds or breeding areas or both. (Blackburnian Warbler)

Winter resident. Present only during winter; usually proceed north with the coming of spring. (American Tree Sparrow)

Summer resident. Nest in the state. (Eastern Kingbird)

Nonbreeding summer resident. Present during the summer months but do not breed; probably immature or unmated. (Bonaparte's Gull)

Postbreeding wanderer. Drift northward (principally but not entirely) after breeding. (Little Blue Heron)

Vagrant. Found out of the normal range. (Western Tanager)

Probable escape or *Escape.* Released or escaped from confinement. (Monk's Parakeet)

Introduced. Released into the state by man, usually for hunting purposes. (Ring-necked Pheasant)

Extirpated. Once present in the state but no longer found and not likely to occur again except as vagrants. (Common Raven)

Extinct. Once present but totally exterminated. (Carolina Parakeet)

Hypothetical. Reported for the state but not properly documented. (Lewis' Woodpecker)

Of the 439 species covered in this book, 35 are hypothetical. That leaves 404 species that have been reliably reported in Illinois within historical times. On the total list, in addition to the 35 hypothetical species, are four extinct birds, four extirpated, and 99 vagrants (some of the latter necessarily arbitrary). Thus some 297 species occur regularly in Illinois.

The numerical status of a species is described by one of seven categories:

Abundant. Occurs in great numbers at a given season and habitat; many individuals may be seen in a day. This category applies to birds with large populations that occur in dominant habitats or several different habitats. (An example is the Common Grackle.)

Common. Occurs in considerable numbers at a given season and habitat; several may be seen in a day. (Gray Catbird)

Fairly Common. Occurs in numbers but to a lesser degree than common; if looked for, one or two may be seen in a day at the correct season and in the right habitat. (Black-billed Cuckoo)

Uncommon. Occurs in small numbers and may be limited by habitat; even if looked for at the correct season and in the right habitat, it may be missed in a day. (Le Conte's Sparrow)

Occasional. Occurs a few times in a year; hard to find, probably limited by habitat or season. (Greater White-fronted Goose)

Rare. Occurs once or twice a year, some years not at all, probably on the edge of its range or in small local populations; can apply to some regular vagrants. (Black Rail)

Very rare. Has occurred only a few times in the state; usually applies to a vagrant. (Say's Phoebe)

All species of birds found in Illinois cannot be neatly pigeonholed into these categories, and what is true for one portion of the state may be totally untrue for another part. For example, the Blue Grosbeak is uncommon in southern Illinois and uncommon to occasional in west-central Illinois but rare in east-central and northern Illinois.

Migrational averages come from four main sources. First is Dreuth's study of Lincoln Park, Chicago (published in Clark and Nice 1950). These averages are designated as "Chicago" in the text. This study is thorough and often quoted, but it is dated; the fieldwork was done from 1928 to 1943. A more up-to-date list of averages for northern Illinois is needed. Dreuth's study is unique because few birds nest in the park and most of the ones found there

are migrants—even birds known as summer residents elsewhere in the state. The second source for migrational averages is Smith (1930), whose dates are actually median dates for Urbana compiled from 1903 to 1922. Third is Craig and Franks (1987), whose dates are median migrational dates for 22 counties in west-central Illinois from 1969 to 1983. Finally, the Sangamon County dates are averages taken from my unpublished study from 1970 to 1987. It is unfortunate, but no averages from the southern part of the state are available. Such a study would be worthwhile and it is hoped that someone will fill this gap. Collection of such data should be at least 10 years in duration and preferably from one observer to ensure accountability. Accountability of sightings is especially difficult in cooperative projects such as the Christmas bird counts and the even less reliable spring bird counts. Data from both counts are sometimes difficult to assess, although they are usually acceptable if looked at in a broad context.

Illinois was lucky to have an early census of the state's birds by Gross and Forbes. It was later recensused by Richard and Jean Graber and published in "A Comparative Study of Bird Populations in Illinois, 1906–1909 and 1956–1958." The present book relies heavily on this landmark study. The Grabers have also completed several fascicles of biological notes on families of birds of Illinois that have proved very valuable (see Literature Cited).

Most records in this volume come from *American Birds* (formerly *Audubon Field Notes*) and the *Audubon Bulletin* with its two offshoots, *Illinois Audubon Bulletin* and *Illinois Birds and Birding.* Seasonal reports from the Illinois Department of Conservation also were used extensively. After a record in the text, identifying initials of observers are given, then the initials of the publication or report, followed by the volume and page number (see Abbreviations, page XVII, and Initials and Corresponding Names of Observers, page 218). Originally, the names of observers were to be mentioned only occasionally, but records are a necessary aspect of this volume and the observers who saw the birds an important part of the record.

Names of birds and order of species used in this book are from the sixth edition of the American Ornithologists' Union *Check-list of North American Birds* (AOU 1983). Subspecies' names are from the fifth edition (AOU 1957). These volumes were also used as sources for breeding and winter ranges.

Two maps are presented, the first to give the principal rivers, counties, and cities of Illinois and the other to show major birding spots in the state.

CONSERVATION IN ILLINOIS

I am probably going to say things in this section that will make some people unhappy. But that is what conservation does: it restricts, when people wish to exploit. Conservation is a sign of our times. Most of the earth's frontiers are gone, and it is time to take care of what we have. Unwittingly we have become caretakers of the earth's remaining resources. I am biased, I admit, in favor of saving as many species of birds in their natural environments in Illinois as is possible. To succeed, there must be major changes in the way we, as the main manipulators of the environment, do things, and especially in the way we think.

Birds do not exist in a vacuum—with the possible exception of pets in cages. Birds need habitats. In Illinois these habitats are woodlands, thickets, weedy fields, ponds, marshes, sloughs, grasslands, and so on. Before Europeans settled this state, it was a mosaic of prairie and woodland. Most of these habitats have been obliterated, or severely fragmented, or polluted. Sheer loss of living space must have lowered the populations of all birds except those associated with agriculture or urban areas. What we need now is to find a way not only to coexist with our remaining native environment but actually to revivify the parts we have already damaged.

I see at least six things that need to be changed or dealt with in a more rational manner.

First, most of today's problems, including the problem of habitat destruction, can generally be traced to overpopulation of this planet by humans. There are now more than five billion members of the single species *Homo sapiens.* But there are only 20 or so California Condors and, for Illinoisans, only 200 Prairie-Chickens. Soon we must agree on how many of each species is enough—even for *Homo sapiens.* When will we come to grips with what is already a near-catastrophe? When will religious leaders face facts? When will politicians deal with them? Population scientists have been pointing out the dangers since 1798, when Malthus published his essay on the principles of populations. China, the world's most populous nation, has started to see the light and to attempt to head off the disaster; will other nations stabilize their populations voluntarily, or by force, or by default? It is a finite planet; there is only so much room. Do we want a variety of organisms, or only a few? The choice can be ours; but it will be made very soon, with or without our help. Once species are gone they are gone forever. Passenger Pigeons will never again blot out the sun in passing.

Second, direct destruction of habitat results from many unnecesssary activities of man. Continued expansion of urban and industrial areas while inner cities crumble is a waste of space and a needless destruction of natural habitat. I know from experience that birding in our expanding urban areas can be very disheartening, as I see habitat after habitat destroyed. I also get the feeling that municipalities cut brush and clear areas simply to have something for people to do; better to let them plant new trees than to destroy the old ones. How many new forests have we planted lately? Dead trees are a boon to many species of birds that rely on them for nesting and shelter, but they are being cut down at an alarming rate, even in so-called parks and natural areas. Underbrush is being senselessly and systematically eliminated, leaving only a few trees with gaps in between—someone's idea of what "looks good." Destruc-

tion of the understory eliminates the bird species that use it. Understory is critical in winter for shelter and in summer for nesting. Unnecessary mowing has been carried out in Illinois for years, not only wasting gasoline but also destroying cover and food needed for grassland species. Mowing around woodland edges destroys the weed and grass seeds birds need for food. The Illinois Department of Transportation recently set aside some areas that are not mowed—a promising trend. Another consequence of woodland destruction or simplification is fragmentation of woodlots, which causes many species of birds to disappear because they are not able to produce enough young. The effects are just beginning to be uncovered by researchers, but target problems include increased cowbird parasitism and proliferation of nest predators, wild and domestic (see Robinson 1987). The more complex the environment the longer predator and prey can coexist. Thus large tracts of woodland are needed for some species to survive. Why not have laws enforcing woodland buffer zones along rivers, the extent of the buffer zone to be correlated with the size of the river? Such a zone would not only serve as a habitat for birds but would also greatly improve the watershed, decreasing pollution and erosion.

Third, intensive agriculture is detrimental to birdlife, especially when all hedgerows are cut down and fields plowed up to the ditch, leaving only a small strip of grass between field and road. It is a situation easily exploited by predators. Certain terrains and certain soil types are not fit for agriculture, but they are put under the plow anyway. Why, when there is an excess of grain? If a landowner lets a forest stand or leaves a field idle, don't we all benefit in the long run? Let the government compensate him under certain conditions if it must. Little or no prairie remains in the Prairie State. Shouldn't every county set aside at least a few areas as natural prairie? It is difficult to appreciate what we cannot see. Few Illinoisans have ever seen a Henslow's Sparrow. This unique bird has been associated with prairies probably for thousands of years yet now is an endangered species because we have left no prairies for it to breed in. If all landowners were required to carefully investigate their own land and know what is there, they might not be so quick to destroy it. Aldo Leopold said, "Many people live on the land, but not by the land." I realize that Illinois is a farming state and that we all benefit from our farmers' ability to produce. But does our farming have to be so intensive that little else can survive?

Fourth, much has been written recently about the cutting of tropical forests. Many of Illinois' most interesting and beautiful birds—more than 100 species—winter where this wholesale destruction is occurring in Central and South America. Plus, of course, many of the native species unique to these bird-rich tropical areas are also being threatened. Overpopulation by *Homo sapiens* is the main force behind this destruction, but other factors contribute to this obvious calamity. Studies are now being conducted on ways to preserve as much of this diversity as possible. Let us hope that some habitats can be saved as parks or nature preserves before it is too late. But ultimately it is not just trees and birdlife that will be destroyed; the climate of the entire globe will be altered—see the excellent books by Myers (1979) and Ehrlich and Ehrlich (1981).

Fifth, in addition to our own population explosion, the animals that associate with us have crossed the survival-of-the-fittest barrier and their populations, too, have exploded. Introduced, or nonnative, animals such as dogs and cats, not to mention European Starlings and House Sparrows, have a definite impact on bird populations. The need to control the pet populations is great. Richard Warner of the Illinois Natural History Survey estimated there were five to six million cats in Illinois (Warner 1985). These mammals are predators, but they are not natural predators. Natural predator numbers are controlled by their prey: if prey numbers drop there is a correlated decline in predator numbers. Not so with cats; they simply keep on taking available prey because they are not wholly dependent on prey but are also fed by people. Thus the relationship between the cat and its prey—birds and mice—is not controlled. Cats, like most people, take from the environment but put nothing back, and the cat population keeps climbing even if its prey populations drop. In city parks, I have noted, cats' prime targets are Ovenbirds and thrushes; one might wish them to specialize in European Starlings and House Sparrows. I cannot help but think that the rise in popularity of pets and the demise of nature are somehow interrelated—if not in reality, then in spirit, in concept. Like much else today, pets represent a movement away from nature. The noblest creatures are those that exist in their natural habitats on their own, independent of—in spite of—man.

And finally, another factor damaging to habitats is the misuse of technology. Since natural habitats have been so reduced in Illinois, one would think that the little we have left would be regarded as sacred. The increasing use of off-road vehicles in forests and other natural areas proves otherwise. Such blatant misuse of technology damages the environment for no good purpose. Could we stop the problem if we instituted lawsuits for ecological damages against the manufacturers and distributors of these machines? The need for landowners, cities, and state and federal governments to end the misuse of these machines is great. Whatever legitimate uses these off-road vehicles serve, their misuse surely far outweighs any benefits. Certainly they should be outlawed on public lands.

In short, our failure to come to grips with the decline of nature has been almost total, and if we are not careful Illinois will lose it all. The general public has failed to understand population dynamics, it has failed to understand predator and prey relationships, and it has failed even to learn what is known. If we went to another planet, what are the most precious things we might find there? Other life forms! Yet here, on the only planet most of us will ever see and the only planet where we know life forms exist, we are destroying them every day. Let us instead choose to preserve this planet's diversity.

Abbreviations

American Birds	AB
Audubon Field Notes	AFN
American Ornithologists' Union	AOU
Chicago Academy of Science	CAS
Field Museum of Natural History of Chicago	FMNH
Illinois Audubon Bulletin	IAB
Illinois Birds and Birding	IB&B
Illinois Natural History Survey	INHS
Illinois State Museum	ISM
Southern Illinois University at Carbondale	SIU
Seasonal Report, Illinois Department of Conservation	SR
United States National Museum	USNM

See also Initials and Corresponding Names of Observers, page 218.

Species Accounts

RED-THROATED LOON

Gavia stellata

RARE MIGRANT

Although Nelson (1876) thought this loon was a very common winter resident on Lake Michigan, it probably has never been numerous in Illinois. The Red-throated Loon differs from the Common Loon on several points: it is usually smaller; its color is a lighter gray; and it has a spotted back and a thin, upturned bill. Appleby et al. (1986) give details on identifying loons. The Red-throated also seems to be more active, diving more often than the Common Loon. It occurs on lakes and large rivers in Illinois. Although it is most numerous on Lake Michigan, the best views of it are often obtained on downstate lakes. It probably eats mostly fish; I saw one take a six- or eight-inch fish at Lake Springfield, November 12, 1983. There are several older specimens for Illinois. One specimen listed in Dinsmore et al. (1984) under Arctic (now Pacific) Loon has been reidentified as a Red-throated Loon. It was taken at Burlington on the Illinois side of the Mississippi River, November 15, 1895, and is in the University of Iowa collection (letters, Goetz and Schrimper, and photos by T. H. Kent, on file ISM).

There are more fall than spring migration records. Early fall arrival dates: Savanna, October 9, 1983 (BSh-SR39:3); Chicago, October 23, 1985 (RB-IB&B2:43); Lake Springfield, October 22, 1976 (HDB). The only multiple count for fall is three at Lake Springfield, October 26, 1984 (HDB). The peak of fall records is in November: Crab Orchard National Wildlife Refuge, November 10-11, 1984 (TF-AB39:59); Alton, November 2, 1984 (BR,CP-IB&B1:13); Decatur, November 11-12, 1985 (RS,RP-IB&B2:43). Late fall departure dates: Olney, December 4, 1985 (LH-IB&B2:43); Knox County, November 22-23, 1983 (MB-SR39:3); Lake Vermilion, December 3, 1983 (SB-SR39:3); Wilmette, November 27, 1985 (RB-IB&B2:43).

Nearly all Red-throated Loons winter in coastal areas. There are no recent winter records for Illinois and very few old ones. However, there is one specimen from Evanston for January 1, 1880 (CAS#5696). Some range maps in field guides show these loons wintering on the Great Lakes, but that is inaccurate. Two Red-throated Loons recorded on Christmas bird counts (Waukegan, 1951, and Cook County,

1956) may have been late fall migrants—if they were identified correctly.

Spring migration starts as early as February. There are several old records from Lake Michigan for that month—February 21, 1915; February 15, 1870 (three found dead); February 13, 1885—and a recent sight record at Chicago, February 21, 1982 (DW,HE-AB36:299). In this respect the Red-throated Loon resembles the Red-necked Grebe, which also returns inland very early from coastal wintering areas. Most records of spring Red-throated Loons are for March and April: Horseshoe Lake, March 11-12, 1988 (ViB,RG); Chicago, March 20, 1982 (HR-AB36:857); La Salle, March 28, 1987 (MB); Spring Lake Conservation Area, April 9, 1987 (TP). The only recent high count for spring is three, McLean County, April 16, 1974 (DBi). This loon has not been recorded on spring bird counts. Latest spring dates have been in May: Chicago, May 20, 1931 (Clark and Nice 1950); Chautauqua National Wildlife Refuge, May 1, 1971 (HDB). Red-throated Loons breed in the Arctic circumpolar.

PACIFIC (ARCTIC) LOON

Gavia pacifica

RARE FALL MIGRANT

A recent decision of the American Ornithologists' Union's Committee on Classification and Nomenclature divided Arctic Loons into two species. Those in Illinois are now called Pacific Loons. Identification of these loons in nonbreeding plumage was already difficult; apparently the only major field mark separating the Arctic and Pacific species in nonbreeding plumage is the absence of a white flank patch in the Pacific Loons. The Pacific species can be distinguished tentatively by smaller size, smaller bill, more rounded head, and gray nape.

All 12 acceptable Illinois records of the Pacific Loon are for fall, from October 29 (Horseshoe Lake, 1986; RG,BR-AB41:94) to December 9 (Lake Springfield, 1980). High count is three at Lake Springfield, November 16, 1980 (HDB). Other records: adult, Alton, November 18-20, 1986 (CP,PS-AB41:94); Clinton Lake, November 3-11, 1984, and two, November 10, 1984 (RS,TP-IB&B1:13); Olney, November 16-17, 1984 (LH-IB&B1:13); Mason

County, November 11, 1985 (LA-IB&B2:43); Carlyle Lake, November 6–26, 1987 (RG). Most Pacific Loons seen in Illinois are immatures. Curiously, none has yet been identified from Lake Michigan; all records are from downstate lakes. Most Pacific Loons winter on the West Coast, a few along the East Coast.

COMMON LOON
Gavia immer

COMMON MIGRANT; RARE WINTER AND NONBREEDING SUMMER RESIDENT

By far the most numerous loon in Illinois, the Common Loon is usually found on large bodies of water, occasionally on ponds and large rivers. Loons apparently are spending more time in Illinois now as a result of the creation of large lakes. The Common Loon comes in a diversity of sizes and shapes, but the daggerlike bill, eye spots, angular head, and large size distinguish it from other loons. Its weird call can be heard especially in spring, usually early in the morning. It can often be lured closer by imitating its call. Although loons migrate at night, they also can be seen migrating in daylight, some flying at fairly high altitudes. Along Lake Michigan migrating loons are a common sight at the right time of year. Occasionally a loon will land by mistake on a wet road surface and be unable to fly again because it needs to tread water to gain flight. Some years die-offs occur along Lake Michigan due to botulism; 1000 loons were found dead in 1963–64 (SR31:3). Excellent divers, Common Loons probably feed on fish in Illinois, but little study has been done of their eating habits.

In spring Common Loons arrive in Illinois about the end of March, reaching peak numbers in early to mid-April. Early spring arrival dates: Des Plaines, March 4, 1982 (PD-AB36:857); Crab Orchard National Wildlife Refuge, March 12, 1986 (DR-IB&B2:86); Horseshoe Lake, March 16, 1985 (HW-IB&B1:79). Average arrival dates: Chicago, April 12 (13 years); west-central, April 15 (10 years); Sangamon County, March 27 (17 years). Maximum counts for spring are low compared with fall: 18, Mississippi Palisades State Park, March 31, 1984 (BSh-SR41:5); 13, La Salle, May 20, 1979 (JH-AB33:775); 16, Evanston, April 27, 1979 (RB-AB33:775). Spring bird counts are done rather late to record high numbers of loons, but Commons have been recorded every year in small numbers (from one to 14). Average spring departure dates: Chicago, May 10 (13 years); Sangamon County, May 11 (17 years).

By mid-May most Common Loons are gone, but a few nonbreeders stay into the summer. They are generally in nonbreeding plumage and are probably one-year-olds. The last breeding pair in Illinois was recorded in 1892 in Lake County. These loons could probably be induced to breed again in northern Illinois if lakes unmolested by people could be provided. Summer records include six at La Salle, 1982 (JH-SR34:2); Lake of Egypt, June 30, 1985 (JR-IB&B2:12); adult, Crab Orchard National Wildlife Refuge, June 12, 1983 (AK-SR38:3); one at borrow pit, Vandalia, July 24, 1981 (F.Kringer-SR30:2); Champaign County, July 1, 1983 (BCho-SR38:3); three, Braidwood, July 12, 1984 (JM-IB&B1:15). Loons begin to return in October or occasionally sooner: Mark Twain National Wildlife Refuge, September 29, 1984 (BR-IB&B1:13); Chicago, September 30, 1981 (PC,HR-AB36:182). Average fall arrival dates: Chicago, November 6 (six years); Sangamon County, October 14 (18 years). Maximum fall counts usually exceed those of spring. The best counts can be made in late evening when these loons gather in a group in the middle of a lake, either to avoid ice or to get ready for night migration. These flotillas may be made up of several family groups. If they do not leave during the night, they will spread out again when daylight comes and move nearer to shore. They also may be seen flying locally in early morning. High counts for fall: 191, Wilmette, October 20, 1985 (RB,MBi-IB&B2:43); 180, Olney, November 15, 1985 (LH-IB&B2:43); 100, Carlyle Lake, November 6, 1987 (DJo,RG); 85, Springfield, November 9, 1986 (HDB); 50, Lake Shelbyville, November 1, 1984 (KF-IB&B1:13); 60, Lake Clinton, November 11, 1979 (RCh-SR23:2). Average fall departure dates: Chicago, November 26 (six years); Sangamon County, December 10 (18 years). Some of these loons stay until they are forced out by freezing lakes.

True winter records for Illinois are rare. Some warm-water (artificial) lakes provide wintering areas; so does Lake Michigan when it does not freeze. Winter records include two at Carlyle Lake, January 24, 1985 (LH,DJo-IB&B1:67); Crab Orchard refuge, January 18, 1985 (JR-IB&B1:67); Dallas City, January 8–11, 1986 (RCe-IB&B2:74); three, Baldwin Lake, February 17, 1985 (JR-AB39:171); Horseshoe Lake, February 14–19, 1983 (SRu,JEa). Christmas bird counts for 1976–85 listed Common Loons in nine of the 10 years. Totals ranged from one to eight; the highest count was seven at Crab Orchard refuge in 1983. Baldwin Lake has had wintering Common Loons annually since 1983 (RG).

YELLOW-BILLED LOON
Gavia adamsii

VERY RARE VAGRANT

The Yellow-billed Loon breeds in the high Arctic and winters along the Pacific Coast from Alaska to California. The only Illinois record was provided by a bird first seen on December 14, 1986, on the Rock River at Rock Falls. About 800 observers from 12 states came to see it. It was picked up dead at Rock Falls on December 30 (see Jones 1987). The specimen (608819), now in the Illinois State Museum, is an immature female that had gravel and fish bones in the gizzard. Features used in the identification were large size, pale yellowish bill, pale grayish head and neck, small eye, auricular patch, double-crested appearance, and white barring across the back. The Yellow-billed Loon has also been recorded in Minnesota and New York.

PIED-BILLED GREBE

Podilymbus podiceps

COMMON MIGRANT; UNCOMMON SUMMER AND WINTER RESIDENT

This little brown hell-diver can be found on nearly any body of water: lakes, ponds, sloughs, rivers, marshes. I once saw a Pied-billed Grebe in a swimming pool, unable to get out because the pool was too short for it to paddle across for takeoff. In its breeding areas the water usually has some emergent vegetation. When it perceives danger, it dives more often than it flies. When it comes back up after a dive it only partly emerges from the water and stays in or at the edge of vegetation so that detecting it is difficult. Many times the only clue to its presence is its cuckoolike call heard from a marshy area. It is very awkward on land because its tarsi are placed so far to the rear.

Even though some Pied-billed Grebes overwinter, there is a noticeable influx fairly early in the year: two, Pekin, February 12, 1984 (LA-SR41:5); St. Clair County, February 21, 1984 (TF-SR41:5); Carbondale, February 17, 1986 (KM-IB&B2:86); Will County, February 26, 1986 (JM-IB&B2:86). Average spring arrival dates: Chicago, April 13 (13 years); Urbana, March 26 (18 years); Sangamon County, March 3 (17 years). Spring bird counts generally come after the peak for this species, but totals have varied from 84 to 393, with northerly counties having the highest totals: Cook County, 105, May 7, 1977 (VK). Maximum counts for spring are not as high as fall counts: 60, Horseshoe Lake, April 8, 1984 (RK-SR41:5); 29, Knox County, April 24, 1984 (MB-SR41:5); 45, Lake Calumet, May 3, 1987 (JL). Most migrants have left by late May.

The Pied-billed Grebe must have been much more numerous before widespread draining was done in the state. Perry (1987) stated that 95 percent of the natural wetlands had been drained or destroyed and that draining was continuing at a rapid pace. On breeding bird surveys for 1965–79, this grebe was found at a rate of 0.1 per route (Robbins et al. 1986). More nesting occurs in northern and central than in southern Illinois. These birds make a floating mat for a nest and anchor it to other vegetation. There are three to nine light buff eggs per clutch. Illinois egg dates are May 5–July 28. The young are nicely marked with a harlequin pattern on the head; this stripe-headed sign of immaturity lingers into fall on some individuals. Very young chicks ride on their parents' backs. Brood numbers recorded include 18 young, Du Page County, July 18, 1984 (JM-IB&B1:15); 20 broods, Palos, July 1, 1981 (PD-SR30:2); 13 broods, Lake Calumet, May 9–July 11, 1981 (JL); five broods, Horseshoe Lake, June 14, 1983 (RG-SR38:3). These grebes have been noted eating fish and crawfish; at times they seem to have trouble swallowing the larger fish they catch.

As early as late June or early July Pied-billed Grebes begin to move around, perhaps because some ponds are drying up. These movements, like the later, more concentrated migration, are associated with cold fronts. The average arrival date for fall in central Illinois is July 29 (16 years). Early fall arrival dates: Jackson Park, July 21, 1982 (PC,HR-SR35:3); Monmouth, July 1, 1985 (MB-IB&B2:43); Cumberland County, August 31, 1984 (RBr-IB&B1:13). Maximum counts for autumn: 400, Mark Twain National Wildlife Refuge, late October 1963 (SV); 560, Lake Springfield, October 1, 1975 (HDB); 70, Savanna, September 22, 1985 (PP-IB&B2:43); 94, Lake Vermilion, October 22, 1984 (SB-IB&B1:13); 65, Riverdale, October 16, 1983 (JL); 75, Horseshoe Lake, November 8, 1983 (BR); 53, Crab Orchard National Wildlife Refuge, October 23, 1985 (TF-IB&B2:43). During migration these birds are often found on open water. Like loons and ducks, they drift in the late evening toward the middle of the lake. They also do less diving and can be counted more easily. The flocks I have seen sitting on the water tended to form lines rather than bunches like coots.

Pied-billed Grebes usually stay in fairly good numbers until the lakes begin to freeze. Christmas bird count totals for 1976-85 ranged from seven in 1977 to 100 in 1983, when Crab Orchard refuge had 72. Other high counts for winter: 25, Olney, January 9, 1985 (LH-IB&B1:67); 18, Lake of Egypt, January 28, 1984 (JR-SR40:4). Except in southern Illinois in mild winters, these grebes can overwinter only where water is kept open by artificial means. Thus overwintering probably is a relatively recent phenomenon in most areas of the state. The Pied-billed Grebe winters as far south as Panama.

HORNED GREBE

Podiceps auritus

FAIRLY COMMON MIGRANT; OCCASIONAL WINTER RESIDENT

Horned Grebes are difficult to find where there is no large body of water, but occasionally they are seen on ponds and sewage lagoons. One was found on a creek in Sangchris State Park, March 29, 1985, evidently having come over the dam. It could not get out of the creek because it did not have enough room for takeoff. Horned Grebes in changing plumage can easily be misidentified as Eared Grebes. Sometimes during migration they give a short, harsh *quark* call. Like other divers they migrate to the coasts in winter and breed mostly in the interior northwest. Nelson (1876) stated that the Horned Grebe "breeds sparingly in small lakes" in Illinois, but it does not do so today and has apparently lost much of its former breeding range in the East. The subspecies in North America is *P. a. cornutus*.

Early arrival dates for fall: Chicago, August 30, 1979 (JL-

AB34:166); Jacksonville, August 27, 1982 (TW,WO-AB37:185); Mendota, September 9, 1984 (JH-IB&B1:13). Average fall arrival dates: Chicago, November 2 (eight years), Sangamon County, October 8 (18 years). Large numbers of these grebes sometimes are seen on Lake Michigan. By October and November they are in their dark and white winter plumage. Maximum counts for fall: 3000, Cook County, November 11–13, 1955 (KB-AFN10:27); 260, Crab Orchard National Wildlife Refuge, November 24, 1982 (JR-SR35:3); 56, Springfield, November 27, 1986 (HDB); 70, Carlyle Lake, November 26, 1983 (RG,BR-SR39:3). Average fall departure dates: Chicago, November 17 (eight years); Sangamon County, December 15 (17 years). These grebes commonly linger into December, especially on warm-water lakes.

A few Horned Grebes winter where there is open water. Like other diving birds, they congregate in the center of the lake in the evening. Christmas bird counts for 1976–85 turned up Horned Grebes in seven of the 10 years, with totals ranging from one (1981) to 33 (1983). High count was at Crab Orchard: 21 in 1983. Other winter records: 76, Baldwin Lake, January 9, 1988 (SRu,M.Peters); four, Charleston, December 31, 1984 (RBr-IB&B1:67); Chicago, December 26–January 1, 1980 (RB,MMd-SR24:2); 12, Baldwin Lake, January 10, 1986 (DR-IB&B2:74). If the lakes freeze, all of these grebes leave.

Early spring migrants are sometimes difficult to distinguish from wintering birds. Early arrival dates: Springfield, February 6, 1987 (HDB); Olney, February 14, 1987 (LH); Horseshoe Lake, February 9, 1984 (CP-SR41:5). Average spring arrival dates: Chicago, April 12 (10 years); Sangamon County, February 28 (17 years). Maximum counts in spring are not as high as fall: 60, Horseshoe Lake, April 8, 1984 (RK-SR41:5); 34, Olney, March 19, 1981 (LH-SR29:3); 30, La Salle County, March 22, 1987 (JH). Sometimes these grebes flock very tightly. Spring birds appear in a number of plumages, from the dark and white to the beautiful breeding plumage. Spring bird count totals are small, ranging from none in 1985 to 17 in 1978; most counts come from the northern counties (VK). Average spring departure dates: Chicago, May 1 (10 years), Sangamon County, April 25 (17 years). Late birds were spotted at Riverdale, May 15, 1982 (JL); Waukegan, May 18, 1986 (LBi-IB&B2:86); Will County, May 9, 1981 (A&JT-SR29:3).

There are a few summer records of nonbreeding Horned Grebes: La Grange Park, July 14–17, 1935 (Pitelka 1935); Champaign, June 4, 1980 (RCh-AB34:781); Prairie Du Rocher, June 13, 1971 (HDB).

RED-NECKED GREBE

Podiceps grisegena

OCCASIONAL MIGRANT

Although this large grebe breeds in the interior of eastern North America, it is about as uncommon in Illinois as the Western Grebe. Red-necked Grebes migrate to the coasts, but most stay to the north of the state and few pass through. Lake Michigan is the most likely spot to find these birds in Illinois. Kennicott (1854) stated that the Red-necked Grebe was known to breed in Cook County, but the breeding area nearest to Illinois today is in Minnesota. Because the immature plumage lasts through the first winter, these dull-colored birds sometimes cause identification problems. In flight, their white wing patches are conspicuous. These grebes are usually seen on large lakes but sometimes on ponds and sewage lagoons. The subspecies in Illinois is *P. g. holbollii*.

Early fall migrants were recorded in Evanston, September 22, 1974 (LB-AB29:64), and Vermilion County, October 8, 1986 (ME-IB&B3:35). Maximum fall counts: six, near Murphysboro, October 31–November 1, 1946 (Bennett 1952); five, Evanston, October 20, 1978 (RB-AB33:182); three, Lake Shelbyville, November 24, 1986 (KF-IB&B3:35). Most records appear to be in October, November, and December. Late fall departures: Springfield, December 23, 1984 (HDB); Horseshoe Lake, December 8–14, 1983 (RG,BR-SR39:4); Carlyle Lake, December 2–9, 1984 (LH,DJo-AB39:172).

True winter records of this grebe are few. They include one from Chicago in the winter of 1940–41 (Ford 1956) and one from Springfield, January 5–10, 1986 (HDB). These grebes linger into December and sometimes return as early as February: Chicago, February 15–16, 1959 (HF-AFN13:296); Springfield, February 10–15, 1978 (HDB); five (the spring high count), Wilmette, February 16, 1977 (LB,GR-AB31:337). Most spring records come in March and April. Late spring departure dates: De Kalb County (spring bird count), May 5, 1984 (VK); Carlyle Lake, April 22, 1984 (LH,DJo-SR41:5). There is one summer record: Max Magraw Wildlife Foundation, June 8, 1967 (Dillon 1968).

EARED GREBE

Podiceps nigricollis

OCCASIONAL MIGRANT AND VERY RARE SUMMER RESIDENT

The Eared Grebe is similar to the Horned Grebe but somewhat dumpier looking, with a peaked head and slightly upturned bill. Nelson (1876) said: "Not uncommon in winter upon Lake Michigan. Several species of grebes and a number of ducks are occasionally taken during winter upon the hooks, set several miles off shore by the fishermen." Although this statement probably refers to Horned Grebes, Eared Grebes were collected early; there is a specimen from Chicago, November 3, 1888. They have undoubtedly increased in the state recently, even breeding. These grebes are mainly found west of the Mississippi River, and like Western Grebes they fly to the Pacific Coast or southern Texas for the winter. They occur on lakes, ponds, and sewage lagoons. The race found in North America is *P. n. californicus.*

Early spring migrants were recorded at Crab Orchard National Wildlife Refuge, March 15, 1987 (DR); Evanston, March 15, 1987 (EW); Horseshoe Lake, March 15, 1984 (JWa,HW-SR41:5). Average spring arrival date in Sangamon County: May 8 (four years). High counts for spring: 14, Olney, May 11, 1981 (LH-SR29:3); 10, Springfield, May 12, 1981 (HDB); five, Carlyle Lake, March 14, 1983 (BR-SR37:4). Eared Grebes have been recorded on spring bird counts four years but in very small numbers (one to three birds). Spring departure dates are from mid- to late May: two, Aledo, May 20–23, 1981 (BB-SR29:3); two, Waukegan, May 7–19, 1983 (JN-SR37:4); Arcola, May 11, 1985 (BCho,RCh-IB&B1:79). Flights sometimes occur in late spring and most or all of these late birds are in their beautiful breeding plumage.

In 1981 the first nesting of this species was recorded in Illinois (Landing and Clyne unpublished). It occurred at Riverdale, where there had been observations of Eared Grebes since 1978. Twelve young were produced from three successful broods. The nest with eggs was first seen June 23, and young were first seen July 16. Other summer records: subadult, Horseshoe Lake, June 5–12, 1983 (TF-SR38:3); Winfield, June 2–7, 1984 (SO-IB&B1:15).

Fall Eared Grebes have occurred as early as August: Urbana, August 5, 1981 (RCh-AB36:182); Jacksonville, August 26, 1982 (PW- SR35:3); Chautauqua National Wildlife Refuge, August 29, 1984 (TP-IB&B1:13). Average fall arrival date in Sangamon County is September 28 (13 years). Maximum counts for fall: five, Crab Orchard National Wildlife Refuge, December 18, 1983 (TF-SR39:4); four, Springfield, October 6, 1983 (HDB); three, Monmouth, October 18–25, 1986 (MB-IB&B3:35).

Very few Eared Grebes have been seen in winter, although some usually linger in December until the lakes freeze. They have been recorded on Christmas bird counts three times: Olney, 1980, and Crab Orchard refuge, 1953 and 1957. One at Baldwin Lake, January 10–11, 1986 (DR,RG-IB&B2:74), was a wintering bird and another—or perhaps the same bird—was there January 9–16, 1988 (SRu,RG,JG).

WESTERN GREBE

Aechmophorus occidentalis

RARE MIGRANT

The long swanlike neck, large body, yellowish bill, and dark and light pattern easily identify this grebe as an *Aechmophorus.* But there may be a problem in distinguishing it from Clark's Grebe. The Western is usually seen alone or in a flock of ducks, rarely with other Westerns. At rest, the Western Grebe lays its neck over its back, with its head under one wing, making it look smaller. It is found on large lakes and occasionally on deep ponds. The first reference

to this bird in Illinois is Musselman's vague statement (1916–17) that Western Grebes were more numerous one fall—he gave no year—than Pied-billed Grebes, which seems highly unlikely. The first and only specimen (definitely *A. occidentalis*) was collected at Swan Lake, Putnam County, December 24, 1921 (Gregory 1923). In this account I will consider all records up to about 1985 to be this species, although a few could be Clark's Grebes.

There are few spring records. Dates range from February 11, 1967, at Glencoe (CC-IAB143:17) to May 22, 1949, at Montrose Harbor (Ford 1956). Most dates are in April and early May. Spring sightings are probably of overmigrants coming from wintering areas on the Pacific Coast and flying east to breeding grounds. Breeding areas nearest Illinois are in western Minnesota and northwestern Iowa. On May 6, 1977, I witnessed a formation display by a pair of Western Grebes on Lake Springfield; two grebes paddling rapidly together across a lake make a spectacular sight (Bohlen 1977). Other spring records: Glencoe, April 4, 1956 (LBi-AFN10:337); Wilmette, April 15, 1973 (RR-AB27:778); Fulton County (spring bird count), May 5, 1979 (VK). There is one summer record: Rockford, June 29–July 2, 1978 (RB-AB32:1167).

These grebes are seen much more frequently in fall than in spring. They seem to have increased in occurrence recently, although this apparent increase may be accounted for in part by observers learning how and where to find them. Certainly they now occur annually in Illinois. Fall dates range from September 6, 1973, Mark Twain National Wildlife Refuge (SV-AB28:59), to December 19, 1986, Carlyle Lake (LH,BR-AB41:286). Most fall Western Grebes are seen in October and November. High counts: six to seven in one day, December 5, 1987, Carlyle Lake (RG-AB42:80), and four, Wilmette, November 12, 1960 (RR-AFN15:44). Some other fall records: two, Clinton Lake, October 19, 1986 (RP-IB&B3:35); Alton, November 1, 1984 (PS-IB&B1:13); Niantic, October 22, 1982 (TP-SR35:3); Crab Orchard National Wildlife Refuge, November 23, 1970 (GC,VK-AB25;65).

CLARK'S GREBE

Aechmophorus clarkii

VERY RARE VAGRANT

Only recently has Clark's Grebe been considered a separate species from the Western Grebe. It is the "light phase" of the two *Aechmophorus* species. It differs from the Western in its bright orange-yellow bill; the Western's bill is greenish yellow. Clark's Grebe also has white rather than dark around the eye, a paler gray back, more white on the flanks, and different calls. There is only one acceptable record for Illinois: Horseshoe Lake, November 24–December 14, 1983 (PS,RG-AB38:207).

NORTHERN GANNET

Sula bassanus

VERY RARE VAGRANT

This seabird comes to land only to nest. It is large, with long wings, a wedge-shaped tail, and a stout conical bill. The only Illinois record of the Northern Gannet comes from the central part of the state: an immature at Powerton Lake near Pekin, Tazewell County, November 19–20, 1983 (Pucelik 1983–84). Immatures are brown with a white V-shaped area at the base of the tail. To catch food, Gannets dive while on the wing, plunging from considerable heights into the water. The bird spotted at Powerton Lake was actively feeding and occasionally resting on the water. At times it was harassed by Herring Gulls. The nearest Gannet nesting sites are dense colonies on rock islands in the Gulf of St. Lawrence. There are several records from other Great Lakes states, especially to the east. These birds winter at sea, mainly off the coast from Virginia to southern Florida. That a Gannet was visiting at a rather small lake near the Illinois River rather than on Lake Michigan can only be regarded as surprising.

AMERICAN WHITE PELICAN

Pelecanus erythrorhynchos

OCCASIONAL MIGRANT IN WESTERN
ILLINOIS; RARE MIGRANT ELSEWHERE IN
THE STATE

Unlike Brown Pelicans, which dive for their food, American White Pelicans tip into the water like dabbling ducks and use their long necks and bills to secure food. They often work in a group when feeding. These large white birds with black wing tips soar on thermals like hawks during migration. They are usually associated with shallow water but also land on larger bodies of water. They can be seen at ponds, gravel pits, and sewage lagoons. A recent female specimen was salvaged near Illiopolis, November 5, 1980 (ISM).

Relatively few of these pelicans are seen in spring in Illinois, and spring arrival dates are late compared with those of pelicans on the Great Plains. The ones seen in Illinois are probably wandering nonbreeders. Recent spring records: two, Rock Falls, May 6, 1985 (BSh,LJ-AB39:306); Carlyle Lake, May 31–June 1, 1986 (CMa-AB40:1208); Bureau County, May 4, 1980 (JH-SR25:3); East Cape Girardeau, May 7–11, 1983 (PK-SR37:4). Flocks are occasionally seen in summer: 20, Fort Kaskaskia, June 14, 1963 (Flieg 1971a); 60, Mark Twain National Wildlife Refuge, June 9–10, 1971 (SV-AB25:863); 16, Baldwin Lake, June 11, 1975 (AB29:979).

There are a few records for July: six, Calumet, July 11–14, 1977 (SM-AB31:1146); two, Mason County, July 8–31, 1985 (KR-AB39:917); Pike County, July 25, 1978 (VK-AB32:1167). But it is not known whether birds seen at this time are early fall migrants or summering nonbreeders. Larger numbers of these pelicans occur in mid- to late September and October: 91, Mark Twain refuge, September 27–October 26, 1985 (DB-AB40:118); 30, Carroll County, October 17, 1984 (BB-AB39:59); 30, Chautauqua National Wildlife Refuge, October 26, 1982 (SR35:3); 23, Hancock County, September 30, 1985 (RAd-AB40:118). Some White Pelicans linger late: Alton, December 12, 1980 (PS,BR-AB35:304); Blandinsville, December 10, 1982 (EFr); Glencoe, November 25, 1982 (MM-SR35:3). And one wintered at Mark Twain refuge, 1982–83 (AB37:306).

BROWN PELICAN

Pelecanus occidentalis

VERY RARE VAGRANT

Brown Pelicans apparently ascend the Mississippi River or its tributaries now and then and are found in Illinois. There are five records of this coastal species for the state: one seen at Lima Lake, October 1873 (Ridgway 1880); one shot near Lacon, May 27, 1903 (Gault 1910); one seen near Quincy in 1913 (Musselman 1950); an adult male specimen (ISM), Fayette County, June 19, 1916; and three observed south of Quincy, April 25, 1948 (Musselman 1950). In addition, one was photographed on the Mississippi River, May 10, 1969, near Montpelier, Iowa (Peterson 1972), and two were sighted near Hamilton on October 18, 1982, but the record was inadequately documented. These pelicans have wandered north to Wisconsin, Michigan, and Ontario. The subspecies found here apparently is *P. o. carolinensis*, from the Gulf Coasts (AOU 1957), but the specimen in the Illinois State Museum should be checked for verification.

GREAT CORMORANT

Phalacrocorax carbo

HYPOTHETICAL

An immature of this East Coast cormorant was reported at Montrose Harbor on December 5, 1947. Although it was observed for half an hour and some description was taken, it was a one-observer sighting (H. T. Dean) and not enough information was gathered to establish a state record (Ford 1956). It has been recorded on Lake Ontario, and there are two unconfirmed records for Indiana (Mlodinow 1984).

DOUBLE-CRESTED CORMORANT

Phalacrocorax auritus

UNCOMMON MIGRANT; RARE SUMMER AND
WINTER RESIDENT

Double-crested Cormorants fly in wedges much like geese, but they do not call. When they are on water, their dark silhouettes are loonlike, but they usually hold their heads at an angle with the bill pointing up. The bill has a hook at the end, and the yellowish orange gular pouch is usually visible. Cormorants dive for food from the surface of the water, not while in flight. They sometimes search for food in groups, perhaps to improve the proficiency of the catch. The food taken is almost entirely fish. Double-crested Cormorants are most numerous along the Illinois and Mississippi Rivers, but overland flights occur during migration and some are seen along Lake Michigan. On some days during migration several flocks can be seen. Like the flights of hawks and other diurnal migrants, these flights are usually associated with clear weather.

Early spring migrants arrive in February, but most Double-crested Cormorants appear in March and April. Early records: Lake Michigan, March 2, 1981 (SR29:3); four, Channahon, February 25, 1985 (JM-IB&B1:79); Horseshoe Lake, March 13, 1977 (JEa-AB31:1007); Olney, March 6, 1984 (LH-SR41:6). Average spring arrival dates: Chicago, April 23 (five years); west-central, April 4 (10 years). Spring bird count totals show an increase in Double-crested Cormorants from none in 1972 to 306 in 1983. These counts probably reflect a real increase in the population. High counts are along rivers; the highest was 126 in Carroll County, May 7, 1983 (VK). Other spring maxima: 1605, Illinois and Mississippi Rivers, March 27, 1980 (RC-AB34:781); 400, New Boston, April 6, 1985 (MB-AB39:306); 286, Rend Lake, April 19, 1986 (DR-IB&B2:86); 249, northeastern Illinois, March 26, 1980 (RC-SR25:3); 1204, from Springfield to Shelbyville and to southern Illinois, April 18, 1983; and 2130, Mississippi and Illinois Rivers north of St. Louis, April 25, 1983 (RC-SR37:4). Most of these cormorants go farther north for the summer, but a few stay in Illinois to nest and a few non-breeders oversummer. Average spring departure dates: Chicago, May 1 (five years); west-central, May 9 (10 years).

Double-crested Cormorants usually nest in colonies over or near water. Many years ago there were nesting colonies in Marshall County of up to 40 pairs associated with Great Blue Herons. A colony with several nests near Havana in 1910 was shot out by fishermen, and there were probably colonies elsewhere. But today the only known colony of any size is at Thomson on the Mississippi River in Carroll County. In 1960 this colony had only seven nests; because of the lack of nest sites, it was thought to be dying out and the Double-crested Cormorant was added to the Illinois endangered species list. The nongame section of the Department of Conservation then put up artificial nesting platforms and the colony began to recover. There were 16 nests in 1978 and more than 110 in 1986. Recently, very small colonies have been found at Rend Lake and Lake Renwick and in Putnam County and Bartonville. Most Doubled-crested Cormorant nests are made of sticks and set in dead trees. There are three to five eggs, oblong and pale bluish with a chalky outer layer. Egg dates are from late April and early May. The young are altricial, leaving the nest after two to three weeks. They learn to swim before they can fly. The earlier drop in numbers of Double-crested Cormorants was due to pesticide thinning of egg-shells, heavy predation, and human disturbance of the birds and their habitats. The 1980s have seen population increases for this species in the Great Lakes region. Summer records away from the known colonies are probably of nonbreeding birds: 10, Crab Orchard National Wildlife Refuge, June 4, 1984 (BCho-IB&B1:15); 10, Lake Calumet, June 14, 1986 (JL); six, Calhoun County, July 3, 1982 (RK-SR34:3). There is some wandering of individuals in June and July.

Earliest arrival dates for fall migrants: Horseshoe Lake, July 5, 1981 (BR-SR31:3); Sanganois, August 11, 1985 (SB-IB&B 2:43); Winfield, July 5, 1984 (MS-IB&B1:13). Average fall arrival dates: Chicago, October 11 (11 years); west-central, September 27 (nine years). Maximum numbers of Double-crested Cormorants seen in fall include 495, Illinois and Mississippi Rivers, October 4, 1982 (RC-SR35:3); 270, Carlyle Lake, November 17, 1985 (LH-IB&B2:43); 270, Rend Lake, November 17, 1985 (LH,TF-IB&B2:43); 350, Illinois Beach State Park, September 26, 1984 (RB-IB&B1:13); 100, Savanna, November 1, 1980 (BSh-AB35:188); 190, Henderson County, October 22, 1983 (MB-SR39:4). Even though the population is making a comeback, these maximum counts cannot compare with such earlier counts as the 12,000 that passed Havana, October 7, 1940 (Mills et al. 1966). Migration continues well into December or until the water freezes. Average fall departure dates: Chicago, November 12 (11 years); west-central, November 23 (nine years).

Christmas bird counts for 1976–85 showed a high total of only 13 Double-crested Cormorants in 1983 and four years without any. The highest count was 58 at Horseshoe Lake in 1950. Wintering birds are not common, but with more warm-water lakes becoming available, wintering may increase. Winter records: three on January 6, 1982, in Tazewell County and one until February 20 (MSw-AB36:299); Pekin, January 12, 1984 (KR-AB38:322); Joliet, January 26, 1984 (JM-AB38:322); two, Kenilworth, January 2, 1961 (Mlodinow 1984); two, Mark Twain National Wildlife Refuge, January 3–10, 1983 (SR36:3); Carlyle Lake, January 20 and 23, 1983 (BR-SR36:3). Most Double-crested Cormorants are presumed to winter along the coasts of the southern United States.

OLIVACEOUS CORMORANT

Phalacrocorax olivaceus

VERY RARE VAGRANT

This cormorant is normally found on the western Gulf Coast and south to South America. There are two records for Illinois. The first, a specimen taken along the Ohio River near Cairo, July 10, 1878 (ISU collection), was reported by Ridgway (1880). The second was an adult at Lake Renwick and in nearby Will County, August 22 to October 5, 1986 (JM-AB41:94). It was photographed and was seen with Double-crested Cormorants, making direct comparisons possible. No Olivaceous Cormorant has ever been seen farther north.

ANHINGA

Anhinga anhinga

VERY RARE VAGRANT

Kennicott (1854) said the Anhinga, a southern bird, was quite common in June in the Cache Bottoms near Cairo. Nelson (1877) said it as was not common. But they agreed that Anhingas perched in dead sycamores near Cairo. Cahn (1930) listed the "Water Turkey," or Anhinga, as a bird of the cypress swamps in southern Illinois and recorded it in 1928 or 1930. In 1942 two were seen in central Illinois, one at Fox Ridge State Park in April or May and the other at Lake Springfield on May 23 (Smith and Parmalee 1955). A male was seen at Stephen A. Forbes State Park, October 8–10, 1968 (Matthews 1969). More recently there have been four records: Big Muddy River, June 4, 1977 (MMo-AB31:1146); Cedar Lake, July 24–26, 1977 (JGa-AB31:1146); Union County Conservation Area, April 28, 1985 (JR-AB39:306); and one photographed, Alexander County, July 5, 1986 (DR-AB40:1208). Thus the number of records seems to be on the increase.

Whether the Anhinga has nested in Illinois is open to question; there are no specific records of its doing so. Anhingas soar on thermals like hawks when migrating; with the right winds they can be drifted northward, especially during postbreeding dispersals.

MAGNIFICENT FRIGATEBIRD

Fregata magnificens

VERY RARE VAGRANT

These graceful tropical birds spend much of their time soaring on thermals. On rare occasions a Magnificent Frigatebird is chased inland by advancing thunderstorms. There are four reports for Illinois. The first involves a mounted specimen, but there is disagreement about whether the bird was on the Illinois or Iowa side of the Mississippi River and whether it was killed in the spring of 1904 (Coale 1910) or August 1903 (Bartsch 1922a). It is assumed that Coale and Bartsch were referring to the same bird, but even that is not certain. The next record is of a frigatebird—species unspecified—seen at Rockford in mid-September 1961 after hurricane Carla passed (DPr-AFN16:36). The third was seen in Alexander County along the Mississippi River, July 19, 1986 (DR-AB40:1208). Then in 1988, after the passage of hurricane Gilbert, an immature was seen by many observers at four localities along Lake Michigan from Jackson Park to Wilmette on September 28. Five other sightings of this tropical bird were reported in the Midwest after that storm.

AMERICAN BITTERN

Botaurus lentiginosus

UNCOMMON MIGRANT; RARE SUMMER AND WINTER RESIDENT

To see this brownish heron, an observer usually must flush it from a marsh. It is also found in wet woodlands and wet weedy fields. Because American Bitterns are secretive, knowledge of their several calls can help to locate them. One call is a pumping sound; another resembles a stake being driven into the ground. These bitterns tend to freeze rather than fly, standing with bill pointed up and blending in with the surrounding vegetation. Frogs apparently are one of their main food items. Mostly nocturnal migrants, these birds occasionally hit wires or television towers, causing some mortality. Goetz observed bitterns migrating by day both along the Chicago lakefront on October 26, 1980, and down the Mississippi River at Alton on September 12, 1982.

Spring migrants usually appear in late March or early April. A few wintering bitterns may be mistaken for early migrants. Early spring arrival dates: three, Oakwood Bottoms, March 25, 1984 (JR-SR41:6); Danville, March 23, 1985 (SB-IB&B1:79); Grand Tower, March 28, 1985 (JR-IB&B1:79). Average arrival dates: Urbana, April 11 (13 years); Chicago, April 29 (13 years); Sangamon County, April 16 (17 years). High counts for spring: 10, Oakwood Bottoms, April 27, 1979 (HD-AB33:776); six, Grand Tower, April 6, 1985 (RP-IB&B1:79). American Bitterns were recorded every year on spring bird counts, with totals ranging from 13 in 1983 to 50 in 1978. Highest count was 10 in Jackson County, May 5, 1973 (VK). Average spring departure dates: Chicago, May 15 (13 years); west-central, May 5 (10 years). Some migrants linger into late May or even June.

American Bitterns were once much more numerous than they are now, especially in northern Illinois, according to Nelson (1876), Cory (1909), and even Ford (1956). These birds breed in wet prairies, prairie sloughs, and marshes, and destruction of such habitats has made the American Bittern an endangered species in Illinois. Recent nesting or apparent nesting has occurred at Beardstown, 1979; Lake County, 1982; Banner Marsh, 1983; Goose Lake Prairie, 1971–73; and several other areas, especially in northeastern Illinois. The bittern's nest is on the ground or on a platform of vegetation. Two to six brown to olive-buff eggs are laid. Illinois egg dates are May 18 to June 16 (Bent 1926).

Unlike other herons, the American Bittern is not prone to postbreeding dispersal in late summer and early fall. In fact, this bittern is more difficult to find in fall than in spring, probably because it is hidden in profuse vegetation.

Early fall arrivals: Henderson County, August 8, 1982 (LMc-SR35:3); on top of a roof, Chicago, August 4, 1983 (DJ-SR39:4); Mark Twain National Wildlife Refuge, August 23, 1981 (SRu-SR31:4). Average fall arrival dates: Chicago, September 8 (13 years); west-central, August 27 (four years). Fall counts of more than a single individual are few: four, Henderson County, September 6, 1982 (LMc-SR35:3); four, Illinois Beach State Park, October 20, 1984 (DJ-IB&B1:13). Average fall departure dates: Chicago, October 25 (13 years); Sangamon County, November 4 (five years).

Winter records are scanty. Some winter bitterns may be cripples; occasionally these birds get caught in traps set for mammals. Others may be late fall migrants. Late records include Urbana, December 2, 1979 (RCh-SR23:3); Moraine Hills State Park, January 23, 1981 (JVS-AB35:304); one caught in trap, Sangamon County, December 17, 1973 (ISM). A few are found on Christmas bird counts: Chautauqua National Wildlife Refuge, 1988; Rockford, 1981; Sand Ridge, Cook County, 1968; Joliet, 1974; and Chicago, 1935.

LEAST BITTERN

Ixobrychus exilis

UNCOMMON MIGRANT AND SUMMER
RESIDENT

This small, secretive heron is found mainly in cattail marshes. Its series of cooing notes, best heard in the evening, are sometimes the only clue to its presence. It may sometimes be seen in flight over marshes, its buffy wing patches conspicuous, or sitting in cattails at the water's edge. Rarely it can be seen standing on a mudflat in the open. The Least Bittern is fairly easy to flush from the vegetation, but at times it will freeze rather than fly. The "Cory's" Least Bittern is a color form that has been collected twice in Illinois: a dark form taken along the Fox River at Cary, McHenry County, May 23, 1914 (Eifrig 1915), and an albinistic female taken near Aurora, June 1, 1909 (Carpenter 1948). The latter specimen is in the Illinois State Museum collection.

Because this bittern is difficult to detect, records are probably not as exhaustive for it as for other heron species. Early arrival dates for spring migrants include Chicago, April 7, 1974 (WK-AB28:807); Danville, April 24, 1985 (SB-IB&B1:79); Kennekuk Cove Park, April 18, 1984 (ME-SR41:6); Urbana, April 26 (Smith 1930). Average spring arrival dates: Chicago, May 14 (four years); Sangamon County, May 14 (11 years). Spring maximum records are nonexistent, but at most three to four birds are seen per day. This bittern's occurrence is very local, and records come mostly from such places as Cook and Lake Counties in the northeast, the Illinois River valley, and Mermet Lake in southern Illinois. Spring migration probably continues into June.

Nests are placed in cattails in marshes, almost always over water. The male helps with nesting activities. Two to five and sometimes as many as seven pale bluish or greenish eggs are laid. Egg dates for Illinois are May 22 to July 10. The young are buff above and white below. Family groups can be seen occasionally standing in cattails. Summer high counts probably reflect family groups: seven, Lake Calumet, August 11, 1980 (MMd-AB35:188); four, Williamson County, July 9, 1983 (JR-AB37:993); twelve, Lake Calumet, July 12, 1981 (JL); 13, Redwing Slough, June 11, 1981 (Harty, JVS-SR30:4).

Migration is even more difficult to detect in fall than in spring because the vegetation is thicker. Least Bitterns have been seen in cornfields, and in Illinois these fields provide many places for them to disappear at this time of year. Fall arrival dates for Jackson Park are August 22, 1981 (HR,PC), and August 29, 1980 (RG,PC). Most migration occurs in September; a television tower kill in Sangamon County, September 3, 1981, shows that migration occurs in early September in central Illinois. Least Bitterns are, however, infrequent victims of these towers. Average fall departure date for Sangamon County is September 20 (four years). Late departure dates: Champaign, November 15, 1982 (BCho-SR35:3); Coles County, November 1, 1986 (LBH-AB41:94); Pere Marquette, November 9, no year given (Comfort 1941); Cook County, November 21, 1976 (RE-IAB180:40).

The Least Bittern winters from the southernmost parts of the United States south to Panama and Colombia.

GREAT BLUE HERON

Ardea herodias

COMMON MIGRANT AND LOCALLY COMMON
SUMMER RESIDENT; UNCOMMON WINTER
RESIDENT DECREASING NORTHWARD

The Great Blue is the largest of the herons found in Illinois and one of the most numerous. It occurs primarily along the major rivers but may also be seen at marshes, lakes, and ponds or anywhere near water. Great Blues migrate singly or in small flocks diurnally, nocturnally, or crepuscularly. Graber et al. (1978) noted a recent serious decline in the Great Blue Heron population of up to 71 percent. Causes of this decline are such human activities as the shooting of adults and young, the destruction of the birds' habitats, and pollution. Windstorms are also a factor. The race *A. h. herodias* is found in most of Illinois, and *A. h. wardi* is present in southern Illinois (AOU 1957). A "Wurdeman's Heron"—an intergrade of *A. h. wardi* and *A. h. occidentalis* (the latter previously known as the "Great White Heron")—was seen by Ridgway (1895) near Mount Carmel from September 11 to 22 (no year given).

Spring migration begins in February: three, Shelby County, February 13, 1983 (KF-SR37:5); 26, Jersey County, February 7, 1987 (RP); four, Tazewell County, February 15, 1984 (KR-SR41:6). But some of these records could refer to wintering birds. Average spring arrival dates: Urbana, March 30 (15 years); Chicago, April 10 (eight years); west-central, March 13 (14 years). High counts for spring are associated with rookeries: 136, Lake Renwick, April 4, 1986 (JM-IB&B2:86); 130, Clear Lake, spring 1987 (MB,KR); 91, Mercer County, May 4, 1985 (PP-IB&B1:79). Spring bird count totals ranged from 144 in 1972 and 1975 to 1445 in 1986. Highest count was 183 in Mason County, May 10, 1980 (VK). Average spring departure dates: Chicago, May 18 (eight years); Sangamon County, May 11 (16 years).

In summer many young herons of nonbreeding age wander and may be present almost anywhere. Breeding bird survey data for 1965–79 singled out Illinois as the only state with significant decreases in Great Blue Herons (Robbins et al. 1986). The mean number of birds per route was 0.3. These herons nest in colonies and occasionally as single pairs. Graber et al. (1978) listed the known colonies in Illinois and gave recent counts of the number of nests. Many colonies have declined or completely vanished. Kleen estimated the total nesting pairs in 1987 as 5340 in 36 colonies. One colony in Massac and Pope Counties had 568 nests. These nesting colonies are being monitored on a yearly basis. Most nests are platforms made of sticks and placed in large trees. Clutches are three to six greenish blue eggs. Illinois egg dates are March 25 to May 17 (Graber et al. 1978). The only data on Great Blue Heron food habits came from nestlings, which were fed mostly gizzard shad, carp, and bluegill.

Great Blue Herons usually disperse northward in July and August after breeding, but some wander as early as late June. Average fall arrival dates in areas where they do not nest include Chicago, August 7 (12 years), and Sangamon County, July 19 (12 years). Maximum counts for fall: 960, Mason County, July 18, 1985 (KR-AB39:917); 112, Crab Orchard National Wildlife Refuge, October 12, 1983 (JR-SR39:4); 305, Rice Lake, August 25, 1985 (MBr-IB&B2:43); 166, Palos, September 7, 1984 (JL). Average fall departure dates: Chicago, October 18 (12 years); west-central, December 16 (10 years); Sangamon County, November 27 (14 years).

Some Great Blue Herons stay on into December or until severe weather hits, and a few winter in Illinois. Christmas bird count totals for the past 10 years ranged from 47 in 1977 to 185 in 1984. Highest count was 86 at Chautauqua National Wildlife Refuge in 1959. More of these herons winter in southern Illinois and along the Illinois River backwaters than anywhere else in the state. Some winter records for northern Illinois are Rockton, January 29, 1983 (DW-SR36:3); 22, Will County, December 22–January 8, 1987 (CMi-IB&B3:66); two, Henderson County, wintered 1985–86 (MB-IB&B2:74); Moline, January 15, 1984 (C.Lieb-SR40:4).

GREAT EGRET
Casmerodius albus

COMMON MIGRANT AND SUMMER RESIDENT ALONG MAJOR RIVERS; UNCOMMON MIGRANT AND POSTBREEDING WANDERER ELSEWHERE IN THE STATE

By 1900 this beautiful and once numerous egret was nearly extirpated from Illinois and the rest of the United States by plume hunters. There were very few records in Illinois between 1900 and 1925. In 1916, when the selling of egret plumes became illegal, the population began a slow recovery (Graber et al. 1978). Numbers reportedly climbed after 1927 near Quincy (Musselman 1932), and nesting was recorded in 1938 in Peoria after a lapse of 35 years (Bellrose 1939). In the late 1930s and the 1940s there were counts of 2300 and 7000 in the Illinois Valley (Graber et al. 1978). But a few decades later Graber and Graber (1978) found this egret again on the decline, with the breeding population dropping by 80 percent between 1973 and 1976. This decline may be due to pollution or other unknown causes.

Great Egrets are distributed nearly worldwide. They always have black legs and a yellow bill, and in breeding plumage they have long plumes on their backs. They are the largest white herons in Illinois, but they are smaller than Great Blue Herons. They are most numerous in the western part of the state, and especially along the Illinois River. They are also found at ponds, at the shallow ends of lakes, and in flooded fields. The race in Illinois is *C. a. egretta*.

Migration apparently is diurnal; flocks flying in V-formation are often observed. Early spring arrival dates: Lake Renwick, March 11, 1986 (JM-IB&B2:86); Rend Lake, March 11, 1981 (RZ-SR29:4); Havana, March 19, 1986 (RBj-IB&B2:86); Rice Lake, March 21, 1987 (LA). Average spring arrival dates: west-central, April 4 (11 years); Sangamon County, April 8 (18 years). High counts for spring: 205, Lake Renwick, April 19, 1987 (JM); 16, Chicago, May 23, 1981 (RB,JL-SR29:4); 22, Palos, May 31, 1986 (CM,JL-IB&B2:86). Spring bird count totals ranged from 39 in 1978 to 311 in 1986, with high counts coming from breeding areas. Highest count was 148, Will County, May 4, 1985 (VK). Average spring departure dates: west-central, April 17 (11 years); Sangamon County, May 7 (11 years). Some migration continues into June.

Great Egrets nest with other heron species, especially Great Blues and Black-crowned Night-Herons. They usually place their nests lower than those of Great Blues. Little is known about the nesting cycle in Illinois, but Graber et al. (1978) list the colonies. In 1987 there were 18, with total pairs estimated at 630 (VK). Great Egrets lay four to five pale bluish eggs. Illinois egg dates are from at least April 5 to June 14. These birds disperse northward after nesting, and egrets from farther south swell the numbers in Illinois.

Fall migrants generally arrive in August, but some egrets show up in nonbreeding areas as early as July. Average fall arrival dates: west-central, August 18 (10 years); Sangamon County, August 5 (11 years). High counts for fall: 538,

Chautauqua National Wildlife Refuge, October 12, 1984 (KR-IB&B1:13); 411, Mark Twain National Wildlife Refuge, September 30, 1985 (HW-IB&B2:43); 300, Rice Lake, September 13, 1986 (MB-IB&B3:35); 365, Brown County, September 12, 1981 (PW,TW-SR31:4); 116, Savanna, August 21, 1986 (SB-IB&B3:35); 135, Palos, September 7, 1984 (JL). Average fall departure dates: west-central, October 20 (10 years); Sangamon County, October 12 (16 years). There are many November records and several for December: Horseshoe Lake, December 26, 1986–January 13, 1987 (JZ-IB&B3:66); Decatur, December 1, 1985 (RP,MD-IB&B2:43); Crab Orchard National Wildlife Refuge, December 14, 1983 (JR-SR39:5); Woodford County, December 6, 1980 (RBj-SR27:3); La Rue Swamp, December 23, 1981 (DH-SR32:2); two, McGinnis Slough, December 5, 1981 (PD-SR32:2). There are also December records from Christmas bird counts in 1953, 1957, and 1972. Great Egrets winter in the southern United States south at least to Mexico.

SNOWY EGRET

Egretta thula

RARE MIGRANT; POSTBREEDING WANDERER
AND LOCAL SUMMER RESIDENT

Snowy Egrets probably have never been common in Illinois, but like Great Egrets they suffered from plume hunting before the turn of the century. The Snowy is a small, slim egret with a black bill, black legs, a yellow loral spot, and yellow feet. Immatures, though a little less distinct than adults, are reasonably easy to identify. This egret's feeding methods are highly variable but usually quite active, including fluttering over the water and running through the water to catch prey. Snowy Egrets are found around lakes, ponds, sloughs, flooded fields, and marshes. In Illinois they are most numerous in the southwest along the Mississippi River to Madison County. The race found in Illinois is the eastern *E. t. thula*.

Spring migrants usually show up in breeding areas, but some overmigrate north of these areas. Early spring arrival dates: Springfield, April 5, 1986 (HDB); two, Horseshoe Lake, April 5, 1985 (BR-IB&B1:79). High counts for spring: 11, Alexander County, May 26, 1985 (JR-IB&B1:79); eight, Horseshoe Lake, May 17, 1981 (PS-AB35:828). Totals on spring bird counts are low, from one to six, and these birds are not recorded every year. Records away from nesting areas include two, Peoria, May 17, 1985 (LA-IB&B1:79); two, New Boston, April 30, 1983 (LMc-SR37:5); Rock Cut State Park, April 27, 1979 (LJ-AB33:776).

Breeding in Illinois occurs near Horseshoe Lake and in the American Bottoms in St. Clair County, but the number of breeding pairs varies from year to year and some years there apparently are none at all. Breeding is suspected at Lake Renwick. In the summer of 1979, 10 to 20 pairs were

at the Pontoon Beach colony (DaJ-AB33:867). They usually nest in trees, laying three to four greenish blue eggs. Little is known about the nesting cycle in Illinois. Northward dispersals in late summer and fall have produced these high counts: 60, Horseshoe Lake, August 2, 1988 (RG); 44, Horseshoe Lake, August 27, 1986 (RG-AB41:94); 39, Horseshoe Lake, August 4, 1985 (SRu-IB&B2:12). Most Snowy Egrets leave the state in September. Late fall records: Mason County, October 14, 1985 (LA-IB&B2:43); two, Clinton Lake, October 20, 1984 (RCh-IB&B1:13); Batavia, October 14, 1978 (AB33:182). Snowy Egrets winter in the coastal United States south to Middle and South America.

LITTLE BLUE HERON

Egretta caerulea

UNCOMMON MIGRANT, BREEDING LOCALLY
IN THE SOUTH; POSTBREEDING WANDERER
THROUGHOUT THE STATE

Little Blue Herons appear in Illinois as dark blue adults, first-year calicos (white with blue in the plumage), or all-white juveniles. They are rather rare away from their breeding areas in southern Illinois except when an extraordinary flight of postbreeding birds occurs. These herons are usually seen where there is shallow water in which to feed and especially in the open sloughs along the Mississippi and Illinois Rivers.

The earliest spring migrants arrive in March: Olney, March 23, 1980 (LH-AB34:781); Union County Conservation Area, March 29, 1986 (TF,DR-AB40:476); Lake Springfield, March 24, 1982 (HDB). Usual arrival dates for breeding areas are in early April. The average spring arrival date is April 24 (13 years) for central Illinois, although the dates vary widely. All Little Blue Herons seen in central and northern Illinois in spring must be overmigrants. Examples of northern records include two, Oquawka, April 26, 1986 (MB-IB&B2:86); three, Green River Conservation Area, May 16, 1981 (BSh-SR29:4); Illinois Beach, May 6, 1981 (JN-SR29:4). Spring bird count maxima are in breeding areas, as would be expected. Totals ranged from 43 individuals in the 1982 counts to 319 in 1973 (VK). Spring and summer maxima from breeding areas include 136, Alexander County, July 7, 1984 (TF,JR), and 400, Pontoon Beach, July 12, 1980 (LW,PS-SR27:3). On May 1, 1983, a tornado smashed through a Little Blue Heron colony in Madison County and killed 59 adults.

The mean number of Little Blue Herons per route in Illinois for the 1965–79 breeding bird surveys was 0.1 (Robbins et al. 1986). There are only three colonies in Illinois—one each in St. Clair, Madison, and Alexander Counties with a total of 125 pairs in 1985 (Kleen)—and the Little Blue Heron is considered an endangered species. In their colonies, these herons usually nest with other species, such as the Black-crowned Night-Heron. They build platform nests, usually placing them fairly low (five to 10 feet) in dense vegetation but occasionally up to 40 feet high. They lay three to six pale greenish blue eggs. Dates for Illinois are not available. The young are semialtricial; they fledge in 35 to 40 days. They can be distinguished from other young white herons by bluish tips on the primaries. Both eggs and young are preyed upon by Fish Crows and raccoons during nesting season. Little Blue Herons feed on fish, crayfish, insects, and frogs.

Postbreeding wandering may begin in early July. The average date for central Illinois is July 30 (15 years). Wanderers include not only herons from southern Illinois but also some from farther south as evidenced by banding recoveries. Records of fall arrival dates: two, Lake Calumet, July 1, 1984 (JL); Palos, July 22, 1980 (SR27:3); two, Oquawka, August 5, 1979 (LMc-SR23:3). Graber et al. (1978) suggest that there is a peak every 20 years in late summer birds moving north. Most of these Little Blue Herons are in juvenile plumage and remain until late August or September. Average fall departure date is August 25 (14 years) for central Illinois. Maximum numbers of individuals for fall include 110, Mark Twain National Wildlife Refuge, early September 1983 (HW-AB38:208); 200, East St. Louis, September 1978 (AB33:182); 31, Havana, August 17, 1986 (RCh-AB41:94); nine, Lake Shelbyville, September 3, 1983 (BCho-SR39:5). Most of these herons are gone by the end of September, but a few linger into October: East St. Louis, October 15, 1978 (HDB-AB33:182); Horseshoe Lake, October 9, 1982 (RG); Lake Renwick, October 6, 1976 (Mlodinow 1984). The Little Blue Heron breeds south to Central and South America and winters from the Gulf of Mexico south.

TRICOLORED HERON

Egretta tricolor

RARE VAGRANT

The Tricolored is a bluish heron with an extraordinarily long bill, a white belly, and a buffy patch on the back. It is found in marshes, lake edges, and flooded fields. The first Illinois record was at Jackson Park, May 22, 1939 (Ford 1956). The second was near Fults, June 2 and July 6, 1968 (Graber et al. 1978). Subsequent records range in dates from April 14 (1985, Lake Calumet, JL) to October 30 (1984, Chicago area, HR-AB39:59). Most of these records are from the Chicago and East St. Louis areas. One to two birds have been at the Lake Calumet area every year since 1981, usually staying through the summer. Records away from these areas include Lake Springfield, October 4–5, 1976 (HDB); Kankakee River State Park, April 16, 1986 (BGl-AB40:476); Henderson County, May 17, 1986 (LMc,MB-AB40:476). This is a southern heron, and since most Tricoloreds in Illinois are recorded in spring, they may be overmigrants. These herons seem to do little postbreeding wandering. Indeed, practically all records are of adult

birds—a very different picture from other heron species that wander into Illinois.

REDDISH EGRET

Egretta rufescens

HYPOTHETICAL

Illinois records of the Reddish Egret, a heron of the southern United States and farther south, are based on remarks of Nelson (1877): "This species was quite common about the borders of lagoons and open marshy situations. They were exceedingly shy and rather solitary, being generally found away from the other species and when startled from a feeding place, instead of going off in company with the others, they usually took another direction." No specimens were taken, however, and it is difficult to believe that this heron was ever common even in 1875 as a postbreeding migrant. The only other record is a sighting reported at the Chain-of-Rocks Bridge, July 29, 1949 (Smith and Parmalee 1955), but the brief description (AFN4:18) does not exclude the possibility that it was a Little Blue Heron.

CATTLE EGRET

Bubulcus ibis

FAIRLY COMMON BUT IRREGULAR MIGRANT; UNCOMMON LOCAL SUMMER RESIDENT

A highly mobile species, the Cattle Egret is believed to have established itself naturally in the New World from its native Africa. There are reports of its presence in South America as early as 1877–82 and in 1911–12 (Palmer 1962). The first records for North America were in 1941 or 1942, and the first Illinois record was at Saganashkee Slough, August 10, 1952 (R.Pringle,CC-AFN6:284). However they arrived, these herons have spread over most of the United States and are now a part of the Illinois avifauna. As their name implies, they associate with cattle and other livestock, using them as beaters to stir up insects that the egrets feed on. Egrets especially favor grasshoppers and flies and such amphibians as toads. Though a Cattle Egret may occasionally be seen perched on a cow's back, the egret apparently does not take ticks off the animal but eats them when they fall off. Cattle Egrets are found on wet or dry pastures, marshes, mudflats, airfields, and golf courses. In spring the buff patches on their crowns, backs, and breasts make them easy to identify. The feathers of the chin always extend along the lower bill and give these egrets a distinctive profile. They usually are seen in flocks and are very tame. The subspecies in the New World is *B. i. ibis*.

The earliest spring migrants arrive in March: Banner, March 9, 1974 (Princen 1975); Carbondale, March 30, 1981 (DR-AB35:828); Wabash County, March 31, 1985

(LH-IB&B1:80). Average spring arrival dates: west-central, April 18 (nine years); Sangamon County, April 24 (13 years). High counts for spring: 275, Madison County, April 19, 1981 (RK-AB35:828); 103, Alexander County, May 26, 1985 (JR-AB39:306); 250 in flocks flying north, Monroe County, May 18, 1983 (BR-SR37:5); 55, Cass County, May 7, 1983 (RQR-SR37:5). Spring bird count totals ranged from 29 in 1972 to 553 in 1983; the highest count was 187 at Union County on May 4, 1985 (VK). Average departure dates for areas where they do not nest are west-central, May 9 (nine years), and Sangamon County, May 14 (nine years). There is some migration into late May or June. Like other herons, Cattle Egrets overmigrate and are found north of their breeding areas in spring.

Cattle Egrets usually nest in colonies with other herons. Their Illinois nesting colonies are at East St. Louis, Lake Renwick, Worley Lake, Alexander County, and Clear Lake. Breeding numbers fluctuate greatly; for example, there were 267 nests at East St. Louis in 1983 but only 13 in 1985. Robbins et al. (1986), using breeding bird survey data, found this egret to be increasing in numbers across North America. The mean number was 0.1 egret per survey route in Illinois. In 1983 an estimated 275 pairs were nesting in Illinois (Kleen 1983) and a high count of 1082 Cattle Egrets was recorded in Alexander County, June 3, 1985 (TF,KR-IB&B2:12). Little is known about the nesting cycle in Illinois. Cattle Egrets lay four to five pale blue eggs. Some of these egrets are seen away from their colonies during the summer: Havana, June 24-27, 1985 (KR-IB&B2:12); Henderson County, June 20, 1980 (LMc-SR26:2); Lake Calumet, June 5, 1982 (RM-SR34:3).

There may be some postbreeding dispersal northward from the more southerly colonies in July and August. These egrets start to move around by July: 25, Springfield, July 20, 1980 (HDB); 32, Carmen, July 15-18, 1984 (MB-IB&B1:13). Average arrival dates for fall migrants: west-central, September 6 (seven years); Sangamon County, August 10 (11 years). High counts for fall: 145, Pulaski County, September 4, 1982 (PK-AB37:186); 200, Henderson County, August 17, 1984 (RCe-AB39:59); 200, Belleville, September 17, 1983 (TF-SR39:5). Average fall departure dates: west-central, October 20 (seven years); Sangamon County, October 1 (11 years). Some of these egrets stay quite late: four, Ware, November 30, 1984 (KPi-IB&B1:13); three, Union County, December 4, 1984 (TF,JR-IB&B1:67); Jackson County, November 23, 1986 (DR-IB&B3:36); Carlyle Lake, December 7, 1975 (CMa-IAB176:29).

GREEN-BACKED HERON

Butorides striatus

COMMON MIGRANT AND SUMMER RESIDENT; VERY RARE WINTER RESIDENT

This small heron is found along creeks, at the edges of ponds and lakes, and in swamps. The Green-backed is one of the few herons that can be seen in city parks, although it rarely nests in them anymore. When flushed at a creek it typically flies up the creek giving its sharp *skeeow* call. It is usually seen alone, sometimes in a small group. It obtains its food by stalking along the edge of the water for fish and crayfish. A specimen taken in Franklin County on August 6, 1979, had grasshoppers in its gizzard.

Spring migrants usually arrive in April, but there are a couple of old March records and one for Carbondale, March 31, 1979 (HD-AB33:776). Early spring arrival dates: Anna, April 6, 1986 (DR-IB&B2:86); Crab Orchard National Wildlife Refuge, April 3, 1985 (JR-IB&B1:80); Jackson Park, April 9, 1981 (RG,PC-SR29:4). Average arrival dates: Chicago, April 28 (15 years); Urbana, April 23 (20 years); Sangamon County, April 16 (18 years). Spring bird count totals ranged from 170 in 1978 to 587 in 1984. All high counts are from northeastern Illinois, perhaps only reflecting the greater number of observers in that area. Highest count was 114, Cook County, May 7, 1983 (VK). Other maxima for spring: 17, Grand Tower, May 27, 1985 (RP-IB&B1:80); 20, Jackson Park, May 18, 1982 (PC,HR-SR33:4); 10, Oquawka, May 27, 1984 (MB-SR41:7). Although migration is mostly nocturnal, a Green-backed Heron soaring like a hawk was seen in daylight on May 7, 1983, in Sangamon County; it was obviously migrating. Others have been seen migrating along Lake Michigan.

As early as 1890 Barns at Lacon felt that Green-backed Heron populations were declining. Graber et al. (1978) show an 80 percent loss in numbers between 1909 and 1958 in Illinois. Robbins et al. (1986) suggest, however, that there have been significant recent increases in the central and eastern United States based on breeding bird survey data for 1965-79. The mean number of birds per survey route in Illinois was 0.5. Green-backed Herons nest solitarily or in small colonies that usually do not exceed 20 to 25 pairs, although Musselman estimated 500 nests at Lima Lake in 1922 (Graber et al. 1978). The nest is a platform of sticks and is usually built in a willow tree. There are two to five pale greenish blue eggs. Illinois egg dates are May 9 to July 3. In late summer family groups can be seen, but Green-backed Herons do not disperse after breeding like other herons. High counts for this season: 73, Cook County, June 8, 1985 (IB&B2:12); 18, Crab Orchard refuge, July 11, 1983 (JR-SR38:4); 60, Lake Calumet, summer 1984 (JL-SR41:7).

Fall migration probably begins in August and it, too, is mostly nocturnal, but I have seen Green-backed Herons migrating in the daytime before an advancing September cold front. Maximum counts for fall: 120, Palos and Lake Calumet, August 3, 1980 (Mlodinow 1984); 50, Big Muddy River, August 29, 1974 (VK,CC); 24, near Peoria, August 11, 1984 (VH-IB&B1:15); 45, Lake County, September 5, 1984 (JL). Average fall departure dates: Chicago, September 21 (14 years); west-central, September 30 (eight years). Some Green-backed Herons linger into November and later, especially in sheltered and warm-water areas. Christmas bird counts produced records in Macon County in

1959, 1983, and 1984; Vermilion County in 1971; Grundy in 1972; Cook/Du Page Counties in 1984; and Marshall County in 1987. The heron in Marshall County stayed until January 3. There is a winter record for Crab Orchard refuge for January 17, 1983 (TF-SR36:3). The Green-backed Heron winters in the southern coastal United States south to northern Colombia and Venezuela.

BLACK-CROWNED NIGHT-HERON

Nycticorax nycticorax

FAIRLY COMMON MIGRANT; UNCOMMON SUMMER AND RARE WINTER RESIDENT

When this chunky heron is encountered it is usually flopping out of some dense vegetation and giving out a *quok*. Black-crowned Night-Herons inhabit marshes, swamps, ponds, lakes, and occasionally sewage lagoons. As the name implies, they feed at night but also in the twilight hours. They migrate mostly nocturnally and can be heard calling as they pass overhead. In daytime they can be seen sitting quietly in trees or dense vegetation, usually at water's edge. Adults in breeding plumage are patterned black, gray, and white with white plumes on the back of their heads. Immatures are streaked buff and brown ventrally; dorsally they are brown spotted with buff. These herons eat mostly fish, including gizzard shad, carp, and sunfish (Graber et al. 1978). Like other large birds that make good targets, they are still being shot by hunters. As a result of habitat destruction as well as shooting, they are on the Illinois endangered list. Black-crowned Night-Herons are nearly worldwide in distribution. The subspecies found in the United States is *N. n. hoactli*. A melanistic Black-crowned was seen at McGinnis Slough on August 7, 1937 (Pitelka 1938).

Though some of these herons spend the winter in Illinois, spring migration is fairly easily discernible. Earliest spring arrival dates: Lake Renwick, March 18, 1984 (JM-SR41:7); Chicago, March 15, 1987 (CM). Average arrival dates: Urbana, April 8 (17 years); Chicago, April 17 (nine years); Sangamon County, April 8 (17 years). High counts for spring: 163, Madison County, May 27, 1981 (RA-SR29:4); 455, Lake Renwick, April 29, 1986 (JM-IB&B2:86); 363, Lake Calumet, May 20, 1987 (JM); 100, Barrington, April 19, 1987 (CM). Spring bird count totals ranged from 86 in 1972 to 931 in 1984; the high count was 378 in Will County, May 5, 1984 (VK). In areas where these herons do not breed, average spring departure dates are Chicago, May 24 (nine years), and Sangamon County, May 15 (15 years).

The Black-crowned, like other heron species, is declining in numbers and has been for the past half-century. In 1987 there were eight known colonies in Illinois, ranging in size from 28 nests at Clear Lake to 659 nests in Madison County. The statewide total was 1900 nesting pairs (VK). Graber et al. (1978) list all the known colonies for Illinois. These herons nest in trees or in marshes, sometimes with other species, including Great Blue Herons, Great Egrets, and Little Blue Herons. They lay three to six greenish blue eggs on a rather flat platform nest. Illinois egg dates are May 10 to June.

After the nesting season part of the population moves north before returning south. This movement usually swells the numbers recorded in Illinois during July and August. Some of these herons have wandered as early as June 23 into Sangamon County. Average fall arrival dates: Chicago, September 13 (nine years); Sangamon County, August 17 (13 years). High counts for fall: 150, Horseshoe Lake, August 17, 1984 (TF-IB&B1:13); 141, Lake Renwick, August 29, 1984 (JM-IB&B1:13); 85, Mason County, August 24, 1986 (TP-IB&B3:36); 200, Horseshoe Lake, September 14, 1979 (BR-AB343:166). Average fall departure dates: Chicago, September 17 (nine years); Sangamon County, October 22 (10 years).

Some of these birds stay on and apparently attempt to overwinter, though the preponderance of December over January and February dates suggests that the lingerers either move on or die off. Black-crowned Night-Herons showed up on Christmas bird counts in seven of the past 10 years, in numbers ranging from one to 14 (in 1984). Highest count was Chicago urban with 12 in 1984. Other winter records: six, Horseshoe Lake, January 27, 1981—but only one by February 7 (BR-AB35:304); 12, Chicago, January 23, 1985 (RB-AB39:172); one or two, Chicago, all winter, 1986–87 (AB41:286); 14, Horseshoe Lake, January 1, 1988 (RG). Recently, a few have overwintered most years at Horseshoe Lake.

YELLOW-CROWNED NIGHT-HERON

Nycticorax violaceus

UNCOMMON MIGRANT AND SUMMER RESIDENT DECREASING NORTHWARD

This night-heron has longer legs than the Black-crowned, and the adults have a distinctive face pattern. Immatures have smaller spots on the back, but the bill and head shape, which are distinctive in Yellow-crowns, are more useful in making an identification. The call note, *quark*, is pitched higher than the call of the Black-crowned. Yellow-crowns are found in swamps and marshes, at the shallow ends of lakes, and particularly at sloughs that are drying up. Ridgway (1895) found their food to be mostly crayfish and frogs. Yellow-crowns are more solitary than some other herons, but they also occur in small groups. I have seen Yellow-crowns migrating at dusk at Lake Springfield. They apparently are more diurnal in their feeding habits than the

Black-crowns. The subspecies found in Illinois is *N. v. vio-lacea.*

Early arrival dates for spring migrants include Oakwood Bottoms, March 22, 1986 (TF-AB40:476); Mark Twain National Wildlife Refuge, March 29, 1986 (HW-IB&B2:86); Palos, March 31, 1963 (LB). Average spring arrival dates: west-central, April 30 (eight years); Sangamon County, April 23 (nine years). High counts for spring: nine, Grand Tower, May 1, 1985 (VK-IB&B1:80); four, Tazewell County, April 23, 1986 (TP-IB&B2:86). Spring bird count totals ranged from 10 in 1972 and 1974 to 35 in 1977; the highest count was 14, Jackson County, May 7, 1977 (VK).

Unlike most herons, the Yellow-crowned usually nests solitarily but will also nest with other heron species or in a small group of Yellow-crowns. It usually nests in trees, lay-ing two to four pale greenish blue eggs. Illinois egg dates are from late April to early June (Graber et al. 1978). Recent nesting areas or suspected areas include 10 to 12 pairs, Grafton, 1977 (JEa-AB31:1147); eight birds, Peoria County, 1981 (VH-AB35:944); 21, Jackson County, July 24, 1986 (DR-AB40:1209); seven adults, Union County, May 28–June 4, 1982 (PK-SR34:4); two nests, Chicago, 1983 (AA-AB37:993); eight birds, Lake Calumet, 1980 (RB- AB34:899); four to five nests with young, Lawrence County, July 8, 1984 (LH,DJo-IB&B1:15).

Fall migration is mostly an exodus from the breeding areas, but there may be some northward dispersal. Average arrival date for fall migrants in Sangamon County is August 22 (eight years). High fall counts: 18, Peoria County, August 3, 1980 (VH-AB35:188); 10, Mark Twain National Wildlife Refuge, September 26, 1981 (RK-AB36:182). Average fall departure dates: west-central, October 9 (three years); Sangamon County, September 24 (six years). Late departure dates: immature, Lake Springfield, November 8, 1979 (HDB,RB); immature, Jackson Park, October 9, 1983 (PC,HR-SR39:5). Yellow-crowned Night-Herons winter south to Costa Rica and Panama.

WHITE IBIS

Eudocimus albus

VERY RARE VAGRANT

The White Ibis breeds in marshes, swamps, and mangroves in the southern United States. Most members of this species seen in Illinois have been immatures, probably individuals dispersing after the breeding season. Nonetheless, two of the 15 records are for spring. One of them was the first Illinois White Ibis record, seven to eight birds seen in May 1878 near Mount Carmel (Ridgway 1895). The other was an adult seen on May 2–3, 1964, at Moredock Lake in Monroe County (George-IAB130:19). All other records are from late summer or autumn (July 4–October 29). Most records are for southern Illinois, but there is one for northern Illinois—Shabbona Lake State Park, July 23–27,

1980 (WS-AB34:899)—and three for central Illinois: Allen-ville, August 11–15, 1980 (RCot-AB35:188); specimens (no date), Quincy (Widmann 1907) and Greene County, August 1917 (Smith and Parmalee 1955). Recent records: immature, St. Clair County, July 31–August 1, 1987 (JM, photograph on cover IB&B3,#3); immature, Jackson County, October 29, 1983 (Nawrot-SR39:5); immature, Alexander County, July 5, 1986 (DR-AB40:1209); two, Lake Carlyle, August 1978 (AB33:182); immature, MacDonough Lake, Madison County, September 8, 1978 (BR-AB33:182); immature, Horseshoe Lake, September 21–23, 1977 (BR,PS,JG).

GLOSSY IBIS

Plegadis falcinellus

RARE VAGRANT

Dark ibises—the Glossy and the White-faced—are fairly easy to separate in spring if the color of the bare parts (facial skin, bill, eye, and legs) can be seen. In fall immatures are very difficult if not impossible to identify. "Field Identifica-tion of White-faced and Glossy Ibises" (Pratt 1976) provides a detailed discussion of the two species, which some authors consider conspecific. Apparently the only supposed Glossy Ibis specimen for Illinois, a male from East St. Louis, February 27, 1880 (Hurter 1881), is actually a White-faced Ibis (see Ridgway 1895).

These long-legged birds with decurved bills occur in marshes and wet fields and at the shallow ends of lakes. They usually breed in coastal areas, but some nest as close to Illinois as Arkansas. Most spring records of the Glossy Ibis occur in May, but one was photographed at Chillicothe on April 14, 1972 (R. Scott, on file ISM). Spring records, some of which are probably questionable as to specific identification, include Horseshoe Lake, May 6, 1951, and Lake Calumet, May 24, 1953 (Smith and Parmalee 1955); Decatur, May 2, 1956 (Chaniot,Mannering-AFN10:337); near Naperville, May 16, 1962, and two, Lake Calumet, May 20, 1962 (Mlodinow 1984); Lake Calumet, May 10, 1969 (CC-AFN23:596); near Havana, May 21, 1976, and near Pecatonica, May 23, 1975 (Bohlen 1978); two, Springfield, May 4, 1982 (HDB); Granite City, May 15, 1984 (PS,RG-AB38:916).

Fall records, probably even more unreliable than spring records, extend from June 28 (1988, Horseshoe Lake, D. Bozzay) to October 21 (1962, Barrington, RR-AFN17:36). Other fall records: Mark Twain National Wildlife Refuge, October 1, 1964 (SV-AFN19:45); one banded and photo-graphed, Cuba, September 13, 1970 (Pointer-AB25:65); East St. Louis, July 22–25, 1971 (JEC-AB25:863); Sangchris, September 9, 1971 (HDB); Union County Con-servation Area, October 13, 1973 (MHm-AB28:59).

Several other birds thought to be *Plegadis* species have been sighted, but unless they are well observed, dark ibises should be identified only to genus. The unidentified birds were seen from August 26 to November 3.

WHITE-FACED IBIS

Plegadis chihi

RARE VAGRANT

The White-faced Ibis is the western counterpart of the Glossy Ibis. The now-missing specimen of Hurter (1881), taken at East St. Louis on February 27, 1880, was first identified as a Glossy, but it was certainly a White-faced if it had a red iris (see Ridgway 1895). There are 11 records of this species in Illinois, 10 of them in spring: Powderhorn Marsh, May 30, 1965 (LB-IAB135:11); two, Peoria, April 24 (one until May 1), 1967, and one near Gorham, May 6, 1972 (Bohlen 1978); Monroe County, May 5–7, 1978 (BR,RA-AB32:1013); one to three, Horseshoe Lake, April 28–May 4, 1980 (AB34:781); three, Mark Twain National Wildlife Refuge, May 3–4, 1980 (HW,PS-AB34:781); Horseshoe Lake, May 16, 1981 (PS-AB35:829); Lawrence County, April 20, 1985 (DJo-AB39:306); Granite City, April 27–29, 1985 (JEa,RBo-IB&B1:80). The only fall record is from Centerville, September 10–22, 1983 (RG,PS-AB38:208). This species is usually found around fresh water. It once bred as close to Illinois as Minnesota and now seems to be regaining some of its historic range.

ROSEATE SPOONBILL

Ajaia ajaja

EXTIRPATED

Most Illinois records of this wader are vague, but Parmalee and Perino (1970) reported that a Roseate Spoonbill skeleton was found at an archaeological site in Calhoun County, a Hopewellian burial mound built about A.D. 150–250. The Spoonbill, an adult, was buried with humans. This spectacular Gulf Coast bird could have been obtained in trade with Indians farther south. A second Illinois record is a specimen from Adams County, April 28, 1887, taken by O. C. Poling (Musselman 1921). This specimen apparently was not preserved. Musselman states that the Spoonbill was "reported to be an occasional resident of southern [Illinois] swamps about 1850." Ridgway (1895) "was informed, in 1879, by a taxidermist whom I have every reason to believe reliable, that some twenty years previously, or about 1859, he shot several specimens about some ponds in the Mississippi Bottoms, below St. Louis." There are no recent records, but the Spoonbill could occur in Illinois as a wanderer; there is a recent Missouri record.

WOOD STORK

Mycteria americana

VERY RARE VAGRANT OR POSTBREEDING WANDERER

This is the only stork that occurs in Illinois, and it has not been seen in 20 years. It nests in swamps and marshes along the Gulf Coasts and wanders north, usually after the breeding season. There are several early fall records: a specimen shot in August on the Sangamon River near Springfield (Kennicott 1854); two specimens taken in Fayette County, July 28, 1898 (ISM); nine birds seen along the Wabash River, September 11, 1888 (Everman 1889); six near East St. Louis, August 10–14, 1879 (Widmann 1880); 50 near East St. Louis, August to September 5, 1880 (Hurter 1881). Nelson (1877) found Wood Storks very common near Cairo from August 11 to September 4, 1875; he saw a flock of 50 near Mound City and collected several. He noted that "they would commence fishing early in the morning and by seven or eight o'clock would be comfortably gorged, when they would gather in small groups on the sandbar and stand dozing in the sun until about noon or after, when some of the members would rise high overhead and soar about with motionless wings in company with the buzzards." Ridgway (1895) frequently saw Wood Storks soaring in broad circles over the Wabash River at Mount Carmel.

Eaton (1926) found decomposed remains in the Little Wabash bottoms on September 6, 1925. He also relates a secondhand sighting of 25 in Lawrence County two weeks earlier. Carson (1926) studied a flock of 50 in Jefferson County from July 30 to August 23, 1925. A Wood Stork was seen at Horseshoe Lake, Alexander County, in September 1941; a small flock was at Du Quoin in early fall 1945; 12 were seen on the Mississippi mudflats in Jackson County, August 3, 1949; and one was at Horseshoe Lake, August 26, 1952 (Smith and Parmalee 1955). There were no more records until 40 were seen in Union County in 1960 (Comfort 1961) and 23 were found at Fults Marsh, August 8, 1963 (Anderson 1964). The most recent records all belong to Musselman and are from central Illinois: Beardstown, September 11, 1966 (AFN21:44); two, Quincy, late May 1967 (AFN21:513); two, Quincy, late September 1967 (AFN22:48).

These interesting birds could occur again, especially in southern Illinois, but numbers in the southern United States are declining. It should be noted that all records are for late summer and fall except the one May record. There are apparently no records from northern Illinois.

GREATER FLAMINGO

Phoenicopterus ruber

HYPOTHETICAL

Flamingos seen in Illinois are certainly escapees from zoos or private collections, although some wild birds apparently wander north (AOU 1983). Available records for Illinois include a Greater Flamingo seen with Great Blue Herons, Putnam County, fall 1981 (SR31:18); one seen in Mason and Fulton Counties, September 28–October 3, 1959 (AFN14:39); and one seen in Chicago, July 28, 1966 (PD).

FULVOUS WHISTLING-DUCK

Dendrocygna bicolor

VERY RARE VAGRANT

This duck is a great wanderer, with records in a majority of states. It has southern affinities, being found in California, Nevada, Arizona, Texas, and Louisiana south to central Mexico. Of five Illinois records, the first is a specimen taken at Chicago, December 4, 1884, by Gault (RG-CAS). The second is of a male killed off Government Pier in Chicago on December 7, 1919 (Moyer 1931). This mounted specimen was never deposited in an institution where it could be examined. The next record was of two birds near Horseshoe Lake, September 2, 1933 (Ernst 1934). On August 24–25, 1974, another Fulvous Whistling-Duck was seen just north of the Big Muddy River, Jackson County, by Madding and Bell. This bird was later seen by several other observers. The last and most spectacular sighting was of 22 birds at Dundee, May 18, 1979. They were photographed by Robert Montgomery. One reported killed in Adams County in 1915 was actually taken in Missouri (Widmann 1909).

This duck inhabits dense marshy areas and is not as much of a tree percher as the Black-bellied Whistling-Duck. It has a long neck and long legs and behaves somewhat like a goose. Its call is a long squealing whistle.

BLACK-BELLIED WHISTLING-DUCK

Dendrocygna autumnalis

HYPOTHETICAL

This striking duck is native to south Texas and south to southern Brazil and northern Argentina. Moyer (1931) reported a Black-bellied Whistling-Duck shot by a hunter and mounted by a taxidermist, but the whereabouts of the specimen is unknown. The bird was reported taken from a tree along the Illinois River near La Salle on September 15, 1930. This long-necked, long-legged species readily perches in trees. In Mexico it is called the *pe-che-che-ne* after the peculiar whistle it gives while on the wing.

TUNDRA SWAN

Cygnus columbianus

OCCASIONAL MIGRANT; RARE WINTER RESIDENT

Tundra Swans migrate mainly east-west, breeding in the Arctic and wintering on the Atlantic Coast. Most pass north of Illinois, but some years moderate-sized flights occur across the northern part of the state. A very few apparently migrate down the Illinois and Mississippi Rivers. Swans fly in V-formations or in lines. They sometimes rest on deep-water lakes, but when feeding they prefer the shallow waters of overflow areas, ponds, or flooded fields. These swans feed on waste corn and aquatic vegetation obtained by using their long necks. Immature Tundras are grayish; adults are white. The Tundra Swan holds its head and neck erect, while the Mute Swan's neck is curved and its head is held downward.

Swans are late migrants in fall, usually not arriving in Illinois until late October or early November. Early arrival records: eight, Mode, October 4, 1984 (KF-AB39:59); three, Belvidere, October 14, 1985 (EB-IB&B2:43); 80, Evanston, October 5, 1986 (RD-IB&B3:36). Maximum counts for fall: 190, Oswego, November 13–14, 1985 (EB-AB40:118); 136, Wilmette, November 28, 1985 (JL,CM-IB&B2:44); 64, Palos, November 3–28, 1984 (JL-AB39:59). Because some Tundras winter in Illinois, late dates of departure are obscured, but most leave by early to mid-December.

As early as 1888 Cooke noted that Tundra Swans occasionally wintered in Illinois. Nowadays some winter where semidomestic waterfowl are given food and a body of water is artificially kept from freezing. Others winter on warm-water lakes. They associate with geese at times and sleep on ice-covered lakes. These swans were noted on seven of the last 10 Christmas bird counts; the high count was 12, Alexander County, 1978. Other winter records: 16, Jasper County, 1981–82 (LH-AB36:299); Peoria, January 22, 1980 (BB-SR24:2); 48, Johnsburg, January 28–31, 1983 (DF-SR36:3); nine, Pittsfield, January 14, 1985 (JF-IB&B1:67).

Spring migration starts as early as February. Spring arrival dates: three, Grand Tower, February 13, 1983 (PK-SR37:5); 18, Lake Sangchris, February 15, 1982 (HDB); four, Carlyle Lake, February 10, 1985 (LH-IB&B1:80). High counts for spring: 600 along Lake Michigan, late March 1979 (AB33:776); 18, Nauvoo, April 9, 1980 (JWar-SR25:3); 15, Boone County, March 31, 1987 (EB); 39, Palos, April 3, 1985 (JM-IB&B1:80). Spring bird counts, though very late (May 4–7) for swans, produced one to two Tundras two years each in Lake County, 1974 and 1983, and McHenry

County, 1972 and 1979 (VK). Spring departure dates: Streator, May 8, 1985 (JMc-IB&B1:80); two, Lake Calumet, May 10, 1958; Kane County, May 11, 1974 (Mlodinow 1984).

TRUMPETER SWAN

Cygnus buccinator

EXTIRPATED; FORMERLY A MIGRANT, A SUMMER RESIDENT, AND, IN SOUTHERN ILLINOIS, A WINTER RESIDENT

The largest waterfowl in North America, the Trumpeter Swan probably disappeared from Illinois as early as the 1880s. Schorger (1964) gives several early accounts of Trumpeter Swans: Marquette (1903) in northern Illinois, June 17, 1673; Liette (1947) in central Illinois, along the Illinois River in August (?) 1702; Kellogg (1903) near Chicago, August or early September (?) 1710; and Peale (1946–47) at the mouth of the Kaskaskia River, June 4 or 5, 1819. Audubon (1929) saw two swans near Little America on the Ohio River, November 15, 1820.

More recently, Musselman (1921) stated that an occasional Trumpeter Swan was reported to nest at Lima Lake in the "early days." Coale (1915) noted that F. Smith of the University of Illinois obtained a specimen from W. N. Butler of Anna in 1880, but it had no data. Cooke (1888) listed spring migrants at Shawneetown, March 19, 1885, and Paris, March 31, 1885, although these and some of the other records could well refer to Tundra (Whistling) Swans. It is believed, however, that most swans seen in summer or early autumn were Trumpeters, since Tundras migrate early in spring and late in fall and are not present in summer.

Trumpeter Swans apparently arrived in mid-March and departed the last of October. They nested at least in northern and central Illinois and wintered casually along the major rivers in southern Illinois.

Wetmore (1935) reported that bones of this species were found near the Fox River, Aurora, Kane County, in late Pleistocene deposits. Parmalee (1958) reported 375 bones, mostly from Cahokia but also from Indian sites in Will and Calhoun Counties. Because Trumpeter Swans become flightless when molting from late June to mid-August, they were easily obtained by the Indians for food and ornaments.

This bird can weigh as much as 38 pounds and has a wingspread of eight to ten feet. Its call is like the notes of a French horn. Although Trumpeters were thought to be close to extinction around the turn of the century, they have made a slight comeback and new populations have been discovered in Alaska. Bellrose (1976) estimated a population of 3600 to 4400 at the end of the breeding season. These swans will probably occur again in Illinois, either as migrants from the north—they have already appeared in winter in nearby Missouri—or as a result of the tentative introduction of individuals at Fermilab in Du Page County. Trumpeters are also being introduced in Wisconsin. It is too soon to assess the status of these birds in Illinois.

MUTE SWAN

Cygnus olor

INTRODUCED; NOW AN UNCOMMON PERMANENT RESIDENT LOCALLY AND A RARE MIGRANT

This is the swan found in zoos, parks, and, more recently, in Illinois in the wild. Mute Swans were released in Fulton County in 1971, and other introductions followed. Some have also escaped from captivity both private and public, so that Mutes are now fairly widespread in Illinois. There may be some migration by feral populations from other states such as Michigan and Wisconsin. Of two Mute Swans seen on the Mississippi River at Grafton from January 6 to February 9, 1985, one had been banded at Eagle, Wisconsin, on July 6, 1984, when it was young and flightless (RG). Bellrose (1976) noted that four of the swans released in Fulton County returned to Traverse Bay, Michigan, their place of origin, in the winter (1971–72) following their release. Adult Mute Swans are distinctive, with a curved neck and raised wings when swimming, an orange bill, and a black face.

At least nine counties have reported from three to 28 Mute Swans on spring bird counts. Highest count was 15 in Edgar County, 1983 (VK). Christmas bird count totals for 1976–85 ranged from four in 1976 to 25 in 1984. Highest count was 20 at Crane Lake in 1984. Breeding now occurs yearly where these swans are established, including Fulton and Du Page Counties.

GREATER WHITE-FRONTED GOOSE

Anser albifrons

OCCASIONAL SPRING MIGRANT; RARE FALL MIGRANT AND WINTER RESIDENT

Although the principal migration corridor of the Greater White-fronted Goose is west of the Mississippi River, in some years the right winds guide fairly large flocks into Illinois. Numbers thus are subject to a substantial year-to-year fluctuation. The subspecies found in Illinois is *A. a. frontalis*, which breeds in the Arctic from western Alaska to northeastern Keewatin. White-fronts—or "Speckled Bellies," as hunters refer to them—are easy to identify at close range but difficult to distinguish from other geese at any distance except when their call can be heard. The call is unique: a high-pitched laugh.

Timing of the Greater White-Front's spring migration varies according to the weather. It can arrive as early as February or a month later, in mid-March. Early spring arrival dates: three, Horseshoe Lake, February 8, 1986 (RG-IB&B2:87); five, Springfield, February 17, 1985 (HDB). Average spring arrival dates: west-central, February 29 (seven years); Sangamon County, March 11 (11 years). The western part of the state, closer to the migration corridor, has more sightings and more birds. High counts for spring: 75, Horseshoe Lake, March 18, 1980 (BR-AB34:781); 58, Wabash County, March 10, 1985 (LH-IB&B1:80); 51, Knox County, March 30, 1985 (MB-IB&B1:80); 21, Walconda, March 26, 1982 (Mlodinow 1984). Spring bird counts are too late in the season to find these geese in any sizable numbers; only one or two individuals were recorded in four of 15 years. Most Greater White-fronts pass through quickly, again depending on suitable weather. They often feed in winter wheatfields and in cornfields left over from the previous year but are especially fond of shallow-water areas and grassflats. Average spring departure dates: west-central, March 22 (seven years); Sangamon County, April 5 (nine years). Occasionally a few individuals linger into May: two, Olney, May 10, 1986 (LH-IB&B2:87); Mendota, May 1, 1984 (JH-SR41:8); Union County Conservation Area, May 6, 1972 (VK-AB26:766). There is one June date, but the origin of the bird is in question: Rochwood, June 6–12, 1982 (BSh-SR34:4).

Far fewer Greater White-fronts are seen in fall. The Illinois and Mississippi River valleys are the places to look for them at this season, since they like the extensive grassflats created by drying lakes. Fall arrival dates: six, Whiteside County, October 11, 1985 (BSh-IB&B2:44); two, Chautauqua National Wildlife Refuge, October 9, 1984 (RBj-IB&B1:13); Crab Orchard National Wildlife Refuge, October 9, 1983 (TF,JR-SR39:6); five, Rend Lake, October 14, 1984 (LH-IB&B1:13). Average fall arrival date for four years in Sangamon County is October 17. Maximum counts in fall: 77, Chautauqua refuge, October 21, 1978 (RBj-AB33:182); 42, Batavia, October 23, 1985 (DCa-AB40:119); 55, Springfield, October 24, 1985 (HDB); 44, Douglas County, October 24, 1985 (RBr-IB&B2:44). Most Greater White-fronts are gone by the end of November. Late fall departure dates: four, La Salle County, November 24, 1985 (LA,JM-IB&B2:44); nine, Carlyle Lake, December 2, 1984 (LH-IB&B1:13); Mark Twain National Wildlife Refuge, November 24, 1982 (BR,RG-SR35:4).

Cooke (1888) stated that in mild years this goose wintered in southern Illinois. Yet today the Greater White-front is rare in winter. Although there are records for eight of the 10 Christmas bird counts for 1976–85, the numbers are low; four in Union County in 1977 was the highest. Other winter records: Jefferson County, January 19, 1985 (JR-IB&B1:67); two, Crab Orchard refuge, January 8, 1983 (JR-SR36:4); three, Canton, January 17, 1987 (MB-AB41:287); Rockford, December 18–February 23, 1984 (DW-SR40:4). Most wintering Greater White-fronts are found among huge concentrations of Canada Geese, although an occasional white-front gets mixed in with domestic fowl at ponds and lakes. One immature arrived at Baldwin Lake in November 1985 and was still there as an adult in March 1988 (RG).

The main wintering areas of the Greater White-fronted Goose are from the Gulf Coast of Texas and Louisiana south to interior Mexico.

BAR-HEADED GOOSE
Anser indicus

HYPOTHETICAL; PROBABLE ESCAPES

A Siberian species that is commonly kept in captivity in the United States, the Bar-headed Goose has been reported a few times in Illinois: Crab Orchard National Wildlife Refuge, December 22, 1961 (AFN16:209); St. Clair County, April 7, 1986 (TF-IB&B2:97); Horseshoe Lake, May 3, 1981 (BR). Sightings of this goose should continue to be reported to see if any patterns emerge.

SNOW GOOSE
Chen caerulescens

FAIRLY COMMON MIGRANT ESPECIALLY IN THE STATE'S WESTERN AREAS; UNCOMMON WINTER RESIDENT DECREASING NORTHWARD

A typical flock of Snow Geese contains white-phase, blue-phase, and a few mixed white and blue birds. Usually in Illinois the blue phase outnumbers the white. In flight, Snow Geese do not have the regular V-formation of Canada Geese but form a U or an irregular mass. They have a more rapid wingbeat than Canada Geese and their call is a high-pitched yelp (Bellrose 1976). Snow Geese breed in the Arctic tundra; those migrating through Illinois come from around Hudson Bay. In Illinois they are found near water, resting on lakes, or feeding in fields, especially on waste corn. I once saw a blue Snow Goose avoid capture by a Bald Eagle by diving into a lake from several feet in the air and staying underwater long enough for the eagle to leave.

Early fall migrants include eight, Jackson Park, September 11, 1983 (PC,HR-SR39:6), and two, Sangamon County, September 16, 1980 (HDB). Average fall arrival dates: west-central, October 15 (10 years); Sangamon County, October 7 (18 years). Peak numbers for fall: 2200, Chautauqua National Wildlife Refuge, November 27-29, 1984 (KR-IB&B1:13); 1000, Baldwin Lake, November 12, 1984 (JR-IB&B1:13); 10,000, Mark Twain National Wildlife Refuge, November 21, 1981 (RK-SR31:4); 21,000, Mississippi and Illinois Rivers, early December 1981 (SR31:5). Departure dates vary with the severity of the weather, but averages are west-central, November 10 (10 years), and Sangamon County, December 1 (14 years).

Some years Snow Geese winter in considerable numbers in Illinois, usually in the west-central and southern parts of the state. They did not start doing so until the 1950s, but by the late 1960s 10,000 to 15,000 were wintering in Illinois (Bellrose 1976). On Christmas bird counts for 1976–85, Pere Marquette State Park had all the high counts except for one year. Christmas count totals ranged from 749 in 1984 to 15,026 in 1979. Highest count for the white phase was 6000 at Pere Marquette in 1962; for the blue phase it was 12,742 at Crane Lake in 1974. Other winter counts: 10,000, Mark Twain refuge, 1980–81 (SR28:2); 1000, Baldwin Lake, 1983–84 (RG-SR40:4); 130, Braidwood, December 22, 1984 (JM-IB&B1:67); 6000, Massac County, February 1, 1986—possibly spring migrants (JR-IB&B2:74). Most of the Snow Geese that pass through Illinois winter on the west Gulf Coast.

Spring migration starts as soon as weather permits in late January or February. Average spring arrival dates: west-central, February 27 (nine years); Sangamon County, March 3 (15 years). High counts for spring: 13,160, Mississippi and Illinois Rivers, March 7–9, 1983 (RC-SR37:6); 1500, Carlyle Lake, March 11, 1984 (LH,DJo-SR41:8); 2000, Kidd Lake, March 2, 1986 (BR,RG-IB&B2:87); 5000, Hancock County, March 10, 1985 (RCe-IB&B1:80). Spring bird counts are taken far past the time of peak numbers for this goose, but some Snow Geese were recorded every spring. Numbers ranged from one in 1972 to 58 in 1984. High counts should be considered very unusual for these dates: 50, La Salle County, May 7, 1977; 56, Pike County, May 5, 1984 (VK). Average spring departure dates: west-central, April 8 (nine years); Sangamon County, March 29 (15 years). Some Snow Geese found in summer must be lost or nonbreeding birds: Saline County, May 28, 1985 (KP-IB&B1:80); Champaign County, 1980 (RCh-SR 26:3); female, mated with domestic African Goose producing three young, Cook County, 1980 (PD-SR26:3); white phase, Cook County, July 14–30, 1976 (RE,LB-AB30:962); blue phase, Deerfield, July 30, 1976 (RE-AB30:962).

ROSS' GOOSE

Chen rossii

RARE MIGRANT AND WINTER RESIDENT

The status of this small goose in Illinois has changed dramatically in the past few years. After the first record, a Ross' Goose bagged by a hunter at Horseshoe Lake, Alexander County, on November 26, 1956 (Smart 1960), there were no other records until 1980. Since then Ross' Geese have been located in flocks of Snow Geese nearly every spring and fall and sometimes in winter. There are now more than 20 records, with dates ranging from November 3 to April 3. This goose has been seen at Baldwin Lake for

at least the past five years. Most Ross' have been seen in central and southern Illinois, but there are two records for northern Illinois. High counts: three, Baldwin Lake, January 4, 1986 (AB40:286); five, Springfield, March 8, 1988 (HDB). Other recent records: two, Massac County, February 1, 1986 (JR-IB&B2:74); two, Wabash County, March 9–10, 1985 (LH, DJo-IB&B1:80); two, Savannah, November 16, 1985 (PP-IB&B2:44); near Streator, March 27–April 3, 1985 (LMc-AB39:306).

The Ross' Goose is much smaller than the Snow Goose and has a smaller, stubbier bill with a purplish warty area at the base. It has a steeper forehead and a short thick neck; it also lacks a grin patch and ocher on the head. The legs are bright pinkish purple. Immatures are whiter than immature Snow Geese and can be identified by size and bill. A blue phase exists, but it has not been reported in Illinois. The Ross' Goose breeds in the high Arctic and winters mostly in California.

BRANT

Branta bernicla

VERY RARE MIGRANT

The Brant is a small Mallard-sized dark goose that breeds in the Arctic and winters along the coasts of North America, Europe, and Asia. A light-bellied form is found in eastern North America and Europe and a dark-bellied form in western North America and Asia. In Illinois the Brant has occurred at least 19 times, with 17 of the records pertaining to the light form. The two dark-form Brant were seen at Lincoln Park, October 9, 1932 (Clark and Nice 1950), and in Rock Island County, October 24, 1977 (PP-AB32:211). Of the Illinois records only two are in spring; both of these birds were seen and photographed in southern Illinois: one on the Illinois levee below St. Louis, May 4–6, 1968 (RA,JEC,JRu-AFN22:532), and one at Baldwin Lake, March 30–April 5, 1987 (VHa). Most of the records come from the Great Lakes area, and all records of more than one bird are from there. High counts include a remarkable 60, McGinnis Slough, November 1943 (Coursen 1947); 17, Evanston, November 12, 1982 (JG-AB37:186); five, Great Lakes, November 14–December 10, 1982 (JL-AB37:186). Most Brant in Illinois are seen in October and November, but one bird stayed at Waukegan until January 1, 1983 (AB37:306). Brant that occur downstate are usually with other geese and stay for a few days feeding in fields. Some old records are questionable because Snow Geese and other waterfowl are sometimes called Brant.

BARNACLE GOOSE

Branta leucopsis

HYPOTHETICAL; PROBABLE ESCAPES

This Eurasian goose occurs rarely in North America, mainly on the East Coast. Some records for this species may be of wild birds, but it is impossible to distinguish them from birds that have escaped from captivity. Nonetheless, observers should continue to report sightings of Barnacle Geese. There are three records for Illinois: two, Lisle Arboretum, December 8, 1968 (PD-IAB 149:15); one with a flock of Snow Geese, Union County Conservation Area, January 3, 1981 (VK-AB35;306); one with Canada Geese, Durand, January 1–30, 1983 (LJ,DW-AB37:309).

CANADA GOOSE

Branta canadensis

COMMON MIGRANT; ABUNDANT WINTER
RESIDENT IN SOUTHERN ILLINOIS
DECREASING NORTHWARD; FAIRLY
COMMON SUMMER RESIDENT

The honking of Canada Geese and their V-formations as they migrate overhead are signs of the changing seasons for many people in Illinois. These geese are found on lakes, ponds, and river overflow areas and in fields. They usually feed in cornfields but also in other small grainfields, pastures, and soybean fields. They feed on many kinds of grasses and weed seeds. Canada Geese have benefited from agricultural practices, and today there are more than ever. Canadas have been introduced into several parts of the state and are breeding and spreading as summer residents. There are several subspecies in Illinois. The most common is *B. c. interior,* the race that winters primarily in southern Illinois. It breeds mainly in marshy bogs on the west coast of James Bay and the southwest coast of Hudson Bay (Bellrose 1976). The Canadas that breed in Illinois are mostly *B. c. maxima,* the "Giant" Canada Goose. The small race found in Illinois is probably *B. c. hutchinsii,* which breeds on the Arctic Coast of the Northwest Territory.

Spring migration is controlled by the weather. Canada Geese move northward during warming periods, even though sometimes the ice is still thick on the lakes. Migration may start as early as late January. In fact, there may be some going back and forth with false springs. Average spring arrival dates: west-central, February 20 (nine years); Sangamon County, February 16 (17 years). Peak numbers: 45,000, Mississippi and Illinois Rivers, March 7–9, 1983 (RC-SR37:6); 42,000, Canton, February 28, 1987 (MB); 13,500, heading south along the Chicago lakeshore, March 14, 1979 (RB-AB33:776); 15,000, Sangnois, March 1, 1986 (RP,MB-IB&B2:87); 12,000, Springfield, March 1, 1986 (HDB). Spring bird counts are taken too late to record peak numbers of Canada Geese, since much of the migration is already past. Spring bird count totals ranged from 309 in 1973 to 5114 in 1986, showing an upward trend in breeding birds in Illinois. Du Page County had the highest count: 1219 on May 10, 1986 (VK). Most migrants leave in April. Average spring departure dates: west-central, May 6 (nine years); Sangamon County, April 18 (16 years).

Both Ridgway (1895) and Nelson (1876) attested that the Canada Goose bred in Illinois but that breeding had declined. Nelson stated that it "formerly bred commonly in the marshes throughout the state, and still breeds sparingly in the more secluded situations." By the time Gault (1922) and Smith and Parmalee (1955) wrote their checklists, however, the Canada Goose was a doubtful breeder in Illinois. The Canada Goose that now breeds in many of the counties is probably not the same race that bred originally. The "Giant" Canada Goose has been introduced in several areas and has spread as a breeding bird in Illinois, becoming very common in some areas. Some summer counts: 250, Winnebago County, 1985; 531, Cook County, 1985; 120, Baldwin Lake, 1985; 105, Du Page County, 1985; 98, Williamson County, 1985 (IB&B2:12). Most nests are depressions in the ground lined with straw, grasses, and down feathers. From one to 12 tan eggs are laid. Illinois egg dates are at least March 24 to June 6. Adults with broods are obvious in late April, May, and June.

Fall migration usually starts in September. One contingent seems to migrate early and a later group only when severe weather forces it to move. This later group sometimes winters in north and central Illinois in mild winters. Average fall arrival dates: west-central, September 9 (nine years); Sangamon County, September 25 (16 years). Because migration is more drawn out in fall than in spring, lower numbers are recorded except in southern Illinois, where these geese winter. High counts for fall: 2000, Batavia, November 8, 1986 (EW-IB&B3:36); 5000, Knox County, November 17, 1985 (MB-IB&B2:44); 1000, Rend Lake, October 31, 1986 (KM-IB&B3:36). Departure dates become obscured in late fall and early winter but usually range from late November to early January.

Bellrose (1976) reports on the increase of these geese in southern Illinois in winter. Before the establishment of Horseshoe Lake as a refuge in 1927, most of them wintered along the Mississippi River between Cape Girardeau, Missouri, and Baton Rouge, Louisiana. In 1928–29 there were just over 1000 geese at the refuge, but by 1932–33 there were 30,000. The population had built up to 90,000 by winter 1948–49, to 200,000 in southern Illinois and nearby Kentucky in the mid-1950s, to almost 300,000 in the 1970s, and to 515,000 in the southern Illinois area in winter 1985–86 (DT-IB&B2:74). Christmas bird count numbers come mostly from southern Illinois, where totals for 1976–85 ranged from 93,360 in 1982 to 467,758 in 1977. Counts from other areas in winter include 8000, Chicago, December 29, 1985 (IB&B2:74); 10,000, Belvidere, January 3, 1982 (SR32:2); 3000, Tazewell County, December 30, 1986 (MB-IB&B3:66); 7400, Fermilab, December 16, 1985 (EW-IB&B2:74).

WOOD DUCK

Aix sponsa

COMMON MIGRANT AND SUMMER
RESIDENT; UNCOMMON WINTER RESIDENT
DECREASING NORTHWARD

This is Illinois' summer duck. It is second only to the Mallard as a hunted species, accounting for 12 percent of the duck harvest. The multicolors and the sleek crest of the adult male make the Wood Duck one of the most beautiful of the waterfowl. It does not like open water, preferring wooded areas with ponds, streams, and swamps; occasionally it is found in marshes and even sewage ponds. It looks odd standing on the high limb of a sycamore; as its name implies, it is one of the few ducks at home in trees. When a bunch of Wood Ducks fly by, winding through the trees with heads arched low, it is the hens that emit the squealing sound. The soft noise made by the drakes is seldom heard. Most of the year these ducks eat acorns and seeds of bald cypress, hickories, buttonbush, and wild millet. In season they eat corn from harvested fields. During the breeding season the hens eat insects.

Because creeks and rivers open up early in spring, these river ducks usually return by late February. The average arrival date for spring migrants in central Illinois is February 27 (17 years). Early arrival dates: two, Chillicothe, February 24, 1984 (LA-SR41:8); two, Crab Orchard National Wildlife Refuge, February 20, 1984 (JR-SR41:8). Wintering birds tend to obscure arrival dates. Spring bird count totals ranged from 371 in 1972 to 1964 in 1986. Most high counts are from the northwest, but the highest is 183, Cook County, May 4, 1985 (VK). Nonetheless, Bellrose (1976) shows the Mississippi, Illinois, and Ohio River areas with the state's densest concentrations of Wood Ducks.

Heavy hunting almost wiped out Wood Duck populations around the turn of the century. After passage of the Federal Migratory Bird Act of 1918, which gave the Wood Duck protection, populations came back. In the early 1940s the Wood Duck was put back on the hunting list, but populations dropped again in the 1950s in the Mississippi Valley. Since the mid-1960s the population has remained fairly high. The Illinois breeding population was estimated at 60,000 in 1965 (Sutherland 1971). In 1972 a stream survey of Wood Ducks by the Illinois Department of Conservation found 4.39 birds and 1.29 nests per mile in the south, 2.14 and 0.84 in the north, and 1.79 and 0.53 in central Illinois. Robbins et al. (1986), using breeding bird survey data, found significant increases in Wood Duck populations in the eastern and central United States. The mean number of Wood Ducks per survey route for 1965–79 in Illinois was 0.04. These ducks nest in natural cavities in trees or in specially erected boxes. Some nest in chimneys, barns, and other available cavities. From six to 14 whitish eggs are laid between March 6 and July 24. Sometimes several hens lay eggs in the same nest. Such "dumping" occasionally produces clutches of up to 40 eggs. Bellrose (1976) noted that the size of clutches in nests declines as the season progresses. He also found that nest success dropped in central Illinois from 49.2 percent in 1938–40 to 39.9 percent in 1958–61. He attributed it to an increase in raccoons, which prey on the eggs and young. Fox squirrels and snakes also cause nest failures by predation. Not long after hatching, young Wood Ducks, at the hen's urging, jump down from the nest entrance, which often is located quite high. The hen then leads the young to the nearest water. Late summer finds young and adult Woodies congregated at basking sites at the edges of lakes and streams.

Fall migration starts in late September and lasts through October and November. Maximum fall counts: 250, Moraine Hills, September 21, 1985 (SH-IB&B2:44); 250, Chautauqua National Wildlife Refuge, September 21, 1984 (KR-IB&B1:14); 500, Palos, October 15 and 21, 1982 (PD-SR35:5). Average fall departure date for Sangamon County is November 19 (15 years).

Most Woodies leave Illinois in winter. But some stay, especially in mild years, the large majority in southern Illinois. Christmas bird count totals for 1976–85 varied radically from winter to winter, with extremes of 27 in 1977 and 771 in 1985. Horseshoe Lake had the highest count: 613 in 1985.

GREEN-WINGED TEAL

Anas crecca

FAIRLY COMMON MIGRANT; UNCOMMON
WINTER RESIDENT DECREASING
NORTHWARD; RARE SUMMER RESIDENT IN
NORTHERN HALF OF THE STATE

This fast flier is the smallest duck in North America. It behaves much like a shorebird, feeding on mudflats and flying in swift synchronous flocks. It is found in emergent vegetation on shallow ponds and pools and sometimes in shallow streams.

Green-winged Teal feed on such plants as nutgrasses, millets, smartweed, and water kemp. They also take some insects and mollusks (Bellrose 1976). The "Eurasian" subspecies, *A. c. crecca*, which has been reported in North America, has not been reliably recorded in Illinois.

Spring migrants sometimes arrive as early as February: La Salle County, February 20, 1983 (LA-SR37:6); Horseshoe Lake, February 7, 1987 (RG); Carbondale, February 12, 1984 (SS-SR41:8); Springfield, February 12, 1984 (HDB). Average spring arrival dates: west-central, March 18 (12 years); Sangamon County, March 4 (18 years). Maximum counts for spring: 300, Henderson County, March 31, 1985 (MB,LMc-IB&B1:80); 300, Havana, April 12, 1986 (RP-IB&B2:87); 107, Woodford County, April 17, 1984 (KR-SR41:8). Spring bird counts are scheduled too late to record peak numbers of Green-winged Teal; totals ranged from 10 in 1974 to 162 in 1976, with 147 tallied in McHenry County on May 8, 1976 (VK). Average spring departure dates: west-central, April 27 (12 years); Sangamon County, April 26 (18 years). Stragglers stay past mid-May: Jackson Park, May 25, 1982 (PC,HR-SR33:5); two, Rochelle, May 30, 1981 (MSw-SR29:5); Lake Calumet, May 25, 1986 (CM-IB&B2:87); nine, Rockford, June 1, 1984 (LJ-SR41:8).

Kennicott (1854), Nelson (1876), and Coale (1912) all listed the Green-winged Teal as a breeder in northeastern Illinois. Boulton and Pitelka (1938a) saw an adult with six young at Palos Park on August 8, 1938. More recent nesting records include eight young, Chicago, July 31, 1966 (CC-AFN20:574); 12 young, Lake Calumet, summer 1979 (RB-AB33:867); five young, Batavia, summer 1980 (RM-AB34:899); six young, Havana, August 10, 1974 (HDB); two broods with 10 and 11 young, Goose Lake Prairie, July 12, 1973 (Birkenholz 1973). Most of these teal nest in boreal forests—which is a survival factor, since duck species that nest in agricultural lands to the south are declining because of habitat losses (Bellrose 1976). Other summer records probably represent nonbreeders: Charleston, June 7, 1977 (LBH-AB31:1007); two, Riverdale, June 23, 1979 (JL-AB33:867); Joliet, June 8, 1984 (JM-IB&B1:15).

Records for late June and early July represent fall migrants, for the males tend to wander after breeding: male, Du Page County, June 25, 1985 (JM-IB&B2:12); four, Lake Calumet, July 14, 1981 (PC,HR-SR31:5). Average fall arrival dates: west-central, September 15 (12 years); Sangamon County, August 1 (17 years). Green-winged Teal in late summer and early fall look very much like Blue-winged Teal; the best distinguishing marks are the Green-wing's smaller size, buffy yellow undertail coverts, and dull-colored tarsi. In flight, of course, the Blue-wing's powder blue patches separate it from the Green-wing, which shows a green speculum. Fall peak counts: 31,000, Illinois and Mississippi Rivers, November 7, 1979 (RC-AB34:167); 1000, Fulton County, October 19, 1985 (RP-IB&B2:44); 200, Nauvoo, November 20, 1983 (AD-SR39:6); 2365, lower Illinois and Mississippi Rivers, December 6, 1982 (RC-SR36:4). Average fall departure dates: west-central, November 15 (12 years); Sangamon County, December 1 (13 years). Green-wings tend to linger in the north until the mudflats are frozen, and some warm-water lakes keep them there even longer. Most of the winter population is in southern Illinois. Christmas bird counts for 1976–85 showed mostly modest totals, from seven in 1976 to 117 in 1982. High count was 357 at Pere Marquette State Park in 1942. Other winter records: 17, Lake Baldwin, January 3, 1988 (RG); 28, Crab Orchard National Wildlife Refuge, January 1, 1985 (JR-IB&B1:67); male, Waukegan, January 9, 1985 (RB-IB&B1:67). Most of these teal winter farther south—as far as central Mexico.

AMERICAN BLACK DUCK

Anas rubripes

FAIRLY COMMON MIGRANT AND WINTER RESIDENT; RARE SUMMER RESIDENT

Sometimes referred to as the Black Mallard, this duck is closely related to the Mallard and hybridizes with it. One of every 22 ducks identified as Blacks in the Mississippi Flyway shows the plumage pattern of both species (Bellrose 1976). Several of these hybrids are reported on Christmas bird counts every year in Illinois. The American Black is an eastern duck, not commonly found west of the Great Plains. Though at times Black Ducks flock with Mallards, at other times they seem to segregate. They often choose the same areas year after year. Black Ducks can be identified easily in flight by their silver wing linings. Sexes can be separated by bill color, which is bright yellow in males and olive green with black mottling in females. Immature males show an olive green bill without the black. American Black Ducks eat plants, including coontail, wild millet, and rice cut-grass, and animal matter such as mollusks and insects, including mayflies and scavenger beetles (Anderson 1959). This duck is declining throughout its range; from 1955 to 1974 there was a greater than 40 percent drop in numbers (Geis et al. 1971). Reasons for the decline are not clear; it may be due in part to hybridization with Mallards.

A few fall migrants arrive by July: Horseshoe Lake, July 12, 1980 (BR-SR27:4); Waukegan, July 24, 1980 (JL-SR27:4); Barrington, July 28, 1986 (CMi-IB&B3:36). Average fall arrival dates: west-central, September 18 (10 years); Sangamon County, September 8 (16 years). High counts for fall: 29,000, Illinois and Mississippi Rivers, November 20, 1979 (RC-AB34:167); 1000, Carlyle Lake, November 16, 1985 (RP-IB&B2:44); 950, Fulton County, October 19, 1985 (RP-IB&B2:44).

These ducks winter in Illinois in varying numbers. They are hardy and can be seen standing on ice with Mallards in midwinter. Christmas bird count totals for 1976–85 ranged from 710 in 1983 to 4453 in 1981. Highest count was 20,000 at Chautauqua National Wildlife Refuge in 1943. Other winter high counts: 11,600, Illinois and Mississippi Rivers, December 6, 1982 (RC-AB37:307); 3000, Goose Lake Prairie, December 26, 1981 (PD-SR32:3).

Most Black Ducks move northward as soon as possible in spring, usually in February. Average spring departure dates: west-central, April 11 (eight years); Sangamon County, April 11 (16 years). Late departure dates: Lisle Arboretum, June 5, 1986 (RW-IB&B2:87); Rend Lake, May 18, 1987 (TF); Mason County, May 27, 1985 (KR-IB&B1:80). Spring bird count totals ranged from five in 1974 to 26 in 1980. Many of the counts came from the Illinois River valley. Highest count was 16, Brown County, May 10, 1980 (VK).

Kennicott (1854) said Black Ducks nest "in the ponds and lakelets." Nelson (1876) noted that one or two pairs nested each year at the Calumet marshes. Coale (1912) wrote that the Black Duck was nesting at Grass Lake in

Lake County in May 1909. Ford (1956) listed three breeding records: McGinnis Slough, adult with 11 young, May 1937, and adult with six young, July 1945; near Orland Park, nine young, May 1944. More recent breeding records include two broods, Barrington, June 13, 1965 (CC-AFN19:551); nest, Powderhorn Marsh, May 29, 1965 (CC); female with four young, Banner Marsh, June 20, 1983 (DBi-SR38:5). Other summer records evidently represent nonbreeders: Union County Conservation Area, June 15, 1982 (PK-AB36:982); Urbana, June and July, 1984 (RCh-IB&B1:15); Winfield, June 4, 1985 (JM-IB&B2:12); Lake Renwick, June 10, 1985 (JM-IB&B2:12); several, Chicago area, 1980 (RB-SR26:3).

MALLARD

Anas platyrhynchos

ABUNDANT MIGRANT AND COMMON WINTER RESIDENT; LOCALLY COMMON SUMMER RESIDENT

These ducks are found in and around rivers, lakes, ponds, park lagoons, even ditches—essentially wherever there is water. Many are semidomesticated; most domestic ducks originated from this species. The Mallard is the common puddle duck of the Mississippi Flyway and is much sought after by hunters. A migration corridor that extends from southeast Saskatchewan to northwestern Illinois and farther south supports the highest density of Mallards—more than two million birds (Bellrose 1976).

Away from the wintering grounds, Mallard numbers begin to increase in spring as soon as open water is available, usually late February. Peak numbers are reached in March, with most migrant Mallards gone by late April. Few maximum spring counts are available for Illinois: 5000, Chautauqua National Wildlife Refuge, February 1, 1986 (LA,MB-IB&B2:74).

Most Mallards breed to the north of Illinois, reaching their greatest abundance in the southern Canadian provinces. Robbins et al. (1986) noted that breeding bird survey data showed a significant increase of Mallards in the eastern United States, including Illinois, which had 1.4 birds per survey route (64 routes) for 1965–79. Apparently more Mallards nest in northern and central than in southern Illinois. Mallards pair up in the fall but do not mate until the next spring. Egg clutches—an average of nine eggs but varying from seven to 16—are found from April through early July; later dates probably represent renesting, since Mallards raise only one brood per year. The smooth, glossy pale green to bluish eggs are laid in a hollow on the ground lined with grasses, leaves, down, and feathers. Occasionally Mallards nest in trees; such a nest was found in Menard County on April 26, 1979 (SR22:3). Eighty-five broods produced 571 young on Fox River in June 1981 (SR30:5). Young are usually seen in late April through July, but half-grown young were seen in Mercer County on October 12,

1980 (BB-SR26:3). The female incubates the eggs and cares for the young. Her distraction displays can sometimes be quite dramatic. The male spends his time loafing and feeding with other males. Loafing areas are an important component of the Mallard's habitat. Occasionally the Mallard hybridizes with other ducks, most frequently with its close relative the Black Duck but also with the Northern Pintail and the American Wigeon. Mallards tend to gather in safe areas to molt, since molting renders them flightless for three or four weeks in mid-June to mid-August. Males molt first and females later because of nest duties. In Illinois Mallards feed on corn, rice cut-grass, coontail, wild millet, and marsh smartweed (Anderson 1959).

Fall migration begins in September. Peak numbers are reached in November or sometimes early December, depending on weather conditions. Maximum fall counts: 20,000, Carlyle Lake, November 16, 1985 (RP-IB&B2:44); 100,000, Crab Orchard National Wildlife Refuge, November 27–28, 1955 (Bush-AFN10:28); 300,000, Chautauqua refuge, December 2, 1958 (KDN-AFN13:296); 1,600,000, Illinois and Mississippi Rivers, November 20, 1979 (AB34:167).

Winter populations also vary with the availability of open water. Wintering Mallards follow a daily rhythm of feeding and resting. In early morning they fly out to feed in grainfields, then return and rest on the ice of a lake, usually near open water, until evening, when they repeat the performance. Christmas bird count totals for 1976–85 ranged from 17,550 in 1980 to 173,000 in 1979. Highest count during those 10 years was 128,000 in Cass and Mason Counties in 1979, but the all-time high count was 650,000 at Chautauqua refuge in both 1942 and 1944. Other maximum winter counts: 8900, Horseshoe Lake, Alexander County, December 18, 1985; 8600, Union County, December 19, 1985; 4000, Marshall County, January 5, 1986 (IB&B2:74). Although Mallards winter in North America as far north as southern Alaska, some go as far south as central Mexico.

WHITE-CHEEKED PINTAIL

Anas bahamensis

VERY RARE VAGRANT

This duck resides in the Bahamas and South America. It is casual in Florida, and there are accidental records for Wisconsin, Texas, Alabama, Virginia, and Delaware (AOU 1983). The only Illinois record for the White-cheeked Pintail was of one shot at Steward Lake, Mason County, November 2, 1968, by D. K. Wilcox. The specimen is in the Illinois State Museum collection. Because the bird was not sexed, its race—and thus its place of origin—could not be determined. The Bahamas race is the one most likely to occur; if it was South American, it probably was not a wild bird. These pintail prefer shallow water with vegetation around the edges.

NORTHERN PINTAIL

Anas acuta

COMMON MIGRANT; UNCOMMON WINTER
AND RARE SUMMER RESIDENT

The drake Northern Pintail weighs less than the Mallard, but it is longer because of its long neck and long central tail feathers. The male pintail's brown head and white breast with an insert of white on the nape are distinctive. Hens, immatures, and eclipse drakes are brownish, but the slender shape, long neck, and gray bill make them fairly easy to identify. In flight the white trailing edge of the pintail's secondaries is a good field mark. The Northern Pintail is most abundant in western North America, but it has increased in numbers in the Mississippi Flyway recently because of a shift in its winter range (Bellrose 1976). This duck is found on lakes, ponds, flooded fields, and marshes. Its food is mostly plants, including rice cut-grass, corn, and wild millet, along with a little animal matter such as snails. Pintail hybridize only rarely with Mallards.

Graceful flocks of Northern Pintail are among the earliest spring migrants. Early spring records include 40, Carlyle Lake, February 1, 1983 (BR-SR37:6); Horseshoe Lake, February 2, 1984 (BR-SR41:8); Henderson County, February 7, 1987 (MB). Average spring arrival dates: west-central, March 12 (13 years); Sangamon County, February 15 (17 years). High spring counts: 1000, Lawrence County, March 14, 1982 (LH-SR33:5); 2000, Kidd Lake, February 23, 1986 (BR-IB&B2:87); 1500, Henderson County, March 9, 1985 (MB-IB&B1:80). Most pintail pass Illinois quickly and go on northward. Spring bird counts are scheduled long past the time for peak numbers of pintail, but some were counted every year (1976–85); the low total was eight in 1982, the high 51 in 1974. Highest count was 26 in Lake County, May 6, 1978 (VK). Average spring departure dates: west-central, April 1 (13 years); Sangamon County, April 10 (17 years).

According to Nelson (1876), the Northern Pintail nested in prairie sloughs near the Calumet River; he found a nest on May 29, 1875. Ford (1956) listed nesting records for McGinnis Slough in 1932 and near Barrington in 1940. More recent nesting records: female with six young, Whiteside County, June 17, 1959 (Shaws-IAB115:7); pair, Woodstock, June 19–21, 1967 (IAB144:17); four young, Goose Lake Prairie, 1973 (DBi-AB27:875); nest with 10 eggs, Goose Lake Prairie, May 14, 1974 (Verner 1975); breeding, Lake Calumet, 1978 (RB-AB32:1167); female with six young, Riverdale, July 14, 1979 (RB-SR22:3); female with 11 young, Riverdale, 1979 (Mlodinow 1984). Other pintail, probably nonbreeders, have been seen in summer: two, Dundee, June 1980 (RM-SR26:3); pair, Havana, June 9, 1987 (RBj); male, Mahomet, June 15, 1987 (RCh); male, Monmouth, June 7, 1986 (MB-IB&B3:13). Fall migration starts early, sometimes in July when not only the females but also the males of all ages are mostly brown. Bellrose (1976) estimated that about 300,000 pintail use the Mississippi River corridor, coming

from Saskatchewan, Manitoba, and the Dakotas. Most head south to the Gulf Coast, but some go southeast to South Carolina. Early fall arrival dates: Alexander County, July 12, 1986 (DR-IB&B3:36); Mason County, July 20, 1974 (HDB). Average fall arrival dates: west-central, September 10 (nine years); Sangamon County, August 23 (18 years). Maximum counts in fall: 151,000, Illinois and Mississippi Rivers, October 30, 1979 (RC-AB34:167); 2500, Nauvoo, November 20, 1983 (AD-AB38:208); 800, Carlyle Lake, November 1, 1986 (RP-IB&B3:35). Northern Pintail are somewhat less common in fall than in spring. Average fall departure dates: west-central, November 11 (nine years); Sangamon County, December 4 (seven years).

Wintering Northern Pintail are found mostly in the southern part of the state, but even in the north small numbers are seen. Christmas bird count totals for 1976–85 ranged from 26 in 1983 to 2140 in 1985. Highest count was 10,075 at East St. Louis in 1955. Other winter records: 1654, Alexander County, December 18, 1985 (IB&B2:74); 50, Horseshoe Lake, January 25, 1981 (RK-SR28:3); 30, Crab Orchard National Wildlife Refuge, January 1987 (DR-IB&B3:66); Lake Calumet, January 29, 1984 (JL); male, Deerfield, wintered 1984–85 (DJ-IB&B1:67).

GARGANEY

Anas querquedula

VERY RARE VAGRANT

This Old World duck has rarely been found in North America. The only Illinois record was of a distinctive male at Fermilab, Du Page County, April 18–23, 1982 (D.Ludwig-AB36:858). It was seen by many observers in a grassy area with marshy ponds, associating with other teal. The Garganey is a small teal, with a wing pattern similar to the Blue-wing's. Females would be difficult to distinguish from other female teal. Some Garganeys seen in the inland and eastern states are suspected escapees from captivity. Most wild Garganeys are thought to arrive in the lower United States via western Alaska, since they are rare but regular visitors to that state.

BLUE-WINGED TEAL

Anas discors

COMMON MIGRANT; FAIRLY COMMON
SUMMER RESIDENT DECREASING
SOUTHWARD; RARE WINTER RESIDENT
DECREASING NORTHWARD

This teal can be recognized in any plumage by its small size and powder blue wing patches. The closely related Cinnamon Teal also has these patches, but it is rare in Illinois. In spring the male Blue-wing has a white crescent on the face, but in fall both sexes and the Cinnamon Teal look much the same. Blue-wings give peeping calls and *kick-kick-kick* call notes. They inhabit the shallow water of lakes, ponds, sloughs, marshes, flooded fields, sewage lagoons, and even drainage ditches and mudflats. Occasionally they are quite tame and will display and court close to observers. They are highly migratory, nesting as far north as Alaska and wintering as far south as Peru and Guyana. There are two races; the one found in Illinois is *A. d. discors*. Blue-winged Teal eat red-rooted nut grass, wild millet, water hemp, and other plants, along with water boatmen and midges (Anderson 1959). The North American average breeding population for 1955-74 was 5,069,000 (Bellrose 1976).

Blue-winged Teal are among the late migrant ducks in spring, usually arriving well after the ice is gone. Early spring arrival dates: four, Carbondale, February 27, 1986 (DR-IB&B2:87); Clinton Lake, February 20, 1983 (RCh-SR37:6). Average arrival dates: Chicago, April 23 (14 years); west-central, March 15 (12 years); Sangamon County, March 11 (17 years). High counts for spring: 400, Havana, April 12, 1986 (RP-IB&B2:87); 225, Alexander County, April 24, 1984 (TF,DJaq-SR41:9); 159, Carlyle Lake, April 8, 1987 (RG). Spring bird count totals ranged from 517 in 1972 to 3594 in 1984; the highest count was 300 in Iroquois County, May 5, 1984 (VK). Average spring departure dates: Chicago, May 14 (14 years); west-central, May 20 (12 years); Sangamon County, May 25 (15 years). Some of these teal linger into late May and June.

In Illinois the Blue-winged Teal breeds mostly in the northern and central areas, but there are some recent breeding records for the south: Jackson County, 1977; Shelby County, 1982; Randolph County, 1985; Wabash County, 1983. Robbins et al. (1986) noted that the average number of Blue-winged Teal per breeding bird survey route in Illinois was only 0.2. Evidence of breeding in Illinois comes mainly from observation of broods, but some nests have been found. Nests are on the ground, usually in marshes or near ponds. Six to 11 white to pale olive eggs are laid. Egg dates for Illinois are from at least May 5 to June 11. In 1981 a brood at Lake Calumet had 19 chicks (JL-SR30:5).

Fall migration is very early, and at this time all these teal are in brown plumage. Although Blue-wings prefer shallow water, occasionally they rest on deeper water; when they do, they tend to stay in very tight flocks. Early fall arrival dates: four, Jackson Park, July 10, 1981 (PC,HR-SR31:5); four, Henderson County, July 19, 1986 (MB-IB&B3:36); three, Charleston, July 21, 1985 (LBH-IB&B2:44). Average fall arrival dates: west-central, August 14 (10 years); Sangamon County, July 26 (17 years). High counts for fall: 42,000, Illinois and Mississippi Rivers, September 11, 1979 (AB34:167); 800, Olney, September 7, 1983 (LH-SR39:6); 500, Monmouth, October 5, 1986 (MB-IB&B3:36). Average fall departure dates: west-central, October 21 (10 years); Sangamon County, November 4 (18 years).

A few Blue-wings stay in Illinois for the winter, usually in mild years and mostly in the south. Some Christmas bird count records for these teal are unreliable, and it is difficult to assess the 103 Blue-wings recorded on the Pere Marquette count in 1939. Some certainly do occur; even Cooke (1888) noted that they were found in winter north to southern Illinois. Some recent winter records: Gladstone, January 12, 1980 (LMc-SR24:2); four, Horseshoe Lake, January 26, 1983 (SRu-SR36:4); Union County, January 7, 1986 (DR-IB&B2:74); Marshall County, January 5, 1986 (MB-IB&B2:74).

CINNAMON TEAL

Anas cyanoptera

RARE VAGRANT

There are more than 20 published records for this beautiful western duck in Illinois. Adult males in breeding plumage are easy to identify, but most other plumages are so much like the Blue-winged Teal that they are difficult to separate. Male Cinnamon Teal have red eyes in all plumages. Wallace and Ogilvie (1977) give details on how to distinguish between the two teal. To make matters worse, hybrids exist; the drakes are fairly obvious and have been recorded at Aledo, April 15, 1975 (photographs ISM), and Meredosia, April 3-5, 1985 (TW,HDB). Most records for Cinnamon Teal are in spring, probably because of the identification problem in fall. Dates of occurrence range from March 18 to April 30 and from August to November 18. There are no summer or winter records. Although Ridgway (1895) said that this bird was taken once or twice in Illinois, no certain records were published until Smith and Parmalee (1955) listed one shot at Dallas City, October 26, 1922. Whereabouts of the specimen was not given. Recent records include Henderson County, April 13, 1979 (AB33:776); Springfield, April 13-17, 1980 (HDB); Evanston and Wilmette, April 3-4, 1981 (JL); Chandlerville, March 25, 1983 (VK-AB37:875); Clinton Lake, March 29 and 30, 1983 (RS,TM- SR37:6); Carlyle Lake, April 18, 1984 (SRu-AB38:917); Crete, April 22, 1985 (ADu-AB39:306); Keysport, March 28–April 9, 1986 (DJo-AB40:477); Evanston, April 30, 1986 (DD,RB 40:477); Buffalo, September 30, 1985 (HDB); pair, Hartford, September 18, 1987 (RG). The subspecies found in North America is *A. c. septentrionalium*.

NORTHERN SHOVELER

Anas clypeata

COMMON MIGRANT; RARE SUMMER AND WINTER RESIDENT

The male Northern Shoveler in breeding plumage is strikingly colorful, but in all plumages the large spatulate bill will identify this duck. In flight it shows powder blue wing patches much like the Blue-winged Teal's. Males when feeding give a low *took, took, took* call. Shovelers are found in shallow lakes, sloughs, flooded fields, ponds, and sewage lagoons. They eat more animal food than any other dabbler, primarily water boatmen, snails, and crustacea (Anderson 1959). But they are still mainly vegetarians, consuming red-rooted nut grass, buttonbush, corn, and coontail. A hybrid Shoveler and Blue-winged Teal was shot at Bureau Junction on April 3, 1905 (Deane 1905).

Some early spring migrants arrive in February: Charleston, February 11, 1987 (RBr); East Alton, February 5, 1983 (RG,SRu); two, Crab Orchard National Wildlife Refuge, February 12, 1984 (SS-SR41:9). Average spring arrival dates: west-central, March 14 (13 years); Sangamon County, March 2 (17 years). Maximum counts for spring: 1000, Carlyle Lake, March 26, 1983 (SRu-AB37:875); 500, Horseshoe Lake, April 3, 1980 (BR-SR25:4); 300, Wabash County, April 6, 1986 (LH-IB&B2:87); 300, Meredosia, April 4, 1985 (MB-IB&B1:80). Shovelers stay later in spring than most other ducks, but spring bird counts have recorded only modest numbers, ranging from 19 in 1986 to 361 in 1984. Highest count was 65 in McLean County, May 5, 1973 (VK). Average spring departure dates: west-central, May 7 (13 years); Sangamon County, May 13 (18 years). Some birds linger into summer.

Nelson (1876) termed the Shoveler a rather common summer resident that deposited eggs in early May. Coale (1912) called it a former breeder in Lake County. Ford (1956) reported that a set of eggs had been taken in Skokie Marsh, June 7, 1890, and listed a set of nine eggs at McGinnis Slough, June 4, 1932. Other breeding records: female with six young, Cook County, July 21, 1968 (IAB150:7); female and three immatures, Goose Lake Prairie, August 8, 1973 (Birkenholz 1975); three broods, Fulton County, June 30, 1973 (HDB). For several other summer records breeding was not certain.

Fall migration begins in August when most Shovelers are in brown plumage: Horseshoe Lake, August 13, 1983 (BR-SR39:7); four, Springfield, August 19, 1986 (HDB). Average fall arrival dates: west-central, September 15 (10 years); Sangamon County, August 26 (18 years). High counts for fall: 3100, Illinois and Mississippi Rivers, November 7, 1979 (AB34:167); 100, Palos, October 19, 1986 (RP-IB&B3:36); 100, Fulton County, October 19, 1985 (RP-IB&B2:44). There is usually a rush of this species to get out before freeze-up in late November or early December. At this time they may be seen on deep-water lakes in tight flocks. Average fall departure dates: west-central, November 7 (10 years); Sangamon County, December 3 (13 years).

Most Shovelers passing through Illinois go southeast. Some winter as far away as Central America. Christmas bird count totals for 1976–85 ranged from six in 1981 to 231 in 1977. Practically all high counts come from southern Illinois; 200 in Union County in 1977 was the highest. A few Shovelers winter in northern and central Illinois: Chicago, January 17, 1987 (JL); Waukegan, January 7,

1984 (SH-SR40:5); 10, Oswego, January 18, 1983 (J.Steele-SR36:4).

GADWALL

Anas strepera

FAIRLY COMMON MIGRANT; UNCOMMON WINTER AND VERY RARE SUMMER RESIDENT

The Gadwall is the only dabbling duck that shows a white speculum in flight, and both sexes show it. These ducks are found on lakes, ponds, overflow areas, marshes, and especially sewage lagoons in colder weather. The Gadwall population has increased since the 1950s, but this duck remains primarily a western species with an important migration corridor along the Mississippi River in Illinois. Gadwalls breed principally in the prairie areas of the Dakotas and Canada. They eat mainly plant food—coontail, algae, marsh smartweed, wild millet—and a little animal food, mostly midge larvae.

Early fall migrants arrive in July: Jackson Park, July 28, 1982 (PC,HR-SR35:5); Mason County, July 21, 1973 (HDB). Average fall arrival dates: west-central, October 2 (nine years); Sangamon County, September 22 (18 years). Maximum counts for fall: 16,000, Illinois and Mississippi Rivers, November 13, 1979 (RC-AB34:167); 700, Springfield, November 1, 1979 (HDB); 195, Crab Orchard National Wildlife Refuge, October 17, 1984 (JR-IB&B1:14); 75, Arcola, October 27, 1985 (RCh-IB&B2:44). Departures are usually in late November or early December, but exact dates are difficult to determine because some Gadwalls winter in Illinois.

Most Gadwalls that pass through Illinois winter in Tennessee or Louisiana. Illinois' small winter population seems to frequent the same areas every year: Christmas bird counts for the past 10 years show Joliet with a constant winter population. Count totals ranged from 159 in 1977 to 402 in 1985. Highest count was 527 at Pere Marquette State Park in 1942. Other winter records: 210, Joliet, January 12, 1985 (JM-IB&B1:67); 43, Henderson County, February 7, 1987 (MB-IB&B3:67); 145, Union County, December 19, 1985 (IB&B2:74).

Spring migration begins in February but is somewhat obscured by wintering birds. Average spring arrival dates: west-central, March 4 (10 years); Sangamon County, February 26 (12 years). High spring counts: 250, Tazewell County, February 13, 1983 (TP-SR37:6); 62, Crab Orchard refuge, March 21, 1984 (JR-SR41:9); 55, Palos, April 5, 1981 (DJ-SR29:5). Spring bird counts are taken past the peak time for Gadwalls, but they were recorded every year (1976–85). Totals ranged from five in 1972 to 75 in 1980; the highest count was 30 in Cook County, May 10, 1980 (VK). Average spring departure dates: west-central, April 24 (10 years); Sangamon County, May 7 (18 years).

Nelson (1876) considered the Gadwall a very rare summer resident, saying he had seen only two or three pairs at that season. No other early observer noted any breeding, but there are some recent breeding records: adult with six young, Riverdale, 1977 (Mlodinow 1984); two females with young, La Salle, July 18, 1982 (JH-SR34:4). Other summer records provide no evidence of breeding: five, Lake Calumet, June 8, 1985 (JL); three, Lake Renwick, June 9, 1985 (JM-IB&B2:13); female, Arcola, June 28, 1986 (RCh-IB&B3:13); pair, Monmouth, June 6, 1983 (MB-SR38:5); Monroe County, June 4, 1983 (PS,RG-SR38:5).

EURASIAN WIGEON

Anas penelope

RARE VAGRANT

This duck is the Eurasian counterpart of the American Wigeon, with which this vagrant from the Old World is usually found. In most cases it is the male that is identified except when a female accompanies a drake. The earliest record was of an adult male shot at Calumet Marsh, April 13, 1876 (Nelson 1876). Of the total of 27 records, all but seven are for spring, mostly March and April. Recent spring records: Meredosia, April 7–8, 1982 (RS-AB36:858); Lake Renwick, April 15, 1987 (JM); Palos, March 25–April 10, 1981 (PD-SR29:5). Fall records, all between September 14 and November 27, seem to have increased in recent years, but that may be due to the use of better optical equipment. Recent fall records: Chicago, November 14–17, 1981 (AA,JL-AB36:183); Palos, October 22–November 27, 1982 (PD,JL-SR35:5); Palos Park, October 12–31, 1986 (PWa,JM-IB&B3:36); Palos, September 22– November 14, 1987 (CM,RP). The one winter record is from near Chillicothe, January 25, 1968 (Princen 1969). Most unusual was the sighting of four Eurasian Wigeon near Mount Zion in March and April 1931 (letter from Gorham at ISM, with photographs at INHS).

AMERICAN WIGEON

Anas americana

COMMON MIGRANT; OCCASIONAL WINTER RESIDENT

The American Wigeon's white crown patch gives this duck the common name of Baldpate. White wing patches in flight, combined with the drake's piping whistle, make these wigeon easy to pick out in flocks of ducks. They fly in fairly compact flocks and have a somewhat erratic flight. They can be found on lakes, ponds, marshes, sloughs, and overflow areas or in fields, where they graze like geese. American Wigeon in Illinois are mostly vegetarian, eating primarily coontail but also rice cut-grass and marsh smartweed. They also eat a little animal food: water boatmen

(Anderson 1959). Wigeon nest in the pothole regions of the north central United States and north through Canada to Alaska. Bellrose (1976) estimated the early fall population in North America at almost 6,500,000. On rare occasions a hybrid American Wigeon and Mallard is seen.

The first spring migrants appear with the opening of water on the larger lakes. Early spring arrival dates: two, Joliet, January 27, 1987 (JM); eight, Springfield, February 1, 1987 (HDB). Average spring arrival dates: Chicago, March 24 (eight years); west-central, March 7 (13 years). High counts for spring: 4000, Lawrence County, March 14, 1982 (LH-SR33:5); 1000, Tazewell County, March 13, 1983 (TP-SR37:6) 400, Horseshoe Lake, March 12, 1986 (RG-IB&B2:87). Fairly low numbers are recorded on spring bird counts because most wigeon have already passed through by then. Totals ranged from two in 1985 to 105 in 1977, when 41 were tallied in Cook County on May 7 (VK). Average spring departure dates: Chicago, April 2 (eight years); Sangamon County, May 5 (18 years). Nelson (1876) referred to the wigeon as a not very rare summer resident that nested about the borders of marshes and prairie sloughs. Ridgway (1895) listed it as known to breed in Illinois. Neither source listed any specific breeding records, however, and apparently there have been none since. There are some summer records of nonbreeding birds: nine, Cook County, June 1, 1964 (Mlodinow 1984); male, Braidwood June 27, 1986 (JM-IB&B3:13); male, Springfield, June 30–July 13, 1985 (HDB); Ogle County, June 23, 1980 (MSw-SR26:3).

Like most dabblers, wigeon return fairly early in fall: Lake Renwick, July 17, 1987 (JM); six, Lake Calumet, August 29, 1987 (JL); Springfield, September 1, 1985 (HDB). Average fall arrival dates: west-central, September 23 (12 years); Sangamon County, September 8 (18 years). High counts for fall: 230,000, Illinois and Mississippi Rivers, November 7, 1979 (RC-AB34:127); 765, Palos, October 28, 1984 (JL); 300, Savanna, October 8, 1983 (BSh-SR39:7); 1500, Mark Twain National Wildlife Refuge, October 7, 1978 (AB33:182); 500, Carlyle Lake, November 1, 1986 (RP-IB&B3:36). Most of the wigeon coming through Illinois winter in the southeastern United States and Louisiana. Departure dates in fall are usually late November and early December.

Only moderate numbers of wigeon winter in Illinois, although in recent years warm-water lakes have provided some habitats to keep them here: 100, Baldwin Lake, winter 1983–84 (RG-SR40:5); 50, Sangchris State Park, January 14, 1983 (HDB). As late as December 6, 1982, 6000 were counted by airplane along the Illinois and Mississippi Rivers (RC-AB37:307), but most of them were late migrants. Christmas bird count totals for 1976–85 ranged from 26 in 1978 to 273 in 1984. Highest count was 500 at Pere Marquette State Park in 1966.

COMMON LOON
Gavia immer

En route from the primordial freshwater lakes of the north where they make their summer home to the southern salt-water bays where they spend the winter, many Common Loons pass over the state. A few in brownish gray and white winter plumage linger until bad weather drives them on. In spring, when returning north, some have attained their full nuptial dress and look much like the birds shown here; many others are molting and are mottled with patches of brownish gray and white.

Adult in nuptial plumage
(sexes similar)

PIED-BILLED GREBE
Podilymbus podiceps

Compared with the elaborate and conspicuous displays of its cousin the Western Grebe, the Pied-billed's courtship might be considered rather subdued. However, courtship among grebes is always a formal affair. When Pied-billeds meet they face each other about a foot apart, stretch their necks high, cock their heads, and pivot in place to present the fluffy white feathers of their undertails, a ritual that they repeat several times before the encounter ends. The presumed male frequently carries a small piece of aquatic plant in its bill.

Adults in nuptial plumage
(sexes similar)

DOUBLE-CRESTED CORMORANT
Phalacrocorax auritus

In the 1800s nesting colonies of Double-crested Cormorants could be found scattered throughout the state, and the overall population was holding its own. Now that we have drained most of the wetlands where they once lived, these relatively unattractive birds, with no great economic value, have dwindled in number and are considered to be mostly uncommon migrants. A few can be found feeding in our larger lakes and streams.

Bluegill
(Lepomis macrochirus)

Adult
(sexes similar)

AMERICAN BITTERN
Botaurus lentiginosus

This well-camouflaged summer resident of cattail marshes is rarely seen except when it carelessly steps into a clearing or is driven to the edge of cover and forced to fly. More frequently its presence is revealed by its unusual pumplike call given in spring.

Adult
(sexes similar)

LITTLE BLUE HERON
Egretta caerulea

In late summer there is a postbreeding northward dispersal of Little Blue Herons. Most are immature birds dressed in white, a plumage they wear for at least a year before they molt into the blue and purple tones of adult birds. Sometimes these visitors are in family groups with the young still begging for food.

Bigeye Chub
(Hybopsis amblops)

Adult
(sexes similar)

Immature

GREEN-BACKED HERON
Butorides striatus

BLACK-CROWNED NIGHT-HERON
Nycticorax nycticorax

The paths of the diurnal Green-backed Heron and the nocturnal Black-crowned Night-Heron frequently cross at the water's edge as they look for food when one's day is ending and the other's is about to begin.

Black-crowned Night-Heron
(sexes similar)

Green-backed Heron
(sexes similar)

TUNDRA SWAN
Cygnus columbianus

En route to and from their nesting grounds in the Arctic and their coastal winter resort on the Atlantic Coast around the Chesapeake Bay, many Tundra Swans follow migration corridors that take them to the north of the state. Each winter, however, a few show up and sometimes stay in winter until all the available open water is covered by ice.

Adult
(sexes similar)

CANADA GOOSE
Branta canadensis

Through the efforts of conservationists a fairly strong breeding population of Canada Geese has been restored to the state. Nowadays, in early spring in areas where significant wetlands are still available, it is not uncommon to see adult Canada Geese accompanied by their newly hatched brood.

Adult
(sexes similar)

Young

WOOD DUCK
Aix sponsa

In early spring even before the leaves appear, pairs of Wood Ducks can frequently be seen high up in the trees along our streams and lakes, investigating every old Pileated Woodpecker hole, natural cavity, or man-made box for a place to nest. After the selection has been made and the hen has laid her clutch of six to fourteen creamy white eggs and begun to incubate them, the male no longer visits the site. But the incubating female usually joins him whenever she leaves the nest to feed.

Adults

(male)

(female)

CANVASBACK

Aythya valisineria

FAIRLY COMMON MIGRANT; UNCOMMON
WINTER AND VERY RARE SUMMER RESIDENT

The Canvasback is a chunky diving duck, highly prized by hunters for its excellent taste. A white back and sloped head make the male easy to identify even at great distances. The female is duller, but the unique profile is the same. Though this duck is found throughout Illinois, it is most numerous along the Mississippi River and relatively scarce along Lake Michigan. The "Can" is found on large rivers, lakes, ponds, open marshes, and sewage lagoons. Anderson (1959) found that the Canvasback eats pondweed, duck potato, and midge larvae. Thompson (1973) noted that 46 percent of the food eaten at Pool 19 on the Mississippi River was mayfly larvae. A hybrid Canvasback and Hooded Merganser was reported at Lake Calumet on July 5, 1968 (CC-IAB152:19).

As soon as rising temperatures start to thaw the ice, Canvasbacks return from their wintering grounds. The few Canvasbacks that winter in Illinois sometimes obscure the early arrivals, but in mild years migrants may return as early as late January. Average spring arrival dates: west-central, February 27 (14 years); Sangamon County, February 13 (16 years). High counts for spring: 15,000, Pool 19, February 22, 1987 (RC-AB41:287); 2500, Mark Twain National Wildlife Refuge, March 2, 1984 (SRu-SR41:9); 2000, Fulton County, February 27, 1983 (VH,LA-SR37:6); 5000, Henderson County, March 2, 1986 (MB-IB&B2:87). Peak numbers are reached fairly early, and these migrants usually do not linger. By spring bird count time, few remain; totals have ranged from one to 12, with most occurring in northern Illinois. Average spring departure dates: west-central, April 14 (14 years); Sangamon County, April 15 (18 years). A few stragglers remain into May.

There is apparently only one breeding record for Illinois, a female with three young at Powderhorn Lake, July 5, 1965 (CC- AFN19:551). Even the early observers did not find the Canvasback nesting in Illinois, although it does breed in central Kansas and rarely in northwestern Iowa. Other summer records include a male at Grand Tower, July 3, 1973 (DH-AB27:875), and a female at Springfield, June 11–16, 1985 (HDB).

Fall migration seems most concentrated in the Mississippi Valley. It is usually October before Canvasbacks are seen in Illinois. Average fall arrival dates: west-central, October 28 (10 years); Sangamon County, October 22 (16 years). Bellrose (1976) states that Canvasbacks arrive at Pool 19 in late October, peak by the middle of November, and remain until forced out by freeze-up, usually in mid-December. He also notes that most of these Canvasbacks go east to winter on Chesapeake Bay but some go south to Florida and Louisiana. When the timing is right I see some of these late "Cans" stopping over at Lake Springfield after they are forced out at Pool 19. High counts for fall: 194,000, Illinois and Mississippi Rivers, November 7, 1979 (RC-

AB34:167); 15,000, Nauvoo, November 20, 1983 (AD-AB38:208); 150, McGinnis Slough, October 20, 1973 (Mlodinow 1984). Average departure dates: west-central Illinois, December 15 (10 years); Sangamon County, December 24 (nine years).

If open water and food are available these ducks will winter in Illinois. Bellrose (1976) says that most of the state's 6500 wintering Canvasbacks reside on the Mississippi River above Alton. Christmas bird count totals for 1976–85 ranged from 35 in 1978 to 735 in 1977. Highest count was 701 at Crab Orchard National Wildlife Refuge in 1977. Other high winter counts: 30,000, Illinois and Mississippi Rivers, January 3, 1983 (RC-AB37:307); 2000, Horseshoe Lake Conservation Area, January 15–28, 1981 (PS-SR28:3); 34, Waukegan, January 1, 1981 (RB-SR28:3).

REDHEAD

Aythya americana

FAIRLY COMMON MIGRANT; OCCASIONAL
WINTER AND RARE SUMMER RESIDENT

These handsome ducks are found on ponds at least as often as on large lakes. They also occur in open marshes and at large rivers. The drake Redhead, although colored somewhat like the Canvasback, has a grayer back and a high forehead, giving it a much different profile. The hen Redhead is mostly brown and can be confused with the hen Ring-necked Duck. Hens occasionally show some albinism. I noted two partial albinos at Lake Springfield, March 6 and 23, 1980, and another was seen at Carlyle Lake, March 18, 1988 (RG). Redheads are usually seen in small flocks; they mingle with other diving ducks. They seem more numerous in spring than in fall and usually are easier to approach for good views. The Redhead's major food items in Illinois are longleaf pondweed, coontail, and midge larvae (Anderson 1959).

Spring migration may occur as early as late January. Average spring arrival dates: Chicago, March 21 (six years); west-central, March 5 (12 years); Sangamon County, February 13 (17 years). There is little chance of confusing migrants with winter residents because so few Redheads winter in Illinois. High spring counts: 1000, Lake County, end of March 1979 (AB33:776); 1000, Olney, March 10, 1980 (LH-SR25:4); 400, Schuyler County, April 1, 1984 (LMc-SR41:10); 700, Fulton County, March 15, 1986 (RP-IB&B2:87); 600, Spring Lake, March 14, 1987 (RP). Spring bird counts come too late for peak numbers; totals have ranged from four to 39, with high counts in northern Illinois and the Illinois River valley. Average spring departure dates: Chicago, April 12 (six years); west-central, April 5 (12 years); Sangamon County, April 24 (18 years). Late departure dates are obscured by summering birds.

Redheads nest sparingly in Illinois in marshy habitat, usually in the north. Breeding records include a pair and

10 young east of Lake Calumet, June 9, 1974 (CC-AB28:909); two family groups in Lake County, summer 1975 (CC,GR-IAB175:27); several nests in Cook and Lake Counties, 1978 (AB32:1168); and one young among a Mallard brood at Lake Calumet, July 14, 1979 (RB,JL-AB33:867). Other summer records indicate possible breeding: one, Springfield, June 11, 1979 (HDB); pair, Lake Calumet, June 9, 1974 (CC-SR2:1); pair, Riverdale, July 4, 1984 (JL); male, Winfield, June 4, 1984 (JM-IB&B1:15); pair, Barrington, June 5–9, 1985 (RB&MBi-IB&B2:13); pair, Starved Rock State Park, June 27, 1985 (JMc-IB&B2:13); Horseshoe Lake, summer 1983 (RG).

Most fall migrants arrive in October, but there are some September records: Peoria, September 1, 1985 (MB,LMc-IB&B2:44); two, Jackson Park, September 16, 1985 (HR-IB&B2:44); Springfield, September 26, 1985 (HDB). Average fall arrival dates: west-central, October 24 (nine years); Sangamon County, October 10 (18 years). Maximum counts for fall: 18,000, Illinois and Mississippi Rivers, November 7, 1979 (RC-AB34:167); 380, Great Lakes, October 2, 1985 (JL,CM); 2240, Illinois and Mississippi Rivers, December 13, 1982 (RC-SR36:5). Bellrose (1976) says that Redheads migrating along the Mississippi River go southeast to the Florida panhandle. Average fall departure dates: west-central, December 3 (nine years); Sangamon County, December 9 (17 years). Some Redheads linger until late December or early January or until freeze-up.

Christmas bird counts verify that few Redheads winter in Illinois. Totals for 1976–85 ranged from nine in 1978 to 55 in 1981. Highest count was 60 at Chautauqua National Wildlife Refuge in 1950.

RING-NECKED DUCK

Aythya collaris

FAIRLY COMMON MIGRANT; UNCOMMON
WINTER AND VERY RARE SUMMER RESIDENT

On the wing this duck looks like a scaup, but it lacks the white stripe. Sitting on water, the drake Ring-neck shows a white slash in front of the wing that is discernible at great distances. Hens are brown and can be confused with other female diving ducks. Ring-necks are usually seen in small groups; they associate with other diving ducks, including scaup, Redheads, and Canvasbacks. Unlike some diving ducks, Ring-necks inhabit swampy areas and seem to prefer shallow sloughs and overflow areas with standing trees and stumps. They are also found on lakes, sewage lagoons, and open marshes. Their major food items in Illinois are coontail, corn, pondweed, and snails (Anderson 1959).

Migration in spring starts as early as February: 13, Springfield, February 12, 1984 (HDB); Charleston, February 11, 1987 (RBr); Chicago, February 12, 1983 (JL). Average spring arrival dates: Chicago, March 27 (seven years); west-central, March 4 (13 years); Sangamon County, February 19 (17 years). High counts for spring: 3000, Pool 19, February 20, 1987 (RC-AB41:287); 1000, Palos, March 21, 1981 (JL); 1000, Olney, March 14, 1984 (LH-SR41:10); 1000, Rice Lake, March 24, 1985 (MB,LMc-IB&B1:80); 300, Crab Orchard National Wildlife Refuge, March 3, 1983 (JR-SR37:7). Spring bird count totals ranged from 13 in 1985 to 572 in 1978. Nearly all high counts were from northern Illinois; the highest was 458 in Cook County, May 6, 1978 (VK). Average spring departure dates: Chicago, April 11 (seven years); west-central, April 18 (13 years); Sangamon County, April 27 (18 years).

The only breeding evidence is a juvenile female seen at Chicago, August 3, 1947 (Springer 1949). There are several other records of Ring-necks seen in summer, but breeding is uncertain: Chicago, July 1978 (JN-AB32:1168); male, Horseshoe Lake, June 1978 (RG); Lake Calumet, June 14, 1979 (JL-AB33:867); male, Powderhorn Marsh, June 30, 1974 (CC-SR2:1); Joliet, June 2–5, 1986 (JM-IB&B3:13); Sangamon County, June–July 20, 1986 (HDB). Most Ring-necked Ducks breed in boreal forests in the northern United States and Canada.

Early fall migration dates are in September: two, Olney, September 21, 1983 (LH-SR39:7); four, Savanna, September 22, 1985 (PP-IB&B2:44). Average fall arrival dates: west-central, October 13 (eight years); Sangamon County, October 7 (17 years). High counts for fall: 116,000, Illinois and Mississippi Rivers, November 7, 1979 (RC-AB34:167); 700, Springfield, November 22, 1983 (HDB); 500, Crab Orchard refuge, November 23, 1983 (JR-SR39:7); 200, Willow Springs, October 19, 1981 (PD-SR31:5). Average fall departure dates: west-central, November 25 (eight years); Sangamon County, December 7 (16 years). Stragglers stay on into late December and early January.

Most of the state's wintering Ring-necks are found in the south. Christmas bird count totals for 1976–85 were moderate, ranging from 27 in 1981 to 442 in 1985. Highest count was 1000 at Murphysboro in 1953. Bellrose (1976) says that many of the Ring-necks migrating through Illinois go south to Florida and the Gulf Coast, and some go as far as Panama.

TUFTED DUCK

Aythya fuligula

VERY RARE VAGRANT

The Tufted Duck, a Eurasian species, is a casual visitor in western Alaska and a rare vagrant in the remainder of the United States. It is found mostly along the coasts and the Great Lakes. Illinois has four records: male, Chicago, December 3, 1972–April 10, 1973 (CC); male, Chicago, December 23–27, 1973, and immature male, Lake Calumet, March 17, 1974 (CC-AB28:646); two pairs, Jackson Park, February 20, 1980 (Mlodinow 1984). These ducks are usually seen with Greater Scaup, and it will be noted that all records were in the Chicago area. They breed in marshy ponds and lakes but winter on larger bodies of water. The prominent feature of this duck is its tuft, present in adult males and to a lesser extent in immature males and females. Otherwise the Tufted Duck looks like a cross between a Greater Scaup and a Ring-necked Duck, having the wing stripe and rounded head of the Greater and a similar side patch and the dark back of the Ring-neck.

GREATER SCAUP

Aythya marila

COMMON MIGRANT AND FAIRLY COMMON
WINTER RESIDENT ALONG LAKE MICHIGAN;
OCCASIONAL MIGRANT AND WINTER
RESIDENT ELSEWHERE IN THE STATE

This duck's status is obscured by its likeness to the Lesser Scaup. The two scaup often fly in mixed flocks and many Greaters go unidentified downstate. Greaters are most numerous on large lakes and rivers but can be seen on ponds and sewage lagoons. Identification of Greater Scaup is fairly easy when they are close and in good light, but many are seen in flocks far out on the water. Points that distinguish the Greater from the Lesser are the broad wing stripe, more extensive in flight than the Lesser's; head shape; bill size; and the sides, which are whiter on sitting Greaters. Balch (1977) discusses these field marks. Greater Scaup breed on tundra and in boreal forests from Hudson Bay west to Alaska. They migrate to and from the Atlantic and Pacific Coasts, with small contingents going to the Gulf Coast. The subspecies in Illinois is *A. m. mariloides*.

Spring migration begins in late January or February: eight, Carlyle Lake, February 13, 1983 (SRu-SR37:7); 40, Pool 19, February 6–7, 1987 (AB41:287); four, Carlyle Lake, January 25, 1984 (BR-SR41:10). High counts in spring: 964, Jackson Park, February 19, 1983 (HR,PC-SR37:7); 1700, Chicago, March 21, 1971 (LB); 40, Horseshoe Lake, April 18, 1982 (RK-SR33:6); 44, Springfield, March 6, 1987 (HDB). Spring bird counts are done too late for peak numbers of Greater Scaup. Totals for 1972–86 ranged from none in 1973 and 1984 to 104 in 1978, when Cook County had the high count of 102 on May 6 (VK). Spring departure dates are usually in late April and early May, with a few birds lingering into summer. Some recent summer dates: pair, Lake Calumet, June 9–July 8, 1979 (RB-AB33:867); two to four, Waukegan, June 1–August 3, 1981 (JN-AB35:944); one, Springfield, May 31–June 25, 1985 (HDB).

Fall migration begins in October: two, Wilmette, October 4, 1986 (JL); 12, Glencoe, October 12, 1983 (DJ-SR39:7); male, Springfield, October 13, 1987 (HDB). High counts for fall: 900, Jackson Park, October 31, 1982 (HR-SR35:5); 787, Jackson Park, November 26, 1985 (HR-IB&B2:44).

Winter numbers are almost as high some years as fall counts. Christmas bird count totals for 1976–85 ranged from 40 in 1985 to 1271 in 1982, when 948 were counted at the Chicago lakefront. Other winter counts: 16, Olney, January 16, 1983 (LH-SR36:5); 60, Horseshoe Lake, winter 1981–82 (RK-AB36:299); 1000, Calumet Harbor, winter 1980–81 (JL); two, Crab Orchard National Wildlife Refuge, January 12, 1985 (TF).

LESSER SCAUP

Aythya affinis

ABUNDANT MIGRANT; UNCOMMON WINTER
AND RARE SUMMER RESIDENT

The Lesser Scaup is probably the most numerous of the diving ducks in Illinois. Huge flocks occur on lakes, ponds, overflow areas, and sewage lagoons during migration. On March 10, 1982, I saw a multitude of specks in the sky that spiraled down to land on Lake Springfield; it was a large flock of Lesser Scaup. Sometimes such flocks make a loud *whoosh* as they pass overhead. Lesser Scaup flock with Ring-necks, Canvasbacks, Redheads, and other diving ducks—sometimes even with puddle ducks. In Illinois the Lesser Scaup spend much of their time resting on water, but occasionally they actively dive for food. Anderson (1959) found that they feed mostly on snails, mussels, and mayflies, along with such plant food as coontail and pondweed. An estimated 1500 waterfowl—75 percent of them Lesser Scaup—died of lead poisoning at Rice Lake in the spring of 1972 (Anderson 1975).

There is an early spring flight of Lesser Scaup as the ice is receding, but most of these divers pass through in March and April. Males move early; females predominate in later flocks. Average spring arrival dates: west-central, March 2 (14 years); Sangamon County, February 15 (15 years). High counts for spring: 30,000, Pool 19, March 4, 1986 (RC-AB40:477); 4000, Rice Lake, March 24, 1985 (MB-IB&B1:80); 4000, Alton, March 23, 1986 (RG); 2630, Crab Orchard National Wildlife Refuge, April 11, 1985 (JR-IB&B1:80); 4000, Springfield, March 27, 1981 (HDB). Spring bird count totals ranged from 66 in 1986 to 2075 in 1978. Most high counts were in the north; the highest was 719 in Cook County on May 6, 1978 (VK). Average spring departure dates: west-central, May 7 (14 years); Sangamon County, May 24 (18 years). Some individuals straggle into late May and June.

There are a few references to nesting by Lesser Scaup in Illinois. Nelson (1876) stated that "their young are hatched from the first to the middle of June." Coale (1912) listed breeding records at Butler's Lake and Grass Lake in June 1909. And a pair nested in central Illinois near Quincy in 1968 (TEM-AFN22:612). Otherwise, records refer to nonbreeding birds: two, Lake Calumet, summer 1986 (RB-IB&B3:13); one to three males, Wabash County, June 5–July 11, 1982 (LH-SR34:4); pair, Champaign County, June 9, 1980 (RCh-SR26:3); male, Joliet, June 20, 1987 (JM); two males, Monmouth, summer 1986 (MB-IB&B3:13).

Some 500,000 Lesser Scaup migrate in a corridor that

starts at the Yukon, passes through Pool 19 on the Mississippi River, and ends in Florida and Louisiana (Bellrose 1976). These birds start showing up in Illinois from mid- to late September. Average fall arrival dates: west-central, October 18 (11 years); Sangamon County, October 8 (18 years). High counts for fall: 447,000, Illinois and Mississippi Rivers, November 7, 1979 (RC-AB34:167); 5000, Chicago, November 16, 1980 (JL); 3730, Crab Orchard refuge, October 28, 1984 (JR-IB&B1:14); 40,000, Nauvoo, November 20, 1983 (AD-AB38:208). These scaup tend to linger until the end of November or early December.

Some Lesser Scaup winter in Illinois where there is open water. Christmas bird count totals for 1976–85 ranged from 109 in 1976 to 984 in 1980, with most high counts coming from the Lake Michigan area. Highest count was 4250 at Sand Ridge in 1971. Most years the numbers are fairly low, however. Other high counts for winter: 450, Illinois and Mississippi Rivers, January 3, 1983 (RC-SR36:5); 164, Waukegan, January 1, 1985 (RB-IB&B1:67); 75, Baldwin Lake, January 10, 1986 (DR-IB&B2:75).

COMMON EIDER

Somateria mollissima

VERY RARE VAGRANT

There are only five records for this sea duck in Illinois, with dates ranging from December 7 to April 12: immature (specimen) near Chicago, December, 1874 (Nelson 1876); adult male, Lincoln Park, Chicago, April 12, 1943 (Clark and Nice 1950); one, Belmont Harbor, Cook County, December 7, 1945 (Ford 1956); male, Chicago, February 1, 1960 (HF,HL-AFN14:312); immature male, Sterling, Rock River, March 11–April 8, 1978 (BSh-AB32:1013). The Common Eider is the largest duck in the Northern Hemisphere. It flies low over the water in an alternating flap and glide flight. An Arctic nester, it migrates to the Atlantic and Pacific Coasts to winter. Four subspecies are found in North America. The race seen in Illinois apparently is *S. m. dresseri* from the northeast. The AOU (1957), however, records the "Pacific" Eider, *S. m. v-nigra*, from as close as Kansas and Iowa, so this race could conceivably occur in Illinois.

KING EIDER

Somateria spectabilis

VERY RARE WINTER RESIDENT

Of the two eiders recorded in Illinois, the King is the one most likely to be seen. This large duck is usually found on large bodies of water in rough weather, although a few Kings have been spotted along the larger rivers. There are

20 records for Illinois, and 13 are from the Lake Michigan area. Not counted are the four or five shot at Calumet Harbor on November 26, 1959 (AFN14:312), since the site was actually about half a mile over the border in Indiana. The southernmost record is of an immature male and two females shot at Rend Lake, November 1973 (Harvey Pitt). All King Eiders recorded to date have been immatures or females.

The range of dates for this winter duck is October 11 (three at Wilmette in 1972, JSa) to April 18 (at Springfield in 1987). Most arrival dates are in mid-November, so October 11 is about a month earlier than any other date. Some King Eiders have stayed in the same area for a considerable time: female, Lake Springfield, February 19–March 17, 1979 (HDB); female, Lake Decatur, February 13–March 26, 1971 (HDB); immature male, Lake Michigan, November 24–December 8, 1986 (AB41:287).

The maximum count undoubtedly is the one reported by Eifrig (1919): "On November 29, 1917, six or seven of this species were shot out of a flock of about thirty, off the Municipal Pier [Chicago]. They were all birds of the year, and one of them is now in my collection." The earliest record for the state is of an adult female collected at Chillicothe on the Illinois River in the winter of 1874 (Nelson 1876). Other records: immature male, taken off Jackson Park, Chicago, December 1, 1908 (DeVine 1909); immature male, Henry, November 21, 1936 (Wheeler 1937); female, Great Lakes Naval Base, December 1974 (Mlodinow 1984); immature male, Calumet Park, March 3, 1968 (LBi,JG,CC-AFN22:444); female, Evanston, December 22, 1985 (RB&MBi-AB40:286).

The King Eider breeds in the Arctic circumpolar region. It migrates to both the East and West Coasts of North America and winters north to where the seas remain free of ice. Very few of these sea ducks come inland, but they probably occur yearly on the Great Lakes, usually in very small numbers.

Although King Eiders are reported to eat mainly mollusks, crustaceans, and echinoderms, in Illinois they have been seen taking small fish. But since they are great divers, they may take food items that observers cannot see.

HARLEQUIN DUCK

Histrionicus histrionicus

RARE MIGRANT AND WINTER RESIDENT ON LAKE MICHIGAN; VERY RARE ELSEWHERE IN THE STATE

A few members of this coastal species winter along the jetties and rocky shores of the Great Lakes. The adult males are a unique slate blue with white and reddish brown markings, while females and immature males are dark brown with white spots on the head. Harlequins look rather like scoters on the water but are smaller, with smaller bills. Occasionally these divers flock with Bufflehead but are usually seen close in to shore along the rocks. At times they are seen with the local Mallards or with coots. In flight they keep their heads up and chests out, looking almost cootlike, but they are much stronger fliers. Harlequin Ducks are seen practically every year on Lake Michigan, with extreme dates ranging from late September to late April. The earliest fall migrant was seen at Evanston on September 22, 1973 (LB-AB28:59); the latest was at Oakhill Cemetery Lagoon on April 29, 1932 (Mlodinow 1984). There are very few downstate records for this duck: specimen, Madison County, October 29, 1880 (Hurter collection); pair, Lake Decatur, April 4, 1926 (Eddy 1927); male, Lake Decatur, December 30, 1955–March 28, 1956 (RS,TN); pair, Lake Springfield, January 7, 1984 (DO); female, Lock 13, Whiteside County, November 13, 1971 (LB,GR-AB26:71). Some recent records for Lake Michigan: Evanston, November 21–early December 1978 (RB-AB33:182); two, Chicago, October 22–25, 1980 (PC-AB35:188); Chicago, March 5– April 4, 1981 (PC,RG,JL-AB35:829); Chicago, January 30, 1982 (JL); Waukegan, November 9-10, 1985 (MS,RB-IB&B2:44). High count for this rare duck was four at Wilmette, October 19, 1959 (Russell 1970).

OLDSQUAW

Clangula hyemalis

COMMON MIGRANT AND WINTER RESIDENT ON LAKE MICHIGAN; RARE ELSEWHERE IN THE STATE

The name Oldsquaw comes from the fact that these ducks are constantly calling. Another name for them, Long-tailed Ducks, obviously derives from the long central tail feathers of the drakes. Most Oldsquaws seen in Illinois are in the white plumage with brown patches since they occur in winter, but sometimes toward spring the browner birds may be seen. They have stubby bills, which in drakes are pinkish on the tip. These divers seem to favor deep water, whether they choose lakes or ponds; occasionally they are seen in the shallower water of sewage lagoons. Oldsquaws can dive quite deep and can stay under water for 30 seconds or more. Some mortality occurs when these ducks are caught in fish nets on Lake Michigan; 15,500 were killed in 1951–52 (Bellrose 1976). A specimen in the Illinois State Museum apparently smashed into a tree at Wilmette, March 26, 1972, when flying in off Lake Michigan in fog. Hull (1915) found that Oldsquaws ate silvery minnows at Chicago, but they also eat crustaceans and mollusks. They nest in the Arctic circumpolar region. Bellrose (1976) estimated a total North American population in early summer of three to four million.

Most early records of Oldsquaws in fall are for late October, but one was observed still in breeding plumage at Lake Decatur, October 1, 1974 (RS). Average fall arrival dates: Chicago, November 1 (16 years); Sangamon County,

November 24 (11 years). Maximum counts in fall: 400, Evanston, November 22, 1979 (RB-AB34:167); 150, Chicago, November 17, 1985 (RB,MBi-AB40:119); seven, Lake Springfield, November 11, 1980 (HDB).

Numbers build up as winter progresses. In Christmas bird counts for 1976–85 all high counts came from Lake Michigan; totals ranged from 27 in 1978 to 1711 in 1982. There has been a definite drop in numbers since the 1950s, however. The highest Christmas count was 17,669 at Chicago in 1952. Other winter counts: 400, Lake Michigan, 1978–79 (AB33:285); 300, Chicago, February 4, 1984 (JL). Downstate records include a pair at Crab Orchard National Wildlife Refuge, December 20–February 27, 1986 (TF-IB&B2:75); seven at Baldwin Lake, February 19, 1983 (JL-SR36:5); and one in Coles County, January 7, 1985 (LBH-IB&B1:67). Bellrose (1976) indicated that at least part of the population that winters on Lake Michigan comes from the west coast of Hudson Bay.

Once in a while an observer can detect Oldsquaws returning in spring from farther south or perhaps from the east. Nonetheless, spring is mostly a time of departure for wintering birds. Maximum spring counts: 65, Winnetka, March 29, 1986 (CM,JL-IB&B2:87); 14, Grundy County, April 3, 1980 (RC-AB34:781); three, Olney, April 11–24, 1984 (LH-SR41:11). Average spring departure dates: Chicago, April 14 (16 years); Sangamon County, March 23 (seven years). Oldsquaws have been sighted on only two spring bird counts, both in Cook County, May 10, 1975, and May 6, 1978 (VK). Other late spring departure dates: Waukegan, May 24, 1970 (CC-AFN24:614); Olney, April 27, 1987 (LH).

BLACK SCOTER

Melanitta nigra

UNCOMMON MIGRANT ON LAKE MICHIGAN; RARE MIGRANT ELSEWHERE IN THE STATE

This dark-winged scoter in female or immature male plumage resembles an oversized Ruddy Duck because of its shape, occasional upturned tail, and whitish cheek patch. Like other scoters, Blacks spend most of their time resting on water. Adult males are seldom seen in fall and only occasionally in spring. Most scoters migrate toward the coasts in a generally east-west rather than north-south migration. Even those that get as far south as the Great Lakes move from there toward the coasts, making the scoters much less numerous downstate. Black (formerly Common) Scoters are usually seen on large bodies of water, but they occasionally occur on sewage ponds. I saw four on an overflow of the south fork of the Sangamon River, November 25, 1985—which was unusual because the water was shallow. The race occurring in Illinois is *M. n. americana,* which breeds in Alaska and scattered areas of Canada and winters on the coasts of North America.

Black Scoters are not very numerous during spring

migration; some years none are seen. Earliest spring records: Chicago, March 1, 1982 (PC-AB36:858); Springfield, April 3, 1986 (HDB). There are no spring concentrations even on Lake Michigan, although four were seen at Evanston, April 24, 1976 (Mlodinow 1984). Late dates for spring: Chicago, May 6, 1978 (JN-AB32:1013); two, Wilmette, June 16, 1964 (RR-AFN18:511).

Fall migration gives observers the best chance to find this sea duck in Illinois. Like the Surf Scoter, the Black seems to show up downstate several years in a row and then to disappear for essentially the same number of years. Early fall arrivals: Waukegan, September 8, 1971 (RR-AB26:71); 32, Chicago, October 2, 1981 (JL). Average fall arrival date for central Illinois is November 5 (11 years). Maximum fall counts: 41, Wilmette, October 25, 1976 (LB,GR); 27, Alton, November 15, 1977 (CS-AB32:211); 40, Chicago, November 4, 1967 (CC-AFN22:48). Average fall departure date for central Illinois is November 22 (five years). Most of these scoters leave toward the end of November, but some are seen in December: Alton, December 22, 1985 (BR-AB40:286); Chicago, December 25, 1979 (RB,JL-SR24:2); specimen, Charleston, December 5, 1970 (LBH-AB25:585); two, Crab Orchard National Wildlife Refuge, December 2, 1984 (JR-IB&B1:67); Lake Springfield, December 12, 1975 (HDB). True winter records seem to be lacking, although Christmas bird counts for 1976–85 showed two in 1980 in Chicago and three in 1977 in Cook and Will Counties.

SURF SCOTER

Melanitta perspicillata

UNCOMMON MIGRANT AND VERY RARE
WINTER RESIDENT ON LAKE MICHIGAN;
RARE MIGRANT ELSEWHERE IN THE STATE

The Surf Scoter is smaller than the White-winged Scoter but about the same size as the Black Scoter, with which it sometimes is seen. At a distance the two white spots on the face of the Surf Scoter tend to merge, and it can be mistaken for a Black. The Surf Scoter, however, has a more sloped head and a heavier bill, and this profile helps separate the two dark-winged scoters. In spring the male Surf Scoter has a highly colored bill and a white patch on the nape. Surf Scoters are usually seen resting on the water, often in a sleeping position with their heads over their backs. When they dive they flip their wings out just before submersion. They occur in small flocks, usually with such other ducks as scaup and Ruddies. The Surf Scoter is confined to North America, breeding in boreal areas of northern Canada. It winters on the Pacific and Atlantic Coasts and rarely south to the Gulf Coast.

Very few Surf Scoters are seen in spring migration. The earliest was seen on February 26, 1978, at Joliet (JF-AB32:358). Most spring records are for March, April, and May, with no large concentrations. Other spring records:

six, Wilmette, March 26, 1982 (JL); Wabash County, May 1–2, 1982 (LH-SR33:6); Alton, May 4, 1985 (BR,SRu,MP-IB&B1:80); Carbondale, May 23–31, 1977 (MMo-AB31:1007); McLean County, April 27–28, 1978 (RCh,JFr-AB32:1013); pair, De Witt County, May 9, 1987 (CB). Spring bird counts showed very small numbers (one or two birds) in only five years.

Although Surf Scoters are seen every fall along Lake Michigan, they (and Black Scoters) exhibit a strange pattern in Sangamon County, where Lake Springfield was monitored daily. From 1970 to 1973, none were recorded; then from 1973 to 1977 they were recorded each year. Then there were none from 1978 to 1983, when they were again recorded each year up to and including 1987. Whether these gaps are related to populations, cold fronts, or observer bias is unknown. Practically all Surf Scoters seen in fall in downstate Illinois are immatures or females. Earliest fall birds were 10 at Waukegan, September 26, 1976 (Mlodinow 1984). Most arrive in October; the average for central Illinois is October 19 (10 years). Maximum counts for fall are much higher than in spring: 55, Wilmette, October 20, 1985 (RB,MBi-AB40:119); 65, Wilmette, October 18, 1986 (JL). No large flocks have been encountered downstate; the maximum was six at Lake Springfield, October 31, 1984 (HDB). Most of these scoters pass through in November. Average departure date for central Illinois is November 10 (seven years).

Wintering records for these ducks are few; most December records are probably of late fall migrants. Possible winter records: two, Jackson Park, January 26, 1981 (PC,RG-SR28:4); Chicago, January 18–19, 1980 (JL,RB-SR24:2); Olney, December 16, 1985 (LH-IB&B2:75); Crab Orchard National Wildlife Refuge, December 2, 1984 (JR); Carlyle Lake, December 19, 1986 (RG).

WHITE-WINGED SCOTER

Melanitta fusca

UNCOMMON MIGRANT AND OCCASIONAL
WINTER RESIDENT ON LAKE MICHIGAN;
RARE MIGRANT AND WINTER RESIDENT
ELSEWHERE IN THE STATE

This large dark sea duck has prominent white wing patches, but these patches in the secondaries can be completely concealed when this scoter is at rest on the water. White-winged Scoter flocks have a distinctive look when they fly low to the water in lines. White-wings are usually found on Lake Michigan, but smaller lakes, large rivers, and occasionally sewage ponds also attract them. They usually move on after resting on the water for a short time. Occasionally some are seen actively diving, although their food habits in Illinois are unknown. White-winged Scoters breed almost circumpolar in tundra. Some also breed in the taiga region, and a few breed as far south as North Dakota. They winter primarily in coastal areas and at sea. The race that occurs in Illinois and most of North America is *M. f. deglandi.*

Sometimes these scoters arrive in the spring before the ice thaws, even as early as late January. Early spring records: Crab Orchard National Wildlife Refuge, late January–February 16, 1971 (DH,F.Reuter-AB25:585); Chillicothe, February 18, 1973 (VH-AB27:623); 35, Jackson Park, February 17, 1982 (PC,HR-SR33:6); six, Springfield, January 19, 1982 (HDB). Average arrival date for central Illinois is February 23 (seven years). Maximum counts in spring vary considerably, since weather factors sometimes bring concentrations. All large counts occur on Lake Michigan: 3000, Lake Michigan, early February 1977 (GR-AB31:337); 1700, Wilmette, February 13, 1983 (JL); 475, Wilmette, March 3, 1984 (JL). Only stragglers are left by April: Waukegan, April 21, 1979 (DJ:AB33:776); three, Chicago, April 26, 1980 (JL). A few occur into May; they have been recorded four years on spring bird counts in small numbers (one to four). One was at Waukegan, May 9–15, 1981 (JN-SR29:6), and a very late female was at Jackson Park, June 13, 1985 (HR-IB&B1:80). Fall migration usually starts in October but sometimes not until November. Average arrival date for central Illinois is November 2 (nine years). There are earlier dates for Lake Michigan: one to four, Chicago, September 9–26, 1980 (JL-SR27:4); Chicago, September 15, 1982 (JL). Maximum counts for fall are much lower than in spring: 25, Wilmette, November 12, 1984 (AA-IB&B1:14); 18, Lake Springfield, October 29, 1984 (DO,HDB). Fall departures dates are less clear because of wintering birds, but the average for central Illinois is November 28 (six years).

White-winged Scoters do not winter every year. Indeed, Christmas bird counts for 1976–85 listed these birds only six out of the 10 years and mostly in low numbers, from one to 33. Highest count was 266 at Chicago in 1970. Other winter records: 1000, Chicago, winter 1978–79 (AB33:286); 760, Wilmette, winter 1983–84 (JL); Charleston, January 1–9, 1985 (RBr,LBH-IB&B1:67); Alton, January 8–10, 1981 (BR-SR28:3); Olney, December 12–22, 1980 (LH-SR28:3).

COMMON GOLDENEYE

Bucephala clangula

COMMON MIGRANT AND WINTER RESIDENT

The Common Goldeneye can be identified before being seen by the whistling sound that its wings make. Drakes are handsome studies in black and white, with a green sheen to the head and a white spot on the face. Females and immatures have brown heads and grayish bodies. Goldeneyes are swift fliers and good divers. They inhabit large bodies of water but can also be found on ponds, sewage lagoons, large rivers, and overflow areas. Bellrose (1976) watched Common Goldeneyes feeding on gizzard shad in the Illinois River valley and timed the dives; they

averaged 30 seconds. These goldeneyes breed in the boreal zone almost circumpolar. The North American subspecies is *B. c. americana.* I have noticed that in the Springfield area these goldeneyes feed on ponds during the day but return to Lake Springfield at night to roost. These ducks show courtship displays toward spring, sometimes beginning in January. In this display the male throws back his head and then swiftly brings it forward, all the while giving a harsh nasal call. Jim Landing found a hybrid Common Goldeneye and Hooded Merganser at Chicago, December 27, 1981. Another was seen at Horseshoe Lake, January 31, 1983 (BR).

Early fall arrivals: Evanston, September 21, 1985 (BHu-AB40:119); Wilmette, October 18, 1986 (JL). Average arrival dates: Chicago, November 22 (16 years); west-central, November 11 (seven years); Sangamon County, November 5 (18 years). Maximum counts for fall: 700, Chicago, November 24, 1979 (RB-SR23:4); 500, Hancock County, November 24, 1985 (AD-IB&B2:44); 500, Springfield, November 9, 1985 (HDB). This migration is sometimes late, with birds arriving only after they are forced out by icy conditions farther north.

Christmas bird count totals for 1976–85 ranged from 2364 in 1983 to 8118 in 1982. Will and Grundy Counties had the high count of 4190 in 1982. Evidence suggests that Common Goldeneye numbers have dropped since the 1950s; the highest Christmas bird count was 5213 at Waukegan in 1951. Other maximum winter counts: 19,000, Illinois and Mississippi Rivers, January 3, 1983 (RC-AB37:307); 1000, Madison County, February 13, 1982 (RK-SR32:3); 1500, Chicago, December 18, 1985 (RB,MBi-AB40:286); 600, Horseshoe Lake, December 6, 1985 (RG-IB&B2:44); 160, Crab Orchard National Wildlife Refuge, December 17, 1983 (SR40:6).

Few of these goldeneyes go much farther south than Illinois, so the return of these birds in spring is usually not impressive. Average spring departure dates: Chicago, April 9 (16 years); Sangamon County, April 10 (18 years). Oddly enough, these goldeneyes have been recorded every year on spring bird counts but in small numbers (one to 30). The highest count, 22 in Marshall County, May 7, 1977, seems somewhat suspect because the next highest is only five and all other high counts are for northern counties.

Several summer records for these goldeneyes are of non-breeding and perhaps of injured birds: Chicago, July 24, 1980 (JL); Roscoe, June 4, 1982 (DW-AB36:982); Lockport, June 2, 1986 (JM-AB40:477); Springfield, June 12, 1988 (HDB).

BARROW'S GOLDENEYE

Bucephala islandica

VERY RARE MIGRANT AND WINTER RESIDENT

This duck has a divided breeding range, in the northwest and the northeast. The northwest component has by far the larger population, and in fact not much is known about the small northeastern population. The adult male Barrow's Goldeneye, with its loral crescent, is fairly distinct from the Common Goldeneye if one can get a good view of it, but immatures and females are difficult to separate. Tobish (1986) provides an aid in identification.

There are at least 25 Illinois records of the Barrow's, but some lack evidence or may be suspect. The dates fall between November 15 and May 3, with three discovered in November, seven in December, three in January, two in February, eight in March, and two in April. Some of these Barrow's were unsexed, but most were identified as males. There were two records of lone females: one shot at Lima Lake, March 27, 1888 (Widmann 1907), and one seen at Chicago, December 16, 1974 (GR-AB29:697). The first Illinois record was of a specimen taken at Mount Carmel in December 1874 (Nelson 1876). Some records are of more than one bird per sighting: seven (two males and a female killed), Quincy, November 15, 1955 (TEM-AFN10:28); about seven (at least three males), Jackson Park, January 13–March 18, 1920 (Ford 1956); five killed, Quincy, November 23, 1923 (Smith and Parmalee 1955). Recent records include an immature male at Chicago, March 24 and 28, 1979 (GN,JL-AB33:776), and an immature male at Great Lakes, March 3, 1985 (RB&MBi-IB&B1:80). These ducks are usually found at large bodies of water with Common Goldeneyes.

BUFFLEHEAD

Bucephala albeola

FAIRLY COMMON MIGRANT AND UNCOMMON WINTER RESIDENT

This very small diver is one of the duck species in which males are black and white. Females and immature males are dark with a white area behind the eyes. Buffleheads occur on big bodies of water but also can be found on ponds and sewage lagoons. They are swift, direct fliers and usually fly low over the surface of the water. Their dives have been timed at about 20 seconds. Except for a few vagrants, the Bufflehead is confined to North America, where its total population has been estimated to be 745,000 (Bellrose 1976). Erskine (1972) noted a decline in the population in the late 1800s and early 1900s, probably a result of over-shooting. Buffleheads breed mainly in mixed coniferous-deciduous forests in Alaska and Canada; a few breed in the northern United States. They eat fish, snails, and insects. They migrate in small to medium-sized flocks, rarely in large numbers. Their migration is mostly nocturnal.

October is the time Buffleheads arrive in Illinois. Early fall arrival dates: Horseshoe Lake, October 8, 1982 (JEa-AB37:186); Illinois Beach State Park, October 8, 1983 (DJ-SR39:8). Average fall arrival dates: Chicago, November 19 (five years); west-central, November 6 (seven years); Sangamon County, October 31 (17 years). Maximum counts for

fall: 7300, Illinois and Mississippi Rivers, November 13, 1979 (RC-AB34:167); 200, Whiteside County, November 14, 1981 (MSw-SR31:5); 150, Springfield, November 12, 1986 (HDB). Although some Buffleheads winter in Illinois, most migrate farther south. Bellrose (1976) shows most of the Illinois migrants going on to the Gulf Coast or the southern Atlantic Coast. Average fall departure dates: Chicago, December 5 (five years); Sangamon County, December 12 (11 years).

Most of the wintering population is on Lake Michigan or the Mississippi River. Some Buffleheads occur in southern Illinois in winter, but most of them are probably very late migrants. Christmas bird count totals ranged from 44 in 1981 to 162 in 1984. Highest count was 75 in Lake County in 1979. Other winter counts: 80, Crab Orchard National Wildlife Refuge, December 6, 1984 (JR-IB&B1:68); 100, Evanston, December 15, 1985 (EW-IB&B2:75); 1445, Mississippi and Illinois Rivers, December 13, 1982, and 160, January 3, 1983 (RC-SR36:5).

Spring migration can be difficult to detect in its early stages because of wintering birds, but late February is the usual time. Average spring arrival dates: Chicago, March 15 (18 years); Sangamon County, February 22 (17 years). Maximum counts for spring: 101, Williamson and Jackson Counties, March 15, 1985 (JR-IB&B1:80); 80, Olney, March 25, 1984 (LH-SR41:11); 45, Lake Shelbyville, March 9, 1986 (KF-IB&B2:87); 58, Springfield, March 29, 1987 (HDB); 80, Spring Lake, April 12, 1987 (MB). Spring bird counts had Buffleheads every year, with totals from five (1981) to 143 (1978). Highest count was 84 in Cook County, May 6, 1978 (VK). Average spring departure dates: Chicago, April 17 (eight years); west-central, April 17 (12 years); Sangamon County, April 24 (18 years).

There are several summer records of nonbreeding birds: Jackson Park, June 12–16, 1981 (PC,HR-SR30:5); Lake Calumet, June 14–23, 1979 (RB,JL-AB33:867); Springfield, June 21–22, 1980 (HDB); Chicago, August 21, 1983 (AB38:208).

HOODED MERGANSER

Lophodytes cucullatus

UNCOMMON MIGRANT AND WINTER RESIDENT DECREASING NORTHWARD; OCCASIONAL SUMMER RESIDENT

The male Hooded Merganser, with a fan-shaped crest and black and white bars on the sides of the breast, is as strikingly colored as the male Wood Duck. Females are much duller but have a loose brownish crest. Hooded Mergansers usually fly low over the water, very fast and direct. Like Wood Ducks, they prefer sloughs, ponds, and wooded creeks but also will sit on open lakes. Most Hooded Mergansers breed in the upper Great Lakes region, but a few breed in Illinois and south to the Gulf states. These mergansers are seldom seen in large flocks; they usually occur singly or in pairs. Their food consists of fish, crustaceans, and aquatic insects.

Spring migration may commence as early as January, but wintering birds obscure the first arrivals. Early spring arrivals: 13, Crab Orchard National Wildlife Refuge, February 3, 1984 (JR-SR41:11); three, Fulton County, February 5, 1981 (VH-SR29:6); two, Chicago, February 18, 1982 (AA-SR33:6); three, Springfield, January 27, 1987 (HDB). Average arrival dates: Chicago, March 30 (eight years); Sangamon County, February 22 (16 years). Numbers are usually low because these birds are in pairs for breeding: 60, Crab Orchard refuge, February 13, 1983 (JR-SR37:7); 14, Chicago, March 22, 1986 (JL). Spring bird counts also show low numbers (one to 44); by then these birds are well into the breeding cycle. The highest count was only three, in Fayette County, May 8, 1982, and Carroll County, May 5, 1984 (VK). Spring departures are obscured by summer birds, but most migrants are gone by mid- to late April.

Nelson (1876) stated that "the last of August 1875, I found several pairs of these birds with partly grown young upon some small lakes in Union County." Loucks (1892) mentioned a nest in Tazewell County, and Coale (1912) said he found nesting at Grass Lake in May 1909. This merganser nests in hollow trees, usually in bottomland forests and swamps, so the nest contents are difficult to assess. The young are usually seen with the adults. Recent nesting records: six young, Jackson Park, 1980; pair at Bartonville, 1981; six nests, Barrington, 1984; 11 young, Union County, 1984; six young, Henderson County, 1984; three broods, Crabtree Nature Center, 1986; female and eight young, Springfield, 1985; female and six young, Banner Marsh, 1985. Females or immatures have been seen in several other areas also; breeding seems to be statewide but local.

Hooded Mergansers move rather late in fall. Average arrival dates: west-central, November 6 (nine years); Sangamon County, October 26 (17 years). In some years after a cold snap, flocks of these wary woodland ducks appear on lakes where good counts can be made. High counts for fall: 1600, Illinois and Mississippi Rivers, November 13, 1979 (RC-AB34:167); 300, Carlyle Lake, November 21, 1987 (SRu); 143, Crab Orchard refuge, November 26, 1986 (DR-IB&B3:37); 150, Springfield, November 22, 1983 (HDB). Fall departure dates are probably in early December or whenever the lakes and rivers begin to freeze.

Most of the Hooded Mergansers that winter in Illinois do so in the south. Some occur early, then apparently drift farther south when severe weather sets in. Christmas bird count totals ranged from 32 in 1978 to 219 in 1982. Highest count was 356 at Crab Orchard refuge in 1957. Other winter records: 100, Crab Orchard refuge, January 24, 1987 (DR-AB41:287); 420, Mississippi and Illinois Rivers, January 3, 1983 (RC-SR36:6); 50, Baldwin Lake, January 2, 1984 (TF-SR40:6). Most Hooded Mergansers winter in the Gulf Coast states.

COMMON MERGANSER
Mergus merganser

COMMON MIGRANT AND WINTER RESIDENT

This large duck brings to mind cold weather and iced lakes with a minimum of open water. Sometimes a flight of 30 or 40 Common Mergansers can be seen flying with shallow wingbeats along a large river, their salmon-colored underparts shining in the sun. Female Common Mergansers are sometimes confused with Red-breasted Mergansers. With experience, the well-delineated throat patch, darker rufous head, and more robust appearance will distinguish the Common Mergansers. These mergansers sit low on the water, usually with their heads thrust somewhat forward. To catch fish they dive below the surface of the water in teams.

Since the earliest writings on Illinois birds (Cooke 1888 and Ridgway 1895), this species has been termed common. It remains so today during winter months, but there has been a decline since the early 1950s on Lake Michigan, evidently correlated with lower populations of certain fish this merganser feeds on. The creation of lakes, particularly cooling lakes, in Illinois has now provided open water all winter, however, and many of these birds have evidently found their way to them. Bellrose (1976) indicates that 20,000 Common Mergansers winter in Illinois. These birds are spread out mainly on large lakes and the larger rivers where ice conditions permit. Some maximum counts for winter: 1390, Crab Orchard National Wildlife Refuge, November 30, 1960 (Bush-AFN15:45); 32,000, Chicago, mid-December 1951 (Mlodinow 1984); 5000, Rend Lake (Christmas bird count), January 1, 1978 (AB32:695); 30,079, Morris-Wilmington (Christmas bird count), December 26, 1981 (AB36:603); 4383, Illini State Park (Christmas bird count), December 22, 1985 (AB 40:834).

Most migration appears to be diurnal; flocks of these mergansers are common flybys in December along lakes and rivers. In fall they are among the latest migrant ducks to arrive. Most arrival dates are in mid-November, but Jim Landing records them almost annually in October along Lake Michigan. His earliest date for Chicago is October 6, 1984, and fair numbers sometimes occur, including 125 at Winnetka, October 27, 1985 (JL). The earliest date for Lake Springfield in Sangamon County is November 8, 1971. George (1968) lists October 20 for southern Illinois. Fall does not usually produce high numbers, but 780 were at Chicago on November 16, 1986 (JL). Common Mergansers stay until early or mid-April: Chicago, April 14, 1985 (JL); female, Lake Springfield, April 23, 1970 (HDB). Although there should be a spring buildup in numbers, few spring maxima are available: 815, Chicago, March 10, 1985 (JL); 400, Channahon, February 23, 1969 (Mlodinow 1984). In spring these birds may tend to choose smaller bodies of water, thus spreading out the population. Some birds (including a few crippled) linger into May, and a few evidently summer in Illinois: pair, Lake Calumet, June 26–August 2, 1970 (CC-AFN 24:690); male, Hampton, June

12–July 10, 1955 (PP-IAB98:15); Waukegan, summered, 1978 (JN-AB32:1168); two, Lake Calumet, summer 1979 (RB-AB33:867); pair, Lake Calumet, July 11, 1986 (JL). There are no breeding records for Illinois. Common Mergansers nest in tree cavities, mostly in the boreal zone of Canada and the mountains of the western United States.

RED-BREASTED MERGANSER

Mergus serrator

COMMON MIGRANT; UNCOMMON WINTER RESIDENT

This merganser is shaggy crested, and the male is quite distinctive in breeding plumage. The females and immatures closely resemble Common Mergansers. The Red-breasted is mainly a coastal species, but the Great Lakes get good numbers during migration, and some Red-breasts usually winter there. The breeding grounds are mainly in Alaska and Canada, but some breed as far south as central Wisconsin. In Illinois they are mostly seen on larger bodies of water. Although they are sometimes seen on sewage lagoons, they definitely depend on deeper water. They eat mostly fish, which they sometimes capture by working as a unit, all diving at the same time.

Fall migrants may arrive as early as September: Chicago, September 5, 1985 (CM-IB&B2:44); Lake County, September 30, 1985 (RB-IB&B2:44). Mid- to late October is more normal, however. Average arrival dates: Chicago, November 7 (16 years); west-central, November 12 (six years); Sangamon County, October 31 (18 years). Maximum counts for fall: 2080, Lake Calumet, December 19, 1987 (JL); 1700, Chicago, November 11, 1984 (JL); 300, Crab Orchard National Wildlife Refuge, November 24, 1982 (JR-SR35:6); 210, Lake Decatur, November 30, 1985 (RP-IB&B2:44). Migrants linger into December or until freeze-up. The average departure date for Sangamon County is December 8 (13 years).

Most wintering Red-breasted Mergansers are on or near Lake Michigan. Christmas bird count totals fluctuate widely, from 31 in 1980 to 2263 in 1984. Highest count was 2798 at Chicago in 1955. Other winter records: 105, Jackson Park, January 23, 1983 (HR-SR36:6); seven, Carlyle Lake, January 29, 1984 (SRu-SR40:6); 49, Waukegan, January 1, 1985 (RB-IB&B1:68).

Spring migrants may arrive as early as February: 78, Jackson Park, February 6, 1983 (HR-SR37:8); Carlyle Lake, February 3, 1987 (RG); three, Chautauqua National Wildlife Refuge, February 15, 1984 (KR-SR41:11). Average spring arrival dates: west-central, March 6 (11 years); Sangamon County, March 2 (17 years). Maximum spring counts: 10,000, Lake Michigan, April 9, 1977 (Mlodinow 1984); 5200, Chicago, March 27, 1982 (JL); 800, Crab Orchard refuge, March 25, 1987 (DR); 400, Lake Springfield, April 11, 1983 (HDB). Spring bird count totals are fairly low because counts are taken well past the peak for

Red-breasts. Totals ranged from 10 in 1972 and 1973 to 1438 in 1978. Highest count was 1342 in Cook County, May 6, 1978 (VK). Average spring departure dates: Chicago, May 7 (16 years); Sangamon County, May 7 (18 years).

Some nonbreeding mergansers straggle into summer: East St. Louis, July 13–August 23, 1978 (RA-AB33:182); nine, Wolf Lake, June 24–July 15, 1984 (JL); Williamson County, June 27, 1985 (JR-IB&B2:13); Starved Rock State Park, June 23, 1985 (JMc-IB&B2:13); two along the Fox River, June 1981 (S.Byers-SR30:6); Cut Rock State Park, June 11, 1980 (DW-SR26:4).

RUDDY DUCK

Oxyura jamaicensis

COMMON MIGRANT; OCCASIONAL SUMMER AND WINTER RESIDENT

This small duck has a white cheek patch and an upright tail. Males in breeding plumage are rust colored, with a bright powder blue bill that looks as if someone painted it on. Females are dull brown with a dark streak on the whitish cheek. Ruddy Ducks are found on lakes, ponds, open marshes, and sewage lagoons in small to large flocks. They have a buzzy flight when flushed by boaters. Otherwise they seldom fly, preferring to dive. I watched two Ruddies land on the ice at Lake Springfield on March 14, 1982; when they tried to leave, they only flopped and scooted on the slick ice. To make matters worse, their struggles attracted some Herring Gulls, which began harassing them; one gull even picked up a Ruddy, but dropped it. Finally the ducks managed to escape and fly away. Ruddies concentrated on the Illinois and Mississippi Rivers feed principally on midge larvae (Bellrose 1976).

Spring migration starts in February: six, Carbondale, February 13, 1984 (TF-SR41:12); three, Chautauqua National Wildlife Refuge, February 15, 1984 (KR-SR41:12); five, Baldwin Lake, February 19, 1983 (JR-SR37:8). Average spring arrival dates: Chicago, March 28 (eight years); west-central, February 22 (10 years). Spring maxima: 20,000, Chautauqua refuge, April 16, 1964 (Bellrose-AFN 18:455); 275, Olney, April 7, 1984 (LH-SR41:12); 9700, Illinois and Mississippi Rivers, early April 1983 (RC-SR37:8); 225, Palos, April 9, 1972 (CC); 1053, Horseshoe Lake, April 1, 1984 (TF-SR41:12). Spring bird counts are too late for peak numbers of Ruddies; totals ranged from 30 in 1974 to 281 in 1978. All high counts are from northeastern Illinois—Cook and Lake Counties (VK). Average spring departure dates: west-central, May 11 (10 years); Sangamon County, May 5 (18 years). Some Ruddies linger all summer but do not breed.

These ducks were noted as breeding in Illinois as early as 1875, when Nelson (1876) saw young at Waukegan. Since then they have nested principally in northern Illinois at Lake Calumet, Baker Lake, Orland, Riverdale, Palos,

Redwing Slough, Winfield, and Hebron. A few breeding records come from much farther south: an old one (1889) for Putnam County and modern ones for Grand Tower, 1973; Horseshoe Lake, 1983; and Arcola, 1985 (Chapel and Applegate 1987). Ruddies nest in ponds or marshes with a lot of emergent vegetation. They build floating nests; the one in Putnam County was made of bullrushes. The female lays six to 10 dull white eggs. Most of the nesting records in Illinois refer to young, which have been noted between June 9 and September 10. The only egg date found was June 17. At Arcola 24 young were produced from four broods. In northern Illinois there is a buildup of nesting birds at Lake Calumet and Riverdale in late summer.

Some early wandering, especially of males, takes place in June, July, and August, but true migration starts in late September and October. Early fall arrival dates: five, Henderson County, September 21, 1985 (MB-IB&B2:45); two, Tazewell County, September 24, 1983 (LA-SR39:9); four, Mendota, September 28, 1985 (JH-IB&B2:45). Average fall arrival dates: west-central, October 16 (10 years); Sangamon County, October 1 (16 years). Maximum counts for fall: 1000, Savanna, October 16, 1982 (BSh-SR35:6); 920, Mississippi and Illinois Rivers, December 13, 1982 (RC-SR36:6); 600, Springfield, October 31, 1984 (HDB); 110, Olney, October 30, 1980 (LH-SR27:6). Average departure dates: west-central December 1 (10 years); Sangamon County, December 9 (16 years).

After December or whenever the lakes freeze up, Ruddy Ducks become scarce. Very few overwinter. Christmas bird count totals for 1976–85 ranged from eight in 1981 and 1977 to 260 in 1979. Highest count was 225 at Chautauqua refuge in 1942. In the north the high count was 17 at Channahon, December 29, 1956 (AFN12:167). Most of the wintering birds are in southern Illinois, although warmwater lakes usually have a few in winter. Other winter records: 25, Horseshoe Lake, January 9, 1983 (BR-SR36:6); three, Joliet, January 26, 1984 (JM-SR40:6). A few wintered in Jasper County in 1980–81 (LH-SR28:3). Ruddy Ducks winter as far south as Honduras.

BLACK VULTURE

Coragyps atratus

UNCOMMON PERMANENT RESIDENT IN EXTREME SOUTHERN ILLINOIS; VERY RARE VAGRANT ELSEWHERE IN THE STATE

This vulture can easily be separated from the Turkey Vulture by its short tail, flatter wing profile, and white patches in the wing tips. It also flaps its wings much more often. Black Vultures are found in swampy woodlands and bluffs; they can often be seen soaring overhead with Turkey Vultures. If much migration occurs, it goes mostly undetected. Some of these vultures overshoot north of their range in spring: Monroe County, May 31, 1983 (KRe-AB37:875);

Will County, April 28, 1985 (JM-IB&B1:81); Horseshoe Lake, April 26, 1984 (JVB-SR41:12); Marshall County, June 22, 1982 (MS-SR34:5); Adams County, March 26, 1961 (TEM-AFN15:414). Other vagrant records are more difficult to explain but may simply be postbreeding dispersals: Fort Chartres, July 28, 1962 (Anderson 1964); one found dead, Lake County, November 18, 1909 (Coale 1912). Black Vultures were seen in low numbers on 14 of 15 spring bird counts. All high counts were in southern counties (Johnson, Pope, Saline); the highest was 26 in Pope County, May 10, 1980 (VK).

Cooke (1888) listed this species as a resident in southern Illinois. Some Black Vultures may migrate farther south in winter, but there are some winter records for Illinois: 31, Johnson County, January 4, 1987 (TF-AB41:287); Crab Orchard National Wildlife Refuge, December 7, 1984 (TF-IB&B1:68); 10, Pope and Massac Counties, winter 1982 (RBr-SR32:4). Christmas bird counts produced four winter records: six, Horseshoe Lake, Alexander County, 1950; two, Murphysboro, 1954; Mermet Lake, 1965; and Union County, 1980.

Several nests have been located, mostly at Dixon Springs or Heron Pond Nature Preserve. The females lay two eggs in shallow caves or cavities in trees. These eggs are light in color with a few brown markings. The only egg date found for Illinois is April 13. Most young have been seen in June.

TURKEY VULTURE

Cathartes aura

COMMON MIGRANT; LOCALLY COMMON SUMMER AND OCCASIONAL WINTER RESIDENT; DECREASING NORTHWARD IN ALL SEASONS

The Turkey Vulture, rather ugly up close and clumsy on the ground, becomes a bird of beauty in flight. It soars on warming thermals, rarely flapping, occasionally teetering, and showing a decided dihedral. Turkey Vultures are associated with areas of heavy timber, but they need pastureland or other open spaces in which to search for food. They seem especially common in hilly areas or bluffs. Sometimes in the morning several vultures can be seen in a large dead tree, all with their wings held out, waiting for thermals. The subspecies found in Illinois is *C. a. septentrionalis*.

Migrating Turkey Vultures often start arriving in Illinois in February: Mason County, February 14, 1987 (LA); Saline County, February 15, 1986 (KP-IB&B2:87); Grafton, February 28, 1981 (HW-SR29:6); two, Shelby County, February 20, 1982 (KF-SR33:6); Batavia, February 28, 1986 (EW-IB&B2:87). Average spring arrival dates: west-central, March 7 (12 years); Sangamon County, March 22 (16 years). Maximum counts for spring: 114, Big River State Forest, March 20, 1986 (MB-IB&B2:87); 65, Mercer County, May 4, 1985 (PP-IB&B1:81); 40, Shelby County,

May 9, 1987 (KF). Spring bird count totals ranged from 293 in 1981 to 1259 in 1985. Most high counts were from the southern part of the state: 90, Pope County, 1977; 93, Pike County, 1982; 102, Jasper County, 1984 (VK). Breeding birds obscure departure dates, but May 15 is probably near the limit.

Graber and Graber (1963) felt that the population was greatly reduced between 1909 and 1956, especially in southern Illinois. Oddly, the central Illinois population increased, from fewer than 7000 in 1909 to 10,000 in 1958, while the southern Illinois numbers dropped from 76,000 in 1907 to 16,000 in 1958. Robbins et al. (1986), using breeding bird survey data for 1965-79, noted a stable population. The mean number of Turkey Vultures per survey route in Illinois was 0.2. Northern Illinois has considerably fewer, but Kennicott as early as 1854 listed these vultures as "known to nest in Cook County." They nest in hollow sycamores and other trees, especially near cypress swamps (Ridgway 1889). Nests have also been found in old barns, hollow stumps or logs, and rock crevices. These vultures lay two eggs, which are whitish with brown spots or splotches. Illinois egg dates are April 27 to June 25 (Hess 1910). Hess mentioned having to lift one female from the nest to collect the eggs. At a Turkey Vulture nest I viewed, the female protested by regurgitation, a distinct deterrent to anyone planning to get close to the nest. Young Turkey Vultures have a blackish head, leading some observers to misidentify them as Black Vultures.

The onset of fall migration is about August 15, but the presence of summering birds makes the actual date uncertain. Maximum counts for fall: 52, Henderson County, October 6, 1985 (MB-IB&B2:45); 60, Lake Shelbyville, October 5, 1984 (KF-IB&B1:14); 60, Johnson County, October 14, 1984 (TF-IB&B1:14); 52 near Newton, October 19, 1980 (LH-SR27:6); 19, Warsaw, October 10, 1982 (AD-SR35:6); seven, Zion, October 6, 1979 (RCo-SR23:5). Average fall departure dates: west-central, October 25 (10 years); Sangamon County, October 15 (14 years).

As early as 1884-85 Cooke (1888) noted Turkey Vultures wintering at Shawneetown. Graber and Graber (1963) suggested that the winter population, almost all of which is in southern Illinois, dropped drastically from 690,000 in 1906-7 to fewer than 16,000 in 1958. But they added that mild years may bring an increase in numbers of wintering vultures and that 1906-7 was a mild winter. Only three Christmas bird counts from 1903 to 1955 listed Turkey Vultures, but they were seen on every count from 1976 to 1985, with totals ranging from 10 in 1976 to 64 in 1982. The highest recent count was 60 in Pulaski County in 1982. In winter these birds can be found in roosts. Their roosts may be traditional, like those in Clark and Crawford Counties, or fortuitous, like those associated with dead livestock or trapping scraps. There are only a few winter records for northern Illinois: Mercer County, January 2, 1961 (AFN15:215); Lisle Arboretum, January 18, 1964 (CC-AFN18:359); one or two, Henderson County, December 7-February 16, 1986 (MB,LMc-IB&B2:75).

OSPREY
Pandion haliaetus
UNCOMMON MIGRANT

There was a near loss of this interesting raptor in the 1960s and 1970s because of DDT poisoning. Numbers seem to have increased since the banning of DDT in 1972. The continued use of this pesticide south of the border may still cause problems, however, since Ospreys spend the winter as far south as Chile, Argentina, and Uruguay. As its colloquial name "Fish Hawk" suggests, this predator eats mainly fish and its fishing abilities can easily be observed at the nearest lake. Occasionally, even though it catches fish with its talons, the Osprey seems to all but disappear below the surface of the water as it plunges in after a fish. Usually, however, its wings are held out of the water so that it can take off again. If a fish is caught, it is carried off head first. The flight profile of the Osprey is distinctive because the crook in its wings gives a cupped effect. The Osprey's call is frequently heard even in migration; it is a series of harsh chipping notes. Ospreys are nearly always found near water—usually lakes but also along rivers and occasionally at ponds. They are widespread, being nearly cosmopolitan. The race in North America is *P. h. carolinensis*. Widmann (1907) reported an albino killed at the Mississippi River near Quincy.

Some early spring arrival dates: Olney, March 10, 1983 (LH-AB37:875); Rend Lake, March 13, 1986 (KPi-IB&B2:87); Charleston, March 29, 1987 (RBr); Horseshoe Lake, March 23, 1984 (BR). Average arrival dates: west-central, April 14 (10 years); Sangamon County, April 19 (16 years). Spring bird counts show an increase in numbers starting about 1978, with totals ranging from three in 1975 and 1976 to 27 in 1985. High count was five in Lake County, May 7, 1983 (VK). Other spring maxima: four, Vermilion County, April 25, 1984 (SB-SR41:12); four, Big River State Forest, April 6, 1985 (MB-IB&B1:81); four, Lake Shelbyville, April 21, 1985 (KF-IB&B1:81). Average departure dates: west-central, May 5 (10 years); Sangamon County, May 10 (15 years). Late spring departure dates: Ware, May 19, 1984 (DJaq-SR41:12); three, Redwing Slough, May 22, 1982 (DJ-SR33:6); Charleston, May 29, 1983 (LBH-SR37:9); Alton, June 2, 1984 (SRu). Some linger into June.

Actual nesting records for the Osprey in Illinois are few. The last record was at Crab Orchard National Wildlife Refuge in 1952 (Bennett 1957). The only other records besides Kennicott's "known to nest in Cook County" (1854) is Louck's reference (1892) to two nests found in the river bottoms in Tazewell County. Ospreys nest in large trees but will accept artificial platforms and thus could be encouraged to nest in Illinois. Other summer records: pair, Will County, 1980 (M.Biggers-SR26:4); Big Muddy River, Jackson County, June 14, 1980 (MSt-SR26:4); Dunlap, June 12, 1982 (MSw-SR34:5); Crab Orchard refuge, June 23 and 29, 1984 (JR-IB&B1:16); Lake Shelbyville, June 6 and

8, 1985 (SR-IB&B2:13). There was a nest on the Kentucky side of the Ohio River in 1986 (LS-IB&B3:13).

Fall migration seems to have more volume than spring, but that may be due to the production of young and to birds lingering longer. Early fall arrivals: Braidwood, July 14, 1983 (JM-SR38:6); three, Rend Lake, July 20–21, 1985 (JR-IB&B2:45); Charleston, July 29, 1985 (LBH-IB&B2:13). Average fall arrival dates: west-central, September 6 (11 years); Sangamon County, August 31 (16 years). High counts: 31, Chicago, September 24, 1985 (RB,MBi-AB40:119); 14, Illinois Beach State Park, October 1, 1981 (RCo-AB36:183); eight, Carlyle Lake, October 4, 1986 (RG); seven, Lake Shelbyville, September 16, 1983 (KF-SR39:9); eight, Savanna, September 22, 1985 (PP-IB&B2:45); 11, Hancock County, September 10, 1986 (RCe,RAd-IB&B3:37). Average fall departure dates: west-central, October 16 (11 years); Sangamon County, October 18 (18 years). Late departure dates: Kane County, November 16, 1981 (JWi-SR31:8); De Witt County, December 1, 1985 (LA,KR-IB&B2:45); Mark Twain National Wildlife Refuge, November 20, 1985 (HW-IB&B2:45).

Winter records are few. Some Christmas bird count records are dubious, especially counts of two in Lake County (1963) and Moline (1955). Other Christmas count records, all singles, are from White Pines, 1953; Murphysboro, 1948; Mercer County, 1985; Quincy and Lisle Arboretum, 1984; and Joliet, 1986. Other winter records, if authentic, are probably of very late fall migrants or injured birds. None have stayed all winter. Bald Eagles in some plumages vaguely resemble Ospreys, depending on the arrangement of the white areas, especially on the head and breast. These oddly plumaged eagles may account for some winter records of Ospreys.

AMERICAN SWALLOW-TAILED KITE

Elanoides forficatus

VERY RARE VAGRANT; FORMERLY FAIRLY COMMON MIGRANT AND SUMMER RESIDENT

Ridgway (1873) noted two of these beautiful, graceful kites at Fox Prairie early in the summer of 1871. Later, in August of the same year at the same place, he saw some sailing about in every direction. He collected specimens and saw full-grown young being attended by parents. A specimen taken at Mount Carmel on August 1, 1870, is in the United States National Museum (Mengel 1965). In late summer 1875, Nelson (1877) noted, the Swallow-tailed Kite was "numerous in the immediate vicinity of Cairo, where I was informed it had been abundant the week previous to my arrival." He added:

At the junction of the Ohio and Mississippi Rivers is a long point

bearing a growth of cottonwoods. The river was so high during my visit that the land was submerged, thus causing a great many grasshoppers to take refuge in the tree tops. This afforded the kites a fine opportunity for capturing their prey, of which they were not long in taking advantage. The kites would first appear about ten o'clock and in a small flock would proceed to work in the following manner: The trees were situated in an oblong patch and the kites would hunt around the border, making a complete circuit. They kept but a few feet above the tree-tops and when a grasshopper was observed, by a turn of the long tail and a sweep of the wings, the bird would dart towards its prey until within reach, when with a sudden upward turn it would reach forth its feet and, grasping the insect, proceed with outstretched wings to feed upon the remains of its victim while passing slowly along with its companions. As each grasshopper was captured the bird's abdomen and tail would brush against the leaves with a loud "swish;" in consequence the feathers upon the abdomen and under tail coverts were badly worn and discolored. Their hunting usually continued until about one o'clock, P.M., when they would leave to return at the usual time the next morning.

Though this kite was most numerous in southern Illinois, it also occurred in central and northern Illinois. A subadult specimen taken at Baden, September 13, 1878, is in the Hurter collection (RA). Loucks (1892) stated that this kite was "very rare, one specimen shot near Pekin and a nest found in Fulton County." Kennicott (1854) listed it as known to nest in Cook County. A male specimen was taken in Lake County, June 5, 1895, and three were taken near Highland Park, March 29, 1905 (Coale 1912). One was observed along Salt Creek near Clinton in early June 1906 (Hull 1913).

Recently there have been two records: at Lodge Park, Piatt County, May 20, 1974 (Clemans and Kulesza 1973–74), and at Rice Lake and Sand Ridge Forest, May 7–10, 1982 (RS,TP,PeP-AB36:858).

Reasons for the decline of this species are unclear. Contributing factors probably include destruction of the prairies, degradation of the bottomlands, and this species' vulnerability to hunters—for these large and rather tame birds undoubtedly made good targets. Today they are mainly confined to the southeastern United States south to South America. The race in the United States is *E. f. forficatus*.

BLACK-SHOULDERED KITE

Elanus caeruleus

VERY RARE VAGRANT

"As to the occurrence of this species in Illinois," Ridgway (1889) stated, "we have little information, the only record being that of the writer's previous lists, based on a pair observed near the river at Mount Carmel during the summer of 1863 or 1864." There are also several records for March 1917 at Rantoul (Ekblaw 1917). But neither Ridgway nor Ekblaw gives any description of the kites. The only satisfactory record for the state is of a Black-shouldered Kite seen northwest of Williamsfield, Knox County, May 9–10, 1987 (Baum 1987). This bird was later seen by several other observers as it perched in dead snags and flew about in an open area with hedgerows. These kites are usually found in the southern and western United States. They have expanded their range recently and have been recorded in several nearby states.

MISSISSIPPI KITE

Ictinia mississippiensis

UNCOMMON MIGRANT AND LOCAL SUMMER RESIDENT IN SOUTHERN ILLINOIS; VERY RARE ELSEWHERE IN THE STATE

This gray falconlike raptor has a very graceful flight and at times soars so high as to be invisible without binoculars. Ridgway (1873) noted numbers of them at Fox Prairie in 1871, and Nelson (1877) said they were abundant in southern Illinois near Cairo and Mound City in 1875. Both writers described this kite's powers of flight and its shyness, although Ridgway managed to collect three specimens in August 1871.

The Mississippi Kite population declined in the early 1900s for unknown reasons. That was about the same time the American Swallow-tailed Kite disappeared from Illinois. The Swallow-tailed had a somewhat more northerly distribution than the Mississippi. The Mississippi Kite has made a slight comeback since about 1960, but it is on the Illinois endangered species list. As a summer resident it is mostly confined to southern Illinois, with possibly a few in west-central Illinois. Other Mississippi Kites seen in the state are either overmigrants in spring or wanderers in summer. Hardin et al. (1977), who studied Mississippi Kites in Union County, estimated 13 pairs there. Another 12 pairs are in Alexander County, and a couple of pairs in Randolph County, making the total breeding population in Illinois about 60 birds. Their food in southern Illinois consists of cicadas, grasshoppers, small toads, beetles, dragonflies, and butterflies (Hardin et al. 1977). Kites need wooded areas for nesting and open areas for foraging.

The earliest spring migrants occur in late April: Union County, April 20, 1984 (DJaq-SR41:12); Union County, April 29, 1985 (KR-IB&B1:81). On spring bird counts these kites were seen every year except 1981, with totals ranging from two in 1974 to 24 in 1986; 11 in Alexander County in 1986 was the highest count. All other years the high counts came from Union County (VK). Spring is the season of overmigrants: two, Cass County, May 21, 1977 (RS-AB31:1007); Springfield, May 18, 1982 (HDB,WO); Channahon, May 5, 1984 (JO-AB38:917); Morgan County, May 13–20, 1984 (PW-AB38:917); up to nine feeding on periodic cicadas, Kennekuk Cove State Park, late May–June 23, 1987 (MC,ME,JSm); Cook County, May 18, 1987 (PS).

In 1977 Hardin et al. found five nests in Union County, most of them near woodlot openings. Most contained one egg, which was incubated in late May and hatched in late June or early July. All young were fledged by August 13, and the parents stayed with the young until they all left the area in early September. Summer is a time of wandering for subadult birds, but some records may be of birds still moving around from spring migration: three to four, Allerton Park, June 7, 1985 (WI-IB&B2:13); two, Sand Ridge State Forest, June 15, 1981 (RBj-SR30:6); Schiller Park, June 14–15, 1983 (DJ-SR38:6); three, Clark County, June 14, 1987 (D.Schuur). There may have been nesting at Sanganois Conservation Area; three adults were seen there on July 29, 1978, and on several other occasions.

Fall migration goes mostly undetected. Late fall dates: 10, Union County, September 2, 1981 (S.Evans-AB36:183); Pere Marquette State Park, September 22, 1956 (DaJ,JEC-AFN11:29). Most Mississippi Kites winter in central South America.

BALD EAGLE

Haliaeetus leucocephalus

FAIRLY COMMON MIGRANT AND WINTER RESIDENT, MAINLY ALONG MAJOR RIVERS AND LAKES; RARE SUMMER RESIDENT

"Along all the larger water-courses in our State the Bald Eagle is a more or less common bird, and may be met with at all times of the year," Ridgway (1889) stated. Illinois is still fortunate to have a large wintering population of Bald Eagles, although the nesting population was nearly extirpated. These huge raptors can be found any winter along the Mississippi and Illinois Rivers and at certain waterfowl refuges in southern Illinois. One of the main problems for Bald Eagles today is illegal shooting, the most frequent cause of death (Evans 1982). But that problem declined significantly during the 1970s (Kaiser et al. 1980). Other problems are loss of habitat—the huge trees used by eagles for nesting and roosting; pesticide poisoning, which causes eggshell thinning; and human disturbances, especially in nesting and roosting areas. The Bald Eagle is a federally endangered species because of a nationwide decline in numbers.

Although these eagles have been found in Illinois every month of the year, there is a definite migration. In fall it starts in August and September but is heaviest in October and November. Early fall arrival dates: immature, Lake Renwick, August 22, 1984 (JM-IB&B1:14); immature, southern Cook County, July 31–August 9, 1981 (PD-SR31:8); three immatures, Savanna, September 22, 1985 (PP-IB&B2:45); Brown County, September 12, 1981 (PW-SR31:8); Charleston, August 24, 1980 (LBH-SR27:6). Aerial counts show groups as early as September 27; 12 adults and five immatures were counted on that day in 1982 along the Illinois and Mississippi Rivers (RC-SR35:7). Forty-three (24 adults and 19 immatures) were there on October 30, 1979 (AB34:167).

Larger counts occur later in winter after these eagles are forced out of the north by frozen water. It is at this time—perhaps as late as early December—that Bald Eagles return to certain areas of the state away from the larger rivers. As the water freezes on the lakes more eagles are forced into the locks and dams that keep the water on the large rivers open. Here they feed on fish that are stunned or killed passing through the dam. Some of the best eagle viewing spots are Lock and Dam 19 at Hamilton, Pere Marquette State Park, Rock Island, Chautauqua National Wildlife Refuge, Horseshoe Lake (Alexander County), Crab Orchard National Wildlife Refuge, and Union County Conservation Area. Christmas bird count totals for 1976–85 ranged from 342 in 1982 to 761 in 1978. Highest count was 198 at Pere Marquette in 1969. Aerial counts include 1400 along the Mississippi and Illinois Rivers on January 20, 1979 (RC-AB 33:286). Other high counts: 71, Carthage Lake, February 2, 1986 (LMc-IB&B2:75); 107, southern Illinois refuges, January 25, 1985 (TF-IB&B1:68); 113, Rock Island, January 24, 1982 (EF-SR32:4); 62, Oquawka, January 7, 1984 (LMc-SR40:7). The ratio of immatures to adults rises from north to south. On waterfowl refuges eagles feed on ducks and geese that have been wounded by gunshot; that sometimes leads to lead poisoning of the eagles—a problem that would be eliminated if hunters switched to steel shot.

By late February or early March, depending on the weather, Bald Eagles are moving north. As in fall, these migrants usually follow streams and rivers. If a large flight of geese occurs in the morning, eagles are usually flying by midmorning or afternoon, depending on the thermals. Aerial surveys show the departure of eagles along the Illinois and Mississippi Rivers: 829, March 18, 1980; 322, March 27, 1980; 88, April 4, 1980 (RC-AB34:782). Actually, migration is somewhat more noticeable away from the rivers, where observers can detect it if they happen to look up at the right moment. As Thoreau said, we who live this plodding life here below never know how many eagles fly over us. Most of the Bald Eagles have gone north by late April.

Many years ago Bald Eagles were reported breeding in scattered areas throughout Illinois, with known sites in the lower Wabash Valley and in Lake, Marshall, Alexander, Gallatin, and Hamilton Counties (Grier et al. 1983). The last known site before recent times was Horseshoe Lake, Alexander County, in 1943 (Bellrose 1944). Then in the late 1970s nest building took place in Jo Daviess County, with actual nesting there in 1982 and 1985, at Horseshoe Lake in 1978, and at Crab Orchard refuge in 1980-86. Several young have been fledged in all of these areas; Robinson (1985) gives the details. In other places, including Pike County and near Lake De Pue, nests have been built but no young produced. Other summer records of nonbreeding individuals include an immature, Lawrence County, June 25, 1978 (DJo- AB32:1168); an adult, Jackson County, June 6, 1980 (JGa-AB34:899); and an imma-

ture, Palos, July 7, 1981 (PC,HR-SR30:6). Bald Eagles have a spectacular courtship flight in which the pair lock talons in midair and descend several hundred feet in a series of somersaults. These eagles build large nests in big trees such as sycamores and cottonwoods. Two or three white eggs are laid in March or April. The offspring take three or more years to attain adult plumage. Until then they are mostly dark brown with scattered amounts of white, usually under the wings and on the breast or back.

With the recent nesting and increases in the wintering population (see Sabine and Klimstra 1985), the Bald Eagle appears to be making a comeback and may eventually be found in numbers similar to those Ridgway witnessed.

NORTHERN HARRIER

Circus cyaneus

COMMON MIGRANT; UNCOMMON WINTER AND RARE SUMMER RESIDENT

Formerly known as the Marsh Hawk, the Northern Harrier is usually seen flying low over grassy fields or marshes with its long wings in a strong dihedral. It possesses a long tail and has a white rump patch in all plumages. Adult males are pale grayish, females brownish with streaks below, and immature birds brown with rusty underparts. Northern Harriers eat a wide variety of mammals, birds, amphibians, and reptiles as well as some insects. Their main diet consists of mice and passerine birds. I once watched a Harrier catch a Killdeer on the wing by flying over it. The larger bird's wings seemed to create a partial vacuum and the Killdeer actually rose to meet the Harrier's talons.

In some years, wintering birds make it difficult to distinguish spring arrivals, but the earliest migrants come in late February or early March. Average spring arrival dates: central Illinois, February 28 (11 years); Chicago, April 7 (seven years). Spring maxima: 30, Evanston, March 22, 1978 (AB32:1014); 24, Springfield, March 22, 1978 (HDB); 47, Lawrenceville, March 12, 1982 (LH-AB36:858); 26, Lake Forest, April 6, 1965 (JPr). Spring bird counts are usually too late to reflect concentrations of Harriers in Illinois. Recent totals have ranged from 11 (1975 and 1981) to 39 (1985). Most Harriers have passed northward by mid-May. Average departure dates: central Illinois, April 30 (17 years); Chicago, April 30 (seven years). Late departure dates: pair, Pope County, June 1, 1986 (TF-IB&B2:88); Perry County, May 27, 1985 (RP-IB&B1:81); Snicarte, May 23, 1985 (KR-IB&B1:81); Banner Marsh, May 29, 1983 (RCh-SR 37:9).

A small remnant of Harriers stays in Illinois to nest. They are considered an endangered species in the state because of their low population, which probably is a result of the destruction of marsh and prairie habitats. Robbins et al. (1986) noted significant declines in the eastern and central United States populations from 1965 to 1979. Recent nesting in Illinois has occurred in Jasper County, Du Page

County, La Salle County, Kennekuk Cove State Park, eastern Pike County, and Goose Lake Prairie. Harriers nest on the ground, making a rim of twigs and lining the nest with grasses. Two to five bluish white eggs are laid between May 4 and July 3. Birkenholz (1975) found that nests were placed in blue joint grass meadows at Goose Lake Prairie.

Fall migrants or wanderers appear by July. Early fall arrival dates: Lake Calumet, July 7, 1981 (PC,HR-SR30:6); female, Lake Clinton, July 6, 1985 (RP-IB&B2:13); Crab Orchard National Wildlife Refuge, July 6, 1983 (JR-SR38:6). Average arrival date for central Illinois is August 30 (18 years). Maximum fall counts usually come from hawk watch areas. Harriers ordinarily do not fly in groups when migrating. Instead, one or two will wheel and glide past a given point, sometimes gliding very high, other times quite low. High counts for fall: 92, Illinois Beach State Park, October 10, 1975 (LB-IAB176:32), and 61, November 5, 1982 (AB37:186); 26, Jasper County, November 7, 1985 (SS-IB&B2:45); 44, Chicago, October 20, 1984 (JL). Exact departure dates are difficult to determine because some Harriers spend the winter.

Graber and Golden (1960), using Christmas bird count data, found no radical change in the Northern Harrier population between 1903 and 1955. Christmas count totals for 1976–85 ranged from 65 in 1979 to 188 in 1976. Highest count was 59 at Bird Haven in 1962. Harriers form communal roosts in winter. One roost at the Lawrenceville airport has had 20 to 30 birds every winter recently. Wintering Harriers are most numerous in the southern portion of the state. They seem to be unevenly distributed in the north and central portions, staying where there are fallow fields but not where extensive plowing of row crops occurs. Like Short-eared Owls, with which they sometimes roost, Harriers are found where meadow mice are plentiful.

The Northern Harrier migrates as far south as Middle America and northern Colombia and Venezuela.

SHARP-SHINNED HAWK

Accipiter striatus

COMMON MIGRANT, UNCOMMON WINTER
RESIDENT, AND VERY RARE SUMMER
RESIDENT

Most active observers have had the experience of "spishing" passerines in close when suddenly they all freeze and stop calling. Usually a small hawk then appears: a Sharp-Shinned looking for a meal. Many times it sits quietly, then darts out after one of the passerines that make up the bulk of its diet. Once, while banding birds near Springfield, I had a bag full of warblers and was taking the birds to put bands on them. I heard something fluttering behind me, and when I turned a Sharp-shinned Hawk was within a foot of me, its eyes trained on the bag of birds. This small accipiter frequently learns to hang around bird feeders in winter and occasionally picks birds off, much to the dismay of

onlookers—but that is one of the drawbacks of the congregation of birds into small areas.

Although it is difficult to distinguish spring migrants from wintering birds, the average spring arrival date for Sharp-shinned Hawks at Chicago is April 12 (nine years); in central Illinois it is March 20 (13 years). Spring maximum counts are always lower than fall counts, suggesting that migrants take different routes in different seasons. Twenty-four at Chicago on April 29, 1959 (HF,HL-AFN13:374), is one of the highest counts for spring. Spring bird count totals ranged from six to 72, with high counts of 10 at Champaign, May 6, 1978, and 12 in Cook County, May 7, 1983 (VK). Spring counts are taken somewhat past the peak for this species. Most have departed for more northerly breeding grounds by mid-May. Average departure dates: Chicago, May 19 (nine years); central Illinois, April 30 (15 years). A few late sightings may include breeding birds: Pomona, May 12, 1984 (JR-SR41:13); Palos, July 3, 1983 (JL-SR38:6); Will County, June 15, 1982 (ADu-SR34:5); immature seen three times, Lake Shelbyville, June 1985 (SR-IB&B2:13).

Definite breeding records for Illinois are few. Ford (1956) mentions one near La Grange in the spring of 1901, and Prentice (Smith and Parmalee 1955) recorded a nest near Rockford in the spring of 1947. But the best evidence comes from Graber and Graber (1980–81): a nest in an area of loblolly pines in Pope County in 1980. The Sharp-shin's nests contain four or five bluish white eggs with brownish markings. Most of these hawks breed in the coniferous zone.

Migration is much more dramatic in fall than in spring. If an elevated spot along one of the state's major rivers can be watched daily from early September to early November, Sharp-shinned Hawks will usually be seen in good numbers. Sometimes they are just specks in the sky, but at other times they fly with a flap-flap and glide just above the trees. The Sharp-shinned can usually be identified by the squared-off tail and—compared with Cooper's Hawk—the lesser bulk before the wings (head and shoulders). The real trick is to distinguish between the female Sharp-shinned and the male Cooper's Hawk, which are very close in size; the male Sharp-shinned is much smaller than either. Average fall arrival dates for Chicago are September 11 (eight years) and for central Illinois, September 11 (17 years). Maximum counts for fall: 257, Illinois Beach State Park, September 26, 1977 (GR-AB32:211); 311, Du Page County, September 28, 1986 (HC-AB41:95); 177, Carlyle Lake, October 4, 1986 (RG-AB41:95); 182, Waukegan, October 3, 1979 (P.Mascuch-SR23:5); 18, Sand Ridge State Forest, September 20, 1980 (RKn-SR27:5); 51, Warrenville, October 11, 1985 (DY-IB&B2:45). Again, it is difficult to distinguish between migrants and wintering birds, but average dates for departure are October 18 (eight years) for Chicago and November 17 (13 years) for central Illinois.

The wintering population is highest in southern Illinois, where the most recorded on a Christmas bird count was 13 at Pere Marquette State Park in 1949. Christmas count totals for 1976–85 ranged from 17 to 44, with a high of five in Carroll/Whiteside Counties on January 4, 1986. Sharp-shinned Hawks winter south to central Panama.

COOPER'S HAWK
Accipiter cooperii

UNCOMMON MIGRANT AND WINTER
RESIDENT; RARE SUMMER RESIDENT

Of the three accipters in Illinois, Cooper's Hawk is the middle-sized one. It usually shows a rounded tail in flight and has a restricted eyeline, if any at all. Details on identification of accipters is in Mueller et al. (1981) and Clark and Wheeler (1987). Kennicott (1854) remarked of Cooper's Hawks: "Common. Follow the [Passenger] pigeons in their migration." The Cooper's is now listed as an endangered species in Illinois because of the state's very thin breeding population. The migrant population seems to have stabilized after a recent decline, which was probably due to the use of pesticides and the loss of woodland habitats. The Cooper's Hawk is found in woodlands, hedgerows, and occasionally open situations. If there is a "chicken hawk," this is it. But since few people raise chickens now, the threat is not great any more. This accipiter's diet includes not only birds but also small mammals and reptiles.

Although Cooper's Hawks winter in Illinois, spring migrants are noticeable because they occur in different areas from those frequented by residents, and migrational behavior is different from hunting behavior. Migrants may appear as early as mid-February, but average arrival date at Urbana is March 24 (10 years) and in west-central Illinois, April 2 (eight years). High counts for spring are low: four, Vermilion County, April 25, 1984 (SB-SR41:13); four, Dundee, May 3, 1983 (RM-SR37:9). Spring bird count totals ranged from six in 1981 to 23 in 1985, but individual counts tallied no more than four (VK).

Murchison (1893) presented a synopsis on the Cooper's Hawk in Illinois, giving nesting data. Recent nesting areas: Winnebago County, 1984; Pomona, 1986; Lockport, 1986; Joliet, 1987; Du Page County, 1987; Cook County, 1981; Woodstock, 1983; Will County, 1980. The nesting population is highest in southern Illinois. Nests are usually in heavy forest, and occasionally these hawks will use an old crow's or squirrel's nest. They lay two to five eggs, which are white, rarely with brownish markings. Illinois egg dates are April 17 to June 27. Young have been noted from June 7 to July 9.

The earliest fall migrants appear in August: Knox County, August 13, 1983 (MB-SR39:10); three, Apple River Canyon State Park, August 22, 1986 (SB-IB&B3:37); Sand Ridge State Forest, August 22, 1987 (KR). Average fall arrival dates: Sangamon County, October 4 (17 years); west-central, September 17 (five years). Fall high counts: 20, Mississippi Palisades State Park, September 27, 1986 (PP-AB41:95); six, Illinois Beach State Park, October 1, 1981

(SR31:6); 12, Carlyle Lake, October 4, 1986 (RG-IB&B3:37). Departure dates are difficult to discern because of wintering birds.

In winter I have noted Cooper's Hawks hanging around blackbird roosts, which I suspect provide ready prey for these bird hawks. Christmas bird counts for 1976–85 ranged from 13 in 1979 to 42 in 1985. No individual Christmas count recorded more than four birds; however, seven were seen on the Pere Marquette count in 1941. Graber and Golden (1960), using Christmas bird count data from 1903 to 1955, noted more Cooper's Hawks from southern Illinois and decreasing numbers northward. These hawks sometimes make the rounds at bird feeders and one occasionally crashes into a window while chasing birds, as at Springfield on December 8, 1980 (ISM).

NORTHERN GOSHAWK
Accipiter gentilis

OCCASIONAL MIGRANT AND WINTER
RESIDENT IN NORTHERN ILLINOIS
DECREASING SOUTHWARD

Adult Northern Goshawks, bluish above and gray below, are quite distinctive, but immatures are difficult to separate from immature Cooper's Hawks. The conspicuous eyeline, if seen, is the best field mark in immature birds. I noted an adult at Springfield on December 1, 1982, with an extended eyeline that gave the impression of eyes on the back of the head. These large hawks are powerful fliers. In Illinois they take such prey as rabbits, pheasants, waterfowl, and other birds. They tend to be associated with larger tracts of forest, roosting especially in conifers, but they have also been seen in fairly open areas and city parks. The Northern Goshawk stages invasions; those on record for Illinois are 1870–71, 1896–97, 1907–8, 1916–17, 1972–73, 1982–83. The last two invasions are well documented. Some invasions had carry-overs into the next winter, evidently birds coming back to the same approximate area. These invasions are related to a decline in prey in the north. The 1972–73 invasion had 85 percent adults, indicating low production of young (Burr and Current 1974). Goshawks may occur every year in northern Illinois, but they have always been scarce or nonexistent in central and southern Illinois except in invasion years. Before the 1972–73 incursion only three records existed for southern Illinois.

While migrating, goshawks usually fly fairly low, just above the treetops. Occasionally they fly higher, wheeling like buteos. Early fall arrivals: Kennekuk Cove Park, September 16, 1987 (MC); Mississippi Palisades State Park, September 27, 1986 (PP-IB&B3:37); Illinois Beach State Park, September 29, 1981 (RCo-SR31:6). Most arrive in October or November. High count for fall is 220 at Illinois Beach State Park, November 3–6, 1982 (AB37:186), including 95 on November 5.

Goshawks tend to set up a territory in one area for most

of the winter. Christmas bird counts for 1976–85 showed Northern Goshawks each year except 1979. Totals ranged from two in 1976 to 41 in 1982. Highest count was eight at Barrington in 1973. Recent winter records for the south: three, Alexander County, December 21, 1982 (SR36:6); Richland County, January 25, 1981 (DJo-SR28:4); Ozark, December 15, 1985 (MG-IB&B2:75).

Spring migration, not as noticeable as fall's, takes place mostly in March and April. Late spring departure dates: Park Forest, May 15, 1982 (VK-SR33:7); Mode, May 1, 1984 (KF-SR41:13).

GRAY HAWK

Buteo nitidus

HYPOTHETICAL

The single Illinois record for the Gray Hawk is based on a statement by Ridgway (1880) that one "was seen, and twice shot at, on the 19th of August, 1871, on Fox Prairie, in Richland Co." It was immediately overhead, he stated. "It was afterwards followed a long distance among the trees which grew in a ravine intersecting the prairie, but finally lost. There can not be the slightest doubt as to the proper identification of the species which I have been well acquainted with for years, and one which could not be mistaken. . . ." There are no other records of this tropical species away from the southwestern United States. It is unfortunate that this specimen was not obtained, since Ridgway did not describe the bird itself.

RED-SHOULDERED HAWK

Buteo lineatus

UNCOMMON MIGRANT, SUMMER RESIDENT, AND WINTER RESIDENT IN SOUTHERN ILLINOIS DECREASING NORTHWARD

The scream of this beautiful buteo was heard in nearly every bottomland woods in the state not long ago. Now most of the central and northern Illinois birds are gone, probably due to loss of habitat, disturbance of nest sites, and use of pesticides. Adult Red-shoulders have a reddish undersurface and almost a checkered appearance above. The tail has very noticeable black and white banding and the wings show a pale crescent patch in flight. Even the immatures have the wing patch and the distinctive shape of this buteo. The call *kee yar* is sometimes imitated by Blue Jays. This hawk spends a lot of its time sitting and waiting for prey, which it then pounces on or flies out and catches. Its prey consists of reptiles, amphibians, small mammals, and birds. The race in Illinois is the nominate form, *B. l. lineatus*.

Though a resident in summer and winter, this hawk

makes a definite migration, usually mixed in with Red-tails, from which it is easily separated by its reddish underparts and broad tail bands. In Sangamon County the average spring arrival date is March 6 (12 years). In some years these hawks are moving by mid-February. High counts are 11, McKee Marsh, March 15, 1985 (SO-IB&B1:81), and 18, Springfield, March 12, 1979 (HDB). Spring bird count totals ranged from 15 in 1980 and 1981 to 57 in 1986. Most high counts were for southern Illinois, but Lake County had the highest: 9 on May 6, 1978 (VK). Migration continues into late May, but by this time most of the migrants are immatures.

As late as 1956 Ford called this hawk a "common summer resident" in the Chicago area, but during the 1960s there was a significant decline in central and northern Illinois. Recently it has nested in various areas, but its stronghold is southern Illinois. Recent nests from north and central: Palos, 1985; Lockport, 1986; Barrington, 1984; Lake County, 1987; Cook County, 1980; Allerton Park, 1988. Most nests are in bottomland forests, 30 to 40 feet high in trees. There are three to five dull white eggs with variable brownish markings. Illinois egg dates are March 3 to May 1.

Although Kennicott described thousands of these hawks migrating in October 1854 (Nelson 1876), the description sounds more like Broad-winged Hawks. Nowadays, fall migration is rather scattered, with some Red-shoulders arriving in August and others continuing into November. High fall counts: seven, Mount Hoy, October 29, 1986 (HC-IB&B3:37); 11, Springfield, November 29, 1978 (HDB); six, Illinois Beach State Park, November 15, 1982 (JG,R.Danley-SR35:7)

Winter populations are low in north and central Illinois, but Christmas bird counts show fairly high numbers in the south. Totals for 1976–85 ranged from 17 in 1979 to 57 in 1982, when 33 were seen in Alexander County. Graber and Golden (1960), in their assessment of hawks on Christmas bird counts, showed 13 at Decatur in 1954 and 12 at Moline in 1955. Counts there today would be lucky to report a single Red-shouldered Hawk.

BROAD-WINGED HAWK

Buteo platypterus

COMMON MIGRANT; UNCOMMON SUMMER RESIDENT

This pint-sized buteo is the most highly migratory hawk in Illinois, going as far south as southern Brazil. No other hawk forms such large flocks; some of these kettles contain hundreds of birds. From the right vantage point at the right season, one can see this hawk rising from its roost as the warming temperatures create thermals. Then it starts to soar at low levels with other Broad-wings. When the right altitude is reached, they all shoot off in their chosen direction and catch another thermal, which the group then circles, forming another kettle. Usually, group after group will pass by in this manner until they have all departed or conditions change. Sometimes they fly so high that they cannot be seen without binoculars. This often quite spectacular migration phenomenon takes place in Illinois principally in mid-April and mid-September, give or take 10 days. Aeronautic personnel should be cognizant of these massive flights, since aircraft could be affected. When Broad-winged Hawks are sitting in the woods in spring they call occasionally. The sound is somewhat like the call of the Eastern Wood Pewee except louder and a bit harsher. When the Broad-wing is hunting, it sits on a horizontal limb and waits for prey, then pounces on it. These hawks take mice, squirrels, chipmunks, small to medium-sized passerine birds, snakes, frogs, crayfish, a variety of larger insects, and earthworms. I watched one take a snake head first and eat it in several chomps on April 21, 1980, at Springfield.

Spring migration starts in April: Pomona, April 4, 1986 (KM-IB&B2:88); Ferne Clyffe State Park, April 3, 1983 (JR-SR37:9); Palos, April 4, 1981 (AA-SR29:7). Average arrival dates: Urbana, April 28 (16 years); west-central, April 17 (11 years). Spring bird counts are taken somewhat late for peak counts of this hawk. All high counts are in northern Illinois, suggesting that the counts are catching the tail end of the Broad-wing's migration. Totals ranged from 47 in 1981 to 250 in 1979, with Iroquois County having the highest count of 150 on May 5, 1979 (VK). Maximum counts for spring: 400, La Salle County, April 25, 1981 (JH-SR29:7); 300, Dundee, May 1, 1979 (RM-AB33:776); 100, Dwight, April 24, 1980 (HRi-SR25:4). A few Broad-wings, mostly immatures, arrive later, but the main flights are usually well synchronized. These hawks stay mainly in forests when they are not flying, but they can also be seen in city parks. They seem to follow river valleys, and the best flights in spring are probably in the Illinois River valley. Average spring departure dates: west-central, May 7 (11 years); Sangamon County, May 21 (17 years). Stragglers linger into June some years.

Broad-winged Hawks nest only in heavily wooded areas in Illinois. Thus the best nesting sites are in northern and southern Illinois and the Illinois River valley in the west-central part of the state. Most recent nests have been found in northern Illinois in the counties of McHenry, Cook, Will, Winnebago, Du Page, Vermilion, Lake, and Iroquois. Robbins et al. (1986), reviewing breeding bird survey data, suggested that a significant increase in the number of Broad-wings occurred between 1965 and 1979 in the United States; however, Illinois data show an average of less than 0.1 bird per route. The Broad-wing's nest is usually placed in the crotch of a tree, and two to three whitish eggs with brownish markings are laid. Egg dates for Illinois are April 25 to May 20. Young have been seen as late as early July. Other summer records may or may not represent breeding birds: Rend Lake, June 7, 1986 (DR-IB&B3:14); two, Mahomet, June 9, 1985 (RCh-IB&B2:13); Thebes, June 29, 1985 (JR-IB&B2:13); Peoria County, June 12, 1982 (MSw-SR34:5).

Fall migration begins in August but usually involves few birds until mid-September. Early arrivals: Normal, August 29, 1984 (DBi-IB&B1:14); Palos, August 1, 1982 (JL); Springfield, August 15, 1984 (HDB); two, Horseshoe Lake, August 18, 1986 (RG). Maximum counts in fall exceed those for spring: 2000, Compton, September 17, 1984 (JH-IB&B1:14); 4395, Bensenville, September 19, 1982 (J&CS-SR35:7); 2800, Mississippi Palisades, September 27, 1986 (PP-AB41:95); 2178 Carlyle Lake, October 4, 1986 (RG-AB41:95); 1600, Jacksonville, September 17, 1981 (PW-SR31:8). I observed a dark-phase Broad-winged Hawk perched at close range on October 5, 1971, at Springfield. Although I know of no other reports, these dark-phase birds should be expected from time to time. They are apparently more numerous in the West. A few Broad-wings linger throughout October. Average fall departure dates: west-central, September 22 (11 years); Sangamon County, October 5 (15 years). There are several November records: Calhoun County, November 17, 1979 (HW-SR23:4); Illinois Beach State Park, November 6, 1976 (GR-IAB180:41); Albany, November 2, 1985 (PP-IB&B2:45); Bell Smith Springs, November 4, 1984 (RAp-IB&B1:14); adult photographed, Springfield, November 30, 1986 (DO,HDB).

Winter records that are not well documented should be given little credence. Weak, sick, or injured birds can survive into winter for a time. A more serious documentation problem, confusion with Red-shouldered Hawks, obscures the true status of this hawk in winter. Winter records: adult, Dundee, January 5, 1984 (RM-SR40:8); Waukegan, December 4, 1978 (JN-IAB188:46); Morton Arboretum, December 15, 1968 (JG,RR); Homer, December 18, 1983 (JSm-SR40:8).

SWAINSON'S HAWK

Buteo swainsoni

RARE MIGRANT; LOCAL SUMMER RESIDENT IN NORTHERN ILLINOIS

The Swainson's Hawk is at the eastern limits of its range in Illinois, where it occupies savanna habitats. A thin relic nesting population gives it an endangered species status in Illinois. This species occurs in two color morphs, a light phase predominating and a dark phase seen only during migration in Illinois. (There are also intermediates, and Clark and Wheeler 1987 describe a third "rufous" phase.) The broad dark trailing edge to the undersurface of the flight feathers is a good field mark for the Swainson's Hawk. It also has a Northern Harrierlike slimness, with long, rather pointed wings. Its principal food is small mammals, but it also consumes insects.

This buteo is one of the most migratory birds of prey, with great flocks gathering at certain places in Central America. Swainson's Hawks winter primarily on the pampas of South America. Early spring arrival dates: Decatur, March 28, 1981 (SS-SR29:7); Mason County, April 2, 1985

(KR-AB39:307). Most spring migrants are seen in April and May: Monroe County, April 26, 1978 (BR-AB32:1014); two, Horseshoe Lake, April 20, 1984 (L.Barber-AB38:917); Whiteside County, May 25, 1986 (LJ-IB&B2:88). There are no spring concentrations, and Swainson's have been recorded on only five of 15 spring bird counts.

Surprisingly, this hawk still has a nesting population in Illinois. It was first recorded nesting in southern Illinois (Richland County) in 1875 by Nelson (Ridgway 1889). Hess (1910) reported a nest near Philo with three eggs on May 5, 1900. All other nests have been in northern Illinois—Winnebago, Boone, and lately Kane Counties. Specimens indicate that De Kalb and Ogle Counties might also be included, and there are summer records from McHenry County. Nest sites are usually in isolated trees in agricultural or grassland areas. One nest containing three eggs was reported near Rockford, May 18, 1947 (Prentice 1949), and three nests were located in Winnebago County in 1958 (AFN12:416). Then in 1973 five nests were found in Kane County, and two of the same nests were used in 1974 (Keir and Wilde 1976). Ten birds and four nests were found in Kane County in 1983 (JM-AB37:993), and nests were still being found there in 1988.

Swainson's Hawks have been seen at their nesting areas as late as September 3, 1984 (AA,IV-IB&B1:14), but a migrant occurred at Brussels as early as August 31, 1980 (PS-AB35:189). Most fall records occur in September and October: Olney, October 5, 1979 (LH-AB34:167); dark phase, Springfield, October 13, 1985 (HDB,TT,DO); Crab Orchard National Wildlife Refuge, October 13, 1982 (JR-SR35:7). There is a specimen record from Waukegan, October 13, 1914 (CAS#15140). Some November records: Carbondale, November 30, 1980 (J.Janacek-AB35:189); Urbana, November 6, 1982 (RCh-AB37:186). There are no satisfactory winter records for this buteo in Illinois.

RED-TAILED HAWK

Buteo jamaicensis

COMMON MIGRANT AND WINTER RESIDENT;
FAIRLY COMMON SUMMER RESIDENT

The plumages of the Red-tailed Hawk are complicated because they show extreme variability. The typical adult of the *B. j. borealis* race—the one that breeds and is most commonly seen in Illinois—has a reddish tail and brown dorsal surface; it is whitish below with a dark belly band. The light-colored plains race, *B. j. krideri*, is a rare migrant and winter resident. The western Red-tail, *B. j. calurus,* which has light, dark, and rufous phases, is an uncommon migrant and winter resident. The "Harlan's" Hawk, *B. j. harlani*, which varies from dark to light but has a peculiar whitish (sometimes reddish) tail, is a rare migrant and winter resident. Mindell (1985) and Lish and Voelker (1986) discuss the variations in Red-tailed Hawks. Adding to the confusion are immature plumages, albinism, melanism, and

size variations. Red-tails inhabit semiopen areas, woodlots, and woodlands. They are the familiar large roadside hawks that sit on fence posts and telephone poles. Unlike Rough-legged Hawks, which sit on the tops of trees, Red-tails usually sit at midheight. Red-tails have a harsh *keeerrr* squeal for a call, most often heard near the nest. They eat a variety of food, from cottontails and tree squirrels to mice, birds, reptiles, and amphibians.

Though many Red-tailed Hawks spend the winter in Illinois, many more go farther south, and definite diurnal spring migration can be seen when the conditions are right. These birds use thermals for migration, wheeling and shooting off in the desired direction. They seem to follow rivers, lakes, and bluff areas. Spring migration usually starts in mid- to late February. High counts for spring: 216, Du Page County, March 30, 1986 (DY-AB40:477); 150, Palos, March 15, 1981 (RB-AB35:829); 123, Springfield, March 12, 1979 (HDB). Spring bird counts probably tally mostly summer residents or late migrants. Totals ranged from 226 in 1972 to 655 in 1985, with the highest count 56 in Du Page County, May 5, 1984 (VK). Spring migration is curtailed by mid-April most years, although immature and nonbreeding birds continue to filter through even in May.

Graber and Graber (1963) estimated the summer population in Illinois in 1957 to be 65,000. Robbins et al. (1986) pointed out that while there had been a significant increase in Red-tails in the rest of North America, only Illinois showed a decrease. The mean number of birds per survey route in Illinois was 0.4. Red-tailed Hawks nest in woodlands, more densely in northern and central Illinois than in southern Illinois. They usually build large, bulky nests in large trees. Two to four eggs are white or buff with variable brownish markings. Illinois egg dates are February 28 to May 12. When the young grow a bit they can usually be seen in the nest, with both parents attending them.

By July and August some Red-tailed Hawks are wandering away from nesting areas, but fall flights do not usually occur until September and October. High counts for fall migrants: 203, Illinois Beach State Park, October 22, 1981 (DFi-SR31:6); 70, Springfield, October 13, 1985 (HDB); 49, Crab Orchard National Wildlife Refuge, October 25, 1983 (JR-SR39:10). There are flights even in November and early December, since some birds do not leave until they are frozen out.

Christmas bird count totals for 1976–85 ranged from 580 in 1979—after severe winters—to 1477 in 1985. Highest count was 115 at Beverly in 1985. Graber and Graber (1963) showed that there had been an increase in Red-tails in southern Illinois in winter and a decrease in northern and central Illinois. Estimates of the winter population in southern Illinois were 90,000 in 1906-7 and 35,000 in 1956-57, a significant drop.

FERRUGINOUS HAWK

Buteo regalis

VERY RARE MIGRANT AND WINTER
RESIDENT

Essentially a raptor of the western Great Plains, the Ferruginous Hawk rarely drifts into Illinois. Many records of this species, including several of my own (Bohlen 1986b), should be considered erroneous because of confusion with "Krider's" Red-tailed Hawk. The critical field mark of the Ferruginous Hawk is feathering of the tarsi to the toes. The Red-tailed Hawk has bare tarsi. The Rough-legged Hawk, with which the Ferruginous probably would not be confused, has similar feathered tarsi. This field mark is difficult to see, however, unless the hawk is close and preferably sitting. The best views are obtained when the hawk lifts its tail to defecate. The red leggings on the adult Ferruginous Hawk are a good field mark, of course, but even some Red-tailed Hawks show light reddish leggings. Another field mark that is useful, especially in immature birds, is the dorsal wing patch. If this patch is on the outer primaries the bird is a Red-tail; if it is on the inner primaries it is a Ferruginous (see Eckert 1982). This large buteo spends much of its time on the ground, while the Red-tailed Hawk prefers to perch in trees or on telephone poles. The Ferruginous Hawk feeds on ground squirrels, which, with its huge mouth, it swallows whole.

The Ferruginous Hawk was first recorded in Illinois in the autumn of 1876 by E. Coues at Rock Island. Apparently no age category or other documenting evidence was given (Coues 1876). The first specimen was taken at Paris on January 19, 1886, by a Mr. Balmer, who said, "He came with a thaw, in a south wind, after our big, big blizzard. I shot him out of a tree after dark, having marked him down for the night. The bird is a male and measured 53 inches in extent" (Cooke 1888). The next record did not occur until April 21, 1939, when a female (CAS) was found shot in Northfield Township, Cook County (Gregory 1948). Then there was a rash of sight records from T. E. Musselman that are not documented or aged (adult or immature): two, Kinderhook, Pike County, February 18, 1953; two, Quincy, September 8, 1957 (AFN12:35); Quincy, December 21, 1958 (AFN13:297); Quincy, October 8, 1961 (AFN16:36). An adult was seen at Wood River, January 20, 1963 (RA-AFN17:328). One (no age class given) was seen at Lisle Arboretum, December 26, 1964 (PD-AFN19:234). Next are my records, all of light-phase immature birds, which should be considered erroneous because tarsi were not checked for feathering. Other recent records: adult, Joliet, December 24, 1971 (LBi,LB,CC-AB26:611); adult, Crane Lake–Sangamon (Christmas bird count), December 19, 1981 (VK,CB,D.Fletcher-AB36:600); no age, Joliet, January 1, 1983 (Mlodinow 1984); adult, Lincoln, January 23 and 30, 1984 (KR).

Future records should be thoroughly documented, especially immatures. Identifiable photographs would help support the documentation. This hawk is probably much rarer in Illinois than the records show.

ROUGH-LEGGED HAWK

Buteo lagopus

COMMON MIGRANT AND WINTER RESIDENT
DECREASING SOUTHWARD

As its name suggests, this Arctic nesting buteo has legs feathered to the toes. In flight the Rough-legged Hawk's large size, long wings held on a slight dihedral, white-based tail, and dark carpal patches are good field marks. This species occurs in light, dark, and intermediate color phases. A study by Schnell (1967) in northern Illinois showed 31 percent dark, 52 percent light, and 17 percent intermediate. In Illinois Rough-legs are primarily winter hawks. They occur mostly in open areas, sitting on telephone poles or fence posts, in the tops of small trees, or on the ground. Their smallish talons are adapted for catching rodents, primarily *Microtus*. They also feed on road kills of such mammals as cottontails, and are sometimes hit by cars. Rough-legs breed in the Arctic circumpolar. The race in Illinois is *B. l. sanctijohannis*.

Rough-legs are somewhat cyclic migrants, depending on prey populations. Very early arrival dates for fall: Banner Marsh, August 31, 1983 (DBi-AB38:208); Dundee, September 11, 1979 (SD-AB34:167); Lake Calumet, September 20, 1981 (JL). Average fall arrival dates: west-central, October 29 (nine years); Sangamon County, November 9 (17 years). High counts for fall: 17, Illinois Beach State Park, November 17, 1982 (AB37:186), and 16, November 6, 1981 (JG-SR31:8); 20, Shelby County, November 28, 1985 (KF-IB&B2:75). Migration lasts into December.

Christmas bird count totals ranged from 126 in 1979 to 434 in 1976; the highest count was 73 at De Kalb in 1971. Southern Illinois has the lowest numbers in winter. Other winter records: 16, Henderson and Mercer Counties, January 28, 1984 (MB,LMc-SR40:8); 53 along 90 miles of Interstate 72, January 10, 1978 (J.Ellis-AB32:358); 20 in pines at Sand Ridge State Forest, February 21, 1982 (RKn-SR32:4).

Occasionally there is a noticeable return in spring of Rough-legs from farther south, but more often the ones that have wintered here simply leave. High counts for spring: 10, Henderson County, March 11, 1984 (LMc-SR41:13); nine, Shelby County, March 24, 1986 (KF-IB&B2:88); five, Carrier Mills, March 16, 1987 (KP). Most Rough-legs leave by April. Average departure dates: west-central, April 19 (seven years); Sangamon County, April 4 (16 years). Spring bird counts have shown this species every year but two. That 11 were counted in Adams County on May 5, 1973, seems very unusual (VK). Late spring departure dates: Buffalo, June 10, 1988 (RS); Palos, May 10, 1986 (PD,JN-IB&B2:88); Mode, May 5, 1984 (KF-SR41:13).

GOLDEN EAGLE

Aquila chrysaetos

RARE MIGRANT AND WINTER RESIDENT

This eagle is seen most frequently along the Mississippi River and at waterfowl refuges in southern Illinois. If hawk watches are manned for lengthy periods in other parts of the state, however, Golden Eagles seem to be regular though rare. This is certainly true of the Sangamon River valley. Unlike Bald Eagles, Goldens do not congregate in roosts but are usually seen singly or in pairs. Nor are they tied to water. They inhabit more open country, where they feed on mammals. At waterfowl refuges they also take wounded ducks and geese much the same as Bald Eagles. Though Nelson (1876) stated that the Golden Eagle "formerly nested throughout the state," there are no egg sets from Illinois. Black (1937) listed 40 specimens taken in Illinois, two of which had dates suggesting possible nesting: Champaign County, June 26, 1900, and Lacon, August 10, 1930. The rest fell within migrational and winter seasons. The race found in North America is *A. c. canadensis*. Clark and Wheeler (1983) discuss identification of Golden Eagles.

Early fall records: Grafton, August 6, 1977 (AB32:211); adult, Lake Calumet, August 15, 1987 (JL); immature, Crab Orchard National Wildlife Refuge, September 21, 1982 (JR-AB37:186). Most fall arrival dates are in late October or November: immature, Rend Lake, October 30, 1987 (TF); two, Savanna, November 29, 1980 (BSh-SR27:6); immature, Winnebago County, October 18, 1981 (DW-SR31:8); Evanston, October 19, 1978 (RB-AB33:183).

Christmas bird counts for 1976–85 showed Golden Eagles every year, with totals ranging from one to eight and the high count four at Union County in 1976. Other winter records: Boone County, January 16–22, 1978 (RGa-AB32:358); Pike County, December 12, 1984 (JF-IB&B1:68); Hidden Springs State Forest, February 11, 1987 (YM-IB&B3:67). Consistent areas in winter for these eagles are the Union County and Crab Orchard refuges, Horseshoe Lake (Alexander County), and some areas along the Mississippi River.

Spring migration takes place mostly in March; the average date for Sangamon County is March 14 (seven years). Late departure dates: Du Page County, April 26–27, 1986 (DY-IB&B2:88); Illinois Beach State Park, May 10, 1972 (GR,RR-AB26:767).

AMERICAN KESTREL

Falco sparverius

COMMON PERMANENT RESIDENT

Although this colorful little falcon is found throughout the state at all seasons, considerable migration can be detected along Lake Michigan and rivers in Illinois. The American Kestrels I have watched migrate along rivers in central Illinois tend to stay just above the treetops. I saw eight together in eastern Sangamon County on September 19, 1982. Enderson (1960) in Champaign County found that spring migration started in early February, peaked between March 4 and April 12, and continued until June. Spring bird count totals ranged from 98 in 1972 to 293 in 1984, with the highest count 43 in Cook County on May 7, 1983 (VK). Few migration dates are available for fall, but migration probably starts in early September and continues until mid-November (Clark and Nice 1950). High counts for fall: 44, Carlyle Lake, October 4, 1986 (RG); 27, Illinois Beach State Park, September 26, 1977 (GR-AB32:212); 25, Waukegan, October 5, 1985 (JL); 14, Henderson County, October 6, 1985 (MB-IB&B2:45); 17, Douglas and Moultrie Counties, September 10, 1981 (RCot-SR31:9).

American Kestrels like to perch on telephone wires and in the tops of trees where they are fairly conspicuous. They have adapted to life on the edges of towns and in cities. Sometimes they are seen near downtown Chicago, and a pair made themselves at home on the State Capitol dome in Springfield for several years. When hunting, this falcon is famous for its hover and pounce. It eats insects, birds, mammals, reptiles, and amphibians. Brodkorb (1928) reported that it eats ants. Its call, a series of *killy* notes, is well known to most observers. The race found in Illinois is *F. s. sparverius*.

The best summer habitats noted by Graber and Graber (1963) were ungrazed grasslands and fallow fields. They also reported a marked reduction in the statewide summer population from 90,000 in 1907 (70 percent of them in southern Illinois) to 78,000 in 1958 (65 percent in central Illinois). Robbins et al. (1986) noted an upward trend from 1965 to 1979 in all areas of the United States except Arkansas and Illinois. More recent short-term studies found a 120 percent increase in Illinois in just one year, 1982 (AB36:982). Apparently there was a drop in numbers in the 1970s but a rise in the 1980s. American Kestrels nest in cavities in trees—especially old flicker nest holes—or structures of any kind with a cavity, including nest boxes. They lay three to five tannish brown eggs with small cinnamon markings. Illinois egg dates are April 15 to June 12. Most young are seen in June, some into August.

Winter populations are fairly high. Graber and Graber (1963) found that the best winter foraging habitats were cornfields, hayfields, small grainfields, and pastures. They noted that winter populations also had shown a decline. In 1906-7 there were 135,000 Kestrels (81 percent in southern Illinois), but by 1957-58 there were only 54,000 (60-70 percent in southern Illinois). Christmas bird count totals for 1976–85 ranged from 549 in 1978 to 925 in 1982, with the highest count 74 in Will/Cook Counties in 1981. Other winter counts: 45, Vermilion County, winter 1985-86 (SB-IB&B2:75); 19, Saline County, December 31, 1985 (KP-IB&B2:75); 22, Lake Calumet, February 20, 1982 (JL).

MERLIN

Falco columbarius

OCCASIONAL MIGRANT AND RARE WINTER
RESIDENT

When a flock of blackbirds in the sky suddenly tightens, balls up, and does some weird gyrations, the observer knows a raptor is close by or in pursuit. I have noted this phenomenon especially when Merlins are present, for they in particular go after birds. In fact, they seem to migrate with late passerine migrants that have large populations, such as White-throated Sparrows, Dark-eyed Juncos, and Yellow-rumped Warblers. Merlins are usually seen in Illinois as flybys, and unless they are close they may be difficult to separate from American Kestrels or other small raptors. Sharp-shinned Hawks sometimes appear to have pointed wings and essentially the same color patterns as Merlins unless viewed closely. But Merlins fly differently, with steady, quick wing flaps. Merlins are also shorter tailed. These falcons are usually seen along the edges of woodlands and in open areas. They may also be seen at mudflats making passes at concentrations of shorebirds. The most common race in Illinois is the eastern *F. c. columbarius*, but *F. c. richardsonii*, the pale interior form, has also been recorded (at Warsaw by Worthen), and Ford (1936) reported a female *F. c. bendirei* collected at Chicago, March 18, 1890. But *bendirei* has apparently been merged with *columbarius*.

Spring migration produces very few Merlins and at times they go undetected. Some early dates may represent winter birds: Mason County, March 2 and 9, 1986 (LA-IB&B2:88); Kennekuk Cove Park, March 25, 1982 (SB-SR33:7); Horseshoe Lake, March 29, 1983 (CP-SR37:9). More usual dates for spring migrants are in April and May. Merlins were recorded on seven spring bird counts in very low numbers (one to three). Other spring dates: Union County, May 10, 1977 (HDB,VK-AB31:1008); two, Lawrence County, April 29, 1982 (DJo-SR33:7); near Carlyle, April 24, 1984 (PS-SR41:14); Lake Calumet, May 9, 1981 (JL); Clinton Lake, April 11, 1987 (RP).

Kennicott (1854) listed the Merlin as "known to nest in Cook County," but there are no definite records of breeding in Illinois.

For Merlins as for Peregrine Falcons, migration is much more noticeable in fall than in spring. Early fall arrivals: Fairmount, August 30, 1984 (JSm-IB&B1:14); Jackson Park, September 9, 1981 (PC-SR31:8); Horseshoe Lake, September 14, 1983 (DB-SR39:12). Average arrival date for central Illinois is September 29 (13 years). High counts by hawkwatchers along Lake Michigan include 36 on September 27, 1981 (DJ-SR31:8), and 33 on October 14, 1982 (AB37:186), at Illinois Beach State Park and 13 at Zion, October 2, 1980 (RCo-SR27:7). Otherwise these birds usually occur as singles. Departure dates are generally in late October and November: Jackson Park, November 11, 1985 (HR-IB&B2:45); Chautauqua National Wildlife Refuge, November 15, 1985 (TP-IB&B2:45); Sangamon County, November 27, 1986 (HDB).

Although Merlins were recorded on eight of the 10 Christmas bird counts for 1976–85, they were seen in small numbers (one to three). The highest count was three at Pere Marquette State Park in 1942. Other winter records: Park Forest, February 1, 1986 (RP-IB&B2:76); Shirland, January 31, 1986 (DW-AB40:286); Quincy, December 27, 1980 (AD-AB35:305); Morton, January 2, 1985 (KR-IB&B 1:68); Jasper County, December 27, 1985 (DJo-IB&B2:76). Merlins winter as far south as Peru and Venezuela.

PEREGRINE FALCON

Falco peregrinus

UNCOMMON MIGRANT AND RARE WINTER
RESIDENT; FORMERLY RARE SUMMER
RESIDENT BUT EXTIRPATED AND NOW BEING
REINTRODUCED

"The Peregrine Falcon is, perhaps, the most highly specialized and superlatively well developed flying organism on our planet today," Thayer (1904) wrote. Yet this beautiful falcon was wiped out as a breeding bird by DDT use, loss of habitat, human disturbance, and indiscriminate shooting in Illinois and the rest of the eastern United States by the mid-1960s. An intensive reintroduction program has put Peregrines back into many states, including Illinois, where they nest on the tops of buildings in Chicago, and Missouri (St. Louis). Whether these populations will survive remains to be seen. The Peregrine Falcon reaches speeds of 200 miles per hour in its dives to catch other birds, which are its main prey. The breeding population in Illinois was *F. p. anatum*, but migrants are predominantly of the highly migratory Arctic race, *F. p. tundrius*. Some migrants may be intergrades. Obviously, the best place to see Peregrine Falcons in Illinois nowadays is along Lake Michigan, but other lakes and rivers are good, too, particularly if there are concentrations of shorebirds or ducks.

Early spring records: Jersey County, March 3, 1984 (CP-SR41:14); Palos, March 22, 1982 (PD-SR33:7); Wilmette, March 3, 1983 (AA,IV-SR37:9); Knox and Warren Counties, March 9, 1987 (MB). Average spring arrival dates: west-central, May 5 (two years); central, April 30 (four years). This falcon was recorded on eight of 10 spring bird counts; the highest count was four in 1983. Spring never produces the numbers fall does, and most Peregrines are seen as singles in spring. Spring departure dates: Arcola, May 23, 1987 (RCh); Rockford, May 14, 1984 (BG,KC-SR41:14); Chicago, May 23, 1986 (JL).

Breeding records for this falcon are few. Nelson as early as 1876 said it was "formerly a rare summer resident." Ridgway (1889) found several pairs nesting in hollow sycamore trees around Mount Carmel in 1878. Widmann (1907) wrote that during the 1880s and early 1890s a few pairs still nested along the Mississippi River near Grand Tower and between Alton and Grafton. More recently, a pair was breeding in Jackson County in 1950 and 1951 (George 1968). It seems to be the last pair for Illinois until the reintroductions. Most Peregrine Falcon nests are on cliffs, but as Ridgway stated, some are in hollow trees. I know of no eggs preserved from Illinois. The most suitable nesting habitats are still those along the bluffs of the Mississippi River.

Migration is much more pronounced in fall than in spring, with Peregrines being seen on days when other raptors are moving, usually behind cold fronts. Early fall arrivals: Vermilion County, August 11, 1982 (MC-SR35:7); Beardstown, August 19, 1985 (KR-IB&B2:45); Clinton Lake, September 1, 1984 (RCh-IB&B1:14). Average arrival dates: Chicago, September 28 (six years); west-central, October 10 (three years); Sangamon County, September 26 (12 years). High counts: 47, Evanston, October 1, 1977 (LB,GR); 23, Evanston, September 25, 1985 (RB-AB40:119); 20, Illinois Beach State Park, September 27, 1981 (RCo-SR31:8); seven, Mississippi Palisades State Park, September 27, 1986 (PP-AB41:95). Departure dates are usually in October, with a thin wintering population obscuring some dates. Late departure dates: Thomson, November 6, 1982 (BSh-SR35:7); Rockford, October 31, 1984 (DW-IB&B1:14); Lake Vermilion, November 30, 1983 (MC,ME-SR39:12); Mahomet, October 28, 1981 (RCh-SR31:8).

Few Peregrines are true wintering birds. Some stay near concentrations of waterfowl, while others concentrate on pigeons in cities. There have never been any large numbers on Christmas bird counts, and some of those counted may have been very late migrants. Six of the Christmas counts for 1976–85 showed Peregrines. The highest count was three at Pere Marquette State Park in 1960. Other winter records: Urbana, February 19, 1983 (RCh-SR36:7); Chicago, January 15, 1986 (MS-IB&B2:76); Kickapoo State Park, January 5, 1986 (Dwe-IB&B2:76); Bismark, January 1, 1984 (IE-SR40:8). Peregrine Falcons winter all the way to the southern tip of South America.

GYRFALCON

Falco rusticolus

RARE MIGRANT AND WINTER RESIDENT

Gyrfalcons are the largest and most powerful falcons on the North American continent. They breed circumpolar and are divided into three highly variable color phases. The darkest phase is found in boreal areas, the gray phase in the lower Arctic, and the white phase predominantly in the high Arctic. Gyrfalcons feed mostly on ptarmigan, but food size ranges from Snow Buntings to geese and arctic hares. In Illinois they are mostly seen pursuing waterfowl. These large-bodied falcons fly with shallow wing beats. They use a level flight to go in directly to catch prey rather than stooping as Peregrine Falcons do. Many times they fly low

to the ground or water. They generally inhabit open areas, where they perch on telephone poles and occasionally in trees but most often sit on the ground. I once watched a Gyrfalcon standing within a few feet of Canada Geese on a mudflat. Whenever it flew over the heads of the geese they would stand still but begin calling. Later the Gyrfalcon was seen pursuing geese in flight.

Starting in 1953, there are 17 records for Illinois, some poorly documented. Burr and Current (1975) summarized the Illinois records up to 1973. That this large falcon went unrecorded in Illinois until 1953 is difficult to imagine, even though most sightings are of short duration. One specimen record is of an immature gray-phase female taken south of Galena, November 3, 1971 (INHS; photographs at ISM). At least eight of the Gyrfalcons seen in Illinois were gray phase. One at Lake Springfield, March 31, 1980 (HDB), was a dark phase. White-phase birds were seen at Arlington Heights, December 20 and 27, 1953 (G.Lukasik-IAB89:8), and Lake Calumet, January 12, 1984 (LB-SR40:8). Other recent records: gray phase, Woodford County, January 23, 1985 (VK-AB39:172); Winnebago County, December 17, 1984 (J.Oar,DW-IB&B1:68). The 11 records for northern Illinois and the six for central Illinois were recorded between October 4 and March 31. The most recent sighting was an adult at the south end of Lake Springfield from October 20 to 24, 1987 (HDB). It was viewed by many observers and photographed.

PRAIRIE FALCON

Falco mexicanus

RARE MIGRANT AND WINTER RESIDENT

This sandy-colored falcon breeds in the western interior and winters from there south to Mexico. There were only nine Illinois records from 1857 to 1959, including some specimens (see Bohlen 1978). Surprisingly, there were more than 17 records from 1978 to 1987. What may be a pair of Prairie Falcons has wintered regularly the past several years at Lawrenceville airport (December 1980 to at least December 1985), and up to four Prairies were there in fall 1982 (LH,DJo-AB37:186). Photographs are on file at the Illinois State Museum. Prairie Falcons have occurred in Illinois between September and May 4. Some recent records: Mark Twain National Wildlife Refuge, November 27, 1979 (BR,PS-AB34:167); Urbana, November 17–29, 1981 (RCh-AB36:183); Alexander County, March 31, 1984 (JR-AB38:917); Winnebago County, November 6, 1985 (DW-AB40:119); Monroe County, April 9, 1986 (RG-AB40:477); Sangamon County, November 9, 1987 (HDB).

Prairie Falcons spend a lot of time on the ground in open areas; they also perch in lone trees and on telephone poles. They are most like Peregrine Falcons, but the black axillars identify the Prairies in any plumage. Prairies also appear larger headed, with less streaking below. They have been observed attacking such birds as Rock Doves and various waterfowl.

GRAY PARTRIDGE

Perdix perdix

INTRODUCED; NOW AN UNCOMMON
PERMANENT RESIDENT IN NORTHERN
ILLINOIS

This game bird is also known as the Hungarian Partridge. It was introduced into the United States as early as 1790 and into Illinois from 1906 through 1927. More than 12,000 were released in the state (Farris 1970). Farris found that 25 northern counties had Gray Partridge populations, with the highest concentrations in Lee and De Kalb. The spread of the Gray Partridge has been west, southwest, and south in Illinois. According to Farris, populations will probably remain low because of the state's too-high summer temperatures and too-abundant rainfall.

Gray Partridge were tallied on every spring bird count, but in small numbers (four to 44). The highest count was 17 in Lee County, May 5, 1973 (VK). Christmas bird counts for 1976-85 showed these partridges for every year but one (1980), with totals ranging from five to 81. Highest Christmas count was 71 in Ogle County in 1983. The Gray Partridge is native to Europe and southwestern Asia. The race in Illinois is *P. p. perdix*. Its main habitat is cultivated fields, hedgerows, and edges. Very little has been reported on nesting in Illinois.

RING-NECKED PHEASANT

Phasianus colchicus

INTRODUCED; NOW A COMMON PERMANENT
RESIDENT IN NORTHERN AND CENTRAL
ILLINOIS BUT RARE IN SOUTHERN ILLINOIS

The pheasant has essentially taken the place of the prairie hen in Illinois, since one disappeared about the time the other was gaining prominence. It was about 1890 that the first introductions of Ring-necked Pheasants took place, and introductions are still occurring, including 32,000 chicks released in 1977. The Illinois pheasant is from mixed ancestry. Warner (1981) found that at least four types were involved: *P. c. colchicus,* the "Caucasus" Pheasant; *P. c. torquatus,* the "Chinese" Pheasant; *P. c. mongolicus,* the "Kirghiz" Pheasant; and a separate species, *P. versicolor,* the Japanese Green Pheasant. Pheasants occur in open habitats but need some cover such as hayfields and other fallow fields for protection and breeding. They also occur in brushy fields, and in winter they sometimes roost in pine groves. Pheasants are dependent on Illinois agriculture, feeding on waste grain. They apparently cannot sustain a population south of 39 degrees latitude in Illinois. Warner traced the pheasant's population fluctuations in his excellent treatise, giving decade by decade accounts. He found that 1900-30 was a period of range expansion, mostly in the northeast but also in east-central Illinois. From 1940 to 1950 there was first a decline in numbers, probably due to adverse spring weather, and then an upswing, particularly in the northeast and east-central regions. In the early 1950s there were 60 pheasants per square mile in northern and 150 in east-central Illinois. The mid-1950s saw a moderate decline. From 1960 to 1970 the pheasant declined even in the east-central area but increased in some peripheral counties. This decline was due to farming practices that left little habitat for the pheasant. It has continued to the present time, compounded by the severe winters of the late 1970s, which saw many dead frozen pheasants in barren fields. Warner also gave annual estimated pheasant kills by hunters in Illinois: 1956-59, 767,000; 1960-64, 907,000; 1965-69, 700,000; 1970-74, 810,000; 1975-78, 522,000.

Pheasants nest on the ground, are single brooded, and lay seven to 15 olive-brown eggs. Available egg dates in Illinois are May 1 to June 27, with young still being seen in early August. Cock pheasants can occasionally be seen sitting in trees and calling; they are polygamous, with six to 12 hens. Pheasants usually do not move more than one or two miles in a given year and have an average lifespan of two years (Warner 1981).

In Illinois the mean number of birds per route on breeding bird surveys for 1965-79 was 13.5 (Robbins et al. 1986). Spring bird count totals ranged from 810 in 1980 (unusually low owing to severe winters) to 1885 in 1974. High counties were Livingston, Will, Ford, and Du Page (VK). Christmas bird count totals for 1976-85 ranged from 396 in 1982 to 1299 in 1976. Highest Christmas count was 209 at Fermilab in 1978.

WILLOW PTARMIGAN

Lagopus lagopus

HYPOTHETICAL

The only evidence that this bird occurred in Illinois is Kennicott's statement (1854) that it was "sometimes found in the timber along Lake Michigan." It seems rather a wild possibility, but two apparently were collected near Racine, Wisconsin, in December 1846 (Cory 1909). The breeding area closest to Illinois is near Hudson Bay, but in winter Willow Ptarmigan are known south to the northern Great Lakes area, most recently in 1964 in Minnesota (Green and Janssen 1975).

RUFFED GROUSE

Bonasa umbellus

PROBABLY EXTIRPATED; VERY RARE IN
NORTHWESTERN ILLINOIS, REINTRODUCED
IN SOUTHERN ILLINOIS

Though never common, Ruffed Grouse once occurred throughout wooded portions of the state. They were apparently extirpated from the state as a result of habitat destruction and hunting, but a few come into the northwest corner from Iowa or Wisconsin during years of high populations. Kennicott (1854) regarded them as common throughout the state. Nelson (1877) said they were "not common" in southern Illinois: "A few were observed in the bottoms. Mr. Ridgway informs me that all the ruffed grouse from this locality possess rufous tails." Specimens from Illinois that I have seen also have the reddish tail. The Illinois State Museum collection includes one from Fayette County, 1889, and another from Baileyville, winter of 1891. A male specimen (FMNH) from Warsaw, January 17, 1892, also has a reddish tail. The extirpated race is *B. u. umbellus*. Eggs were taken at Kankakee, May 2, 1888, and Lake County, May 8, 1893 (Ford 1956). There are three egg sets in the state museum: 15 from near Lacon, May 12, 1905; 14, Grant Park, May 6, 1905; and seven, Fulton County, April 21, 1889.

Considering these dates, the grouse seems to have disappeared from Illinois just after the turn of the century. There were records from the north after that—Winnebago County in 1929-31 (Smith and Parmalee 1955)—but the Ruffed Grouse was essentially gone until reintroductions were tried in southern Illinois by the Department of Conservation. Three attempts seem to have failed: Pope County, 1953-58 and 1967, and Alexander County, 1972. It is hoped that the most recent attempt, in Union County in 1982, will succeed. The birds were brought in from Indiana, and they have already bred in Illinois (Thomas 1987). Three were seen during the Christmas bird count in Union County in 1985. Ruffed Grouse seen recently in northern Illinois include two in Stephenson County on the spring bird count, May 8, 1982 (VK), and one in Jo Daviess County, fall 1977 (G.Hubert-AB32:212). These northern birds are found on steep hillsides in birch tree areas; they roost in junipers.

GREATER PRAIRIE-CHICKEN

Tympanuchus cupido

RARE AND LOCAL PERMANENT RESIDENT IN
SOUTHERN ILLINOIS

Greater Prairie-Chickens were an integral part of the tall-grass prairie in Illinois. When the prairie, which covered about 60 percent of the state, was destroyed, so were the chickens. Actually, they increased in numbers at first—until the late 1860s or so—because the wooded sections of the state were opened up. Prairie-Chickens were still present in 74 counties in 1912, but just 21 years later there were none west of the Illinois River. By 1940 they were reduced to the Green River bottoms of Lee County, the Kankakee River drainage, and the gray prairie area of southeastern Illinois. The last northern birds disappeared from Lee County about 1960 (Lockart, no date). Today this grouse of the tallgrass prairie exists only in Jasper and Marion

Counties on managed sanctuaries, a remnant population of 200 in the spring of 1986.

As early as 1854 Kennicott noted:

For a few years after the settlement of this region the prairie hens were rapidly on the increase. But when the country became thickly populated, the breaking up of their breeding places, the havoc made by guns in summer, and traps in winter, and worst of all the destruction of their eggs by burning the prairie late in spring, has caused their numbers as rapidly to decrease; and it is to be feared they will soon become as rare here as at the east [the Heath Hen]. . . .

Several times the hunting season was closed, even as early as 1887, but the effects of the changing habitat overshadowed those of hunting. In 1933, when hunting was stopped, an estimated 25,000 prairie-chickens were still in Illinois. Now there are only 200.

Males display in spring on bare booming grounds, strutting, dancing, and giving various calls. These displays occur from January to June but primarily in April and May. (They also have a territorial display in fall.) The hens appear and mate with one or several cocks, each of which defends a certain portion of the territory. The hens lay 12 to 17 olive buff eggs that usually have a few darker spots. Illinois egg dates are April 20 to June 6. Another threat to the prairie-chicken population in Illinois comes at this time from pheasants. These nonnative birds lay their eggs in the chickens' nests, and since pheasant eggs hatch a couple of days earlier than prairie-chicken eggs, the hens abandon the nests to raise the young pheasants and leave their own to die. Pheasants also seem to harass prairie-chickens. Sanderson, of the Illinois Natural History Survey, stated that the introduction of the pheasant was a likely factor in the demise of the prairie-chicken.

In the fall these chickens gather in flocks and are found in stubble or grass or along fencerows. Occasionally they even sit in trees. They feed on waste grain, weed seeds, and buds of trees.

The Greater Prairie-Chicken is on the Illinois endangered species list. The loss of this species would be a great blow to the people of Illinois.

SHARP-TAILED GROUSE

Tympanuchus phasianellus

EXTIRPATED

Not much is known about this grouse in Illinois, since it was extirpated very early. Kennicott (1854) wrote that it was "not uncommon, formerly" and indicated that it was known to nest in Cook County. Ford (1956) mentions that it was abundant in northern Illinois south to Chicago from 1840 to 1845 and that several fine specimens were secured in Chicago in 1844. A specimen from Geneva, collected before 1894, is in the Chicago Academy of Science (Ford et al. 1934). Nelson (1876) stated that "if this species now occurs it is extremely rare," but "in the fall of 1863 or 1864, while two gentlemen were shooting prairie chickens near Waukegan, they found and secured a covey of these birds, numbering fourteen individuals." A specimen of an adult male from Rock Island County, June 29, 1901, is in the Putnam Museum in Davenport, Iowa. Some Sharp-tailed Grouse were released in Fulton County, but the introduction did not succeed. This grouse is known to interbreed with the Greater Prairie-Chicken.

WILD TURKEY

Meleagris gallopavo

EXTIRPATED BUT REINTRODUCED; NOW AN UNCOMMON PERMANENT RESIDENT IN SOUTHERN ILLINOIS AND BECOMING ESTABLISHED IN NORTHERN AND CENTRAL ILLINOIS

Wright (1915) summarized the early accounts of large numbers of Wild Turkeys in Illinois. Marquette in 1669–70: "There is fine hunting of Turkeys"; Binnetau in 1699: "Game is plentiful such as ducks [and] Turkeys"; La Honton in 1703: "The River of the Illinois is intitled to riches, by virtue of the benign climate, and of the great quantities of ... Turkeys that feed on its brinks"; Vivier in 1750: "Wild turkeys abound everywhere in all seasons, except near the inhabited portions"; Brown in 1817: "Wild turkeys abound in the hilly districts of Illinois"; Vigne in 1832: "Wild Turkeys are there very plentiful." But by October 1903, five Wild Turkeys killed in Clinton County were thought to be the last in Illinois (Felger 1909). Ferry, however, saw a flock near Olive Branch in 1907 (Cory 1909), and there were rumors of turkeys in Union County as late as 1935 (Smith and Parmalee 1955).

The Illinois Department of Conservation released several thousand game farm turkeys between 1954 and 1958, but this reintroduction effort failed. Then, starting in 1959, 65 wild-trapped turkeys from Mississippi, Arkansas, and West Virginia were released in southern Illinois. Such releases continued to 1967 and resulted in the successful reestablishment of a turkey population (Calhoun and Garver 1974). Illinois had its first turkey season in 67 years in 1970 when hunting was allowed in three counties: Alexander, Union, and Jackson. Other southern Illinois counties with turkeys are Pope, Randolph, Williamson, Saline, Gallatin, Monroe, and Hardin. The turkey has also expanded its range and, with new releases, is now found in several other areas of the state. Additional counties on spring bird counts include Kane, Henry, Du Page, McHenry, Adams, Marshall, and Schuyler. Spring count totals ranged from two in 1977 to 79 in 1985. The highest count was 35 in Marshall County in 1982 (VK). Christmas bird counts also have shown some new counties with turkeys, including Jersey, Calhoun, Cook, Carroll, and Whiteside. Numbers on

Christmas counts for 1976–85 ranged from seven in 1976 to 144 in 1985, with the highest count 65 at Pere Marquette State Park in 1985. Numbers on both spring and Christmas counts are increasing. Turkeys have also been reported in Vermilion, Pike, Brown, and Henderson Counties.

Turkeys are most often found in heavily wooded areas, but they also inhabit semiopen woodlands and cultivated areas next to woodlands. They feed on acorns, nuts, fruits, and insects such as grasshoppers. They roost in trees, usually over water or in steep ravines. Their nests are on the ground in dead leaves; there are eight to 12 eggs, pale buff with reddish brown spots. Nesting apparently begins in mid-March, but few data are available to determine egg dates for Illinois. The race found in Illinois is *M. g. silvestris*.

NORTHERN BOBWHITE

Colinus virginianus

COMMON PERMANENT RESIDENT DECREASING NORTHWARD

Just about everyone knows the *bobwhite* call of this plump brown bird. The Northern Bobwhite is found in shrubs, orchards, hedgerows, hayfields, grassy fields, and pastures. Familiar along rural roads, it can be seen on fence posts in spring giving its call notes. It can live near people, but its nest and young are vulnerable to people's pets, and this vulnerability increases when people simplify the Bobwhite's habitats. The Bobwhite eats mostly vegetable matter, including grain, seeds, and fruits. About 16 percent of its diet is insects, including beetles, grasshoppers, bugs, and caterpillars (Judd 1905).

Although Bobwhites are found throughout the state, the population is highest in southern Illinois and lowest in northeastern Illinois. Graber and Graber (1963) estimated the June statewide population for 1909 at 842,000. For 1958 it was 662,000—80 percent of them in southern Illinois. The decrease is probably due to habitat loss. The Grabers found that grassland pasture, the most significant habitat for the Bobwhite, had decreased greatly by 1957. In a 15-year study (1955–69), Preno and Labisky (1971) found Bobwhites most abundant in the southern and western sectors of Illinois. Lows occurred in the population in 1956, 1961, and 1965, and highs in 1958, 1964, and 1969. The Bobwhite population seems to fluctuate fairly dramatically from year to year and season to season. Preno and Labisky reported an average of 2,127,000 Bobwhites shot annually by Illinois hunters from 1956 to 1969—a very high figure that does not seem to jibe with other population estimates. They also concluded that despite intensive environmental degradation in Illinois the Bobwhite population had increased substantially during the study period. Breeding bird surveys for 1965–79 showed decreases in Bobwhite populations in the eastern United States, with significant decreases in Illinois and 14 other states. This decline was caused largely by the severe winters of 1976-78, and it shows up in spring and Christmas bird counts. What significance the prior depletion of habitat played in these stressful winters is unknown. The mean number of birds per breeding bird survey route in Illinois was 31.5 (Robbins et al. 1986).

Spring bird count totals ranged from 429 in 1979 to 2318 in 1986. The 1979 figure represents the low point following severe winters, while the 1986 figure demonstrates good recovery. Some very open areas, however, had still not recovered by 1987, and these areas probably should be closed to Bobwhite hunting to help the recovery. The highest spring count was 188 in Bureau County, May 4, 1974 (VK).

Bobwhites nest on the ground, making a depression, lining it with grasses, and pulling some taller vegetation over the nest to conceal it. Most available Illinois egg dates are in May and June, but Bent (1932) gives the dates as late April to Mid-October. The eggs are white and probably number from nine to 19 (based on a small sample). The young mature fast and stay together until the following spring.

The plumage of the Northern Bobwhite is quite variable. There are three erythristic specimens in the Illinois State Museum collection, evidently from a small population in Sangamon County collected from 1958 to 1973. These birds are a rich reddish brown, and one has a white breast.

In fall, winter, and early spring the Bobwhite occurs in coveys. Christmas bird counts show the low ebb due to the severe winters of the late 1970s, with only 301 tallied in 1979 compared with 1328 in 1976. The highest Christmas count was 416 at Chillicothe in 1974. Graber and Graber (1963) found the January statewide population always higher than the June population: an estimated 2,082,000 in January 1907 and 2,235,000 in January 1958.

The Northern Bobwhite ranges south to northwestern Guatemala and has been introduced widely.

YELLOW RAIL

Coturnicops noveboracensis

RARE MIGRANT

The presence of this elusive bird is difficult to prove without a diligent search. Though the Yellow Rail occurs in marshes like other rails, it is more often found in wet grassy fields. At Sangchris State Park it favors a grassy field with clumps of old grass intermingled with shallow pools of water. Finding a Yellow Rail takes a lot of tramping and results in wet feet, since each puddle needs to be walked. These rails will sometimes flush 10 to 15 feet away and at other times right underfoot. I saw one run into a clump of grass and peer back out at me. Once kicked up they are difficult to flush again. Yellow Rails occur in drier habitats, too, and have been seen by persons burning prairies (Bartel

1978) and cutting clover fields. Most Yellow Rails are identified on the wing by the white wing patches, small size, and buffy color. They are seldom seen on the ground.

If Yellow Rails ever nested in Illinois they apparently do not do so anymore. Nelson (1876) stated that a set of six eggs and the parent bird were taken at Winnebago, May 17 (no year, Smithsonian collection). Widmann (1907) noted that Worthen found Yellow Rails during the breeding season near Warsaw. Coale (1912) called them rare summer residents in Lake County. They now breed north of Illinois, as close as southern Wisconsin. The race in the United States is *C. n. noveboracensis,* the only other race, *C. n. goldmani,* being restricted to one valley in Mexico.

The average spring arrival date for Sangamon County is April 11 (nine years). There are a few March dates: Urbana, March 31, 1924 (Packard 1958); Sangchris State Park, March 29, 1977 (HDB). This rail was detected seven of 15 years on spring bird counts in very low numbers (one to five). The three reported in Lee County in 1974 should be questioned in the absence of documentation (VK). Most records in spring are for April and May: Champaign, May 7, 1982 (BCho-SR33:7); Horseshoe Lake, May 4, 1980 (PS-SR25:5); Moline, April 19, 1981 (CS-SR29:7); Crab Orchard National Wildlife Refuge, April 8–19, 1987 (DR,TF). One of the latest dates for recent sightings is May 22, 1984, at the Green River Conservation Area (BSh-SR41:14).

If spring is a tricky time to find this rail, fall with its profusion of vegetation presents even greater obstacles. In fall the Yellow Rail inhabits hayfields and other agricultural areas as well as marshes, spreading out the population. Early fall arrival dates: television tower kill, Olney, September 12, 1977 (LH-AB32:212); Gilbert Lake, September 11, 1965 (JEC,SV-AFN20:54); Beach, September 13, 1926 (Brodkorb and Stevenson 1934). There are no high counts for fall. Late departure dates: Geneva, November 1, 1891 (Ford et al. 1934); Chicago, October 18, 1980 (RG-AB35:189); television tower kill, Springfield, October 24, 1971 (ISM).

BLACK RAIL

Laterallus jamaicensis

RARE MIGRANT AND RARE SUMMER RESIDENT

Rails are noted for being difficult to detect, but the Black Rail is the most elusive of all. To add to its mystique, it has a weird *kick-ke-doo* call, which it gives mainly at night. It will make a scolding sound in reaction to a tape of its own call. Black Rails are found in marshy vegetation, usually in shallow water but also in wet hayfields and pastures. One was found in summer in Mason County in rushes and sedges. The subspecies in Illinois is the eastern form, *L. j. jamaicensis.* Though this rail probably was never common in Illinois, destruction of marsh habitat has made it an endangered species in the state.

Most of the records for this rail come in spring, especially in May. There are a few April records: Rockford, April 8 and 13, 1959 (DPr-AFN13:375). Other recent spring records: possibly four, Vermilion County, May 5, 1979 (AB33:776); Fairmount, May 30, 1984 (JSm-AB38:917); Grundy County, May 24, 1985 (JH,JMc-AB39:307); specimen, Chicago, May 19, 1984 (FMNH).

There are several Illinois nesting records. The first record was of 10 eggs found near the Calumet River on June 19, 1875 (Nelson 1876). Hess (1910) found a nest with two eggs near Philo, May 30, 1901. Musselman (1937) banded two young in Adams County on August 22, 1932, and saw another immature on July 25, 1936. More recently, summer records have occurred at Banner Marsh, June 16–28, 1983 (DBi-SR38:7), and Snicarte, June 20–21 and 25, 1975 (RS,HDB). The Black Rail's nest resembles a meadowlark's, and the eggs are creamy white with reddish spots.

Even less is known about the fall migration than about spring's. The only relatively recent record is of one Black Rail found dead at Chicago in early September 1964 (Bohlen 1978). Other fall records are from Crab Orchard National Wildlife Refuge, October 15, 1949, and Rockford, September 25, 1950 (Smith and Parmalee 1955); Chicago, October 15, 1903, and Canton, October 27, 1894 (Bent 1926). Black Rails winter along the Gulf Coast.

CLAPPER RAIL

Rallus longirostris

HYPOTHETICAL

This coastal species rarely comes inland, but it has been recorded in Nebraska and several eastern states. The only Illinois report is one listed from near Rockford on August 5, 1916, without further comment (Nature Study Society of Rockford 1917–18).

KING RAIL

Rallus elegans

OCCASIONAL MIGRANT AND SUMMER RESIDENT

Even though the King Rail is fairly large, it is usually difficult to see because it stays in heavy marsh vegetation. Occasionally it comes into the open on a mudflat or at the edge of cattails in shallow water. Its call is a loud clacking most often heard at dawn or dusk. The King Rail's population has been dropping over a long period, probably due to a loss of aquatic habitat. Its status should be determined by census, and if warranted it should be placed on the state's endangered species list. The race found in Illinois is *R. e. elegans*.

Early arrival dates are for April: Grand Tower, April 14, 1985 (JR-IB&B1:81); Savanna, April 12, 1986 (BSh,LJ-IB&B2:88); Sanchris State Park, April 6, 1974 (HDB). Average spring arrival dates: Chicago, May 9 (eight years); Sangamon County, April 23 (seven years). Because of the drop in numbers and the difficulty of detection, spring bird count totals are quite low (one to 12), though this rail was recorded every year (VK). High counts: six, Decatur, April 19, 1973 (RP); four, Madison County, May 17, 1980 (PS-SR25:5); four, Lake County, May 18, 1980 (JG-SR25:5). Migrants are present until mid- to late May. Dreuth recorded one on May 25, 1931, along the Chicago lakefront (Clark and Nice 1950).

In view of its rarity today, the many old nest records for this species in Illinois testify to a definite decline. Nevertheless, some areas still have nesting birds: East St. Louis marshes (declining, RG), Beardstown, Chain O'Lakes State Park, Goose Lake Prairie, Lake Calumet, Negro Lake, Volo Bog, Tinley Park, and Banner Marsh. Like most rails, Kings nest in marshes on clumps of vegetation with additional vegetation pulled over to form a canopy. Beecher (1942) found four nests in lake sedge (*Carex lacustris*). The females lay from six to 13 eggs, which are pale buff with a few reddish or purplish spots. Illinois egg dates are April 29 to July 6. The young are black; they can leave the nest soon after hatching. Two specimens of juveniles are in the Illinois State Museum collection, one from Hancock County collected on July 29, 1932, and the other from Havana collected on July 22, 1985. Both specimens show the dark coloration ventrally.

Very few King Rails are seen in fall. Apparently many migrate fairly early, and dense vegetation conceals others. Many records are for July and August. Late records: Lake Calumet, October 2, 1983 (JL); two, Joliet, September 2, 1981 (JM-SR31:9); Pecatonica, September 20, 1900 (specimen ISM).

Winter records are very rare: a crippled King Rail at Rock Island, December 26, 1960 (IAB117:15), and a bird at Chillicothe, January 2, 1967 (BPr-AFN21:253). King Rails winter regularly in the Gulf states south into Mexico.

VIRGINIA RAIL

Rallus limicola

FAIRLY COMMON MIGRANT; FAIRLY COMMON SUMMER RESIDENT DECREASING SOUTHWARD; RARE WINTER RESIDENT

This rail is not as common as the Sora, but it can be seen every year if an observer is willing to wade through enough marshes. The Virginia Rail is rusty, with a fairly long bill, a gray face, and white under the tail coverts, which it exposes by flicking its tail when nervous. It seems to prefer to run rather than flush, staying in cattails or wet grasses and occurring less often than the Sora in drier habitats. Its common call is the *ki dick* series with grunting sounds at the end.

Some spring migrants may arrive in March, but early records may include wintering rails: Springfield, March 19, 1987 (HDB); Havana, March 29, 1987 (LA). Average spring arrival dates: Chicago, April 29 (seven years); west-central, May 2 (nine years); Sangamon County, April 12 (18 years). Spring bird count totals ranged from 11 in 1972 to 68 in 1982. High counts: 32, Lake County, May 8, 1982; 22, Will County, May 4, 1985; 17, Cook County, May 5, 1979; 15, Carroll County, May 5, 1984 (VK). Average spring departure dates: Chicago, May 1 (seven years); Sangamon County, May 10 (17 years). Late departures are usually difficult to distinguish from summering birds, but most migrating Virginia Rails are gone by mid- to late May.

The Virginia Rail breeds locally throughout the state but more consistently in northern Illinois. Some recent evidence of breeding: 16 pairs, Chain O'Lakes State Park, summer 1982 (SH,JN-AB36:982); present in three marshes in Kane County, 1980 (RM-SR26:5); young, Macon County, July 5, 1985 (RP-IB&B2:13); several pairs, Lake Calumet, 1982 (RM-SR34:5); young, Springfield, 1983 (HDB); young, Bloomington, 1979 (DBi-SR22:4); young, Joliet, 1983 (JM-SR38:7). These rails nest on the ground in marshes by building up vegetation around a cuplike nest. Eggs number seven to 12 and are cream-colored with some reddish brown spots. Illinois egg dates are May 5 to June 18. The chicks are blackish. Later, when the immatures are about the size of adults, they are colored like the adults but with blackish areas, especially ventrally. Young seem most abundant in late June and July.

Fall migration probably begins in August, but Virginia Rails are much more difficult to detect in fall than in spring. Early arrival dates: Chicago, August 15, 1933 (Clark and Nice 1950); Sangchris State Park, August 13, 1970 (HDB). The average arrival date for Sangamon County is September 23 (11 years). There are no high counts for fall. Departure dates are obscured by wintering birds, but most migrants are gone by late October or early November. Some are killed at television towers; the latest such kill was at Springfield, November 12, 1972 (ISM).

Any rail seen in winter is usually of this species. Virginias tend to stay where there is open water, so wintering in Illinois may be a recent phenomenon. In Christmas bird counts for 1976–85 they were encountered five years: Chautauqua National Wildlife Refuge, 1976; Cook County and Chautauqua refuge, 1980; Decatur and Barrington, 1983; Springfield, 1984; Joliet, 1985. On all previous Christmas counts they had shown up only five years. Some actually make it through the winter, but others must be frozen out. They are sometimes caught in traps set for muskrats. Late winter records: Rockford, December 28–January 28, 1984 (KBr-SR40:8); Will County, February 25, 1982 (PD-SR32:5); Du Page County, January 15–February 15, 1981 (JSt-AB35:305). The Virginia Rail winters as far south as central Guatemala.

SORA
Porzana carolina

COMMON MIGRANT; FAIRLY COMMON SUMMER RESIDENT IN NORTHERN ILLINOIS DECREASING SOUTHWARD

Soras are the most numerous rails in Illinois and the easiest to flush from their marshy habitat. When a Sora is flushed, this small chickenlike bird usually flies straight up, feet dangling and short wings flapping, and goes only a short distance before flopping back into the vegetation. Soras do a lot of running before and after they are rousted up. They are found not only in marshes but also around ponds, the shallow ends of lakes, flooded fields, and occasionally drier places, such as hayfields. The best way to detect Soras is by their whinnying call. They also give a plaintive note and some sharp call notes. With practice these calls can be imitated, and Soras will respond to them. On occasion—usually in early morning or late evening—they actually come out into the open and walk around on mudflats.

Soras seem to be such poor fliers that it is difficult to imagine them as long-distance nocturnal migrants. They do have a propensity for hitting television towers, power lines, and tall buildings and getting hit by automobiles. Sometimes the first indication that they are migrating is a dead Sora found on the road. The earliest spring Soras arrive in March. I have a record for March 12, 1977, at Sangchris State Park, but the central Illinois average is April 2 (18 years). Dreuth (Clark and Nice 1950) at Chicago found April 27 to be the average arrival date (11 years). Other early dates: Palos, March 21, 1985 (KB); Danville, March 23, 1985 (SB); Warren County, March 29, 1985 (MB-IB&B1:81). Spring bird counts show all the highs in northern Illinois: 109, Cook County, May 5, 1979; 95, Lake County, May 8, 1982. Count totals ranged from 102 in 1975 to 571 in 1984 (VK). Other maximum counts: 28, La Salle County, May 5, 1984 (SR41:14); 10, Oakwood Bottoms, April 18, 1983 (TF-SR37:10). Migrants leave by mid- to late May, some going as far north as southern Alaska. Average spring departure dates: Chicago, May 13 (11 years); central Illinois, May 19 (18 years).

Even though George (1968) indicates that the Sora is a rare summer resident, there are no breeding records for southern Illinois. Beecher (1942) found 54 nests at Fox Lake, Lake County, in 1937 in cattail, sedge, and blue joint grass—an average of one nest every 1.78 acres. The Sora's nest is cuplike with plants pulled over the top to keep out the sun and hide the nest. Eggs number four to 14 and are buff with sparse darker brown spotting. Illinois egg dates are May 26 to August 5. The black downy young can leave the nest in one or two days. Immature birds are brownish compared with the gray and dark brown adults. Of 42 specimens in the Illinois State Museum collection, 33 were taken in fall, 26 of them in immature plumage.

Soras either wander south or begin fall migration early, perhaps because ponds or wet areas are drying up. They move on cold fronts like other nocturnal fall migrants. The earliest arrival date for Sangamon County is July 21, 1982, with an average of August 9 (14 years). Dreuth's average for Chicago is September 16 (12 years). Other early fall arrival dates: Knoxville, July 11, 1985 (MB); Jasper County, July 30, 1985 (SSi-IB&B2:13). Maximum counts for fall are lower than spring counts, but that could be because the vegetation is much thicker, the birds vocalize less, and migration is more prolonged. Maximum fall counts: 25, Palos, September 5, 1976 (Mlodinow 1984); 21, Joliet, September 22, 1984 (JM-IB&B1:14); 25, Chautauqua National Wildlife Refuge, August 29, 1976 (RS); seven, Mark Twain National Wildlife Refuge, September 24, 1983 (SRu-SR39:12). Most Soras have departed by late October. Dreuth's average for Chicago is October 1 (12 years), and the average for central Illinois is October 8 (16 years). Latest dates: three, Shelby County, October 30, 1984 (KF); Lake Carlyle, October 28, 1984 (LH-IB&B1:14); Long John Slough, November 6, 1976 (Mlodinow 1984). A specimen was collected 15 miles south of Springfield on November 11, 1914 (ISM).

Several references give southern Illinois as a wintering area for this rail, but there is very little supporting evidence. Only one Christmas bird count record is known: Rantoul, December 25, 1912 (*Bird-Lore* 14:40). Soras winter as far south as northern South America.

Although the Sora is considered a game bird, no population census exists for the species and no accurate harvest figures are available (Odom 1977). Two other species of rails are considered endangered in Illinois, and two have low populations. Since the habitat for these birds is nearly depleted and still declining, rail hunting in Illinois should be made a thing of the past.

PURPLE GALLINULE

Porphyrula martinica

RARE VAGRANT; VERY RARE SUMMER
RESIDENT IN SOUTHERN ILLINOIS

With its purplish breast, greenish back, bluish frontal plate, and yellow legs, the Purple Gallinule is more brightly colored by far than either the American Coot or the Common Moorhen. It is a southern bird that appears to reach Illinois primarily by overmigration, since 24 of the approximately 35 records are for spring. Even though most of these gallinules are found in marshes and at lakes, some have turned up in buildings and in backyards. Spring birds occur in April and May; the extreme dates are April 7 and May 27. The oldest record is of a Purple Gallinule at Englewood, June 1, 1885 (CAS#4099). Recent spring records: Waukegan, May 10, 1978 (JN-AB32:1014); Granite City, April 7, 1983 (A.Evens-AB37:876); Greenville, April 11, 1983 (CMa-AB37:876); near Alton, May 5–27, 1984 (R.Edwards,PS-AB38:917); Mermet Lake, May 26, 1985

(LH-AB39:307); Chicago, April 7, 1981 (SR29:7); Palos, April 29, 1984 (PD-SR41:14).

Because the Purple Gallinule has nested in Illinois only at Mermet Lake, it is on the Illinois endangered species list. Mermet Lake is shallow, with a lot of emergent and floating vegetation, especially American lotus, on which these long-toed birds can walk. Waldbauer and Hays (1964) recorded the first nesting evidence: two downy young with an adult in 1963. A nest with eight eggs was found there on June 19, 1973 (MHm,MSy-AB27:876). Other summer records are without evidence of breeding: Evanston, June 11 and 15, 1977 (JG,LY-AB31:1147); Union County Conservation Area, July 11–18, 1987 (TF,DR); Moredock Lake, June 8, 1963 (WG,DE-AFN17:464).

Fall records are quite scarce and probably represent dispersal of immatures: one immature collected, Bellwood, September 22, 1925 (Eifrig 1927); immature, Palos, October 30, 1982 (PD-AB37:186); Omaha, August 7, 1980 (RBr-AB35:189); immature, Thomson, October 30 and November 6, 1982 (BSh-SR35:7).

COMMON MOORHEN

Gallinula chloropus

UNCOMMON MIGRANT; LOCALLY
UNCOMMON SUMMER RESIDENT IN
NORTHERN ILLINOIS DECREASING
SOUTHWARD

This cootlike gallinule is shy, staying in or near emergent vegetation, and thus is much more difficult to see than the American Coot. The red shield of adult Common Moorhens easily separates them from American Coots, with which they are occasionally seen. The immature Moorhen, like the adult, has a brownish back and a white fringe along the side. Nelson (1876) referred to the Common Moorhen as an abundant summer resident in Illinois marshes and prairie sloughs, but it is not abundant anywhere in the state today because much of its habitat has been destroyed.

Moorhens seem to arrive in spring at varying times, perhaps because of the difficulty in detecting them and the varying availability of habitat in a given locality. Early spring arrival dates: Lake Calumet, April 9, 1977 (Mlodinow 1984); Springfield, April 11, 1985 (HDB); Mermet Lake, April 11, 1986 (DR-IB&B2:88). Average spring arrival dates: west-central, May 8 (six years); Sangamon County, May 9 (nine years). Maximum counts for spring are low; 19 at Lake Calumet, May 23, 1987 (WM), is the highest. Spring bird count totals ranged from five in 1972 to 189 in 1979, with 167 at McHenry County, May 5, 1979, by far the highest count. The next highest was 65 at Cook County, May 10, 1986 (VK).

In Illinois this gallinule nests most commonly in the northeast. It is especially prevalent at Lake Calumet, Powderhorn Marsh, Eggers Marsh, Redwing Slough, and the marshes in the East St. Louis area. It nests elsewhere only haphazardly when the appropriate habitat is present. Most nests are in marshes and are made of dead plants and other debris. The female lays six to 12 eggs that are buff with dark spots. Illinois egg dates are May 20 to June 27. The young are black with some blue over the eye and a reddish bill. A young bird was seen at Lake Calumet as late as September 23, 1979 (JL).

Fall migration is even less noticeable than spring migration. High counts for fall: 37, Chicago, August 14, 1983 (JL-AB38:208); nine, Arcola, August 31, 1986 (SB-IB&B3:39); 12, Lockport, August 17, 1983 (JM-SR39:12). Late spring departure dates: Olney, November 14, 1980 (LH-SR27:7); Lake Calumet, November 30, 1981 (JL-AB36:183); Fulton County, November 9, 1982 (BPr-AB37:186). An injured bird was seen at Illinois Beach State Park, January 1, 1975 (JSa).

AMERICAN COOT

Fulica americana

ABUNDANT MIGRANT; COMMON SUMMER
RESIDENT IN NORTHERN ILLINOIS
DECREASING SOUTHWARD; UNCOMMON
WINTER RESIDENT IN SOUTHERN ILLINOIS
DECREASING NORTHWARD

Few people realize that this familiar bird is a member of the rail family. Its other name, mud hen, suits its habits, for it often forages on mudflats, though it is also found wherever there is water, even on golf courses, airfields, and lawns. American Coots run in herds where there is short grass near water. On water they usually sit in compact flocks, flying only when they are approached closely or nearly run down by motorboats. Migration is nocturnal; in fact, seeing a flock of migrant coots in flight is unheard of. This propensity for night flight killed several hundred coots at Spring Lake when an intense cold front came in during the day on December 8, 1985, and instead of leaving, as diurnal migrants would have done, the coots stayed until nightfall. By then it was too late, and they froze to the ice. Coots also fly into television towers, power lines, and buildings during migration. They eat a wide variety of aquatic plants and animals, some of which they get by diving. Coots make several different grating cackles and croaks, mostly in their marshy breeding areas. Several recent sightings in Illinois of what were termed Caribbean Coots were probably of American Coot variants (see Clark 1985). The race in North America is *F. a. americana*.

Spring migation starts as soon as the ice breaks up, with small numbers appearing as early as February: Charleston, February 19, 1987 (LBH); 25, Baldwin Lake, February 17, 1984 (TF-SR41:14); eight, Springfield, February 17, 1982 (HDB). Average spring arrival dates: Chicago, April 4 (11 years); west-central, March 4 (12 years). High counts for spring: 420,000, Mississippi and Illinois Rivers, April 11,

1983 (RC-SR37:10); 1365, Palos, March 30, 1985 (JL); thousands, Spring Lake, April 12, 1987 (MB). Spring bird count totals ranged from 442 in 1986 to 5866 in 1982; the high count was 5000 in Iroquois County, May 8, 1982 (VK). Most coots have moved farther north by mid- to late May, with some nonbreeding stragglers hanging on into summer in favored spots.

Nesting coot records include hundreds of young, Horseshoe Lake, 1983 (RG-AB37:993); 20 broods, Arcola, 1985 (RCh-AB39:918); 46 young, Havana, 1985 (KR-IB&B2:14); 40 nests, Lake Calumet, 1982 (RM-SR34:6); and 50 nests, Jackson County, 1973 (VK,DH-AB27:779). Some nests are in such fortuitous places as flood overflow areas. Coot nests are built on the ground near water or on vegetation in the water, usually in cattails. They contain from five to 15 dull buff eggs with dark spots or specks. Illinois egg dates are May 20 to June 25. The young are dark with reddish orange on their heads; the color lightens to gray as the chicks become older.

Early fall arrival dates: Lake Renwick, August 3, 1985 (JM-IB&B2:45); Randolph County, August 13, 1983 (JR-SR39:12). Average arrival dates: Chicago, October 3 (15 years); west-central, September 24 (nine years). High counts for fall: 852,000, Illinois and Mississippi Rivers, November 7, 1979 (RC-AB34:167); 31,650, Pool 19, October 27, 1985 (RCe-AB40:119); 9000, Carlyle Lake, November 1, 1986 (RP-IB&B3:39); 2000, Clinton Lake, October 26, 1985 (RCh-IB&B2:45). Average departure dates for fall: Chicago, November 21 (15 years); west-central, November 15 (nine years). When lakes freeze, coots are forced out, although once in a while a tardy bird will be seen walking around on the ice.

Totals on Christmas bird counts for 1976–85 ranged from 50 in 1985 to 726 in 1981. Highest count was 1200 at Chautauqua National Wildlife Refuge in 1972. Numbers in winter fluctuate, depending on the severity of winter and the availability of open water. Coots that are present in early winter are not necessarily there at the end of winter. Winter populations are highest in southern Illinois: 600, Crab Orchard National Wildlife Refuge, January 31, 1987 (DR-AB41:287); 200, Olney, January 4, 1982 (LH-SR32:5).

LIMPKIN

Aramus guarauna

HYPOTHETICAL

A unique large rail- and cranelike bird of the tropics, the Limpkin is an unlikely bird for Illinois, even as a vagrant. It is found in Georgia, Florida, and farther south, with vagrant records for Texas and Maryland. The only report for Illinois is in Cory (1909), in a letter written by Hess: "A limpkin was taken here (Philo, Champaign Co., Ill.) in 1896. I have the wings of this bird yet." If these wings are still extant, their whereabouts is unknown.

COMMON GOLDENEYE
Bucephala clangula

This fast-flying hardy duck is a regular visitor from the north. Many flocks of Common Goldeneyes spend the winter throughout the state. Both these ducks and their cousins the Barrow's Goldeneyes are known as "whistlers," a name that refers to the particularly loud and musical whistling sound produced by their wings in flight. This sound has an extraordinary carrying power that announces their approach before they come into sight.

Adults

(male)

(female)

RED-BREASTED MERGANSER
Mergus serrator

The majority of Red-breasted Mergansers prefer to spend the winter months feeding on the animal life they can find along the coasts and in saltwater bays. Each year, however, a few of these birds can be found wintering on the Great Lakes and elsewhere in the state.

Adults

(male)

(female)

RUDDY DUCK
Oxyura jamaicensis

About the time the new green leaves of the cattail (*Typha* sp.) are emerging at the edges of our ponds and lakes, Ruddy Ducks in full breeding plumage are passing through on the way to their nesting grounds on the northern plains. In the fall when these chunky little ducks are on their way south, males and females are dressed in a drab mottled brown. In this plumage, however, adult males can still be distinguished from their mates by the white patches on their cheeks that persist throughout the year.

Adults

(male)

(female)

TURKEY VULTURE
Cathartes aura

These ugly black birds of prey are miraculously transformed into soaring creatures of beauty when they take to the skies—an activity that roosting Turkey Vultures usually delay until the air has been warmed by the morning sun and the thermals have begun to rise. Frequently these vultures gather in small groups to feed and roost.

Adult
(sexes similar)

OSPREY
Pandion haliaetus

For years anglers have unjustly accused Ospreys of being a negative influence on the populations of many species of their favorite game fish. The fish in the talons of this Osprey is a River Redhorse (*Moxostoma rufum*), one of several species of so-called trash fish upon which these fish hawks prey, but which few fishermen prize.

Adult
(sexes similar)

NORTHERN HARRIER
Circus cyaneus

It takes a male Northern Harrier up to three years to attain the pure silver-gray plumage of an adult bird. During this time, both the adult females and their young are dressed in shades of brown and rust. Consequently the chance of seeing an adult male in full gray plumage hunting on a windswept marsh can vary seasonally but is never more than about one in four.

Adult
*(male; female is brown—both have
the distinctive white rump)*

ROUGH-LEGGED HAWK
Buteo lagopus

These hawks of the Canadian tundra are only winter visitors to the state, and their highly variable plumage causes much confusion when they arrive. Some Rough-legged Hawks are dressed in black while others are very light trimmed in various shades of brown. Audubon once noted of a series of specimens he examined that no two were alike. The bird here is of the most common color phase. The winter diet of the Rough-legged Hawk is primarily voles (*Microtus*).

Adult
(sexes similar)

AMERICAN KESTREL
Falco sparverius

Silent most of the year, the American Kestrel becomes quite vocal and conspicuous in spring when courtship begins. Courtship includes a series of circling flights and dives performed by the male. These movements usually end in a graceful balancing act on the uppermost branch of a tree, where the female waits. The Kestrel is one of the few North American hawks that nest in cavities in trees.

Adults

(male)

(female)

RUFFED GROUSE
Bonasa umbellus

The drumming of the Ruffed Grouse has been heard every month of the year. In early spring, however, about the time the flowers of the Hepatica (*Hepatica acutiloba*) and Snow Trillium (*Trillium nivale*) appear, the male Ruffed Grouse's efforts to attract a mate begin in earnest as he displays and drums on a favorite resonant log.

Adult
(male; sexes similar)

SANDHILL CRANE

Grus canadensis

UNCOMMON MIGRANT AND VERY RARE
SUMMER RESIDENT IN NORTHERN ILLINOIS;
RARE MIGRANT ELSEWHERE IN THE STATE

Sandhill Cranes in Illinois are mostly seen flying overhead during spring and fall migrations. High fliers, they usually go unnoticed unless an observer is looking for them. Most of them nest northwest of Illinois and winter in Georgia and Florida, with stopovers in spring and fall at Jasper-Pulaski Fish and Wildlife Area in Indiana (Walkinshaw 1960). As many as 12,000 were at Jasper-Pulaski in October 1979 (SR:23:6). When passing over Illinois most of these cranes stay on a line from Jasper-Pulaski to Chain O'Lakes State Park. Since they usually move in fair weather, few are seen on the ground. A few turn up in other parts of Illinois when the winds cause them to veer off course. A probable Mississippi Valley contingent of this population has been extirpated. The Sandhill Crane is a large bird that flies with neck extended and legs trailing behind, taking on a distinctive profile. Its voice has been called loud and ringing; it is a musical trumpeting that carries long distances. Sandhill Cranes are found in grasslands, marshes, and fields, especially cornfields, and on the edges of swampy areas and lakes. The subspecies in Illinois is *G. c. tabida*, although *G. c. canadensis* (Little Brown Crane) once occurred here, as evidenced by bones found in a kitchen midden pit in Jackson County (Baker 1937).

Spring migration begins in late February and March: 14, Newton, February 24, 1987 (LH); 13, Forest Glen Preserve, February 25, 1987 (MC,ME); 10, Charleston, March 3, 1984 (KWa-SR41:15); Lake Clinton, March 14, 1981 (RCh-SR29:7). High counts for spring: 2000, Cook County, March 17, 1986 (PD,JN-IB&B2:88); 724, Lake Calumet, March 10, 1985 (JL,CM-AB39:307); 500, Lombard, March 22, 1980 (JC-SR25:5); 1497 and 1623, Mount Hoy, March 16 and 19, 1987 (DY). Usually by May most of this migration is over. Late dates: Starved Rock State Park, May 23, 1985 (JH-IB&B1:81); 20, Lockport, April 16, 1987 (JM); two near Lexington, April 25, 1981 (DBi-SR29:7); two, Winthrop Harbor, May 20, 1981 (JN-SR29:7). Spring bird counts, though done well after the peak of crane migration, recorded Sandhills in 11 of 15 years. All maximum counts were from northern Illinois (Lake, McHenry, and Will Counties) and ranged from one to 14 birds.

Sandhill Cranes probably bred fairly commonly in Illinois until about 1890 (Johnsgard 1983). The last nest found was in Champaign County in 1872 (Gault 1922). Recently they began nesting again, as a few spilled over into Illinois from Wisconsin. Recent breeding records include two downy young with parents on May 24, 1979, in Lake County (Greenberg 1980); adults with young on May 27, 1981 (VK,MSw-AB35:945), nested in summer 1982 (JN-AB36:982), and nested in summer 1986 at Chain O'Lakes State Park (RHe-AB40:1210); and one nest in McHenry

County, summer 1986 (WSc-AB40:1210). Other summer records: two, Illinois Beach State Park, June 25, 1981 (SH,JN-SR30:7); probable nesting, two adults and one immature near Thomson, August 10, 1985 (LJ-IB&B2:14). Sandhill Cranes nest on the ground in large marshy areas. The nest is a pile of vegetation in which are laid two brown eggs with darker brown markings.

Fall migration begins in mid-September: 28, Palos, September 15, 1984 (JL-IB&B1:14); Dundee, September 22, 1981 (SD-SR31:9); 18, Flossmoor, September 18, 1982 (PH-SR35:8). Maximum counts for fall: 1030, Flossmoor, October 3, 1982 (PH-SR35:7); 585, Lake Calumet, October 6, 1985 (JL-IB&B2:45); 400, Willow Springs, September 28, 1981 (PD-SR31:9); 400, Palos, November 21, 1983 (PD-SR39:12). Most Sandhills are gone by late November.

Winter records are few, but occasionally a crane will attempt to winter with domestic fowl because handouts of food are available. Winter records: Knoxville, January 28, 1983 (MB-SR36:7); immature, Baldwin Lake, February 2–March 14, 1984 (VHa-SR40:8); Horseshoe Lake, January 4, 1986 (RA-IB&B2:76); immature, Crab Orchard National Wildlife Refuge, January 8–February 25, 1985 (JR-IB&B1:68). Oddly, Sandhill Cranes were not recorded on Christmas bird counts until 1983, when three were spotted on the Will/Cook count. Then they were found at Pere Marquette (1984) and in Union County (1985).

WHOOPING CRANE

Grus americana

VERY RARE MIGRANT

Nelson (1876) said this crane was "once an abundant migrant, but is now of rare occurrence in this vicinity. Along the Illinois River and more thinly settled portions of the state it is still common during the migrations, and a few pairs breed upon the large marshes in Central Illinois." Evidence to back up these assertions is slim. There are four specimens: Chicago, June 1858 (Baird et al. 1858); male, Champaign County, March 27, 1871; two, Jo Daviess County, April 1891. But there are no specific breeding records. Ford (1956) lists the Whooping Crane as not common from 1867 to 1887 in the Chicago region. A record is listed in Bent (1926) for Mount Carmel, March 6 (no year). Loucks (1892), in "Birds of Peoria and Tazewell Counties, Illinois," said this crane was "a rare migrant. Only a very few have been shot here." In 1958 an adult was seen and photographed near Hull, Pike County. It stayed, feeding in a cornfield near a slough, from October 16 to November 5 (Mills and Bellrose 1959). There are a few other recent reports: adult, two miles south of the Wisconsin line near Lake Geneva, April 19, 1964 (Groth 1964); four, Flossmoor, October 20, 1981 (R.&J.Orr-SR31:9); two, Blue Island, March 23, 1982 (listed in Mlodinow 1984 but rejected by IORC). At Flossmoor and Blue Island the Whooping Cranes were reported to be flying with Sandhill Cranes.

Whooping Cranes have made a slight comeback in the past few years in North America. They breed in Canada and winter at Aransas National Wildlife Refuge in Texas. An introduced flock summers in Idaho and winters in New Mexico.

BLACK-BELLIED PLOVER

Pluvialis squatarola

COMMON MIGRANT ALONG LAKE MICHIGAN; UNCOMMON MIGRANT ELSEWHERE IN THE STATE

This large plover is common on the East and West Coasts and to a lesser degree inland. In Illinois it is common only along Lake Michigan, the state's only "coast." It inhabits the sandy beaches with Sanderlings and Ruddy Turnstones. It can also be found at mudflats and in wet fields if rains provide large pools of water. Occasionally it occurs in dry fields, but not nearly as often as the Lesser Golden-Plover, which is smaller than the Black-bellied and arrives earlier in spring.

The Black-bellied Plover in its springtime breeding plumage is one of the best-looking shorebirds, with a striking black and white pattern. Its mellow *kee-o-wee* call allows easy identification in flight. Spring arrival is usually in May, but some Black-bellies are seen in April: Polo, April 30, 1884 (Cooke 1888); Chicago, April 26, 1940 (Clark and Nice 1950); Springfield, April 30, 1982 (HDB). Spring bird counts usually occur somewhat before the peak for this species. Most high counts come from the northeast: 200, McLean County, May 5, 1973; 248, Vermilion County, May 6, 1978. Other spring maxima: 500, Waukegan, May 11, 1947 (Dumont 1947): 750, Lake County, May 21, 1966 (J.Probst). Nineteen were counted at Jacksonville in west-central Illinois, May 17, 1954 (WO). Migration continues into June: two, Lake Calumet, June 12, 1978 (Mlodinow 1984); Dickson Mounds, Fulton County, June 3, 1973 (HDB).

This plover, known in the Old World as the Grey Plover, breeds on the tundra in the circumpolar region. The few summer records for Illinois are of nonbreeders or more probably late or early migrants. Fall migration begins in July, although Dreuth's average date of arrival for Chicago was August 24 (Clark and Nice 1950). Early migrants: Lake Calumet, July 15, 1972 (CC-AB26:865); four adults, Evanston, July 31, 1964 (RR). As with most Arctic shorebirds, the adults migrate before the immatures in fall, although there is little in the Illinois records to substantiate this fact. Migration dates probably vary from year to year depending on cold fronts, but the earliest birds should be adults still in breeding plumage and the latest should be immatures in gray plumage. Peak counts in fall are somewhat less than in spring: 200, Lake Calumet, September 9,

1969 (LC-IAB148:19); 100, Wolf Lake, August 16, 1959 (AFN14:40); 40, Banner, September 28, 1985 (RP,MB-IB&B 2:50). For some reason these shorebirds tend to stay late, with the majority leaving by late October. Average departure date for Chicago is October 30 (14 years) and for central Illinois November 1 (12 years). Late departure dates: Crab Orchard National Wildlife Refuge, November 30, 1960 (Bush-AFN15:45); Chicago, November 26, 1938 (Clark and Nice 1950); Jacksonville, November 29, 1973 (WO,HDB); Lake Calumet, December 22, 1973 (KB-AB28:378).

The Black-bellied Plover winters on both coasts from British Columbia and New Jersey south to northern Argentina and central Chile.

LESSER (AMERICAN) GOLDEN-PLOVER

Pluvialis dominica

COMMON MIGRANT

When Lesser Golden-Plovers first appear in spring, they are still in their brownish winter plumage. Thus they blend in well with the plowed fields as they follow the plow to get grubs and other insects. When a flock is feeding in a field they spread out in a fairly even pattern. These plovers are also seen in stubble fields and flooded fields, at mudflats, and along the lakeshore. When they rise up they give their whistled *queedle* and fly off with strong, swift wingbeats. As the season progresses, their underparts become black bordered by a bold white mark extending from the forehead down to the sides of the breast. They breed on tundra in the Arctic. The golden-plover in Illinois may someday be redesignated as the American Golden-Plover. Knox (1987), Pym (1982), and Connors (1983) discuss identification and taxonomy of the various golden-plovers. Observers should examine these birds for such forms as the Pacific and the Greater Golden-Plover, especially when they occur at odd seasons.

Lessers have an elliptical migration route, with the majority coming through interior North America in spring. In Illinois they are more numerous on the east side of the state. Early arrival dates: 30, Cumberland County, March 17, 1984 (RBr-SR41:15); Richland County, March 17, 1981 (LH-AB35:829); Alton, March 3, 1986 (RG-IB&B2:88). Average arrival dates: west-central, April 21 (eight years); Sangamon County, March 29 (18 years). High counts: 6000, Champaign County, April 13, 1979 (RCh-AB33:777); 1000, Mount Hoy, May 10, 1987 (DY); 5000, Ford County, April 16, 1981 (RCot-SR29:8); 5000, Mount Zion, May 5, 1983 (SS-SR37:10); 2500, Bismark, March 26, 1986 (SB-IB&B2:88). Spring bird count totals ranged from 631 in 1986 to 24,800 in 1978, with high counts coming from the east north-central counties, including Livingston, La Salle, Marshall, Will, Kankakee, and Whiteside.

Highest count was 8000 in Livingston County, May 6, 1978 (VK). Average spring departure dates: west-central, May 10 (eight years); Sangamon County, May 6 (16 years). Late departure dates: five, La Moille, June 10, 1984 (JH-SR41:15); Alexander County, June 3, 1985 (TF,JR-IB&B1:82).

A few of these golden-plovers evidently spend the summer; they should be checked closely, however, to make certain of the species. Summer records: Alexander County, June 26, 1978 (MMo-AB32:1168); Springfield, June 11–July 16, 1984 (HDB); two, La Moille, June 26, 1981 (JH-SR29:8).

Most plovers go toward the East Coast in fall and then make long flights to South America, wintering as far south as Chile and Argentina. In fall, therefore, golden-plovers are most numerous in Illinois along Lake Michigan. Only a few move farther downstate. Adult migrants precede immatures, as is usual with shorebirds. Early fall arrival dates: two, Alexander County, July 5–19, 1986 (DR-IB&B3:39); Chautauqua National Wildlife Refuge, July 1, 1987 (KR); Urbana, July 17, 1982 (RCh-SR35:8). Average arrival dates: Chicago, August 25 (12 years); central Illinois, August 26 (15 years). High counts for fall: 500, Evanston, October 9, 1985 (RB-AB40:120); 100, Will County, September 19, 1983 (MS-SR39:13); 150, Chautauqua refuge, October 3, 1982 (TP-SR35:8). Average departure dates: Chicago, October 14 (12 years); central Illinois, October 13 (15 years). Lesser Golden-Plovers linger late some years: Lawrence County, November 23, 1980 (LH-SR27:7); two, Mermet Lake, November 22, 1986 (TF,DR-IB&B3:39); Rice Lake, November 18, 1987 (KR).

SNOWY PLOVER

Charadrius alexandrinus

VERY RARE VAGRANT

Although this small plover breeds as close as central Kansas there were no Illinois records until recently. These were at Lake Springfield, May 7, 1986 (Bohlen 1986a), and near Dickson Mounds, Fulton County, May 10–11, 1987 (KR,MB). The birds were seen on cinder flats and dry mud, and both were photographed. There were earlier records from Minnesota, Wisconsin, Indiana, and Missouri, so the Illinois records were overdue. The Snowy Plover has a light sandy back and black legs. It inhabits beaches, dry mud, and salt flats. Its two races are difficult to tell apart. The Illinois birds could have come from the Gulf Coast or from farther west.

WILSON'S PLOVER

Charadrius wilsonia

HYPOTHETICAL

This southeastern coastal plover is rarely seen away from beaches and tidal areas. Although the Illinois records may

be correct, none is supported by more than one observer or documented thoroughly enough to warrant adding Wilson's Plover to the state list: Glencoe, May 16–26, 1962 (AFN16:418); Mark Twain National Wildlife Refuge, May 14, 1977 (possibly as many as four!); Illinois Beach State Park, August 30, 1987. There are vagrant records from Minnesota, Ohio, Arkansas, and Pennsylvania.

SEMIPALMATED PLOVER

Charadrius semipalmatus

FAIRLY COMMON MIGRANT

This perky little plover is easily recognized. It looks like a small single-ringed Killdeer and has a distinctive *che-wee* call. In Illinois it frequents flooded fields and mudflats, almost always staying on the drier flats and usually away from vegetation. It is seen singly or in small flocks, occasionally in larger flocks. On mudflats it runs and then stops to pick up food in typical plover fashion. Semipalmated Plovers breed on tundra in Alaska and northern Canada and winter on the southern coasts of the United States south to central Chile and Argentina. Although Nelson (1876) referred to breeding Semipalmated Plovers in Illinois, they must actually have been early or late migrants, as the Semipalmated breeds nowhere near Illinois.

Early spring arrivals: Chicago, April 17, 1941 (Clark and Nice 1950); 15, Sanchris State Park, April 17, 1977 (HDB); two, Kidd Lake, April 22, 1987 (RG); three, Alexander County, April 20, 1985 (JR-IB&B1:82). Average spring arrival dates: Chicago, May 1 (nine years); west-central, May 3 (eight years); Sangamon County, May 1 (18 years). Maximum counts for spring: 100, Rend Lake, May 26, 1987 (LH); 200, Wabash County, May 6, 1985 (LH-AB39:307); 70, Alton, May 10, 1986 (SRu-IB&B2:88). Spring bird count totals ranged from 20 in 1973 to 917 in 1986. High count was 123 in Lawrence County, May 8, 1982 (VK). Average departure dates: Chicago, May 26 (nine years); west-central, May 26 (eight years); Sangamon County, May 31 (17 years). Some years these birds are still going north in June, although some records could be of nonbreeding summer birds: Springfield, June 18, 1978 (HDB); two, Hancock County, June 4, 1978 (VK-AB32:1168); three, Rend Lake, June 7, 1986 (DR-IB&B2:88); five, Peoria, June 3, 1985 (LA-IB&B1:82).

Fall migration begins in late June or July. As with other Arctic shorebirds, the adults arrive first. Early fall arrival dates: Chicago, July 5, 1980 (JL); Jackson Park, June 23, 1985 (HR), and Waukegan, June 23, 1985 (JL-IB&B2:50); Horseshoe Lake, July 4, 1985 (JR,TF-IB&B2:50). Average arrival dates: Chicago, August 3 (15 years); west-central, July 31 (eight years); Sangamon County, July 21 (18 years). Maximum counts for fall: 50, Chautauqua National Wildlife Refuge, September 11, 1976 (HDB); 100, Waukegan, August 27, 1961 (CC); 60, Lake Calumet, August 2, 1981 (JL). Average fall departure dates: Chicago, October 6 (15 years); west-central, September 29 (18 years). The latest date for this shorebird is November 10–December 1, 1973, at Waukegan (CC-AB28:647). Other late dates: Alton, October 31, 1982 (PS,RG-SR35:9); Peoria, October 23, 1983 (VH-SR39:13).

PIPING PLOVER

Charadrius melodus

RARE MIGRANT; VERY RARE (EXTIRPATED) SUMMER RESIDENT ALONG LAKE MICHIGAN

This light-colored plover blends beautifully with the sand. Thus it is the ghost of the sand dunes—not only figuratively but almost literally. The Piping Plover is now on both the federal and state endangered species lists. Only 17 to 19 breeding pairs remain in all of the Great Lakes areas from a historic population of 644 to 802 pairs (Russell 1983). This special shorebird's decline is due to storm erosion and increased vehicular and recreational use of its beach habitat and to industrialization. It is closely tied to sandy spits along larger rivers and lakes and to mudflats. Usually seen in association with Semipalmated Plovers, the Illinois Piping Plovers are members of the inland race, *C. m. circumcinctus*.

Early arrival dates for spring: Chicago, April 17, 1986 (RD-IB&B2:88); Waukegan, April 17, 1977 (JN-AB31:1008). Average arrival dates: Chicago, April 28 (seven years); central Illinois, May 1 (three years). High counts for spring: seven, Horseshoe Lake, April 18, 1981 (JEa-AB35:829); six, Illinois Beach State Park, April 21, 1974 (Mlodinow 1984); three, Meredosia, May 23, 1983 (TW-SR37:11); three, Waukegan, April 25, 1982 (JN-SR33:8). Spring bird counts show small numbers (one to three) for only six years. Two counts had three: Lake County, May 4, 1974, and Franklin County, May 10, 1980 (VK). Dreuth found that the average departure date at Chicago was May 14 (seven years). One was seen at Arcola, May 22, 1987 (BCho).

Nelson (1876) wrote that the Piping Plover was a "very common summer resident along the Lake Shore, breeding on the flat, pebbly beach between the sand dunes and shore.... some thirty pairs were breeding along the beach at this place [Waukegan], within a space of two miles, and I afterwards found the birds as numerous at several points along the shore." The places Nelson described, along with Wolf Lake and Lake Calumet, were the nesting areas in Illinois. A dramatic population decline in the Illinois dune area occurred in the 1940s, closely paralleling military and recreational buildup in the area. At this same time Lake Calumet became heavily industrialized (Russell 1983). Russell estimated the historical breeding population in Illinois to be 125 to 130 pairs. By 1955 all had disappeared, but a pair nested at Waukegan in 1973, raising three young, and again in 1979, raising four young. Since then none have nested in the state, and this unique bird must be considered

extirpated as a breeding species. The Piping Plover usually lays four buffy eggs that have black markings. Available Illinois egg dates are May 30 to June 12. Other summer records: Waukegan, June 4–20, 1981 (JL,J.Bockrath-SR30:8); Waukegan, all summer, 1978 (LB-AB32:1168).

Fall migration begins in July: Springfield, July 14–15, 1985 (HDB); Montrose Harbor, July 19, 1981 (JL); Jackson Park, July 28, 1981 (PC,HR-SR31:9); East St. Louis, July 23–24, 1979 (BR-AB33:867). Average arrival dates for fall: Chicago, August 16 (five years); central Illinois, July 31 (seven years). Maximum counts for fall are low: three, September 16, 1979 (MSc-SR23:6), and five, September 4, 1973 (SV-AB28:60), Mark Twain National Wildlife Refuge. Average departure dates: Chicago, August 27 (five years); central Illinois, September 14 (two years). Sometimes these plovers stay late: Mendota, November 9–21, 1982 (JH-SR35:9); Illinois Beach State Park, November 10, 1973 (CC-AB28:60); La Salle, November 13, 1982 (LA-AB37:187).

KILLDEER

Charadrius vociferus

COMMON MIGRANT AND SUMMER RESIDENT; UNCOMMON WINTER RESIDENT DECREASING NORTHWARD

If a person knew only one kind of shorebird, the Killdeer would probably be the one. It is the most widely distributed shorebird in North America. A vociferous bird, it is usually the first to alert other birds on a mudflat to a perceived danger with its emphatic *kill-deer*. In fact, it goes through this act so often that I sometimes wonder if it is a ploy to get rid of competition. I have noticed that the Killdeer is not only the first to fly away but also the first to return to the feeding grounds. Killdeers are found in open country such as fields, preferably with bare ground or very short vegetation, as well as on mudflats. It also inhabits areas close to people: airfields, golf courses, sewage ponds, gravel roads, and wet ditches. The race found in North America is *C. v. vociferus*. The other race is found in South America.

The Killdeer is a harbinger of spring, usually arriving in February or March. Early spring arrival dates: Chillicothe, January 27, 1984 (LA-SR41:15); Pere Marquette State Park, February 1, 1986 (RG); Richland County, February 3, 1987 (LH). Average arrival dates: Urbana, March 1 (20 years); Chicago, March 19 (16 years); Sangamon County, February 23 (17 years). The vicissitudes of weather account for some spring concentrations, and fairly high numbers can occasionally be counted by watching the river valleys that Killdeers pass over in their diurnal migration. Maximum spring counts: 125, Adams County, March 16, 1985 (AD-IB&B1:82); 274, Chicago, April 4, 1982 (JL); 95, Springfield, April 10, 1982 (HDB). Spring bird counts showed a fairly steady increase in Killdeer totals from 1972 (502) to 1986 (2926), which may be attributable more to enthusiastic support for the spring counts than to any real population increase. The highest count was 330 in Cook County on May 10, 1980 (VK).

Killdeers undoubtedly nest in every county. Graber and Graber (1963) found a northward trend in the population between 1909 and 1957. The total June population for Illinois was an estimated 406,000 in 1909, 326,000 in 1957, and 524,000 in 1958. Robbins et al. (1986), using breeding bird survey data for 1965-79, noted that Killdeers had shown strong increases in the eastern and central regions of the United States. The mean number of birds per survey route in Illinois was 3.3. Kleen (SR22:4) found a 50 percent increase by 1979 over a nine-year average in southern Illinois. Killdeers nest on the ground in gravelly, rocky, or short grass areas, making a depression in the substrate and occasionally lining it with debris. The clutch is usually four buffy eggs with heavy black markings that make them difficult to see. In at least one case the young were fledged from a nest on a gravel roof, but only after five attempts (PD-SR22:4). Illinois egg dates are March 30 to June 27. Young have been reported as early as April 20 and as late as July 24. Adult Killdeers are famous for their distraction display, or "broken-wing trick," with which they lead a potential predator away from the nest. High counts for summer: 675, Chicago, July 28, 1985 (JL); 227, Cook County, June 8, 1985 (IB&B2:14): 70, Lake Vermilion, June 22, 1983 (SB-SR38:7); 300, Horseshoe Lake, July 17, 1980 (BR-SR27:7); 171, southwestern Illinois, June 29, 1985 (JR-IB&B2:50). Some of these counts represent concentrations of postbreeding Killdeers at choice locations.

Some fall migration probably occurs as early as late June or July. Fall concentrations: 320, Chicago, August 14, 1983 (JL); 113, Tazewell County, November 13, 1981 (MS-SR31:9); 300, Lake Vermilion, October 10, 1984 (SB-IB&B1:15); 180, Hancock County, October 27, 1984 (RCe-IB&B1:15). Average fall departure dates: Chicago, October 30 (16 years); west-central, December 4 (10 years); Sangamon County, December 20 (11 years). Some Killdeers stay well into January before finally being forced out by extreme weather.

Graber and Graber (1963) found that the Killdeer's optimum winter habitat was clover and alfalfa fields and that most of Illinois' wintering Killdeers were in the south. They are also found at cattle feedlots, open sewage lagoons, warm-water lakes, and other areas with open water. The Grabers estimated winter populations at 157,000 for both 1906-7 and 1956-57 but only 11,000 for 1957-58, probably showing that the size of the winter population is closely linked to the severity of the weather. Christmas bird count totals for 1976-85 ranged from 10 in 1977 (a severe winter) to 304 in 1982. The highest counts were also in 1982: 100 at Union County and 99 at Alexander County.

BLACK-NECKED STILT

Himantopus mexicanus

VERY RARE VAGRANT OR MIGRANT

Nelson (1876) called this bird "an exceedingly rare visitant," adding that there "is a fine specimen of this species, taken in McLean County, Ill. . . . in the collection of the Illinois Natural History Society, at Normal, Ill." The present location of this specimen is unknown. Ridgway (1881 and 1889) stated that the Black-necked Stilt was mostly a transient but bred in some localities; it was on record only as a summer visitant to Illinois but undoubtedly bred in some portion of the state. In neither citation does Ridgway make a case for his conjectures by giving records.

There are six recent records: Chicago, August 28–September 2, 1959 (HL,HF-AFN14:40); Lake Calumet, August 23–September 7, 1968 (CC,JG-AFN 23:65); specimen INHS, East St. Louis, August 21–August 31, 1969 (JEC-AFN 24:54); near Havana, May 18, 1986 (RP,MD); Peoria, May 24, 1988 (LA, VH); one photographed, Lake Calumet, June 10, 1988 (F.Stoop,JM). This large, slender, black and white shorebird with long reddish legs is found in the western and southeastern United States and south as far as northern South America. Illinois sightings are probably the result of overmigration or mirror-image reversal during migration. Unlike some other rare migrants, this flashy shorebird is unlikely to be overlooked. It is usually found at shallow ponds or mudflats.

AMERICAN AVOCET

Recurvirostra americana

RARE MIGRANT

Nelson (1876) summed up the status of this large shorebird: "A rare migrant. Generally occurs in small parties the last of April and first of May, and during September and the first of October. Frequents the borders of marshy pools." The numbers and records seem to have dropped after that time, as Ford (1956) recorded this species as accidental. But now these orange-headed black and white shorebirds are seen in regular numbers and fairly large flocks. Nonbreeding American Avocets are gray-headed, while juveniles show some orange on the head. In females the long bill is more upturned than in males. American Avocets occur in Illinois at large expanses of mudflats, sandbars, lake edges, and grassy pools. I have seen flocks of these birds floating on an open lake, but they seldom swim in this manner. They often feed in water up to their bellies and work as a team to secure food, sweeping their bills from side to side.

Early spring migrants: Clinton Lake, April 18, 1987 (RCh); 19, Decatur, April 15, 1983 (SS-SR37:11); Springfield, April 15, 1988 (HDB). The average arrival date in Sangamon County is April 21 (five years). High counts for spring: 22, Rockford, April 28, 1984 (LJ-AB38:917);

23, Springfield, April 23, 1983 (HDB). Late spring departure dates: two, Chicago, June 6, 1981 (JL); Waukegan, May 29, 1987 (JN); Round Lake, June 2, 1973 (LB-AB27:876).

Early fall migration is composed of returning adults: Chicago, July 5, 1980 (JL); Starved Rock State Park, June 28, 1985 (JM-IB&B2:50); Springfield, July 4, 1988 (HDB); Horseshoe Lake, July 4, 1978 (RG). The average arrival date for central Illinois is August 12 (13 years). That date is misleading, however; in species such as shorebirds that have migrations divided by age classes, arrivals and departures should be considered separately for each age class, but the data rarely present themselves adequately to do this. High counts for fall: 20, Illinois Beach State Park, October 20, 1984 (DJ-AB39:60); 20, Barrington, September 19, 1985 (N.Gresey-AB40:120); 13, Banner, September 25, 1985 (VH-IB&B2:50). Late fall departure dates: Nauvoo, November 9, 1986 (RCe-AB41:95); six, East St. Louis, November 1, 1979 (BR-AB34:168): Chicago, November 2, 1979 (Mlodinow 1984).

The American Avocet breeds mostly in western North America and winters from southern coastal areas in the United States to Central America.

GREATER YELLOWLEGS

Tringa melanoleuca

FAIRLY COMMON MIGRANT

The larger of the two yellowlegs also has a larger bill that is usually somewhat upturned. It uses this bill to sweep through shallow water to obtain minnows. Brooks (1967) found that Greater Yellowlegs eat dragonfly larvae and predaceous diving beetles and snails, along with smaller quantities of other aquatic animals. The Greater Yellowlegs gives a loud three-note *whew* that is more forceful and clearer than the Lesser Yellowlegs' call. This call will alert an observer that Greater Yellowlegs migrants are passing overhead. Apparently their migration is mostly diurnal. These larger sandpipers are found at mudflats, grassy pools, flooded fields, and sewage ponds.

Spring migration starts fairly early: three, St. Clair County, March 11, 1986 (TF-IB&B2:88); Mercer County, March 21, 1987 (MB); Pope County, March 14, 1985 (JP-IB&B1:82). Average spring arrival dates: Chicago, April 14 (15 years); Sangamon County, March 29 (17 years). High counts for spring: 90, Kidd Lake, March 27, 1987 (RG); 43, Sangamon County, May 2, 1987 (HDB); 21, Knox County, May 5, 1984 (MB-SR41:15). Spring bird count totals ranged from 35 in 1972 to 952 in 1984. The highest count was 84 in McHenry County on May 5, 1983 (VK). Average departure dates: Chicago, May 11 (five years); Sangamon County, May 14 (18 years). Some Greater Yellowlegs tend to linger late in spring: Horseshoe Lake, June 2, 1983 (RG); Shelby County, June 13, 1970 (HDB); Rend Lake, May 25, 1986 (TF-IB&B2:88); Oquawka, June 12, 1983 (LMc-SR37:11). Nelson (1876) thought this bird bred

in northern Illinois and he even listed the collection of eggs from a nest, but the Greater Yellowlegs actually breeds well north of the United States border.

Early fall migration arrivals: Lake Calumet, June 20, 1985 (JL); Springfield, June 24, 1980 (HDB). Average arrival dates: Chicago, August 22 (nine years); Sangamon County, July 15 (17 years). Maximum fall counts for Greater Yellowlegs are much lower than for Lesser Yellowlegs: 500, Banner, October 9, 1985 (TP-AB40:120); 80, Evanston, October 9, 1985 (RB-IB&B2:50); 61, Lake Calumet, October 25, 1981 (JL); 43, Winfield, October 30, 1984 (JM-IB&B1:15). Average fall departure dates: Chicago, October 18 (nine years); Sangamon County, November 8 (18 years). Late departure dates: Carbondale, November 24, 1984 (JR-IB&B1:15); Chautauqua National Wildlife Refuge, November 25, 1983 (LA-SR39:13); Springfield, December 3, 1987 (HDB). The Greater Yellowlegs winters from the southern United States to the southern tip of South America.

LESSER YELLOWLEGS

Tringa flavipes

COMMON MIGRANT

The Lesser Yellowlegs is a smaller version of the Greater Yellowlegs, but there are subtle differences, especially in bill size and call. The Lesser Yellowlegs' appearance changes somewhat at various times of the year with age and molting (Wilds 1982). Like other shorebirds, the Lesser bobs its head and is an active feeder. It is one of the prime mudflat shorebirds, feeding mostly in shallow water off the flats. Sometimes it also feeds on the flats by picking. The Lesser Yellowlegs' diet is fairly broad compared with other shorebirds. Brooks (1967) found that in September its main food items were midge flies, water boatmen, and predaceous diving beetles, but by October it was feeding mostly on water boatmen (59 percent). This sandpiper sometimes occurs in large flocks. In spring Lesser Yellowlegs are found with Pectoral Sandpipers in flooded fields. A partial albino Lesser Yellowlegs was observed at the Calumet sewage plant, October 2, 1983 (JL).

Early arrival dates for spring: Springfield, February 25, 1977 (HDB); East St. Louis, March 10, 1987 (J.Loomis); three, St. Clair County, March 11, 1986 (TF-IB&B2:88). Average arrival dates: Chicago, April 28 (six years); west-central, March 29 (eight years); Sangamon County, March 28 (17 years). High counts for spring: 200, Kidd Lake, May 3, 1987 (RG); 130, Alexander County, May 5, 1984 (TF-SR41:16); 150, Rockford, May 6, 1985 (DW-IB&B1:82); 160, Alton, April 13, 1986 (RG). Spring bird count totals ranged from 170 in 1972 to 2120 in 1984. The highest count was 208 in Winnebago County on May 5, 1979 (VK). Average spring departure dates: west-central, May 14 (eight years); Sangamon County, May 24 (18 years). Late departure dates: Eldon Hazlet State Park, June 3, 1985 (KR-IB&B1:82); Springfield, June 7, 1985 (HDB).

Nelson (1876) believed that Lesser Yellowlegs bred in the Chicago area and asserted that he saw their young in July 1874. No other breeding records have occurred. Some Lessers do appear in Illinois in summer, but the records may be of very early fall migrants: Horseshoe Lake, June 16, 1977 (JEa-AB31:1148); two, Springfield, June 22, 1985 (HDB); four, Havana, June 17, 1985 (KR-IB&B2:50). Average arrival dates for fall: west-central, July 11 (eight years); Sangamon County, July 9 (18 years). Sometimes large numbers of these shorebirds are attracted to extensive mudflats and may stay for prolonged periods. Maximum fall counts: 15,000, Rice Lake, August 4, 1987 (KR-AB42:82); 3050, Chicago, August 11, 1984 (JL); 1750, Mason County, July 29, 1985 (KR-AB39:918); 1890, Lake Calumet, July 28, 1985 (JL). Average departure dates: west-central, November 7 (eight years); Springfield, October 26 (17 years). Late departure dates: Chautauqua National Wildlife Refuge, November 28, 1983 (KR-SR39:13); Crab Orchard National Wildlife Refuge, November 17, 1984 (TF); Henderson County, November 17, 1984 (MB-IB&B1:15). Lesser Yellowlegs winter from the Gulf Coast south to Tierra del Fuego.

SOLITARY SANDPIPER

Tringa solitaria

COMMON MIGRANT

This sandpiper is well named, for it is frequently found apart from other shorebirds. Though it is seldom met with in flocks of any kind, an optimum habitat sometimes attracts several Solitaries. They inhabit the wooded edges of mudflats, woodland pools and ponds, sewage lagoons, stream edges, and occasionally open mudflats. They teeter or bob just like several other shorebirds, and their call notes, *peet-weet,* can be heard when they fly. Their tail pattern in flight is especially distinctive. The Solitary Sandpiper nests in coniferous forests in Alaska and Canada. It has the unusual nesting habit of laying its eggs in the deserted nests of passerines. The great majority of Solitary Sandpipers in Illinois belong to the race *T. s. solitaria,* but at least one record, taken at Grand Chain, is of the more northwestern form, *T. s. cinnamomea* (Conover 1944).

Early spring arrival dates: Skokie, March 28, 1976 (Mlodinow 1984); Jackson County, March 23, 1985 (JR-AB39:307); Chicago, March 29, 1986 (DP-AB40:478). Average spring arrival dates: Urbana, April 23 (16 years); Chicago, April 30 (14 years); Sangamon County, April 15 (18 years). Spring bird count totals ranged from 133 in 1973 to 867 in 1979. The 1979 high count of 378 (McHenry County) may be flawed, however, because it is nearly four times the next highest count. In situations where inordinately high counts occur, written explanations are necessary. Other high counts: 91, St. Clair County, May 6, 1978 (VK); 60, Danville, May 3, 1985 (SB-IB&B1:82); 24, Rockford, May 6, 1985 (DW-IB&B1:82); 24, Knox

County, May 9, 1987 (MB). Average spring departure dates: Urbana, May 21 (16 years); Chicago, May 15 (14 years); Sangamon County, May 20 (18 years). Some Solitary Sandpipers linger late, which led some earlier observers to consider them breeders in Illinois. Nelson (1876) stated, "I have several times taken young of this species just able to fly, and have observed the adults throughout the breeding season." Unfortunately, these specimens are no longer extant. The breeding area nearest Illinois is in northern Minnesota. Late dates for spring: Springfield, June 5, 1984 (HDB); Arcola, May 27, 1987 (BCho); Crab Orchard National Wildlife Refuge, May 26, 1987 (DR); Lake Calumet, June 4, 1977 (RB).

No sooner have these birds gone north than early fall migrants—the adults—begin returning. Early arrival dates: Bartonville, June 26–27, 1985 (KR-IB&B2:50); Alexander County, June 29, 1985 (JR-IB&B2:50); Springfield, June 28, 1980 (HDB). Average fall arrival dates: Chicago, August 17 (12 years); west-central, July 14 (10 years); Sangamon County, July 7 (18 years). Maximum counts for fall: 422, Lake Calumet, July 28, 1985 (AB39:918); 250, Lake Calumet, July 26, 1981 (JL); 45, Danville, August 4, 1984 (SB-IB&B1:15); 65, Chautauqua National Wildlife Refuge, August 7, 1971 (HDB). Average dates of departure: Chicago, September 18 (12 years); Sangamon County, September 28 (17 years). Late departure dates: Springfield, October 27, 1986 (HDB); Lake Vermilion, October 22, 1983 (SB-SR39:14). Solitary Sandpipers winter from the Gulf Coast south to Peru, Argentina, and Uruguay.

WILLET

Catoptrophorus semipalmatus

OCCASIONAL MIGRANT

Nelson (1876) referred to this bird as a rare summer resident, but there is no evidence of breeding in Illinois. It apparently bred in Minnesota and Iowa, however, so the potential was there. The Willet is a fairly large shorebird but not very flashy until it flies, revealing a dramatic black and white pattern on the wings. It is a noisy bird, giving several calls. The best known is its *pill-will-willet.* It occurs singly or in flocks of up to 20 birds at mudflats, flooded fields, beaches, sandbars, and grass flats. The frequency of sightings of this species in Illinois seems to be increasing. The race found in Illinois is the western form, *C. s. inornatus.*

Early spring arrival dates: Jackson Park, March 17, 1980 (Mlodinow 1984); Sangchris State Park, April 9, 1977 (HDB); Pulaski County, April 6, 1974 (Haw-AB28:808). The average arrival date in central Illinois is April 30 (19 years). High counts are usually from single flocks: 28, Horseshoe Lake, May 2, 1981 (BR-AB35:829); 35, Chicago, April 24, 1985 (RB-IB&B1:82); 27, Peoria, April 29, 1983 (LA-SR37:11). Willets were seen on spring bird counts in 14 of 15 years (they were absent in 1975), with totals ranging from one to 50 (1984). The highest count was 31 in Lake County, May 5, 1984 (VK). The central Illinois average departure date is May 13 (10 years). Some Willets are seen into June: Lake Calumet, June 14, 1981 (RB,JL-SR29:8); Evanston, June 6, 1981 (RGu-SR29:8).

Fall arrivals appear in late June, and in some cases it is difficult to distinguish them from spring migrants. Early fall arrival dates: three, Starved Rock State Park, June 28, 1985 (JM-IB&B2:50); Kidd Lake, June 30, 1983 (RG-SR38:7). In central Illinois the average arrival date is July 28 (seven years). High counts for fall: 16, Illinois Beach State Park, July 8, 1981 (JN- AB35:945); 13, Chautauqua National Wildlife Refuge, July 13, 1987 (KR); 10, Chicago, August 3, 1983 (JL). Most Willets are gone by the end of September. Late departure dates: Douglas County, November 3, 1984 (RCh-AB39:60); four, Lake Vermilion, October 24, 1983 (MC-AB38:209). The Willet winters from the coastal areas of the southern United States south to South America.

SPOTTED SANDPIPER

Actitis macularia

COMMON MIGRANT; COMMON SUMMER RESIDENT DECREASING SOUTHWARD

A peculiar flight, low over the water with stiff, cupped wings, is diagnostic for the Spotted Sandpiper. In spring and summer this teetering shorebird shows spots ventrally, but immatures and fall adults are white below. Its call note is *peet-weet,* sometimes with several *weet*s at the end. Spotted Sandpipers are found singly or in twos or threes, usually apart from other shorebirds. Their habitat is rocky shores, mudflats, beaches, rocky creeks, and even small pools of water. They occasionally catch their food on the wing by jumping up at swarms of gnats.

Early spring arrival dates: Crab Orchard National Wildlife Refuge, March 28, 1987 (DR); Carbondale, April 6, 1986 (DR-IB&B2:89); Springfield, April 11, 1985 (HDB). Average arrival dates: Chicago, May 2 (16 years); central Illinois, April 18 (19 years). Spring bird count totals ranged from 127 in 1973 to 686 in 1986. The highest counts were 111, Moultrie County, May 7, 1977; 118, La Salle County, May 8, 1982; and 158, Cook County, May 7, 1983 (VK). Migration probably continues until late May.

Nelson (1876) stated that the Spotted Sandpiper "breeds in abundance among the small sandhills along the Lake shore. Near Waukegan, the first of June, 1876, I saw Mr. T. H. Douglas secure over two dozen of their eggs in considerably less than an hour. The nests were generally placed under a small shrub or in a thin tuft of grass and the eggs could be seen several yards away." Spotted Sandpipers nest on the ground in a depression, not always near water, and line the nest with grasses and plant stems. Parent sandpipers occasionally land in the top of a small tree and scold when an observer is near the nest. There are usually four, some-

times three eggs that are buff with blackish markings. Illinois egg dates are May 30 to June 21. Most young are out of the nest by mid- to late June. They are sand brown above and white below, with a black dorsal stripe and pinkish legs. There is more nesting in northern and central than in southern Illinois. Gravel pits and sewage lagoons are favored spots away from Lake Michigan.

Fall migration starts in mid- to late July. High counts: 39, Lake Calumet, July 26, 1986 (JL); 25, Spring Lake, July 29, 1985 (KR-IB&B2:50); 16, Lake Shelbyville, September 16, 1983 (KF-SR39:14). Average departure dates: Chicago, September 18 (16 years); central Illinois, October 12 (17 years). Late departure dates: Mississippi River Lock and Dam 18, November 2, 1986 (AB41:95); Chicago, November 20, 1965 (FB-AFN20:54). The Spotted Sandpiper winters from the coastal southern United States to the West Indies and South America.

UPLAND SANDPIPER

Bartramia longicauda

UNCOMMON MIGRANT AND SUMMER RESIDENT

This "field plover," associated with the prairies in Illinois, had to adapt to other habitats as the prairies vanished. For a while it did well on pasturelands and hayfields. But then came mechanization and the practice of plowing up to the ditch, farming every inch. As a result the Upland Sandpiper is on the Illinois endangered species list. Earlier this bird was hunted nearly to extinction by market hunters but bounced back after it received protection. Cooke (1888) noted that thousands passed over on migration—certainly not the case today. Upland Sandpipers have been pushed into corners here and there and survive as only a small remnant, like the prairie itself. They live in grasslands adjacent to airfields and in the larger pastures and hayfields that remain.

Upland Sandpipers appear suddenly in early to mid-April. They announce themselves with a call that is like a wolf whistle, with flight songs, and with a characteristic fluttering flight and raised wings when sitting on a fence post. Although Bent (1929) gave very early spring dates for Illinois (and very late ones for fall), I believe some or all of them may refer to yellowlegs. Early arrival dates: three, Union County Conservation Area, April 5, 1986 (KM-IB&B2:89); Vermilion County, April 10, 1986 (SB-IB&B2:89); Newton, April 5, 1977 (KA-AB31:1008); Champaign County, April 11, 1981 (RCh-SR29:8); Cook County, April 14, 1981 (A&JT-SR29:8). Average arrival dates: Chicago, May 2 (five years); Urbana, April 18 (six years); Sangamon County, April 22 (15 years). Maximum counts for spring: 500, Olney, April 7, 1962 (PN-AFN16:419); 134, Joliet Arsenal, May 6, 1986 (BGl-AB40:478); nine, Wabash County, April 19, 1981 (LH-SR29:8); 12, Vermilion County airport, May 31, 1985 (SB-

IB&B1:82); 24, Tinley Park, May 7, 1983 (AA-AB37:11). Spring bird count totals ranged from 16 in 1980 to 95 in 1984. The highest count was 46 in Crawford County, May 5, 1984 (VK).

These sandpipers are most numerous as nesting birds in the north and central parts of the state. They are found in open field habitats such as pastures, hayfields, fallow fields, grainfields, and especially red clover fields. Graber and Graber (1963) found that the population distribution had changed between 1909 and 1957, with the north losing and central Illinois gaining. The statewide population was 283,000 in 1909 and 177,000 in 1958. It must be well below the 1958 figure by now. Some of the population loss is due to the decline of pastureland, in both quality and acreage. Robbins et al. (1986) noted that breeding bird survey data for 1965–79 showed an increase for the Upland Sandpiper in the eastern and central United States but a decrease in Illinois. The mean number of birds per survey route in Illinois was 0.3. Carl Becker compiled breeding records for 29 counties in 1979–80 (SR26:6). This sandpiper nests by lining a hollow in the ground with grasses or leaves. It lays three to four rather large tan eggs that have dark brown spots. Available Illinois egg dates are mid-May to mid-June. The young are precocial, and family groups can be seen in June and July.

Upland Sandpipers gather at staging areas in July and August before departing southward: 24, Vermilion County, July 28, 1984 (SB); 19, Tazewell County, July 17, 1985 (KR-IB&B2:50); 12 near Orion, early August 1979 (PP-SR23:7); nine flybys, Jackson Park, July 17, 1981 (PC,HR-SR31:10). These sandpipers leave fairly early, and most are gone by mid-September. Average dates of departure: Chicago, August 29 (four years); central Illinois, August 27 (12 years). Late departure dates: Fermilab, September 11, 1981 (MS-SR31:10); Chicago, September 24, 1937 (Clark and Nice 1950); Chandlerville, October 2, 1971 (HDB).

Long-distance migrants, these sandpipers winter in South America as far south as central Argentina and Uruguay.

ESKIMO CURLEW

Numenius borealis

NEARLY EXTINCT

Although Nelson (1876) stated that the Eskimo Curlew was "rather common during the migrations," little has been written about it in Illinois. Evidence of its occurrence comes from a few nineteenth-century specimens: Cook County, April 10, before 1834 (British Museum); female, Summit, August 11, 1872 (Harvard College); two, McLean County, September 1879 (Cincinnati Museum of Natural History); Cook County, April 1880 (CAS#15324); Fayette County, March 30, 1894 (ISM). This migrant apparently arrived in March and April and passed on without much delay. Nelson said it returned the last of September and in October and frequented wet prairies with golden-plovers.

The bulk of the migration range was to the west of Illinois in spring and along the Atlantic Coast in fall. A few Eskimo Curlews—perhaps immatures—passed through in the fall, as do golden-plovers. Cory (1909) stated that these curlews were still common in 1895, but by 1900 they were rare, even in their prime range. In Illinois the last record was by Gault of eight at Lincoln Park, May 22, 1923, but these might have been Whimbrels.

Eskimo Curlews were destroyed primarily by hunters. The curlews fed on grasshoppers and crowberries and got so fat they were called Doughbirds. They nested in northwestern Mackenzie and wintered in South America from south-central Brazil to southern Argentina and Chile. Recent sight records indicate that a few individuals may still survive.

WHIMBREL

Numenius phaeopus

RARE MIGRANT ALONG LAKE MICHIGAN AND VERY RARE MIGRANT ELSEWHERE IN THE STATE

Kennicott (1854) said the Whimbrel was common, and Cooke (1888) said it was "a common migrant in most parts of the Mississippi Valley." If so, most of this population was extirpated early. Nelson and Ridgway both thought the Whimbrel was rare. Today most of the records come from the Lake Michigan area, which means there is some east-west movement of this shorebird to and from the East Coast. Downstate residents might never see it. The Whimbrel rarely lingers, and many of the records along Lake Michigan are of flybys. Whimbrels are recorded yearly, usually in small numbers. They are found at mudflats, but they prefer beaches or grassy areas with shallow water. The Whimbrel is grayer than other curlews and has a call of short, rapid whistles. It breeds in the Arctic circumpolar region and winters from southern coastal areas south to southern Chile and Brazil. The subspecies in Illinois and most of the United States is *N. p. hudsonicus*.

The earliest spring records are for April: Waukegan, April 16, 1977 (JN-AB31:1008); Madison County, April 24, 1969 (RA,PB-AFN23:596); Kankakee, April 22, 1981 (TG-SR29:8). High spring counts: 15 near Bondville, April 29, 1971 (Grabers); 19, Waukegan, May 18, 1980 (JN-AB34:782); 12, Illinois Beach State Park, May 26, 1980 (JG-AB34:782); 15, Waukegan, May 27, 1985 (RB-IB&B1:82). Most spring records are for May, but some Whimbrels are seen quite late in spring: Lake County, June 16, 1935 (Bujak 1935); La Moille, June 3–5, 1984 (JH-AB38:917); Chicago, June 7, 1986 (JL). Recent downstate spring records: two, Monroe County, May 26, 1983 (SRu-AB37:876); Wabash County, May 7, 1986 (LH-AB40:478); Springfield, May 18, 1987 (HDB).

Fall migrants return as early as July: Chicago, July 18–19, 1981 (JL); Waukegan, July 30, 1978 (JN-AB32:1169); three, Waukegan, July 25–August 7, 1981 (JN-AB35:945);

Chicago, July 26, 1980 (JL,CC-SR27:7). High count for fall is 22, Chicago, September 15, 1982 (JL). Late fall dates: pair, Lincoln Park, October 18, 1923 (Stevenson 1929); Illinois Beach State Park, September 27, 1986 (SB-IB&B3:39). Recent downstate fall records: Chautauqua National Wildlife Refuge, August 4, 1980 (VK,CB-SR27:7); Rend Lake, September 21, 1986 (TF-IB&B3:39).

LONG-BILLED CURLEW

Numenius americanus

VERY RARE MIGRANT

Nelson (1876) said this curlew was "formerly very abundant during the migrations, and a common summer resident. Now rather uncommon in the migrations and a very rare summer resident. A pair nested on the Calumet Marshes in spring of 1873. More numerous on the large marshes in Central Illinois. Arrives the last of April and departs in October." Kennicott (1854) also noted that the Long-billed Curlew was abundant on the large prairies in the middle of the state and indicated that it was known to breed in Cook County. Cooke's statement (1888) that it occasionally was found in winter in southern Illinois is difficult to believe. There are surprisingly few old records for this bird: two males and one female specimen, Lake Calumet, September 22, 1889 (Stoddard 1921a); specimen, Cook County, July 1889 (ISM); Fernwood, Cook County, October 13, 1885 (Cooke 1888); Tazewell County, no date (Loucks 1892); Beach, June 18, 1922 (Ford 1956). There are only three recent records: one photographed, Villa Grove, April 20-24, 1962 (H.W.Norton- AFN16:419); Camargo, April 21, 1963 (P.Norton-AFN17:408); one seen by several observers and photographed near Meredosia, April 2-3, 1985 (Jones 1985).

The Long-billed Curlew is found on prairies and meadows farther west and in coastal areas at beaches and mudflats.

It winters along the southern coasts south to Costa Rica. The race occurring in Illinois was presumably *N. a. americanus* (Ford 1956).

HUDSONIAN GODWIT

Limosa haemastica

RARE MIGRANT

This large shorebird occurs in the state every year, usually in small numbers. Its main migration route in spring is west of the Mississippi River, and in fall it goes to the East Coast and then southward. It breeds in the Arctic in Alaska and Canada and winters in South America from Chile to Tierra del Fuego. Hudsonian Godwits are a bright rust ventrally in spring but mostly gray in the fall. Like all godwits they have long, slightly upturned bills. They are found singly or in small flocks at flooded fields and mudflats at lakes and shallow ponds.

Spring migrants arrive as early as April: Wabash County, April 19, 1981 (LH-AB35:830); five, Winnebago County, April 19, 1986 (DW-IB&B2:89); Horseshoe Lake, April 21, 1982 (BR-SR33:8). High counts for spring: 25, Springfield, May 14, 1988 (HDB); 39, Rochelle, May 15, 1980 (LJ-AB34:782); 18, Horseshoe Lake, May 19, 1981 (PS,BR-AB35:830); 17, Meredosia, May 23, 1983 (TW-SR37:11). Late departure dates: Lake Calumet, June 23, 1956 (Levy-AFN10:387); Springfield, June 7, 1978 (HDB); Harrisonville, May 28, 1984 (RG-SR41:16).

Fewer birds are seen in fall. The earliest appear in August: Winthrop Harbor, August 24, 1978 (JN-AB33:183); Lake Calumet, August 25, 1984 (JL). High fall counts: eight, Lake Calumet, August 30–September 3, 1984 (JL); four, Chautauqua National Wildlife Refuge, October 10, 1983 (LA-AB38:209); six, Havana, October 6, 1985 (RP,MD-IB&B2:50). Late fall dates: Starved Rock State Park, October 28, 1985 (JH,JM-IB&B2:50); Horseshoe Lake, October 15, 1978 (BR-AB33:183); Carbondale Reservoir, October 17, 1970 (VK-AB25:65).

MARBLED GODWIT

Limosa fedoa

RARE MIGRANT

Ridgway and Nelson both thought the Marbled Godwit was common in Illinois, but if that was true in the nineteenth century it is not true today. This godwit is, however, a fairly regular migrant through Illinois, with a few seen every year. It looks much like a Long-billed Curlew with its buffy coloring and cinnamon wing linings, but it has a straight or upturned bill. When feeding, these godwits go into the water up to their bellies and jab their long bills into the mud. They are usually found at extensive mudflats, beaches, shallow ponds, and flooded fields. The Marbled Godwit breeds on the wet prairies of the interior United States and Canada and winters mostly in coastal areas south as far as Peru and northern Chile.

The earliest spring records are for April: Sangchris State Park, April 7, 1980 (HDB); Horseshoe Lake, April 13, 1987 (SRu). High counts for spring: 17 near Havana, April 20, 1975 (RBj); 13, Springfield, April 21, 1981 (HDB); five, Rochelle, May 15, 1980 (LJ-AB34:782); five, Starved Rock State Park, May 5, 1985 (JH-IB&B1:82). Late spring departure dates: Lake Calumet, June 3, 1978 (TC-AB32:1014); Thomson, May 18, 1967 (Shaws).

Fall migrants arrive by July: Rend Lake, July 20-21, 1985 (JR,LH-IB&B2:50); Lake Calumet, July 23-27, 1980 (JL). Most fall birds occur in August and September. The high count for fall is low: three, Chautauqua National Wildlife Refuge, August 26, 1983 (TP-SR39:14). Late dates: Charleston, October 9-18, 1978 (LBH-IAB188:46); Evanston, October 4, 1978 (LB-IAB188:46).

RUDDY TURNSTONE

Arenaria interpres

COMMON MIGRANT ALONG LAKE MICHIGAN;
OCCASIONAL MIGRANT ELSEWHERE IN THE
STATE

These harlequin-patterned shorebirds are striking in their breeding plumage, but in fall they are rather plain until they take flight. Their call notes are *tuk-a-tuk*. Their stout, pointed bill is used to probe and turn over stones and other objects on the beach as they search for food. Ruddy Turnstones can be found on mudflats, but they seem to prefer the drier parts. They choose sandy spits or rocky jetties when they are available. Lake Michigan is their prime abode in Illinois. They probably migrate from the coasts toward the Great Lakes instead of taking the conventional north-south migration routes. Turnstones breed in the high Arctic and winter from the Gulf and Atlantic Coasts south to South America. The subspecies found in Illinois is *A. i. morinella*.

Early arrival dates for spring: Lawrence County, April 19, 1985 (LH-IB&B1:82); Mark Twain National Wildlife Refuge, April 25, 1987 (HW). Maximum spring counts: 350, Illinois Beach State Park, June 1, 1966 (Bohlen 1978); 100, Chicago, May 14–26, 1980 (JL,PC-SR25:6); 31, Peoria, May 26, 1986 (LA-AB40:478); 25, Rend Lake, May 19, 1987 (LH); 20, Meredosia, May 21, 1983 (TP-SR37:11); 63, Waukegan, May 23, 1982 (JN-SR33:9). Turnstones linger late in spring, and some actually summer in Illinois. Late dates for spring: East St. Louis, June 15, 1979 (JEa-AB31:1148); Chicago, summered, 1986 (JL); four, Chicago, June 18 1985 (I.Benjamin-IB&B1:82).

Fall birds, led by adults still in breeding plumage, begin to arrive in July: Lake Calumet, July 8, 1979 (RB-SR23:7); two, Springfield, July 30, 1979 (HDB); three, Chautauqua National Wildlife Refuge, July 21, 1985 (TP-IB&B2:50); Horseshoe Lake, July 25, 1978 (RG). High counts in fall are much lower than in spring, suggesting that these birds go toward the coasts at higher latitudes in fall. High fall counts: 19, Chautauqua refuge, September 5, 1971 (PW,HDB); 12, Chicago, September 3, 1980 (JL); six, Horseshoe Lake, August 29, 1981 (YB-SR31:10). Late departure dates: three, Chicago, December 6, 1978 (RNi-AB33:183); Evanston, November 17, 1985 (EW-IB&B2:50); two, Granite City, October 8, 1981 (RK-SR31:10).

RED KNOT

Calidris canutus

RARE MIGRANT

Most of the Illinois records of this plump shorebird come from the Lake Michigan area. Red Knots prefer beaches and sandbars but can be found on extensive mudflats. One was seen in a wet sod field at Springfield. In spring Knots have reddish underparts like dowitchers, but their short bill and their rump and tail pattern easily separate them. In fall they are mostly gray, but lighter than most other shorebirds, and the distinctive plump shape and tail pattern are still diagnostic. Knots feed by probing. They nest in the Arctic and winter from the southern United States to the tip of South America. The race found in Illinois is *C. c. rufa*.

Knots have not been recorded in Illinois before May. The one at Rend Lake on May 2, 1987, was very early (DR,TF). Most arrival dates are in mid- to late May. High counts: 48, Waukegan, May 19, 1983 (JN-SR37:11); four, Meredosia, May 23–24, 1983 (TW-SR37:11); 22, Waukegan, May 27, 1985 (CM,JL-AB39:307). The latest record for spring is Waukegan, June 9, 1978 (JN-AB32:1014). The first Knots to return in fall are adults still in breeding plumage. Early fall arrival dates are in July: Rend Lake, July 28, 1986 (DR-AB40:1210); Chicago, July 30, 1979 (RB,JL-AB33:868); Mark Twain National Wildlife Refuge, July 30, 1980 (HW-SR27:8). High counts for fall: six, Horseshoe Lake, August 15, 1978 (AB33:183); 10, Waukegan, September 6, 1969 (Mlodinow 1984); six, Peoria County, September 23–October 1, 1978 (VH-AB33:183). Although higher maximum counts occur in spring, the best chance to see Red Knots is in fall because they linger longer. Departure dates are in late September and early October. Late records: Chicago, December 2, 1978 (LB-AB33:183); Springfield, October 25, 1985 (HDB); Chicago, October 29, 1983 (JL-SR39:14); Alton Dam, November 6–7, 1981 (BR).

SANDERLING

Calidris alba

COMMON MIGRANT ALONG LAKE MICHIGAN;
OCCASIONAL MIGRANT ELSEWHERE IN THE
STATE

A flock of small, stocky, whitish shorebirds running along a beach or dashing to and retreating from the waves is almost certain to be Sanderlings. In spring the Sanderling has varying amounts of rust in its plumage and may look quite different. It shows a broad white wing stripe in flight and gives out its *twick* call. Sanderlings feed along beaches and mudflats by probing or pecking. They are difficult to find downstate but can sometimes be seen on sandbars and wide open flats. They breed in the Arctic circumpolar region.

Most arrival dates are for May, though one still very whitish Sanderling was seen at Springfield on April 24, 1988 (HDB). Average spring arrival dates: Chicago, May 15 (nine years); central Illinois, May 15 (12 years). Most high counts are along Lake Michigan: 55, Waukegan, May 29, 1981 (JN-AB35:830); 36, Rend Lake, May 18, 1987 (TF); 20, Springfield, June 3, 1981 (HDB). Spring bird count totals have ranged from five to 36, with most high counts coming from northeastern Illinois (VK). Southern Illinois records are scarce. One was seen in Wabash County on May 15, 1982 (LH-SR 33:9). Average spring departure dates: Chicago, May 27 (nine years); Sangamon County, May 29 (six years). Migration continues into June: Waukegan (possibly a fall migrant), June 22, 1980 (JL); Jackson Park, June 6, 1983 (HR-SR37:16).

Fall migrant adults begin to appear not long after the spring migrants have departed. Many nonbreeding birds remain on the winter range. Early fall arrivals: Chautauqua National Wildlife Refuge, June 30, 1987 (KR); Waukegan, June 23, 1985 (JL); three, Jackson Park, July 13, 1987 (HR). Average fall arrival dates: Chicago, August 7 (16 years); central Illinois, August 13 (14 years). High counts for fall: 100, Waukegan, July 24, 1980 (JL-AB34:900); 90, Chicago, October 18, 1983 (JL); 30, Chautauqua refuge, September 19, 1979 (DF-AB34:168); 44, Big River State Forest, September 17, 1983 (LMc,MB-SR39:14); 28, Granite City, September 6, 1984 (RG); 13, Rend Lake, August 18, 1987 (TF). Average departure dates: Chicago, November 4 (16 years); central Illinois, October 4 (16 years). Late departure dates: Waukegan, November 16, 1985 (JL,CM-IB&B2:50); Waukegan, December 1, 1968 (Bohlen 1978); La Salle County, November 7, 1982 (JH-SR35:9); Pere Marquette State Park, December 22, 1979 (BR). Sanderlings winter in the Hawaiian Islands and coastal areas of the United States south to the southern tip of South America.

SEMIPALMATED SANDPIPER

Calidris pusilla

COMMON MIGRANT

This is the lightest colored of the peeps, or small sandpipers. It tends to grays and whites with dark legs and bill. As the name Semipalmated implies, the toes have partial webbing. These sandpipers are found at mudflats and other open wet areas. They tend to stay away from the grassy areas preferred by Least Sandpipers. Along Lake Michigan they can be found on the beaches.

Semipals arrive later in spring than the other common peeps, usually in May, although there are some April dates: Springfield, April 25, 1985 (HDB); Horseshoe Lake, April 26, 1986 (RA); Danville, April 29, 1986 (SB-IB&B2:89). The average arrival date for Chicago is May 15 (seven years) and for central Illinois, May 6 (17 years). Peak numbers in spring usually come after the spring bird counts, but some have been recorded every year. The more northern counts are somewhat dubious, however, because of the early dates. The high for a spring bird count was May 10, 1986, when 44 counties recorded 664 birds, with 259 in Alexander County (VK). Other maximum counts: 250, Lake Calumet, May 27, 1974 (Mlodinow 1984); 500, Alton, May 18-19, 1986 (RG); 451, Rend Lake, May 16, 1986 (DR-IB&B2:89). This bird lingers longer than most other birds in spring, staying well into June. Jim Landing had five on

June 15, 1984, at Lake Calumet. The average departure date in spring for Springfield (17 years) is June 7, with June 16, 1976, the latest. Forty Semipals were at Waukegan on June 12, 1977 (JN-AB31:1148). These sandpipers breed in the high Arctic.

Not long after the last spring migrants leave, the first adults return in the fall. Most of them apparently have failed at nesting; in the short Arctic summer only one attempt is usually made. A few may summer in suitable localities in Illinois; one spent the summer at Waukegan in 1977 (JN-AB31:1148). Landing's average for returning adults at Chicago (six years) is July 12, while the average return date for immatures is August 16. For central Illinois the average return date (16 years) is July 19. Some early arrival dates: 10, Starved Rock State Park, July 9, 1985 (JM); Chautauqua National Wildlife Refuge, July 6-7, 1985 (KR-IB&B2:50). Some maximum counts for fall: 428, Lake Calumet, August 2, 1981 (JL); 600, Chautauqua refuge, July 29, 1985 (KR-AB39:918); 130, Lake Shelbyville, August 1, 1985 (SR,KJ-IB&B2:50). Although Semipals arrive later than Least Sandpipers in fall, they leave earlier. Average departure dates: Chicago, October 7 (14 years); central Illinois, September 28 (17 years). The latest date for Chicago is October 22, 1936 (Clark and Nice 1950); for central Illinois, October 31, 1984.

It is easy to misidentify peeps in fall because different age groups of the same species may look as different as separate species. Semipalmated and Western Sandpipers are practically indistinguishable except by bill length, call notes, and a few other clues (see Veit and Jonsson 1984). Semipalmated Sandpipers leave all of the states in winter except Florida and travel as far south as Argentina and northern Chile.

WESTERN SANDPIPER

Calidris mauri

OCCASIONAL SPRING MIGRANT AND UNCOMMON FALL MIGRANT

The status of the Western Sandpiper in Illinois is unclear because of its close resemblance to other peeps, especially the Semipalmated Sandpiper. Western Sandpiper females have longer bills than other peeps with a down curve near the end, making them easier to identify. This peep feeds in deeper water more often than other small sandpipers. The call note is a high *cheep,* somewhat like the White-rumped Sandpiper's call. Recent field guides and Grant (1984) discuss other differences. Early observers in Illinois thought this shorebird was rare; Bartel and Pitelka (1939) give a history of records to 1939. Their distribution does seem spotty, suggesting that they choose only certain mudflats, probably because of food preferences.

Western Sandpipers arrive late in spring, usually along

with the more numerous Semipalmated Sandpipers. Early spring arrival dates: two, Spring Lake, April 27, 1986 (TP-IB&B2:89); Lawrence County, April 28, 1984 (DJo-SR41:16). Average arrival date for central Illinois is May 21 (11 years). Spring bird counts have produced low totals (from none to 12). High counts for spring: 10, Jackson County, May 10, 1986 (VK); 10, Waukegan, May 18, 1985 (DW-AB39:307); 10, Lake Calumet, June 2, 1981 (RG,PC-AB35:830). Numbers in spring are lower than in fall. Average departure date for central Illinois is June 2 (nine years). Late departure dates: Waukegan, June 7, 1987 (JN); three, Rend Lake, June 4, 1977 (MMo-AB31:1008); nine, Illinois Beach State Park, June 12, 1982 (JL-SR33:9).

Early fall arrivals: four, Starved Rock State Park, July 8, 1985 (JM-IB&B2:51); Richland County, July 17, 1983 (LH-SR39:14). Average fall arrival date for central Illinois is July 28 (17 years). High counts for fall: 65, Waukegan, September 7, 1978 (LB-AB33:183); 20, Rend Lake, July 28, 1985 (LH-IB&B2:51); 35, Chautauqua National Wildlife Refuge, July 25, 1987 (KR). The central Illinois average departure date is September 16 (15 years). Late departure dates: Jackson Park, November 5, 1984 (HR-IB&B1:15); Rend Lake, October 30, 1987 (TF); Chautauqua refuge, November 1, 1975 (HDB). The Western Sandpiper winters from the southern coasts of the United States south to northern South America.

LEAST SANDPIPER

Calidris minutilla

COMMON MIGRANT

This is the smallest sandpiper, browner than other peeps and with yellowish legs. It is found on mudflats and in wet grassy areas. Its flight call is *kree-eet*. Kennicott (1854) listed the Least Sandpiper as known to nest in Cook County. One was building a nest near the Calumet River on June 5, 1875, but did not complete it, according to Nelson (1876). Actually, Least Sandpipers nest much farther north, usually on the tundra.

Early spring migrants: Monmouth, March 29, 1986 (MB-AB40:478); Crab Orchard National Wildlife Refuge, March 29, 1985 (JR-IB&B1:87); Springfield, March 27, 1977 (HDB). Average arrival dates: west-central, April 28 (nine years); Sangamon County, April 21 (18 years). Maximum counts for spring: 140, Carbondale, May 8, 1986 (DR-IB&B2:89); 200, Henderson County, May 20, 1985 (MB,BW-IB&B1:87); 200, Rend Lake, May 8, 1987 (TF). Spring bird count totals ranged from 66 in 1973 to 3087 in 1976; 1500 were counted in Mason County on May 8, 1976 (VK). Average spring departure dates: west-central, May 17 (nine years); Sangamon County, May 24 (18 years). Late departure dates: Illinois Beach State Park, June 12, 1976 (Mlodinow 1984); three, Carlyle Lake, June 3, 1985 (KR-IB&B1:87); Springfield, June 5, 1988 (HDB). Few Least

Sandpipers linger into June as Semipalmated and Western Sandpipers do.

This small sandpiper returns earlier and stays longer in the fall than most other sandpipers. Early fall migrants: five, Lake Calumet, June 25, 1987 (JL,CM); Jackson County, June 29, 1985 (JR-IB&B 2:51). Average arrival dates: west-central, July 12 (nine years); Sangamon County, July 2 (19 years). High counts for fall: 1000, Banner, October 12, 1985 (TP-AB40:120); 515, Lake Calumet, July 24, 1983 (JL-AB37:994); 500, Chautauqua National Wildlife Refuge, July 27, 1984 (KR-AB38:1026). Average fall departure dates: west-central, September 29 (nine years); Sangamon County, November 4 (18 years). Some years these birds linger so late they can be seen standing on the early-morning ice. Late dates and winter records: two, Springfield, December 15, 1981 (HDB); Alexander County, December 29, 1976 (MMo,D.Klem-AB31:338); Chautauqua refuge, January 1, 1975 (RS,HDB); Chillicothe, December 6, 1981 (LA-AB36:299). The Least Sandpiper winters from the coastal southern United States south to South America.

WHITE-RUMPED SANDPIPER

Calidris fuscicollis

UNCOMMON SPRING MIGRANT AND RARE FALL MIGRANT

The White-rumped Sandpiper is one of the larger peeps and, as its name indicates, it shows a white rump in flight. Like the Baird's Sandpiper, it has noticeably long wings. It gives a high *jeet* call note as it flies. White-rumps feed on mudflats, but more often they stay just off the flat in very shallow water. In spring they usually appear with the similar Semipalmated Sandpiper. The White-rumps have a distinctive pattern of fine streaking on the breast and sides. Like some other shorebirds, White-rumped Sandpipers have an elliptical migration route. Most are seen in Illinois in spring, when they take the interior. In fall, when they go down the East Coast, very few are seen in the state. These sandpipers nest on the Arctic tundra and winter in South America south to Cape Horn.

Spring White-rumps arrive relatively late. April dates are unusual: Springfield, April 25, 1985 (HDB); Lawrence County, April 29, 1984 (LH-SR41:17). Average spring arrival dates: west-central, May 25 (six years); Sangamon County, May 10 (18 years). Spring bird counts are too early for peak numbers, and White-rumps are not recorded every year. Totals ranged from one in 1973 to 51 in 1986. Highest counts were 26 in Union County, May 6, 1978, and 27 in Alexander County, May 10, 1986 (VK). Maximum counts for spring: 50, Rend Lake, May 19, 1987 (LH); 100, Meredosia, May 21, 1983 (TP-AB37:876); 52, Madison County, May 20, 1986 (RG,SRu-AB40:478); 52, Monroe County, May 25, 1983 (RG). Average departure dates for spring: west-central, May 31 (six years); Sangamon County, June 1 (17 years). This sandpiper typically stays into mid-

June: two, Chicago, June 14, 1986 (JL-IB&B2:89); two, Rockford, June 10, 1984 (LJ-SR41:17); Springfield, June 21, 1982 (HDB).

Presumably, July records are of returning White-rumps, but they may be nonbreeding summering birds: Joliet, July 24, 1984 (JM-IB&B1:15); Wabash County, July 8, 1982 (LH-SR35:10); male specimen, Sangchris State Park, July 28, 1976 (ISM#606450). There are some August and September records of adults mostly in winter plumage: Horseshoe Lake, August 29, 1979, and September 5, 1986 (RG). Late birds are mostly juveniles, but observers need to give details on age classes so that a clearer picture can be drawn from their sightings. Hayman et al. (1986) and Prater and Marchant (1977) give aids for determining ages of shorebirds. Some late records: Lake Vermilion, October 3, 1983 (SB-SR39:15); Waukegan, November 26, 1982 (RB-SR35:10); two juveniles, Batavia, October 15–27, 1986 (MS-IB&B3:40); juvenile, Hartford, October 29–31, 1982 (RG,PS,BR). In fall more records come from the northern part of the state, since the birds move eastward from there.

BAIRD'S SANDPIPER

Calidris bairdii

OCCASIONAL SPRING MIGRANT AND
UNCOMMON FALL MIGRANT

Except for their long wings these shorebirds are about as nondescript as they come. Most Baird's Sandpipers seen in Illinois are fall juveniles, which are distinctly buffy with scaly backs. Adults are usually identified by a process of elimination. In spring most adult Baird's Sandpipers pass to the west of Illinois on the central plains, while in fall they favor the East and West Coasts. Immatures, however, sometimes occur in numbers in Illinois. They are found at mudflats, often on back areas in short grasses. They also frequent beaches, sandbars, and short grass areas away from water such as golf courses and airfields. They breed in alpine tundra in the Arctic and winter in South America south to Tierra del Fuego.

Given the correct conditions, spring migrants may arrive as early as March: Springfield, March 26, 1977 (HDB); Jacksonville, March 19, 1977 (WO,BA,RQR). Average arrival dates are in late April or May: west-central, May 11 (seven years); Sangamon County, April 30 (11 years). Counts in spring are low: 15, Havana, May 5, 1986 (RP-AB40:478); eight, Springfield, April 27, 1983 (HDB). They were recorded on 11 of 15 spring bird counts; the highest total was 46 in 1983. Rock Island County had the highest count, with 32 on May 7, 1983 (VK). Most Baird's Sandpipers are gone by mid-May. Some June sightings are questionable; they were more likely White-rumped than Baird's Sandpipers: 14 at Batavia, June 1, 1985 (IB&B1:87), and two at Rend Lake, June 7, 1986 (IB&B2:89).

Fall migration produces many more Baird's, some as early as July: Lake Calumet, July 21, 1985 (RB,JL-IB&B2:51);

Horseshoe Lake, July 17, 1983 (SRu-SR39:15); two, Alexander County, July 26, 1986 (DR-IB&B3:40). Average fall arrival dates: Chicago, August 19 (12 years); Sangamon County, August 20 (18 years). Maximum counts for fall: 29, Waukegan, September 13, 1978 (JN-AB33:183); 21, Rend Lake, September 16, 1986 (LH-IB&B3:40); 19, Madison County, August 28, 1987 (RG). Average departure dates: Chicago, October 4 (12 years); Sangamon County, October 6 (17 years). These shorebirds linger quite late at times, given the right conditions: Havana, December 2, 1972 (PW); two, Waukegan, November 23, 1978 (JN-AB33:183); Carlyle Lake, November 6, 1987 (DJo,RG); Tazewell County, November 11, 1982 (LA-SR35:10).

PECTORAL SANDPIPER

Calidris melanotos

COMMON MIGRANT

As this chunky brown sandpiper heads for the tundra it makes stops in Illinois at flooded fields, mudflats, and wet pastures. At a grassy pool of water Pectoral Sandpipers "freeze" with heads up, and an observer may think there are only a few until they begin to move again. Then there may be 40 to 50 or more running through the grass, or they may take wing in synchronous flight. They seem quite pugnacious, threatening each other and calling. The males are noticeably larger than the females. The Pectoral's *kriik* flight note is well known to shorebirders.

When these sandpipers arrive in spring, they sometimes can be seen standing on ice in early morning. Early spring arrival dates: Alton, March 8, 1983 (RG); Springfield, March 11, 1986 (HDB); five, Lake County, March 29, 1986 (JL). Average arrival dates: Urbana, April 8 (eight years); Sangamon County, March 23 (17 years). Fifteen years of spring bird counts had totals ranging from 390 in 1972 to 4156 in 1979, with the highest count 800 in Sangamon County, May 5, 1979 (VK). These birds, like most shorebirds, will be present if the right habitat is available, and in spring that takes rain to create flooded fields. Other high counts for spring: 500, Mahomet, May 8, 1982 (RCh-SR33:9); 360, Jackson County, March 31, 1985 (JR-IB&B1:87); 1500, Beckmeyer, April 19, 1984 (RG,BR); 350, Monroe County, May 3, 1987 (RG). Although most Pectoral Sandpipers move through rather early, a few linger late in spring. The average departure date for central Illinois is May 22 (17 years). Some are recorded into June: Green River Conservation Area, June 7, 1982 (BSh-SR33:9); Lawrence County, June 2, 1985 (LH-IB&B1:87); Springfield, June 5, 1979 (HDB).

Fall migration is not far behind the last spring departures. The first wave is adult birds returning from the Arctic. Adults are grayish, while immatures are more rusty, especially on the breast. Both adults and immatures have the streaks sharply cut off on the breast. Early fall arrivals: Lake Calumet, June 30, 1981 (RG,PC-SR31:11); two, Manito,

July 5, 1984 (KR-IB&B1:20); Crab Orchard National Wildlife Refuge, July 5, 1985 (JR-IB&B2:51); Sangchris State Park, June 24, 1987 (HDB). Average fall arrival date for central Illinois is July 12 (17 years). Numbers soon escalate; in some areas Pectorals outnumber all other shorebirds combined. These sandpipers probe in the mud for their food, mainly Diptera and amphipods, along with some plant materials. They feed belly deep in mud, occasionally swimming in shallow water. Maximum counts in fall are higher than in spring: 5000, Chautauqua National Wildlife Refuge, August 14, 1984 (TP-AB39:60); 2050, Chicago, August 11, 1984 (JL); 2000, Banner, September 28, 1985 (TP-AB40:120). Pectorals stay fairly late; the average departure date for central Illinois is October 31 (17 years). Other departure dates: Knox County, November 6, 1983 (MB-SR39:15); Carbondale, November 25, 1984 (JR-IB&B1:20); two, Alton, November 8, 1984 (CP-IB&B1:20). The few December records are of very late migrants; none have overwintered: Crab Orchard refuge, December 5, 1960 (L.Hood-AFN15:333); Lake Calumet, December 31, 1954 (KB-IAB93:12); south of Lacon, December 30, 1979 (BPr-AB34:525).

Pectoral Sandpipers winter in southern South America from Peru and southern Brazil south to central Chile and southern Argentina.

SHARP-TAILED SANDPIPER

Calidris acuminata

VERY RARE VAGRANT

This Asian species has been recorded in Illinois only twice. The Sharp-tailed Sandpiper is closely related to the Pectoral Sandpiper, which it resembles. The Illinois birds, however, were both immatures, which are distinctive, with buffy breast and chestnut cap. They were seen and photographed at Chautauqua National Wildlife Refuge, September 28–29, 1974 (Bohlen and Sandburg 1975), and Chicago, October 6, 1985 (JL-IB&B2:50). This species has been recorded in several eastern states and is seen yearly on the West Coast.

PURPLE SANDPIPER

Calidris maritima

RARE MIGRANT ALONG LAKE MICHIGAN

This coastal species has been recorded in Illinois only at Lake Michigan. The Purple Sandpiper inhabits rocky areas along the lake, jetties, and occasionally beaches. It seems to prefer rocks covered with algae. Most sightings are for late fall, when these sandpipers are gray with orange legs and orange at the base of the bill. Of some 22 records, the only one for spring is of four Purple Sandpipers at

Wilmette, March 14, 1961 (RR-AFN15:415), although three seen in June were probably late spring migrants: Cook County, June 1895 (Cory 1909); Camp Logan, June 2, 1951 (Smith and Parmalee 1955); Chicago, June 30, 1979 (RB,JL- AB33:868). All other records were between October 27 (1976, Waukegan) and January 3 (1987, Waukegan), with November having the most. Recent records: Chicago, November 29–December 7, 1980 (RB,JL-AB35:305); Waukegan, November 21–22, 1981 (DJ-AB36:183); Wilmette, November 17, 1985 (GR,SB-IB&B2:51). A specimen mentioned in Cory (1909), from Cook County, November 7, 1871, is in the Illinois State Museum collection.

Purple Sandpipers breed in the Arctic and winter along the East Coast, rarely along the Gulf Coast. They are closely related to the Rock Sandpiper of the West Coast.

DUNLIN

Calidris alpina

UNCOMMON SPRING MIGRANT AND
COMMON FALL MIGRANT

The reddish back and black belly of the spring Dunlin make this medium-sized shorebird easy to identify. In fall only the thick, drooping bill is a good clue, because the plumage is mostly grayish brown. Dunlins both pick and probe for food at mudflats and beaches. They breed in the Arctic and winter on the Gulf and Atlantic Coasts. The subspecies found in Illinois is *C. a. pacifica*.

Occasionally Dunlins appear early in spring, still in dull plumage. Early arrival dates: Tazewell County, March 24, 1985 (LA-AB39:308); Rend Lake, April 4, 1987 (TF); Springfield, April 2, 1977 (HDB). Most arrive fairly late. Average arrival dates: west-central, May 2 (eight years); Sangamon County, May 6 (18 years). Numbers are lower and more irregular in spring than in fall: 200, Waukegan, May 28, 1979 (RB-AB33:777); 80, Fulton County, May 17, 1983 (TP-SR37:16); 279, Rend Lake, May 18, 1987 (TF); 63, Henderson County, May 20, 1985 (MB,BW-IB&B1:87). Spring bird count totals have ranged widely, from 11 in 1973 to 409 in 1981. High count was 182 in Cook County, May 9, 1981 (VK). Average departure dates: west-central, May 18 (18 years); Sangamon County, May 23 (17 years). Some years the flight extends into June: three, Waukegan, June 21, 1986 (JL-IB&B2:89); Starved Rock State Park, June 2, 1985 (JH-IB&B1:87); Chicago, June 30, 1979 (JL).

Dunlins are usually the last shorebirds to arrive in fall. There are a few early dates, however: Granite City, August 24, 1986 (SRu-IB&B3:40); Waukegan, July 4 and 22, 1972 (GR-AB26:866); East St. Louis, September 3, 1983 (PS-SR39:15). Average arrival dates: Chicago, October 3 (12 years); Sangamon County, October 6 (18 years). Maximum counts for fall: 1200, Evanston, October 24, 1973 (GR-AB28:60); 200, Rend Lake, October 27, 1985 (LH-IB&B2:51); 500, Rice Lake, October 17, 1987 (RP). Some years bring good flights along Lake Michigan. Average fall departure dates: Chicago, October 31 (12 years); Sangamon County, November 16 (17 years). Dunlins are fairly hardy birds, and some linger into early winter: Waukegan, December 14, 1980 (JL); Tazewell County, December 28, 1982 (MSw-SR32:5); Charleston, December 5, 1985 (RBr-IB&B2:76); Chicago, December 18, 1980 (RB,JL-SR27:8); Chicago, early January 1972 (HB-AB26:612).

CURLEW SANDPIPER

Calidris ferruginea

VERY RARE VAGRANT

Principally a Eurasian species, this shorebird has also bred in northern Alaska. The first state record of the Curlew Sandpiper occurred in southern Illinois at Rend Lake, July 23, 1976 (Peterjohn and Morrison 1977). Since then seven more records have been added, all in northeastern Illinois: Lake Calumet, July 22–26, 1979 (RB-AB33:868); Chicago, July 29, 1979 (LB-AB33:868); Waukegan, July 31, 1979 (GR,JN-AB33:868); Wolf Lake, May 23, 1980 (KB-AB34:782); Vermilion County, May 16–19, 1986 (SB-AB40:478); Lake Calumet, August 24–September 1, 1986 (JPo-IB&B3:40); Lake Calumet, July 18–24, 1987 (KH,JL). Several of the birds were photographed. All were in the distinctive breeding plumage characterized by chestnut head and underparts. Other field marks include a white rump and decurved bill. In late fall most of the plumage is gray.

STILT SANDPIPER

Calidris himantopus

OCCASIONAL SPRING MIGRANT AND
COMMON FALL MIGRANT

Although most Stilt Sandpipers apparently migrate up the Mississippi Valley in spring, few are seen. Shorebird migration is generally a hurried affair at this time, especially the tundra species, which linger late in the south and then fly almost directly to their breeding grounds. The Stilt Sandpiper breeds in the Arctic north of the tree line. When it arrives in Illinois in spring it is distinctively barred ventrally and has a rusty cheek patch. Its fairly long drooping bill and long greenish legs also help distinguish it from the Lesser Yellowlegs, with which it associates. Its call is *whu* or *kriik*. In flight the Stilt Sandpiper has a humped-backed appearance. It frequents small pools and extensive mudflats, usually feeding off the flat in shallow water.

These birds usually arrive in May, but there are a few April arrivals: Sangamon County, April 2, 1978 (HDB); Marshall County, April 18, 1982 (LA-SR33:9); Charleston, April 20, 1986 (LBH-IB&B2:89); Pope County, April 27, 1986 (DR-IB&B2:89); Mason County, April 14, 1985 (KR-

IB&B1:87). The average arrival date for central Illinois is May 11 (14 years). Maximum counts for spring: 27, Kidd, May 18, 1983 (RG); 10, Oquawka, May 17, 1986 (MB-IB&B2:89); 11, Wabash County, May 10, 1985 (LH-IB&B1:87). Most of these sandpipers pass through after spring bird count time; only small numbers have been seen, and in seven of 15 years there were none. This migration lasts through May and sometimes into June. The average spring departure date for central Illinois is May 22 (10 years). Late departures: Springfield, June 1, 1983 (HDB); Dundee, June 7, 1983 (RM-SR37:16).

Hardly have the spring migrants departed than fall birds begin to appear. Jehl (1973) pointed out that gonadal regression occurs about a week after the egg clutch is completed and renesting then appears to be impossible. Adults that have nest failures probably start drifting south with cold fronts. As with most shorebirds, the adults arrive first. Early arrival dates: Lake Calumet, June 28, 1986 (JL); Havana, July 8, 1985 (KR-IB&B2:51); Springfield, June 28, 1980 (HDB). The average arrival date for central Illinois is July 15 (17 years). These fall Stilts are still in breeding plumage and are easily recognized. Immatures tend to show up about early to mid-August. Then, with immatures in fresh juvenile plumage and adults molting, identification becomes more complicated the rest of the fall, since Stilts can look very much like Lesser Yellowlegs. If examined closely, however, they can still be identified fairly easily by the drooping bill and plumage characters. They have a distinctive feeding manner, probing as they wade in water usually up to the belly and sometimes submerging the head. Since fall migration is much more leisurely than spring migration, numbers tend to build up in favored localities, making fall maxima higher: 200, Horseshoe Lake, August 29, 1979 (RG); 196, Chautauqua National Wildlife Refuge, August 6, 1984 (KR-AB39:60); 95, Argo, August 11, 1979 (RB-SR23:7); 91, Chicago, September 3, 1984 (JL); 60, Chautauqua refuge, October 3, 1982 (DW-SR35:10). Departure dates probably vary with mudflat conditions and weather, but Stilts usually stay fairly late. The average departure date for central Illinois is October 5 (16 years). Late departure dates: Skokie Lagoon, November 2, 1971 (GR-AB26:72); Lake Springfield, November 1, 1984 (HDB); Tazewell County, October 24, 1981 (MSw-SR31:11); two, East St. Louis, October 31, 1982 (RG,PS).

The Stilt Sandpiper winters chiefly in South America from Bolivia and Brazil south to northern Chile and Argentina.

BUFF-BREASTED SANDPIPER

Tryngites subruficollis

VERY RARE SPRING MIGRANT AND
OCCASIONAL FALL MIGRANT

This buffy sandpiper is not usually found on mudflats but on the short grassy areas that grow up on the drier flats. It also has adapted to airfields, golf courses, and sod fields.

Mlodinow (1984) notes that Buff-breasted Sandpipers are found on beaches along Lake Michigan, and Goetz found them on sandbars in the Mississippi River. When feeding, several work as a team, getting in a line to work the insects, which they pick at or dart around and grab with their bills. They show white wing linings in flight. On the ground they are almost dovelike, but with longer yellow legs. Males are noticeably larger than females. Immatures can be recognized by whitish edgings on the back feathers rather than the buff edgings of adults and a different scapula and wing covert pattern (see Prater and Marchant 1977). These sandpipers breed on the tundra in the Arctic.

There are only a few spring records, as the bulk of these sandpipers migrate to the west of Illinois on the Great Plains. Spring dates: specimen (CAS), Cook County, April 1906 (Ford 1956); Jackson Park, April 27, 1921 (Lewis 1921); Monroe County, May 25, 1985 (RG-AB39:308); two, Illiopolis, April 26, 1987 (HDB); three near Carlyle Lake, May 7, 1987 (RG). Since Buff-breasteds do not usually come into mudflats, some may be overlooked in spring.

Fall migration is not as early for Buff-breasteds as for some other shorebirds, and numbers vary widely from year to year. Early arrival dates: two, Lake Calumet, July 28, 1985 (JL); Springfield, July 28, 1987 (HDB). The average arrival date for central Illinois is August 23 (15 years). High counts for fall: 44, Will County, August 30, 1983 (JM,DW-AB38:209); 32, Madison County, September 6, 1984 (RG,PS); 26, Rend Lake, September 8, 1985 (LH-IB&B2:51); 34, Chicago, September 3, 1984 (JL). The average departure date for central Illinois is September 16 (13 years). Late departure dates: Rend Lake, October 13, 1985 (TF-IB&B2:51); five, Tazewell County, October 10, 1981 (MSw-SR31:11); Springfield, October 8, 1983 (HDB).

Buff-breasted Sandpipers are very long distance migrants, wintering in Paraguay, Uruguay, and northern Argentina.

RUFF

Philomachus pugnax

RARE MIGRANT

An Old World species, the Ruff is now colonizing North America. It has bred in northwestern Alaska. Its plumage is variable, especially in breeding adult males; they may be black, white, or cinnamon. In winter both males and females (Reeves) are rather plain birds that resemble yellowlegs. Through 1987 there were 42 records for this shorebird in Illinois. The earliest was one seen at Calumet, July 18–25, 1949 (Smith and Parmalee 1955). The Lake Calumet area continues to be the spot in the state where Ruffs are seen most often.

The 16 spring records occurred between April 6 (Lawrence County, 1980, LH,DJo-AB34:782) and May 19 (Monroe County, 1984, PB-AB38:918). All were singles. Other recent spring records: Urbana, May 9, 1980 (RCh-AB34:782); Decatur, April 10, 1982 (RS-AB36:858); Spring

Lake, May 6, 1986 (PW,RQR-AB40:478); Lake Calumet, May 14, 1986 (RB-AB40:478).

Some return early in fall, and July 4 is the time to start looking for Ruffs. The 26 fall records range from June 29 (Lake Calumet, 1976, CC and LC) to November 9 (Pekin, 1987, LA). The only multiple count is two at—where else?—Lake Calumet, August 25, 1986 (AB41:96). Other fall records: Urbana, July 17–25, 1979 (RCh-AB33:868); Horseshoe Lake, September 21, 1985 (VB,E.Larson-IB&B2:51); Waukegan, August 13, 1981 (JWi-AB36:183). Ruffs are found at mudflats, wet grassy areas, and flooded fields.

SHORT-BILLED DOWITCHER

Limnodromus griseus

UNCOMMON MIGRANT

The trouble with dowitchers is that they all look alike. Only after several studies of collected birds did researchers learn that there are three subspecies of *Limnodromus griseus*, the Short-billed Dowitcher, plus the separate species *Limnodromus scolopaceus*, the Long-billed Dowitcher. Each form has age and sex classes that present identification problems, and in fall all these classes have their own times for migration. In Illinois, fortunately, only the inland *griseus* subspecies, *L. g. hendersoni*, occurs as a migrant (the eastern *L. g. griseus*, to complicate things a bit, may occur as a vagrant). The main problem, then, is to separate the inland race of the Short-billed Dowitcher from the Long-billed Dowitcher (see Jehl 1963, Conover 1941, Rowan 1932, and Wilds and Newlon 1983 for clarification). The best clue is the flight notes: *tu tu tu* in the Short-billed and *keek* in the Long-billed. Though both dowitchers are salmon-colored in spring and gray later in fall, adult Short-bills generally migrate through Illinois too early in fall to show the gray plumage and the later-migrating juveniles are much rustier than juvenile Long-bills. Most or all Short-billed Dowitchers look rusty ventrally. These birds are found at mudflats and in shallow water, where they are constantly probing into the mud with their long bills. They breed on the tundra and wet meadows of Alaska and Canada.

Identification during spring migration is relatively easy, since Short-bills usually arrive in May after most Long-bills have left. Even then there are problems, however, for sometimes the migrations overlap, or an observer can miss either species. Early spring arrival dates for Short-bills: 27, Chicago, April 27, 1986 (JL); Rend Lake, April 27, 1987 (TF). The average arrival date for central Illinois is May 8 (16 years). High counts: 65, Springfield, May 10, 1988 (HDB); 70, Peoria County, May 12, 1986 (TP,LA-IB&B2:89); 60, Monmouth, May 20, 1985 (MB,BW-IB&B1:87); 60, Chicago, May 5, 1985 (JL). Spring bird count totals ranged from three in 1972 to 306 in 1980. Highest count was 59 in Lake County, May 10, 1980 (VK).

The average departure date for central Illinois is May 19 (17 years). Late departure dates: Alexander County, June 8, 1985 (JR-IB&B1:87); Lake Calumet, June 14, 1981 (RB,JL-SR29:9).

Fall migration starts in late June or early July as adult females depart and leave the males to care for the young (Jehl 1963). Early fall arrival dates: 31, Lake Calumet, June 27, 1982 (JL); two, Chautauqua National Wildlife Refuge, June 28, 1987 (KR); Springfield, June 30, 1986 (HDB). The average arrival date for central Illinois is July 13 (16 years). Maximum counts for fall: 500, Lake Calumet, July 14, 1987 (CM); 80, Banner, September 28, 1985 (RP-IB&B2:51); 90, Chautauqua National Wildlife Refuge, July 22, 1987 (KR); 50, Rend Lake, September 5, 1985 (LH-IB&B2:51). The average departure date for central Illinois is September 8 (13 years). Late departure dates: Chicago, October 24, 1986 (JL-AB41:96); four, Havana, October 19, 1985 (RP-IB&B2:51); East St. Louis, October 1, 1982 (RG,PS-SR35:10). Late dowitchers should be examined carefully because October is usually the time for Long-bills. The Short-billed Dowitcher winters from southern coastal United States south to South America.

LONG-BILLED DOWITCHER

Limnodromus scolopaceus

UNCOMMON MIGRANT

This dowitcher is somewhat less common than the Short-billed and is not recorded every spring, though it is numerous in fall. This pattern suggests that Long-bills follow an elliptical migration route that takes them west of Illinois in spring. Their *keek* flight note is the best means of identification. Long-bills can also be identified on plumage characters by using a combination of field marks only (see Wilds and Newlon 1983). They inhabit mudflats and shallow water areas much as the Short-bills do.

Long-billed Dowitchers arrive earlier in spring than Short-bills. Early spring arrivals: three, Charleston, April 3, 1986 (LBH-IB&B2:89); Wabash County, April 4, 1982 (DJo-SR33:9); Whiteside County, April 6, 1986 (LJ-IB&B2:89). High counts: 21, Springfield, April 30, 1981 (HDB); 15, Oquawka, April 28, 1984 (MB-SR41:17); 26, Peoria, May 5, 1986 (LA-IB&B2:89). Long-bills were recorded on spring bird counts in nine of 15 years, with totals ranging from one to 53. Highest count was 26 at Bureau County, May 7, 1983 (VK). May is late for these migrants. Late dates: Lake Calumet, May 9, 1981 (JL-SR29:9); three, Havana, May 10, 1984 (HDB,VK).

Fall migration is complicated because different age groups arrive at different times. Adults arrive first, usually in August (the adult Short-bills arrive in late June and July). Immatures arrive in late September (immature Short-bills arrive about mid-August, so there is overlap). Early fall arrival dates: Havana, July 19, 1987 (KR,MB); Springfield, August 2, 1986 (HDB); Lake Calumet, August 6, 1983 (JL).

High counts for fall: 200, Rice Lake, October 20, 1987 (KR); 100, Banner, October 5, 1985 (MB-AB40:120); 93, Chautauqua National Wildlife Refuge, October 9, 1983 (TP-AB38:209); 48, Chicago, October 6, 1984 (JL). The later birds are immatures in grayish plumage. Late departure dates: eight, Mark Twain National Wildlife Refuge, November 24, 1978 (RG); Crab Orchard National Wildlife Refuge, November 23, 1982 (JR-SR35:10); four, Springfield, November 17, 1987 (HDB); one probable (dowitcher sp.?), Mark Twain refuge, December 6, 1981 (AB36:299).

The Long-billed Dowitcher winters from the southern United States south to Guatemala.

COMMON SNIPE

Gallinago gallinago

COMMON MIGRANT; RARE SUMMER RESIDENT; UNCOMMON WINTER RESIDENT IN SOUTHERN ILLINOIS DECREASING NORTHWARD

Common Snipes have a long bill, stripes on the head, and a cryptically colored back. They are found in open wet spots in grassy bogs, on mudflats, in wet fields, and even in roadside ditches. When flushed they fly in a zigzag pattern, or they may crouch low and remain motionless until the perceived danger has passed. If one snipe is seen, the observer should scan for others that are probably present but well camouflaged. Their call while flying is a grating *scaip*. These snipes have a courtship flight called winnowing in which they do aerial acrobatics and the outer tail feathers produce a series of rapid hollow noises. They feed by probing into mud with their long bill, eating mostly earthworms but also insects and some marsh plants. The race in most of North America is *G. g. delicata*.

Wintering snipes make it somewhat difficult to distinguish very early spring migrants. Early dates: East St. Louis, February 18, 1983 (JEa-SR37:16); three, Crab Orchard National Wildlife Refuge, March 6, 1986 (DR-IB&B2:89); Sangchris Lake, March 7, 1987 (HDB). Average arrival dates: Urbana, April 2 (12 years); Chicago, April 16 (11 years). Maximum counts for spring: 150, Lake Calumet, April 11, 1981 (JL); 95, Mason County, April 17, 1985 (KR-IB&B1:87); 63, Vermilion County, March 28, 1986 (SB-IB&B2:89); 73, Mark Twain National Wildlife Refuge, April 4, 1987 (HW). Spring bird count totals ranged from 29 in 1972 to 271 in 1984, with the high count 63 in Jasper County, May 5, 1984 (VK). Average departure dates: Urbana, April 29 (12 years); Chicago, May 2 (11 years). Migration probably continues until mid-May.

Snipes nest on the ground in wet grassy areas in Illinois. There are usually four dark buff eggs with black markings. Illinois egg dates are April 24 to May 10. A nest with young was reported at Illinois Beach State Park on May 21, 1972 (LB,JSa-AB26:767). Much more information is needed on the Illinois nesting cycle. Summer birds were noted at Goose Lake Prairie, 1982; Fulton County, 1983; Randolph County, 1985; and Sangchris State Park, 1985.

Fall migration can begin early: two, Lake Calumet, June 24, 1983 (JL); Springfield, July 20, 1985 (HDB). Average arrival dates: Chicago, September 6 (14 years); central Illinois, August 20 (18 years). Maximum counts for fall: 200, Pekin, November 10, 1987 (KR); 200, Rice Lake, November 1, 1987 (LA,MB); 90, Tazewell County, November 9–11, 1981 (MSw-SR31:10). Average departure dates: Chicago, October 20 (14 years); west-central, November 24 (12 years).

Totals on Christmas bird counts for 1976–85 ranged from 42 in 1984 to 97 in 1976. The highest Christmas count was 65 at Mermet in 1966. Snipes occasionally winter even in the northernmost counties of Illinois, but in small numbers and only where they find open water. Sewage lagoons, natural springs, and shallow ditches with a source of warm water provide areas in which wintering snipes can survive.

AMERICAN WOODCOCK

Scolopax minor

COMMON MIGRANT; UNCOMMON SUMMER AND RARE WINTER RESIDENT

Unlike most other shorebirds, the American Woodcock is found in the woods or along woodland edges. It is chunky and buff-colored, with a long bill and rounded wings. Its dorsal surface is cryptically colored for camouflage, and it usually flushes only at close approach. It has a distinctive flight, going straight up before flying away, thus avoiding tree limbs. American Woodcocks give a twittering sound in flight. When they are displaying, at dusk or dawn along wooded edges in open areas, they give a *bzeep* call from the ground and fly high into the air with twittering notes. At the apex they "sing," then flutter to the ground near the spot where they began. The American Woodcock uses its long bill to probe in moist soil for earthworms. Its eyes are so far back on its head that it can see behind itself.

These woodcocks are early spring migrants, arriving with the first warm southerly winds. They may not be detected, however, unless they are heard calling or seen displaying. Observers must make a special effort at dusk or dawn. Early spring arrival dates: Carbondale, February 1, 1986 (TF-IB&B2:94); Shelby County, February 18, 1983 (KF-AB37:876); Chicago, February 19, 1984 (JL). Average arrival dates: Chicago, March 29 (12 years); west-central, March 8 (12 years). Spring bird count totals ranged from 30 in 1972 to 202 in 1986, with high counts of 25 in Lake County, May 6, 1978; 18 in McHenry County, May 5, 1979; and 29 in Knox County, May 10, 1986 (VK). Dreuth recorded a migrant at Chicago as late as May 24, 1940 (Clark and Nice 1950).

These birds not only arrive early, they also nest early,

and some nests fail because of late snowstorms. They nest on the ground in the woods or near openings. The nest is a hollow lined with plant material. There are three to four buff-colored eggs with brown and gray markings. Illinois egg dates are March 31 to June 12. I have recorded young as early as April 21 at Springfield. The young American Woodcock is a miniature of the adult but with incongruously big feet and bill.

Early fall migration is obscured by the summer populations. Sightings become more frequent in late October and November, probably indicating peak numbers at that time. According to Musselman (1945), "About three miles northeast of Perry, in a creek valley, some two or three hundred woodcock have been having a great time feeding." These birds were present beginning November 13, 1944, and a few stayed until November 26. Woodcocks are usually seen singly; if Musselman's identification is correct, the concentration must have been caused by a peculiar weather pattern and an excellent feeding area. Snipes are more apt than woodcocks to congregate in numbers. Average fall departure dates: west-central, November 8 (nine years); Sangamon County, November 11 (17 years). Late departure dates are usually in mid- to late November. There is a hunting season on this shorebird; in fall 1986, hunters bagged 15,514 American Woodcocks in Illinois (Ellis and Mahan 1987).

There are a few winter records, but it is doubtful that these birds stayed all winter: Crab Orchard National Wildlife Refuge, January 6, 1985 (ABa-AB39:173); Calhoun County, December 19, 1987 (DM); Union County Conservation Area, January 19, 1985 (IB&B2:76); Chicago (Christmas bird count), December 26, 1983 (AB38:642). They were recorded three times on Christmas bird counts for 1976–85. Oddly, four were reported on the Peoria count in 1970. American Woodcocks winter in the southern United States.

WILSON'S PHALAROPE

Phalaropus tricolor

UNCOMMON MIGRANT; RARE SUMMER RESIDENT IN NORTHERN ILLINOIS

The Wilson's Phalarope breeds much farther south (in the interior West) than the other two phalaropes and is not pelagic. It has a longer neck, a larger bill, a white rump and tail, and no wing stripe. Thus it is easily separated from the Red-necked and Red Phalaropes. In fall it looks more like a small yellowlegs. The male-female roles are reversed in this genus, and in spring the females have the brighter plumage. When the Wilson's Phalarope feeds, it moves around quickly, usually picking insects off the surface of the mud; it also swims—usually in shallow water—and spins. These feeding behaviors make it easy to pick out of a crowd, even at long distances.

Since the main migration of this species is to the west of

Illinois, numbers vary considerably from year to year, probably depending on winds. Early spring arrival dates: Lawrence County, March 28, 1985 (GB-AB39:308); Lee County, April 6, 1986 (BSh,LJ-IB&B2:94). Average arrival dates: west-central, May 2 (eight years); Sangamon County, May 2 (15 years). High counts for spring: 39, Crab Orchard National Wildlife Refuge, May 6, 1978 (AB32:1014); 17, Alexander County, May 5, 1984 (TF-SR41:17). Spring bird count totals ranged from none in 1983 to 225 in 1978. Highest count was 45 in Madison County, May 6, 1978 (VK). Average spring departure dates: west-central, May 7 (eight years); Sangamon County, May 22 (13 years). Late departure dates: two, Wabash County, June 1, 1986 (DJo,GB-IB&B2:94); Seaton, June 4, 1983 (MB-SR37:17).

Nelson (1876) said he found these phalaropes nesting about damp prairies and on grassy marshes from May 25 to June 25 in northern Illinois. The eggs—usually four and looking much like Killdeer eggs but with more numerous dark markings—are laid in a depression that is sometimes lined with fine grasses. In the late 1950s and early 1960s and again in 1981, Wilson's Phalaropes nested at Lake Calumet on cinder flats, producing eight flying young by July 26 in 1981. But deteriorating conditions at Lake Calumet and degradation of prairie wetlands in general in Illinois have placed this shorebird on the state's endangered species list. Adults have been seen at several other places in northern and central Illinois in summer, but nesting has not been proven.

Wilson's Phalaropes migrate early in the fall. Earliest dates: Horseshoe Lake, July 1, 1984 (DB-IB&B1:20); Springfield, June 30, 1986 (HDB); Arcola, July 4, 1987 (RCh). Average arrival dates for fall: west-central, August 13 (six years); Sangamon County, July 22 (14 years). High counts: 30, Lake Calumet, August 18, 1979 (JL-AB34:168); 22, Chautauqua National Wildlife Refuge, August 30, 1984 (KR-AB39:61). Average departure dates: west-central, September 1 (six years); Sangamon County, September 13 (10 years). Late departure dates: Peoria, October 16, 1981 (LA-SR31:10); Chautauqua refuge, October 16, 1983 (LA-SR39:16); Chicago, October 12, 1985 (JL-IB&B2:51). This phalarope winters principally in western South America.

RED-NECKED PHALAROPE

Phalaropus lobatus

RARE SPRING AND OCCASIONAL FALL MIGRANT

This essentially pelagic shorebird is able to land on the surface of the water and swim. Its breeding range is circumpolar, and it comes inland to Illinois only during migration between the Arctic and the Atlantic and Pacific Oceans. The Red-necked, the smallest of the three phalaropes, has a needlelike bill. Its flight is erratic and its call is *krit*. The females are more brightly colored than the males. Phalaropes have a distinct method of feeding: they spin in the water and pick food off the surface. A female collected off a puddle north of Springfield on May 22, 1977, had a gizzard full of Coleoptera of the Hydrophilidae family.

Spring migrants usually do not arrive until mid-May: Lawrence County, May 15, 1980 (LH-SR25:6); Bureau County, May 16, 1980 (JH-SR25:6); Jacksonville, May 11, 1974 (WO,PW). The average arrival date for central Illinois is May 21 (four years). These phalaropes were recorded on spring bird counts only two years, in low numbers and on very early dates: two, Ogle County, May 9, 1981; De Kalb County, May 5, 1984 (VK). The spring maximum was six in Whiteside County, May 19, 1979 (BSh-AB33:777). Late departures for spring: Round Lake, May 28, 1979 (RB-AB33:777); Springfield, June 1, 1986 (HDB,TT); two, Meredosia, May 23, 1983 (TW-SR37:17).

Most fall Red-necks apparently are juveniles, but observers should try to determine the ages of more of these birds at this season to be sure. The earliest fall arrivals are in July: three, Lake Calumet, July 26, 1981 (JL); Horseshoe Lake, July 26-31, 1980 (PS-SR27:8). The average arrival date for central Illinois is August 25 (13 years). More regular in fall than in spring, the Red-necked Phalarope is most numerous in September. Maximum fall counts: 26, Chautauqua National Wildlife Refuge, August 30, 1984 (KR-IB&B1:20); 13, Rice Lake, September 3, 1986 (TP-AB41:96); nine, Banner, September 28, 1985 (RP-AB40:120); nine, Evanston, September 3, 1973 (LB,GR-AB28:61). Fall migrants are usually seen in shallow water just off the mudflats, but they also land on the deeper water of lakes and sewage ponds. The average fall departure for central Illinois is September 19 (seven years). Late departure dates: three, East St. Louis, October 11, 1978 (RA-AB33:183); two, McGinnis Slough, October 22, 1939 (Boulton and Beecher 1940); Palos, October 22, 1984 (JM-IB&B1:20); Lock 13, Whiteside County, November 13, 1970 (Shaws-IAB157:28). The Red-necked Phalarope winters at sea.

RED PHALAROPE

Phalaropus fulicaria

VERY RARE SPRING AND RARE FALL MIGRANT

Of the three phalaropes, the Red is the most pelagic and the least numerous in Illinois. It looks most like the Red-necked Phalarope but plumper, with a grayer and less streaked back and a thicker bill. Occasionally Red Phalaropes are seen on mudflats. But they swim more than the other phalaropes and are found more often on the open, deeper water of lakes, sewage lagoons, and ponds. I sometimes see one swimming in the middle of Lake Springfield. They fly off erratically for a while and then land on the water again. At such great distances they are easily missed. Observers should look carefully for them on lakes at the correct seasons.

There are apparently only two spring records, and both lack documentation: one hit by a car near Salem, April 30, 1970 (W.Jones-IAB155:16), and a female in breeding plumage at Lyndon, May 25, 1971 (BSh-AB25:752).

Fall migration is usually late, though there are a few early records: Lake Calumet, September 8, 1987 (JL); adult female, Lake Calumet, July 23, 1949 (Ford 1956); male specimen, north of Waukegan, September 10, 1938 (Pitelka 1938a); Havana, September 14-15, 1985 (RP-AB40:120). These early birds must have been adults, since the adults migrate before the immature birds. Red Phalaropes have occurred in Illinois only as singles; no flocks have been recorded. Most records are for late September, October, and November. Some recent records: Horseshoe Lake, October 1-3, 1977 (BR,PS-AB32:212); Waukegan, November 24-28, 1978 (LB,JN-AB33:183); Baldwin Lake, September 21, 1980 (RK-AB35:189); Banner, October 2-5, 1985 (RS-AB40:120). The latest record is for Frank Holten State Park, December 27, 1952 (AFN7:135). The Red Phalarope winters at sea.

POMARINE JAEGER

Stercorarius pomarinus

RARE FALL MIGRANT

When an immature Pomarine Jaeger arrived at Lake Springfield and stayed around from September 7 to 12, 1983, it chased off most of the gulls. It spent much of its time either sitting on the water or chasing other birds—not only gulls but also terns, crows, and even an Osprey and a Barn Swallow. Another Pomarine at Alton Dam, November 7-9, 1979 (BR-AB34:168), actually flew above some gulls and knocked them into the water. Sometimes these jaegers alternate between sitting on the water and catching their own fish. They look like dark gulls on the water with their long wings sticking up over the back. Other recent records: Wilmette, September 17, 1978 (AB33:183); one photographed, Olney, November 9-11, 1979 (LH-AB34:168); third-year bird, Alton, July 9-12, 1981 (YB-AB35:945); immature dark phase, Carlyle Lake, November 18–December 2, 1982 (BR,RG-AB37:187); Chicago, October 6, 1983 (JL); Crab Orchard National Wildlife Refuge, December 18, 1982 (MM-SR36:7); Glencoe, October 14, 1974 (GR,RR); adult near Kampsville, August 31, 1962 (Starett); two, Carlyle Lake, November 10-17, 1985, with one lingering until November 20 (LH,RG-IB&B2:51). Two early records: an adult seen near Chicago, October 9, 1876 (Nelson 1876), and one off Lincoln Park, Chicago, October 16, 1921 (Sanborn 1922). A distal portion of a left humerus of a Pomarine Jaeger was found in a Fulton County Middle Mississippian site dated about A.D. 1100-1250 (Parmalee and Speth 1981). The Pomarine Jaeger breeds in the Arctic and winters at sea. Because jaegers are difficult to identify, photographs should be taken whenever possible and complete descriptions made on the spot.

PARASITIC JAEGER

Stercorarius parasiticus

RARE FALL MIGRANT

Though Parasitic Jaegers are more numerous than the two other jaegers found in Illinois, they are still rare. They are seen regularly along Lake Michigan in fall, but there are no verified spring records. These agile and fast "sea hawks" streak in to harass gulls and terns, trying to make them drop their food so the jaegers can pluck it out of midair. The best spots to watch for these birds along Lake Michigan are Gillson pier, Northwestern landfill, Montrose, and Illinois Beach State Park. They also appear, though unpredictably, on large rivers and lakes downstate, most notably at Carlyle Lake and Chautauqua National Wildlife Refuge. Most of the Parasitic Jaegers seen in Illinois are immatures, in either the light or the dark phase. The difficulties in identifying these birds are legendary. Usually they are flybys and it is difficult to get good views of the tail feathers and other field marks. Several books and articles have been written on identification, including Harrison (1983) and Olsen and Christensen (1984).

Most Parasitic Jaegers are seen in October and November in Illinois, but a few have occurred in September and one record is for December. Early and late records: Chicago, September 9, 1972 (RR-AB27:68); two, Evanston, September 17, 1978 (RB-AB33:183); Lake Clinton, September 22, 1984 (RCh-IB&B1:20); Chicago, December 23, 1973 (Mlodinow 1984). High counts are all from Lake Michigan: nine, Wilmette, October 25, 1986 (JL); five, Evanston, October 14, 1974 (LB). Several specimens have been taken: one along the Mississippi River near Keokuk, Iowa, October 6, 1896 (Praeger 1925); one off Chicago, November 5, 1922 (Ford 1956); three off Chicago, October 29, 1926 (Eifrig 1927); one somehow hit by a car, Lake Calumet, October 27, 1976 (LB-IAB180:44). The Parasitic Jaeger breeds in the Arctic and winters at sea.

LONG-TAILED JAEGER

Stercorarius longicaudus

VERY RARE FALL MIGRANT

The first of only two Illinois records of the Long-tailed Jaeger is of a decayed bird picked up on the shore of the Mississippi River at Cairo in November 1876. Unfortunately the skeleton was not kept and we are left to ponder whether W. H. Ballou made a correct identification (Ridgway 1889). The other record comes from a mounted immature specimen now at Southern Illinois University at Carbondale that was collected at Nashville, Washington County, on October 21, 1893. The Long-tailed is the smallest of the jaegers, but immatures are difficult to separate from the other species even at close range. It breeds in the Arctic and winters at sea. Although there are several inland records, it is considered the most pelagic of the three jaegers.

GREAT SKUA

Catharacta skua

HYPOTHETICAL

Ridgway (1895) listed this oceanic species as accidental in Illinois, but he gave no justification of this status. The American Ornithologists' Union (1983) lists the Great Skua as accidental in Missouri and the New York–Ontario region.

LAUGHING GULL

Larus atricilla

RARE MIGRANT

Cooke (1888) noted of this coastal species that "a few pass up the Mississippi during the summer as far as southern Illinois." Ridgway also suggested that this gull was present in Illinois, but later (1895) he stated that it may not have been, adding: "Franklin's Gull have been mistaken for it?" At any rate no specific records were listed until the careful observer Dreuth saw a Laughing Gull at Lincoln Park, Chicago, on August 30, 1935 (Clark and Nice 1950). I took a specimen of an adult male at Lake Springfield on May 27, 1971 (ISM#604789). It remains the only specimen record for Illinois. With well over 60 records, however, this species' occurrence is increasing in Illinois, for reasons unknown.

Apparently Laughing Gulls migrate up the Mississippi Valley to Illinois in the spring, although they also show up in eastern Illinois, perhaps following the Ohio, Kaskaskia, or Illinois River. Laughing Gulls arrive in late April, May, or even June. The earliest date for spring is April 16, 1972, at Montrose Harbor, Chicago (LB,CC,GR-AB26:767). At least 21 published records for spring include Lake Baldwin, April 18, 1978 (RA- AB32:1015); three, Waukegan, May 14, 1978 (JN-AB32:1015); two, Macoupin County, May 10, 1980 (MSt-AB34:782); three, Rend Lake, May 16–17, 1986 (DR,TF-AB40:478); and six, the maximum count for spring, Monroe County, April 27, 1973 (KW-AB27:779). Laughing Gulls associate with gulls of other species and are found on beaches and sandbars, at lakes, and along rivers.

Some of these gulls stay all summer. Nesting seems imminent, since an attempt was noted at Lake Erie (Tranaer and Campbell 1986). Of 14 published records for June and July, all are in the north and central parts of the state, including five, the maximum count for summer, Nauvoo, June 12, 1971 (JF-AB25:864); three, Chicago, June 21–July 7, 1981 (AB35:945); Urbana, July 28, 1981 (RCh-AB35:945); two adults, Springfield, July 10, 1985 (HDB);

Barrington, June 8, 1948 (Smith and Parmalee 1955). Some Laughing Gulls in juvenile plumage appear in August, perhaps as a result of the dispersal of the young of the year.

Fall has brought at least 29 records, ranging from August 4 to November 20. Most of these gulls apparently leave the state in September and October, but there are also some November records: Evanston, mid-November 1965 (JW,RR-AFN20:54); Chicago, November 18, 1972 (LB,GR-AB27:69); three, Alton Dam, September 8–9, 1985 (PS-AB40:120); Carlyle Lake, November 20, 1985 (BR-AB40:120); five, the maximum fall count, Clinton Lake, August 30, 1986 (RCh-AB41:96). Two records for December are probably of very late migrants rather than wintering gulls: immature, Lake Springfield, December 13–22, 1980 (HDB); adult, Chautauqua National Wildlife Refuge, December 28, 1986 (HDB).

Although the Laughing Gull is similar to the Franklin's Gull, it is larger and has a longer bill that is usually somewhat downturned. In winter or immature plumage it has less black on its head. Its tail can be used as an indicator of age: completely banded the first year, partially banded the second year, and all white in adults. In spring, of course, adults lack the white separating the black tip from the gray upper wing. Goetz (1983) gives more aids to identification.

FRANKLIN'S GULL

Larus pipixcan

OCCASIONAL SPRING AND UNCOMMON FALL MIGRANT

Of the two medium-sized hooded gulls, this one is most likely to be seen in Illinois. Franklin's Gulls breed in the northern interior west of the Mississippi River, and most of them migrate through the Great Plains.

Spring arrival times vary, probably depending on winds. When these gulls arrive early (late March to mid-April), they are mostly breeding adults with a rosy blush on their breasts. If strong westerlies blow later, immatures (nonbreeders) straggle through from May to early June. Some years bring influxes of both adults and immatures; other years there are few if any of these "prairie doves." Early spring arrival dates: Horseshoe Lake, March 13, 1987 (RG); Wilmette, March 24, 1963 (RR-AFN17:408); two, Lake Springfield, March 27, 1975 (HDB). Maximum counts for spring are lower than for fall, although a few counts are atypical: 48, Lake Springfield, May 17, 1986 (HDB); 125, Keokuk, May 19, 1986 (RCe-AB40:479). Franklin's Gulls are scarcer farther north: seven, Chicago, June 1981 (RB,JL-SR30:8). They can be found on lakes and along rivers but even more often at extensive mudflat areas and flooded fields. They follow the plow in spring, though rarely in fall. A few spring migrants, usually immatures, sometimes straggle into summer: two, Lake Springfield, July

4, 1977 (HDB); one or two at five Illinois locations, June or July 1980 (AB34:900).

As early as July wandering adult or immature Franklin's Gulls start arriving in Illinois: seven, Waukegan, July 27, 1977 (Mlodinow 1984); adult, Lake Springfield, July 21, 1982 (HDB); adult, Elsah, July 22, 1986 (RG); first-year bird, Lake Springfield, August 2, 1986 (HDB). Fall migration reaches its peak in mid-October and early November when pure flocks of Franklin's Gulls stop by lakes, principally in central Illinois: 100, Mark Twain National Wildlife Refuge, mid-October 1978 (RA-AB33:183); 24, Chicago, October 20, 1982 (PC,HR-AB37:187); 80, Lake Springfield, November 10, 1983 (HDB); 62, Clinton Lake, October 20, 1984 (RCh-AB39:61); 150, Havana, October 19, 1985 (RP-AB40:120); 100, Carlyle Lake, October 25, 1985 (BR-AB40:120). Fall migration also varies with the weather. Big flocks usually arrive with or precede a cold front and stay only briefly before moving on. When they settle on a lake and rest, they stay in a compact flock; many times they do not attempt to feed. Some Franklin's may stay on for a few days, but by mid- to late November almost all are gone. Late departure dates: Lake Springfield, November 28, 1983, and December 2, 1977 (HDB).

There are a few winter records: Chicago, December 26, 1959 (Huxford-AFN14:202); adult, Lake Springfield, December 23, 1975, to January 6, 1976 (WO,D.Allyn); specimen, Orion, December 15, 1960 (ISM); adult, Hamilton, January 16–17, 1987 (VK,RCe). The Franklin's, one of the most migratory of our gulls, usually winters along the Pacific coast of South America south to Chile.

LITTLE GULL

Larus minutus

RARE MIGRANT ALONG LAKE MICHIGAN
AND VERY RARE ELSEWHERE IN THE STATE

An Old World species that recently colonized North America, the Little Gull, oddly enough, chose the Great Lakes region. It breeds only in Wisconsin, Michigan, Ontario, and Churchill, Manitoba. It follows an essentially east-west migration route, wintering along the Atlantic Coast. In Illinois it is usually found in harbors and along Lake Michigan. Downstate records are few. It is often seen with Bonaparte's Gulls, which it closely resembles. The adult Little Gull, however, has dark underwings, with wing tips that are more rounded than the Bonaparte's and lack the white wedge and black border. Immature Little Gulls, more difficult to separate, have a black M on the wings and a dark cap (see Grant 1986 for details). The first Illinois Little Gull was recorded in spring, at Lincoln Park, Chicago, April 29, 1938 (Boulton and Pitelka 1938). But fall records are more numerous. These gulls arrive fairly early some autumns: Chicago, August 30, 1978 (LB-AB33:183); Waukegan, August 14, 1985 (RB,MBi-IB&B2:52). They are more regular in late October and November, sometimes

staying into December and even early January. Recent fall records: six to eight, Chicago, December 25, 1979 (RB,SM-AB34:278), with some staying until January 6, 1980; three, Chicago, until December 19, 1984 (AB39:173); Waukegan, October 29, 1985 (RB,MBi-IB&B2:52); three, Zion, November 26, 1983 (TP-SR39:16). Given the right conditions, this species may occasionally winter; one was at Zion on February 14, 1981 (JN-SR28:5).

Most spring migrants arrive in April: Jackson Park, April 2-3, 1986 (HR-IB&B2:94); Chicago, April 8-9, 1983 (RDe-SR37:17); Waukegan, April 25, 1985 (RB,MBi-IB&B1:87). Late spring dates are in May: Chicago, May 18–19, 1981 (RB,JL-AB35:830); Chicago, May 28, 1942 (Clark and Nice 1950). The few inland and downstate records include Frank Holten State Park, November 14 and 15, 1962 (RA-AFN17:37); Crab Orchard National Wildlife Refuge, April 9, 1976 (BP-AB30:849); Barrington, December 26, 1982–January 2, 1983 (CW-AB37:307); Carlyle Lake, April 18 and 24, 1984 (SRu-AB38:918); Decatur, November 29, 1985 (RS,RP-AB40:120); Carlyle Lake, October 23–30, 1987 (RG).

COMMON BLACK-HEADED GULL

Larus ridibundus

VERY RARE VAGRANT

This Old World species, which is most similar to the Bonaparte's Gull, has recently colonized North America. The first breeding record for the New World was in Newfoundland in 1977. The Common Black-headed Gull was first recorded in Illinois at Quiver Lake, February 10, 1973 (Bohlen and Kleen 1973-74). Nine other Illinois records since that time show no regular pattern: Chicago, July 15, 1976 (LB); Evanston, September 29, 1978 (GR-AB33:183); Waukegan, June 1–3, 1981 (GR-AB35:830); Chicago, October 24, 1981 (JL-AB36:184); Chicago, May 5, 1982 (RG,PC-AB36:859); Evanston, July 2, 1982 (SM-SR34:6); Horseshoe Lake, December 4, 1985–January 4, 1986 (BR,RG-AB40:287); Crab Orchard National Wildlife Refuge, December 13, 1987 (R.Danley,DR); Alton, September 10–22, 1988 (DB,J.Cook). Found with other gulls on lakes and rivers, the Black-headed is separated from the Bonaparte's Gull by its dark underprimaries, light-colored bill, larger size, and heavier flight.

BONAPARTE'S GULL

Larus philadelphia

COMMON MIGRANT, UNCOMMON WINTER
RESIDENT, AND RARE NONBREEDING
SUMMER RESIDENT

This is the most common small hooded gull in Illinois. Bonaparte's Gulls are dainty, almost ternlike, and adults can be identified at any distance by a white wedge in the outer wing. Many times Bonaparte's feed in flocks, hovering just above the water, with a bird now and then hitting the water to come up with a fish. Sometimes they are quite noisy, giving a nasal *cherr.* They nest in old birds' nests in open coniferous forests. In Illinois they sometimes land on wires or posts, but they are usually seen on mudflats or sandbars or in tight flocks on lakes. They are most numerous along Lake Michigan.

Returning south in fall, the Bonaparte's Gull is usually in winter plumage, which lacks the black hood. Some years a few return early, even in July or August: eight, Chicago, July 30, 1983 (JL); two, Rice Lake, August 28, 1986 (TP-IB&B3:40); five, Illinois Beach State Park, July 25, 1987 (JN); Hartford, August 13, 1983 (RG). The mass movement occurs in October and November. Average fall arrival dates: Chicago, August 2 (16 years); Sangamon County, September 25 (17 years). High counts for fall: 3100, Wilmette, December 10, 1983 (AA-SR39:16); 2000, Chicago, November 27, 1980 (RB-SR27:8); 500, Carlyle Lake, December 9, 1983 (RG); 500, La Salle County, November 10, 1985 (JM,JH-IB&B2:52). Average departure dates: Chicago, December 11 (16 years); Sangamon County, December 19 (12 years). Some Bonaparte's leave as late as mid-January; 140 were at Baldwin Lake on January 3, 1988 (RG), but all were gone by January 9.

This small gull does not like ice and rarely stands on it with other gulls. If there is a large amount of open water, it will attempt to winter. Its main wintering area is Lake Michigan, since downstate lakes usually freeze sometime in December or January. Christmas bird counts are probably early enough to reflect late migrants. Totals for 1976–85 counts ranged from eight in 1977 to 1520 in 1979. The highest count was 1000 at Waukegan in 1942. Few of these birds stay all winter. Most winter south to the Gulf and into Mexico.

A few spring migrants arrive as the ice is retreating, but most Bonaparte's arrive in late March and April, when they are in full breeding plumage. Early spring arrival dates: two, Crab Orchard National Wildlife Refuge, February 28, 1986 (DR-IB&B2:94); Clinton Lake, February 21, 1987 (RCh). Average arrival dates: Chicago, March 31 (16 years); Sangamon County, March 22 (17 years). High counts for spring: 1230, Chicago, April 18, 1984 (RE-SR41:18); 270, Crab Orchard refuge, April 11, 1984 (JR-SR41:18); 120, Spring Lake, April 20, 1986 (TP-IB&B2:94). Spring bird counts, though taken past the peak for the Bonaparte's, showed totals ranging from 20 in 1986 to 3712 in 1974. All high counts were in Cook and Lake Counties (VK). Average spring departure dates: Chicago, May 26 (16 years); Sangamon County, May 8 (17 years).

Some of these gulls, nonbreeders, stay into summer. Nelson (1876) said they sat in the summer on fishermen's stakes half a mile from the Lake Michigan shore. Summer records: seven, Waukegan, 1978 (AB32:1169); 11, Chicago, June 26, 1982 (JL); Springfield, June 20–July 3, 1979 (HDB).

MEW GULL
Larus canus
VERY RARE VAGRANT

The Mew Gull looks much like the Ring-billed Gull in all plumages. It breeds in western Canada and Alaska and winters along the West Coast. With only four records for Illinois, all in the 1980s, this gull must have been overlooked in the past even though it is very rare. Illinois records: Moline, December 19–31, 1982 (PP-SR36:7); Rend Lake, October 7, 1984 (DJo,LH-IB&B1:20); Carlyle Lake, February 12–March 8, 1986 (BR-IB&B2:76); Chicago, April 11, 1987 (LB,JL). The subspecies recorded in Illinois is *L. c. brachyrhynchus,*, but the East Coast species, *L. c. canus,* apparently could also occur. Lauro and Spencer (1980) discuss identification of immature Mew Gulls.

RING-BILLED GULL
Larus delawarensis
COMMON MIGRANT AND WINTER RESIDENT;
RARE SUMMER RESIDENT

The Ring-billed Gull has yellow legs and a dark mark across the bill. It is smaller and somewhat less hardy than the Herring Gull, and because it takes less time to reach maturity it has fewer plumages for the observer to deal with. The Ring-billed nevertheless shows much variation, and occasionally albinistic birds are seen: Montrose Harbor, December 15–30, 1984 (JL); Springfield, November 17–28, 1984 (HDB). In spring many Ring-billed Gulls show a rosy blush on their breast. These gulls can be seen wherever there is water, including lakes, rivers, and flooded fields. They also follow the plow and frequent garbage dumps, airports, and golf courses. They roost on lakes and fly out daily—sometimes considerable distances—to feed in fields. They stay around lakes that have kills of shad and other rough fish. They also need resting areas such as sandbars, islands, and mudflats. Lakes lacking these refinements usually have far fewer gulls.

Fall migration begins fairly early, although a few of these birds seen at various localities could be summering immatures. Early arrivals: Springfield, June 21, 1983 (adults) and July 27 (immatures); two, Madison County, July 4, 1985 (JR-IB&B2:52); Henderson County, July 20, 1985 (MB-IB&B2:52); 64, Chautauqua National Wildlife Refuge, July 6, 1984 (KR-IB&B1:20). Average fall arrival dates: Chicago, August 30 (16 years); west-central, August 23 (nine years); Sangamon County, August 2 (17 years). High counts for fall: 5000, Springfield, November 25–26, 1983 (HDB); 4000, Carlyle Lake, December 8–13, 1983 (BR-SR39:17); 1000, Horseshoe Lake, November 30, 1985 (IB&B2:52); 1200, Chautauqua refuge, September 19, 1984 (SB-IB&B1:20); 1000, Peoria, October 2–3, 1981 (MSw-SR31:11). Dreuth gives November 30 (16 years) as the average departure date for Chicago. Like other gulls in winter, the Ring-billed fluctuates in numbers depending on the severity of the weather. Many Ring-bills go farther south in midwinter, only to return on the heels of the melting ice. Christmas bird count totals for 1976–85 ranged from 1865 in 1985 to 11,505 in 1981. The highest count was 12,000 at Peoria in 1967. Other high counts for winter: 4000, Mississippi River from Alton to Grafton, January 6, 1985 (RG,PS-IB&B1:68); 1000, Crab Orchard National Wildlife Refuge, January 31, 1987 (DR); 3000, Carlyle Lake, December 15, 1982 (RG,PS-SR36:7).

Average arrival dates for spring: Chicago, March 16 (13 years); west-central, March 8 (10 years); Sangamon County, February 17 (12 years). It is often difficult to distinguish spring migrants from wintering birds. To do so, numbers must be monitored daily. Spring high counts: 2500, Carlyle Lake, March 25, 1983 (BR,RG-SR37:17); 5000, Decatur, March 5, 1986 (RP-IB&B2:94); 5000, Crab Orchard refuge, March 1, 1986 (DR-IB&B2:94); 3000, New Boston, March 29, 1985 (MB-IB&B1:87). Though spring bird counts are done past the peak for the Ring-billed Gull, totals ranged from 326 in 1973 to 9092 in 1985. Most high counts came from Cook County, with the highest 7682 on May 4, 1985 (VK). The average departure date for Sangamon County is May 25 (14 years).

The Ring-billed Gull was first found breeding in Illinois at Lake Calumet on July 6, 1975. Some 800 birds, including 71 young, were counted. This colony continued to grow yearly, with several thousand individuals there by 1987. Nesting occurred at La Salle in spring 1979 (JH-AB33:777). At least four nests were found at Waukegan, June 11, 1981 (WS-SR30:8). Eight fledglings were at Starved Rock State Park, June 29–July 8, 1985 (JMc-IB&B2:14). Other summer records: two, Lake Shelbyville, summer 1983 (KF-SR38:8); 17, Rend Lake, summer 1986 (DR-IB&B3:14); 19, Marshall County, June 4, 1982 (MSw-SR34:7); 11, East St. Louis, June 29, 1980 (RA-SR26:7). Ring-billed Gulls will probably continue to increase in Illinois as summer residents.

CALIFORNIA GULL

Larus californicus

RARE VAGRANT

As Illinois birders become more sophisticated, optical devices more powerful, and field guides more accurate, the California Gull becomes more numerous. Adult Californias are not especially difficult to identify if the observer looks for a back that is somewhat darker than Ring-billed Gulls' backs, red on the bill, dark eyes, and greenish yellow legs. Immatures are much more difficult, since they take three years to reach adult plumage, with identifiable first-year, second-year, and third-year plumages in between (see Grant 1986).

The first California Gull in Illinois was recorded at Jack-son Park the first week in March 1940, but it was not well documented (Lewy, *Bird-Lore*, May-June 1940). The second record was not added until a first-year bird was seen at Chicago, October 26, 1974 (LB,GR,LC). Nine more records were accumulated between 1980 and 1987, with fall dates ranging from July 9 (1985, Springfield, HDB) to November 13 (1981, East Alton, BR-AB36:184) and spring dates ranging from February 24 (1985, Rend Lake, DJo-AB39:173) to March 8 (1987, Rice Lake, LA,TP,KR). In spring California Gulls fly east from their winter quarters on the Pacific Coast to breed inland. Those seen in Illinois may be individuals that overshoot their breeding range. The fall Californias are probably vagrants going in the wrong direction. Other recent records: East Alton, October 17–30, 1981 (BR-AB36:184); Alton, October 31, 1982 (RG,PS-AB37:187); Springfield, July 30–31, 1985 (HDB); Alton, October 4, 1986 (RA-IB&B3:40). Jehl (1987) pointed out that this species has two races: the small, dark-mantled *L. c. californicus*, which breeds in the Great Basin, and the larger, paler *L. c. albertaensis*, which breeds in the northern United States and south-central Canada. They have about equal chance of vagrancy in Illinois, but perhaps at different seasons.

HERRING GULL

Larus argentatus

COMMON MIGRANT AND WINTER RESIDENT; RARE SUMMER RESIDENT

To the beginning observer, all "sea gulls" may look alike, but the student of gulls knows that there is not only a great diversity among species but also a great variety in plumages within species. The Herring Gull exemplifies this variety, taking four years or more of changing plumages to reach maturity (see Grant 1986). These gulls are most abundant in Illinois along Lake Michigan and the larger rivers and lakes. They also frequent garbage dumps and flooded fields. They form flocks at night and roost on the water, often in association with ducks and geese. Although Herring Gulls take a lot of fish, especially shad, they will eat almost anything. I have seen them kill and eat ducks, usually weak and sick ones. They dominate and take food away from smaller gulls and also squabble among themselves. The subspecies found in Illinois is *L. a. smithsonianus*.

The Herring Gull migration is regulated by ice conditions. These birds need both ice to rest on and open water for feeding. In the absence of either condition they move on. In some mild years few are seen in southern Illinois. Herring Gulls also move around with alternating periods of ice buildup and warming during winter. Some arrive very early in fall: Springfield, July 7, 1984 (HDB); Channahon, July 1, 1985 (JM-IB&B2:52); two, Chautauqua National Wildlife Refuge, July 20, 1985 (KR-IB&B2:52). Average fall arrivals: west-central, September 2 (10 years);

Sangamon County, August 31 (18 years). Most Herring Gulls do not arrive until November or later, depending on the weather. High counts for fall: 450, Chicago, July 19, 1981 (JL-SR31:11); 100, Alton, November 28, 1983 (RG-SR39:17); 5000, Lake Calumet, September 20, 1984 (JL); 200, Decatur, November 24, 1985 (RP-IB&B2:52).

Total numbers on Christmas bird counts for 1976-85 ranged from 6121 in 1982 to 17,897 in 1978. Highest count was 10,890 at Peoria in 1978. Other high counts for winter: 4500, Madison County, December 26-January 7, 1986 (RG-IB&B2:76); 5000, Lake Calumet, winter 1980-81 (JL); 1000, Pekin, December 15, 1984 (LA-IB&B1:68).

Most of these gulls go north fairly early as the ice breaks up. Later birds are usually immatures that have wintered farther south than the adults. Average departure dates for the few stragglers: west-central, March 30 (nine years); Sangamon County, May 1 (17 years). Late departure dates: two, Springfield, June 5, 1982 (HDB); Alexander County, May 26, 1984 (JR,TF-SR41:18); Rend Lake, May 30, 1987 (TF). Spring bird counts are much past the peak for this winter species. Totals ranged from 172 in 1976 to 5810 in 1986, with 4869 at Cook County in the latter year (VK).

Even in the early years Herring Gulls summered in the Chicago area (Nelson 1876), but it was not until 1976 that the first nesting attempt was recorded, at Lake Calumet. The first successful nesting there was in 1978, with three nests. Then the numbers soared to 600-700 birds by summer 1985. Other nest sites: Baker Lake (two pairs), Crabtree Nature Center (one pair), and Palos. Birds summering in other areas are nonbreeders: 16, Lockport area, June 7-July 13, 1985 (JM-IB&B2:14); immature, Dallas City, June 21, 1985 (VK-IB&B2:14); adult, Springfield, June 19, 1978 (HDB); two, Moline, summer 1982 (PP-SR34:7).

THAYER'S GULL

Larus thayeri

OCCASIONAL MIGRANT AND WINTER RESIDENT

This bird epitomizes the significance that a shade of difference can make in gull identification. Richard Sandburg and I watched an immature gull for two days in December 1974 before deciding it was indeed a Thayer's Gull. The Thayer's plumages closely parallel the Herring Gull's, but the Thayer's is smaller than the Herring and has lighter wingtips, darker eyes, and a notably smaller bill. Several papers have been written on identification of this gull, including Gosselin and David (1975) and Lehman (1980 and 1983). The first Illinois specimen of a Thayer's Gull was taken at Chicago on March 27, 1876 (Dwight 1925). In the intervening years this gull has had a checkered nomenclatural career. Since 1973 it has been considered a full species closely related to the Herring Gull, but recently it was found to interbreed with the "Kumlien's" Gull (AOU 1983). Landing (1985) gives a history of this species in Illinois.

The earliest fall Thayer's Gulls arrive in October: Chautauqua National Wildlife Refuge, October 6, 1984 (LA-IB&B1:20); Madison County, October 21, 1981 (BR-SR31:11); Lake Calumet, October 17, 1984 (JL). Most arrive in November. High counts into winter: nine, Chicago area, January 24, 1987 (JL); nine, Alton, winter 1985-86 (AB40:287); 16 between St. Louis and Alton, winter 1983-84 (RG-AB38:323); six, Peoria, December 28-February 2, 1982 (MSw-AB36:300). Late departure dates in spring: immature, Waukegan, May 21, 1986 (RB,LBi-AB40:479); two, Chicago, April 30, 1986 (JL,CM).

These gulls seem to choose the same sites every year: at Lake Michigan, the Illinois and the Mississippi Rivers, and to a lesser extent some of the larger reservoirs. Records away from these areas include Union County, December 30, 1977 (HDB); Lawrence County, March 18, 1987 (DJo); and Crab Orchard National Wildlife Refuge, January 31, 1987 (DR-IB&B3:68). Thayer's Gulls breed in the Arctic and winter primarily on the Pacific Coast.

ICELAND GULL

Larus glaucoides

RARE MIGRANT AND WINTER RESIDENT

Taxonomically, the Iceland Gull remains an enigma. Its plumages parallel those of the Glaucous Gull, but the Iceland has two forms: the nominate *L. g. glaucoides*, which breeds on coastal Greenland, and *L. g. kumlieni*, which has darker markings in the wingtip and breeds in northeast Canada. Most Iceland Gulls seen in Illinois are the latter form, the "Kumlien's." Some authorities think the "Kumlien's" and the Thayer's Gull may be conspecific. There is still more cause for confusion: albinistic birds and possible hybrids. At any rate, the Iceland Gull, perhaps in both forms, occurs in Illinois mostly along Lake Michigan and the Illinois and Mississippi Rivers, seldom on downstate lakes. Apparently there are no records of this gull south of East St. Louis in Illinois. It is on the hypothetical list for Kentucky (Mengel 1965). Iceland Gulls usually appear with flights of Herring Gulls during cold Arctic blasts and are most easily found at periods of maximum ice. Sometimes Icelands frequent garbage dumps with other gulls. Given the good possibility of confusion with Glaucous and Thayer's Gulls, observers should take great care in identification (see Grant 1986 for clarification).

Early arrival dates in fall: Illinois Beach State Park, November 15, 1987 (JN); Alton Dam, November 19, 1980 (TB,RK-AB35:189); Chicago, November 16, 1986 (JL). Most Icelands arrive in December or January and some as late as February, which is not unusual for northeastern species, such as Great Black-backed Gulls and eiders. The maximum count for Iceland Gulls is six at Waukegan, April 22-23, 1978—although this date seems very late (JN-AB32:1015). Most of these gulls are seen singly. Records for "Kumlien's" Gulls include Chicago, January 5, 1985 (DJ-IB&B1:68); Lake Calumet, February 5, 1987 (JL); and

Alton, January 21–22 and 29, 1984 (BR,RG-SR40:9). Most Icelands depart by March. Late departure dates: Waukegan, May 15, 1978 (JN-AB 32:1015); Chicago, May 21, 1982 (JL). All late records should be examined with care, as many gulls at this time show very worn primaries that make misidentifications easy.

LESSER BLACK-BACKED GULL

Larus fuscus

RARE MIGRANT AND WINTER RESIDENT

Considering that the Lesser Black-backed Gull went unrecorded in Illinois until 1980, there has been a veritable explosion of sightings during this decade, with 18 acceptable records by the end of 1987. This European species, which is increasing its numbers in North America, has three recognized subspecies. The main one occurring in Illinois is *L. f. graellsii*, which has a dark gray mantle. *L. f. fuscus* and *L. f. intermedius* have also been recorded in North America and could eventually occur in Illinois.

The first Illinois record was of an adult at Chicago, April 27–28, 1980 (PC-AB34:782). The range of dates for records is October 6 (1984, Chautauqua National Wildlife Refuge, LA,MB-AB39:61) to April 28. There are two definite winter records: Dolton, January 5, 1985 (RB,MBi-AB39:173), and Carlyle Lake, December 30–January 6, 1987 (BR-AB41:288). Most records are for November, December, and February, suggesting that they are of late fall and early spring migrants. A sampling of other recent records: Quad City, February 6–16, 1987 (PP-AB41:288); Springfield, November 16, 1987 (HDB); Decatur, November 24–December 14, 1983 (RS); Granite City, December 30–31, 1980 (AB35:305).

SLATY-BACKED GULL

Larus schistisagus

VERY RARE VAGRANT

The occurrence of this Asian gull was one of the most unexpected events in Illinois birding history. In the wake of a blast of arctic air known as the Siberian express, a Slaty-backed was found near Lock 27 on the Mississippi River on December 20, 1983. It stayed along a 19-mile stretch of the river until January 29, 1984. Viewed by nearly 1000 birders from 24 states, it was also photographed many times. Slaty-backed Gulls are fairly large, dark mantled, light eyed, and pink legged, with a distinctive wing-tip pattern. Goetz, Rudden, and Snetsinger (1985–86) give a good account of this sighting. These three birders conducted an excellent investigation of an unknown bird in severely trying conditions to record the first verified occurrence of this species in eastern North America. The Slaty-backed Gull is normally found in Asia on the coasts of the North Pacific and the Bering Sea south to Japan. In North America

it is found in western Alaska. There are also records from Vancouver Island and Washington State.

WESTERN GULL

Larus occidentalis

VERY RARE VAGRANT

This West Coast species is very rarely seen inland. In fact, it has never been recorded farther east than Illinois. A Western Gull was seen at Lincoln Park, Chicago, on October 19, 1927, and was collected on November 17 (CAS#1663). It was a near-adult male, identified as a member of the *L. o. wymani* race (Wright and Komarek 1928). A second record, a sight report from Chicago on February 18, 1950, is undocumented. All large dark-backed gulls should be identified with care; this specimen was first thought to be a Great Black-backed Gull.

GLAUCOUS GULL

Larus hyperboreus

OCCASIONAL MIGRANT AND WINTER RESIDENT ALONG LAKE MICHIGAN AND THE LARGER RIVERS AND LAKES; RARE ELSEWHERE IN THE STATE

Glaucous Gulls, the largest of the white gulls, usually stand out in a crowd. They are almost always found near big water and particularly standing on the ice, where they dominate the lesser gulls in struggles over fish. Immature Glaucous Gulls can be fairly dusky, but they have white wing tips. Their proportions are larger and their bill heavier than the Iceland Gull's. It takes them four years to obtain adult plumage. Bellrose (1938) collected a Glaucous specimen on the Illinois River near Ottawa on April 13, 1936 (CAS). This species nests along the Arctic coasts. The race found in Illinois is the nominate, *L. h. hyperboreus*.

Early fall arrival dates: immature, Chicago, July 19, 1981 (JL); along Lake Michigan, August 19, 1978 (AB33:183); Chicago, September 22, 1984 (JL). Most of these gulls arrive in November or later. High counts for fall: seven, Lake Calumet, February 9, 1977 (CC,LB,GR-AB31:338); four, Peoria, January 2, 1977 (DBi-AB31:338); nine to 12, Lake Calumet, December 30, 1980 (RB-AB35:305); 11, St. Louis to Alton area, winter 1983–84 (RG-AB38:323). Records away from the usual areas: Decatur, February 24–25, 1986 (RP,MD-IB&B2:76); Baldwin Lake, January 18, 1986 (R.Coles-IB&B2:76); Crab Orchard National Wildlife Refuge, February 21, 1985 (TF-IB&B1:69). Most of these gulls leave when the ice breaks up, usually in late February or March. Late spring departure dates: Springfield, May 15, 1982 (HDB); Chicago, June 4, 1982 (JL-AB36:983); three, Waukegan, April 22, 1978 (JN-AB32:1015).

GREAT BLACK-BACKED GULL

Larus marinus

RARE MIGRANT AND WINTER RESIDENT

The Great Black-backed is North America's largest gull. Its expanding population has resulted in an increased number of records in Illinois, but it has been present for many years, since Nelson (1876) found it "not uncommon on Lake Michigan." Adults are fairly easy to identify, but younger gulls can be difficult. Some plumages of immature Herring Gulls look much the same as immature Great Black-backs. These birds become adults by their fourth winter (see Grant 1986 for details). Great Black-backs are found mostly on Lake Michigan or nearby waters and to a lesser extent on the larger rivers and lakes. The record of an adult specimen taken at Crystal Lake in 1916 was pointed out by Ross Silcock (letter, December 1985). The only Great Black-backed specimen from Illinois, it is in the Hastings Municipal Museum in Nebraska (#2522).

These gulls usually do not arrive until November or December, but there are some earlier records: adult, Rice Lake, August 22–26, 1987 (KR,MB,JW); adult, Chautauqua National Wildlife Refuge, September 13, 1987 (KR,LA); Alton, November 7–9, 1985 (BR,CP-AB40:121). Occasionally more than one bird is counted: four, Lake Calumet, January 24–25, 1987 (JL,DW-IB&B3:68); seven, Chicago, March 2, 1986 (JL-AB 40:479); three, Granite City, December 28, 1985–January 7, 1986 (BR,RG); two, Carlyle Lake, January 3–February 1, 1987 (LH,BR-AB41:288). Spring departure dates usually coincide with the breakup of the ice, but some Great Black-backs stay later: immature, La Salle County, April 20, 1986 (JH-AB40:479); Chicago, April 7, 1979 (RCh, JPo-AB33:777). Southern Illinois records are scarce south of St. Louis: subadult, Baldwin Lake, January 22, 1983 (BR-SR 36:8); adult, Crab Orchard National Wildlife Refuge, February 5-8, 1976 (BP-AB30:726).

BLACK-LEGGED KITTIWAKE

Rissa tridactyla

RARE MIGRANT AND WINTER RESIDENT

This pelagic species migrates through Illinois and sometimes winters in small numbers. It is usually seen along Lake Michigan, but a good number of records also come from downstate lakes. The Black-legged Kittiwake is usually tame, not having learned to avoid people since it spends most of its time at sea. Kittiwakes nest on the steep cliffs of coastal or oceanic islands. In Illinois they occasionally sit on buildings—simulated cliffs—with pigeons. The immature plumage is more distinctive than the adult, and practically all kittiwakes observed in Illinois are immatures. Good field marks include a W pattern on the wings, a dark collar (less evident on second-winter birds), a rather heavy short

bill, short dark legs, and a black tip on the tail. Kittiwakes were recorded early. Nelson (1876) referred to a kittiwake that wintered at Chicago in 1870. A specimen was taken at Chicago on December 9, 1896 (CAS#4062), and an immature female was collected at Meredosia Lake, November 25, 1898 (FMNH). The building of artificial lakes opened more habitats to these northern gulls. Eddy (1927) noted several during a severe cold spell in December 1923 at the newly created Lake Decatur. The subspecies in Illinois is *R. t. tridactyla*, the Atlantic form.

Fall records are much more numerous than spring records. Two extremely early fall records are from Montrose, September 2, 1978 (Mlodinow 1984), and Springfield, August 25, 1984 (HDB). October records are few: Clinton Lake, October 24, 1981 (RCh-SR31:12); East Alton, October 29, 1982 (RG-AB37:187). Most kittiwakes arrive on wintry blasts in November or later. High counts: 15 flybys at Evanston, November 27, 1980 (RB-SR27:9); five, Wilmette, November 26, 1983 (DJ-SR39:17); three, Carlyle Lake, December 9–15, 1983 (BR-AB38:323). Very late or wintering birds: two, Evanston, January 5, 1980 (RB,JL,SM-AB34:278); Carlyle Lake, January 14, 1984 (BR-AB38:323); Decatur, January 4, 1986 (RP-AB40:287); East St. Louis, January 12, 1980 (RA- AB34:278).

The few spring records may indicate that some kittiwakes take an alternate route or that most make a fast overflight, like other pelagic species that are casual in fall but extremely rare in spring: adult, Fulton, February 19, 1977 (BSh-AB31:338); Rend Lake, April 5, 1987 (RP); Springfield, April 1–8, 1971 (HDB).

ROSS' GULL

Rhodostethia rosea

VERY RARE VAGRANT

The appearance of a Ross' Gull in Illinois was most unexpected. This species is rarely found away from saltwater except when it breeds, mainly in Siberia. Its primary winter range remains unknown, but it is thought to winter in open waters in the Arctic (AOU 1983). The Illinois record occurred at Chicago on November 19, 29, and 30 and December 1, 1978 (see Balch et al. 1979). This gull probably came from a small colony at Churchill, Manitoba, that was discovered in 1980 (Chartier and Cooke 1980). It had a rosy blush to the underparts, a distinctive black area around the front of the eye, a short black bill, a wedge-shaped tail, and a light mantle. Richard Biss took several identifiable photographs (on file ISM). The Ross's Gull also has records from Massachusetts (1975, 1981, 1984), Colorado (1983), Oregon (1987), Connecticut (1984), and Minnesota (1984).

SABINE'S GULL

Xema sabini

RARE FALL MIGRANT

Day-to-day coverage of Lake Michigan and other lakes in Illinois has shown that this primarily pelagic gull occurs almost every fall, usually in September and October. Of some 33 Illinois records, only one is for spring. Nelson (1876) reported it:

while collecting on the lake shore near Chicago, the first of April, 1873, I saw ... this bird in a small pool of water on the beach. At first I supposed it was a Bonaparte's Gull, and was about passing it, when it arose, and as it passed toward the Lake I saw it was something new to me and fired. It flew a few rods and fell into the lake.... It was in perfect breeding dress, as was shown by the black markings on the head ... a gale from off shore soon drifted it from sight.

Some 15 other records up to 1974 are all for fall, except for one Sabine's at Waukegan Harbor, January 9, 1949, and an adult at Greenwood Beach, July 24-30, 1954 (Smith and Parmalee 1955). Worthen took three specimens in September 1900 along the Mississippi River, one of which had data: "male, Warsaw, September 15, 1900" (Fleming 1912). The only other specimen was an immature taken at Lake Springfield, September 25, 1974 (ISM). Most birds are immatures recorded between September 9 and November 10. Three records are multiple sightings: three (adult and two immatures), Wilmette, November 10, 1985 (RB,MBi-AB40:121); seven, Carlyle Lake, September 23-28, 1986 (LH,BR-AB41:96); seven immatures, Lake Springfield, September 18, 1988 (HDB).

Since 1974 there have been 13 fall records. This gull actually seems to appear on downstate lakes earlier than on Lake Michigan, but that may be due to the randomness of the sightings. The Sabine's Gull is small, with a very distinctive pattern in flight: dark primaries and brownish back and forewing set off a white triangle in the rear part of the wing. It also has a small bill, forked tail, and ternlike flight. Any late fall or winter birds thought to be Sabine's Gulls should be checked carefully, since immature Black-legged Kittiwakes have been confused with this species. Other recent Illinois records: Urbana, September 25, 1980 (RCh-AB35:189); immature, Springfield, October 8, 1985 (HDB); Chautauqua National Wildlife Refuge, September 30, 1984 (TP,RQR-IB&B1:20); Horseshoe Lake, September 19, 1987 (DB,RG); Rice Lake, October 4, 1987 (LA,KR); Chicago, October 25, 1982 (RDe-SR35:11). The Sabine's Gull breeds in the Arctic and winters at sea south to Peru.

IVORY GULL

Pagophila eburnea

HYPOTHETICAL

This small white gull breeds in the high Arctic and winters mainly in Arctic waters within the drift ice and along the edges of the pack ice (Harrison 1983). The only Illinois report was made at Waukegan Harbor on January 1, 1949, by several members of the Chicago Ornithological Society. They noted that the gull had black tarsi, but no plumage notes were taken. This record is very likely correct, but very little description was recorded for such a rare bird and certainly not enough to form the single basis of a state record. Three other Ivory Gulls were recorded on the Great Lakes from Wisconsin and Michigan in 1947-49. One of them was collected (Ford 1956) and should lend some credence to the Illinois record.

GULL-BILLED TERN

Sterna nilotica

HYPOTHETICAL

This coastal species was listed in Illinois by Nelson (1876) and Ridgway (1895), but they gave no records. The American Ornithologists' Union *Checklist of North American Birds*, 6th edition (AOU 1983), lists this gull as casual in Illinois. There are three known sight records: Wilmette, August 10 and 15, 1960 (Russell et al. 1962); Chicago, August 15 and 26, 1959 (HF,HL-AFN14:40); Waukegan, August 13, 1967 (K.Eckert,RR-AFN21:578). But notes were made on only the last observation and by just one person. More documentation (preferably photographs) is needed to add this species to the state list.

CASPIAN TERN

Sterna caspia

UNCOMMON MIGRANT

The largest tern in Illinois, the Caspian can be distinguished by its large red-orange bill and black cap. Immatures have a less solid black cap but can still be easily identified. Its call is loud and rasping, and it captures food by diving while on the wing. The Caspian Tern, a wide-ranging species found Holarctic, is named for the Caspian Sea. It nests in colonies, many of which are on islands in the Great Lakes north of Illinois.

Spring migrants usually arrive in April. Early arrival dates: Long John Slough, April 7, 1968 (PD-AB22:532); two, La Salle County, April 7, 1985 (JH,JMc-IB&B1:87); Lake Springfield, April 8, 1984 (HDB). Average spring arrival dates: Chicago, May 4 (four years); Sangamon County, April 24 (16 years). Caspian Terns will be consistently seen only where there is a large body of water, especially one with a beach or similar area where they can rest. They sit with gulls and are large enough to hold their own with these aggressive birds. Caspians are especially numerous along Lake Michigan, although the larger rivers also attract them, especially those with exposed sandbars. Maximum counts for spring: 25, Horseshoe Lake, May 15, 1986 (EL-

IB&B2:94); 71, Monroe County, May 20, 1984 (JEa-SR41:19); 30, Lake Springfield, May 12, 1980 (HDB). Late spring departure averages: Sangamon County, May 25 (16 years); Chicago, May 16 (four years). Departure dates are sometimes obscured by summering birds: Waukegan, June 2, 1985 (CM-IB&B1:87); Horseshoe Lake, June 8, 1982 (BR-SR33:10); Baldwin Lake, June 4, 1983 (RK-SR37:17). Some years Caspian Terns do not occur in numbers until late May or early June. These terns are probably late migrants but may be nonbreeding birds, as some stay all summer.

Breeding was suspected at Lake Calumet when two adults and three fledged young were seen from June 26, 1976, to the end of summer (Mlodinow 1984) and again when a similar group was seen on July 14, 1979 (RB-AB33:868). No nests were found, however. Adults continue to feed their young south of the breeding grounds. I have seen young birds begging for food from adults at Lake Springfield several times in July, and this behavior has been seen in Illinois into September (RG). The young birds give a characteristic high squeal call when they beg. Other summer records: six, Waukegan, summered, 1978 (JN-AB32:1169); eight, Chicago, June and July 1984 (JL); 14-18, Waukegan, summered, 1985 (JL); four, Marshall County, June 21, 1982 (MSw-SR34:7); four, Mississippi River at Moline, June 17, 1982 (PP-SR34:7).

Some of the terns seen in summer are undoubtedly very early fall migrants, for Caspians begin to return by mid- to late June and migration is well under way by July. Early fall records: 73, Waukegan, July 25, 1981 (JN-AB35:945); four, Jackson Park, June 26, 1984 (HR-IB&B1:20); nine, Springfield, July 17, 1980 (HDB); 35, Starved Rock State Park, July 8-11, 1985 (JM-IB&B2:52); three, Chautauqua National Wildlife Refuge, July 11, 1985 (KR-IB&B2:52). Average arrival date for Chicago is August 31 (11 years)—which is late by recent standards—and for Sangamon County, July 20 (18 years). Maximum counts for fall are higher than for spring: 100, St. Louis area, September 17-22, 1977 (JEa-AB32:213); 140, Waukegan, August 30, 1978 (AB33:183); 185, Chicago, August 22, 1981 (AB36:184); 50, Carlyle Lake, September 16, 1984 (LH-IB&B1:20); 24, Hamilton, September 4, 1985 (RCe-IB&B2:52). Caspian Terns stay fairly late, with an average departure date for Sangamon County of October 6 (17 years) and for Chicago of October 4 (11 years). November dates are few: La Salle County, November 16, 1985 (JMc-AB40:121), and Rend Lake, November 2, 1985 (TF,LH-IB&B2:52). There are no winter records for Illinois as suggested by Nelson (1876). Caspian Terns winter in coastal areas from the southern United States south to northern Colombia and Venezuela.

ROYAL TERN
Sterna maxima
VERY RARE VAGRANT

Even though Nelson (1876) listed this coastal species as an exceedingly rare summer visitant to Lake Michigan and Cooke (1888) termed it a summer resident in Illinois, they may have mistaken it for the Caspian Tern, as Ridgway (1895) suggested. Two records are substantiated for Illinois: one Royal Tern photographed at Lake Calumet on September 7, 1985 (AS,RHu,JL-AB40:121), and one photographed at Chicago on July 13, 1988 (RHu). Gantlett and Harris (1987) discuss in detail the identification of all the large terns. An undocumented sight record came from Crab Orchard National Wildlife Refuge, September 5, 1962 (Bohlen 1978).

ROSEATE TERN
Sterna dougallii
HYPOTHETICAL

This Atlantic Coast species has been reported from Illinois several times: two, Jackson Park, May 7-18, 1934 (Ford 1956); Jacksonville, April 17, 1954 (Smith and Parmalee 1955); Crab Orchard National Wildlife Refuge, May 7, 1961 (AFN15:415); Wilmette, May 1967 (Mlodinow 1984). None of these records provide sufficient evidence to add the Roseate Tern to the state list. There is a specimen record for Indiana (Stoddard 1917). This bird is difficult to separate from the Forster's Tern, which also has a long tail.

COMMON TERN
Sterna hirundo
COMMON MIGRANT AND RARE SUMMER RESIDENT ON LAKE MICHIGAN; FAIRLY COMMON MIGRANT ELSEWHERE IN THE STATE

The Common Tern is found on the larger lakes and moves in larger flocks than the Forster's Tern. It is shorter legged, grayer ventrally, and has a redder bill, shorter tail, and darker primaries than the Forster's Tern. Its call is *kee-ar* or a series of *kip* notes. Like most terns, Commons dive from the wing, sometimes working in a group, to catch fish. The race in North America is *S. h. hirundo*. Scarceness of habitat and the resultant low breeding populations have put both the Common and the Forster's Terns on the Illinois endangered species list.

Common Terns usually arrive later in spring than Forster's Terns. Early arrival dates: four, Chicago, April 12, 1985 (JL-IB&B1:87); seven, Lake Vermilion, April 23,

1984 (SB-SR41:19); four, Peoria County, April 30, 1981
(LA-SR29:10). Average arrival dates: Chicago, April 29 (16
years); Sangamon County, May 6 (17 years). High counts
for spring: 1000, Chicago, May 14, 1981 (AB35:830); 700,
Waukegan, May 18, 1986 (CM,JL-AB40:479); 52, Springfield, May 11, 1981 (HDB); 30, Fulton County, May 29,
1983 (BCho-SR37:17). Spring bird count totals ranged from
40 in 1973 to 2179 in 1977. Cook and Lake Counties had
all the high counts, and 1446 in Lake County on May 7,
1977, was the highest (VK). Average departure dates: Chicago, May 25 (16 years); Sangamon County, May 20 (17
years). Migration continues into June some years.

Common Terns nest in colonies, choosing from time to
time small islands off the Lake Michigan shore. But even in
the nineteenth century Nelson (1876) noted that such nesting had declined. Lyon (1937) found a small colony along
Lake Michigan in 1935 and 1936 and collected a set of
eggs on July 19. The birds used the colony at least until
1940, when the highest number of nests was a dozen. The
only colony in recent years was at Waukegan, starting in
1977. Most years nesting failed for several reasons, including predators and offroad vehicles. The colony was successful in 1979 (30 nests plus young), 1982 (16 young), and
1983 (21 young). Common Terns nest on the sand or
gravel, producing two to three deep buff eggs with black
markings. Other summer records are of nonbreeding birds:
Horseshoe Lake, June 20, 1980 (BR-SR26:7); three, Dallas
City, June 21, 1985 (VK-IB&B2:14).

Fall migration begins in July: two, Lake Shelbyville, July
15, 1984 (JM-IB&B1:21) Chautauqua National Wildlife
Refuge, July 7, 1987 (KR); Olney, July 22, 1984 (LH-
IB&B1:21). Average fall arrival dates: Chicago, August 4
(13 years); central Illinois, August 8 (16 years). High counts
in fall are lower than in spring, even along Lake Michigan,
suggesting an eastward deflection of the migration route
at this season. High counts: 60, East St. Louis, September
15, 1977 (RA-AB32:213); 35, Carlyle Lake, September 23,
1986 (LH-IB&B3:41); 283, Waukegan, September 5, 1987
(JN). Average fall departure dates: Chicago, October 20 (13
years); central Illinois, October 5 (14 years). Late dates of
departure: Baldwin Lake, November 23, 1984 (LA-
IB&B1:21); East Alton, October 29, 1983 (BR-SR39:17);
Illinois Beach State Park, November 3, 1970 (LB). The
Common Tern winters from the southern United States
south to South America.

ARCTIC TERN

Sterna paradisaea

HYPOTHETICAL

This long-distance migrant occasionally occurs inland, with
records for Minnesota and Indiana. The one Illinois report
is a one-observer sighting of a first-year immature at
Springfield, October 3, 1986 (HDB). Grant and Scott (1969)
discuss identification of juvenile terns.

FORSTER'S TERN

Sterna forsteri

COMMON MIGRANT; OCCASIONAL SUMMER
RESIDENT IN NORTHEASTERN ILLINOIS

Common and Forster's Terns look very much alike, and
considerable confusion exists in the literature concerning
these two terns in Illinois. Forster's Terns are found on
lakes and rivers and at ponds, sewage lagoons, and marshes.
They sit on flats, buoys, and pilings and occasionally rest
on the water. The most numerous of the white terns in
Illinois away from Lake Michigan, they have two calls, a
nasal *zaaap* and a *kyarr*. Immatures have a black patch
around the eye and ear that is distinctive, and they lack the
dark bar on the leading secondary coverts shown
prominently by Common Terns. Adult Forster's differ from
Common Terns in having an orangish bill, longer legs, and
"frosted" primaries.

Forster's are usually the earliest terns to arrive in spring:
Charleston, April 3, 1986 (LBH-IB&B2:94); Chicago, April
4, 1982 (MDa-AB36:859); Alton, April 5, 1986 (RG-
IB&B2:94). Average spring arrival dates: Chicago, April 29
(eight years); Sangamon County, April 15 (18 years). Maximum counts for spring: 500, Jackson Park, May 8, 1983
(HR-SR37:17); 32, Crab Orchard National Wildlife Refuge,
May 5, 1985 (KR,TF-IB&B1:87); 34, Lake Vermilion, May
2, 1986 (SB-IB&B2:94). Spring bird count totals ranged
from 53 in 1973 to 1245 in 1977. All high counts were
along Lake Michigan, with 930 in Lake County, May 9,
1987, the highest (VK). Forster's, including some "portlan-
dica" birds, continue to migrate into June. Late dates: Rend
Lake, June 7, 1986 (DR-IB&B2:94); two, Waukegan, June
10, 1981 (JN-SR29:10); five, Kidd, June 4, 1983 (RG,PS-
SR37:17). Nelson (1876) gives a good account of nesting
Forster's Terns at Grass Lake, where nests were on masses
of floating plants. These terns will also nest on muskrat
houses and floating logs and in old grebe nests. Nelson
found clutches of two and three eggs, which are buff
marked with black; young and eggs were found in mid-
June. Today Forster's nest only at Chain O'Lakes State Park;
16 pairs nested there in 1982 (JN-AB 36:983). Many birds
have been seen elsewhere in summer, but breeding has not
been recorded: four, Oquawka, June 23, 1979 (LMc-
AB33:868); 90, Chicago, June 13, 1982 (JL-SR34:7); three,
Lake Shabbona, June 20, 1980 (MSw-SR26:7).

These terns start moving south with the first cold fronts
in late June and early July. Adults arrive first: two, Rice
Lake, June 30, 1987 (KR); Lake Calumet, July 4, 1980 (JL);
Springfield, June 23, 1982 (HDB). Average fall arrival dates:
west-central, August 18 (seven years); Sangamon County,
July 17 (17 years). High counts for fall: 180, Lake County,
July 6, 1985 (JL-AB39:918); 32, Lake Renwick, September
7, 1986 (JM-IB&B3:41); 105, Chicago, September 4, 1983
(JL). Average departure dates: west-central, September 10
(seven years); Sangamon County, October 14 (18 years).
Late departure dates: Channahon, November 11, 1983
(JM-SR39:17); East Alton, December 22, 1984 (RA,PB-

IB&B1:69); Lake Vermilion, November 3, 1984 (SB-IB&B1:21). The Forster's Tern winters from coastal southern United States south to Costa Rica.

LEAST TERN

Sterna antillarum

OCCASIONAL MIGRANT AND LOCAL SUMMER
RESIDENT IN SOUTHERN ILLINOIS; RARE
MIGRANT AND POSTBREEDING WANDERER
ELSEWHERE IN THE STATE

The Least Tern, only a little larger than the Purple Martin, has a distinctive feeding method of plunging into the water after small fish. It gives a harsh *kit* and a squealing *zreeep* call. Adults have a yellow bill and feet, but immatures have a black bill and brownish mottling on the head and back. The Least Tern rests on sandbars and mudflats. It is an endangered species in Illinois because its nesting areas have been flooded and people have overused its sandbar habitats. For a while this tern was considered conspecific with the Little Tern of Europe, but recent studies proved otherwise (see Massey 1976). The subspecies in Illinois is the interior race, *S. a. athalassos*.

Spring migration is very late, mainly in mid-May. Early arrival dates: Morgan County, May 7, 1977; Mercer County, May 5, 1979; Pope County, May 10, 1980 (spring bird count, VK). Least Terns found away from the Ohio and Mississippi Rivers in spring are overmigrants: La Salle, May 28, 1978 (JH-AB32:1015); Waukegan, June 3, 1978 (DJ,RB-AB32:1169); Meredosia, May 23, 1982 (RS-AB36:859); immature, Waukegan, May 27, 1985 (JL-AB39:308); Peoria, June 5, 1986 (LA-IB&B2:94). Immatures that appear in spring are nonbreeders; most of these "portlandicas" stay on the wintering grounds. Migration continues well into June: Springfield, June 16, 1987 (HDB); Baldwin Lake, June 21, 1980 (RK-SR26:7).

Hardy (1957) lists the Illinois colonies of this small tern: questionable nesting, Bird Point, Alexander County (Bartsch 1922); Gabaret Island, Mississippi River (Widmann 1898); Mosenthein Island, Mississippi River; and Bell Island, Ohio River. The only recent nesting area is in Alexander County, where 18 nests were found in 1986 (A.West-IB&B3:14). These terns place their eggs—usually two or three, pale or olive buff and speckled or streaked with darker colors—in a shallow depression in sand or gravel. Butler (1897) reported Least Terns breeding at Wolf Lake on the Indiana border, with three eggs seen, on June 5, 1882, and at Hyde Park on May 27, 1875. They do not nest in these areas now.

These terns begin postbreeding dispersal in July. Sometimes adults and young stay together, as I have seen adults feeding immatures at Lake Springfield. Early fall arrival dates: Cook County, July 16, 1981 (PD-AB35:945); Waukegan, July 24, 1985 (JL-IB&B2:52); two, Beardstown, July 30, 1982 (PW,WO-SR35:11); Cordova, July 8, 1980 (BB-SR27:9). These birds are not seen in any numbers away from their nesting areas. Late dates of departure: immature,

Rend Lake, September 9, 1984 (LH-IB&B1:21); three, East St. Louis, September 5, 1977 (JEa-AB32:213); Orland Park, September 19, 1948 (Ford 1956). Least Terns winter along the coast of South America from Colombia to eastern Brazil, but the exact winter range of the interior race is unknown.

LARGE-BILLED TERN

Phaetusa simplex

VERY RARE VAGRANT

On July 15, 1949, at the northeast end of Lake Calumet, A. L. Campbell and his wife observed a Large-billed Tern. This bird stayed on until September 20 and was viewed by many observers from Chicago (see Zimmermann 1949). It was also photographed, but not with a large lens. The photographs, drawings, and a description are on file at the Illinois State Museum.

The Large-billed Tern is a very distinctive bird, with a large yellow bill and a wing pattern similar to that of an immature Sabine's Gull. It is native to South America, breeding along the larger river systems and ranging to the seacoast in the nonbreeding season. It has occurred as far north as Panama, Bermuda, Cuba, and Aruba. Besides the Illinois sighting, there is a sight record from near Youngstown, Ohio, May 29, 1954 (McLaughlin 1979). Skins in the Field Museum of Natural History were examined, and the Lake Calumet bird was determined to be the most southerly subspecies, *P. s. chloropoda* because of the brightness of the yellow legs. Although there is a chance that this bird escaped from a zoo, several zoo curators contacted at the time knew of none in captivity.

BLACK TERN

Chlidonias niger

COMMON MIGRANT, COMMON SUMMER
RESIDENT IN NORTHERN ILLINOIS, AND
RARE SUMMER RESIDENT IN CENTRAL
ILLINOIS

Skimming the surface of a pond or marsh, the Black Tern looks like a large dark swallow. These terns inhabit larger lakes and rivers, but overflow areas and sewage lagoons are also good places to see them in migration. When feeding, they work in loose flocks. I have seen them feeding on adult mayflies when large emergences occur. Adults are mostly dark in spring, but both they and the immature birds are grayish by early fall. A large flock at Springfield on August 14, 1980, had Black Terns in all plumages, from dark black to gray. The nonbreeding birds, or "portlandicas," usually stay on the wintering grounds; they are common, for example, in the Bay of Panama in summer. The race in North America is *C. n. surinamensis*.

WILD TURKEY
Meleagris gallopavo

Before conservationists restored the Wild Turkey to its former range, the largest of North America's upland game birds was extirpated from most midwestern states. Today it is again possible to see a turkey gobbler and one of his mates (he is polygamous) foraging in a patch of blooming Bloodroot (*Sanguinaria canadensis*) on the side of a hill.

Adults

(male)

(female)

NORTHERN BOBWHITE
Colinus virginianus

Few who venture into the field have not experienced the heart-stopping explosion into flight of a covey of Bobwhites from beneath their feet. This tactic often leaves a predator unable to focus on a single victim and allows the entire covey to escape. Sometimes, in a flurry of rustling leaves and muttering musical chirps, the covey will choose to run a short distance before bursting into flight one or two at a time.

Adults

(male)

(female)

(male)

(female)

(female)

BLACK RAIL
Laterallus jamaicensis

VIRGINIA RAIL
Rallus limicola

The presence of the seldom-seen Black and Virginia Rails is frequently revealed only after danger has provoked one of them to call out an alarm, an action that usually stimulates answers from every corner of the marsh. Censuses of the calls of the different species of rails are sometimes the only way to evaluate a population.

Black Rail
(sexes similar)

Snapping Turtle
(Chelydra serpentina)

Virginia Rail
(sexes similar)

SANDHILL CRANE
Grus canadensis

In earlier days nesting Sandhill Cranes could be found foraging in remote, yet-undrained marshes. Here they fed on bulbs, tubers, seeds, and leaves of plants as well as a wide variety of insects, small reptiles, amphibians, mammals, and occasionally birds. Today the Sandhill Crane is considered to be mostly a migrant in the state. Many large flocks are observed in spring and fall in northern Illinois.

Adult
(sexes similar)

LESSER GOLDEN-PLOVER
Pluvialis dominica

KILLDEER
Charadrius vociferus

RUDDY TURNSTONE
Arenaria interpres

DUNLIN
Calidris alpina

During spring migration a wide variety of North American shorebirds pass through the state. Many stop to rest and feed but appear to be in a hurry to reach their Arctic nesting grounds. Having the same general requirements—mudflats and shorelines—many of these shorebirds are seen feeding with the Killdeer, a resident of the state.

Killdeer
(sexes similar)

Ruddy Turnstone in nuptial plumage
(sexes similar)

Lesser Golden-Plover in nuptial plumage
(sexes similar)

Dunlin in nuptial plumage
(sexes similar)

BONAPARTE'S GULL
Larus philadelphia

FORSTER'S TERN
Sterna forsteri

Historically the status of these two birds has been somewhat ambiguous. The Bonaparte's Gull was considered America's smallest gull until 1962 when a small group of Little Gulls (*Larus minitus*), previously considered stragglers from Europe, were discovered nesting in Canada. The Forster's Tern was not recognized as a separate species from its cousin the Common Tern until 1831. Frequently traveling side by side, the Forster's and the Bonaparte's follow our larger rivers as they migrate north.

Bonaparte's Gull in nuptial plumage
(sexes similar)

Spottail Shiner
(Notropis hudsonius)

Forster's Tern in nuptial plumage
(sexes similar)

MOURNING DOVE
Zenaida macroura

Like so many other birds whose nests are vulnerable to predators, the Mourning Dove hides its nest among the thick foliage and thorny branches of a small tree or shrub such as the Wild Rose (*Rosa* sp.). These locations are usually revealed only by the activity of the adult birds, which increases and makes them more noticeable to the predator's watchful eye after the eggs have hatched.

Adults

(male)

(female)

BLACK-BILLED CUCKOO
Coccyzus erythropthalmus

YELLOW-BILLED CUCKOO
Coccyzus americanus

About the time the downturned deep brown-purple blossoms of the papaw (*Asimina triloba*) appear, Black- and Yellow-billed Cuckoos are returning to the state—an event that, because of the quiet, somewhat secretive nature of both species, is sometimes overlooked. Listening for the call of the bird farmers know as the rain crow is a good way to detect the presence of cuckoos.

Yellow-billed Cuckoo
(sexes similar)

Black-billed Cuckoo
(sexes similar)

COMMON BARN-OWL
Tyto alba

The facial disks that make up most of the Common Barn-Owl's heart-shaped face are in reality feather-covered flaps of skin that form the front of the enormous opening of their ear canal. Although these owls can see extremely well with very little light, their acute hearing allows them to hone in on their prey when it can only be detected by sound. The Barn-Owl's diet is primarily small rodents.

Adult
(sexes similar)

White-footed Mouse
(Peromyscus leucopus)

In Illinois the Black Tern probably uses the Mississippi and Illinois River valleys as its main migration routes in spring. Some years these migrants appear in numbers over a broad front, but in other years very few are detected away from the rivers. Early spring arrival dates: Olney, April 21, 1984 (LH-SR41:19); Chicago, April 26, 1981 (LA-SR29:10). Average arrival dates: Chicago, May 7 (13 years); Sangamon County, May 5 (19 years). High counts for spring: 700, Henderson County, May 17, 1986 (MB-AB40:479); 160, Oquawka, May 22, 1982 (LMc-AB36:859); 148, Harrisonville, May 18, 1983 (RG-SR37:18); 200, Peoria County, May 11–15, 1981 (VH,LA-SR29:10). Spring bird count totals ranged from three in 1985 to 824 in 1983; 140 were counted in Warren County, May 7, 1983 (VK). Average spring departure dates: Chicago, May 22 (13 years); Sangamon County, May 26 (15 years). Black Terns are seen into June, some years in fair numbers.

Although old Illinois breeding records come only from Putnam and Henry Counties, the Black Tern's breeding range may once have encompassed the whole state, since Audubon (1835) noted breeding as far south as Kentucky. Today the Black Tern is declining and is on the Illinois endangered species list because of habitat destruction and human disturbance of marshes. Recent nesting areas: Lake Calumet, Antioch, Redwing Slough, Moraine Hills State Park, Busse Reservoir, Powder Mill, Dundee, Barrington, and Round Lake Marsh. Black Terns build a well-formed nest of material taken from surrounding vegetation, usually placing it only a couple of inches above the water. They lay two to three brownish eggs with heavy black markings. Illinois egg dates are May 11 to July 28.

Sometimes the fall migrants appear on downstate lakes with cold fronts in June. At this time, they are all adults. Early arrivals: Chautauqua National Wildlife Refuge, June 28, 1987 (MB); Baldwin Lake, July 3, 1985 (TF-IB&B2:52); two, Springfield, July 5, 1980 (HDB). Average fall arrival dates: Chicago, August 2 (16 years); Sangamon County, July 16 (19 years). High counts for fall: 350, Chautauqua refuge, September 12, 1983 (TP-SR39:17); 116, Horseshoe Lake, August 20, 1983 (TF-SR39:17); 400, Waukegan, August 3, 1968 (Mlodinow 1984); 38, Alexander County, August 16, 1986 (DR-IB&B3:41). Average fall departure dates: Chicago, September 19 (16 years); Sangamon County, September 22 (17 years). Late departure dates: Chicago, October 27, 1983 (HR-AB39:209); Crab Orchard National Wildlife Refuge, October 18, 1985 (SO-IB&B2:52); Springfield, October 12, 1972 (HDB). The Black Tern winters from Panama south to Peru and Surinam.

ANCIENT MURRELET

Synthliboramphus antiquus

VERY RARE VAGRANT

This Pacific Ocean species has been found twice in Illinois—oddly enough, on the same date, 21 years apart. The first

was an injured bird found alive on a road in McDonough County on November 16, 1961. It later died, and the specimen is in the Illinois State Museum (Balding 1964). The second Ancient Murrelet was found swimming and diving in Lake Michigan off Wilmette on November 16, 1982. It was seen again by many birders on November 20 and 21, 1982, and was photographed (Rosenband 1983). Rosenband noted that the bird spread its wings before diving in characteristic alcid fashion. Munyer (1965) discusses the inland records of Ancient Murrelets (there were 24 at the time) and concludes that they appear because of strong storms and poor visibility that force them off course and inland during their migrations. Ancient Murrelets breed on the coasts and offshore islands of the North Pacific from Japan to the western United States. They winter on the open ocean from the Komandorskiye (Commander) Islands south to Fukien, Taiwan, and the Ryukyu Islands and from the Pribilof Islands to northern Baja California.

ROCK DOVE

Columba livia

INTRODUCED; NOW AN ABUNDANT PERMANENT RESIDENT

Rock Doves, better known as pigeons, were introduced to North America at Nova Scotia in 1606-7 by Lescarbot. Their introduction into what is now the United States took place about 1621 (Long 1981), and they have long since spread to all areas of the country. In Illinois cities, where they nest on buildings, they are so numerous as to be pests, their droppings causing sanitation and health problems. In rural areas they feed on waste grain and nest on bridges, overpasses, barns, and grain elevators and sometimes in trees. Pigeon plumages vary greatly, and some pigeons have been bred to bring out certain qualities and colors.

Their nesting season lasts practically the whole year, sometimes induced by artificial lighting. Usually two white eggs are laid. Available Illinois egg dates are March 17–September 12. Robbins et al. (1986) noted a significant increase in pigeons in eastern North America based on breeding bird survey data for 1965–79. The mean number of birds per survey route in Illinois was 15.8.

Spring bird count totals ranged from 2238 in 1972 to 7492 in 1985, with a high count of 1674 in Cook County, May 10, 1986 (VK). Christmas bird count totals for 1976–85 ranged from 14,361 in 1978 to 23,675 in 1982. Chicago urban had all the high counts; the highest was 9,000 in 1982.

RINGED TURTLE-DOVE

Streptopelia risoria

HYPOTHETICAL—PROBABLE ESCAPES

The Ringed Turtle-Dove, from Africa or Eurasia (AOU 1983), was first recorded in Los Angeles in 1909 (Long

1981). It now has established populations in California, Florida, Texas, and Alabama. Several records in Illinois are presumably of escaped birds. Nesting records: Beardstown, 1964 (TEM-AFN19:45); pair with fledglings, Joliet, mid-June 1985 (IB&B2:14). Other records: three, Springfield, August 23, 1957 (AFN11:408); Highland Park, June 17, 1967 (IAB144:17); Decatur, July–December 1973 (RS); Ogle/Lee Counties Christmas bird count, December 31, 1978; Joliet Christmas bird count, December 19, 1980; Rock Island/Henry Counties Christmas bird count, December 18, 1982, and December 6, 1983. The Ringed Turtle-Dove occurs in open woodlands, usually in parks near people.

MOURNING DOVE

Zenaida macroura

ABUNDANT MIGRANT AND SUMMER RESIDENT; COMMON WINTER RESIDENT

Mourning Doves have one of the broadest geographical and ecological distributions of any birds in Illinois. They thrive in open habitats and are tied to agriculture because they feed on waste grain. Their prime foods in Illinois are foxtail grass, corn, wheat, spurges, crabgrass, prairie grass, and croton (Hanson and Kossack 1963). Two races are found in Illinois, the eastern *Z. m. carolinensis* and the western *Z. m. marginella,* along with many apparent intermediates (see Aldrich and Duvall 1958). *Marginella* evidently occupied the original prairie peninsula in Illinois and *carolinensis* the more wooded areas, but this distribution was muddled after farming began.

Although Mourning Doves are present all year in Illinois, they have definite migrations. These migrations are difficult to see, but bird banders have proved that they do occur. I have seen flocks of doves that seem to be migrating at dusk. Spring migration takes place during the last half of April, but flocks of migrating doves have been observed as late as May 1 at McClure (southern Illinois) and mid-May at Elgin (Hanson and Kossack 1963). Dreuth at Chicago saw them as early as March 12, 1938; his average arrival date was March 27 (16 years). His average spring departure date was May 18 (also 16 years), and the latest individual was seen on June 1, 1940 (Clark and Nice 1950). Doves were reported moving south in spring at Jackson Park—perhaps a reverse migration—with 112 counted on April 13, 1983, and 70 the next day (PC,HR-SR37:18). Spring bird count totals ranged from 4374 in 1972 to 9541 in 1986, with a high count of 731 in Cook County in 1986 (VK).

Graber and Graber (1963) noted a 19 percent decline in the state's breeding population between 1909 (2,438,000) and 1957 (2,000,000). Most of the decline was in the south, causing a shift to the north in the population. Robbins et al. (1986), using breeding bird survey data for 1965–79, reported a significant increase in the number of Mourning Doves across the continent and a northward expansion of the breeding range. Nineteen states had increases, while only three showed declines: Oregon, Indiana, and Illinois. They also said that dove mortality due to severe winters in the late 1970s was obvious. The mean number of birds per survey route in Illinois was 37.5. Summer habitat for doves consists of edge shrubbery, hedgerows, clover fields, grasslands, orchards, marshes, urban areas, and fallow fields. Mourning Doves usually nest in trees, building a platform of sticks that looks as if it would blow out of the tree with the first gust of wind. I have found several nests placed on the ground, usually in clover fields. The female lays two white eggs, which sometimes are visible through the poorly constructed nest. Doves nest very early and very late; normal dates are from late March to September. Hunt (1978) found young nestlings in Coles County in early November and indications of eggs being laid as early as March 18. Doves have several broods per year. Preno and Labisky (1971) calculated that each pair fledged 2.4 young, making the total annual Illinois production 2,400,000 birds. (They also figured that hunters shot an average of 1,545,000 doves each year between 1955 and 1969.) By July flocking occurs, usually in tandem with the wheat harvest.

Many of the late summer birds are migrants from north of Illinois. A drop in temperature after mid-August causes doves to migrate south. They leave northern Illinois by mid-September (Preno and Labisky 1971). Dreuth in Chicago had early migrants on August 3, 1936, with an average arrival date of September 20 (11 years). High counts for fall: 450, Palos, July 16, 1981 (PC,HR-SR31:12); 250, Bismark, November 21, 1983 (SB-SR39:18); 200, Springfield, August 18, 1985 (HDB); 600, Durand, late July 1950 (Hanson and Kossack 1963). The average departure date in Chicago was October 14 (11 years).

Taber (1930), studying banded bird recoveries, showed that Illinois birds migrate to Georgia, northern Florida, Louisiana, and Texas to winter. A few have been recovered as far away as Mexico, Guatemala, and Honduras (Hanson and Kossack 1963). But many stay for the winter in Illinois, mostly in the southern part. Graber and Graber (1963) found that the Mourning Dove winter population in 1906–7 was 350,000, whereas in 1957–58 it was 1,200,000. These doves wintered farther north in the 1950s than they did in the early part of the century. The population varies more in winter, with the northern edge of dependable weather in Illinois being at latitude 40 degrees. Most of the Mourning Doves were in cornstalk habitat in 1906–7, but a change in agricultural methods eliminated this habitat. With the recent increase in bird feeders, many are probably using residential habitat now. Doves tend to feed near roads during inclement weather; it is not uncommon for them to suffer frostbitten toes, and mortality is high at this time. Christmas bird count totals for 1976–85 ranged from 3579 in 1977 to 8444 in 1976. The highest count was 1438 in Richland County in 1975.

PASSENGER PIGEON

Ectopistes migratorius

EXTINCT

When one approaches the country of the Illinois, one sees during the day, clouds of doves, a kind of wood or wild pigeon. A thing that may perhaps appear incredible is that the sun is obscured by them; these birds live only on the beechnuts and acorns in the forests, and are excellent in autumn; sometimes as many as 80 of them are killed with one shot. (Bossu 1768)

Passenger Pigeons were once the most numerous of all the world's birds, but these large doves were driven to extinction by man. The last Passenger Pigeon died in captivity at the Cincinnati Zoological Gardens on September 1, 1914. Passenger Pigeons had been abundant migrants in Illinois, common summer residents in the north, and uncommon summer residents in the central part of the state. Apparently they also occasionally wintered in southern Illinois, and perhaps even farther north.

Spring migration dates for northern Illinois were March 15 to mid-April (Nelson 1876). Other northern Illinois spring dates: Evanston, February 11, 1882; Galena, March 17, 1846; Hanover, February 14, 1882; Highland Park, February 6, 1882; Freeport, April 4, 1867. Central Illinois spring dates: Carthage, March 12; Charleston, February 3, 1882; Ellsworth, February 6, 1882; Virden, February 11. Southern Illinois arrival dates may be confounded by wintering birds: St. Clair County, February 11, 1882; Robinson, March 10, 1883; Wabash Valley, January 15 (Schorger 1955). Thus it seems that some migration took place as early as January or February, but the peaks, when hordes of pigeons flew over, were apparently in late March and early April. Like other early migrants, wild pigeons were influenced by the weather and moved around frequently in search of food.

Although Passenger Pigeons nested in huge colonies, isolated pairs and small colonies of a dozen or so pairs also occurred. Breeding records for Illinois are scanty. Pike found a colony on April 28, 1806, on an island in the Mississippi River off Pike County, and 298 squabs were captured in a few minutes (Schorger 1955). These pigeons were formerly abundant residents along the Des Plaines River west of Lake Forest; two nests and three eggs were collected there in June 1879 (Coale 1912). Loucks (1892) stated that a nest was found near Peoria. The last breeding record occurred in the spring of 1893 (Deane 1895). Since Passenger Pigeons nested in Kentucky and farther south I see no reason why they would not have nested in southern Illinois, but I can find no records. A Passenger Pigeon egg in the Illinois State Museum collection was taken from a woods north of Waukegan on April 17, 1879, by W. B. Porter. The presence of an immature bird in the collection, taken in Fayette County, May 20, 1893, could indicate breeding in southern Illinois.

Northern Illinois fall records: Bryn Mawr, September 30, 1901 (latest specimen); Freeport, September 12, 1866; Grand Crossing, August 21, 1886; Lake Forest, August 7, 1895; Palatine, October 15, 1874; Baileyville, August 24, 1891 (specimen ISM). Central Illinois fall records: Charleston, September 24, 1878; Jerseyville, September 6, 1896; Middlegrove, September 5, 1876; Virden, October 5. Southern Illinois fall records: Belleville, October 5, 1854; Ohio River mouth, October 16, 1700, and October 24, 1807 (Schorger 1955). No numbers are given, and the early literature lacks any description of the huge migrations in Illinois except the one by Bossu quoted above.

Winter records exist for all three sections of the state. Ridgway (1874) called the Passenger Pigeon a resident in southern Illinois, especially in mild winters. There are December records for Waukegan and January records for La Salle and Lee Counties.

Cory (1909) stated that "as late as the year 1882, wild Pigeons were very abundant in Illinois and Wisconsin; but about that time their numbers began to decrease very rapidly. Besides the thousands which were shot, immense numbers were caught in nets on their breeding grounds, with the result that in 1895 it had become a rare bird." Apparently the last published record of this pigeon in Illinois is the one for the specimen from Bryn Mawr in 1901. Eifrig (1944) asserted that he saw a Passenger Pigeon with a Mourning Dove at Cowling, Edwards County, on April 10, 1911, that he saw one at River Forest on May 1, 1923, and that he saw a pair on May 2, May 11, May 16, and July 18, 1923. There were other visual reports in 1911 (Hodge 1912). Schorger (1955 and 1973) gives a detailed account of the Passenger Pigeon's natural history and extinction.

COMMON GROUND-DOVE

Columbina passerina

RARE VAGRANT

The normal range of this small dove is the extreme southern United States and Mexico. Its appearance in Illinois must be part of a fall dispersal flight similar to that of the Groove-billed Ani. Most of the 10 records for the Common Ground-Dove in Illinois occurred in late fall and only one in spring: Crab Orchard National Wildlife Refuge, October 1964 (Rice and Rose); two near Harrisonville, May 23, 1970 (W.Krause-IAB155:28); male (specimen SIU collection), Lake Chautauqua, Jackson County, November 10, 1974; Brown County, August 17, 1975 (RQR); Springfield, November 23, 1975 (HDB); specimen (ISM collection, head and wings only) killed by cat, Carbondale, November 26, 1977 (McNerney and Biggers); two, Sangchris State Park, November 7 and 11, and one, November 24, 1979 (HDB); Marshall County, November 20-21, 1979 (DC,VH-AB34:168); one questionable, Chicago, September 27, 1980

(Mlodinow 1984); Union County Conservation Area, December 23, 1981 (MH,VK-AB36:300). Vagrant records also come from Kansas, Iowa, Indiana, southern Ontario, Pennsylvania, and New York. The subspecies seen in Illinois is probably *C. p. passerina*, but the Southern Illinois University specimen should be examined to make sure. Escaped cage birds might account for some records. These diminutive doves have rusty primaries and short dark tails. They eat seeds on the ground.

MONK PARAKEET

Myiopsitta monachus

HYPOTHETICAL—PROBABLE ESCAPES

Fairly large and mostly green, the Monk Parakeet has a pointed tail, gray breast, and blue primaries. Native to south-central South America, it can endure fairly cold temperatures and thus can survive in the Illinois climate. Some Monk Parakeets have been released by pet owners in the United States who thought them too noisy, and some have escaped. Most of those seen on the loose have been in cities, usually in the Chicago area, where many people feed birds and where it is warmer than in open country. These parakeets build fairly large communal nests and roosts of sticks placed in trees or in man-made structures. A nest with four adults produced three young at Hinsdale in July 1973 (Larson 1973). Parakeets have been in Jackson Park since 1979, and in fall 1987 eight nests were reported there. Other records: 20, Cook County, October and November 1981 (PD-SR31:18); two with a nest, Carlock, 1973 (Larson 1973). Four specimens are in the Illinois State Museum collection, three from Joliet taken October 30, 1974, and one from Sangamon County taken September 28, 1980. These parakeets are considered fruit and farm pests in their normal range and therefore are being eliminated when they occur in Illinois. But in fact their maliciousness toward people has yet to be demonstrated in the Northern Hemisphere, though it is possible that they compete with native bird species (see Long 1981).

CAROLINA PARAKEET

Conuropsis carolinensis

EXTINCT

The Carolina Parakeet, Illinois' only native parrot, was lost forever, apparently through people's greed and ignorance and a fatal habit of the bird itself. These parakeets were unevenly distributed in the state, and whether they were present all year is uncertain. They were probably common residents in southern Illinois decreasing northward. They nested and roosted in hollow trees, particularly sycamores.

Their favorite food was cockleburs, but they also liked hackberries and other fruits. Some people considered them orchard pests and shot them. Unfortunately, if one parakeet was shot the rest of the flock would remain around it—and thus all could eventually be killed. This behavior apparently facilitated their demise, though another theory is that the expansion of the Evening Grosbeak's range eastward and the resultant competition for food was a contributing factor.

Very early evidence of the presence of the Carolina Parakeet in Illinois comes from two archaeozoological sites (Parmalee 1958 and 1967). At Cahokia, in Madison and St. Clair Counties, nine bills, a tarsometatarsus, and two ulnae were found that date between A.D. 900 and 1500. At the Irving site in Pike County (A.D. 525–1025), a complete left coracoid was found.

Early travelers gave accounts of the Carolina Parakeet in Illinois, although some are a bit vague. The first such account came in 1673 from Father Marquette on the Illinois River: "We have seen nothing like this river that we enter, as regards its fertility of soil, its prairies and woods; its cattle, elk, deer, wildcats, bustards, swans, ducks, parroquets, and even beaver" (Thwaites 1896). In 1702 Pierre de Liette remarked: "Three leagues from the fork [of the Illinois River] is the river Mazon (Mason) which signifies the tow, where flocks of parakeets of fifty to sixty are found. They make a very strange noise. They are a little bigger than turtledoves" (Quaife 1947). John James Audubon had this to say in December 1810 at the mouth of the Cache River between Pulaski and Alexander Counties: "Though the trees were entirely stripped of their verdure, I could not help raising my eyes toward their tops, and admiring their grandeur. The large sycamores with white bark formed a lively contrast with the canes beneath them; and the thousands of Parroquets, that came to roost in their hollow trunks at night, were to be objects of interest and curiosity" (Audubon 1942). In 1833 Patrick Shirreff visited Springfield along the Sangamon River and wrote: "The forests abounded with green coloured paroquets, which fluttered about with a disagreeable noise, in flocks of six or seven" (Shirreff 1835).

T. E. Musselman related one of the last sightings, which occurred on April 21, 1884. Two men from Adams County, while crossing a dried marsh at the approach to Kates Lake, saw an old dead pecan tree that seemed to be covered with green and yellow leaves. On closer approach, a flock of 30 to 50 "parrots" flew screaming from the dead branches; they circled overhead, then alighted in a cocklebur patch that covered the overflow field (McKinley 1978). Loucks (1892) noted in "Birds of Peoria and Tazewell Counties" that the Carolina Parakeet was "now extinct but formerly found here. Mr. H. H. Fahnestock informs me that he has seen them years ago along the [Illinois] river."

Four specimen records exist for Illinois. The earliest was an adult male collected at Cairo about 1834 (possibly on April 29) by J. K. Townsend and now in the United States National Museum. The second specimen was collected by

R. Kennicott in 1857 (or 1855) in Union County (or Union, McHenry County). It is in the Chicago Academy of Science collection. An adult female collected from the Illinois River on May 8, 1879, is in the Delaware Natural History Museum; it is from the collection of Matthew Clugston. The last is a specimen from a collection in the Aurora Historical Museum, supposedly collected locally sometime around the 1880s.

The state's final record, a sighting, came from an unlikely place: the sand dunes of Lake Michigan near Chicago on June 11, 1912 (Bent 1940). The last specimen was taken in Florida in 1913, and the last Carolina Parakeet died in the Cincinnati Zoo in 1918. Although the river bottoms still support cockleburs for food and large sycamores for roosting, the Carolina Parakeet is no longer there to use them and its loud calls and splashes of green and yellow are gone forever.

BLACK-BILLED CUCKOO

Coccyzus erythropthalmus

FAIRLY COMMON MIGRANT; UNCOMMON SUMMER RESIDENT IN NORTHERN ILLINOIS DECREASING SOUTHWARD

This cuckoo, though it arrives earlier than the Yellow-billed Cuckoo, is more difficult to detect because it stays in denser foliage and is quieter. There are also fewer Black-billed Cuckoos: Graber and Graber (1963), in their statewide census, found a ratio of one Black-billed to 14 Yellow-bills. Adult Black-bills show a red eye ring, a smaller amount of white in the tail, and little rufous in the wing. They inhabit forests, orchards, and woodland edges. The call is a fast rhythmic cucucu. They occasionally call at night.

The arrival of Black-bills is somewhat irregular from year to year. Some years they do not arrive until late May or early June. Early arrival dates: Springfield, April 30, 1986 (HDB); west-central, April 28 (Craig and Franks 1987). Average arrival dates: Chicago, May 11 (14 years); Urbana, May 13 (20 years). Spring bird count totals ranged from seven in 1984 to 185 in 1981. High spring bird counts: 15, Du Page County, May 9, 1981; 12, Cass County, May 10, 1975 (VK). Average departure dates: Chicago, May 28 (14 years); Sangamon County, May 27 (18 years). Late departure dates: Chicago, June 22, 1985 (JL-IB&B1:87); Buffalo, June 17, 1984 (HDB).

Most of the nesting population is in the northern part of the state. Breeding bird survey data for 1965–79 showed that the mean number of birds per route in Illinois was 0.4 (Robbins et al. 1986). The nest is usually at medium height and is better made than the Yellow-bill's nest. There are two to five light bluish eggs. Illinois egg dates are May 28 to August 2. Southern Illinois records include a nest at Lake

Shelbyville in June 1985 (SR-IB&B2:14) and one to four birds at Carlyle Lake all summer 1985 (TF-IB&B2:14).

Early fall migrants: two, Williamson County, July 8, 1984 (TF-AB 38:1026); Lawrence County, July 6, 1980 (LH-SR 27:9). Average arrival dates for fall: Chicago, August 15 (13 years); central Illinois, August 15 (19 years). There are high counts of only two or three birds for fall. Average departure dates: Chicago, September 21 (13 years); west-central, September 17 (five years). Late departure dates: Savanna, October 29, 1977 (BSh-AB 32:213); Carbondale, October 31, 1982 (KM-AB 37:187); Springfield, October 27, 1983 (HDB). Black-billed Cuckoos winter in South America.

YELLOW-BILLED CUCKOO

Coccyzus americanus

COMMON MIGRANT AND SUMMER RESIDENT

This rather large bird with a long tail can go unnoticed because it is sluggish and tends to stay in dense vegetation. Its song, if it can be called that, is a series of ka notes followed by slower and longer notes at the end. Old-timers referred to the cuckoo as the Raincrow and thought that its call forecast rain. The Yellow-billed Cuckoo is found in woodlands, along woodland edges, and in orchards and other open wooded situations. It has a habit of dropping low when it flies, and in so doing it is frequently hit by automobiles. This bird is also noted for flying into picture windows. Although it has been accused of eating other birds' eggs, this cuckoo is beneficial because it eats large numbers of caterpillars and especially fall webworms. When periodical cicadas emerge, this bird feeds on them.

The Yellow-billed Cuckoo waits until late to arrive on the state's breeding grounds. Early spring arrival dates: Richland County, April 27, 1985 (LH-IB&B1:87); Chicago, April 29, 1936 (Clark and Nice 1950); Urbana, April 27 (Smith 1930). Most migration is in May; average dates are Chicago, May 18 (16 years); Urbana, May 5 (18 years); and Sangamon County, May 8 (18 years). Spring bird count totals ranged from 38 in 1984 to 540 in 1982; the highest count was 45 in Pike County, May 9, 1981 (VK). Spring migration continues to about mid-June. An influx was noted at Chicago in June 1980 (SR26:7), and a migrant was at Chicago on June 13, 1984 (JL).

Graber and Graber (1963) noted a decline in these cuckoos between 1909 and 1957, which they attributed to a decrease in orchards (only 10 percent of the 1909 acreage was left by 1957) and the destruction of hedgerows. They estimated that the total Illinois population was 383,000 in 1909 and 92,000 in 1957. The Yellow-billed Cuckoo is most abundant in southern Illinois; numbers decrease northward. Robbins et al. (1986) found significant increases in the east and central regions between 1965 and 1979 on breeding bird surveys. The mean number of birds per survey route in Illinois was 4.5. The nest is placed from medium height to fairly low in vegetation and looks like a well-made dove's nest. The female lays two to five light bluish or greenish blue eggs. Egg dates in Illinois are May 21 to August 30. Parents will sit tight and allow an observer to approach closely before they will leave the nest. Sometimes young are found late, as on September 7, 1979, in Mason County. Some of the highest Yellow-billed Cuckoo counts are in summer: 15, Lake Kinkaid, June 5, 1983 (JR-SR38:8); 18, Pine Hills, June 28, 1986 (DR-IB&B3:14); 70 territories, Lake Shelbyville, July and August 1986 (SR-IB&B3:14); 16, Henderson County, June 10, 1984 (MB-IB&B1:16). Immatures of the Yellow-billed and Black-billed species look very much alike, and even bill color is an unreliable marker at this age.

Actual fall migration is difficult to detect. Yellow-billed Cuckoos migrate at night, since a few have been killed at television towers, but some may also migrate in daytime. Average dates of departure: Chicago, September 16 (16 years); west-central, October 16 (eight years). Most are gone by mid-October, but sometimes these birds stay quite late, looking rather odd sitting in leafless trees: Clinton, November 11, 1979 (RCh-AB34:168); one found dead, Chicago, November 22, 1982 (G.Sadock-SR35:11); Riverton, November 7, 1982 (HDB); Crab Orchard National Wildlife Refuge, November 16, 1982 (JR-SR35:11); Kankakee County, November 6, 1983 (RCh-SR39:18).

Yellow-billed Cuckoos winter from northern South America south to Peru, Bolivia, and northern Argentina.

GROOVE-BILLED ANI

Crotophaga sulcirostris

VERY RARE FALL VAGRANT

This relative of the cuckoos is found in southern Texas and from Mexico south to Central and South America. Records from states adjacent to Illinois point to fall dispersal flights by Groove-billed Anis, which look superficially like Common Grackles, with a floppy or loose tail and a large ridged bill on which grooves are usually visible at close range. Differentiating between Smooth-billed and Groove-billed Anis in the field can be difficult (see Balch 1979).

The Groove-billed Ani's place in the fauna of Illinois is based on five acceptable records, including a specimen and some photographs. All but one of the records are from the Chicago lakefront: Olive Park, October 6, 1979 (JL-AB34:168); Evanston, October 13, 1979 (RE-AB34:785); Montrose Harbor, September 27, 1981 (JL-AB36:184), and September 24-25, 1982 (JL,CM-AB37:187); and the first Illinois specimen (ISM), a window kill from Galesburg, September 28, 1987 (MB,B&A Stephens). Two other records from southern Illinois may be correct, but both birds were first identified as Smooth-billed Anis, which, unlike Groove-bills, are not known to vagrate to any extent: Carbondale, November 12, 1978 (AB33:184); Beall Woods State Park, October 10, 1979 (AB34:168).

COMMON BARN-OWL

Tyto alba

OCCASIONAL PERMANENT RESIDENT

Medium-sized, light in color, and with a heart-shaped face, the Common Barn-Owl has adapted somewhat to living near people. It is found in rather open areas, and it nests and roosts in man-made structures. The call of this owl is a shrill rasping hiss. Nearly every small town and some farms had Barn-Owls up to the early 1960s, when the population declined rapidly, possibly because of the use of pesticides in rodent control and the loss of foraging and nesting habitats (Bowles 1981), shooting, and road kills. Spiers (1940) also noted that extremely cold temperatures cause mortality in these owls. The decline could have been a combination of all these factors, and now they are on the Illinois endangered species list. Their main food item is voles, but they also eat other mammals and birds. The Barn Owl's range is nearly cosmopolitan. The race in the United States is *T. a. pratincola*.

Barn-Owls originally nested in hollow trees but now also nest in barns, steeples, grain elevators, and abandoned buildings. They use no nest materials except occasionally owl pellets. There are four to nine roundish white eggs. Illinois egg dates are March to June 3. Young have been seen as late as September.

Barn-Owls migrate, and at times there appear to be large influxes, as Coale (1925a) suggested after 20 were brought in to be mounted in one fall in Chicago. Bent (1938) noted that a banded Barn-Owl from Illinois was recovered in Mississippi. Because the Barn-Owl population is so low, this migration is now mostly undetectable. Recent records for this owl: Murphysboro, January 26, 1977 (MT-AB31:338); one illegally shot, Logan County, October 8, 1977 (AB32:213); Charleston, April 13, 1978 (LBH-AB32:1015); Chicago, November 25, 1982-January 25, 1983 (AA-AB37:187); nest, Pulaski County, June 11, 1983 (JWh-AB37:994); one in barn, Will County, August 17, 1987 (JM). Spring bird counts showed Barn-Owls only four years, with two in Cook County on May 10, 1975, the highest number (VK). Christmas bird counts for 1976-85 had these owls only four years; all were found in northern Illinois.

EASTERN SCREECH-OWL

Otus asio

COMMON PERMANENT RESIDENT

These small owls have reddish and gray phases (dichromatism), and some are intermediate. Owls of either phase may be paired or both may occur in the same clutch. Both phases are found throughout Illinois. Many Eastern Screech-Owls are killed along roads, especially when snow covers the ground. Schorger (1954) found that the color-phase percentages of 235 owls killed along roads from

Madison, Wisconsin, to Freeport, Illinois, were 38.7 red and 61.3 gray. He also found a melanistic Screech-Owl in Stephenson County on October 28, 1938. Of 73 specimens from Illinois in the Illinois State Museum collection, 41 are red phase and 32 gray. Two subspecies are found in Illinois, *O. a. naevius* in the north and central and *O. a. asio* in the south, but the exact dividing lines are not known and, to complicate matters, *naevius* wanders southward in winter. Apparently little true migration occurs. Screech-Owls are found in all kinds of Illinois woodlands and even in residential areas and city parks. The greater use of wood to heat homes and the manicuring of parklands have depleted their nesting trees in some areas. They eat a variety of insects, small birds, mammals, reptiles, and amphibians. Although Eastern Screech-Owls do occasionally screech, their common call is a whinnying or wavering series of notes. They can be counted by their responses to imitations of their calls, for they will call back at night and sometimes in daylight. Caution should be used in daylight, however, because their roosting spots may be revealed, leaving them open to harassment by Blue Jays and other birds. Though they call at all seasons, August seems to be their most vocal time. Screech-Owls roost in conifers, cavities in trees, and occasionally buildings.

Eastern Screech-Owls are probably more numerous than many observers believe. Spring bird count totals ranged from 25 in 1972 to 88 in 1985. High counts: 20, Pike County, May 9, 1981; 16, McHenry County, May 4, 1974; 14, Lake County, May 8, 1982; 12, Champaign County, May 4, 1985 (VK). Christmas bird count totals for 1976–85 ranged from 135 in 1983 to 222 in 1976. High counts: 47, Chicago North Shore, 1982; 27, Sangamon County, 1980; 21, Beverly, 1978; 20, De Kalb, 1976.

Nesting usually takes place in hollow trees, but these owls will accept specially made boxes or take over Wood Duck boxes. They lay three to seven rounded white eggs; most clutches total five. Illinois egg dates are April 3 to May 27. Most young are fledged in May and June.

GREAT HORNED OWL

Bubo virginianus

COMMON PERMANENT RESIDENT

At dusk or dawn this large owl may be seen sitting on an exposed perch such as a telephone pole or in the top of a tall tree. Even in silhouette its size and its ear tufts make identification easy. Great Horned Owls have yellow eyes and rusty underparts with black barrings. They give low hoots that carry considerable distances. Females can be distinguished by voice, since their hoots are pitched lower than the males'. Females are also larger. With their big talons Great Horns take large prey, including such mammals as opossums, skunks, woodchucks, squirrels, and even domestic cats. They also prey on a variety of birds, some as large as Great Blue Herons, and almost anything else they can kill.

Plumages vary widely in color, and there are several distinct subspecies. The breeding race in Illinois is *B. v. virginianus,* but two other races have occurred. Records for the subarctic, light-colored *B. v. wapacuthu* include a specimen, possibly from Chicago, the last of December 1874 (Nelson 1876); specimen, Bureau County, April 6, 1886 (Ribeau 1891); and sight records—which might be difficult to confirm—from Chicago, January 27–February 4, 1973 (LB,CC-AB27:624), Matteson, January 7–March 11, 1984 (PH-SR40:10), Orland Park, January 30, 1983 (J.Peterson-SR36:8), and Chicago, December 1, 1979 (JL). One specimen of the interior race, *B. v. occidentalis,* was taken at Waukegan, November 25, 1927 (Ford 1956). Migration of the breeding form would be difficult to prove without a banding and recovery program.

These owls nest in old crow, hawk, and squirrel nests. They will also nest in tree cavities, especially where a limb has broken off, and even in buildings. Two to three round white eggs are laid very early in the season. Illinois egg dates are January 28 to March 8. When the young are out of the nest they give a screeching call similar to a Barn-Owl's call.

Totals on spring bird counts ranged from 33 in 1972 to 207 in 1984. Some high counts: 33, Pike County, May 8, 1982; 14, Alexander County, May 7, 1977; 17, Jasper County, May 5, 1984; 12, Ogle County, May 10, 1975 (VK). Christmas bird count totals for 1976–85 ranged from 152 in 1976 to 291 in 1984. High counts were 52 at Beverly in 1977 and 1983. Crab Orchard National Wildlife Refuge recorded 21 in 1984.

SNOWY OWL

Nyctea scandiaca

OCCASIONAL WINTER RESIDENT
DECREASING SOUTHWARD

A few of these diurnal owls, which breed in the tundra circumpolar, show up nearly every winter, especially in northern Illinois. The invasion years are somewhat cyclic depending on the availability of prey farther north. One of the first Illinois observations of Snowy Owls was reported by Kennicott (1854), who said that "during the very cold and stormy weather, I frequently saw them capture prairie hens." From the meager data available, it appears that the major invasion years were 1876–77, 1882–83, 1889–90, 1892–93, 1896–97, 1901–2, 1905–6, 1909–10, 1917–18, 1926–27, 1930–31, 1949–50, 1974–75, 1976–77, 1978–79, and 1980–81. Other possible irruptions took place in 1967–68 and 1987–88.

Snowy Owls occur in open areas, such as plowed fields, fallow fields, lake edges, airfields, and golf courses, and sometimes in cities. They perch on the ground, on higher areas such as knolls, and on more elevated perches, such as telephone poles, bridge abutments, barns, haystacks, and fence posts. Goetz observed one that was flushed from the ground by a person walking a dog in Jackson Park; it then perched for several hours atop a 14-story building. Sometimes these owls can be seen sitting on the ice of a frozen lake. In Illinois they feed on a variety of birds and mammals, mostly voles, although no intensive study of their feeding habits has been done.

Christmas bird counts for 1976–85 showed Snowy Owls every year except 1977, with totals ranging from one to 14 (1980). Highest Christmas count was eight at Calumet City–Sandridge, December 27, 1980. In the winter of 1980–81 at least 59 Snowy Owls were seen in Illinois (VK-SR28:7), including one at Union County Conservation Area, November 19, 1980 (AB35:190)—one of the few records from extreme southern Illinois.

The earliest recent fall Snowy Owl occurred at Montrose, October 4–10, 1974 (T.Gatz-AB29:67). Usually, arrival dates are in November: Rockford, November 2, 1980 (LJ-SR27:9); McHenry County, November 11, 1981 (DF-SR31:13); Coles County, November 21, 1984 (M.Covalt-IB&B1:21). After establishing a winter territory an owl may stay all winter or only a few days. Many Snowy Owls become confused by traffic and are killed on the roads. Others apparently succumb to starvation. A male (ISM#607245) found dead near New Berlin, December 10, 1980, had no fat, an empty gizzard, and a heavy infestation of Mallophaga (bird lice).

Spring departures are usually in March. Available late dates: La Salle, April 1, 1984 (JH-AB38:918); Lake Calumet, May 9, 1964 (Mlodinow 1984); Wolf Lake, April 17, 1966 (LB); Mossville, March 29, 1981 (LA-SR29:10).

NORTHERN HAWK-OWL

Surnia ulula

VERY RARE WINTER RESIDENT

This gray-brown, long-tailed, diurnal owl breeds in the boreal forests and only rarely wanders south in winter to Illinois. Kennicott (1854) listed it among the Illinois birds without comment. Seven records exist for Illinois, but some have no documentation. Nelson (1876) called the Northern Hawk-Owl a rare winter resident and mentioned a specimen collected in Kane County, September 1, 1869. That seems very early for this winter owl. Sanborn (1930) thought this specimen was destroyed in the great Chicago fire. He gave details on another specimen that is still preserved at the Field Museum of Natural History, a female taken at Chicago, December 3, 1922. Arthur Rueckert, who collected that specimen, saw another at Chicago on November 27, 1928, but reported no details. The only record for central Illinois is a sighting by Musselman (1948) near Clayton, Adams County, in January 1947. This bird stayed for three weeks, roosted on the root of a large tree along a creek bank, and was observed eating rabbits and starlings. A Hawk-Owl was observed at Rockford on April 24, 1950, and another was seen at Lisle Arboretum, April

28, 1953 (Smith and Parmalee 1955). Neither record is well documented, and the date of the latter bird was listed incorrectly in Smith and Parmalee. There is a mention of a Hawk-Owl at Chicago about February 14, 1965, without a specific date or any observers listed (AFN19:384).

BURROWING OWL

Athene cunicularia

RARE VAGRANT

A peculiar owl with long legs, this species nests in the ground in abandoned mammal burrows. It is diurnal and is usually seen sitting on the ground, rock piles, or fence posts. The principal range of the Burrowing Owl is the western United States and Florida. The race found in Illinois is probably *A. c. hypugea,* the western form. Two of the 15 Illinois records are specimens, but their present whereabouts are unknown: male near Hamilton, April 9, 1930 (Lambert 1930); Chicago, March 27, 1953 (IAB86:2). Dates of the 10 spring records range from March 27 (1952, Lake Calumet) to May 6 (1950, Chicago). April has the most, with seven. The four fall records range from July 12 (1980, Indiana border, AB35:190) to December 1 (1982, Evanston, JG-SR35:11). There is one winter record for McLean County, January 25–March 30, 1988 (DBi). Other recent records: Lake County, April 26, 1984 (RHe-AB38:918); Jasper County, April 6–17, 1985 (AB39:310); Cerro Gordo, August 6–September 5, 1983 (TM).

BARRED OWL

Strix varia

COMMON PERMANENT RESIDENT
DECREASING SOMEWHAT NORTHEAST

The Barred Owl is fairly large, lacks ear tufts, and has brown eyes. It is the "hoot owl" that calls from the woods, giving a series of eight or nine hoots or caterwauls. It will often call in response to loud noises or an imitation of its own call. On dark, gloomy days it calls in the late afternoon. Its main habitat is bottomland forest, but it also occurs in upland woods and sometimes roosts in conifers in winter. Barred Owls are mostly nocturnal, but occasionally they are seen in the daytime, especially when they have young to feed. They eat primarily mice, but they also take other mammals, birds, reptiles, amphibians, fish, insects, and even spiders and crawfish. Nelson (1876) called this bird a rare species in northeastern Illinois, but Ford (1956) termed it uncommon. The race in Illinois is the nominate form. Like most owls, the Barred nest early, with egg dates ranging from February 25 to April 30 (Bent 1938). They usually nest in a cavity of a tree but will also use old hawk nests. There are two to three round white eggs. The young, giving out a squeaky hiss as they beg for food, are fairly easy to find after they come out of the nest. In the Marshall County Conservation Area, 13 young were fledged in the summer of 1982 (MSw-AB36:983).

Totals on spring bird counts ranged from 48 in 1972 to 264 in 1986, with high counts of 30 in Pike County in 1978 and 1982 and Alexander County in 1985 (VK). Christmas bird count totals for 1976–85 ranged from 58 in 1977 to 122 in 1980. The highest count was 18 in Alexander County in 1984.

GREAT GRAY OWL

Strix nebulosa

HYPOTHETICAL

Kennicott (1854) listed this northern owl as rare and Nelson (1876) called it a very rare winter visitant, but neither gave any records. A Dr. Lambert is supposed to have collected a Great Gray Owl near Rockford about 1930, but the specimen cannot be located (Smith and Parmalee 1955). The largest owl in North America, the Great Gray is usually confined to extensive coniferous forests. There is a recent record from northeastern Iowa, February 15, 1974 (Dinsmore et al. 1984).

LONG-EARED OWL

Asio otus

UNCOMMON MIGRANT AND WINTER RESIDENT; RARE SUMMER RESIDENT

In Illinois Long-eared Owls are usually found by checking coniferous groves where they roost by day. Whether they occur singly or, more usually, in small groups, they choose the densest, darkest parts of the grove in which to roost. These areas can be recognized by the white wash and accumulation of pellets, which they drop one per day per owl. At times an observer can approach closely enough to obtain good views of the owls, but at other times they fly before being seen. When sitting they stretch their bodies and their ear tufts upright to camouflage themselves. It is best not to flush them very frequently because crows will find and harass them and they may leave. At times, especially during migration, Long-eared Owls sit in deciduous trees, usually next to the trunks so that they blend in with the bark. This owl has a variety of call notes, including low-pitched hoots and catlike meows. It hunts strictly at night in open fields or forests. The great majority of its food comprises small mammals, such as voles and mice. It also takes some birds. Detailed accounts of its food habits are given in Graber (1962a) and Birkenholz (1958). The race found in Illinois is *A. o. wilsonianus*, the eastern form. Occasionally this nocturnal owl is seen migrating

along Lake Michigan during the day. It is then difficult to separate from the Short-eared Owl, which is more often a daytime migrant. Balch (1978a) discusses ways to identify these birds in flight. The earliest fall migrants arrive in October: Jackson Park, October 1, 1984 (HR-IB&B1:21), and October 18, 1982 (PC-SR35:11); Matteson, October 29, 1982 (PH-SR35:11); Normal, October 30, 1984 (DBi-IB&B1:21). November is more usual, especially farther south: three, Mossville, November 22, 1980 (LA-SR27:9); two, Urbana, November 21, 1981 (RCh-SR31:13).

Long-eared Owls were recorded every winter on Christmas bird counts for 1976–85, with totals ranging from six in 1984 to 36 in 1976. The highest count was 38 at Rockford in 1961. Other winter records: 200, Morton Arboretum, January 1955 (AC-AFN9:261); 10, Stark County, December 28, 1981 (LA-SR32:6); six, Orland Park, January 9, 1983 (PD-SR36:8); three, Lawrenceville, January 5, 1986 (LH-IB&B2:76); Calhoun County, February 19, 1984 (Hoell-SR40:10); Charleston, January 14–February 3, 1980 (LBH-SR24:3). Wintertime Long-ears are most numerous in northern Illinois.

Spring migration goes mostly undetected, but departure dates are usually in March. Late dates of departure: Urbana, April 18, 1982 (BCho-SR33:10); Jackson Park, April 24, 1982 (PC,HR-SR33:10); Bismark, April 2, 1983 (SB-SR37:18). Spring bird counts, which are in May, have recorded Long-eared Owls only four years, always in small numbers.

Though a sizable breeding population once resided in Illinois, the Long-eared Owl is now an endangered species in the state. Its decline was likely caused by loss of habitat. Loucks (1892), Ford (1956), and Strode (1890) listed several old breeding records. Recent breeding records include Carlyle, 1977 (M.Jantzen-AB31:1008); Vermilion County, 1983 (SB-AB37:994); and Lawrence County, 1986 (DJo-AB40:1211). These owls nest in old crows' nests, usually in conifers but sometimes in dense deciduous trees. They lay four to eight roundish white eggs. Illinois egg dates are March 9 to May 7. Other summer records may indicate nesting: one hit by car, Carbondale, June 11, 1977 (MMo-AB31:1148); Montrose, July 18, 1976 (LB-AB30:963).

SHORT-EARED OWL

Asio flammeus

UNCOMMON MIGRANT AND WINTER RESIDENT; RARE SUMMER RESIDENT

A crepuscular species, the Short-eared Owl is found in open country, usually in fallow fields and marshy areas. Short-ears sometimes fly in the daytime when it is very overcast but are usually seen at dusk or dawn showing their butter-flylike flights over fields. They generally roost in grassy fields but occasionally in short pines. They occur as single birds, small groups, or even in large numbers. They are counterparts of Northern Harriers, sometimes even roosting with them. In Illinois they are usually nonvocal. Their food consists of voles, mice, and other small mammals, a few birds, and some insects (Munyer 1966 and Graber 1962a). Once probably the most abundant owl species in Illinois (Nelson 1876), it is now considered endangered, mainly because of today's clean farming practices and the destruction of prairie habitat. The Short-eared Owl is a cosmopolitan species. The nominate race is found in Illinois.

Early fall arrivals: Evanston, October 3, 1979 (DJ-SR23:8); Illinois Beach State Park, October 15, 1982 (JG-SR35:12); three, Lawrenceville, November 1, 1980 (LH-SR27:9); Springfield, October 8, 1979 (HDB). Dreuth's earliest arrival date for Chicago was August 17, 1934, and his average date was September 28 (11 years). The average arrival date for central Illinois is November 13 (eight years). There are flights along Lake Michigan some years; 13 were noted in Cook County on October 14, 1973 (LB-AB28:61).

Short-eared Owls were recorded every year on Christmas bird counts for 1976–85, with a range of six (1982 and 1985) and 35 (1981). The highest Christmas count was 38 at Rockford in 1950. Other maximum counts in winter: 150 near Mattoon, February 1964 (Irwin 1964); 54, Pike County, February 7, 1986 (LS-IB&B2:77) 14, Silver Springs State Park, December 20–March 12, 1981 (Oram,Steele-SR28:7); 12, St. Clair County, mid-February 1982 (RK-SR32:6). Short-ears winter as far south as central Mexico.

Some migrants from farther south start to appear in Illinois in March and April. High counts for spring: 13, St. Clair County, March 3, 1986 (TF-IB&B2:94); 20, Lake Calumet, March 18, 1979 (IAB190:29). Short-ears occurred on five spring bird counts in small numbers (one to six). Average departure date for spring in central Illinois is April 4 (10 years). Late departure dates: Vermilion County, May 1, 1979 (MC-AB33:777); Carroll County, May 14, 1980 (RN-SR25:6); Springfield, April 30, 1982 (HDB).

Short-eared Owls nest in wet prairie on the ground among tall grass or reeds. They lay four to eight roundish white eggs. Illinois egg dates are April 1 to May 10. The only recent nesting occurred at Goose Lake Prairie in 1973, when two young were raised (DBi-AB27:877). Other summer records may indicate breeding: Green River Conservation Area, June 14, 1982 (M.Brown-SR34:7); one killed, Fulton County, July 20, 1981 (MSt-SR30:9); seven, McHenry County, into June 1981 (DF-SR30:9); Perry County, June 19, 1977 (MMO,MT-AB31:1148); Mode, summer 1985 (KF-AB39:919); Pike County, June 1986 (LS-AB40:1211); three, Lake Calumet, June 12–July 15, 1976 (LB-AB30:963). Short-eared Owls breed as far north as Alaska and northern Canada.

BOREAL OWL

Aegolius funereus

VERY RARE WINTER RESIDENT

The Boreal Owl is a little larger than the Saw-whet Owl and differs in bill color and facial disk. It is also somewhat

more diurnal, feeding in low light. It breeds in the boreal forests of Canada, Alaska, and the northern Rocky Mountains. Boreal Owls infrequently stage invasions of the northern states in winter. Five old records for Illinois are probably valid, but the whereabouts of some of the specimens are not known: one flew against a store window, Rockford, October 15, 1884 (Dickinson 1885); one caught in a barn near Sycamore, last week of January 1887 (Wyman 1915); one shot with an air gun, Kenilworth, December 26, 1902 (Deane 1903); one collected, Cicero, December 1902 (Deane 1903a); one female found dead in the street (CAS#15083), Chicago, March 5, 1914 (Coale 1914). A recent record in Mlodinow (1984) contains insufficient documentation and should be considered invalid.

NORTHERN SAW-WHET OWL

Aegolius acadicus

UNCOMMON TO RARE MIGRANT AND WINTER RESIDENT; VERY RARE SUMMER RESIDENT

Even when this small owl is present in a given area, it will probably not be found except by intensive search or by accident. Nocturnal, it roosts by day in thick vegetation, such as pines, cedars, and tangles of vines. Usually it sits low in trees but sometimes as high as 20 to 30 feet. The Northern Saw-whet Owl is utterly tame and can usually be picked up off a branch and put back without much disturbance—though this is not recommended unless the owl is to be banded. The trick is finding one. A thorough search of pines too often proves fruitless. Graber (1962a) found that these owls roost near the edges of pine plantations that have extensive woodlands nearby. The observer should look for white wash on the trunks of pines, for pellets, and for the mobbing actions of smaller birds to give the Saw-whet's position away. Details on these and other methods of detection are given by Swengel (1987). The call of these owls is a whistled too, too, too in long series. Apparently they call most often in late winter and spring. Graber (1962a) found that 70 percent of Saw-whets' prey is deer mice. They also take house mice, voles, and—particularly toward spring—small birds, probably because migrants are so abundant at that time. The subspecies in Illinois is A. a. acadicus. Of five specimens in the Illinois State Museum collection, one is dated December 16, 1909, from Aurora; four others are road or window kills in Sangamon County from November 11 to March 15. One male weighed 101.1 grams, while three females weighed 87.4, 89.2, and 101.4 grams.

Early fall migrants occur in October: Chicago, October 9, 1983 (SP-SR39:18); Dundee, October 2, 1977 (B.Turner-AB32:213); Winnebago County, October 8, 1981 (LJ-SR31:13); Carbondale, October 14, 1988 (DR). One banded at Arnold, Minnesota, on October 2, 1981, was recovered at Horseshoe Lake a few weeks later, on October 27. High counts for this species are virtually nonexistent. The best method of detecting migrant Saw-whets is by netting. Lee Johnson banded 12 in Winnebago County, October 8–November 15, 1981.

Seven Christmas bird counts for 1976–85 produced Saw-whets. Most were in northern Illinois, including two at Chicago urban in 1983. Farther south, one was counted at Beverly in 1977 and one at Pere Marquette in 1980. Because so few records come from southern Illinois, the presence of two Saw-whets (one banded) at Ozark, February 2–March 1, 1986, is of special interest. A male specimen in the Illinois Natural History Survey collection came from Albion, Edwards County, March 6, 1957.

Spring migration probably starts in late February or early March. Late spring migrants: one banded, Rockford, April 21, 1984 (LJ-SR41:20); Jackson Park, April 14, 1980 (PC-SR25:6); Urbana, March 16, 1980 (RCh-SR25:6).

Although specific breeding records are few, evidence suggests that Saw-whets nest in Illinois in very small numbers. Coale (1877a) listed these records: a female caught in a pine tree, Chicago, June 23, 1874; three adults shot, Chicago, July 1874; a young female shot, Chicago, June 15, 1875; one young brought in alive, Chicago, July 10, 1875; and another young shot from a poplar tree, July 16, 1875. Gault (1922) referred to a nest in Marion County in 1890, and three young were captured from a willow thicket along the Mississippi River near Quincy, April 28, 1951 (Musselman 1951). One was shot and another captured near Evanston, June 26, 1932 (Ford 1932). An adult, June 4, and a juvenile, June 18, 1966, were seen at Allerton Park (Roth 1967). A juvenile was seen in southern Cook County, June 12, 1982 (PD-AB36:983), and another was at Joliet, July 1, 1982 (JM-AB36:983). Further searches for this diminutive, secretive owl may yield more nesting records.

COMMON NIGHTHAWK

Chordeiles minor

COMMON MIGRANT AND SUMMER RESIDENT

In the sand areas of Mason and Henderson Counties some Common Nighthawks still nest on the ground. Most of these nighthawks, however, have adapted to life in the city, nesting on rooftops. They glide above the buildings on pointed wings, showing their white wing patches and giving their nasal *peent* or *beerp* call notes. Their flight is often erratic, and the male displays by dives and sudden upward surges. These aerial displays produce a booming noise made by the wings. Common Nighthawks are usually crepuscular but some can be seen migrating in the daytime. When perched, they sit lengthwise on horizontal branches, where their cryptic coloration makes them difficult to see. They usually sit higher than other goatsuckers, although at times they sit on the ground. There is considerable variation in nighthawk populations, and at least three subspecies have occurred in Illinois. The main breeding form is *C. m. minor,*

but *C. m. chapmani* breeds in southern Illinois and *C. m. sennetti,* which breeds to the northwest, has been recorded on migration. Oberholser (1914) also listed the western form, *C. m. howelli,* for Illinois.

The first spring Common Nighthawks appear in April: Carbondale, April 21, 1986 (KM-IB&B2:94); Springfield, April 21, 1987 (HDB); Kendall County, April 26, 1974 (Mlodinow 1984). Average spring arrival dates: Urbana, May 7 (20 years); Chicago, May 17 (11 years); west-central, May 4 (15 years). High counts for spring: 110, Big River State Forest, May 23, 1987 (MB); 125, Quincy, May 17, 1982 (AD-SR33:10); 100, Rockford, May 30, 1958 (LJ-AFN12:358). Spring bird count totals ranged from 57 in 1978 to 986 in 1976; the highest count was 117 in Macon County, May 8, 1976 (VK). Flocks were still migrating at Dundee on June 5, 1983 (RM-SR37:18).

Robbins et al. (1986) found no definite trend in Common Nighthawk populations based on recent breeding bird survey data. The mean number of these nighthawks per survey route in Illinois was 0.2. Nighthawks build no nests; they nest on the ground or on flat roofs. The female usually lays two whitish or buff eggs heavily marked with darker colors. Illinois egg dates are at least May 25 to July 13. People often find young nighthawks on the streets, but unless they are in immediate danger they should be left so that the parents can attend them.

Fall migration generally starts with the passage of the first cold front in August, but migrants are sometimes difficult to distinguish from locally summering birds. The average fall migrant arrival date for Sangamon County is August 18 (12 years). Maximum counts for fall are higher than in spring: 3000, Chicago, August 29, 1985 (AA-AB40:121); 1000, Petersburg, September 14, 1981 (CB-SR31:13); 2430, Danville, August 31, 1982 (ME-SR35:12); 1000, Waukegan, August 20, 1980 (JN-SR27:9). Average departure dates: Chicago, September 11 (11 years); west-central, October 1 (seven years); Sangamon County, October 7 (18 years). Several stragglers are reported nearly every year, some of which seem to have come back north on southerly flows of air: Kane County, October 23, 1982 (J.Steele-SR35:12); Springfield, October 26, 1986 (HDB); Rockford, October 10, 1978 (AB33:184); Blue Island, October 11, 1959 (KB-AFN14:41). Common Nighthawks winter in South America.

CHUCK-WILL'S-WIDOW

Caprimulgus carolinensis

UNCOMMON MIGRANT AND SUMMER RESIDENT IN SOUTHERN ILLINOIS DECREASING NORTHWARD

This nocturnal woodland species is best detected by its distinctive calling of its common name. It is larger and browner than the Whip-poor-will, and where the two nest in the same area the Chuck takes the more open spaces on the forest edge and the Whip the wooded habitat. Chucks are often associated with pine groves in Illinois; they prefer upland areas. Many of the Chuck-will's-widows that occur in northern Illinois are probably overmigrants; one was recorded there as early as 1910, on May 5 at Hinsdale (Craigmile 1934–35). Mlodinow (1984) noted 20 records for the Chicago area. Like all goatsuckers, the Chuck has a small bill but a huge mouth, so it can capture flying insects on the wing. Occasionally it takes small birds, too. Oddly, a female wandered into a building at Springfield on May 11, 1979, and perched on a ledge for the whole day. Early spring arrival dates: Coles County, April 28, 1981 (R.Funk,LBH-SR29:10); specimen, Willow Springs, April 26, 1967 (CAS); Sand Ridge State Forest, April 23, 1986 (RBj-IB&B2:94); Jackson County, April 20, 1987 (DR). George (1968) listed an early arrival date of March 30 for southern Illinois. Spring bird count totals ranged from two in 1983 to 47 in 1977. All high counts came from southern Illinois: 24, Alexander County, May 7, 1977; 18, Pope County, May 5, 1979; 16, Union County, May 8, 1982 (VK). Recent overmigrants: Decatur, May 16, 1977 (RP-AB31:1008); Waukegan, May 28, 1978 (JN-AB32:1015); Vermilion County, May 27, 1986 (MC-IB&B2:94).

Chuck-will's-widows nest on the ground, laying two whitish eggs with gray or purplish blotches and brown spots. They have nested in Sand Ridge State Forest since 1979 and occasionally other areas in central Illinois, including Peoria County, 1963, and Pike County, 1966. One Chuck was in Henderson County, June 9, 1984 (MB-AB38:918). Two were calling at Palos Hills throughout June 1985 (RB,MBi-IB&B2:14). Little is known about the nesting cycle in Illinois.

Fall migration goes almost undetected. George (1968) listed the late date of September 19 for southern Illinois. One Chuck was at Springfield flying around an outside light on September 13, 1971 (HDB). Chuck-will's-widows winter from the southern United States south to Colombia.

WHIP-POOR-WILL

Caprimulgus vociferus

COMMON MIGRANT AND SUMMER RESIDENT

Even though this is the famous night-calling bird of song and poetry, few people have actually seen one. Although Whip-poor-wills occasionally call off and on all night, they call most regularly at dawn and dusk. These goatsuckers inhabit open woods and feed over brushy pastures and along woodland edges. They catch moths and other flying insects on the wing by opening their large mouths. They sometimes sit in the road, where their eyes glow red in the headlights, and unfortunately they are frequently hit by cars.

Whip-poor-wills are fairly early spring migrants: Pope County, March 23, 1975 (RGr-AB29:698); Pope and Saline Counties, March 30, 1986 (TF,KP-AB40:479); Chicago, April 8, 1981 (RB-SR29:10); Springfield, April 7, 1977 (HDB); Urbana, March 30 (Smith 1930); specimen, Fayette County, April 7, 1893 (ISM-E.F.Steinhauer). Average spring arrival dates: Chicago, April 27 (10 years); Urbana, April 24 (19 years); Sangamon County, April 18 (17 years). Cooke (1888) found that the Whip-poor-will averaged about 20 miles per day during spring migration in 1884. The total number of Whips on spring bird counts ranged from 192 in 1972 and 1973 to 698 in 1982. High counts—all from southern and western Illinois—included 86, Pike County, May 8, 1982, and 92, Alexander County, May 7, 1977 (VK).

Bjorklund and Bjorklund (1983), after taking a census of Whip-poor-wills in Sand Ridge State Forest (3000 hectares), Mason County, estimated 202 territories in 1981 and 158 in 1983. They found that June is the best time for censusing, even though Whip-poor-wills call from April to August. Nights with light winds and moonlight seemed best for calling. Other breeding counts: 60 in southern Shelby County (KF) and 53 at Lake Shelbyville in 1985 (SR-IB&B2:14). The mean number of Whips on 64 breeding bird survey routes in Illinois for 1965–79 was 0.5 (Robbins et al. 1986). Whip-poor-wills may be declining in some areas, leaving their distribution in the state somewhat spotty or local. These cryptic birds nest on the ground, using oak leaves on which to lay two whitish eggs that have faint spots or blotches. Holland, who took 27 clutches of eggs in Knox, Henderson, and Warren Counties, found that Whips nest in open areas of woodlands or along woodland edges, usually near a hazelnut thicket. His egg dates are May 16–June 11. A nest at Siloam Springs State Park had two eggs by May 10, 1980 (SR18:133). Barns, who collected at Lacon, gave egg dates of May 9–June 15.

There is a cessation of song in August, then Whip-poor-wills resume calling briefly in September. Dreuth detected a fall migrant in Chicago as early as August 26, 1941 (Clark and Nice 1950). No large counts are available for fall because of the difficulty of detection. Usually the only Whips seen are those flushed. In some cases they can be detected by the mobbing behavior of smaller passerines. I found a Whip-poor-will sitting 13 feet up in a pine tree at Oak Ridge Cemetery in Springfield on September 26, 1982, by watching some scolding warblers, vireos, and kinglets. Even though I walked completely around the tree and the passerines kept jumping all around the Whip, it did not fly off. Most departure dates for fall migrants are in September and early October. The average date for central Illinois is September 16 (11 years). Late dates of departure: Athens, September 18, 1980 (VK-AB35:190); Mode, September 27, 1985 (KF-IB&B2:52); Monroe County, October 5, 1980 (RK-SR27:9); Jackson Park, September 27, 1981 (RG-SR31:13); Forest Glen, October 5, 1983 (SB-SR39:18); female specimen (SIU) near Cobden, October 6, 1967.

Whip-poor-wills winter on the Gulf and southern Atlantic Coasts and south as far as western Panama.

BLACK SWIFT

Cypseloides niger

HYPOTHETICAL

This large swift is found in the western mountains. All three reports from Illinois fail to give adequate details to form state records: one, Saganashkee Slough, September 5, 1953, and four, Evanston, early September 1953 (Smith and Parmalee 1955); Chicago, May 15, 1956 (Wasson 1956). Vagrant records exist for Texas and Florida. Black Swifts winter in the Neotropics, but the exact areas are unknown. These interesting birds nest under waterfalls and in sea caves.

CHIMNEY SWIFT

Chaetura pelagica

COMMON MIGRANT AND SUMMER RESIDENT

These short, stubby-tailed birds are generally taken for granted, since they can be seen at any time during daylight hours in the warmer months, flying overhead on stiff wings. But when they depart in fall the sky seems empty and the cold of winter just around the corner. This swift's rapid chatter of notes is familiar to almost everyone, though some people may not realize that they know it. The Chimney Swift is one of the birds that have benefited from people's presence, because it adopted chimneys for nesting. However, fewer and fewer chimneys are available. Some Chimney Swifts, such as those in the Cache River bottoms in southern Illinois, still use hollow trees for nesting. Graber and Graber (1963) noted that ecological changes had favored this bird: for every 100 acres of urban habitat in 1909 there were 6.0 swifts; in 1958 the average had increased to 24.4 swifts. Robbins et al. (1986) found a slight but significant increase in Chimney Swifts on breeding bird surveys for 1965–79. Occasionally fairly large numbers of swifts are killed by carbon monoxide poisoning in chimneys (see Deane 1908 and Musselman 1950a). I have found as many as 100 killed by cars on cold and rainy spring days when swifts fly low to glean insects at the dam at Lake Springfield. Chimney Swifts feed almost exclusively on insects, taking most of them from the air but also gleaning them from leaves in the tops of trees (George 1971a).

Migrating spring swifts usually arrive in mid-April, but there are some exceptions: Carbondale, March 30, 1986 (DR-AB40:479); west-central, March 22, no year given (Craig and Franks 1987); Fulton County, April 6, 1980 (KM-AB34:782); Chicago, April 1, 1972 (BT-AB26:767). Average spring arrival dates: Urbana, April 20 (18 years); Chicago, May 6 (16 years); west-central, April 13 (14 years). Total numbers on spring bird counts ranged from 2837 in 1972 to 9987 in 1983. The highest count was 1000 in

Grundy County, May 7, 1977 (VK). Other high counts: 1000, Horseshoe Lake, May 8, 1984 (TF,KR-SR41:20); 750, Lake Vermilion, May 3, 1983 (SB-SR37:18).

For nests, Chimney Swifts glue sticks to the walls of chimneys with their saliva. The female lays two to six white eggs. Illinois egg dates are May 15 to July 3 (Bent 1940). Young occasionally fall out of the nest and are found on the hearth. More than 300 swifts were using a chimney at Chicago, June 26, 1982 (JL-SR34:8).

In fall, flocks of swifts fly over ponds and lakes. Large concentrations can also be seen at dusk swirling around chimneys, which the swifts then drop into one at a time at fairly high speeds. Maximum counts for fall: 5000, Jackson Park, September 3, 1981 (PC,HR-SR31:13); 1200, Madison County, September 21, 1983 (RG,PS-SR39:18); 3700, Danville, October 8, 1985 (ME-IB&B2:52). Average departure dates for fall: Chicago, September 12 (16 years); west-central, October 18 (nine years); Sangamon County, October 14 (17 years). Swifts usually leave on a rigid schedule about mid-October. In 1925, however, hundreds stayed late for some unknown reason; 500 were found dead at Edwardsville on November 14 that year, and late birds were seen up to November 16 at Quincy and November 14 at Lawrenceville (Widmann 1928). Other late dates: Carbondale, November 23, 1974 (DK-AB29:67); two, Lawrence County, October 25, 1983 (LH-SR39:18); west-central, November 6, no year given (Craig and Franks 1987).

The whereabouts of the Chimney Swifts' winter home was unknown until rather recently. It is now known that they migrate to Peru, northern Chile, and northern Brazil.

RUBY-THROATED HUMMINGBIRD

Archilochus colubris

COMMON MIGRANT AND FAIRLY COMMON SUMMER RESIDENT

The smallest bird in eastern North America and the only hummingbird found regularly in Illinois, the Ruby-throated inhabits woodlands, wood edges, weedy areas, gardens, and anywhere else it can find flowers to feed on. In fall a jewelweed patch in the woods is a good place to see Ruby-throated Hummingbirds; at times 10 or 15 might be found in a single patch. In spring and summer they favor columbine and trumpet vine. Except for some squeaks and clicks they do little vocalizing, but the buzzing of their wings may attract an observer's attention. They are usually seen in flight, but they also spend a considerable time perched, usually near the tops of dead branches. In their interesting pendulum display flight, the male flies back and forth in an arc over the female. These hummingbirds are very aggressive, fighting among themselves for space and often attacking other birds in their territories. A well-placed hummingbird feeder can attract Ruby-throats for close looks and photo sessions.

The earliest spring migrants arrive in April: Richland County, April 11, 1981 (LH); Chicago, April 11, 1981 (DP-AB35:830); Carbondale, April 12, 1985 (KM-IB&B1:88). Average arrival dates: Urbana, May 9 (20 years); Chicago, May 16 (16 years); west-central, May 4 (15 years). Maximum spring counts: 14, Massac County, May 4, 1985 (DR-IB&B1:88); 26, Alexander County, May 8, 1987 (PK). Spring bird count totals ranged from 21 in 1978 to 548 in 1986, reflecting the considerable fluctuation in hummingbird numbers from year to year. The highest spring count was 43 in Schuyler County on May 10, 1986 (VK). Dreuth's latest migrant at Chicago was June 2, 1940 (Clark and Nice 1950).

The mean number of Ruby-throats per breeding bird survey route in Illinois was 0.3 (Robbins et al. 1986). Twenty-two territories were located at Lake Shelbyville in June and July 1986 (SR-IB&B3:15). The nests—little cups saddled on a limb and containing two white eggs—are difficult to locate in the dense vegetation, but occasionally a female will fly directly to a nest. Illinois egg dates are May 31 to July 3. A female was spotted on a nest in Alexander County on May 9, 1987 (ID).

The Ruby-throats that go farther north for the summer start returning by August. Average fall arrival dates: Chicago, September 2 (nine years); Sangamon County, August 11 (six years). High counts for fall: 38, Vermilion County, September 6, 1986 (SB-AB41:96); 20, Olney, August 28, 1983 (LH-SR39:18); 17, Champaign County, September 3, 1984 (RCh-IB&B1:21). High counts seem to be declining, and it may be that the population of these fragile birds has decreased in the past decade. Average fall departure dates: Chicago, September 25 (nine years); Sangamon County, September 28 (18 years). Hess (1910) said that many of these hummingbirds "stay in the fall until caught by the frost. I have found them hanging quite dead in the vines after a sharp October night frost." Late departure dates: Urbana, November 7, 1979 (IM-AB34:168); Charleston, November 3, 1984 (LBH-AB39:61); Mode, October 20, 1985 (KF-IB&B2:52). The Ruby-throated Hummingbird winters from southern Texas south to central Costa Rica.

BLACK-CHINNED HUMMINGBIRD

Archilochus alexandri

HYPOTHETICAL

This western hummingbird has been reported once from Illinois: a male at Beall Woods the first week in August 1967. The details were not sufficient, however, to add the Black-chinned to the state's bird list. No reports have come from elsewhere in the Midwest, but this hummingbird has been recorded in Florida and Massachusetts and occurs annually in Louisiana.

RUFOUS HUMMINGBIRD

Selasphorus rufus

HYPOTHETICAL

Two immature female birds that may have been Rufous or Allen's Hummingbirds have been seen and photographed in Illinois. The first was at a feeder in Virden from August to November 24, 1986. Goetz (1987) discusses this event in detail. The second bird was also at a feeder, at Macomb from at least August 29 to 31, 1988 (EFr,DO). These hummingbirds can be identified only by photographs, since the photos stop the action. Even then they usually can be identified only to superspecies. The main identification points lie in the shape and coloration of the tail feathers. But because Rufous and Allen's Hummingbirds in immature and female plumages are so similar, neither could be eliminated in these two instances, although Rufous is the most likely to occur and seems to be indicated by some minor points. Rufous Hummingbirds have been seen in Wisconsin, Michigan, Indiana, Kentucky, and Missouri.

BELTED KINGFISHER

Ceryle alcyon

COMMON MIGRANT; UNCOMMON SUMMER AND WINTER RESIDENT

This unique bird is found in Illinois around ponds and lakes and along streams and rivers. Its harsh rattling calls, bluish and white pattern, and fairly large size make it conspicuous. Females have a chestnut vest, but otherwise male and female are colored much alike. Belted Kingfishers catch fish by diving from a perch or a hovering position. They were once persecuted by fishermen because of their diet, but today they are protected. They take mostly fish under six inches long and cause trouble only at fish hatcheries, where screened pools avert the problem. The subspecies in Illinois is the eastern *C. a. alcyon*.

Spring migration is detectable only after severe winters, since these kingfishers stay north as long as there is open water. They start moving north as early as February. Average spring arrival dates: Urbana, March 17 (20 years); Chicago, April 1 (16 years); Sangamon County, March 19 (12 years). Spring bird count totals ranged from 91 in 1972 to 365 in 1986; the highest count was 43 in Cook County, May 10, 1986 (VK). A migrant was at the Chicago lakefront as late as May 31, 1937 (Clark and Nice 1950).

No long-term changes were found in kingfisher populations using breeding bird survey data for 1965–79. The mean number of birds per survey route in Illinois was 0.2 (Robbins et al. 1986). These birds burrow into high banks, sometimes up to 15 feet deep, to lay their six to eight white eggs. Illinois egg dates are May 6 to June 8. Nest contents are usually very difficult to determine, but when the young come out they line up on a limb to be fed by the adults.

Even less is known about the timing of fall migration than of spring's, but in both seasons migration seems to be diurnal. Dreuth noted in his study of Lincoln Park, Chicago, that the average arrival date in fall was August 6 and the average departure date October 18 (both for 16 years).

Any extensive open water in winter may induce a kingfisher to stay. Christmas bird count totals for 1976–85 ranged from 110 in 1983 to 203 in 1984. The highest count was 28 at Forest Glen in 1965. Belted Kingfishers winter as far south as northern South America.

LEWIS' WOODPECKER

Melanerpes lewis

HYPOTHETICAL

This interesting western woodpecker is the subject of two undocumented Illinois sight records. One Lewis' Woodpecker was reported on the north side of Chicago, May 26, 1923 (Hine 1924) and the other was reported at Argo, Cook County, May 14, 1932 (Ford 1956). Although these records may be correct, no specimens, photographs, or written descriptions are available on which to make a judgment. The Lewis' Woodpecker has been reported from Missouri, Iowa, Wisconsin, Kansas, Arkansas, and Oklahoma, with extreme records from Rhode Island and Massachusetts.

RED-HEADED WOODPECKER

Melanerpes erythrocephalus

COMMON MIGRANT AND SUMMER RESIDENT; COMMON WINTER RESIDENT DECREASING NORTHWARD

The bold pattern of the Red-headed Woodpecker is so distinctive that this bird is familiar to most people. It prefers woodland edges, open areas within woodlands, or even open areas with isolated trees or telephone poles. Burned places, areas with dead trees (as in Dutch elm disease), and inundated spots with killed trees provide an especially good habitat for Red-headed Woodpeckers. They do a lot of fly-catching, feed on the ground, and bore into trees to obtain food. In summer their food is mostly insects, especially Coleoptera and Lepidoptera. In winter they store and eat acorns, and the availability of the mast crop determines whether they winter in a given locality. They also eat waste grain, mostly corn, from fields next to woods or sometimes along roads. This habit of feeding along roads leads to the accidental killing of many Red-heads by motorists. Red-heads are usually noisy and aggressive, fighting in particular with Red-bellied Woodpeckers and European Starlings when not squabbling among themselves. The eastern race, *M. e. erythrocephalus,* is found in Illinois.

Because many Red-heads winter in Illinois and some spring migration is probably nocturnal, the movement occurs with little fanfare. It may begin as early as February some years. Average arrival dates: Chicago, April 28 (16 years); west-central, March 29 (13 years); Sangamon County, April 19 (11 years). High counts come from spring bird counts, which have totaled from 2400 in 1985 to 4564 in 1974. The highest count was 337 in McDonough County, May 5, 1979 (VK).

Graber and Graber (1963) found Red-headed Woodpeckers throughout the state in summer, with a June population in 1909 of 1,270,000 but down to 134,000 in 1958. They surmised that the drop was due to the introduction of the European Starling and to subtle changes in habitat. Illinois had a mean of 6.9 birds per breeding bird survey route for 1965–79 (Robbins et al. 1986). Kleen in 1979 (SR22:5) noted a 300 percent increase in the number of Red-heads in southern Illinois on a nine-year average. These woodpeckers excavate holes in the trunks of trees or telephone poles and occasionally use bluebird boxes for nesting sites. The three to six roundish white eggs are laid on the floor of the cavity with no nest. Illinois egg dates are at least May 9 to July 10 (Bent 1939). Young Red-headed Woodpeckers have gray heads and are sometimes seen late in the season, occasionally into the following year.

Fall migration is mostly diurnal and usually much more obvious than spring migration. In fall these woodpeckers can be seen with Blue Jays as they follow watercourses south. They fly fairly low, just above the treetops. The larger river valleys are good places to see this migration. Some Red-heads apparently migrate by night, as they are killed at television towers in small numbers. Average arrival dates of fall migrants: Chicago, August 30 (16 years); Sangamon County, September 9 (six years). Average departure dates: Chicago, October 12 (16 years); Sangamon County, October 19 (nine years).

The winter population in Illinois varies considerably from year to year. Some years hardly any are present; other years many obviously migrate only to the state's major river valleys. Yet occasionally many seem to winter near their summer homes, making a habitat change from open areas to forests, mostly in the bottomlands. Graber and Graber (1963) noted that Red-heads wintered farther north in 1956–57 than in 1906–7. In January 1907 an estimated 38,000 were all in southern Illinois, whereas in January 1957 the estimated 92,000 were mostly in central and southern Illinois. The very next year, in February 1958, there were 424,000 and 98 percent of them were in southern Illinois. Thus most of the central Illinois population had migrated to southern Illinois. Christmas bird count totals for 1976–85 ranged from 580 in 1978 to 1894 in 1976. The highest count was 700 at Pere Marquette State Park in 1950. All the highs came from southern Illinois and the Illinois and Mississippi River valleys.

RED-BELLIED WOODPECKER

Melanerpes carolinus

COMMON PERMANENT RESIDENT
DECREASING NORTHWARD

The Red-bellied Woodpecker is one of the southern Illinois species that have steadily expanded their populations northward. Graber and Graber (1963) noted that in 1907–9 Red-bellieds were breeding only in southern Illinois but by 1957–58 they were found throughout the state. They remain most abundant in southern Illinois, but central Illinois has about equal numbers per forest area. The estimated Red-bellied population was 103,000 in 1907, all in southern Illinois, and 198,000 in 1957, mostly in southern and central Illinois. Robbins et al. (1986) noted a rising population trend throughout the Red-bellied's range. The mean number of birds per breeding bird survey route in Illinois for 1965–79 was 2.9. In one year, from 1978 to 1979, the southern Illinois population declined by 20 to 40 percent (VK-SR22:5), probably a temporary drop due to the severe winter.

Red-bellied Woodpeckers are a forest species, utilizing both upland and bottomland. They compete with Red-headed Woodpeckers, and usually the Red-heads dominate. Although the two species tend to stay apart both ecologically and geographically, some overlap occurs. Red-bellieds are also found in some residential areas and parks. They feed on acorn mast, fruits, and insects such as beetles and ants. The race found in Illinois is *M. e. zebra,* although Mengel (1965) considered all Kentucky specimens *M. c. carolinus.* The exact subspecies needs to be determined from a large series of Illinois specimens.

It is questionable whether this woodpecker does much migrating. Certainly some dispersal takes place. One seen flying south at Sangchris State Park, October 1, 1980, appeared to be migrating. The Grabers have noted Red-bellieds flying with other diurnal migrants in fall. Goetz saw them on a regular basis at Jackson Park, and they appeared to be migrating along Lake Michigan both in May and in October and November. And a Red-bellied or two have been killed at television towers, but they may have been local birds killed in daytime fog. Spring bird count totals ranged from 596 in 1972 to 1521 in 1986, an increase that is probably attributable to the presence of more observers rather than a change in population. The highest spring bird count was 132 in Jasper County, May 5, 1984 (VK).

Red-bellied Woodpeckers nest in excavated cavities in dead trees. They usually choose a limb rather than the trunk. Red-bellieds compete not only with Red-headed Woodpeckers but also with European Starlings for nest sites, especially in woodlots that have been simplified or fragmented. The female lays three to five rounded white eggs. Illinois egg dates are April 1 to June 23.

Graber and Graber (1963) noted that the Red-bellied population had increased in winter. They speculated that in southern and central Illinois this increase was due to local production of young. In northern Illinois, however, the increase was greater than production of offspring would warrant, and where these "extra" birds come from is unknown. Red-bellieds, though still principally woodland birds, forage more often in the open in winter, and some are killed along the road while feeding on waste grain. Christmas bird count totals for 1976–85 were fairly constant, ranging from 1355 in 1978 to 2018 in 1982. The highest count was 331 at Union County in 1982.

YELLOW-BELLIED SAPSUCKER

Sphyrapicus varius

COMMON MIGRANT; FAIRLY COMMON
WINTER RESIDENT DECREASING
NORTHWARD; RARE SUMMER RESIDENT

Of all the woodpeckers, Yellow-bellied Sapsuckers have the most definite migration pattern. Night migrants, they travel considerable distances; some winter as far south as Panama. In Illinois they are found in woodlands, both deciduous and coniferous. Their tree-drilling pattern is easy to identify, for the holes are placed in rows. They feed on the sap and the cambium of trees, and they can damage or kill the trees when they feed on them extensively. They also eat insects and fruits. Yellow-bellied Sapsuckers are generally located by sight, but their catlike call or squeal sometimes gives their position away. Imitation of this note will induce them to call back.

Much has been written about the occurrence of Red-naped Sapsuckers in Illinois. As early as 1876 Nelson wrote that "males in spring often have the white nuchal band tipped with red much as in var. nuchalis." Dreuth recorded one such bird at Chicago on April 27, 1930 (Clark and Nice 1950). Four others marked with red napes are listed from Chicago by Landing (1987), and I saw one at Springfield. All these birds are now considered variations of the Yellow-bellied Sapsucker (see Landing).

Even with winter birds present in Illinois, increased numbers of Yellow-bellieds can be detected during spring migration. Average arrival dates: Urbana, March 26 (20 years); Chicago, April 1 (15 years); Sangamon County, March 28 (17 years). High counts for spring: 35, Chicago, April 14, 1985 (CM-AB39:308); 24, Chicago, April 18, 1982 (JL-AB36:859); 16, Springfield, April 13, 1982 (HDB). Spring bird count totals ranged from 25 in 1986 to 134 in 1973; the highest count was 39 in Cook County in 1973 (VK). Average spring departure dates: Urbana, May 11 (20 years); Chicago, May 4 (15 years); Sangamon County, April 28 (18 years). The latest departure date was Chicago, June 7, 1982 (SP-SR33:11).

A thin population of these sapsuckers has nested in Illinois since the earliest records were kept. Kennicott (1854) noted that the Yellow-bellied was known to nest in Cook County. Cooke (1888) stated that two nests were found at Danville in 1884. A nest was reported in Marshall County in 1888. Two sets of eggs were taken from a nest in

Tazewell County (Loucks 1892). Other nests were recorded in Putnam County in 1922, Cook County in 1949, and the Henderson State Forest (three nests) in 1955. More recently, nesting occurred at Palisades State Park in 1985 (Guth 1986) and Kennekuk Cove State Park in 1986 (MC-AB40:1211). Sapsucker egg dates in Illinois are April 20 to June 3 (Bent 1939). Fall migration begins in September. Early arrival dates: Chicago, September 7, 1941 (Clark and Nice 1950); Springfield, September 7, 1988 (HDB). Average arrival dates: Chicago, September 15 (16 years); Sangamon County, September 24 (18 years). High counts for fall: 16, Chicago, October 6, 1985 (JL,CM); 13, Jackson Park, October 6, 1983 (PC,HR-SR39:19); 12 at a television tower kill, Springfield, October 14, 1985 (ISM). Average departure dates: Chicago, October 18 (16 years); west-central, October 19 (seven years).

In winter these birds tend to frequent residential areas, parks, and cemeteries in the central and northern parts of the state. In the south they are usually found in bottomland forests. Christmas bird count totals for 1976-85 ranged from 60 in 1978 to 185 in 1972. The highest count was 77 at Union County in 1976, and all recent high counts have come from southern Illinois.

WILLIAMSON'S SAPSUCKER

Sphyrapicus thyroideus

VERY RARE VAGRANT

An uncommon bird anywhere, the Williamson's Sapsucker is a strange record in Illinois. Native to the mountains of western North America, it is found especially in fir and lodgepole pine (AOU 1983). In winter it migrates to lowland areas and has occurred as far east as Minnesota, Kansas, and east central Texas. The one Illinois record was of a distinctive male at a residential area in Chicago on April 17, 1985. It was first seen by D. Yarbrough and later by several Chicago birders and was documented by Dave Johnson and Jim Landing. Though hybrids between the Williamson's and the Red-naped Sapsuckers are found, this bird appeared to be a normal Williamson's. This species exhibits strong sexual dimorphism, with the female looking somewhat like a flicker. Williamson's Sapsuckers winter as far south as west central Mexico.

DOWNY WOODPECKER

Picoides pubescens

COMMON PERMANENT RESIDENT

The smallest woodpecker in Illinois, the Downy closely resembles the bigger Hairy Woodpecker. Graber and Graber (1963) found Downies four times more numerous than Hairy Woodpeckers in Illinois. Downies occur in woodlands, on woodland edges, and sometimes in fairly open areas such as weed patches and cornfields. Though they are mostly sedentary, they seem to increase in numbers at certain times of the year, reflecting either partial migration or a dispersal of some sort. These woodpeckers readily come to feeders and monopolize the suet, giving way only to larger woodpeckers. They feed on cornstalks, obtaining corn borers, and on ragweeds, evidently getting cocoons of Lepidoptera. They also eat ants, grasshopper eggs, and beetles, especially wood borers. Their vegetable food includes corn and poison ivy berries. The race found in Illinois is *P. p. medianus*.

Graber and Graber (1963) estimated the breeding population in Illinois in 1957 to be 287,000 and found central Illinois forest to have the highest density. Robbins et al. (1986), using breeding bird survey data, found an increase in Downy numbers in Illinois, with a mean of 1.5 birds per survey route. Spring bird count totals ranged from 701 in 1972 to 2185 in 1984. Counts are highest in the northern counties, probably owing to the presence of more observers. The highest count was 243 in Cook County, May 5, 1984 (VK). Downy Woodpeckers nest in forests, usually in willows and elms but also in other trees as long as they are dead or have dead limbs. The female lays three to six white eggs in a tree cavity. Illinois egg dates are March 30-June 3. Young have been seen out of the nest by early June.

The 1906-7 winter population in Illinois was estimated to be 322,000, whereas in 1957-58 it was 507,000, a substantial increase. About 60 percent of the winter population was in southern Illinois (Graber and Graber 1963). Christmas bird count totals for 1976-85 ranged from 2720 in 1979 to 4146 in 1980. The highest count was 374 in Union County in 1982. Numbers seem to have dropped slightly in the harsh winters of the late 1970s.

HAIRY WOODPECKER

Picoides villosus

FAIRLY COMMON PERMANENT RESIDENT

This woodpecker is a larger version of the Downy, adapted to larger prey. Lacking the Downy Woodpecker's black on the white outer tail feathers, the Hairy is fairly easy to identify because of its larger bill and loud, sharp *peek* notes.

In North America, a race of the Hairy Woodpecker is found wherever there are trees. It is distributed from the boreal forest south to western Panama. The nominate race is found in Illinois. Hairy Woodpeckers are essentially nonmigratory, though at times in winter there seem to be more of them, probably because they are much easier to detect during that season. In Illinois they inhabit woodlands but can also be found in wooded sections of towns and city parks. That they can survive in city parks is amazing, since they tend to have low populations. For more than a decade a pair has been residing in Springfield's Washington Park even though it is far from any woods.

Hairy Woodpeckers are most numerous on spring bird counts in northern Illinois, perhaps because more observers participate in the counts there. Maximum counts: 34, Cook County, May 10, 1980; 34, Lake County, May 5, 1984; 14, Marion County, May 8, 1976—the only year a southern count was highest (VK).

The mean number of Hairy Woodpeckers on breeding bird survey routes in Illinois (64 routes) is 0.1 (Robbins et al. 1986). Three to six eggs are laid in tree cavities excavated by these woodpeckers. Available egg dates are May 2 (four eggs), May 3 (three eggs), May 20 (four eggs), May 29 (six eggs). I saw fledged young with a female at Riverton on August 1, 1982.

There are no maximum counts for fall. Most winter data come from Christmas bird counts. Maximum counts for 1976–85 were mostly from Chicago North Shore (58, December 29, 1984; 69, December 26, 1981) and Union County (87, December 22, 1982; 62, January 3, 1981). Graber et al. (1977) found a decline since 1900 in numbers of Hairy Woodpeckers on Christmas counts.

WHITE-HEADED WOODPECKER
Picoides albolarvatus
HYPOTHETICAL

The only reference to this species in Illinois is by Musselman (1916–17) from near Quincy: "From the westland we have recorded the Oregon Junco, and White-headed Woodpecker...." He gives no description or other remarks. This woodpecker has not been recorded away from western North America.

THREE-TOED WOODPECKER
Picoides tridactylus
HYPOTHETICAL

The only sighting of this rare woodpecker in Illinois was reported by Russell (1983–84): a male seen in a spruce grove along Lake Michigan south of Glencoe on March 6, 1898, by F. Dayton. The observer approached to within 10 feet of the bird and was able to note its call and its three toes, yellow crown, and black back crossed with white. Though open to doubts because only one observer was present and the notes are not very extensive, the record is probably correct. Three-toed Woodpeckers have been seen as close to Illinois as southern Wisconsin.

BLACK-BACKED WOODPECKER
Picoides arcticus
VERY RARE WINTER RESIDENT

This boreal species occasionally has flight years that bring a few of these birds into Illinois. They are usually found in conifers but also in elms and other dead trees. They feed by stripping the bark off the trees and boring in after wood-boring beetles. Records for the Black-backed Woodpecker come mainly from northern Illinois, with a few from central Illinois. Extreme dates are September 12 (1913, near Glenview) and May 19 (1957, Chicago). The first state record was reported by Nelson (1876) from Chicago, no date given. The largest invasion was in the mild winter of 1920–21, when about 15 Black-backs were seen (Eifrig 1921). Records from central Illinois: Rantoul (Christmas bird count), December 25, 1917 (*Bird-Lore* 20:41); two, Peoria, January 11, 1925 (Starrett 1936); Peoria, November 19, 1965 (IAB137:4); female, Normal, October 22, 1965 (specimen, ISU). The only recent record was a female at Thorn Creek Forest, January 5–March 1986 (B.Bartleman-AB40:287). Usually tame, Black-backed Woodpeckers can be detected by their loud sharp call or the noise they make as they strip bark from the trees.

NORTHERN FLICKER
Colaptes auratus
COMMON MIGRANT; COMMON SUMMER RESIDENT AND COMMON WINTER RESIDENT DECREASING NORTHWARD

Although the Northern Flicker is a woodpecker, it looks and behaves somewhat differently. Mostly brown with a conspicuous white rump patch, it spends a lot of time on the ground, apparently looking for ants, its favorite food. It also consumes ground beetles, Hemiptera, Orthoptera, and such fruits as blackberries, poison ivy berries, and wild black cherries (Graber et al. 1977). Males have a black mustache, and older females do not, but immatures of both species possess this mark. The Northern Flicker has two forms. The western form, *C. a. cafer,* formerly the "Red-shafted" Flicker, occurs rarely in Illinois, and most "Red-shafts" are probably intergrades. Recent "Red-shafted" records: Woodstock, December 31–January 1, 1981 (DF-SR28:7); Peoria, September 29, 1987 (LA); one banded, Palos Park, March 2, 1979, and recaptured, January 8, 1980 (KB-AB34:278); Alexander County, January 2, 1987 (RP,MD-AB41:288). Two subspecies of the "Yellow-shafted" form occur. *C. a. luteus* is the breeding form in Illinois; the northern form, *C. a. borealis,* occurs as a migrant and in winter (Ford 1956).

Next to the Yellow-bellied Sapsucker, the Northern Flicker is the most migratory of the woodpeckers. It migrates both diurnally and nocturnally. In daylight the migrants are in loose flocks and move like Blue Jays and Red-headed Woodpeckers, just above the treetops and usually along watercourses. Though Northern Flicker migrants are seen as early as February, the average arrival dates are Chicago, March 28 (16 years), and west-central, March 13 (11 years). Some maximum spring counts: 100-115, Chicago, March 29–April 5, 1986 (JL); 24, Henderson County, March 29, 1986 (MB-IB&B2:94); 40, Palos, April 8, 1984 (PD-SR41:20). Spring bird count totals ranged from 1471 in 1972 to 3566 in 1983. All high counts were in northern counties, with 533 in Cook County the highest on May 7, 1983 (VK).

The Northern Flicker population declined sharply between 1909 (2,279,000) and 1957 (300,000), according to Graber and Graber (1963). They thought the causes were loss of savanna habitat and introduction of the European Starling, which competed for nest cavities. In summer, northern Illinois has the highest population of Northern Flickers. Robbins et al. (1986) also noted a continuing decrease in the population using breeding bird survey data for 1965-79. The mean number of birds per survey route in Illinois was 4.2. Flickers nest in fairly open situations in trees scattered through grasslands, on forest edges, and in residential areas. Five to 12 white eggs are laid on the floor of the tree cavity excavated by the flickers. Illinois egg dates are April 30–May 30 (Bent 1939).

Flicker migration in fall may start fairly early, in late July or early August. It is not usually obvious until September-except along Lake Michigan, where 15 were seen at Jackson Park on August 8, 1987 (HR). High fall counts: 160, Chicago, September 10, 1980 (JL); 50, Carlyle Lake, October 5, 1986 (RG-IB&B3:41); 90, Dundee, September 15, 1981 (SD-SR31:13). The average departure date for Chicago is October 23 (16 years).

Southern Illinois has the largest flicker population in winter. Favored habitats at this time are cornfields, shrub areas, forests, and pastures. Graber and Graber (1963) estimated that the state population was 544,000 in January 1907 and 202,000 in January 1957. Totals on Christmas bird counts for 1976-85 ranged from 469 in 1983 to 16,343 in 1980. Most high counts came from the south except for two central counts: Springfield with 154 in 1979 and Crane Lake with 167 in 1978. The highest count was 259 in Union County in 1980. The few existing band recoveries indicate that flickers banded in Illinois winter in northeastern Louisiana and northwestern Alabama (Graber et al. 1977).

PILEATED WOODPECKER

Dryocopus pileatus

UNCOMMON PERMANENT RESIDENT IN HEAVILY FORESTED AREAS

This crow-sized woodpecker, with its flaming red crest and loud call, is mostly restricted to heavily forested bottom-lands in Illinois. Most abundant in the south, it is virtually unknown in many other parts of the state. Its presence can be discerned by its loud drumming and the large oval holes it leaves in trees. The loud flickerlike call can be distinguished with practice; an imitation of it sometimes prompts a Pileated to call back. The main food of this woodpecker is ants and wood-boring beetles, though it also eats a wide variety of insects and wild fruit.

The Pileated Woodpecker is mostly sedentary. In spring and early winter, however, there seem to be local dispersals. I have noted them in "new" areas during these seasons in Sangamon County, and so has Goetz in the St. Louis area. Occasionally one of these large woodpeckers is mistaken for a crow and shot. The Pileated Woodpecker population underwent a reduction about the turn of the century, but since then it has made a comeback, although it is still rare in some northern areas, including Chicago. Of two subspecies, the northern *D. p. abieticola* may now be extirpated in Illinois (see Graber et al. 1977), while the southern *D. p. pileatus* is the breeding form.

Spring bird count totals ranged from 57 in 1972 to 166 in 1986. Southern counties provided all the high counts; the most frequent and highest was Union County with 23 on May 5, 1984 (VK).

The mean number of Pileated Woodpeckers noted by Robbins et al. (1986) on breeding bird survey routes in Illinois was 0.1. They also found that the Pileated population had remained stable. This woodpecker may in fact be making inroads in certain portions of the state, especially in Vermilion, Shelby, Winnebago, and Coles Counties. In Sangamon, Macon, and Champaign Counties only a remnant population seems to be holding on along the major rivers. Pileated Woodpeckers nest in large trees, particularly sycamores, in bottomland forests. Little is known about the nesting cycle, but usually four white eggs are laid between April 20 and May 6. The nest hole is usually oval, and young are occasionally seen sticking their heads out to beg for food.

Totals on Christmas bird counts ranged from 99 in 1983 to 272 in 1982. The high counts for 1976-85 were all in southern Illinois, with the highest 104 in Union County in 1982. Recent records from areas where they are rare: pair, Winnebago County, December 18-21, 1983 (LJ,DW-SR40:11); Joliet, April 23-29, 1987 (JM); Willow Springs, winter 1977-78 (LB-AB32:359).

IVORY-BILLED WOODPECKER

Campephilus principalis

EXTIRPATED AND NEAR EXTINCTION

"Descending the Ohio," Audubon (1831) wrote, "we meet with this splendid bird for the first time near the confluence of that beautiful river and the Mississippi." Only two other reports of the Ivory-billed Woodpecker in Illinois are known. One comes from Ridgway (1889): "The writer has a distinct recollection of what he believes to have been this species in White County, some forty miles south of Mount Carmel." The other is from Gault (1922): "the present writer feels quite certain of hearing its call note in a swamp near Ullin, Pulaski County in the fall of 1900." Other evidence of this woodpecker's existence in Illinois includes a tarsometatarsal bone found in midden deposits at Cahokia dated A.D. 1000–1200 and one upper and two lower bill sections at a Sauk-Fox cemetery in Rock Island County (Parmalee 1967). A female was collected at Forest Park in St. Louis, Missouri, on May 8, 1886 (Hahn 1963).

The Ivory-billed Woodpecker inhabited extensive forests of oak-gum bottomland and cypress-tupelo, which southern Illinois still possesses. Rumors are still heard of the Ivory-bill in the southern United States, and a very close relative, the Cuban Ivory-billed Woodpecker (C. imperialis), has just been rediscovered.

OLIVE-SIDED FLYCATCHER

Contopus borealis

UNCOMMON MIGRANT

This flycatcher has a larger bill and is more distinctively vested than the Eastern Wood-Pewee. It looks large headed and may show white at the rump edges. The typical place to look for an Olive-sided Flycatcher is high up in dead snags, usually in dead trees near the forest's edge. Often using the same perch for several days, this bird sallies forth, catches an insect, and then returns to the perch. Its song, a whistled *quick-three-beers*, is commonly given during migration.

Olive-sided Flycatchers arrive late in spring. Early arrival dates: Warrenville, April 26, 1981 (MS-SR29:11); Springfield, May 1, 1975 (VK). Average arrival dates: Chicago, May 21 (seven years); Urbana, May 12 (20 years); Sangamon County, May 13 (19 years). High counts are low for this usually solitary bird: eight, Lake Shelbyville, June 3, 1985 (SR-IB&B1:88); four, Urbana, May 28, 1986 (RCh-IB&B2:94). Spring bird count totals ranged from none in 1974 to 22 in 1983; these counts occur well before the peak of this species' migration. The high count was five in Cook County, May 7, 1983 (VK). Average spring departure dates: Urbana, May 25 (20 years); Sangamon County, May 30 (17 years). Late dates go well into June: Forest Glen, June 11, 1984 (DWe-SR41:20); Jackson Park, June 8, 1985 (HR-IB&B1:88). A specimen was taken at Wolf Lake on June 11, 1909 (CAS#466).

This flycatcher leaves so late in spring and returns so early in fall that some early writers thought it nested in Illinois. The closest breeding area is in northern Wisconsin. Early fall migrants: Springfield, July 30, 1978 (HDB); Waukegan, August 3, 1979 (AB34:168). Average arrival dates: west-central, August 25 (10 years); Sangamon County, August 13 (18 years). Fall high counts: five, Mason County, September 8, 1973 (HDB); 10, central Illinois, September

7, 1957 (Graber et al. 1974). Average departure dates: west-central, September 14 (10 years); Sangamon County, September 18 (18 years). Late departure dates: Jackson Park, October 5, 1981 (HR-SR31:13); Springfield, September 29, 1979 (HDB). The Olive-sided Flycatcher winters in the mountains of South America.

WESTERN WOOD-PEWEE

Contopus sordidulus

HYPOTHETICAL

Phillips et al. (1966) said that Eastern and Western Wood-Pewees are two of the most difficult North American species to separate using morphological characters. In fact, three of the four records for Illinois are known to be based on calls, and I suspect the other one is also: adult, Springfield, October 8, 1982 (Bohlen 1983); immature, Lincoln Park, Chicago, September 30, 1983 (Landing 1984); Chicago, late September (no year given); Urbana, May 26, 1984 (RCh-AB 38:918). Three are one-observer records. The other is of an immature bird, and immatures sometimes tend to give strange songs or calls. A tape recording or a specimen will be required to add this difficult-to-identify species to the state list. Since the Western Wood-Pewee breeds as close as North and South Dakota and there are records from Iowa and Wisconsin, the Illinois records are probably correct.

EASTERN WOOD-PEWEE

Contopus virens

COMMON MIGRANT AND SUMMER RESIDENT

What this dull-colored flycatcher lacks in plumage it makes up for in song. Its melancholy *pee-a-wee* cannot help but bring to mind a summer woodland. These pewees sing all day, even on the hottest days when no other sound comes from the woods. They are found in uplands, bottomlands, along the edges of woods, and occasionally in towns and parks.

Pewees usually arrive in Illinois in early May, although there are some April dates: Urbana, April 22 (Smith 1930); Springfield, April 21, 1973 (HDB). Average arrival dates: Urbana, May 2 (14 years); Chicago, May 13 (16 years); Sangamon County, May 3 (18 years). Spring bird count totals ranged from 69 in 1978 to 914 in 1986. The highest count was 55 in Jackson County, May 7, 1977 (VK). Higher numbers usually occur later in May, after the spring counts. Some one-observer records: 20, Chicago, May 28, 1982 (JL); 30, Vermilion County, May 29, 1983 (SB-SR37:18); 33, Giant City State Park, May 12, 1984 (DR-SR41:20). Migration continues into June but can usually be detected only in certain parks in which pewees are not known to nest. Two such birds were seen in Chicago, June 13, 1984 (JL).

Robbins et al. (1986) found a slight but significant decline in pewee numbers across the continent. The mean number per breeding bird survey route in Illinois (1965–79) was 2.4. Even though pewees forage beneath the canopy, their nests are usually so high that the contents are difficult or impossible to observe. The nest, built of weeds, bark strips, grasses, spider webs, and lichens, is placed on a horizontal limb. The easiest way to find one is to watch a pewee until it flies to its nest and sits. The female lays two to four creamy white eggs with reddish brown markings at the larger end. Illinois egg dates are late May to mid-July. Rusty wingbars distinguish immatures from adults, whose wingbars are white. Eastern Wood-Pewees eat mostly insects, including Diptera, Hymenoptera, Coleoptera, and Lepidoptera.

Much early fall migration goes undetected except when a pewee is killed by flying into a television tower or one is seen out of habitat, as along a hedgerow. Three pewees in the Illinois State Museum collection from the Springfield towers were killed, two on September 2, 1981, and one on August 25, 1976. Pewees seem to hold onto their territories quite late, as they have been seen chasing migrant warblers at least into September. Maximum counts in fall: 18, Springfield, August 29, 1981 (HDB); 13, Vermilion County, August 22, 1985 (SB-IB&B2:52). Average fall departure dates: Chicago, October 1 (16 years); Sangamon County, October 13 (17 years). Late departure dates: Crab Orchard National Wildlife Refuge, October 15, 1983 (JR-SR39:19); Springfield, November 8, 1972 (HDB). Starlings imitate the call of Eastern Wood-Pewees quite well, so late or early pewee records should not be based on the call without seeing the bird.

Eastern Wood-Pewees winter mainly in South America from Colombia and Venezuela south to Peru and western Brazil.

YELLOW-BELLIED FLYCATCHER

Empidonax flaviventris

COMMON MIGRANT

This small flycatcher resembles the other *Empidonax* species but is somewhat easier to identify because of its yellow wash ventrally and its greenish back. Light examples can be difficult to separate from the Acadian Flycatcher, which is larger and has a bigger bill. Most *Empidonax* can be identified, but it takes experience and close leisurely looks at the birds to do so. The best way to obtain experience is to work with a bird bander who handles large numbers of birds and to check museum skins. Several articles in *Birding* discuss *Empidonax* identification; see Whitney and Kaufman (1986a). The Yellow-bellied Flycatcher has several songs. Most notable are the *che-bunk,* which is similar to the Least Flycatcher's song, and the *pr-weee,* a peweelike

song. This flycatcher flicks both wings and tail as it flies from perch to perch. It is found in woodland and edge habitats.

Warm weather is usually well established before this flycatcher returns to Illinois, usually in mid-May. Early spring arrival dates: Urbana, May 4 (Smith 1930); Chicago, May 7, 1943 (Clark and Nice 1950). Average arrival dates: Chicago, May 17 (15 years); Urbana, May 14 (18 years); Sangamon County, May 14 (17 years). Few show up on spring bird counts since they arrive so late. The highest total was only 16, on May 7, 1983, and several years none were seen (VK). Maximum counts occur later: 12, Illinois Beach State Park, May 25, 1964 (JPr); 16, Lake Shelbyville, May 25, 1985 (SR-IB&B1:88); nine, Chicago, June 1, 1984 (JL). Average departure dates: Sangamon County, June 1 (17 years); Chicago, May 29 (15 years). Late departures: Blue Island, June 8, 1984 (KB-SR41:20); Chicago, June 12, 1982 (JL); Starved Rock State Park, June 13, 1983 (RGu-SR37:18); Villa Grove, June 11, 1983 (RCh-SR37:18); Lake Mermet, May 30, 1982 (LH-SR33:11). Two dates are so late that they may be early fall migrants: Lake Shelbyville, June 20, 1985 (A.Raim-IB&B2:14), and a female found dead at Palatine, June 24, 1948 (Ford 1956). The Yellow-bellied Flycatcher nests in boreal forests in the northern United States and Canada.

These flycatchers are capable of returning early because they molt on the wintering grounds. The early birds are adults in worn plumage; immatures return later. Yellow-bellied Flycatchers are not as easy to detect in fall as in spring because they call much less often and tend to sit in shaded areas in forests. Early fall arrivals: Jackson Park, August 6, 1983 (PC-SR39:19); Springfield, July 26, 1983 (HDB). Average arrival dates: Chicago, August 15 (15 years); Sangamon County, August 12 (18 years). Maximum counts for fall are nonexistent, although bird banders surely catch a good number at this season. Average departure dates: Chicago, September 19 (15 years); Sangamon County, September 29 (17 years). Most leave by the end of September, but a few linger into October: Springfield, October 13, 1975 (HDB). One very late bird at Springfield, November 13, 1980 (HDB), was photographed.

Yellow-bellied Flycatchers winter in Middle America from Mexico south to western Panama.

ACADIAN FLYCATCHER

Empidonax virescens

COMMON MIGRANT AND SUMMER RESIDENT IN CENTRAL AND SOUTHERN ILLINOIS DECREASING NORTHWARD

The Acadian is a flycatcher of bottomland interior forests. It is best detected by its explosive call, *pit-see,* or the call it gives near its nest, *peet.* It sometimes calls as late as mid-September. Though it resembles the other *Empidonax* species, the Acadian has a large bill and long wings with more yellow and olive green than others breeding in the same areas; see Whitney and Kaufman (1986a) for details.

Acadian Flycatchers usually arrive rather late in spring. Early arrival dates: one banded, Springfield, April 29, 1974 (HDB); southern Illinois, April 26 (George 1968). Average arrival dates: Urbana, May 12 (nine years); Sangamon County, May 9 (18 years). High counts for spring: 24, Giant City State Park, May 11, 1985 (DR-IB&B1:88); 11, Vermilion County, May 19, 1985 (SB-IB&B1:88). Spring bird count totals ranged from 32 in 1978 to 207 in 1986. The highest count was 47 in Jackson County, May 10, 1975. All high counts came from southern Illinois except 12 in Vermilion County, May 9, 1981 (VK). Recent records from northern Illinois: Rockford, May 19, 1984 (LJ-SR41:20); two, Lake County, May 30, 1982 (JL-SR33:11); Palos, May 31, 1986 (CM,JL-IB&B2:94). Some Acadians are still migrating in June: one banded at Chicago, June 1, 1983 (SP-SR37:18), and one in a city park at Springfield, June 5, 1979 (HDB).

Graber et al. (1974) felt that the Acadian population had dropped about 1930, especially in northern Illinois, but had later made a slight gain. Robbins et al. (1986), using more recent data (from breeding bird surveys for 1965–79), also noticed a slight decline and then some recovery. The mean number of Acadians per survey route in Illinois was 0.4. These flycatchers nest along deeply shaded watercourses in bottomlands, making well-constructed but ragged nests that resemble debris caught in trees after a flood. The two to five eggs (most often three) are creamy white with sparse brownish spots. Illinois egg dates are at least May 30 to June 20. The nests are subject to a fairly high incidence of Brown-headed Cowbird parasitism. I once saw a black snake taking eggs from an Acadian Flycatcher nest in Coles County. Nesting has been recorded recently in northern Illinois at Woodstock, Palos, Joliet, Apple River Canyon State Park, Sugar River, Mississippi Palisades State Park, and Lake County.

Because of identification problems, fall migration goes mostly undetected. The average departure date for Sangamon County is August 22 (16 years). A migrant was banded at Chicago on August 25, 1982 (SP-SR35:12). Late departure dates: three, Beall Woods, September 20, 1983 (LH-SR39:19); southern Illinois, October 2 (George 1968). The Acadian Flycatcher winters from Nicaragua south to northern South America.

ALDER FLYCATCHER

Empidonax alnorum

FAIRLY COMMON MIGRANT

It is almost impossible to distinguish this flycatcher from the Willow Flycatcher in the field except by voice. The Alder Flycatcher is of the *fee-bee-o* song type. Occasionally in fall the Alder will call *bic,* as opposed to the Willow's *whip.* With experience the two flycatchers' calls are rather easy to tell apart. Alder Flycatchers nest north of Illinois as close as central Wisconsin. Graber et al. (1974) said there is no firm evidence that they nest in Illinois. They are usually seen along forest edges and hedgerows during migration.

Spring migration is late, usually starting in late May and extending into July. Early arrival dates: Green River Conservation Area, May 11, 1986 (JH-IB&B2:94); Lawrence County, May 13, 1982 (LH-SR33:11). High counts for spring: 13, Lake Shelbyville, May 28, 1985 (SR-AB39:308); five, Mahomet, May 25, 1981 (RCh-AB35:830). Late departure dates: Lake Calumet, July 7, 1984 (JL); Volo Bog, June 27, 1983 (SH-SR38:10); Springfield, July 6, 1981 (HDB).

The best evidence about fall migration is obtained from television tower kills and bird banding. Kills have occurred between August 31 and October 7, 1959 (at Orion; Peterson 1959). Sight records: Madison County, September 2, 1983 (PS,RG,SRu-SR39:19); Springfield, September 13, 1987 (HDB). Alder Flycatchers winter in South America, but the limits are unknown except for Peru.

WILLOW FLYCATCHER

Empidonax traillii

COMMON MIGRANT AND COMMON SUMMER RESIDENT DECREASING SOUTHWARD

Only by songs and calls can the Willow and Alder Flycatchers be separated. Morphologically they are very much alike, and many plumage and measurement characters overlap. Even specimens in the hand are very difficult to identify. Whitney and Kaufman (1986) discuss identification details and present photographs of these similar birds. The Willow Flycatcher's song is *fitz-bew.* It inhabits scrub and brushy areas, especially those with willow trees.

Migration is difficult to detect unless the migrants are singing. Early spring arrival dates: Chicago, May 2, 1985 (CM-IB&B1:88); Alexander County, May 10, 1986 (JR-IB&B2:94). Average arrival dates: west-central, May 14 (nine years); Sangamon County, May 17 (18 years). High counts: eight, Chicago, May 26, 1987 (CM); eight, Lake Shelbyville, May 28, 1985 (SR-IB&B1:88). Migration continues well into June: Chicago, June 5, 1984 (JL).

Some early observers felt that the Willow Flycatcher was an orchard species, but today it is associated with willow-lined streams and hedgerows. The mean number of Willows per breeding bird survey route in Illinois was 0.6 (Robbins et al. 1986). Nests are placed from three to 25 feet high in small trees. They are neat cups resembling Yellow Warblers' nests. The three to four eggs are creamy white with a few brownish spots. Illinois egg dates are June 12 to July 7. Brown-headed Cowbirds infrequently lay their eggs in this flycatcher's nest. Lately, Willow Flycatchers have been noted more frequently in southern Illinois in summer. Recent records: Williamson County, 1983; Jackson County, 1985; Baldwin Lake, 1981; Richland County, 1980; Rend Lake, 1985; and White County, 1983.

Fall migration is difficult to detect. It probably starts in July. The average departure date for Sangamon County is August 18 (15 years), which is probably early because it was based on birds singing on territory. However, birds giving the *whip* call note and showing very little eye ring are also identifiable. One was identified at Jackson Park, September 29, 1983 (PC-SR39:19). A television tower kill of one adult occurred in central Illinois on September 21, 1966 (Graber et al. 1974). Most tower kills appear to be of the more northerly Alder Flycatcher. The Willow Flycatcher winters from central Mexico south to Panama.

LEAST FLYCATCHER

Empidonax minimus

COMMON MIGRANT; UNCOMMON SUMMER
RESIDENT IN NORTHERN ILLINOIS
DECREASING SOUTHWARD

The Least Flycatcher is small and grayish with a prominent white eye ring. It is usually seen on forest edges but can also be found in the interior of woods. It is best identified by its *che-beck* song. Its call note is *wit*. Leasts are the most numerous of the *Empidonax* species in Illinois and usually the first to arrive in spring. With close study, an experienced observer should be able to identify a nonsinging Least Flycatcher.

Early spring migrants: Springfield, April 20, 1987 (HDB); Chicago, April 25, 1986 (JL). Average arrival dates: Chicago, May 10 (14 years); Urbana, April 30 (16 years); Sangamon County, April 26 (18 years). High counts: 29, Jackson Park, May 21, 1983 (PC,HR-SR37:19); 20, Springfield, May 12, 1984 (HDB); 21, Chicago, May 14, 1986 (EW-IB&B2:94). Totals on spring bird counts ranged from 36 in 1978 to 485 in 1986, with the high 69 in Cook County on May 10, 1986, and Lake County on May 7, 1983 (VK). Average departure dates: Urbana, May 26 (16 years); Chicago, May 27 (14 years); Sangamon County, May 27 (18 years). Migration continues into June: Springfield, June 11, 1981 (HDB); Jackson Park, June 8, 1981 (HR-SR29:11); Rockford, June 3, 1984 (LJ-SR41:21).

Apparently this flycatcher once bred more commonly in Illinois than it now does. There are a few recent records as far south as Siloam Springs State Park. Other possible breeding records: Aurora, 1980; Champaign, 1986; Kickapoo State Park, 1981; Palos, 1984; Mississippi Palisades State Park, 1985; Rockford, 1987; six pairs, Chain O'Lakes State Park, 1982; five pairs, Des Plaines River, 1982; Marshall County, 1982; Will County, 1982. Little is known about the nesting cycle in Illinois. The nest is usually in a small tree near the end of a limb. Three or four eggs are laid from May 20 to July 3 (Graber et al. 1974).

Fall migration starts extremely early because the adults molt on the wintering grounds (see Hussell 1980). Imma-

tures migrate later and can be separated from adults by their buffy rather than white wingbars. Early arrival dates: Springfield, July 10, 1980 (HDB); Urbana, July 23, 1983 (RCh-SR39:19); Chicago, July 21, 1987 (JL). Average arrival dates: west-central, September 2 (seven years); Sangamon County, July 30 (18 years). Maximum counts are low for fall because of identification problems: nine, Jackson Park, October 4, 1983 (PC,HR-SR39:19); eight, Springfield, September 2, 1985 (HDB). The best counts should come from television tower kills and bird banders. Average departure dates: west-central, September 14 (seven years); Sangamon County, October 8 (18 years). There are some very late dates for this flycatcher: Springfield, November 9, 1976 (HDB): male collected near Crane Lake, December 15, 1973 (Bohlen and Funk 1974); Springfield, October 26–November 3, 1987 (HDB). The Least Flycatcher winters from northern Mexico south to Honduras and Nicaragua.

EASTERN PHOEBE

Sayornis phoebe

COMMON MIGRANT; UNCOMMON SUMMER
AND RARE WINTER RESIDENT

On the first warm days of March these brownish flycatchers come back to Illinois, bobbing their tails and saying their name with a nasal buzz. Sometimes there is no doubt that they are migrating, since they fly low for long distances over open areas. Eastern Phoebes arrive before there is much greenery in the woods, and sometimes they pay for their early arrival when late snowstorms and cold temperatures stall them where little food is available. Although these flycatchers eat mostly insects, they also feed on some fruits and rarely on small fish (Graber et al. 1974). They are found on forest edges, along streams, and at their nesting sites at bridges, bluffs, and isolated buildings.

Eastern Phoebes are among the first insectivorous birds to return in spring. Early arrival dates are known even from the earliest state records: Shawneetown, March 5, 1885 (Cooke 1888). Recent early dates: two, Crab Orchard National Wildlife Refuge, February 20, 1983 (JR-SR37:19); Jackson Park, March 9, 1983 (CMq-SR 37:19); Harrisburg, March 8, 1986 (KP-IB&B2:94). Average arrival dates: March 28, Chicago (15 years), and March 17, Urbana (20 years) and Sangamon County (17 years). Spring bird count totals ranged from 174 in 1978 to 456 in 1986, with west-central counties having the highest counts: 24, Madison, May 6, 1972; 18, Jersey, May 4, 1974; 23, McDonough, May 9, 1981; 31, Adams, May 4, 1985; 36, Calhoun, May 10, 1986 (VK). One-party counts for spring include 17, Jackson Park, April 13, 1983 (PC,HR), and 15, Giant City State Park, March 19, 1983 (JR-SR37:19).

Robbins et al. (1986) say that the severe winter of 1976–77 destroyed Eastern Phoebe populations in the northern portions of their winter range, but in Illinois there was only a moderate lowering of numbers. The mean number per breeding bird survey route in Illinois for 1965–79 was 0.8. Eastern Phoebes often nest near people, building their rather shallow nests on bridges and buildings fairly low to the ground. The female generally lays five eggs (sometimes two to six), which are white and usually unmarked. Illinois egg dates are late April to early July. Frequently there are two broods. Phoebe nests are usually heavily parasitized by Brown-headed Cowbirds except in extreme southern Illinois (Graber et al. 1974), where these cowbirds may be unable to exploit the heavily wooded tracts.

Eastern Phoebes probably begin migrating south by August, but migration is much more leisurely in fall than in spring. Dreuth gave August 4, 1938, as an arrival date, and one Eastern Phoebe was banded on August 26, 1983, at Chicago (SP-SR39:19). In many parts of the state it is difficult to distinguish migrants from summer residents. Maximum counts are lower in fall than in spring: eight, Springfield, October 13, 1982 (HDB); six, Chicago, October 29, 1976 (Mlodinow 1984). Although these phoebes seem to be mainly diurnal migrants, I found one male at a television tower kill near Springfield on October 11, 1985. In fall these phoebes are sometimes seen with mixed flocks of migrants feeding along wood edges or in weedy fields. Fall vocalizations are mostly limited to a chip note that sounds much like a Swamp Sparrow or a chipmunk. Most Eastern Phoebes are gone by late October; Dreuth gave October 23 (16 years) as the average departure date for Chicago, and the average for central Illinois is November 4 (17 years). Late departure dates: Rockford, November 9, 1980 (LJ-AB35:190); Springfield, November 25, 1973 (HDB).

Several winter records of the Eastern Phoebe may be very late fall migrants rather than wintering birds, since most are in December. Some recent winter records: Libertyville, January 1, 1982 (Mlodinow 1984): Chicago, December 22–January 7, 1980 (RB-AB34:278); two, Alexander County, December 21, 1982 (SR36:8); Union County, December 22, 1982 (PW-SR36:8); La Rue, December 21, 1983 (MSt-SR40:11); three, Alexander County, December 18, 1985 (DR). Most Eastern Phoebes winter in the Gulf states south to Oaxaca and Veracruz.

SAY'S PHOEBE

Sayornis saya

VERY RARE VAGRANT

Nelson (1876) noted that two Say's Phoebe specimens taken at West Northfield, Illinois, by R. Kennicott were registered in the catalogue but were missing from the museum at Northwestern University. There are seven other records from Illinois: Mermet (Christmas bird count), December 30, 1966 (RM,L.Hood-AFN 21:255); Thorn Creek Woods, May 5, 1973 (Bohlen 1978); one photographed, Evanston, September 23, 1978 (GR-AB33:184); Beverly, December 26, 1978–January 1, 1979

(JF-AB33:286); Illinois Beach State Park, September 25–26, 1982 (JR,JL-AB37:188); Springfield, November 30, 1984–January 13, 1985 (HDB); Chicago, October 1, 1985 (K.Swagel-AB40:121). The nearest nesting area is in northwestern Iowa, and there are many vagrant records for eastern North America. Say's Phoebes tend to stay near buildings; the Beverly bird was captured in a henhouse, and the one in Springfield was at a sewage disposal plant. Others have been near water or open barren areas. The Say's Phoebes found in Illinois are presumably members of the nominate race.

VERMILION FLYCATCHER

Pyrocephalus rubinus

VERY RARE VAGRANT

This brilliantly colored little flycatcher is widespread from the southwestern United States to Central and South America. Four Illinois records are all for spring: male, Urbana, spring 1962 (Graber et al. 1974); male, Chicago, May 4, 1973 (PaW-AB27:780); female, Chicago, April 8–12, 1981 (JL-AB35:830); male, Chicago, April 15–22, 1986 (KH-AB40:479). Vermilion Flycatchers like to perch on fences and other structures as well as the lower branches of trees. They have been recorded in nearby states, including Minnesota, Ohio, Kentucky, Tennessee, and Missouri. Missouri has some fall records (September–November), so they could occur at that season in Illinois also. The race in Illinois has not been determined, but it is probably *P. r. mexicanus*.

ASH-THROATED FLYCATCHER

Myiarchus cinerascens

VERY RARE VAGRANT

Only one Illinois record exists for this western North American species. On November 2, 1973, an Ash-throated Flycatcher was found in a city park in Springfield. It stayed mostly in oaks, where it fed by picking insects off the vegetation. Fairly low temperatures (23 degrees F) and snow occurred, and the bird was collected on November 9. The specimen, a female that proved to be *M. c. cinerascens,* was placed in the Illinois State Museum collection.

The species that make up the *Myiarchus* complex can be very difficult to distinguish from one another. In this case, the Ash-throated had to be separated from the Nutting's Flycatcher. Even pale, smallish Great Crested Flycatchers may approach the coloration of Ash-throated Flycatchers. In late fall all flycatchers should be examined with care, for this is the season when vagrants tend to appear. Few, if any, additional noncoastal records exist for this species east of the Mississippi River, although there are several East and Gulf Coast records (see Bohlen 1975).

GREAT CRESTED FLYCATCHER

Myiarchus crinitus

COMMON MIGRANT AND SUMMER RESIDENT

Except for their loud call of *creeep*, many Great Crested Flycatchers would go unnoticed even though they are fairly large birds, since they tend to stay in the dense leafy parts of trees. They have a wide, flat bill that can be heard snapping as it sallies after insects. Besides flycatching, these birds pick insects off foliage at midheights to high in the trees. Their food includes Diptera, Hemiptera, Hymenoptera, and Lepidoptera (Graber et al. 1974). The subspecies in Illinois is the northern race, *M. c. boreus.*

The earliest spring migrants appear in mid-April: southern Illinois, April 12 (Graber et al. 1974); Chicago, April 10, 1977 (Mlodinow 1984); Springfield, April 20, 1980 (HDB). Average arrival dates: Urbana, May 1 (20 years); Chicago, May 4 (16 years). Spring bird count totals ranged from 172 in 1978 to 1651 in 1986. Some high counts: 138, Cook County, May 10, 1980; 44, Mason County, May 8, 1976; 45, Alexander County, May 4, 1983 (VK). Dreuth gave May 26 (16 years) as an average departure date for Chicago and June 2, 1940, as the latest departure date (Clark and Nice 1950). Great Crested Flycatchers nest in both upland and bottomland woods. They stay mostly in forest interiors, with a preference for oaks. Robbins et al. (1986) noted an increase in Great Crested numbers based on breeding bird survey data, though earlier accounts noted a decline due to habitat destruction. The mean number of birds per survey route in Illinois was 2.3. These flycatchers nest in natural tree cavities, old woodpecker holes, or nest boxes. They have a unique habit of including a snake skin in the nest. The three to seven eggs are creamy white, heavily marked with streaks and irregular blotches of purple. Egg dates for Illinois are May 24 to June 26. Young are out of the nest and obvious in late June and July. Birds at Springfield were showing molt in mid-August.

Fall migration is fairly difficult to detect. Some years a slight increase in numbers can be noted berore they depart. Dreuth (Clark and Nice 1950) recorded arrival in Chicago by August 19, 1942, and an average arrival date of August 28 (12 years). Few if any high counts are available for fall. Average departure dates: Chicago, September 9 (12 years); west-central, September 14 (seven years). Late dates of departure: Jackson Park, October 25, 1981 (HR-AB36:184); Vermilion County, October 7, 1986 (SB-AB41:97); Springfield, October 8, 1983 (HDB). The Great Crested Flycatcher winters from Florida south to Colombia and Venezuela.

WESTERN KINGBIRD

Tyrannus verticalis

RARE MIGRANT AND VERY RARE SUMMER RESIDENT

Western Kingbirds are found in open, austere places, usually perched on fences or telephone wires or the dead branches of a lone tree. Since Illinois is mostly open agricultural land, these kingbirds could occur almost anywhere. They are particularly fond of golf courses and open parks. Other yellow-bellied kingbirds, such as the Cassin's or the Tropical, may wander to Illinois, but the Western is the only one with a black tail and white outer tail feathers. The first Illinois record was at Highland Park, June 6, 1924 (Coale 1924), and the second was at Niles Center, June 10, 1935. In both cases, specimens were taken, but their whereabouts are now unknown. Anderson (1968) saw a kingbird that he thought was a hybrid Eastern and Western in the American Bottom, June 2, 1968.

Early arrival dates for spring migrants: Chicago, April 19, 1986 (CM-IB&B2:94); Scott County (spring bird count), May 4, 1985 (VK); Alton, May 8, 1986 (CP-IB&B2:94). All other spring records are for May and are of single birds except where they breed. Other recent spring records: Jo Daviess County, May 16, 1986 (RCh-AB40:479); Homer, May 23, 1982 (JSm-AB36:859); Lawrenceville, May 17, 1981 (LH-AB35:830); Hancock County, May 12, 1984 (RAp-AB38:918).

A number of records in June and July seem to be wandering birds: Union County Conservation Area, June 10, 1982 (PK-AB36:983); Lake Calumet, June 14-15, 1986 (JL); Spring Lake, July 4, 1985 (KR-AB39:919); near Taylorville, June 6, 1984 (MH-IB&B1:17); Freeport, June 19, 1985 (DW-AB39:919). Several nest sites have been found: a nest near Kilbourne, June 1965, and young and adults near Bath, August 14, 1967 (Graber et al. 1974); young and adults near Winnetka, August 13, 1970 (AFN24:690); three young, Alton, 1984 (AB38:1026); nest, Charleston, 1985 (S.Steele,LBH-AB39:919); nest, Alton, 1986 (AB40:479). A pair resided at the Alton site four years in a row (RG).

Fall migration starts in August: Chicago, August 21, 1980 (RG-AB35:190); Jacksonville, August 29, 1982 (RQR-AB37:188); Macoupin County, August 30, 1987 (DC). No concentrations form away from nest sites, but five Westerns were seen in the Chicago area between August 28 and September 12, 1978 (AB33:184). Late fall departure dates: Clinton Lake, September 14, 1985 (RCh-AB40:121); Fairmont, September 15, 1986 (JSm-AB41:97); Quincy, October 8, 1957 (TEM-AFN12:36); Springfield, October 23, 1948 (WO). One Western Kingbird attempting to winter south of Springfield was seen from November 29 to January 10, 1983 (C.Curby).

The Western Kingbird winters from southern Mexico to Costa Rica.

EASTERN KINGBIRD

Tyrannus tyrannus

COMMON MIGRANT AND SUMMER RESIDENT

Kingbirds will defend their territory against anything that flies, including hawks and eagles. They have been seen pulling feathers out of the backs of fleeing hawks. Nevertheless, Hess (1910) noted that an angry Yellow Warbler made a kingbird do a hasty retreat. White-breasted with white-tipped tails, Eastern Kingbirds are found in open and semiopen areas, especially pastureland, where they sit on wires and fences. They feed on Coleoptera, Lepidoptera, Hymenoptera, and spiders (Graber et al. 1974); they also eat some fruit, such as wild black cherries. A partial albino kingbird, snowy white except for a dark spot on the forehead and dark wings and tail, was seen east of Springfield.

In spring some of the first migrants can be found in the tops of trees in forests if the weather is still chilly. At other times loose flocks of downed kingbirds can be seen sitting on the ground in fields. Early spring arrival dates: Crab Orchard National Wildlife Refuge, April 8, 1972 (VK,GC-AB26:767); Edwardsville, April 15, 1983 (BR-SR37:19). Average arrival dates: Chicago, May 6 (16 years); Urbana, April 27 (20 years). High counts for spring: 45, Union County Conservation Area, May 5, 1983 (VK-SR37:19); 36, Springfield, May 14, 1981 (HDB); 100, Evanston, May 30, 1978 (Mlodinow 1984). Spring bird count totals ranged from 238 in 1978 to 2801 in 1986. Some high counts: 152, McDonough, May 10, 1986; 121, Adams, May 7, 1977; 99, Alexander, May 4, 1985. Migration continues into June.

Graber and Graber (1963) found a decrease in this flycatcher's estimated breeding population for Illinois from 662,000 in 1909 to 307,000 in 1957. They attributed the decline to a loss of pastures and orchards and the spraying of roadsides with herbicides and insecticides. Robbins et al. (1986), using breeding bird survey data, also found a decline through 1975 but then a slight gain in population. The mean number of birds per survey route in Illinois was 4.0. Eastern Kingbirds are most abundant in northern Illinois in summer, decreasing southward. Cook County had 116 kingbirds on June 8, 1985 (IB&B2:14). Kingbirds nest toward the end of a horizontal branch, often over water. They also use fence posts or stumps. The nest is substantial, with a deep cup in which the female lays three to six whitish eggs with dark marks mostly at the larger end. Illinois egg dates are May 2 to July 27 (Bent 1942). Fledged young appear from late June to mid-July.

During fall migration these kingbirds start to behave as they do in the tropics, congregating in loose flocks and feeding around lake edges. Migration may start in late July, but birds seen then may also be family groups. By early to mid-August they are certainly moving. High counts for fall: 50, Lilly, August 19, 1977 (DBi-AB32:213); 46, Hancock County, August 22, 1985 (RCe-IB&B2:53); 30, Chicago, August 9, 1981 (JL); 28, Springfield, August 14, 1980 (HDB). Average departure dates: Chicago, August 31 (16 years); central Illinois, September 21 (18 years). Late departure dates: Chicago, October 4, 1983 (JM-SR39:19); Springfield, October 4, 1986 (HDB); Cass County, October 16, 1971 (RQR-AB26:72). The latest date in Illinois by far was at Goose Lake Prairie, December 9, 1979 (KB-AB34:278).

The Eastern Kingbird winters in South America from Colombia south to northern Chile and northern Argentina.

SCISSOR-TAILED FLYCATCHER

Tyrannus forficatus

RARE VAGRANT

This flycatcher is unmistakable because of its long tail, gray body, and salmon-colored wing linings, though some young Scissor-tailed Flycatchers have much shorter tails. The earliest of at least 38 records for this southwestern species in Illinois was near Peoria in the spring of 1885 (Loucks 1892). Most of the records (32) are for spring or summer, suggesting overmigrants, and only six are for fall. Spring dates range from April 15 (1967, Neponset, AFN21:513) to July 26 (1954, south of Chicago, Smith and Parmalee 1955). Fleig (1971a) mentioned two birds in the American Bottom that might have bred in 1967, and the chances of this species nesting in Illinois are good. Scissor-tails nest as close as north-central Missouri, with isolated nestings in Tennessee and Iowa. Fall dates ranged from September 5–9 (1982, Belleville, TF-AB37:188) to October 26 (1984, Belleville, B.Stumpf,TF-AB39:61). Recent records: Winnetka, May 22, 1987 (M. Merrick); Douglas County, July 4, 1978 (ELo-AB32:1169); Pike County, May 20, 1979 (JF-AB33:777); Richland County, July 1, 1979 (LH-AB33:868); Clinton Lake, October 12, 1982 (TP,PeP-AB37:188); Macomb, May 5, 1984 (EFr-AB38:918); Normal, October 25, 1984 (JHe,DBi-IB&B1:21); Winnebago County, June 11, 1986 (DW-IB&B3:14). Scissor-tailed Flycatchers winter from the Gulf states south to Costa Rica.

HORNED LARK

Eremophila alpestris

COMMON PERMANENT RESIDENT

Horned Larks are birds of the open country, preferring bare ground or short vegetation. Mechanized agriculture in Illinois has favored these birds so much that one wonders how they existed when tall-grass prairie covered the unwooded portions of the state. They must have used barrens and areas leveled by fire or water. Today they are found in open fields and pastures, at golf courses and airports, and along roadsides. Like other larks they fly high into the air in spring and give their call notes or sing their song, a tinkling sound sometimes of long duration. They eat grain, grass seeds, and insects in varying percentages depending on the season. Occasionally they will come to seed that is spread out on the ground. In snowy weather they are found around feedlots. A ground feeder in Logan County attracted 150 during the winter of 1981–82 (SR32:6). Albinism sometimes occurs in Horned Larks; I have seen at least two examples and another was photographed near Mattoon in May 1987 (ISM-Atterberry). At least two races of this widespread variable bird are found in Illinois. The breeding form is the "Prairie" Horned Lark, or *E. a. praticola*, of which the type was taken in Richland County. The northern form, *E. a. alpestris,* is larger and darker; it is seen fairly regularly in winter. The northwestern Arctic race, *E. a. hoyti,* and other forms probably also occur in winter.

Although the Horned Lark's resident status suggests that it is a sedentary bird, it undertakes considerable migration and wandering, especially in the colder months. Changes in vegetation heights also must cause some moving around. Horned Larks are frequently seen flying overhead, but it is difficult to tell local movements from migrations. There is still much to be learned about their migrations in Illinois. Spring bird count totals ranged from 1623 in 1973 to 4264 in 1985. All high counts came from the central or north-central portions of the state; the highest was 484 in McDonough County, May 6, 1978 (VK).

Graber and Graber (1963) found that Horned Larks increased their numbers more dramatically from 1909 to 1957 than any other Illinois bird. The statewide summer population in 1909 was estimated at 842,000; in 1957 it was 5,621,000. In summer most of the population is in the northern and central parts of the state. Breeding bird surveys for 1965–79 showed a stable population, with a mean number per survey route in Illinois of 37.9. Horned Larks nest on the ground, usually lining a cuplike depression. They nest very early, sometimes when there is still snow on the ground. Illinois egg dates are February 29–July 6. The female usually lays four pale greenish eggs, which are peppered with light brown. Young may be seen quite early; I have a record from Sangamon County for April 3. Fledged young present identification problems; some have been misidentified as longspurs or pipits. These larks become most noticeable in winter, since they tend to come up to roads during snows. They feed with Lapland Longspurs and Snow Buntings. The population in winter 1906–7 was estimated at 2,416,000, and in 1956–57 it was 9,175,000, more evidence of a dramatic population growth (Graber and Graber 1963). Some Horned Larks are displaced from northern to central and southern Illinois in winter. Christmas bird count totals for 1976–85 ranged from 2377 in 1982 to 17,329 in 1985. The highest count was 5000 at Urbana in 1957. Other large counts: 50,000 estimated between Decatur and Carlyle, February 15, 1986 (RP-AB40:287); 600, Tazewell County, February 8, 1985 (KR-IB&B1:69); 350, Union County, December 18, 1983 (JR-SR40:11).

PURPLE MARTIN
Progne subis

COMMON MIGRANT AND SUMMER RESIDENT

Since people put up houses for the Purple Martin, it lives near them and is well known. Martins are large swallows that catch their insect prey on the wing with graceful sweeps and dives. Their whole diet is insects, including dragonflies, wasps, grasshoppers, and butterflies. They forage over open areas, especially near or over water but also over fields and forests and around towns. The race found in Illinois and the rest of eastern North America is *P. s. subis.* Martins are among the few birds that arrive early in spring and leave early in fall. The early arrival may be due to the former scarcity of nest sites, before people started putting up houses for them. Some observers, however, mistake European Starlings and other birds for Purple Martins, so some early records are suspect. A very early spring record for Metropolis is February 24, 1923 (Conley 1926). Other early arrivals: Shelby County, March 8, 1987 (KF); 14, Rend Lake, March 3, 1986 (KPi-IB&B2:94). These early birds are sometimes exposed to cold periods and snow that proves fatal. Thirteen were found dead at Effingham after a snowstorm on April 8, 1982 (J.Ellis-SR33:11). Most Purple Martins arrive in late March and early April. They tend to gather over bodies of water with other swallows on cold or rainy days during migration. Average arrival dates: Chicago, April 11 (16 years); Urbana, April 9 (18 years); west-central, March 31 (15 years). An early spring high count is 340 at Chicago, April 17, 1982 (JL). As these birds spread out to breeding colonies, high counts are usually difficult to obtain. Spring bird count totals ranged from 1761 in 1973 to 4444 in 1978; Cook County had the highest count with 705 on May 8, 1976 (VK).

Though Purple Martins once nested in natural cavities in rocks and trees, they rarely do so now that an industry exists to produce their very own nest boxes. Many are produced at Griggsville, Illinois. People like to have these birds nearby because of their beauty and grace and their appetite for flying insects. Robbins et al. (1986) found increased numbers of Purple Martins in eastern and central North America using breeding bird survey data for 1965–79. The mean number per survey route in Illinois was 5.6. Martins nest in colonies of varying sizes, usually limited by the availability of nest sites. The female lays three to six white eggs. Illinois egg dates are mid-April to July 13. Two colonies in Shelby County produced 93 and 200 young in 1982 (KF-SR34:8). House Sparrows and starlings compete with martins for nest sites, so nest boxes should be closed for the winter until the martins return in spring.

After nesting, martins form large roosts at staging sites away from the nesting colonies: 10,000, Waukegan, August 10–22, 1982 (JN-SR35:12); 10,000, Lawrence County, August 18, 1984 (LH-IB&B1:21); 9000, Chicago, August 14, 1986 (EW-IB&B3:41); 4500, Keokuk, Iowa, July 28, 1985 (RCe-AB39:919). Average fall departure dates: Chicago, September 10 (16 years); central Illinois, September 11 (18 years). I have watched small flocks of 20 to 30 martins migrating south in fall in the evening, but I do not know whether they continue on into the night. Most Purple Martins are gone by the end of September, but there are a few October records: Mark Twain National Wildlife Refuge, October 10, 1981 (SRu-SR31:14); Carlyle, October 30, 1984 (CP-AB39:61); Shelby County, October 15, 1986 (KF-IB&B3:41); Lake Calumet, October 13, 1986 (EW-IB&B3:41); Lake Springfield, October 16, 1977 (HDB). This long-distance migrant winters in South America.

TREE SWALLOW

Tachycineta bicolor

COMMON MIGRANT; COMMON SUMMER RESIDENT IN NORTHERN ILLINOIS DECREASING SOUTHWARD

This swallow is the hardiest of the six species found in Illinois. I have seen Tree Swallows skim over ice-covered ponds in early spring. Their plumage is metallic green and white, their call a twitter, with notes of *cheet* and *trit* also given. Closely associated with water, these swallows are found at lakes, rivers, and marshes. When stopped by cold fronts during spring migration, hundreds of Tree Swallows may be seen flying constantly just above the water of lakes and ponds.

Spring migration starts early: Mermet, March 8, 1986 (TF- AB40:479); two, Lake Calumet, March 7, 1987 (JM, CM); two, Crab Orchard National Wildlife Refuge, March 6, 1986 (DR-IB&B2:94). Average spring arrival dates: Chicago, April 25 (15 years); Sangamon County, March 20 (17 years). Maximum counts in spring: 800, Crab Orchard refuge, April 16, 1986 (DR-IB&B2:94); 600, Chicago, April 16–21, 1983 (IV-SR37:19); 800, Kennekuk Cove Park, April 21, 1982 (SB-SR33:11); 1000, Kidd Lake, April 22, 1987 (RG). Spring bird count totals ranged from 743 in 1975 to 13,503 in 1978, when 5040 were seen in Jersey County (VK). The average departure date for both Chicago and Sangamon County is May 15 (15 and 16 years).

Most Tree Swallows continue on north of Illinois, but some stay to nest, especially in the northern part of the state. There are also nesting populations along the major rivers, including the Illinois and Mississippi. This species increased its numbers in the eastern and central regions of the United States between 1965 and 1979 (Robbins et al. 1986). The mean number of Tree Swallows per breeding bird survey route in Illinois was 0.4. These swallows nest in cavities in trees—usually trees standing in water—and in Wood Duck and bluebird boxes. They must compete with many other cavity nesters, including the introduced House Sparrow. They nest either in colonies or singly. The female lays four to seven white eggs. Illinois egg dates are May 4 to July 10 (Graber et al. 1972). In Cook County, 35 nests produced 118 young, or 3.37 per nest (PD-SR34:8). At Palos Park, 24 nests produced 80 young; at Flossmoor, 22 nests produced 81 young (KB-SR34:8).

Fall migration begins in July: Clinton Lake, July 21, 1984 (RCh-IB&B1:21); Charleston, July 19, 1977 (LBH-AB31:1149). The average arrival date for central Illinois is August 3 (16 years). This migration is protracted, usually with a buildup of birds in favored areas. In mid-October the movement becomes general on a broad front as these swallows flee colder temperatures. High counts: 10,000, Olney, October 10, 1978 (LH-AB33:184); 12,000, Henderson County, October 4, 1986 (MB-AB41:97); 7000, Chautauqua National Wildlife Refuge, September 21, 1985 (RP-AB40:121); 3000, Alexander County, September 13, 1986 (DR-IB&B3:41). Average fall departure dates: west-central, October 25 (eight years); Sangamon County, November 1 (18 years). Late departure dates: Union County, November 19, 1983 (JR-AB38:210); Crab Orchard refuge, December 8, 1983 (TF-AB38:324); Plainfield, December 16, 1984 (JM-IB&B1:69). Tree Swallows winter from the Gulf Coast south to Costa Rica.

VIOLET-GREEN SWALLOW

Tachycineta thalassina

VERY RARE VAGRANT

The only Illinois record of this western North American species is a male specimen collected in the Calumet region of Chicago, May 4, 1897, by George F. Clingman. Oddly, the collector apparently did not know what kind of bird it was, since he asked Coale (1925) to identify it. Coale found it to be *T. t. lepida*, the widespread race that breeds as close to Illinois as southwestern South Dakota and western Nebraska. The specimen, given to Bryn Mawr High School, is no longer extant. Vagrant records also come from Missouri, Minnesota, Nova Scotia, New Hampshire, and Florida (AOU 1983).

NORTHERN ROUGH-WINGED SWALLOW

Stelgidopteryx serripennis

COMMON MIGRANT AND SUMMER RESIDENT

This brown-backed swallow is associated with river systems in Illinois. It can be seen cruising up and down streams in search of insects, giving its harsh *trrit* call notes. Like other swallows it can also be seen in migration over lakes and ponds during inclement weather. The Rough-winged Swallow has a wide distribution; the race found in Illinois is *S. s. serripennis*.

Spring migrants arrive fairly early: St. Clair County, March 21, 1986 (TF-IB&B2:95); Giant City State Park, March 28, 1985 (JR-IB&B1:88); Sangchris State Park, March 26, 1977 (HDB). Average arrival dates: west-central, April 16 (15 years); Sangamon County, April 9 (18 years). Maximum counts for spring: 80, Jackson Park, May 9, 1987 (HR); 200, Lake Calumet area and Palos, May 9, 1964 (Mlodinow 1984). Spring bird count totals ranged from 547 in 1972 to 6468 in 1983. High count was 1575 in Carroll County, May 7, 1983 (VK).

These swallows are found along watercourses with high banks because they burrow 10 inches to three feet into the banks to nest. They nest either singly or in a loose colony. The white eggs number four to eight. Illinois egg dates are May 7 to June 14 (Graber et al. 1972). Summer high counts: 200, Alexander County, June 29, 1985 (JR-IB&B2:15); 160, Chautauqua National Wildlife Refuge, July 11, 1985 (KR-IB&B2:15); 150 pairs, Starved Rock State Park, June 1983 (RGu-SR38:10). These swallows may leave the breeding areas very early in July.

Most of the fall migration occurs on the larger rivers and may go virtually undetected in some parts of the state. Maximum counts for fall: 2000, Mark Twain National Wildlife Refuge, September 28, 1986 (SRu-AB41:97); 2500, Union and Alexander Counties, October 8, 1984 (JR-IB&B1:21); 700, Chautauqua refuge, August 17, 1985 (RP-IB&B2:53). Average departure dates: west-central, October 4 (10 years); Sangamon County, September 25 (17 years). Late departure dates: Alexander County, October 31, 1982 (JR-AB37:188); Horseshoe Lake, Alexander County, November 22, 1985 (RBr-IB&B2:53); Mode, November 1, 1984 (KF-IB&B1:21); Coles County, November 3, 1983 (RBr-SR39:20). In fall, care must be taken to avoid confusing Rough-wings with immature Tree Swallows. The Rough-winged Swallow winters from the southern United States south to Panama.

BANK SWALLOW

Riparia riparia

COMMON MIGRANT AND LOCALLY COMMON SUMMER RESIDENT

This brown-backed swallow has a brown neck band. It is smaller and daintier with a darker back than the Rough-winged Swallow. Its flight is more fluttery than other swallows', and its call is a dry, weak rattle. Bank Swallows are found in open areas, over fields, along rivers, and over lakes and ponds. The subspecies in North America is *R. r. riparia*.

Early spring arrivals: three, Springfield, March 29, 1987 (HDB); three, Springfield, March 31, 1985 (HDB). Average arrival dates: Urbana, April 20 (16 years); west-central, April 19 (12 years). Maximum counts for spring: 250, Henderson County, May 23, 1987 (MB); 250, Hamilton, May 24, 1987 (AD); 250, Knox County, May 7, 1983 (MB-SR32:19). Spring bird count totals ranged from 556 in 1973 to 5464 in 1983, with the highest count 2100 in Carroll County in 1983. All high counts came from the west side of the state except one in Shelby County in 1979 (VK).

Bank Swallows have a spotty distribution in summer because they are limited by available nest sites. These sites are most often banks associated with watercourses, but they

also use cuts made for roadways and mounds of sand at gravel pits. Robbins et al. (1986) noted little change in this swallow's population for 1965–79 using breeding bird survey data. The mean number of birds per survey route in Illinois was 0.8. Bank Swallows nest in colonies that contain 20 to 2000 pairs. Recent nestings: 2000 nests, Dallas City, summer 1982 (VK-AB36:983); 1500 pairs, Henderson County, summer 1978 (VK-AB32:1170); 355 nesting holes, Charleston, summer 1983 (LBH-SR38:10); 200 nesting holes, Horseshoe Lake, summer 1983 (RG-SR38:10). The nest holes average two or three feet deep. Three to seven white eggs are laid between May 7 and July 9.

Fall migration begins early, by mid-July, and groups of these swallows can be seen at this time sitting on wires, in roads, on sandbars, and on the sides of sandpiles. Maximum counts for fall: 3800, Hancock County, August 9, 1986 (RCe-AB41:97); 2000, Mark Twain National Wildlife Refuge, September 23, 1980 (HW-AB35:190); 1000, Chautauqua National Wildlife Refuge, August 18, 1985 (SB,RCh-AB40:121). Average departure dates: west-central, September 15 (nine years); Sangamon County, September 14 (18 years). Late departure dates: Springfield, October 19, 1985 (HDB); Illinois Beach State Park, October 25, 1975 (GR,LC). The Bank Swallow winters principally in South America as far south as northern Chile.

CLIFF SWALLOW

Hirundo pyrrhonota

FAIRLY COMMON MIGRANT AND RARE SUMMER RESIDENT

This swallow has a square tail and a buffy rump. Its call notes, often in flight, are creaking or grating. It is found in open country, usually near water, but it also forages over fields. Forbes (1883) found that Cliff Swallows eat Coleoptera and Hemiptera, and Graber et al. (1972) saw them feeding on midges. I observed them foraging in a soybean field near Buffalo on September 16, 1980; they were actually fluttering among the plants picking off insects. The race in Illinois is *H. p. pyrrhonota*.

Most spring migration is in late April and May. There are a few very early records: Clinton Lake, March 16, 1985 (RCh-AB39:308); Springfield, March 30, 1985 (HDB); Crab Orchard National Wildlife Refuge, April 6, 1986 (DR-AB40:479). Average arrival dates: Chicago, May 11 (six years); west-central, April 30 (10 years); Sangamon County, April 23 (17 years). Maximum spring counts: 400 per hour at Waukegan, May 9, 1978 (AB32:1015); 100, Urbana, May 14, 1980 (RCh-SR25:7); 70, Aledo, May 19, 1980 (BB-SR25:7). Ten thousand were seen in northwestern Illinois on May 19, 1968, a year that brought a big spring influx (Graber et al. 1972). Spring bird counts show great fluctuations in numbers from year to year, with 48 in 1975 and 2370 in 1983. The highest count was 650 in Carroll County, May 7, 1983 (VK). Although some Cliff Swallows stay to nest, most go farther north. Average departure dates:

Chicago, May 15 (six years); Sangamon County, May 22 (18 years).

These swallows declined as a nesting species in Illinois, primarily because of competition from House Sparrows for nesting areas. Unpainted barns on which to attach their adobe mud nests are also harder to find, and they are now using dams, highway bridges, and other such structures for nest sites. Robbins et al. (1986) found their numbers to be increasing again. The mean number per route on breeding bird surveys for 1965–79 in Illinois was 0.2, making the Cliff the least common of our summer swallows. Cliff Swallows nest colonially. They construct globes of mud in which three to six whitish eggs with darker markings are laid between May 20 and June 23 (Graber et al. 1972). Summer records: several hundred nests, Pope County, May 28, 1983 (VK-SR38:11); 114, Victoria, June 17, 1986 (MB-IB&B3:15); three colonies (71 nests) under a bridge, Lake Shelbyville, summer 1985 (KF-IB&B2:15); 50 nests, Apple River Canyon State Park, summer 1979 (BB-SR22:5); 33 nests, Fox River at Dundee, summer 1985 (RM-IB&B2:15); 20 pairs, Crab Orchard refuge, June 2, 1984 (BCho-IB&B1:17).

Migration in fall begins early: flock, Normal, July 14, 1977 (T.Marquardt-AB32:213); Chautauqua National Wildlife Refuge, July 18, 1984 (KR-IB&B1:21); 20, Lake Calumet, July 9, 1982 (KB-SR35:13). Migration is diurnal, and at times mass movement is obvious, usually associated with the approach of cold fronts. On clear days Cliff Swallows may fly over at fairly high altitudes and pass unnoticed. The average arrival date for Sangamon County is July 16 (17 years). Maximum counts for fall: 1100, Illinois Beach State Park, September 27, 1981 (DJ-SR31:14); 800, Clinton, August 2, 1980 (RCh-SR27:10); 1000, Vermilion County, September 10, 1986 (AB41:97); 300, Monmouth, August 14, 1983 (MB-SR39:20). Two Cliff Swallows collected near Buffalo on August 26, 1980, were both in molt, indicating that they migrate while molting. Cliff Swallows in heavy molt closely resemble Rough-winged Swallows, since the rump patch is obscured. Average fall departure dates: west-central, September 17 (nine years); Sangamon County, September 23 (18 years). Late departure dates: Urbana, October 9, 1977 (JFr-AB32:213); Crab Orchard refuge, October 14, 1986 (DR-IB&B3:41); Jackson Park, October 5, 1983 (PC-SR39:20); Springfield, October 21, 1988 (DO). The Cliff Swallow winters from Panama south to Tierra del Fuego.

BARN SWALLOW

Hirundo rustica

ABUNDANT MIGRANT AND SUMMER
RESIDENT

This swallow, with its wide distribution and its penchant for living close to people, is familiar not only to most residents of rural Illinois but also to most people in the Northern Hemisphere. Seen gliding over meadows and ponds in early April, it is a harbinger of spring.

The earliest spring arrival records are for March: Crab Orchard National Wildlife Refuge, March 21, 1972 (VK-AB 26:767); Saline County, March 5, 1986 (TF-AB 40:479). But early April is the expected arrival time. Sometimes Barn Swallows are caught by late snowstorms, although no mortality has been noted. I observed a Barn Swallow flying north into a snowstorm at Sangchris State Park in early April. Apparently these swallows also reverse migrate: a large movement of several species of swallows, including Barn Swallows, was observed at Waukegan, all flying south on May 9, 1978 (AB 32:1015). These swallows are conspicuous along roadsides and are therefore among the most numerous birds on spring counts every year. Maximum counts: 1203, Jersey County, May 6, 1978, and 3526, Carroll County, May 7, 1983 (VK). Some 1400 flew past Chicago on May 23, 1982 (JL-AB36:859).

In summer the Barn Swallow is the most abundant swallow in Illinois. Graber and Graber (1963) reported that in 1907–9 it was more numerous in northern Illinois, but by 1957–58 it was more numerous in southern Illinois. The Barn Swallow was not only increasing in numbers but was also extending its range toward the Gulf of Mexico. The Grabers estimated the Illinois population as 300,000 in June 1909 and 910,000 in June 1957. The mean number of birds per breeding bird survey route for 1965–79 was 23.5 (Robbins et al. 1986). Most nests are placed on man-made structures, including barns, houses, culverts, and bridges. From four to six eggs constitute a clutch, five being the most common. Barn Swallows apparently have double or triple broods. Many young are killed by automobiles when first fledged.

Like other swallows, Barn Swallows start fall migration early, usually in July and August. They can be seen at this time near water and in cut hayfields; they roost with other swallows in cornfields and marshes. Maximum fall counts are scarce, but 200 were seen at Lake Vermilion on September 30, 1985 (SB-IB&B2:53). Most Barn Swallows are gone by mid-October. There are a few November records: Lincoln Park, Chicago, November 6, 1971 (HDB,CC-AB26:72); Pekin, November 20, 1983 (LA-AB38:210); two, East St. Louis, November 11–12, 1986 (RG-IB&B3:41); two, Olney, November 20, 1984 (LH-IB&B1:21).

An early winter record places two Barn Swallows at the Carbondale Reservoir on December 29, 1954 (Brewer, Ellis,Bell-AFN9:261). Another was at Lake Springfield on December 10, 1988 (HDB,DO). Barn Swallows usually winter in Central and South America.

GRAY JAY

Perisoreus canadensis

HYPOTHETICAL

A jay of the northern woods and mountains of the West, the Gray has no satisfactory records from Illinois. Nelson (1876) speculated that "before the pine forest extending along the Lake shore, in the northern extreme of the state, was destroyed, this species was in all probability a regular winter visitant." Loucks (1892) reported one in Peoria in winter. The only other report was of a Gray Jay at a feeder in Highland Park on January 1, 1959 (AFN13:190); no details were given. There are records for Wisconsin and Iowa.

STELLER'S JAY

Cyanocitta stelleri

VERY RARE VAGRANT

Apparently this jay of the western mountains sometimes wanders erratically in fall and winter in search of food. Because the three Illinois records are for late spring and summer, the birds may have been escaped pets. The first record was of a bird shot at Lincoln Park, Chicago, June 12, 1911 (CAS). This bird had been seen eating Yellow Warbler nestlings. It was identified as *C. s. macrolopha* (Woodruff 1912). The second Steller's Jay was caught at Highland Park, July 13, 1952, by Downing and found to be *C. s. annectens* (Smith and Parmalee 1955). The last is a sight record from Palos Hills Forest Preserve, May 25, 1965 (PD-IAB135:12). The nearest breeding area is western Nebraska. There is a specimen record from Quebec.

BLUE JAY

Cyanocitta cristata

COMMON PERMANENT RESIDENT

Although the Blue Jay has a bad reputation as a destroyer of other birds' eggs and young, its beautiful plumage and interesting habits make it well worth studying. It is aggressive, always in the thick of the action when a hawk or an owl is present to harass. Blue Jays are the first to spy out and report an observer entering a woods, using their raucous calls to alert other wildlife. They have a wide vocabulary, including one call that sounds like a Red-shouldered Hawk. Usually in groups of three or four, these jays can invade and hold on to a feeding station for long periods. They eat a wide variety of food, including nuts, corn, domestic and wild fruits, insects, carrion, and especially acorn mast. In winter they tend to roost early, sometimes by midafternoon. Many times I have startled them from their winter afternoon roosts in small oak trees still bearing leaves. Two forms of the Blue Jay are found in Illinois: *C. c. bromia* in northern and central and *C. c. cristata* in southern Illinois. The northern form is also found in southern Illinois in winter.

Although Blue Jays are present all year, they have definite migrations in spring and fall. These movements are diurnal and at low elevations, usually just above the treetops. Flocks of five to 100 birds fly loosely in a line and pass by the same point at intervals. Some days large numbers can be recorded; other days, only a few. The flight line usually follows rivers, hedgerows, wood edges, or lake shores. In spring, jay migration has been recorded from March 14 to June 7. Fall flights occur from early September to early November. Spring bird count totals ranged from 4665 in 1972 to 13,446 in 1984 (VK). Other high counts include 2,000 in one hour, Mason County, September 22, 1973 (VK, HDB); 300, Chicago, May 21, 1981 (JL); 350, Big River State Forest, September 15, 1986 (MB-IB&B3:41); 230, Madison County, October 3, 1982 (RG-SR35:13); 350, Marshall County, October 1, 1983 (LR-SR39:20).

Graber and Graber (1963) found that the summer Blue Jay population had declined greatly in Illinois between 1909 and 1957 while shifting from mostly forested to mostly residential areas. The June population in 1909 was 1,557,000; in 1957 it was only 470,000. The drop was most precipitous in the south (81 percent). Breeding bird surveys for 1965–79 showed slight but significant decreases in the eastern United States but increases in the central states. The mean number of Blue Jays per breeding bird survey route in Illinois was 9.9 (Robbins et al. 1986). Jays nest in forests, residential areas, orchards, and wherever else trees are available. Nests are usually fairly low, averaging 12.4 feet high, and are usually placed in the crotch of a tree. The eggs, four or five, are olive to bluish green with dark markings. They are laid between April 12 and July 12 in Illinois.

In winter over 80 percent of the state's Blue Jay population is in southern Illinois (Graber and Graber 1963). The winter population, too, has declined, from 833,000 in 1906-7 to 570,000 in 1957-58. Christmas bird counts for 1976–85 showed probable winter kill or additional southward displacement as a result of the harsh winters of the late 1970s. Christmas count totals ranged from 3891 in 1978 to 8317 in 1985. Highest count was 1158 at Meredosia in 1984. Blue Jays store food for the winter, and their distribution is regulated by the availability of acorns, their principal food.

SCRUB JAY

Aphelocoma coerulescens

VERY RARE VAGRANT

This sedentary species is found in western North America and Florida. Vagrant records are few, but it has reached southwestern Nebraska and central Kansas. One Scrub Jay stayed at Illinois Beach State Park from at least September 29 to October 30, 1984 (see Chapel and Chato 1986), a dispersal year for several western corvids, including Scrub Jays. This elusive jay stayed in an oak-pine area, where it was seen by many observers and was photographed by Joe Milosevich. Because of its duller coloration the bird was identified as a member of the interior race, *A. c. woodhouseii,* which resides closest to Illinois in the interior western states. The bird could have escaped from captivity, of course, but the evidence indicates that it was wild.

CLARK'S NUTCRACKER

Nucifraga columbiana

HYPOTHETICAL

Irruptions of this jay of the western mountains sometimes bring it east. The two biggest flights occurred in the winters of 1894 and 1972–73. Illinois reports of the Clark's Nutcracker: one shot, Gross Point (Cook County), October 9, 1894 (Coale 1911); one seen, Whiteside County, May 8, 1909 (Maxwell 1921); one seen, Carrollton, November 4, 1972 (letter from Sarah Vasse on file ISM). None of the reports meets the requirements for a state record, although two of them came during irruption years and are probably correct. The specimen from Gross Point cannot be located. The Clark's Nutcracker has established vagrant records in Minnesota, Iowa, Wisconsin, Michigan, Ontario, Pennsylvania, Missouri, and Arkansas.

BLACK-BILLED MAGPIE

Pica pica

VERY RARE VAGRANT

Kennicott (1854) said the Black-billed Magpie was "not uncommon in winter." If so, its status has changed dramatically. Graber et al. (1987) stated that there were only about 30 records for Illinois. The earliest specific record was at Chicago, October 17, 1892 (Dunn 1895). The magpie is a western species that occasionally drifts eastward in winter. It apparently invaded Iowa in 1921 and 1934 (Dinsmore et al. 1984). Black-bills have appeared in Illinois between mid-September (1974, Barrington) and May 16 (1896, Knoxville), most of them in the northeast corner or the western part of the state. Recent records: Dundee, October 21, 1981 (RM-AB36:184); Vermilion County, May 8, 1982 (SB-SR33:11); Illinois Beach State Park, October 11, 1980 (Mlodinow 1984). Some were probably escaped pets. Magpies inhabit open country or brushy areas.

AMERICAN CROW

Corvus brachyrhynchos

COMMON PERMANENT RESIDENT

The flapping of a crow across the desolate landscape is a familiar sight in Illinois in winter. A resourceful bird, the American Crow has managed to survive even though it has been pursued by man with firearms, TNT, poisons, and traps. It is a large passerine, and nearly everyone is familiar with its *caw* note. Crows inhabit open or semiopen areas. They usually stay on the periphery of woodlands, where their quarrelsome habits let an observer know that they have found a Great Horned Owl to harass. They eat mostly corn in winter and summer but also eat sumac, poison ivy, and insects in season. Crows are commonly seen along highways and roads because they eat dead animals killed by motorists. I have seen crows at television tower kills, not only eating the dead birds but also hiding their carcasses under clods of dirt and corncobs, presumably for later consumption. Crows also eat a variety of other items, including eggs and nestlings of other birds. The crows in Illinois belong to the nominate subspecies, *C. b. brachyrhynchos.*

Crows migrate, but it is difficult to distinguish between local movements and migrations. Spring migration begins in February or March, and banded birds from Illinois have been recovered in Ontario and Michigan. Large roosts break up and the populations spread out in early spring. Spring bird count totals ranged from 2321 in 1972 to 8841 in 1984, with the highest count 923 in Cook County, May 10, 1986 (VK).

Graber and Graber (1963) found that Illinois crow populations had declined from an estimated 1,227,000 in June 1909 to 342,000 in June 1957. Why they declined is unknown, but a reduction in food sources is thought to be one reason. Robbins et al. (1986), using breeding bird survey data for 1965–79, saw a slight but significant increase in the crow population in the eastern United States. Illinois averaged 20.3 crows per survey route.

Crows build a substantial nest of sticks and usually line it with bark. The female lays two to seven eggs; four or five make up the usual clutch. The eggs vary from greenish blue to pale blue and are marked with darker colors of varying intensity. Illinois egg dates are March 16 to May 22, and only one brood is produced per season. Two hundred crows gathered at Lockport as early as June 3, 1984 (JM-IB&B1:17).

Fall migration is composed mainly of crows flying into Illinois from farther north or northern Illinois crows migrating to central Illinois. These movements occur from October to December. Crows establish large roosts in conifer plantations or wooded areas, sometimes near towns or cities. Some 100 crows have a small roost in Washington Park near downtown Springfield. Other roosts: 10,000, Rockford, 1986–87 (EW-AB41:289); 12,000, Henderson and Mercer Counties, November 8, 1985 (MB-AB40:122); 25,000, Keokuk area, 1985–86 (RCe-AB40:289); 10,000, Cass County, January 2, 1985 (VK-AB39:173); 8300, Vermilion County, 1984–85 (AB39:173); 8000, Aurora, 1977–78 (PD-AB32:359); several thousand, Alton vicinity, 1982–88 (RG). Christmas bird count totals for 1976–85 ranged from 16,662 in 1979 to 62,305 in 1985, with the highest count 29,837 at Meredosia in 1985. Graber and Graber (1963) said that central Illinois—the major corn-growing region—had the largest crow population in winter. January populations in Illinois were estimated at 4,805,000 in 1907 and 1,387,000 in 1957, a 71 percent decline. Since some winter crows come from areas outside Illinois, this decline must have occurred over a broad geographic area.

GREAT HORNED OWL
Bubo virginianus

Few predators are willing to take on the powerfully protective spray of the striped skunk (*Mephitis mephitis*). The Great Horned Owl, however, appears to be one that will. In fact, the high number of recorded instances of its preying on skunks may indicate that it even relishes the skunk as a food item.

Adult
(sexes similar)

WHIP-POOR-WILL
Caprimulgus vociferus

During brief pauses in the seemingly never-ending calls of the Whip-poor-will—a sound synonymous with warm summer nights in the country—these mysterious birds of the night take short, erratic flights through the woods in pursuit of a wide variety of flying insects, including the Luna Moth (*Actias luna*), upon which they feed.

Adults

(male)

(female)

CHIMNEY SWIFT
Chaetura pelagica

Each evening for several weeks during fall migration, small bands of twittering, fast-flying Chimney Swifts gather in the air over the place where they plan to roost. As the light fades their numbers grow, until sometimes more than a hundred birds can be seen circling, criss-crossing, and then dropping into the chimney, where they will spend the night.

Adults
(sexes similar)

RUBY-THROATED HUMMINGBIRD
Archilochus colubris

In late summer after their young have fledged, Ruby-throated Hummingbirds gather where there are nectar-producing plants. A favorite that grows in low wet places, along streams, and in ditches along country roads is the Jewelweed (*Impatiens capensis*). Here hummingbirds pass the summer days feeding, preening, and belligerently defending the choicest flowers.

Adults

(male)

(female)

BELTED KINGFISHER
Ceryle alcyon

The Belted Kingfisher is a conspicuous resident of the state, frequently announcing its presence with a harsh, clattery-rattling call. Kingfishers are particularly noisy during courtship and when tending their young. Much of their time is spent perched above water on a low-hanging branch waiting for an unsuspecting fish to swim into range. Sometimes they spot their prey by hovering almost motionless over a quiet pool.

Adults

Creek Chub *(female)*
(Semotilus atromaculatus)

(male)

DOWNY WOODPECKER
Picoides pubescens

PILEATED WOODPECKER
Dryocopus pileatus

The Downy and the Pileated, the smallest and the largest of our woodpeckers, occupy different ecological niches of the same woods. They usually come in close contact with each other only when a particularly attractive food item such as the wild grape (*Vitis* sp.) draws them to the same location.

Pileated Woodpecker
(male; female has less red on head)

Downy Woodpecker
(male; female has no red on head)

ACADIAN FLYCATCHER
Empidonax virescens

GREAT CRESTED FLYCATCHER
Myiarchus crinitus

When looking for a place to live, small mammals such as this Southern Flying Squirrel (*Glaucomys volans*) have no trouble competing with most cavity-nesting birds and might even make a meal of the displaced tenant's eggs and young when this takeover occurs. If a noisy dispute develops between the rival occupants, neighbors such as the Acadian Flycatcher come to see what the fuss is all about.

Great Crested Flycatcher
(sexes similar)

Acadian Flycatcher
(sexes similar)

HORNED LARK
Eremophila alpestris

WATER PIPIT
Anthus spinoletta

As the forests of the Midwest have been cut and transformed into open fields, the occurrence of both the Horned Lark and the Water Pipit has increased. During migration flocks of as many as a hundred birds of either species may be seen feeding in short-cropped or newly plowed fields. Because of their preference for barren conditions, the two species are often found side by side.

Horned Lark
(male; female duller,
horns less prominent)

Water Pipit
(sexes similar)

CLIFF SWALLOW
Hirundo pyrrhonota

BARN SWALLOW
Hirundo rustica

In areas of the state where Barn Swallows and Cliff Swallows both nest, they can frequently be seen together fluttering like butterflies at the edge of mud puddles in dirt roads or along the muddy banks of streams, gathering mouthfuls of the material they need to build their masonry nests.

Barn Swallow

(male)

(female)

Cliff Swallow
(sexes similar)

FISH CROW

Corvus ossifragus

UNCOMMON MIGRANT AND SUMMER
RESIDENT ALONG THE MISSISSIPPI AND
OHIO RIVERS IN SOUTHERN ILLINOIS

Though Parmalee (1967) reported that Fish Crow bone fragments from Randolph County were at least 10,000 years old, no Illinois sight records were established for this crow before 1962. The range of this species in the Mississippi Valley may wax and wane with climatic or other conditions. Neither Widmann nor Ridgway, both excellent observers, recorded the Fish Crow, so its modern presence in Illinois is believed to be a recent phenomenon. Although the Fish Crow is generally somewhat smaller than the American Crow, the sizes overlap. The best means of identification is the voice, which in the Fish Crow is a doublet nasal *cah-cah* or *car-car*. Observers should be aware that young American Crows sound somewhat like Fish Crows. Not much is known about Fish Crows in Illinois. They inhabit the floodplains of the larger rivers in southern Illinois. In other states they are tied to heron colonies, where they feed on eggs, although that is yet to be demonstrated in Illinois.

Early spring arrivals: 13, Alexander and Union Counties, March 5, 1974 (VK,HDB); eight, Alexander County, March 16, 1985 (JR-IB&B1:88); Union County, March 15, 1980 (RCh-SR25:7); two, Horseshoe Lake, March 27, 1982 (VB,SRu-SR33:11). Spring bird counts showed small numbers of Fish Crows every year, ranging from four in 1982 to 32 in 1972; high counts (with 14 the highest) came from Union, Monroe, Pope, Alexander, and Gallatin Counties (VK). Other high counts: 100, Tamms, April 12 (Graber et al. 1987); 17, Monroe County, May 12, 1968 (RA-IAB147:28). The northernmost points these crows have reached are Pike County, 1987 (JF), and Mason County, 1988 (RP,MD).

Fish Crows are believed to nest in Illinois, but no nest has been located. Parents with fledged young were at Granite City on July 4, 1983 (RG-SR38:11).

Maximum counts in fall: 54, Madison County, September 2, 1983 (RG-AB38:210); 45, Monroe County, September 27, 1986 (RG-AB41:97); 30, Jackson County, October 10, 1984 (JR-AB39:62). The latest date for fall is East St. Louis, October 31, 1981 (RK-AB36:184). Whether these birds go undetected because they quit calling or whether they actually migrate is not known. They have not been recorded on Christmas bird counts. Goetz has seen flocks that appear to be migrating in both spring and fall near St. Louis.

COMMON RAVEN

Corvus corax

EXTIRPATED; FORMERLY UNCOMMON
PERMANENT RESIDENT

Raven bones have been discovered at several sites in Illinois, suggesting that this species was once distributed statewide

(Parmalee 1957, 1958, 1967; Parmalee and Bogan 1980). Kennicott (1854) stated that it was common throughout the state and marked it as known to nest in Cook County. Nelson (1876) wrote:

Formerly a not uncommon resident; now occurs only in winter and is rare. Frequents the sand hills along the Lake shore from the last of October until spring. The first of November, 1875, I saw several specimens near Waukegan, where they were repeatedly seen flying along the Lake shore, and also eating the dead fish found there.

And Ridgway (1889) noted:

The Raven is a very local and nowhere abundant bird in Illinois. The writer has seen it only in the bottoms of the Big Creek and about the borders of Fox Prairie, in Richland County, where, up to 1871 at least, one or two pairs might be seen at almost any time, usually soaring in circles over the timber.

Nelson (1877) found that a Raven had been killed at Fox Prairie in the summer of 1875. Several specimens are still in collections: a female, Meredosia, October 23, 1892 (FMNH); Fayette County, January 10, 1901 (ISM). Others specimens are mentioned in the literature: Waukegan, October 15, 1875 (Ford 1956); Hamilton, before 1907 (Widmann 1907). There are sight records from Highland Park, spring 1908 (Coale 1912), and Waukegan, May 12, 1926 (Grasett 1926). The most recent record is from Chicago, October 13, 1953 (Smith and Parmalee 1955). Since then not even vagrants have occurred, but the Raven might be seen again if populations increase in neighboring states such as Wisconsin. The subspecies found in Illinois was *C. c. principalis*.

BLACK-CAPPED CHICKADEE

Parus atricapillus

COMMON PERMANENT RESIDENT IN
NORTHERN AND MOST OF CENTRAL
ILLINOIS

This cheery, energetic little bird brightens even the most dismal winter scene. It is a favorite at feeding trays, sometimes becoming quite tame. Often more Black-capped Chickadees are visiting an area than suspected; 49 were banded at one feeder in Morgan County on February 13, 1982 (VK-SR32:6). At all times of the year these chickadees are constant companions of other species in woodlands. Warbler flocks can be detected by listening for the chickadees that forage with them. In winter, flocks of chickadees, titmice, creepers, nuthatches, woodpeckers, and others form feeding flocks. These chickadees are easily "spished up" and seem curious about the observer. Not only does the Black-capped call *chick-a-dee-dee;* it also whistles *fee-bee* in spring, as opposed to the Carolina Chickadee's usual four-syllable *fee-bee, fee-bay*. Chickadees are mostly associated with woodlands but also occur in shrub and residential areas, especially parks. The race found in Illinois is *P. a. atricapillus* of eastern North America.

Spring bird count totals ranged from 665 in 1972 to 4297 in 1984. The highest count was 679 in Du Page County, May 5, 1984. No drop in numbers was apparent on spring counts following the severe winters of the late 1970s.

Graber and Graber (1963) estimated the statewide chickadee population—Carolinas as well as Black-caps—to be 600,000 in 1957, with the northern Illinois population, which would be all Black-caps, accounting for 82,000. Breeding bird surveys for 1965–79 found an increase in the chickadee population in several states, including Illinois (Robbins et al. 1986). The mean number of birds per survey route in Illinois was 1.0. These chickadees nest in cavities in trees or fence posts and in bluebird boxes. The female lays six to eight whitish eggs that have brownish markings, usually concentrated toward the larger end. Illinois egg dates are April 20–June 21. Young have been seen from May 9 to July 10. A high count in summer was 371 in Cook County, June 8, 1985 (IB&B2:15).

Chickadee distribution in Illinois is somewhat complicated (see the Carolina Chickadee account for boundaries). If there is a Black-capped migration into southern Illinois it is not well documented. Bennett (1952) stated that the Black-capped Chickadee was a winter resident, irregular in numbers, while George (1968) listed it as a common winter resident in southern Illinois. Graber and Graber (1963) saw indirect evidence of migration because of a decline in winter populations (chickadee species?) in the north and a gain in the south. Nonetheless, specimen evidence for this migration is apparently lacking. Mengel (1965) lists the Black-capped Chickadee as a "species recorded on inadequate grounds" for Kentucky. Farther east these chickadees have definite invasion years, but such invasions have not been proved for Illinois. In winter, chickadees broaden their habitat, going into fallow fields, corn stubble, and other more open areas, usually adjacent to woodland. Christmas bird counts showed lower numbers in the late 1970s, with gains in the 1980s. The range of totals for 1976–85 was 5577 in 1978 and 9400 in 1980. The highest count was 1061 at Chicago North Shore in 1982.

CAROLINA CHICKADEE

Parus carolinensis

COMMON PERMANENT RESIDENT IN
SOUTHERN ILLINOIS AND THE EASTERN
EDGE OF CENTRAL ILLINOIS

The Carolina Chickadee is closely related to the Black-capped Chickadee, and in Illinois areas where these two species meet, some individuals hybridize. Brewer (1963) studied chickadees in these areas and found that the boundary counties were Madison, Bond, Fayette, Shelby, Moultrie, Champaign, Ford, and Kankakee. Although Carolina Chickadees are probably more sedentary than Black-

caps, there are a few records north of this line: five, Pere Marquette State Park, December 21, 1974 (TB-AB29:416); specimen, Lake Forest, December 25, 1890 (Woodruff 1907); Decatur, December 28, 1968 (AFN23:296); one banded and photographed, Tinley Park, December 11, 1972 (Mlodinow 1984). Sight reports are probably open to question because of the known hybrids. Near Urbana, apparently, very few chickadees of either species are found, and this hiatus acts as an isolating mechanism to prevent hybridization (see Brewer 1963). The race of Carolina Chickadee in Illinois is *P. c. extimus*. The Carolina has various vocalizations, and some overlap with the Black-cap's songs. The Carolina appears smaller than the Black-capped Chickadee, with smaller wing and tail measurements. It also exhibits color differences, including a white area in the wing and a different-shaped black bib. The Carolina Chickadee is a woodland species but sometimes forages in more open areas, especially in winter.

Spring bird counts showed 36 counties with this chickadee in 1986. The range of totals was from 239 in 1978 to 685 in 1984, when 142 were seen in Jasper County.

Graber and Graber (1963) found the estimated summer population of Carolinas in southern Illinois to be greater in 1957–58 (300,000–400,000) than in 1907–9 (78,000). Robbins et al. (1986), using 1965–79 breeding bird survey data, found little change in the Carolinas' population. The mean number of Carolinas per survey route in Illinois was 0.5. Brewer (1963) thought that Carolinas were moving north at the expense of the Black-caps. Carolinas nest in the same places chosen by Black-caps, even using bluebird boxes. The female lays six to eight eggs, which are slightly smaller than Black-capped eggs and much the same color. Illinois egg dates are April 18–26.

Christmas bird counts for 1976–85 showed a range of totals from 567 in 1977 to 1706 in 1982. All high counts came from extreme southern counties, including Union, Alexander, and Williamson. The highest count was 676 in Union County, 1982.

BOREAL CHICKADEE

Parus hudsonicus

VERY RARE WINTER RESIDENT IN
NORTHERN ILLINOIS

A native of boreal forests with a preference for spruce and occasionally willow thickets, this chickadee rarely makes it to northern Illinois, and records are few. The first reference was by Nelson (1876), who cited a secondhand report that a Dr. Velie had observed Boreal Chickadees at Rock Island. Ferry (1907) collected a female at Beach on November 5 and saw another near Lake Forest on November 10, 1906. Woodruff (1907) secured two more females near Waukegan on November 8, 1906. Several Boreal Chickadees were seen at the Wilmette Harbor area in November 1951 and January and February 1952 (Smith and Parmalee 1955). More recently one was photographed at Fulton,

November 19, 1961 (PP-AFN16:41), and another was seen at a feeder in Dixon during February 1963 (JK-AFN17:329). These chickadees have invasion years, but they rarely wander out of coniferous areas. The Boreal Chickadee has a squeaky chickadee note that is different from that of the Black-capped Chickadee. Boreals seen in Illinois belong to the interior race, *P. h. hudsonicus,* which breeds from the tree limit in north-central Alaska and the northern Canadian interior south to northern Minnesota and Michigan.

TUFTED TITMOUSE

Parus bicolor

COMMON PERMANENT RESIDENT
DECREASING NORTHWARD

This vocal little bird most often gives its *peto* call, but in spring it broadens its range to include several whistled songs. Tufted Titmice are mainly woodland birds, keeping more to the woods than chickadees do. They may be found in both upland and bottomland forests foraging with chickadees, nuthatches, kinglets, woodpeckers, and other birds of the season. They also come readily to feeders and may be observed in residential areas and city parks. Titmice seem to be mostly sedentary, but some apparently migrate. Mlodinow (1984) states that on very rare occasions they have been observed in diurnal migration along Lake Michigan. They tend to expand northward but occasionally their distribution is cut back by severe winters. Therefore, numbers fluctuate in northern Illinois from year to year.

Spring bird count totals ranged from 963 in 1972 to 2488 in 1984. All high counts came from southern or central Illinois, with the highest 152 in McDonough County on May 5, 1984.

Graber and Graber (1963) noted a very low Tufted Titmouse summer population in northern Illinois: only 0.6 bird per 100 acres compared with 20 per 100 acres in southern Illinois. They also found an increase in the estimated titmouse population in southern Illinois from 324,000 in 1907 to 550,000 in 1957. The estimated statewide population in 1958 was 756,000. Robbins et al. (1986) found variations in breeding bird survey data for 1965-79 and concluded that the population had been hurt by the severe winters of the late 1970s. The mean number of titmice on survey routes in Illinois was 3.7. Kleen (SR22:6) reported figures showing southern Illinois populations down 75 percent on a nine-year average in 1979. Numbers were considered to be increasing in the Rockford area in 1983-84 (LJ-SR40:11). Titmice nest in cavities much as chickadees do, excavating their own nests or choosing old woodpecker holes or accepting nest boxes. The female lays four to nine whitish eggs with fine speckling. Holland, from 11 nests, found one parasitized with a Brown-headed Cowbird's egg in Knox County in 1947. Egg dates for Illinois are April 30–May 23. Young are seen from early May to August.

The Grabers found lower statewide populations in winter than in summer. Estimates were 670,000 for January 1957 and 470,000 for February 1958. Whether these lower figures are due to migration or some other factor is not known. The 1976-85 Christmas bird count totals ranged from 1413 in 1979 to 2377 in 1982. High counts were mostly from southern counties, with a few from west-central Illinois. Horseshoe Lake, Alexander County, had the highest: 470 in 1982.

RED-BREASTED NUTHATCH

Sitta canadensis

UNCOMMON MIGRANT AND WINTER
RESIDENT; RARE SUMMER RESIDENT

The high nasal call of this small nuthatch announces its presence in coniferous areas. It becomes very agitated at the imitation of a screech-owl's call and will come within a few feet of the observer. Smaller size, a dark area through the eye, and rusty underparts separate the Red-breasted from the White-breasted Nuthatch. Female Red-breasts have gray crowns and males have black. These nuthatches can be seen on the cones of various conifers, feeding on the seeds; or they may be spotted on the trunks of trees, coming down head first and inspecting the bark for insects and insect eggs. The Red-breasted is a favorite at feeders, where it takes suet and sunflower seeds. It hides some of the seeds in the bark of trees for later consumption.

Fall migration may start as early as August. Early fall dates: Sand Ridge State Forest, August 17, 1985 (RCh-IB&B2:53); Barrington, August 18, 1985 (RPi-IB&B2:53); Vermilion County, August 17, 1982 (JSm-SR35:13); Jackson Park, August 19, 1981 (PC,HR-SR31:14). There are heavy flight years for these nuthatches and other years when very few are seen. This has long been the case; Coale (1912) stated that "in September, 1878, immense flocks passed through Lake County." Average fall arrival dates: Chicago, September 16 (15 years); central Illinois, September 17 (17 years). High counts for fall: 200, Lisle Arboretum, November 17, 1957 (Grow-AFN12:35); 50, Chicago, September 4, 1981 (RD-SR31:14); 19, Big River State Forest, November 16, 1986 (MB-IB&B3:41); 15, Crab Orchard National Wildlife Refuge, November 8, 1986 (DR-IB&B3:41). Some Red-breasts winter, while others go farther south.

In winter these nuthatches are almost always seen in coniferous areas. Their numbers fluctuate widely, with 1976-85 Christmas bird count totals ranging from 40 in 1979 to 350 in 1981. The highest count was 188 at Crab Orchard refuge in 1975. In winter 1959-60 the high count was 300 at White Pines State Park (JK-AFN14:313). Daily counts in winter usually do not exceed five to 10 birds, since the habitat is restricted in Illinois.

Spring migrants can usually be detected when these nuthatches begin to be seen in deciduous woodlands instead of conifers. Average spring arrival dates: Chicago, May 1 (11 years); central Illinois, April 23 (nine years). Totals on spring bird counts ranged from five in 1980 to 192 in 1982. Most high counts came from northern Illinois, with 37 in Cook County, May 8, 1982. Average spring departure dates: Chicago, May 18 (11 years); central Illinois, May 11 (14 years).

Like some other irrupting boreal species, the Red-breasted Nuthatch occasionally stays and breeds in Illinois. This is nothing new; Nelson (1876) noted a pair at Chicago with full-grown young in July and a pair feeding nestlings the last of April 1874 at Evanston. Recent breeding records: Sterling (pair with four young), 1970 (BSh); Urbana (female with one young), 1977 (Polk 1979–80); Lisle Arboretum (three young fledged), 1986 (EW-IB&B3:15); Dundee (pair with two young), 1985 (RM-AB39:919). Other summer records that may represent breeding: Sand Ridge State Forest, 1980 (RBj-AB34:901); Illinois Beach State Park, July 10, 1981 (JN-AB35:946); Du Page County, June 17, 1985 (JM-IB&B2:15).

WHITE-BREASTED NUTHATCH

Sitta carolinensis

COMMON PERMANENT RESIDENT

The White-breasted is the larger of the two nuthatches seen in Illinois, and the more prevalent one. It nests in deciduous woodlands. Occasionally it is found in towns and parks. Fairly static in numbers, White-breasted Nuthatches seem to be most numerous in the major river valleys. If migration occurs in this species it has not been well demonstrated in most areas of the state. The presence of a few in fall and spring at Jackson Park, Chicago, may be evidence of migration or dispersal. Banding of individuals would probably be the best method to study movements in this species. Its diet mostly consists of insects, nuts, and acorns. It forages in true nuthatch fashion by coming down tree trunks head first. White-breasts are usually found in the company of chickadees, titmice, woodpeckers, creepers, and other woodland birds in season. The race found in most of Illinois is *S. c. cookei;* southern Illinois may be in the transitional zone between *cookei* and *carolinensis.*

Spring bird count totals ranged from 270 in 1972 to 1283 in 1984. All high counts came from northern and central Illinois, with the highest count 83 in Will County, May 5, 1984 (VK). Numbers on Christmas counts are even higher, probably because White-breasts are easier to see in winter and more secretive during the breeding season. Totals on Christmas counts for 1976-85 ranged from 1511 in 1976 to 2698 in 1982. Highest count was 245 in Union County in 1982.

The White-breasted Nuthatch population increased in Illinois, according to breeding bird survey data for 1965–79; the mean number of birds per survey route was 0.4. Most nuthatch nests I have observed are in knotholes in rather large trees, but these birds also nest in old woodpecker holes and even birdboxes. The female lays six to nine white eggs spotted with reddish brown. Illinois egg

dates are at least April 7 to May 11. High counts in summer: 48, Lake Shelbyville, summer 1985 (SR); 45, Cook County, June 8, 1985 (IB&B2:14).

BROWN-HEADED NUTHATCH

Sitta pusilla

HYPOTHETICAL

This nuthatch inhabits pine woods in the southeastern United States. The only Illinois record is contained in a letter written by E. S. Currier (DuMont 1935):

I cannot find where the Brown-headed Nuthatch has ever been recorded from Iowa and therefore I will report an unusual flight or visit of these birds to Keokuk during May, 1893. On May 9 early in the morning I saw one in town and in the afternoon, while out of town a few miles, I saw five others. I shot two of them but the shot were too large and mutilated them so they could not be made into skins. On May 10 I saw three more in town during the early morning. On May 12 two were seen in Hancock County, Illinois, across from Keokuk. Two were seen in Keokuk on May 13. These are my only Iowa observations.

Widmann (1907) saw one in St. Louis on May 6, 1878. A record also comes from Whiting, Indiana, April 6, 1932 (Mumford and Keller 1984). More recently one was seen in Milwaukee from October 1971 to January 1972 (AB26:69&608). Since there does seem to be some dispersal of this small nuthatch, more records from Illinois are not out of the question, although it is hoped that they will be better documented.

BROWN CREEPER

Certhia americana

COMMON MIGRANT AND WINTER RESIDENT; OCCASIONAL SUMMER RESIDENT

This interesting little brown bird feeds by spiraling up tree trunks and pulling insects out of the bark with its tweezer-like bill. It has a high *see* call note that attracts an observer's attention—a good thing, because the Brown Creeper blends in with the bark and is difficult to see. The song is unexpectedly pleasant, almost warblerlike but not loud. The subspecies found in Illinois is *C. a. americana,* the widespread eastern form. The Brown Creeper eats insects; a male from Springfield collected on December 18, 1975, had about equal amounts of spiders and Homoptera along with one Coleoptera in its gizzard.

Even with winter residents present, an increase in Brown Creeper numbers is usually noticeable in spring. Dreuth in Chicago found that this increase came about April 1 (the average date over 15 years). High spring counts: 30, Kicka-poo State Park, April 10, 1985 (SB-IB&B1:88); 16, Chicago, March 28, 1986 (JL). Spring bird counts, taken past the time of maximum abundance for the Brown Creeper, showed a low of 19 individuals in 1977 and a high of 204 in 1984. Practically all high counts were in northern Illinois; the highest was 59 in Cook County, May 5, 1984 (VK). Departure dates are somewhat uncertain because of the presence of summering birds, but averages are Chicago, May 3 (15 years); Urbana, May 1 (20 years); and Sangamon County, April 23 (17 years).

Although Kennicott (1854) stated that the Brown Creeper was known to nest in Cook County, Cooke (1888) believed there were no breeding records for Illinois. One Brown Creeper was observed at Olive Branch on the trunks of cypress and tupelo on August 11, 1907 (Ferry 1907a). Not until 1963 was the Brown Creeper again noted in summer in Illinois, but since then numerous records have occurred. The Brown Creeper's breeding habitat is cypress swamps in southern Illinois and floodplain forests in the rest of the state. More than likely a thin breeding population has been present in Illinois all along but was mostly overlooked. Actual nests are few; those discovered were in trees behind loose bark. Nests were found at Keithsburg in 1966 (Greer 1966), in Sangamon County along the Sangamon River in the 1970s and Lick Creek in 1982 (HDB), at Ryerson Forest Preserve in 1978 and MacArthur Woods in 1980 (Mlodi-now 1984), and in Coles County in 1980 (LBH-AB34:901). Other areas where summer birds have been found are the bottoms of the Cache, Kankakee, Mississippi, and Illinois Rivers. Mark Swan counted 24 territories in Marshall and Woodford Conservation Areas in 1982 (SR34:9). The nest-ing population is low enough that the Brown Creeper has been placed on the Illinois endangered species list. George (1971) thought that this southern breeding population should be examined carefully, since it might constitute an undescribed form.

Fall migrants, when they can be separated from summer-ing individuals, begin arriving in September. Average arrival dates: Chicago, September 20 (16 years); west-central, Sep-tember 29 (10 years). High counts for fall are few: 14, Jackson Park, October 3, 1981 (RG,PC-SR31:14); 30, Chi-cago, September 26, 1982 (JL). Twelve Brown Creepers were television tower casualties in Sangamon County on October 14, 1985 (ISM). Departure dates are obscured most years by wintering birds.

In winter Brown Creepers are usually found in flocks with chickadees, titmice, woodpeckers, nuthatches, and kinglets. Christmas bird counts for 1976–85 showed a low total of 330 in 1985 and a high of 785 in 1982. High counts were 86 in Alexander County, 1982, and 74 in Rock Island County, 1980. The highest Christmas count ever was 103 at Chicago urban on December 27, 1967 (AFN22:268). No portion of the state appears to dominate in numbers, but numbers do vary drastically from year to year in given localities.

ROCK WREN
Salpinctes obsoletus
RARE VAGRANT

The Rock Wren is a rather large wren with a dull brown back and whitish, lightly streaked underparts. It stays near the ground and fans its tail, which has buff-colored corners. It usually inhabits arid areas with rocks and brush in west-ern North America. In Illinois the Rock Wren has been found around burned tree stumps, concrete dams, and log piles. There are nine Illinois records: Urbana, May 30, 1926 (Hyde 1927); specimen (ISM), Normal, November 2, 1970 (Birkenholz and Weigel 1972); near Olive Branch, December 30, 1974–January 28, 1975 (VK); Horseshoe Lake, Octo-ber 11–19, 1978 (PS,BR-AB33:184); Montrose, September 29, 1979, Chicago, October 4–6, 1979, and Illinois Beach State Park, October 8, 1979 (Mlodinow 1984); Lock and Dam 13, September 28, 1986 (RPi-IB&B3:41); Montrose Harbor, October 8–9, 1988. The nominate race is found in Illinois.

CAROLINA WREN
Thryothorus ludovicianus
COMMON PERMANENT RESIDENT IN
SOUTHERN ILLINOIS DECREASING
NORTHWARD

The presence of this wren is usually announced by its loud, clear song, *tea-kettle, tea-kettle, tea-kettle, tea.* The Carolina Wren is a skulker that stays low in the brush and undergrowth in woodlands and in vines and thickets in resi-dential areas. "Spishing" will usually bring it out into the open at least temporarily to give its buzzy scolding notes, and then this rufous bird with the prominent white eye stripe can be seen. Like most wrens, it switches its tail and cocks it over its back. The bill is rather long and decurved, designed for plucking insects out of crevices. The Carolina Wren is essentially a southern bird that has extended its range northward. Carolinas are most numerous in bottom-land woods. In severe winters the population may be deci-mated and Carolinas may then be scarce for years before regaining their numbers. That tends to make them irregular migrants, though most of the time migration is difficult to prove in this species. Two were seen migrating along Lake Michigan on October 1, 1982 (JL). The subspecies in Illinois is the nominate form.

Robbins et al. (1986) noted a long-term increase in the Carolina Wren population in Illinois using breeding bird survey data for 1965–79. The mean number of Carolinas per survey route was 1.4. These wrens nest in a variety of natural and man-made situations, from tree cavities to hanging planters. Goetz found a nest in a handlebar bag on an old bicycle leaning against his house in 1988, and five young were fledged. The Carolina builds a bulky nest with or without a dome. The female lays four to six whitish eggs, finely speckled with reddish brown. Illinois egg dates are April 18 to July 28. There is more than one brood per season. Young may be out of the nest by late April or early May.

Both the spring and the Christmas bird counts showed a drastic reduction in the Carolina Wren population as a result of the severe winters of the late 1970s. On the spring 1976 count 757 birds were seen, but the next spring there were only 63. The total dropped to 31 in 1979 before increasing moderately to 61 in 1980. By 1986 there were still only 320, suggesting about half recovery. Christmas bird counts showed the same trend, with 800 in 1976, only 33 in 1977, and a low of 13 in 1979. Partial recovery was indicated by the 200 counted in 1984, and by 1987 the recovery was nearly complete. Carolina Wrens that survived these winters usually did so by attending feeders and roosting in outbuildings and garages. Hard icy snow often covered their food sources. The woodland wrens suffered the most mortality—sometimes 100 percent. High counts on spring bird counts: 61, Marion County, May 8, 1976; 58, Jackson County, May 10, 1975; 50, Pike County, May 5, 1973 (VK). High counts on Christmas bird counts: 209, Union County, 1975; 86, Pere Marquette, 1976; 54, Alexander County, 1984.

BEWICK'S WREN

Thryomanes bewickii

OCCASIONAL MIGRANT AND SUMMER
RESIDENT IN SOUTHERN ILLINOIS
DECREASING NORTHWARD; RARE WINTER
RESIDENT

This wren's song is like the Song Sparrow's but thinner and more musical, ending in a trill. The Bewick's Wren also has a scolding note, a buzzing *dzz*. It is a fairly large wren, but it is slender, with a prominent white stripe over the eye and a long tail with white in the corners that it switches back and forth or cocks over its back. It is found in brushy places and in rural areas around outbuildings and brush piles. Ridgway (1889) called it the House Wren of southern Illinois but noted that the true House Wren competed with the Bewick's and took over most of its range. The present scarcity of the Bewicks's Wren has put it on the Illinois endangered species list. The nominate form breeds in Illinois, but the Appalachian race, *T. b. altus,* has been taken in Chicago (Aldrich 1944). Apparently some observers have confused this wren with the Carolina Wren, but to what extent is difficult to assess.

Bewick's Wrens arrive early in spring; some spring birds are overmigrants, since most of the remaining population nests in southern Illinois. Early arrival dates: Springfield, March 12, 1986 (HDB); Chicago, April 13, 1980 (E.Abeles-

AB34:782). Average arrival dates: Urbana, March 25 (20 years); Springfield, April 7 (11 years). There are no high counts because these wrens occur only in ones and twos. On spring bird counts they were found in 13 of 15 years; the highest count was seven (?) in Jefferson County, May 10, 1986 (VK). Most records of Bewick's Wrens are for spring.

With the drastic drop in this wren's population, it is now a rare breeding bird in the state. Recent nests were found at Marion, 1987; Wild Cat Bluff National Preserve, 1981; Elsah, 1983; Godfrey, 1984; and Geneva, 1976. Nests are placed in or under such man-made structures as a tool box on a tractor that was used during the nesting season, a newspaper tube, a water wagon, a ditch digger, a split-rail fence, bird boxes, and especially outbuildings. In natural situations tree cavities are chosen. The female lays five to seven or more white eggs finely speckled with reddish brown. Illinois egg dates are May 5 to June 16. Young are seen out of the nest from May 20 to August 6.

There are few fall records, but late dates are Urbana, September 23, 1985 (RCh-AB40:122); Geneva, September 29, 1970 (Mlodinow 1984); and Mason County, November 23, 1973 (HDB).

Christmas bird counts show that the Bewick's Wren was much more common in earlier years. Few have been recorded recently in winter: two, Murphysboro, 1955; Olney, 1958; Decatur, 1960; Pere Marquette, 1969; Crab Orchard National Wildlife Refuge, 1984; Crane Lake, 1982. Bewick's Wrens wintered at Carbondale in 1984–85 (AB39:173).

HOUSE WREN

Troglodytes aedon

COMMON MIGRANT AND SUMMER
RESIDENT; RARE IN WINTER

Its bubbling song, nervous activity, and habit of living close to people endear this little brown bird to many. Two forms of this widespread species have been found in Illinois: the grayer western *T. a. parkmanii* and the inland *T. a. baldwini,* which seems to be an intergrade between *aedon* and *parkmanii* (see Mengel 1965) and probably forms the breeding population in Illinois. These wrens are found not only in residential areas but also in woodlands, thickets, forest edges, orchards, and other semiopen areas. Like most wrens, they scramble about scolding in brush piles and thickets, usually staying near the ground and coming out into the open only when singing. They can be "spished up" for a few seconds' worth of scolding with their tails cocked up.

House Wrens usually arrive in mid-April. Average spring arrival dates: Chicago, April 29 (16 years); Urbana, April 21 (20 years); Sangamon County, April 16 (18 years). Some arrive as early as March: Clarksburg, March 16, 1982 (KF-AB36:859): Urbana, March 26 (Smith 1930); Springfield, March 31, 1986 (HDB). Spring bird count totals ranged from 765 in 1978—low because of winter kills—to 4178 in 1986. High counts are mainly from northern and central counties; the highest was 284 in Cook County, May 10, 1986 (VK).

Despite some winter kills in the late 1970s, House Wren populations have increased across the continent. The mean number of House Wrens on Illinois breeding bird survey routes for 1965-79 was 6.3 (Robbins et al. 1986). The House Wren is apparently uncommon to rare in some areas of southern Illinois, and the north-south disparity was even greater in Ridgway's time. In fact, the House Wren may have expanded southward relatively recently. It has adapted fairly well to people and therefore is thriving. For nesting it uses bird boxes that people put up for it, takes over bluebird boxes, or makes do with any enclosed space that has an entrance of the right size. This wren is notorious for puncturing other birds' eggs, especially the eggs of species it competes with for nest sites. In woodlands it seeks out natural cavities or other cavities such as woodpecker holes. The male House Wren is often polygamous and constructs several nests in which the females lay four to eight eggs. These eggs vary in color but are usually buff with small reddish brown dots that give the eggs a cinnamon-peppered look. Available Illinois egg dates are May 11–August 7. House Wrens usually have two broods, so that by the end of summer the population seems to soar and eight or 10 wrens can be found in one brush pile. The young are fed insects, which constitute 98 percent of the House Wren's diet. Two specimens from the Springfield area showing molt were found on August 27 and September 30 (ISM collection).

House Wrens apparently start their fall migration fairly early, as there was a television tower kill east of Springfield on September 3, 1981. Fall maxima: 26, Mount Zion, August 31, 1985 (RP-IB&B2:53), and Springfield, September 12, 1985 (HDB); 25, Horseshoe Lake, October 5, 1983 (SRu-SR39:20). Average fall departure dates: Chicago, October 9 (16 years); central Illinois, October 28 (17 years). Some House Wrens linger into November: Springfield, November 16, 1981 (HDB).

Of several winter records, most are from the south. A few are from northern and central Illinois. Christmas bird counts for 1976-85 showed only two years with House Wrens: one wren in 1982 (Will County) and seven wrens in 1983-84 (four in Alexander County and one each in Calhoun, Sangamon, and Union Counties). Other winter records: two, Beall Woods, November 28 and December 26, 1982 (LH-SR36:9); Energy, February 4, 1983 (JR-SR36:9); two, Crab Orchard National Wildlife Refuge, December 23, 1964 (AFN19:232). Most of the population winters from the northern portions of the Gulf states south to Mexico.

WINTER WREN

Troglodytes troglodytes

COMMON MIGRANT AND UNCOMMON
WINTER RESIDENT DECREASING
NORTHWARD

The smallest wren in North America, the Winter Wren is widespread, occurring in Eurasia as well. It is very dark reddish brown, with a short tail and black bars on the belly and undertail coverts. It is usually found near water, especially in forests with many downed trees. Along streams it occurs in logjams. Occasionally it is seen in brushy areas or even open fields. The Winter Wren has a very prolonged song that is loud for the bird's size. It sings its series of tinkling trills and warbles while it is in Illinois on migration and even in the dead of winter. Its two-note chip sounds much like the Song Sparrow's chip note. When "spished up" from a log pile, it sits and bounces while chipping at the observer and occasionally breaks into song. The race found in Illinois is *T. t. hiemalis*.

Spring migrants start returning in March, although they are difficult to distinguish from wintering birds. Average arrival dates: Chicago, April 16 (nine years); Urbana, March 28 (19 years). High counts: 12, Sterling, April 8, 1984 (BSh), and nine, Crab Orchard National Wildlife Refuge, April 23-24, 1984 (JR-SR41:22); 13, Illinois Beach State Park, April 3, 1976 (Mlodinow 1984). Totals on spring bird counts ranged from one in 1973 to 20 in 1980; early May, when the counts are done, is past the peak for this species. The high count was seven in Winnebago County, May 10, 1980 (VK). Average spring departure dates: Urbana, May 1 (19 years); Chicago, April 23 (nine years). The few summer records include no observations of nesting: singing males, Starved Rock State Park, June 6-14, 1983 (RGu-AB37:994); one near Woodstock through July 20, 1980 (DF-SR26:9). The nearest breeding area is in southern Wisconsin.

Early fall migrants: Chicago, September 9, 1981 (JL); Georgetown, September 9, 1987 (MC); Springfield, September 8, 1974 (HDB). Average fall arrival dates: Chicago, October 1 (11 years); west-central, September 30 (eight years). Maximum fall counts: 150, Chicago, October 12, 1985 (FS-AB40:122); 11, Springfield, October 23, 1983 (HDB). Departure dates are not clear, but average dates are Chicago, October 25 (11 years), and west-central, October 28 (eight years). These small wrens linger in many areas until they are pushed out by heavy snows. They can survive in northern areas that have log piles near open water.

Totals on Christmas bird counts for 1976-85 ranged from 19 in 1981 to 122 in 1984. The highest count was 30 in Alexander County in 1984. Counts in the late 1970s showed decreased numbers due to severe winters, but the Winter Wren's decline was not as dramatic as the Carolina Wren's. Some northern Illinois records for winter: Chicago, February 12-28, 1983 (IV-SR36:9); Mississippi Palisades State Park, January 6, 1985 (RPi-IB&B1:69); Rockford, all winter 1986-87 (DW-IB&B3:68).

SEDGE WREN

Cistothorus platensis

UNCOMMON MIGRANT AND SUMMER
RESIDENT; VERY RARE WINTER RESIDENT

These small buffy wrens seemingly have an unorthodox spring migration. Some appear in April and May, others not until July or August. It may be that they all arrive at the same time but some go unnoticed until they begin to sing on territories. Whatever the case, Sedge Wrens are not very noticeable in spring, yet seem easily found later in summer. Their song starts slow and ends in a chattering trill, somewhat like a weak Dickcissel song. For such small birds the song is fairly loud, and these wrens are known to sing in the heat of the day and all night. The call note is a distinctive *tick*. These wrens are found in wet grasses, sedge marshes, weedy fields, clover, alfalfa fields, and shrub areas. They are often difficult to see except when flushed. They appear grayish brown as opposed to the reddish brown of the Marsh Wren, but the two species have the same weak fluttering flight of short duration. Sedge Wrens are fairly easily "spished up" and can occasionally be approached closely. The race that occurs in Illinois and the rest of North America is *C. p. stellaris*.

Early spring migration dates: Granite City, April 6, 1986 (RA-AB40:479); Chicago, April 22, 1983 (MS-SR37:19); Jackson Park, April 27, 1985 (HR-IB&B1:88). One Sedge Wren heard singing at Mark Twain National Wildlife Refuge on March 5, 1983, may have overwintered (SRu). Average spring arrival dates: Chicago, May 8 (seven years); west-central, April 29 (five years); Sangamon County, May 5 (13 years). Spring bird count totals ranged from one in 1979 to 55 in 1976. The highest count was 14, McLean County, May 4, 1974 (VK).

Robbins et al. (1986) noted that Sedge Wren numbers were declining across the continent. The mean number of Sedge Wrens per breeding bird survey route in Illinois for 1965–79 was 0.1. Time of nesting varies, perhaps in response to summer rains. Summer records: 13 pairs, Champaign County, summer 1981 (RCh-AB35:946); 10 locations in southern Illinois south to Jackson County, summer 1986 (AB40:1211); 15 territories, Lake Shelbyville, summer 1986 (SR-IB&B3:15); 16 pairs, Chain O'Lakes State Park, summer 1982 (JN,SH-SR34:9). Sedge Wrens build a globular nest with a side entrance. They build several dummy nests in addition to the one in which the eggs are laid. Unlike the Marsh Wren's dark eggs, the Sedge Wren's four to seven eggs are white and unmarked. Available egg dates for Illinois are June 1 to August 3, but recently fledged young were seen at Mark Twain National Wildlife Refuge as late as October 2, 1982 (BR-AB37:188), suggesting later dates.

Maximum counts for fall: 19, Horseshoe Lake, October 5, 1983 (SRu-SR39:20); 15, Chicago, October 10, 1983 (MS-SR39:20); seven, Mahomet, October 28, 1981 (RCh-SR31:14); six, Lockport, September 16, 1982 (JM-SR35:13). Average fall departure dates: Chicago, October 8

(11 years); Sangamon County, October 14 (18 years). Late dates of departure: Crab Orchard National Wildlife Refuge, November 22, 1982 (JR-AB37:188); Olney, November 3, 1977 (LH-AB32:213); Mahomet, November 8, 1981 (RCh-AB36:184); Jackson Park, November 9, 1982 (PC,HR-35:13).

Sedge Wrens rarely winter in Illinois. Most winter records come in December and may be very late fall migrants. Christmas bird counts for 1976–85 found only four Sedge Wrens. The highest count was two at Pere Marquette State Park in 1972. The Sedge Wren winters as far south as northern Mexico.

MARSH WREN

Cistothorus palustris

FAIRLY COMMON MIGRANT; UNCOMMON
SUMMER AND RARE WINTER RESIDENT

Since the Marsh Wren stays in dense vegetation, it is usually heard—with its sputtering song or its double-noted call of *tsuk-tsuk*—before it is seen. With careful watching it may be glimpsed, and an imitation of its notes will sometimes induce it to sit up in the cattails. If flushed, it flies weakly for a short distance, then plunges back into the vegetation. Marsh Wrens cling to reeds sideways, and occasionally they have each foot on a different reed, spread-eagle style. As might be expected, Marsh Wrens inhabit mostly marshes, but they may also be found in weedy fields and shrub areas during migration. These wrens feed mainly on insects and their larvae. The subspecies breeding in Illinois is *C. p. dissaeptus*, although others may occur during migration and in winter, notably *palustris*. There is a size dimorphism, with males being larger.

Early spring arrival is usually in April; Marsh Wrens seen in March could be wintering individuals. Early spring records: Chicago, March 25, 1986 (RD-AB40:479); Knox County, April 5, 1987 (MB); Urbana, April 13, 1982 (RCh-SR33:12). Average arrival dates: Chicago, May 9 (12 years); west-central, May 5 (10 years); Sangamon County, April 29 (18 years). Spring bird count totals ranged from 17 in 1974 to 150 in 1986, with two counties reporting highs of 38 in 1986 (VK). Many Marsh Wrens go farther north to breed. Even though much marsh habitat has been destroyed, a number of breeding birds remain, particularly in northern Illinois. Breeding records: 50 pairs, Chain O'Lakes State Park, summer 1982 (JN,SH-AB36:984); 43, Du Page County, June 4–July 2, 1985 (JM-IB&B2:15); 41 males, Lake County, June 16, 1984 (SH-IB&B1:18); six pairs, Goose Lake Prairie, summer 1982 (DBi-SR34:9). The males build several domelike nests, but the females later build the nests in which they lay eggs. These nests are usually attached to cattails over water. Clutch size is four to six, and the eggs are brown. Illinois egg dates are May 26 to July 27 (Bent 1948). There is more than one brood per year.

Fall migration begins in late August, although few dates are available: Chicago, August 24, 1936 (Clark and Nice 1950); Sangamon County, August 22, 1981 (HDB). The average arrival date for central Illinois is September 14 (16 years). High counts for fall are few: nine, Crab Orchard National Wildlife Refuge, October 14, 1984 (JR-IB&B1:21); 14, Horseshoe Lake, October 11, 1982 (RG-SR35:13); 25, Jackson Park, September 30, 1979 (Mlodinow 1984). Marsh Wrens have been killed by flying into television towers in the fall, but not in large numbers. Average dates of fall departure: Chicago, October 6 (11 years); west-central, October 8 (four years); Sangamon County, October 31 (17 years).

Ridgway (1889) noted that Marsh Wrens were sometimes winter residents. They are still found in winter in cattails where some open water remains. Christmas bird counts for 1976–85 found these wrens five years in low numbers (one to six). The highest single count was two on several counts. Other winter records: Springfield, wintered 1986–87 (HDB); Horseshoe Lake, February 26, 1983 (SRu-SR36:9).

GOLDEN-CROWNED KINGLET

Regulus satrapa

COMMON MIGRANT AND WINTER RESIDENT

Next to hummingbirds, the Golden-crowned Kinglet is one of the smallest birds in Illinois. Males have red-orange crowns, females yellow. Their *see-see-see* call notes are often difficult to hear and, if heard, to distinguish from the Brown Creeper's calls. Golden-crowns are usually associated with conifers, but in migration they are just as often found in deciduous trees. They breed in northern coniferous forests south as close to Illinois as central Michigan. They also breed in the mountains of Tennessee and North Carolina. These kinglets are fairly tame, and "spishing" can sometimes bring them within arm's reach. They feed in small flocks and associate with other woodland species of the season, including creepers, nuthatches, warblers, and chickadees. Though they sometimes feed high in the trees, they also can be seen fluttering near the ground. The eastern race, *R. s. satrapa*, occurs in Illinois, but the western form, *R. s. olivaceous*, has occurred as a vagrant as close as northern Indiana (Wetmore 1940).

Wintering birds tend to obscure early spring arrival dates. Average arrival dates: Chicago, March 31 (16 years), west-central, March 29 (15 years); Sangamon County, March 23 (17 years). High counts for spring: 95, Vermilion County, April 10, 1985 (SB-AB39:308); 52, Big River State Park, March 29, 1985 (MB-IB&B1:88); 42, Lisle Arboretum, March 28, 1986 (EW-IB&B2:95). Spring bird counts are too late for peak numbers, but these kinglets were recorded every year except 1986 in totals ranging from one to 80. The highest count was 45 in Cook County on May 5, 1984 (VK). Average departure dates: Urbana, April 26 (20 years); Chicago, April 29 (16 years); Sangamon County, April 22

(18 years). Some Golden-crowns linger late, and perhaps the late ones should be checked as possible members of the western subspecies: two, Lisle Arboretum, June 2, 1987 (EW); Chicago, May 27, 1943 (Clark and Nice 1950); Marshall County, May 12, 1984 (LA-AB38:919); Massac County, May 7, 1977 (VK); Springfield, May 18, 1972 (HDB). Cooke (1888) mentioned that Golden-crowned Kinglets remained all summer in thick swamps at Polo. In 1988 three nesting attempts were noted at Lisle Arboretum.

The earliest fall migrants arrive in mid-September: Peoria County, September 16, 1983 (LA-SR39:21); Chicago, September 17, 1980 (PC,RG-AB35:190); Chicago, September 21, 1985 (JL,CM). Average fall arrival dates: Chicago, September 24 (16 years); Sangamon County, September 28 (18 years). Most return in October: 500, Chicago, October 20, 1985 (JL); 53, Carlyle Lake, October 30, 1985 (RG-IB&B2:53); 75, Springfield, October 20, 1983 (HDB). Average departure dates are less certain than arrival dates because of the presence of wintering birds: Chicago, November 8 (16 years); west-central, November 5 (11 years).

The greatest numbers of wintering Golden-crowns are usually in southern Illinois, but the lack of observers there limits the counts. Severe winters kill off many of these kinglets. I have found them dead in coniferous forests, their primary winter habitat. Christmas bird count totals ranged from 100 in 1978—a low ebb due to harsh weather and high mortality—to 793 in 1982. The highest count was 206 at Chicago in 1974. Other winter counts: 152, Union County, December 22, 1982 (SR36:9); 189, Crab Orchard National Wildlife Refuge, December 28, 1974 (AB29:411); 99, Pere Marquette State Park, December 17, 1983 (AB38:648); 111, Chautauqua National Wildlife Refuge, December 22, 1984 (AB39:634). Golden-crowned Kinglets winter south to northern Mexico.

RUBY-CROWNED KINGLET

Regulus calendula

COMMON MIGRANT; UNCOMMON WINTER RESIDENT IN SOUTHERN ILLINOIS DECREASING NORTHWARD

This very small greenish kinglet has an eye ring, two wing bars, and, in the male, a red crown patch that can be completely concealed. When the male is excited by a predator, by competition, or by an observer "spishing," it erects this crown patch. I discovered while banding that in a small percentage of Ruby-crowned Kinglets this patch is orange. The song is a musical warble, somewhat like the song of a Winter Wren but shorter. The call is a distinct two-note *tic* given at all seasons. These small birds feed by fluttering at the tips of branches. They inhabit deciduous woodlands more often than Golden-crowned Kinglets do; but Ruby-crowns are found in conifers, too, especially in winter, and in fruit trees and gardens in urban areas. The subspecies in

Illinois is the eastern form, *R. c. calendula,* which breeds from northwestern Alaska to north-central Wisconsin.

Arrival of spring migrants is usually noticeable, since few of these kinglets winter in Illinois. Average arrival dates: Urbana, March 28 (20 years); Chicago, April 11 (16 years); Sangamon County, March 30 (17 years). Spring bird count totals ranged from 201 in 1981 to 2840 in 1984. The high count was 494 in Cook County on May 5, 1984 (VK). Other high counts: 100, Illinois Beach State Park, April 26, 1986 (CMi-IB&B2:95); 45, Chicago, May 7, 1987 (JL,CM); 24, Springfield, April 15, 1985 (HDB). Average departure dates: Urbana, May 15 (20 years); Chicago, May 20 (16 years); Sangamon County, May 19 (17 years). Some late records: Jackson Park, June 1, 1983 (RG); Chicago, June 1, 1986 (JL); Springfield, June 4, 1983 (HDB).

Fall migration begins in September, although there are a few August dates for this kinglet, including one in central Illinois, August 24, 1904 (Graber et al. 1979). Average fall arrival dates: Chicago, September 14 (16 years); Sangamon County, September 14 (18 years). Maximum counts for fall: 135, Chicago, October 6, 1985 (JL); 60, Springfield, October 20, 1983 (HDB); 50, Henderson County, October 9, 1983 (MB-SR39:21). Average departure dates are confounded by wintering Ruby-crowns. Migrants are frequently killed at television towers in the fall.

Sightings are more numerous in early than in late winter, suggesting either that some of these kinglets migrate very late or that some die during the winter. Christmas bird count totals for 1976–85 held fairly steady, ranging from 29 in 1983 to 80 in 1978. All high counts were from southern Illinois. The highest were 49 in Alexander County in 1984 and 53 at Crab Orchard National Wildlife Refuge in 1975. Ruby-crowns occur in very low numbers in central and northern Illinois, usually in sheltered areas such as woodlands near warm water and dense evergreens. Occasionally they appear at bird feeders. Ruby-crowned Kinglets winter as far south as Guatemala.

BLUE-GRAY GNATCATCHER
Polioptila caerulea

COMMON MIGRANT; SUMMER RESIDENT IN SOUTHERN ILLINOIS DECREASING NORTHWARD

The Blue-gray Gnatcatcher usually announces itself by its high, thin, buzzy call, although it also has a warbled song. In spring the male has a black line over the eye that extends to the forehead. The gnatcatcher's tail is very long for such a small bird, and it flicks the tail frequently, switches it from side to side, or cocks it like a wren. These gnatcatchers forage from midheight to high in the forest. Like kinglets they are easy to "spish" into close range. The nominate race is found in the eastern United States.

The earliest spring reports come in March: Christian County, March 30, 1985 (RP-AB39:308); Pomona, March

27, 1984 (TF-SR41:22); Mermet Lake, March 28, 1987 (TF). Average spring arrival dates: Chicago, May 1 (15 years); Sangamon County, April 11 (19 years). High counts for spring: 70, Union and Jackson Counties, April 18, 1987 (RP); 106, Massac County, May 5, 1984 (DR-SR41:22); 25, Siloam Springs State Park, April 18, 1981 (AD-SR29:12). Spring bird count totals ranged from 287 in 1972 to 1289 in 1979, with high counts of 115 in Carroll County, May 5, 1984, and 111 in Alexander County, May 7, 1977 (VK). Dreuth recorded a migrant at Chicago as late as May 26, 1931 (Clark and Nice 1950).

The gnatcatcher's nest is usually fairly high, saddled on a horizontal branch. It is a well-made cup kept together with spider webs. The three to five eggs are blue with reddish brown spots. Illinois egg dates are at least May 19 to June 16. Many nests are too high to see the contents. Most nesting occurs in bottomland forest, but gnatcatchers occasionally nest on the forest edge or rarely in residential areas. Recent nesting in northern Illinois: McHenry County, 1986; Joliet, 1987; Barrington, 1982; Ogle County, 1980; Illinois Beach State Park, 1981. High counts in summer: 18, Kinkaid Lake, June 11, 1983 (JR-SR38:11); 41, Lake Shelbyville, summer 1985 (SR-IB&B2:15).

Fall migration is early. Most species that arrive early in spring leave late in fall, but not the gnatcatcher. Its migration in Illinois is mostly made up of birds leaving the breeding grounds, since few gnatcatchers nest north of Illinois. Early arrivals occur in mid- to late August. There are no high counts for this season. Average fall departure dates: west-central, September 13 (eight years); Sangamon County, September 7 (16 years). Late departure dates: Monmouth, October 16, 1977 (LMc-AB32:214); Urbana, October 9, 1977 (RCh-AB32:214); Decatur, October 12, 1985 (MD, RP-IB&B2:53). The Blue-gray Gnatcatcher winters from the southern United States south to Guatemala and Honduras.

EASTERN BLUEBIRD
Sialia sialis

COMMON MIGRANT AND SUMMER RESIDENT; COMMON WINTER RESIDENT IN SOUTHERN ILLINOIS DECREASING NORTHWARD

Once a common sight, the handsome Eastern Bluebird is not well known today except among birdwatchers. It formerly was found in towns and around dwellings, but now it is entirely rural because of the introduction of the House Sparrow, which competes for its nesting sites. The Eastern Bluebird can still be seen along rural roads, perching on fences and telephone wires. The intense blue of the back and the robinlike breast in males is worth a drive in the country to see.

The Eastern Bluebird arrives in February and March. The average arrival date for Urbana (20 years) is February 23

(Smith 1930) and for Chicago (16 years) March 19 (Clark and Nice 1950). These birds appear as singles or pairs or in small groups. Some years they arrive too early and are decimated by severe blizzards and cold temperatures. As a consequence some can be found dead in their roosting sites. Population fluctuations, apparently continuing phenomena due to winter kill and other factors, have occurred at least twice on a dramatic scale in the past 40 years. Spring bird count totals show a decline due to the severe winters of the late 1970s. From 1972 (when the spring bird counts started) to 1976, counts were fairly high, reaching 763 birds in 1976. Then numbers began to drop and reached a low of 11 in 1978. The recovery took five years; by 1983 totals reached 625 and by 1986 they surpassed the 1972–76 level, with 94 counties reporting 1374 birds. High counts were 134 in Adams County, May 4, 1974, and 196 in Crawford County, May 10, 1986 (VK). Decimation and recovery are also obvious from an examination of Christmas bird counts.

Graber and Graber (1963) estimated the June population to be 460,000 in 1909 (70 percent in southern Illinois) and 220,000 in 1957 (80 percent in southern Illinois). But in June 1958 the population was only 50,000. They found the highest number in pastures, with 8.3 birds per 100 acres. Eastern Bluebirds are also found in open woodlands, orchards, and roadside edges. Robbins et al. (1986) stated that the population had been low since the harsh winter of 1958. The mean number of bluebirds per breeding bird survey route in Illinois for 1965–79 was 2.0 (64 routes). Eastern Bluebirds usually produce four or five light blue eggs; some are white. Illinois egg dates are mid-April to August. There are usually two broods. A large percentage of bluebirds now use man-made nesting boxes. Observers place several of these boxes over routes called bluebird trails and use them to gather data about the birds. These boxes helped in the recovery of bluebirds from the winter kills of 1972–76. House Wrens, chickadees, House Sparrows, Eurasian Tree Sparrows, and many other bird species and mammals compete for the use of these boxes.

Families of bluebirds can be seen feeding in open areas. I observed a family, including spot-breasted immatures, pouncing on insects from some bales of hay. Bluebirds eat mostly insects, including cutworms, beetles, crickets, and grasshoppers. In winter they switch to fruits such as mistletoe, grapes, sumac, haws, and holly (Graber et al. 1971).

Fall migration begins in late September, but it is often difficult to distinguish migrants from local nesters. During fall bluebirds can easily be detected in early morning by their distinctive flight calls; points of land along lakes can sometimes produce good counts of these birds passing overhead. They can also be seen along roadsides with migrant Chipping Sparrows, Yellow-rumped Warblers, and occasionally Eastern Phoebes. These species seem to form loose foraging flocks in fall. Maximum counts for fall: 48, Illinois Beach State Park, September 29, 1985 (JL); 81, Lake Shelbyville, October 5, 1984 (KF). The latest fall departure date for Springfield is December 15, 1976, and the average (13 years) is November 15.

The majority of the wintering bluebird population is in southern Illinois. The Grabers' study (1963) showed about 680,000 bluebirds in both January 1907 and January 1957. Wintering birds in northern and central Illinois combined numbered fewer than 25,000. Christmas bird count maxima: 110, Michael, December 28, 1947 (AFN11:92); 83, Olney, December 26, 1966 (AFN21:251); 74, Union County, December 30, 1976 (AB31:691); 69, Crab Orchard National Wildlife Refuge, December 15, 1984 (AB39:635). Not only do severe winters limit the bluebird's numbers; pesticides sprayed in orchards and other areas may also cause heavy losses in certain southern areas. Some Eastern Bluebirds winter south to eastern Mexico, and there are sedentary breeding populations of this species as far south as north-central Nicaragua.

MOUNTAIN BLUEBIRD
Sialia currucoides
VERY RARE VAGRANT

Nelson (1876) noted that there was a specimen of the Mountain Bluebird from East Dubuque, but upon examination Ridgway (1907) decided it was a discolored female Eastern Bluebird. A report also comes from Peoria County, May 10, 1969, with few details (Princen 1970). But two Illinois records are backed by photographs. The first acceptable record of this western North American species was at Sangchris State Park near Springfield, April 9–11, 1982 (Bohlen 1982). This female stayed near the concrete dam on the Sangamon-Christian county line—not unusual behavior for the Mountain Bluebird, which inhabits rather austere areas—and fed by the hover-and-pounce method. This bird was probably east of its intended range, having been drifted there during migration by high westerly winds. The second sighting occurred at Lake Le-Aqua-Na State Park in Stephenson County, near the Wisconsin border, on January 8, 1983 (HDB,RS). This male fed on juniper berries and sat on a telephone wire along a road. Photographs of the two birds, taken by Jack Armstrong and Mark Harris, are on file at the Illinois State Museum. A third record was of a female seen in Mason County on December 13, 1987 (LA,KR). There are records of Mountain Bluebirds from surrounding states, and they winter casually as close as eastern Kansas. Some hybridization occurs between this species and the Eastern Bluebird.

TOWNSEND'S SOLITAIRE
Myadestes townsendi
RARE VAGRANT

This western montane species is usually seen in winter in Illinois, but the state's 13 records run from October 22

(1985, Chicago, RB,MBi-AB40:122) to April 8 (1977, Sterling, BSh-AB31:1009). The first record was of a specimen taken at Waukegan, December 16, 1875 (Ford 1956). Another specimen, a male, was taken at Springfield on February 21, 1978, having been seen there since January 15 (ISM). Some Townsend's Solitaires stayed in the same locality for extended periods, including one at Beall Woods from December 17, 1969, to February 22, 1970 (Bohlen 1978). Nine records come from northern, two from central, and two from southern Illinois. The Solitaires recorded in April could be spring migrants. The breeding area closest to Illinois is in northwestern Nebraska. Solitaires feed on berries of red cedar, hawthorn, and crabapple. Other recent records: Chicago Navy Pier, November 19–22, 1977 (MM-AB32:214), and Crab Orchard National Wildlife Refuge, January 25, 1979 (S.Hossler-AB33:286).

VEERY

Catharus fuscescens

COMMON MIGRANT; OCCASIONAL SUMMER RESIDENT IN NORTHERN AND PARTS OF CENTRAL ILLINOIS

This thrush has a tawny back and fewer spots than other brown-backed thrushes; these spots are concentrated in the throat area. The Veery's song is flutelike and descending, while its call note sounds much like that of the Gray-cheeked Thrush. Veeries sing frequently in the early morning but even more toward dusk. They are found in woodlands. Graber and Graber (1973) found them nesting in a sandy hill habitat with low damp areas of oak and a floor covering of low bush blueberry. The Veeries that breed and are common migrants in Illinois belong to the grayer western race, *C. f. salicicola*. The more reddish migrants belong to the eastern race, *C. f. fuscescens*. Others are obvious intergrades of the two races.

Most spring migrant Veeries do not arrive until late April or May. The earliest records come from Des Plaines Conservation Area, April 15, 1981 (JSt-AB35:830), and Springfield, April 20, 1976 (HDB). Average spring arrival dates: Urbana, April 29 (18 years); Chicago, May 5 (16 years); Sangamon County, May 1 (17 years). Spring bird count totals ranged from 48 in 1974 to 528 in 1983, when Cook County tallied 256 on May 7 (VK). Other high counts: 60, Chicago, May 18, 1957 (Mlodinow 1984); 15, Jackson Park, May 10, 1982 (PC,RG); 14, Springfield, May 14, 1981 (HDB). Average spring departure dates: Urbana, May 25 (18 years); Chicago, May 23 (16 years); Sangamon County, May 23 (16 years). Late departure dates: Chicago, June 12, 1983 (JL); Park Forest, June 5, 1985 (AD-IB&B1:88); Normal, June 19, 1973 (DBi-AB27:877).

A thin and local nesting population is found mostly in northern Illinois, although some appear to be moving into central Illinois. Recent summer records: several, Middle Fork, 1981 (SB-AB35:946); Coles County, 1982–83 (LBH);

Lake Shelbyville, 1985 (AR-AB39:919); Sand Ridge State Forest, 1985–86 (RBj-AB39:919); three pairs, Allerton Park, 1979 (Graber-SR22:6); 16 pairs, Chain O'Lakes State Park, 1982 (JN,SH-AB34:10); eight males, Palos, 1983, and six males, Joliet, 1983 (JM-SR38:12); nine pairs, Starved Rock and Matthiessen State Parks, 1983 (RGu-SR38:12). Recent nests: with cowbird egg, Joliet, June 6, 1985 (JM-IB&B2:15); adult feeding three young and a cowbird, Kennekuk Cove Park, July 6, 1984 (ME-IB&B1:18); one Veery egg and one cowbird egg, Winnebago County, June 14, 1957 (IAB108:9); two young and one cowbird, Kankakee County, June 23, 1972 (Graber and Graber 1973).

Fall migration is rather unspectacular, probably because the majority of Veeries overfly Illinois or deflect east. Early fall arrival dates: Springfield, August 19, 1977 (HDB); Chicago, August 22, 1941 (Clark and Nice 1950). Average arrival dates: Chicago, August 29 (six years); west-central, September 1 (six years); Sangamon County, August 29 (18 years). High counts for fall: 17, Springfield, September 3, 1981 (HDB); 59, television tower kill, Sangamon County, September 2, 1971. Average departure dates are early, as this species does not linger in fall: Chicago, September 6 (six years); west-central, September 4 (six years); Sangamon County, September 20 (17 years). Late departure dates: Forest Glen Preserve, October 16, 1981 (MC-SR31:14); Jackson Park, September 25, 1983 (HR); Chicago, September 22, 1983 (SP-SR39:21). The Veery winters in South America.

GRAY-CHEEKED THRUSH

Catharus minimus

COMMON SPRING MIGRANT; UNCOMMON FALL MIGRANT

Like the Swainson's Thrush, the Gray-cheeked has a plain back; a view of the facial area is usually required for identification. The Gray-cheek's call note, a somewhat nasal *weer*, distinguishes it from the Swainson's Thrush but not from the Veery, except for observers with extensive practice. The Gray-cheeked sings occasionally on spring migration, as do other thrushes; its flutelike song is descending, while the Swainson's is ascending. The Gray-cheeked is found in woodlands of all types. It breeds mainly in spruce forests in the far north, even as far northwest as Siberia. The race found in Illinois is *C. m. minimus*, although the smaller eastern race, *bicknelli*, has been reported a few times: Highland Park, September 6, 1909, and Warsaw, May 24, 1884 (Coale 1916). Gray-cheeks feed on insects, including ants, caterpillars, and Coleoptera; fruits such as elderberry and pokeberry; and molluscs.

This nocturnal migrant can be identified by its calls as it flies overhead. Mid-April is about the earliest this thrush has been reported: Jackson Park, April 19, 1987 (HR); Springfield, April 18, 1985 (HDB). Average spring arrival dates: Urbana, April 29 (19 years); Chicago, May 4 (16 years); Sangamon County, April 28 (18 years). Spring bird count totals ranged from 28 in 1978 to 612 in 1976, with the high count 105 in Cook County, May 7, 1983 (VK). For southern Illinois 52 at Giant City State Park, May 12, 1984 (DR-SR41:22), is a significant number. Spring departure averages: Urbana, May 25 (19 years); Chicago, May 25 (16 years); Sangamon County, May 26 (16 years). Several June records suggest that this thrush lingers and then makes long flights into the far north to breed. June records: Vermilion County, June 14, 1978 (MC-AB32:1015); two, Chicago, June 3, 1984 (JL); Springfield, June 4, 1982 (HDB).

This is another species that deflects eastward in the fall and consequently becomes less numerous in southern and western Illinois. Depending on the winds, it can be either rather common or very difficult to find. Earliest fall records are for August: Springfield, August 22, 1977 (HDB); Chicago, August 21, 1938 (Clark and Nice 1950). Average fall arrival dates: Chicago, September 4 (15 years); Sangamon County, September 5 (18 years). Maximum counts for fall are few: 10, Urbana, September 15, 1981 (BCho-SR31:14); 12, Chicago, September 27, 1983 (JL); 145 at a television tower, Sangamon County, September 16–17, 1958 (Parmalee and Parmalee 1959). Average departure dates: Chicago, October 5 (15 years); Sangamon County, October 3 (18 years). Some Gray-cheeks stay until mid-October or later: Olney, November 12, 1978 (LH-AB33:184); Jackson Park, October 23, 1982 (HR-SR35:13); Springfield, October 18, 1983 (HDB). One was reported on a Christmas bird count at Peoria, December 18, 1982 (AB37:616). Gray-cheeked Thrushes winter in South America and north to Costa Rica.

SWAINSON'S THRUSH

Catharus ustulatus

COMMON MIGRANT

This plain-backed thrush has the buffy eye ring, although not all Swainson's Thrushes show the eye ring and the back color varies. These disparities are partly explained by the presence of at least two subspecies in Illinois, *C. u. incanus* and *C. u. swainsoni*. Swainson's Thrushes breed in the northern United States, Alaska, Canada, and the mountains of the western United States—*incanus* in the northwest and *swainsoni* in the east. In Illinois Swainson's tend to outnumber all other migrant brown-backed thrushes. The *bot* call note instantly separates these thrushes from all others. Found in woodlands of all types during migration, they eat ants, caterpillars, and Coleoptera in spring but mostly fruit, such as grapes, wild cherries, elderberries, and blackberries, in fall (Forbes 1903).

A few Swainson's Thrushes arrive fairly early some years. The earliest spring arrival dates are Illinois Beach State Park, April 3, 1976 (Mlodinow 1984); Keithsburg, April 14, 1984 (MB-SR 41:22); Jackson Park, April 15, 1983 (HR); Springfield, April 14, 1974 (HDB). Average arrival dates: Chicago, April 28 (16 years); Sangamon County,

April 22 (18 years); Urbana, April 25 (20 years). Spring bird count totals ranged from 49 in 1978 to 1593 in 1983. This wide range probably reflects differences in timing of migrations, but this species does show wide fluctuations in numbers from year to year. Highest spring count was 490 in Cook County, May 7, 1983 (VK). Other high counts: 51, Giant City State Park, May 12, 1984 (DR-SR41:22); 46, Jackson Park, May 7, 1983 (RL,PC-SR37:20); 38, Springfield, May 14, 1981 (HDB). Migrating Swainson's Thrushes can be heard calling as they fly over at night. They also are commonly heard singing in woodlands and parks in Illinois in May. Migration continues into June. Departure date averages: Chicago, May 28 (16 years); Sangamon County, May 31 (16 years); Urbana, May 27 (20 years). Late departure dates: Chicago, June 12, 1983 (JL); Urbana, June 6, 1982 (BCho-SR 33:12); Normal, June 12, 1973 (DBi-AB 27:887).

Fall migration usually begins in August, but there are a few July records, including one at Shirland, July 29, 1972 (LJ-AB27:69). Early fall arrival dates: Blue Island, August 22, 1985 (KB-IB&B2:53); Normal, August 25, 1977 (DBi-AB32:214); two, Waukegan, August 4, 1963 (CC); Jackson Park, August 11, 1982 (PC). Average arrival dates: Chicago, August 26 (16 years); Sangamon County, August 29 (18 years). Maximum counts for fall tend to occur along Lake Michigan, where hordes of migrants are pushed up against the lakefront: 200, Chicago, September 2, 1980 (JL); 150, Chicago, September 4, 1981 (JL); 67, Jackson Park, September 2, 1982 (PC,HR-SR35:13); 25, Chicago, October 1, 1983 (JL). Downstate concentrations seem to occur only at television tower kills: 107, Sangamon County, September 16–17, 1958 (Parmalee and Parmalee 1959). Average departure dates: Chicago, October 7 (16 years); Sangamon County, October 9 (17 years). Late departure dates: Chicago, November 15, 1984 (PC,HR-AB39:62); Dundee, November 15, 1982 (RM-SR35:13); Springfield, October 26, 1980 (HDB). There are several winter records, some poorly documented: Winnetka, November 28, 1949–January 2, 1950 (Ford 1956); Lisle Arboretum, December 2, 1961 (CC); Evanston, December 27, 1981 (Mlodinow 1984); western Mercer County, January 3, 1965 (AFN19:238), and January 2, 1986 (AB 40:839).

The Swainson's Thrush is a long-distance migrant that winters from Mexico south to Peru, Bolivia, Argentina, and Paraguay.

HERMIT THRUSH

Catharus guttatus

COMMON MIGRANT; UNCOMMON WINTER RESIDENT DECREASING NORTHWARD

The Hermit Thrush has a rusty tail, which it cocks up and drops slowly. Its call note is a low *chuck*, but it rarely sings its beautiful flutelike song in Illinois. It is the earliest arriving and latest departing of the brown-backed thrushes. The

Hermit is found mainly in woodlands. It eats insects, principally Coleoptera, Lepidoptera, and ants (Forbes 1903). In fall it eats wild fruits. It breeds in the coniferous zone in Alaska, Canada, the northern United States, and the western mountains. The race usually found in Illinois is *C. g. faxoni*, but the western forms, *C. g. guttatus* and *C. g. sequoiensis*, have also been reported from Illinois (Ford 1956).

Wintering birds can somewhat obscure the arrival of spring birds, but spring migration usually occurs in late March. Average arrival dates: Urbana, March 31 (18 years); Chicago, April 1 (16 years); Sangamon County, March 30 (17 years). Maximum counts for spring: 185, Chicago, April 22, 1983 (JL); 30 banded, Chicago, April 25, 1984 (SP-SR41:23), 40, Sterling, April 17, 1975 (BSh). Spring bird counts are past the peak for this thrush, but totals ranged from 45 in 1981 to 204 in 1984. Almost all the high counts were in the north; the highest was 96 in Cook County, May 5, 1984 (VK). Average spring departure dates: Urbana, May 5 (18 years); Chicago, May 9 (16 years); Sangamon County, May 6 (17 years). Late spring departure dates: Jackson Park, June 4, 1983 (HR-SR37:20); Green River Conservation Area, May 17, 1987 (JH); Chicago, May 22, 1983 (JL).

A few Hermit Thrushes return very early from the north in mid-August, but most arrive in late September. Early arrival dates for fall: Chicago, August 12, 1983 (SP-SR39:21); Wilmette, August 13, 1962, Evanston, August 19, 1977, and Wilmette, August 21, 1966 (Mlodinow 1984). Average fall arrival dates: Chicago, September 21 (16 years); Sangamon County, September 30 (18 years). High counts for fall: 125, Chicago, October 9, 1983 (JL); 135, Chicago, October 12, 1985 (RB,JL-AB40:122); 40 television tower kills, Sangamon County, October 14, 1985; 30, Vermilion County, October 16, 1983 (JSm-SR39:21). Average fall departure dates: Chicago, October 28 (16 years); Sangamon County, November 16 (18 years).

Hermit Thrushes winter in small numbers in north and central Illinois and somewhat larger numbers in southern Illinois. They inhabit dense wooded areas, especially in ravines and other sheltered places. Christmas bird count totals for 1976–85 ranged from seven in 1978 to 64 in 1982. Highest count was 32 at Horseshoe Lake, Alexander County, in 1983. Other late winter records: Clinton Lake, January 31, 1987 (RP,MD-IB&B3:68); Evanston, February 17, 1987 (EW-IB&B3:68); Peoria, January 1–February 14, 1982 (E.Pearson-SR32:7); Shelby County, February 6, 1983 (KF-SR36:9).

WOOD THRUSH

Hylocichla mustelina

COMMON MIGRANT AND SUMMER RESIDENT

This brown-backed thrush has more spots and is somewhat plumper than the other thrush species. Its mellow, flutelike song comes from the woods at dawn and dusk. Along the Mississippi River bluffs the Wood Thrush sings from wooded ravines (RG). Its call notes are a harsh series of *pits*, which identify it in fall when it does not sing. It usually stays on or near the ground in heavily wooded bottomlands, making it difficult to see. It eats mostly insects, millipedes, and some fruit.

Although there are a few March records of these migrants, including a Wood Thrush photographed at Westville, March 29, 1975 (DWa-AB29:699), most of them arrive in late April. One was seen at Chicago on April 18, 1987 (CM). Average spring arrival dates: Urbana, April 30 (20 years); Chicago, May 7 (14 years); Sangamon County, April 25 (18 years). The only maxima are from spring bird counts, in which the totals ranged from 282 in 1978 to 1251 in 1986. High counts were from the northeastern and southern parts of the state; 85 in Vermilion County, May 10, 1986, was the highest (VK). Dreuth at Chicago noted that the average departure date for spring migrants was May 19; the latest migrant was seen on May 31, 1940 (Clark and Nice 1950).

Robbins et al. (1986), using breeding bird survey data, found that Wood Thrush populations had decreased in some areas of the United States and increased in others. In Illinois 1.1 was the mean number of birds per survey route for 1965–79. Earlier Wood Thrush populations must have been greater because there was more bottomland forest. These thrushes nest from low to medium height in trees, building rather bulky nests like those of robins. The three to five eggs are bluish like robins' eggs. Illinois egg dates are May 3–July 10 (Bent 1949). Nests are heavily parasitized by cowbirds; one Wood Thrush nest at Lake Shelbyville had 11 cowbird eggs in it (SR-IB&B2:15). I have noted Wood Thrushes in molt from mid-July to early September.

Dreuth found fall migrants at Chicago as early as September 6 (1931). His average arrival date was September 9 (10 years). I noted a migrant at Springfield on September 11, 1985. There are no large counts for fall; at television tower kills Wood Thrushes are found only in small numbers. Average fall departure dates: Chicago, September 28 (10 years); Sangamon County, October 5 (18 years). Late fall departure dates: Blue Island, October 28, 1983 (KB-AB38:210); Kennekuk Cove Park, November 2, 1986 (ME-IB&B3:46); Forest Glen Preserve, November 4, 1981 (MC-SR31:14); Dixon, November 15, 1969 (Bohlen 1978). There is one Christmas bird count record: Pere Marquette State Park in 1976. Wood Thrushes winter from southern Texas south to northwestern Colombia.

AMERICAN ROBIN

Turdus migratorius

ABUNDANT MIGRANT AND SUMMER RESIDENT; UNCOMMON WINTER RESIDENT DECREASING NORTHWARD MOST YEARS

Since the American Robin lives in residential areas, it is well known and appreciated by most people. It also occurs in woodlands, orchards, parks, and more open areas such as pastures. Its song is a loud caroling, and several robins often sing together to produce their famous dawn and dusk choruses in spring and summer. Several different calls are given—for example, while in flight or in conflict. That robins eat earthworms is well known, but they also ingest larvae of March flies, cutworms, tussock moth egg masses, ground beetles, wireworms, cankerworms, and seventeen-year cicadas, among others. In summer, fall, and winter they also eat the fruit of wild grape, black cherry, hackberry, dogwood, multifora rose, pokeberry, elderberry, persimmon, and red cedar (Graber et al. 1971). During spring snowstorms, robins commonly come up to the road-sides, where many are killed. They are frequently killed on roads at other times, too; in a listing I kept for 1985 in Sangamon County, robins were the most frequent avian victims. Even more serious is mortality caused by insecticide poisoning, although it appears to be on the wane. The race of the American Robin in Illinois is *T. m. migratorius*. The subspecies *T. m. achrusterus* is listed in AOU (1957), but see Mengel (1965). Albinism in the robin seems fairly frequent; there are three albinistic specimens in the Illinois State Museum collection from Mason, Morgan, and Sangamon Counties.

Spring migration may start as early as mid-January, with the peak in February and March. Average arrival dates: Urbana, February 20 (13 years); Chicago, March 9 (16 years); west-central, February 19 (14 years). Migration apparently is both in daylight and at night. Armstrong (1920) reported several hundred robins in migration at Chicago, March 19, 1920, and 2615 were seen heading south (reverse migration) at Jackson Park, April 14, 1983 (PC,HR-SR37:20). In the spring of 1982 a late snowstorm caused thousands to be killed on the roads. Concentrations of 900 occurred at Jackson Park, March 24, 1982 (PC,RG-SR33:13), and at Springfield, April 10, 1982 (HDB). Spring bird count totals ranged from 9219 in 1972 to 33,506 in 1986. The highest count was 3483 in Cook County, May 5, 1984, with all high counts coming from the northern part of the state (VK).

Graber and Graber (1963) estimated June populations for the robin to be 1,900,000 in 1909 and 1,500,000 in 1957. The numbers greatly increased in residential areas but dropped in other habitats. Robbins et al. (1986), using breeding bird survey data for 1965–79, found a strong and significant increase in Illinois, and the mean number of robins per route was 36. Robins nest in a variety of places, from trees and bushes to man-made structures. The nest is a solid cup of mud and plant materials, plus string and other junk. There are usually four bluish eggs, but there may be three to seven. Illinois egg dates are April 18 to July 20, and there is usually more than one brood per year. The young have a spotted breast, which they may retain as late as mid-October. After nesting, robins revert to the woods and become "wilder" birds, traveling in flocks that feed mostly on fruit.

The beginning of fall migration is difficult to determine; it may start as early as late July or August (Graber et al. 1971). Few fall counts are available: 500, Shelby County, October 25, 1986 (YM-IB&B3:46); 350, Urbana, Novem-

ber 19, 1986 (SB-IB&B3:46); 900, Jackson Park, August 19, 1980 (PC); 220, Springfield, October 11, 1986 (HDB); 4000 migrating, McGinnis Slough, October 21, 1978 (Mlodinow 1984). Numbers begin to drop in November. Average fall departure dates: Chicago, November 21 (16 years); west-central, November 30 (10 years).

Most of the wintering population is in southern Illinois, but some years there are also high numbers in central and northern Illinois. The wintering population is growing; Graber and Graber (1963) estimated 100,000 in January 1907 and 1,366,000 in January 1957. Christmas bird count totals for 1976–85 ranged from 409 in 1978 to 5333 in 1985. For seven of the 10 years the high counts were from northern Illinois; the highest was 1970 at Chicago North Shore in 1985. Robins form roosts at many times of the year, but especially in winter. These roosts are usually in conifers. I noted about 1000 using a coniferous area at Springfield in 1979–80.

VARIED THRUSH

Ixoreus naevius

VERY RARE WINTER RESIDENT

This beautiful western thrush is usually seen at feeders or associated with coniferous trees or berry bushes. Varied Thrushes are usually shy, preferring to stay in heavy cover except when they are at feeders. They normally feed on the ground and are frequently seen flipping dead leaves over in search of food. Even though their principal range is the West Coast of North America, they probably occur every winter in Illinois in small numbers, but some may go undetected or unreported.

The Varied Thrush has been reported in Illinois at least 30 times between November 21 and May 1. The first record was of a male at Blue Island on April 26, 1929 (Bartel 1932). Then four were reported in the 1950s, four in the 1960s, 12 in the 1970s, and nine so far in the 1980s. The majority of the records are from northern Illinois (23), with six from central Illinois and only one from the upper part of southern Illinois—Brussels, December 18–26, 1976 (JEa-AB31:338). No Varied Thrushes have been reported south of this Calhoun County site, although that may be due to a scarcity of observers in the south. No specimen has been taken in Illinois, but some of these thrushes were photographed and the photographs are on file at the Illinois State Museum. Some recent records: Peoria, February 5–29, 1980 (C.Rist,VH-AB34:278); Winthrop Harbor, April 20–May 1, 1980 (JN-AB34:784); Plato Center, November 22–January 17, 1982 (AB36:300); Crane Lake, December 21, 1985–January 1, 1986 (JF,R.Mudd-AB40:288); St. Joseph, December 4–9, 1986 (RCh); Springfield, January 14–March 2, 1987 (HDB); Elgin, January 11–February 24, 1987 (JM-IB&B3:68).

GRAY CATBIRD

Dumetella carolinensis

COMMON MIGRANT AND COMMON SUMMER
RESIDENT; RARE WINTER RESIDENT

The song of the Gray Catbird is varied. It usually sings a phrase just once, unlike the Brown Thrasher, which sings each phrase twice, or the Northern Mockingbird, which sings the same phrase three times or more. The Catbird intersperses several catlike sounds through its song. The scold note is a heavy-breathing *kaah*. In fall the Catbird also has a warblerlike chip note that may take the warbler seeker a while to track down.

The Catbird tends to stay low in the brush but reacts well to an observer's "spishing" and "squeaking" by jumping up to higher branches and scolding back. Catbirds like wooded areas, especially the edges; they are seldom found in the interiors. They haunt residential areas; this species is a prime example of a Neotropical migrant that can be encouraged to nest in backyards if suitable habitat is provided. In spring Catbirds eat mostly insects, including ants, caterpillars, crane flies, ground beetles, and spiders (Forbes 1880). In fall they are fond of wild grape, elderberry, mulberry, black cherry, and especially pokeberry, as shown at close range by the purplish stains on these birds. The breeding race in Illinois is *D. c. carolinensis*, but the western race, *D. c. ruficrissa*, may well occur as a migrant (see Graber et al. 1970).

The first Catbirds begin to arrive in Illinois about April 20, with the majority coming in May. Average arrival dates: Urbana, April 26 (16 years); Chicago, May 3 (15 years); Sangamon County, April 27 (18 years). Spring bird count totals ranged from 289 in 1978 to 4152 in 1986. The wide range is probably due to differences in the timing of migrations. The highest spring count was 705 in Cook County, May 7, 1983 (VK).

Graber and Graber (1963) found that the Catbird population declined considerably from 1909 to 1957. The statewide population in 1958 was estimated at 220,000. Robbins et al. (1986) noted some increases and a few decreases in numbers of Catbirds in the United States using breeding bird survey data for 1965-79. In Illinois the mean number per survey route was 3.6. A summer high count of 300 was tallied in Cook County, June 8, 1985 (IB&B2:15). The Catbird builds its nest fairly low to the ground in thickets; the eggs, usually four, are dark green. Illinois egg dates are May 14-July 11. In late summer young Catbirds boost the population, making the species seem ubiquitous in their favored habitats. Bird banders identify young Catbirds by the dull gray iris, the light-colored palate, and the loose texture of the undertail coverts. Adults, which usually molt in late summer, have deep reddish eyes and black palates. When in molt these birds become sedentary and are difficult to see. Even banders catch mostly the young, which are more mobile in late summer.

In late September and early October concentrated numbers of Catbirds can be seen, especially along linear habitats such as hedgerows and railroad rights-of-way. Catbirds are frequently victims of television tower kills, proving that they migrate at night; 25 were killed in Sangamon County, October 4, 1983. Fall high counts: 28, Vermilion County, September 15, 1985 (SB-IB&B2:53); 30, Fulton County, October 1, 1986 (KM-IB&B3:46); 28, Chouteau Island, September 18, 1987 (RG). Average departure dates: west-central, October 13 (10 years); Chicago, October 8 (16 years); Springfield, October 25 (18 years). By late October most Catbirds have gone south, although a few seem to linger into November and even fewer try to winter. Christmas bird counts for 1976-85 showed a few Catbirds every year. Six were reported in 1980. Just as many are recorded in northern as in southern Illinois. Many of these Catbirds must be very late migrants. Catbirds winter as far south as Panama.

NORTHERN MOCKINGBIRD

Mimus polyglottos

COMMON PERMANENT RESIDENT IN
SOUTHERN AND PARTS OF CENTRAL
ILLINOIS; UNCOMMON TO RARE ELSEWHERE
IN THE STATE

The Northern Mockingbird is a southern species that is extending its range northward. It occasionally suffers losses during severe winters. Musselman (1938) stated that mockingbirds were irregular migrants before 1930 in western Illinois but became common following the mild winter of 1936. Graber and Graber (1963) showed that even though the state population—most of it in southern Illinois—dropped, Northern Mockingbird numbers increased in central Illinois from 5000 in 1907-9 to 31,000 in 1957. Mockingbirds occur in fairly open habitats such as scrub edges, residential areas, orchards, and farmyards. They especially prefer multiflora hedges, and their extension northward may be correlated with plantings of these hedges. Unfortunately, multiflora is now out of favor and the species that depend on it will become less numerous. Mockingbirds are noted for their songs and their mimicking of other birds and sounds. They also have a distinctive call note, a harsh *chuck*. The subspecies in Illinois is the eastern form, *M. p. polyglottos*.

Though some mockingbirds stay for the winter, others migrate. Average spring arrival dates: Urbana, April 26 (16 years); Sangamon County, April 2 (seven years). Dreuth noted migrants in April and May at Chicago (Clark and Nice 1950). I noted a spring migrant as early as February 28, 1982, in Sangamon County. Recent northern Illinois spring records: Park Forest, April 26, 1985 (ADu-IB&B1:88); a migrant, Jackson Park, May 29, 1981 (RG-SR29:11); McHenry County, April 6, 1986 (CMi-IB&B2:95); Chicago, April 28-29, 1984 (SP-SR41:23). Totals on spring bird counts ranged from 230 in 1978 to

784 in 1974. Low counts in the late 1970s were the result of severe winters; by 1986, when 740 were seen, numbers were getting back to normal. All high counts came from southern Illinois; the highest was 79 in Perry County, May 4, 1985 (VK).

Graber and Graber (1963) estimated summer populations, all in southern Illinois, of 386,000 in 1909 and 89,000 in 1957—a significant decline, even though the population was expanding northward at the same time. Using breeding bird survey data for 1965-79, Robbins et al. (1986) noted a significant decline in mockingbird numbers in Illinois and other states. The mean number of mockingbirds per survey route in Illinois was 5.5. Mockingbirds build a bulky cup nest, usually fairly low in a bush or thicket. The three to six eggs are pale blue to greenish blue with reddish brown markings. Illinois egg dates are April 8 to July 4. Recent nesting has occurred in several counties outside southern Illinois: Grundy, Champaign, Tazewell, Menard, Vermilion, Shelby, Sangamon, Will, Henderson, Mason, and Marshall. Immature mockingbirds have faintly streaked breasts, but the white in the wing and tail makes them easy to identify.

Fall migration is even less understood than spring migration. I have seen mockingbirds that seem to be migrating diurnally, including one that was moving with Blue Jays. High counts in fall are low: six, Mason County, September 11, 1983 (MB,LMc-SR39:21); five, Springfield, August 10, 1986 (HDB). Obviously, counts from southern Illinois could improve these numbers.

Wintering birds obscure late departure dates. Graber and Graber (1963) estimated populations of 63,000 in January 1907 and 39,000 in January 1957, all in southern Illinois. Christmas bird counts for 1976-85 showed a drop in numbers due to severe winters in the late 1970s: only 84 in 1979 and 489 in 1976. Winter numbers have apparently not returned to the pre-1976 level, suggesting that while migrant mockingbirds survived, wintering ones did not. The highest count was 199 at Crab Orchard National Wildlife Refuge in 1972. All the high counts were in southern Illinois. Some winter records for northern Illinois: Jackson Park, January 1, 1984 (M.Sidney-SR40:12); McHenry County, December 20-January 1987 (CMi-IB&B3:68); Waukegan, December 17, 1981 (SH-SR32:6); Lisle Arboretum, January 13, 1982 (R.Wason-SR32:6).

SAGE THRASHER

Oreoscoptes montanus

VERY RARE VAGRANT

This thrasher resides in western North America and rarely strays east. There are three Illinois records: Lincoln Park, Chicago, May 11, 1940 (Clark and Nice 1950); one photographed, Winnetka, December 26, 1969-March 8, 1970 (JA-photograph on file ISM); one photographed, Evanston, October 24, 1974 (GR,LB,RR-AB29:67). Other vagrant records of the Sage Thrasher come from Wisconsin,

Ontario, Massachusetts, and North Carolina. It is usually found in brushy areas or thickets.

BROWN THRASHER

Toxostoma rufum

COMMON MIGRANT AND SUMMER RESIDENT; UNCOMMON WINTER RESIDENT IN SOUTHERN ILLINOIS DECREASING NORTHWARD

The Brown Thrasher is a hedgerow and thicket species that tends to stay low and to skulk in the underbrush. When it sings its loud song, usually repeating each phrase twice, it sits high in a tree and the song carries a long distance. These thrashers are typically seen on roadsides in Illinois, running or flying alongside cars and not infrequently being killed before they can get out of the way. They forage on the ground in leaf litter. They especially eat Coleoptera in spring, but from summer on they feed mainly on fruit, seeds, and grain. The subspecies in Illinois is the eastern *T. r. rufum*.

Spring migration usually begins in March. Average arrival dates: Urbana, March 27 (19 years); west-central, March 31 (10 years); Sangamon County, March 25 (18 years); Chicago, April 18 (16 years). Thrashers seen on very early dates may be wintering. Spring bird count totals ranged from 1997 in 1972 to 4585 in 1984; 305 in McDonough County on May 5, 1984, was the highest count. Other high counts: 37, Jackson Park, May 7, 1983 (SR37:21); 18, Springfield, April 22, 1982 (HDB); 60, Chicago area, April 30, 1966 (Mlodinow 1984).

The state's estimated summer Brown Thrasher population declined greatly between 1909 and 1957, from 1,558,000 to 431,000, perhaps because of the reduction of orchards and the destruction of hedges (Graber and Graber 1963). Robbins et al. (1986) found no long-term trend for these thrashers in 1965-79 breeding bird survey data. The average number per survey route in Illinois was 6.9. A cuplike nest made of sticks is usually placed low in a bush or thorn tree. The female lays two to six pale blue eggs that are heavily speckled all over with fine reddish brown markings, making the eggs appear light brown. Illinois egg dates are at least April 29 to July 11. Cowbird eggs have been found in thrashers' nests, but not to any great extent.

Fall migration is difficult to detect, at least until September or October when their migration becomes more obvious. They can be seen more easily in hedgerows and railroad rights-of-way, moving with Catbirds and various species of sparrows. High counts for fall: 40, Chouteau Island, September 18, 1987 (RG); 25, Chicago, October 1, 1983 (JL); 14, Springfield, September 17, 1983 (HDB). Average departure dates: west-central, October 29 (10 years); Sangamon County, November 11 (18 years); Chicago, October 12 (16 years).

In winter Brown Thrashers are found in sheltered areas where heavy brush protects them; many also attend feeders. Christmas bird count totals for 1976-85 ranged from 15 in 1979 to 54 in 1982, with 31 at Horseshoe Lake in 1983 the highest count. All high counts were from southern Illinois. Northern records for winter: four, Chicago North Shore (Christmas bird count), December 23, 1972 (AB27:368); Morris, December 26, 1983 (PD-SR40:12); Chicago, February 13, 1983 (IV-SR36:9); Arlington Heights, winter of 1981-82 (TC-SR32:6).

WATER PIPIT

Anthus spinoletta

IRREGULAR AND UNCOMMON MIGRANT

When kicked up from a field, a flock of Water Pipits climbs high into the sky and then drifts back down in stairstep fashion before landing. These pipits are open-country birds, ocher and brown, thin-billed, with white outer tail feathers. Flocks contain up to 50 or 100 birds. Their habitat is stubble fields, clover fields, fallow fields with fairly short vegetation, and lake shores, especially along the wrack line. They like wet areas in fields and are found around the edges of large puddles. Their distinctive flight notes help the observer detect them as they fly overhead. They breed in the Arctic and in alpine meadows. The Water Pipit has several subspecies; the one occurring in Illinois is *A. s. rubescens*.

In spring the Water Pipit tends to show a divided migration pattern. An early population—usually the larger one—arrives in mid-March and a later population in early May. An observer may miss the early population some years and will record the later arrival dates. In my records for Sangamon County and central Illinois I did that in four of 16 years, so that in 12 years the average arrival date was March 18 and in 16 years it was March 28. The west-central Illinois average date is April 25 (eight years). The earliest spring dates are Lincolnwood, March 11, 1964 (CC); 45, Pope County, March 9, 1984 (JP-SR41:23); Sangchris State Park, March 3, 1983 (HDB). Maximum counts for spring: 50, Middlefork Waterfowl Area, April 28, 1985 (SB-IB&B1:88); 50, Richland County, March 28, 1984 (LH-SR41:23); 21, Rice Lake, March 26, 1983 (LMc,MB-SR37:20); 30, Grayslake, May 12, 1977 (DJ); 40, Urbana, May 3, 1981 (RCh-SR29:12). Spring bird count totals ranged from two in 1972 to 85 in 1978 (VK). In early April 1982 a late snowstorm forced many pipits up to the roads and some mortality occurred. Average spring departure dates: west-central Illinois, May 9 (eight years); Sangamon County, April 30 (15 years). Late spring departure dates: Chicago, May 24, 1937 (Clark and Nice 1950); Waukegan, May 26, 1983 (JG-SR37:20); Springfield, May 24, 1988 (HDB); Jackson Park, May 20, 1978 (RG).

Fall migration does not show the divided effect of the spring migration and is more leisurely. Water Pipits will sometimes take insects on the wing in swallow fashion while migrating. Two central Illinois specimens showed gizzard contents for April of Coleoptera, Hemiptera, Lepidoptera, Homoptera, Diptera, and a spider and for November, Homoptera (aphids). Early fall arrival dates: one banded, Calumet sewage plant, August 21, 1950 (KB); Chicago, September 14, 1985 (JL). Average arrival dates: Chicago, September 27 (nine years); west-central, September 27 (six years); Sangamon County, October 10 (15 years). High counts for fall are higher than for spring: 110, Horseshoe Lake, November 12, 1982 (RG,BR-SR35:14); 75, Rockford, October 28, 1972 (JD-AB27:69); 125, Bismark, October 23, 1985 (SB-IB&B2:53); 100, Will County, October 19–November 3, 1985 (MS,JM-IB&B2:53). Water Pipits stay late, especially in mild years. Average fall departure dates: Chicago, October 18 (nine years); Sangamon County, November 14 (16 years). Latest departure dates are in December: Chicago, December 24, 1936 (Clark and Nice 1950); Lake of Egypt, December 18, 1984 (JR-IB&B1:70); three, New Athens, December 4, 1983 (TF-SR39:22); three, Murphysboro, December 26, 1953 (AFN8:159); Princeton, December 28, 1961 (IAB121:8-9).

Even though Cory (1909) and others considered the Water Pipit a winter resident in southern Illinois, there are few if any true winter records. One pipit flying south near Carlyle Dam, January 7, 1987 (RS,RB,MBi,HDB), is the latest winter record. Water Pipits winter from the Gulf states south to Guatemala and El Salvador.

SPRAGUE'S PIPIT

Anthus spragueii

RARE MIGRANT

This bird is very difficult to find in Illinois. The only way to see a Sprague's Pipit is to walk through many open short-grass fields during the correct seasons: from April 1 to May 1 and from October 1 to late November or, depending on the weather, early December. In fall Sprague's Pipits are associated with cold fronts, especially when cold and snowy weather hits in their breeding areas in Canada's Prairie Provinces, Montana, and the Dakotas. The fields they inhabit have short grass with bare spots; if there is a knoll, they usually sit just off the crest. These pipits like dry fields, not wet ones as Water Pipits do. Sprague's Pipits do not flock like Water Pipits; even when several Sprague's are in the same field, each will probably be alone. When flushed a Sprague's Pipit rockets skyward, flies to the other end of the field, and drops out of the sky like a stone, then levels off near the ground to settle down. This behavior is diagnostic. When seen on the ground this buffy-streaked bird walks around, looking like a miniature Upland Sandpiper. Graber (1957) describes the call note as *chink-chink*.

Some spring records could be of immature Horned

Larks, since these larks and other birds have been misidentified as Sprague's Pipits: near Chicago, April 17, 1966 (FB-AFN20:514); two, Grant Park, April 21, 1983 (Mlodinow 1984); near Woodstock, May 6, 1968 (Fiske 1968); near Jacksonville, April 22, 1972; Springfield, April 26, 1976 (HDB).

Fall records: Rockford, October 30, 1950 (VanDuzer, McMaster-AFN5:19); Springfield, October 19, 1975 (HDB); near Decatur, October 20, 1975 (RS); five on a golf course, Springfield, October 22, 1975 (HDB,VK); Springfield, October 1, 1976 (HDB); Springfield, October 30, 1982 (HDB).

The Grabers found several of these pipits wintering in southern Illinois in large alfalfa fields. Their records: three to five on January 10, 1957, near Cora and at least four on January 13, 1957, and six or seven on March 16, 1957, at Omaha. The stomach of one of the collected birds contained spiders, curculionid weevils, and Lepidoptera larvae (Graber 1957). Sprague's Pipits winter from the southern Great Plains south to central Mexico.

BOHEMIAN WAXWING

Bombycilla garrulus

IRREGULAR AND RARE WINTER RESIDENT IN NORTHERN ILLINOIS DECREASING SOUTHWARD

The Bohemian Waxwing is a larger, grayer version of the Cedar Waxwing. It has white and yellow in the wing and rusty undertail coverts. Its call notes are similar to the Cedar Waxwing's but with a rougher, burry quality. Bohemians wander in search of berries and fruit, including mountain ash, juniper, barberry, highbush cranberry, and apple. I watched one at Sterling feed on sap dripping from a broken limb. Bohemians often travel with Cedar Waxwings.

The southernmost record for the state is a Bohemian Waxwing specimen collected at Villa Ridge, December 18, 1879 (Ridgway 1889). Otherwise most records have come from northern Illinois, with a few from the central part of the state. Occasionally there are large flights; in 1875–76 an immense flock was seen on the shore of Lake Michigan at Waukegan (Nelson 1876). Some 1500 passed over the pines at Beach in early winter 1919 (Coale 1920). Lyon banded 131 Bohemian Waxwings at Waukegan in March and April 1932 (Ford 1956). Seventy-five were at Lisle Arboretum in March 1962 (Swink). More recently, numbers have been small and occurrences infrequent: two, Lake Forest, December 26–30, 1977 (LB-AB32:359); Danville, February 28, 1978 (ME-AB32:359); Lisle Arboretum, February 21–26, 1987 (EW-AB41:289). Extreme dates: Waukegan, November 22, 1969 (CC-AFN24:55); Lisle Arboretum, November 4, 1964 (Mlodinow 1984); Lake Forest, May 7, 1983 (Mlodinow 1984); Chicago, May 24, 1916 (Ford 1956). Recent records for central Illinois: spec-

imen, Springfield, December 22, 1972 (ISM); Decatur, December 23, 1972 (HDB).

CEDAR WAXWING

Bombycilla cedrorum

COMMON BUT ERRATIC MIGRANT; UNCOMMON SUMMER AND WINTER RESIDENT

Flocks of these sleek, brown, crested birds are usually found around fruiting trees. In fact, their migrations and wanderings are so bound up with these trees that they seem to behave much like some tropical frugivorous birds, following a timetable different from that of the insectivores. When Cedar Waxwings are flying overhead they can be detected by their high hissing notes. Waxwings got their name from the red waxy tips on their wings. These red tabs seem to be randomly acquired. Among the 41 specimens in the Illinois State Museum collection, 11 of 24 males and 8 of 17 females had red tabs. Even a bobtailed young male had small red tabs on its wings. Dates on the specimens showed that the red tabs occur throughout the year. Cedar Waxwings are common victims of window kills; occasionally a whole flock crashes into a window in which they have seen trees reflected.

If spring migration is watched closely over several years, it will be seen that Cedar Waxwings have a split migration most years. Flocks usually start arriving in late January or early February and continue until late March to mid-April. Then there is a gap during which few if any birds are seen. A second migration begins in early or mid-May and continues into late May, early June, or even mid-June. Unless one makes daily observations, these waxwings will simply seem erratic (see Bohlen 1974). This double migration northward was also noted by Brewster (1906) in eastern Massachusetts. The Cedar Waxwing is a polytypic species, with three races—which might account for the split migration, since both the eastern and northern races should pass through Illinois. Spring bird count totals show wide fluctuations, ranging from 19 to 1399 waxwings. The maximum count was 596 in Du Page County, May 9, 1981 (VK). Other spring maxima: 467, Richland County, January 21, 1981 (LH-SR29:12); 750, Danville, March 1, 1985 (SB-AB39:309); 900, Jackson Park, May 29, 1981 (PC,RG-SR29:12).

Cedar Waxwings probably nest in all Illinois counties, though not commonly. Robbins et al. (1986) found that the mean number of Cedar Waxwings on the 64 Illinois breeding bird survey routes (1965–79) was 0.9. They also found that Cedar Waxwing numbers are increasing in the eastern United States. These waxwings like fairly open woodland and will nest in residential areas. The female lays three to five pale blue eggs that have dark spots, usually most abundant toward the larger end of the egg. Illinois egg dates are June to August. Some nests are in loose colonies; four nests were found within a few yards of each other at Kickapoo State Park in 1981 (SB-SR30:13). Streaked young or immature birds have been noted from June to mid-December. Timing of nesting, like other phases of the Cedar Waxwing's life cycle, is tied to the availability of fruit. Although the young are fed for a while on insects, fruit is soon added to their diet, most often mulberry, cedar berry, wild cherry, and crabapple. I saw waxwings feeding on periodical cicadas that emerged in 1972 and 1973 in the Springfield area, and Joe Milosevich saw them flycatching at Joliet on July 12, 1984 (IB&B1:18).

Fall migrants were detected as early as July 24, 1980, at Waukegan (JL-AB34:901). Dreuth listed August 2, 1936, as the earliest date for Chicago (Clark and Nice 1950) and August 14 (15 years) as the average. The average for central Illinois is August 26 (16 years). Evidently the double migration does not occur in fall, or perhaps it is obscured. Maximum fall counts: 600, Waukegan, August 24, 1975 (Mlodinow 1984); 200, Galesburg, September 21, 1983 (MB-SR39:22); 2920, Illinois Beach State Park, October 20, 1984 (DJ); 3000 (over three days), Urbana, October 19–21, 1984 (RCh-AB39:62); 155, Union County, November 12, 1983 (JR-SR39:22). Some years fall migration tapers off in late November; other years flocks of waxwings stay on until all the fruit is gone; and sometimes they overwinter.

Christmas bird count totals for 1976–85 ranged from 404 in 1977 to 2462 in 1979. The highest single count was 655 in west Mercer County in 1956. Other winter maxima: 246, Chicago, December 29, 1985 (IB&B2:78); 347, Pere Marquette State Park, December, 22, 1979 (AB-34:529); 397, Horseshoe Lake, December 20, 1983 (AB38:645). Some Cedar Waxwings winter as far south as central Panama.

NORTHERN SHRIKE

Lanius excubitor

UNCOMMON WINTER RESIDENT IN NORTHERN ILLINOIS AND VERY RARE WINTER RESIDENT ELSEWHERE IN THE STATE

The differences between the Northern and Loggerhead Shrikes are subtle, and many of the supposed identifying marks have points of overlap (see Balch 1977–78). With care and experience, however, these species can be separated in the field. The Northern Shrike is circumboreal in open deciduous and coniferous woodlands. In Illinois it occurs during the cold months in open woodlands and hedgerows, usually perching in the tops of trees, although it will also perch on utility poles and other man-made structures. It seems to prefer marshy situations with scattered larger trees among many smaller trees. In these areas it takes mice and small birds, sticking them on thorns. A

definite year-to-year fluctuation in shrike numbers occurs, but the reason is unclear. Davis (1949), using Christmas bird count data from several states, including Illinois, concluded that emigration of Northern Shrikes from 1930 to 1947 occurred at intervals of five or six years and was not synchronous with invasions of Snowy Owls. The subspecies found in Illinois is presumed to be *L. e. borealis,* of northeastern North America.

Early migrant arrivals in fall: Winfield, October 8, 1984 (MS-IB&B1:21); Illinois Beach State Park, October 7, 1981 (DJ-SR31:15). These shrikes occur singly and have fairly large, wide-ranging territories. Karl Bartel banded one at Palos in November 1981, then retrapped it in fall 1982 and on January 13, 1983 (SR36:10). Christmas bird counts for 1976–85 had high totals of 22 in 1976, 18 in 1981, and 21 in 1985; lows were two in 1979 and three in 1982. The highest individual count was four, in Cook County in 1973 and Lake County in 1985. These shrikes rarely reach central Illinois: Petersburg, February 27, 1982 (CB-AB36:301); Decatur, January 4, 1986 (RP-AB40:288); Snicarte, January 1 and 26, 1986 (LA-IB&B2:78); Knox County, December 13, 1986 (MB-IB&B2:78). The presence of a specimen in the Steinhauer collection (ISM) that was taken in Fayette County, March 27, 1896, suggests that this species once ranged farther south. In fact, Mengel (1965) listed it as a casual winter visitor for Kentucky.

Late spring departures: Grayslake, March 15, 1978 (DJ-AB32:1016); Wadsworth, March 27, 1986 (SH-AB40:480); Chain O'Lakes State Park, March 23, 1981 (F.Harty-SR29:12). The latest spring record is from Blue Island, April 16, 1932 (Bartel and Reuss 1932).

LOGGERHEAD SHRIKE

Lanius ludovicianus

COMMON PERMANENT RESIDENT IN SOUTHERN ILLINOIS; OCCASIONAL MIGRANT AND SUMMER AND WINTER RESIDENT ELSEWHERE IN THE STATE

An interesting and unique bird, the Loggerhead Shrike unfortunately is losing in its struggle to survive in a world dominated and manipulated by people. The northern and central Illinois populations are already mere remnants, and even the southern Illinois population has started to decline. The northern and central decline was steady from about 1900 to 1957; then a precipitous drop occurred, and the shrike population has not recovered (Graber et al. 1973). This shrike is now on the Illinois endangered species list. Among the probable reasons for the decline are loss of hedgerows and pasturelands and the use of pesticides.

Loggerhead Shrikes in Illinois belong to the race *L. l. migrans,* although other subspecies may occur during migration or in winter. Shrikes inhabit open country, sitting on wires and fence posts and in the tops of small trees. In their peculiar flight they drop from the perch, then fly with an undulating motion. They have several calls; the most common one is harsh, but even it is given infrequently. Their prey includes several kinds of larger insects, small mammals, birds, reptiles, and amphibians. They feed by impaling their prey on thorns and fences; as a consequence they are often called butcher-birds. The stomach of a shrike taken near Decatur on June 16, 1976, contained only insects: Hemiptera, Coleoptera, and Lepidoptera.

Even though shrikes are found at all seasons, a definite migration occurs throughout the state. Spring arrival dates: two, Mercer County, February 27, 1983 (MB-SR36:10); Leroy, March 30, 1982 (RCh-SR33:13); Winnebago County, March 29, 1981 (DW-SR29:12); Decatur, March 23, 1986 (RP-IB&B2:95). Average arrival dates: Chicago, March 30 (seven years); Urbana, March 18 (20 years); Sangamon County, March 21 (14 years). All the high spring bird counts are in southern Illinois; Pope County had 21 on May 10, 1980. Count totals ranged from 51 in 1978 to 146 in 1986 (VK). Robbins et al. (1986) continued to find significant decreases in the Loggerhead Shrike's populations with data gathered on the breeding bird surveys for 1965–79. The mean number of shrikes per survey route in Illinois was 0.7. Shrikes nest in Osage orange, locust, red cedar, and crabapple. The female lays five to seven grayish eggs with brownish spots. Egg dates for Illinois are March 24 to May 29. Thirty-five pairs of shrikes were located in portions of Wayne, Clay, and Jasper Counties in 1986 (BL-AB40:1211). Other nesting is scattered across the state, but the main numbers are in the south.

Fall migration is fairly difficult to detect, but some years it apparently begins as early as July or August. There are no fall maxima; in fact, observers in northern and central Illinois are lucky to find one Loggerhead Shrike at this season. Burnside (1987) listed a shrike that was banded in northern Illinois in April 1960 and recaptured in northwestern Tennessee in November of the same year. The average fall departure date for Sangamon County is October 15 (eight years). Late departure dates: Chicago, September 28, 1980 (JL-SR27:11); Warren County, November 17, 1984 (MB-IB&B1:21); Whiteside County, October 24, 1981 (BSh-SR31:15).

In winter these shrikes occur in very small numbers in northern and central Illinois, with higher concentrations in the south. Christmas bird count totals for 1976–85 ranged from 39 in 1981 to 112 in 1982. The highest count was 48 in Alexander and Pulaski Counties in 1982.

EUROPEAN STARLING

Sturnus vulgaris

INTRODUCED; NOW AN ABUNDANT
PERMANENT RESIDENT

European Starlings were introduced into North America in 1890–91 in New York City. Immensely successful, they are now considered pests because they compete with the native fauna; damage buildings, crops, and feed stock; and carry disease (Long 1981). This species is dark and chunky with a stubby tail. In breeding plumage it shows some iridescence and its bill is yellow. At other times the bill is dark and the black plumage is speckled with white. Immatures are gray-brown.

The first record in Illinois was of seven or eight starlings at Urbana in January and February 1922 (Ford 1956). A flock of 63 was seen at Quincy on September 21, 1929 (Musselman 1930), indicating that they had spread across the state in considerable numbers by then. They are now among the most abundant birds in Illinois. Although they are present all year, there are definite migrations. Davis (1970) described their migrations for western Illinois. Spring migration begins the first week of March, Davis said, but the flocks are not large, as they are in fall, and they occur over longer periods of time. During the nesting season starling numbers are low, Davis noted, because they are spread out in nesting pairs. In June fledged young form into flocks, and in July some juveniles may be seen flying north. Fall migration starts in August and peaks in late September and early October; a second peak comes when immatures go south in late October. Flock sizes decline in winter as a result of weather movements, and in late February resident flocks show another decline when they break up into pairs.

Graber and Graber (1963) noted that there were no starlings in Illinois in 1909 but estimated the 1957 summer population at 3,100,000 and the winter population at 11,000,000, 90 percent of which was in southern Illinois. Starlings are found in almost all habitats except heavily forested areas. The fragmented forests of central Illinois are overrun with them. The mean number of starlings per breeding bird survey route in Illinois for 1965–79 was 98.5 (Robbins et al. 1986). Cavity nesters, European Starlings compete with native species, especially bluebirds and woodpeckers, for nest sites. The female lays five to seven light blue eggs. Available Illinois egg dates are April 10–June 12. These birds are not only aggressive but also adaptable; it is not uncommon in cold weather to see them standing on chimneys to keep warm. Like Brown-headed Cowbirds, they use cattle as beaters to obtain food. In late fall, after the Chimney Swifts have left, I have seen them take over the swifts' niches and catch flying insects over the city. They also seem to watch Cedar Waxwings and other fruit eaters find fruiting trees and then take them over. Starlings mimic many other birds, including pewees, Killdeer, and bobwhite, but they usually give themselves away by emitting a squawk or a squeal of their own.

Starlings form huge roosts; a roost at Champaign had 175,000 starlings in winter 1981–82 (RCh-SR32:7). Most high numbers on Christmas bird counts come from roosts. Totals on counts for 1976–85 ranged from 60,514 in 1983 to 1,503,629 in 1977. The highest count was 950,000 at Springfield in 1977. Spring bird counts show much smaller numbers because there are no large roosts in spring. Totals on spring counts ranged from 14,936 in 1972 to 29,825 in 1976. Most high counts came from northern Illinois; the highest was 3533 in Cook County on May 10, 1986.

WHITE-EYED VIREO

Vireo griseus

COMMON MIGRANT AND SUMMER RESIDENT
DECREASING NORTHWARD

This thicket vireo is heard much more often than seen. It has a definitive song, *chick-a-weeo-chick*, which is so ventriloquial that the singer is difficult to find. An inhabitant not only of thickets but also of bottomland forests, forest edges, and brushy woodlands, the White-eyed Vireo can be lured into view by "spishing."

White-eyes sometimes arrive fairly early in spring: Union County, April 6, 1985 (RP-AB39:309); Carbondale, April 7, 1986 (TF-IB&B2:95); Pere Marquette, April 12, 1986 (HW-IB&B2:95); Springfield, April 8, 1977 (HDB); Chicago, April 27, 1984 (JL-SR41:23). Average spring arrival dates: Urbana, April 29 (six years); Sangamon County, April 21 (18 years). Totals on spring bird counts ranged from 192 in 1981 to 460 in 1977 and 1986. All high counts came from the south with the exception of Vermilion County, which had the high count four years. Highest count was 135 in Jackson County, May 7, 1977 (VK). A count of 62 at Giant City State Park, May 12, 1984 (DR-AB38:919), is extraordinary for such a limited area. Some migration or wandering continues until late May or early June, as I have records of these vireos, usually males, for June 4, 1986, and May 26, 1978, at Springfield. A female killed at a television tower was found east of Springfield on May 12, 1986.

The White-eyed Vireo is essentially a southern bird, and its stronghold in Illinois is in the south. It has been found in low numbers in northern Illinois since the earliest records were kept, but Dreuth, in his study of Lincoln Park, Chicago, never recorded it (Clark and Nice 1950). Scrub birds such as the White-eyed Vireo move around from year to year, perhaps because of succession in their breeding habitat. Graber et al. (1985) noted no change in the size of the Illinois population between 1907 and 1957. Robbins et al. (1986) recorded an upward trend in the United States of 1.2 percent per year as the population increased from 1972 to 1974 and then stabilized. The mean number of White-eyes per breeding bird survey route in Illinois for 1965–79 was 0.6. Nests are usually cuplike, suspended in a forked branch close to the ground. They are frequently parasitized by Brown-headed Cowbirds. The vireo's eggs—usually four—are white with a few small dark spots. Illinois egg dates are late April to late June. Summer maxima: 24 males, Vermilion County, June 1983 (SB-SR38:13); 12, Kinkaid Lake, June 5, 1983 (JR-SR38:13); seven, Warren and Henderson Counties, summer 1979 (LMc-SR22:6); 20, Lake Shelbyville (645 acres), summer 1985 (SR-IB&B2:15). Some northern occurrences: three males, Des Plaines, May 31–June 23, 1982 (JM,JO-SR34:10); two, Palos, June 24, 1982 (JL-SR34:10); three, Dan Wright Woods, June 1, 1985 (SH-IB&B2:15); male, Jackson Park, June 27, 1985 (HR-IB&B2:15). White-eyed Vireos molt in August and early September. After a pause in their singing they start again and sing for a brief time in September.

Maximum counts for fall are few: seven, Vermilion County, September 15, 1985 (SB-IB&B2:53); eight, Crab Orchard National Wildlife Refuge, September 11, 1983 (JR-SR39:22). The average departure date for central Illinois is September 22 (15 years). Late dates for October: Mode, October 20, 1985 (KF-IB&B2:53); Alexander County, October 5, 1984 (TF-IB&B1:21); two, Crab Orchard refuge, October 9, 1982 (JR-SR35:14); Forest Glen Preserve, October 5, 1983 (SB-SR39:22).

It comes as a surprise to see December records for this species, especially from northern and central Illinois: two, Chicago North Shore channel, December 13–18, 1982 (RR,JG-AB37:308); one north of Springfield, December 21, 1986 (VK). Most White-eyed Vireos winter from the Gulf Coast south to northern Nicaragua and the Cayman and Swan Islands.

BELL'S VIREO

Vireo bellii

UNCOMMON MIGRANT AND SUMMER
RESIDENT

The distinctive, loud chattering song is the best indication that this rather drab bird is present. The Bell's Vireo is difficult to detect because it stays at low to moderate heights usually in thick vegetation. It is found most often along open willow-lined streams and in shrub areas, roadside brushy situations, and prairie areas with small trees. The Bell's Vireo, a southwestern species, is on the northeastern edge of its range in Illinois. The population seems to fluctuate greatly from year to year, partly because plant succession eliminates or creates its desired habitat. Some areas of Illinois, especially in the north, seem not to have this vireo. In southern Illinois the White-eyed Vireo, which has similar habits, may compete with the Bell's Vireo. The race in Illinois is *V. b. bellii*.

The first spring migrants are usually found in early May. They should theoretically enter the state from the southwest. Early arrival dates: Springfield, April 27, 1976 (HDB); Richland County, April 29, 1986 (LH-AB40:480). Average arrival dates: Sangamon County, May 8 (16 years); west-central, May 7 (10 years). Totals on spring bird counts ranged from 11 in 1974 to 46 in 1982 and 1986. The highest count of 14 on May 6, 1972, seems out of place in McHenry County (VK).

Bell's Vireos may have become more numerous in certain portions of the state, for Nelson (1876) mentioned only one specimen and Coale (1912) did not list the species. But Ridgway and others farther south thought it was rather common in prairie areas. Robbins et al. (1986) noted sharp declines in some areas based on breeding bird survey data for 1965–79. The mean number of birds per survey route in Illinois was 0.3. Some areas in Illinois have fairly good populations: 20, Goose Lake Prairie, 1982 (DBi-AB36:984); 14, Des Plaines Conservation Area, 1982 (JM,JO-AB36:984); 16 pairs, Lake Shelbyville, 1985 (RAp,RCh-

IB&B2:15); 18 males, Homer, 1986 (RCh-IB&B3:15). Bell's Vireos nest low to the ground, usually on the outside edge of vegetation. Like other vireo nests, the Bell's nest is a suspended cup of woven weeds and plant fibers. There are three to four mostly white eggs; some have a few fine spots at the larger end. Illinois egg dates are May 25 to July 6 (Bent 1950).

In late August and early September Bell's Vireos seem to have a resurgence of song. The high count for fall is 11 in Vermilion County, August 28, 1985 (MC-AB40:122). Average departure dates: Sangamon County, September 6 (15 years); west-central, September 1 (three years). Late departure dates: Springfield, September 29, 1984 (HDB); Urbana, September 23, 1981 (BCho-SR31:15); Union County, September 21, 1986 (DR-IB&B3:46). A very late straggler was seen near Barrington on November 14, 1964 (CW-IAB133:4). Bell's Vireos winter from northern Mexico south to Honduras.

SOLITARY VIREO

Vireo solitarius

UNCOMMON MIGRANT AND VERY RARE
SUMMER RESIDENT

This nicely marked vireo has a song like the Red-eyed Vireo's but less harsh and slower, with longer pauses. The Solitary Vireo inhabits woodlands and edges, staying from medium to moderately high in the trees. It is quiet, moves slowly, and occurs in small numbers, making it difficult to detect. Solitary Vireos breed north of Illinois in Canada and the northeastern United States. The race in Illinois is the eastern *V. s. solitarius*.

Early spring migrants: Vermilion County, April 13, 1986 (SB-IB&B2:95); Carbondale, April 14, 1986 (TF-IB&B2:95). Average arrival dates: Chicago, May 8 (13 years); Urbana, April 29 (14 years); Sangamon County, April 27 (18 years). Totals on spring bird counts ranged from 20 in 1973 to 130 in 1975. High counts were 19 in Cook County, May 10, 1975, and 29 in Champaign County, May 5, 1984 (VK). Average departure dates: Chicago, May 23 (13 years); Urbana, May 20 (14 years); Sangamon County, May 21 (16 years). Some Solitaries linger late: Springfield, May 30, 1973 (HDB); Chicago, May 31, 1938 (Clark and Nice 1950).

Summer records for the Solitary Vireo are few. A singing male was seen at Sand Ridge State Forest on July 1, 1977 (DBi-AB31:1149). A nest in the same area in 1979 and 1980 is the only evidence of nesting attempts for the state; both attempts failed because of cowbird parasitism (see Bjorklund 1979–80 and 1980–81). A male was seen at the Marshall County Conservation Area on June 6, 23, and 24, 1982 (MSw-SR34:11).

Fall migration is rather late, but some of these vireos arrive early: Springfield, August 29, 1977 (HDB). Average arrival dates: Chicago, September 14 (14 years); Sangamon County, September 14 (17 years); west-central, September

15 (10 years). High counts for fall: 12, Knox County, September 26, 1982 (MB-SR35:14); 15, Springfield, October 14, 1985 (HDB). Average departure dates: Chicago, October 7 (14 years); Sangamon County, October 27 (18 years). Solitary Vireos sometimes linger late, and early November records are not unusual. Late dates: Dwight, November 27, 1979 (DF-AB34:169); Springfield, November 16, 1982 (HDB); Volo Bog, November 28, 1967 (RR); one eating berries, Dixon, November 24, 1960 (Shaws-IAB117:6). Solitary Vireos winter from the Gulf states south to Costa Rica.

YELLOW-THROATED VIREO

Vireo flavifrons

UNCOMMON MIGRANT AND SUMMER
RESIDENT

One of the brighter colored vireos, the Yellow-throated forages fairly high and is slow moving. Usually its song, which has a slow, burry quality with long pauses, announces its presence. The call note, similar to the Solitary Vireo's, is a *cha-cha-cha* (Graber et al. 1985). The Yellow-throated Vireo is a woodland interior species that prefers large trees. It feeds on Lepidoptera, Hemiptera, and other insects. Though not rare, it occurs in low numbers.

Spring migrants usually arrive in April, but one occurred at Springfield on March 28, 1975 (HDB). Other early spring arrival dates: Pomona, April 10, 1986 (KM-AB40:480); Big River State Forest, April 13, 1985 (MB-AB39:309); Urbana, April 14, 1981 (RB-AB35:831). Average arrival dates: Chicago, May 5 (six years); Urbana, May 4 (19 years); Sangamon County, April 22 (18 years). Spring bird count totals ranged from 41 in 1978 to 309 in 1986. Highest counts were 24, Johnson County, May 5, 1984, and 36, Carroll County, May 10, 1986 (VK). Migration probably continues into late May, but the presence of summer birds obscures most spring departure dates. Dreuth had one at Chicago on May 28, 1929 (Clark and Nice 1950).

Robbins et al. (1986) noted a stable population for this vireo; however, there must have been an earlier drop in numbers with the loss of woodland. The mean number of birds per breeding bird survey route in Illinois was 0.2. Most nests are placed high, so that little information is available on the nesting cycle. The nest is a deep rounded cup that holds three to five white eggs with dark spotting at the larger end of the egg. Illinois egg dates are at least late May to mid-July. Molting occurs in August and also during fall migration, since some Yellow-throated Vireos killed at television towers are still showing traces of molt.

Fall migration probably starts in early September: Chicago, September 1, 1930 (Clark and Nice 1950); west-central, September 3 (Craig and Franks 1987). High counts in fall are few: eight, Union County, September 21, 1986 (DR-IB&B3:46); five television tower kills, Sangamon County, September 17, 1980 (ISM). Average departure dates: Sangamon County, September 29 (18 years); Chicago,

September 13 (10 years). Late departure dates: Peoria, October 17, 1981 (MSw-SR31:15); two, Springfield, October 14, 1985 (ISM); Charleston, November 16, 1974 (LBH-AB29:67); Jackson Park, October 8, 1979 (RG). The Yellow-throated Vireo winters from central Mexico to Colombia and Venezuela.

WARBLING VIREO

Vireo gilvus

COMMON MIGRANT AND SUMMER RESIDENT

This mostly gray vireo has no wing bars, but it has a nice warbled song that it sings frequently. The call note is a wheezy, scolding *twee*, which is much like the call note of the Philadelphia Vireo. The Warbling Vireo tends to stay fairly high in tall trees. It inhabits open woods and is usually found along streams and beside ponds and lakes. Graber et al. (1985) noted that these vireos were associated with silver maples as well as cottonwoods and willows. They eat mostly Lepidoptera and Coleoptera in spring, but they feed on fruit, including elderberries and pokeberries, when it is available. The race in Illinois is the eastern, *V. g. gilvus*.

The earliest spring migrants arrive in mid-April: Jersey County, April 15, 1972 (HDB); seven, Union County, April 16, 1986 (DR-IB&B2:95). Average arrival dates: Chicago, May 9 (14 years); west-central, April 25 (15 years); Sangamon County, April 23 (18 years). Spring bird count totals ranged from 209 in 1980 to 1473 in 1986. Most high counts came from counties bordering the Mississippi River; the highest was 78 in Carroll County, May 8, 1982 (VK).

In southern Illinois Ridgway (1915) noted a drop in the Warbling Vireo's population. No one has recorded any further decline, and Robbins et al. (1986), using breeding bird survey data, found increases in the east and central United States. The mean number of birds per survey route in Illinois was 1.9. Warbling Vireos usually nest high in trees, making a hanging cup nest bound to twigs at the rim and laying three to five white eggs that show little or no spotting. Available egg dates for Illinois are at least May 23 to June 16. Cowbirds frequently parasitize this vireo's nest.

A specimen in the Illinois State Museum collection from Sangamon County, August 30, 1980, shows some molt. Migration begins at least by September 2, since a Warbling Vireo was killed at a television tower on that date in Sangamon County. Compared with some other vireos, however, the number of Warbling Vireos killed at television towers is not great, suggesting that not all of their migration is nocturnal and that they may funnel down the major rivers on their southward journey. High counts are low in fall: 10, Springfield, September 2, 1983 (HDB); seven, Carroll County, August 21, 1986 (SB-IB&B3:46). Average departure dates: Chicago, September 5 (14 years); west-central, September 13 (eight years); Sangamon County, September 30 (18 years). Late departure dates: television

tower kill, Sangamon County, October 14, 1985 (ISM); Decatur, October 13, 1985 (RP-IB&B2:54); Springfield, October 15, 1977 (HDB). Warbling Vireos winter from northern Mexico south to El Salvador.

PHILADELPHIA VIREO

Vireo philadelphicus

FAIRLY COMMON MIGRANT

A bird of soft yellow and olive pastels, this vireo looks most like the Warbling Vireo. However, the Philadelphia has dark lores and more yellow ventrally, especially on the undertail coverts. Bird banders will notice that the outer primary is longer than that of the Warbling Vireo. The Philadelphia sings like a Red-eyed Vireo except that its song is somewhat higher and slower. Its call note is much like the Warbling Vireo's. It inhabits woodland, foraging from medium to high in the canopy. It has been seen eating fruit of the dogwood (Graber et al. 1985), and stomach contents have included Coleoptera and Lepidoptera.

Early spring arrival dates are in late April: Springfield, April 24, 1987 (HDB); Monroe County, April 26, 1984 (PS-SR41:24). Average arrival dates: Chicago, May 19 (15 years); Urbana, May 12 (19 years); west-central, May 5 (10 years). High counts for spring: 12, Chicago, May 15, 1985 (CM); 12, Lake Shelbyville, May 30, 1985 (SR-IB&B1:89). Spring bird count totals ranged from one in 1974 to 72 in 1983; the highest count was 18 in Du Page County, May 8, 1982 (VK). Average spring departure dates: Chicago, May 27 (15 years); Urbana, May 21 (19 years); Sangamon County, May 28 (16 years). Some of these vireos are seen into June: Springfield, June 4, 1976 (HDB); Chicago, June 7, 1983 (JL). A reference by Nelson (1876) to two pairs breeding at Mazon Creek, 60 miles south of Chicago, on July 1, 1874, must refer to Warbling Vireos. The breeding area closest to Illinois is in northeastern Minnesota.

Fall migration starts in August: Chicago, August 18, 1941 (Clark and Nice 1950); Rend Lake, August 16, 1986 (RP-IB&B3:46); Carroll County, August 21, 1986 (SB-IB&B3:46). Average arrival dates: Chicago, September 9 (15 years); Sangamon County, August 30 (17 years). High counts for fall: 14 killed at a television tower, Macon County, September 27, 1972 (Seets and Bohlen 1977); 12 killed at a television tower, Sangamon County, October 14, 1985 (ISM). Average fall departure dates: Chicago, September 24 (15 years); Sangamon County, October 7 (18 years). Late departure dates: Springfield, October 31, 1985 (HDB); Illinois Beach State Park, October 22, 1965 (JP). This vireo tends to be less common in southern Illinois in fall, but whether this is owing to detectability or migration route is unknown. One was seen in Gallatin County, September 6, 1986 (DR-IB&B3:46). The Philadelphia Vireo winters from Guatemala south to central Panama.

RED-EYED VIREO

Vireo olivaceus

ABUNDANT MIGRANT AND COMMON
SUMMER RESIDENT

If Red-eyed Vireos were not such incessant singers they would be difficult to detect. Their fairly dull coloration and the high position they occupy in the canopy help to keep them out of sight. Their song, which is sung over and over, is somewhat like the American Robin's, but more monotonic. A harsh nasal call note is given, especially around the nest. The Red-eyed Vireo is a woodland species that occurs in migration wherever there are trees. Its food is insects, including Lepidoptera, Diptera, and Coleoptera, and such fruits as woodbine, black cherry, wild grape, pokeberry, and multiflora rose (Graber et al. 1985).

Early spring arrival dates are in mid-April: Pomona, April 13, 1985 (JR-AB39:309); Springfield, April 19, 1981 (HDB). Average arrival dates: Urbana, May 6 (20 years); Sangamon County, April 24 (17 years); Chicago, May 14 (16 years). High counts for spring: 18, Joliet, May 23, 1985 (JM-IB&B1:89); 23, Starved Rock State Park, May 30, 1985 (RGu-SR37:20); 20, Springfield, May 14, 1981 (HDB); 36, Giant City State Park, May 11, 1985 (DR-IB&B1:89). Totals on spring bird counts ranged from 159 in 1978 to 1266 in 1986; the highest counts were 20 in Jackson County, May 8, 1976, and 77 in Vermilion County, May 10, 1986 (VK). These vireos are still migrating in June: 15, Chicago, June 5, 1983 (JL).

Red-eyed Vireos breed in both upland and bottomland forests, city parks, cemeteries, even residential areas, though in small numbers. They must have been more numerous when there were more forested areas in Illinois, but Robbins et al. (1986) found that the population was still doing well, with increases continentwide on breeding bird surveys for 1965–79. The mean number of Red-eyes per survey route in Illinois was 0.7. The nest is cuplike and suspended with twigs at its rim. It is placed from two to 45 feet high (Graber et al. 1985). The female lays three to five finely speckled white eggs. Illinois egg dates are early May to at least June 15. Cowbirds take a heavy toll on this species by frequently parasitizing the nests. Immature Red-eyed Vireos have brown eyes and adults red, although the certainty of this information has been questioned (Parkes 1988).

Fall migration starts in August. The average arrival date for Sangamon County is August 22 (10 years). Nocturnal migrants, Red-eyed Vireos suffer heavy mortality at television towers; 153 were killed at Springfield on September 2, 1972. Few other high counts for fall are available. Peak numbers occur in late August and September, with dwindling numbers in early October. Average fall departure dates: Chicago, October 4 (16 years); west-central, October 3 (11 years); Sangamon County, October 14 (18 years). Late departure dates: Chicago, October 19, 1974 (GR,RR-AB29:67); Springfield, November 30, 1973 (HDB). These vireos occur more on forest edges in fall and forage somewhat lower than they do in spring. They are more numerous in eastern than in western Illinois in fall. They winter in South America east of the Andes in the Amazon Basin.

BACHMAN'S WARBLER

Vermivora bachmanii

HYPOTHETICAL

The Bachman's Warbler is certainly America's rarest songbird, and it may be extinct. An individual of this species was last observed on April 30, 1966, at Birmingham, Alabama, and no nest has been found since 1938. The species occurred in bottomland swamps of the southeastern United States, possibly including southern Illinois.

No specimen or photograph of the Bachman's Warbler exists for Illinois, though there are a few sight records. Southern Illinois is very close to the area in southeastern Missouri where this warbler's nest was first discovered (Widmann 1907). The first indications of its presence in Illinois came from Gault (1922):

Listed here as new to Illinois on the authority of Robert Ridgway, who states positively of having found it in the vicinity of Mount Carmel, Wabash County, during the spring or breeding season of 1878, while investigating the bird-life of that locality in company with William Brewster. Considering the supposed extreme rarity of this warbler, and the fact that no specimen was taken, it was not thought advisable at that time to publish the record, fearing it might be seriously questioned; and the above statement until now never has appeared in print. Future investigations doubtless will clearly establish the fact of its being a regular summer resident within our borders, though perhaps limited as to numbers, and of very local distribution, in the extreme southern portions of the state.

According to Smith (1941) a specimen was collected at Decatur in 1899, but it cannot now be located. If this specimen really existed, the bird was collected outside its normal range and habitat. Fawks (1936) felt that he had two sight records of the Bachman's Warbler from Rock Island County, one on May 14, 1935, and the other on May 21, 1926. His description does not, however, exclude the Hooded Warbler, which he did not have on his list of warblers. Overmigrants of either species were possible.

One of the more plausible records came when Bush found a singing male in a swampy woodland at Crab Orchard National Wildlife Refuge on April 25, 1951, and gave a short description of it (AFN4:245). Graber et al. (1983) discuss a bird they saw and heard that they believed to be a Bachman's Warbler in swampy forest near Cache on July 20, 1958.

The Bachman's Warbler wintered on Cuba and the Isle of Pines.

BLUE-WINGED WARBLER

Vermivora pinus

UNCOMMON MIGRANT AND SUMMER
RESIDENT

Yellow with bluish wings, this warbler sings several songs, the most common of which is the very distinct ascending buzz, descending buzz. Blue-wings forage from middle to lower levels in vegetation. They prefer rather open situations such as forest edges and brushy hillsides but are also seen in upland and bottomland forests during migration. This species interbreeds with the closely related Golden-winged Warbler, producing a wide variety of offspring. Two generalized forms have been named: the "Brewster's" Warbler, which is rare, and the "Lawrence's" Warbler, which is very rare in Illinois. Some recent records of the "Brewster's" hybrid: Mississippi Palisades State Park, May 9, 1982 (BSh); Urbana, June 8, 1982 (BCho-SR33:13); Boone County, May 17, 1983 (E.Burstatte-SR37:21); Vermilion County, May 1, 1986 (SB,MC-IB&B2:95). Some recent "Lawrence's" hybrid records: Tazewell County, May 23, 1986 (RBj-IB&B2:95); Lake County, May 17, 1983 (JG-SR37:21); Chain O'Lakes State Park, June 5, 1982 (JN-SR34:11). A "Lawrence's" territorial male was at Palos in summer 1987 and 1988. Most "Lawrence's" records come from northern Illinois. In my intensive study of the birds of Sangamon County (1970–88), I have noted the "Brewster's" seven times from May 2 through 11 and September 3 through 17, with one male specimen taken north of Springfield on May 5, 1977 (ISM). I have never found a "Lawrence's" in Illinois.

Early spring migration dates for the Blue-winged Warbler: three, Pomona, April 16, 1986 (DR-IB&B2:95); Richland County, April 16, 1986 (LH-IB&B2:95); three, Urbana, April 21, 1985 (RCh-IB&B1:89). Average arrival dates: Urbana, May 4 (nine years); west-central, May 4 (10 years); Sangamon County, April 29 (16 years). High counts for this uncommon migrant are usually only one to four per day. Exceptions: 10, Lake Shelbyville, May 14, 1985 (SR-IB&B1:89); eight, Cook County, May 9, 1982 (AA-SR33:13). Spring bird count totals ranged from 32 in 1972 to 154 in 1986. The highest count was 28 in Cook County, May 10, 1986 (VK). Average departure dates: Urbana, May 21 (nine years); west-central, May 11 (10 years); Sangamon County, May 11 (16 years). A few are seen into late May: Knox County, May 31, 1987 (MB).

Some Blue-wings stay in Illinois to breed, especially in the northeast and south. This species may have expanded its range northward near the turn of the century at the expense of the Golden-winged Warbler. Dreuth had only two spring records for Chicago, in 1938 and 1943, while Carpenter had at least two specimens, from Polo on May 14, 1906, and Aurora on May 19, 1910 (ISM). Recent numbers for summer: six pairs, Chain O'Lakes State Park, 1982; nine pairs, Mississippi Palisades State Park, 1985; five pairs, Lake County, 1982; three, Pike County, 1980; eight males, Pope County, 1986. The nests are usually on or near the ground and contain four to six white eggs finely speckled with brown, mostly at the larger end. Illinois egg dates are May 2 to June 14.

Some Blue-wings must start wandering during or before molt, as one in partial molt was at Springfield on July 15, 1980. Average arrival dates for fall migrants: west-central, August 30 (three years); Sangamon County, August 23 (12 years). Maximum counts for fall are nonexistent. Very few of these warblers are killed at television towers, but there are two for Sangamon County: September 2, 1981, and October 4, 1983, a late record (ISM). The average departure date for Sangamon County is September 13 (12 years). Other late departures: Mississippi Palisades State Park, September 27, 1986 (PP-IB&B3:46); Crab Orchard National Wildlife Refuge, September 17, 1982 (JR-SR35:14); Windsor, November 11, 1986 (YM). Blue-winged Warblers winter from central Mexico south to central Panama.

GOLDEN-WINGED WARBLER

Vermivora chrysoptera

FAIRLY COMMON MIGRANT; RARE SUMMER
RESIDENT IN NORTHERN ILLINOIS

Although gold wing bars are present in all plumages, the male Golden-winged Warbler has black face and throat markings while the female has gray. The Golden-wing's primary song is a buzzy note followed by *zee-zee-zee*. These brightly colored warblers feed at midheight in both upland and bottomland forests. They breed mainly north of Illinois as far as southern Manitoba. Where the breeding ranges meet, Golden-winged and Blue-winged Warblers hybridize (see the Blue-winged Warbler account).

Early spring migrants arrive in April: Jackson Park, April 20, 1986 (RL-IB&B2:95); three, Decatur, April 18, 1976 (RS). Average arrival dates: Urbana, May 6 (16 years); Chicago, May 11 (9 years); Sangamon County, May 2 (18 years). High counts are low: eight, Henderson County, May 8, 1987 (MB); 10, Chicago, May 6, 1986 (EW-IB&B2:95). Spring bird count totals ranged from 16 in 1978 to 170 in 1975, with the highest count 30 in Cook County, May 10, 1986 (VK). Average departure dates for spring: Urbana, May 19 (16 years); west-central, May 18 (14 years); Sangamon County, May 17 (17 years). Some migrants staggle into June.

Ridgway (1889) stated that Golden-wings were breeding in Richland County, and Poling (Butler 1897) found them nesting in the Mississippi bottoms. Both of these places are farther south than the present breeding range, although there are sight records of a Golden-winged Warbler from Siloam Springs State Park, June 19, 1982 (AD-SR34:11), and a female from Vernon, June 19, 1979 (Graber et al. 1983). Most other summer and nesting records come from northern Illinois. Recent records: pair carrying food, Palos Park, July 9, 1986 (SH-IB&B3:15); nested, Illinois Beach State Park, 1981 (SH,JN-SR30:14); one to five pairs, Lake

County, 1982 (SH-SR34:11); male, Will County, June 6–29, 1982 (ADu-SR34:11). Little is known about the nest or the eggs in Illinois. Golden-wings generally nest in deciduous woodlands with thick undergrowth. The nest is placed on or near the ground, and the female lays four to five eggs, which are whitish with darker spots.

Early fall arrival dates: Champaign, August 10, 1985 (RCh-IB&B2:54); adult female, Springfield, July 22, 1988 (HDB). Average arrival dates: Chicago, August 27 (13 years); Sangamon County, August 24 (18 years). High counts for fall: 10, Lake County, September 11, 1984 (SH-IB&B1:21); nine, Springfield, September 5, 1985 (HDB). Average departure dates: Chicago, September 11 (13 years); Sangamon County, September 22 (18 years). Late departures: Chicago, October 26, 1956 (Mlodinow 1984); Springfield, October 3, 1971 (HDB). Golden-winged Warblers winter from Yucatan south to Colombia and Venezuela.

TENNESSEE WARBLER

Vermivora peregrina

ABUNDANT MIGRANT

In May Tennessee Warblers are probably more numerous than any other woodland species in Illinois. Their often-repeated song, a loud staccato of notes almost like a sewing machine, is heard everywhere in forests, parks, even residential areas. In fall, though still found in woodlands, they also frequent weed patches and more open areas. The Tennessee Warbler's color is among the dullest of the warblers, mostly gray and olive in males but more yellowish in females and immatures. In spring 1981 I saw several of these warblers carrying small sticks, which they were using to probe into flowers, presumably for insects. The Tennessee Warbler nests mostly in Canada in coniferous and deciduous woodland.

Early spring records are in mid-April: Chicago, April 17, 1982 (MDa-AB36:860); Henderson County, April 17, 1982 (LMc-AB36:860); Carbondale, April 17, 1986 (DR-AB40:480). Average spring arrival dates: Chicago, May 12 (15 years); west-central, April 27 (15 years). High counts for spring: 200, Springfield, May 16, 1981 (HDB); 104, Shelby County, May 9, 1987 (KF); 200, Piatt County, May 11, 1986 (RCh-AB40:480). Spring bird count totals ranged from 154 in 1978 to 4170 in 1986, with the highest count 418 in Cook County, May 10, 1986 (VK). Average departure dates: Urbana, May 21 (13 years); Sangamon County, May 28 (16 years). Some Tennessees straggle late in spring: Woodstock, June 1, 1984 (DF-SR41:24); Chicago, June 23, 1981, and Jackson Park, June 18, 1981 (PC,HR-SR29:12); Monmouth, June 26, 1982 (LMc-AB36:984); Lockport, June 8, 1987 (JM).

Some early fall migrants are seen in July, indicating that they probably migrate before their molt, which is in July. Recent records: Springfield, July 10, 1986 (HDB); two (including a singing male), Jackson Park, July 16–30, 1982

(PC,HR-SR34:11); Winnebago County, July 20, 1981 (LJ-AB36:185); Charleston, July 21, 1986 (LBH-AB40:1211). Average fall arrival dates: Chicago, August 21 (16 years); Sangamon County, August 18 (18 years). Fall maximum counts: 206 banded, Cook County, August 30–September 11, 1982 (KB-AB37:188); 80, Warsaw, August 27, 1986 (RCe-AB41:97); 50, Urbana, October 4, 1986 (BCho-IB&B3:46); 75, Springfield, September 3, 1981 (HDB). Large numbers of Tennessee Warblers are killed at televisions towers, including 107 in Sangamon County, September 17, 1958 (Parmalee and Parmalee 1959). Average fall departure dates: Chicago, October 11 (16 years); west-central, October 8 (10 years). Some of these warblers stay quite late: Savanna, November 1, 1980 (BSh-SR27;11); Charleston, December 13, 1979 (LBH-AB34:278); La Salle County, November 6, 1983 (JH-SR39:22); Urbana, November 26, 1984 (BCho-IB&B1:21). There is a winter record for Charleston, January 27–March 6, 1975 (LBH-AB29:699). Tennessee Warblers winter from central Mexico south to Colombia and Venezuela.

ORANGE-CROWNED WARBLER

Vermivora celata

UNCOMMON MIGRANT AND VERY RARE WINTER RESIDENT

Although the Orange-crowned is dull of plumage for a warbler, its greens, grays, and dull yellows make it a fairly handsome bird when viewed close up. The orange in the crown is almost always hidden but can occasionally be seen. The Orange-crowned Warbler inhabits deciduous vegetation, usually at lower to midheight on the edges of woodlands. Like most *Vermivora*, it probes into flower heads on trees. Its infrequent, rollicking, chippinglike song usually goes unnoticed and is difficult to learn and separate from the songs of other species. It breeds in Canada, Alaska, and the mountains of the western United States. This interesting species has four races in North America. The nominate form occurs in Illinois.

Orange-crowned migrants arrive early in spring—about mid-April—and have usually passed through the state by mid-May. The earliest date for Springfield is April 1, 1983; this bird may have wintered close by. Another early date is April 13, 1982, for Jackson Park (T.McLarnan-AB36:860). Maximum counts for spring: 69, Du Page County (spring bird count), May 10, 1980 (VK); six, Lake Shelbyville, May 19, 1985 (SR-IB&B1:89); nine, Chicago, May 4, 1986 (JL). Some records are later than mid-May, and these might be expected in extreme northern Illinois. But two June dates, if correct, are certainly past the usual spring departure date. One was on June 2 (Ford et al. 1934), but I have not been able to find any further data on it. The other was a singing male in blackjack oak woodland at Big River State Forest, June 5, 1982 (LMc-AB36:860).

In fall the Orange-crowned Warbler usually arrives in late September. Earlier birds should be identified with great care, since several other species—including dull Nashville Warblers, immature Yellow Warblers, yellowish Tennessee Warblers, and even immature female Cape May Warblers—could easily be mistaken for Orange-crowns, since they are greenish, show streaking, and have obscured wing bars. Immature Orange-crowns may show buffy wing bars. Early arrival dates like these should be documented: July 28, probably 1901, Glen Ellyn (Gault 1901); August 28, 1895, Chicago, specimen taken by Gault (Woodruff 1907); August 23, 1926, Chicago (Brodkorb 1926); August 29, 1938, Chicago, recorded by Dreuth (Clark and Nice 1950); August 20 (year unknown) and August 26, 1941, Chicago (Blake and Smith 1941); two, August 31, 1978, Wilmette (Mlodinow 1984); August 28, 1982, Chicago (HR-AB37:188); one banded, August 25, 1984, Chicago (SP-AB39:62). Average arrival dates for fall: Chicago, September 24 (16 years); central Illinois, September 27 (18 years). The Orange-crowned chooses even less woody habitats in fall than in spring. It can also be found in weedy and brushy areas. It comes easily to "spishing" and usually gives a rather sharp chip note, which can be recognized with some practice. Occasionally Orange-crowned Warblers will be seen with flocks of White-throated Sparrows in late fall. Immature Orange-crowns can be distinguished at close range by their grayish heads and whitish eye rings as opposed to the adults' olive heads with yellow above the eyes (see Bohlen and Kleen 1976). Maximum counts for fall: 20, Springfield, October 21, 1981 (HDB); 19, east of Springfield (television tower kill), October 14, 1983 (ISM). Average departure dates: Chicago, October 16 (16 years); central Illinois, November 10 (18 years).

Orange-crowns typically stay until early November, and a few attempt to winter in very sheltered areas. A sizable number of winter records include Chicago, December 29, 1975 (SM-AB30:428), and January 7, 1980 (AB34:278); Joliet, December 23, 1981 (JM-AB36:301); one to three, Chicago, December 6–19, 1982 (RR,JG-AB37:308); Forest Glen, January 16, 1983 (M.Resch-AB37:308); Crab Orchard National Wildlife Refuge, January 18, 1983 (JR-AB37:308); Lawrence County, February 6, 1983 (LH-AB37:308); two, Chicago, December 16–17, 1983 (Mlodinow 1984); Chicago, December 15, 1984 (RB-AB39:174); Horseshoe Lake, Alexander County, December 18, 1984 (AB39:637); Pere Marquette, December 15, 1984 (JEa-AB39:640).

NASHVILLE WARBLER
Vermivora ruficapilla

COMMON MIGRANT AND VERY RARE
SUMMER RESIDENT

A fairly small warbler, the Nashville is olive and yellow with a gray head and white eye ring. Females are paler ver-

sions of the males. Although the males may show a chestnut patch on the crown, it is usually concealed. These rather nondescript warblers feed both high in the trees and, especially in fall, low in weed patches and second growth. Their song usually is in two parts but has several variations, some easily confused with the songs of other warblers. The Nashville Warbler may flip its tail, but not as constantly as the Palm Warbler. The subspecies in Illinois is the eastern *V. r. ruficapilla.*

Early spring arrivals: Oakwood Bottoms, April 16, 1986 (DR-IB&B2:95); Springfield, April 16, 1977 (HDB). Average arrival dates: Urbana, May 1 (20 years); Chicago, May 5 (16 years); Sangamon County, April 23 (18 years). Nashvilles are among the more numerous of the warblers in spring. Maximum counts: 50, Springfield, May 20, 1981 (HDB); 26, Lake Shelbyville, May 14, 1985 (SR-IB&B1:89); 28, Lisle Arboretum, May 9, 1987 (EW). Spring bird count totals ranged from 138 in 1978 to 1597 in 1975; the highest was 324 in Cook County, May 10, 1986 (VK). Average spring departure dates: Urbana, May 27 (20 years); Chicago, May 22 (16 years); Sangamon County, May 22 (16 years). Some Nashville Warblers linger even into June: Braidwood, June 3, 1985 (JM-IB&B1:89); Springfield, June 10, 1980 (HDB); Chicago, June 7, 1982 (SP-SR33:14).

Nelson (1876) listed the Nashville Warbler as a rare summer resident, but there are few specific nest records. Smith (1888) reported finding 20 nests in Fulton County that averaged five eggs per clutch. If that is correct, it means that a population of Nashvilles existed in the 1870s that is gone now. Tuttle (1918) found a nest in Lake Forest that had five eggs in mid-June. Pitelka (1940) saw a female carrying food in Lake County, June 17, 1938. The only recent summer records are of a singing male in Lake County in 1962 (RR-AFN16:480) and another at Bath, June 25, 1983 (R.Vogel-AB37:995).

Fall migrants may arrive in mid-August: Springfield, August 17, 1986 (HDB); two, Jackson Park, August 18, 1982 (HR). Average fall arrival dates: Chicago, August 31 (16 years); Sangamon County, August 28 (18 years). High counts for fall: 66, Springfield, October 14, 1985 (HDB); 28, Monmouth, October 1, 1983 (MB-SR39:22). A big push usually comes with cold fronts in October as these warblers move south to escape the colder weather. Average departure dates: Chicago, October 8 (16 years); Sangamon County, October 28 (18 years). Some linger well into November: Blue Island, November 24, 1985 (KB-AB40:122); Monmouth, November 10, 1982 (LMc-SR35:14); Chicago, November 25, 1983 (DW-SR39:22).

A few records exist for winter, probably representing very late migrants: Champaign, December 15, 1976 (DFr-AB31:338); Monmouth, December 9, 1979 (LMc-AB34:279); Charleston, January 6, 1975 (LBH-AB29:699). Three records come from the Chicago North Shore channel: December 12–January 2, 1983; December 29–January 2, 1976; and two, December 16–17, 1983 (Mlodinow 1984). Nashville Warblers normally winter from southern Texas south to central Honduras.

VIRGINIA'S WARBLER

Vermivora virginiae

HYPOTHETICAL

This western species is closely related to the Nashville Warbler. In the one report from Illinois, a Virginia's Warbler was seen by nine observers at Evanston, May 6, 1979 (Mlodinow 1984). Unfortunately, the documentary evidence was inadequate and conflicting. Virginia's Warblers have been found in Ontario and New Jersey. In their normal range they inhabit woodland and scrub.

NORTHERN PARULA

Parula americana

COMMON MIGRANT; COMMON SUMMER
RESIDENT DECREASING NORTHWARD

The Northern Parula is difficult to see, since it is small, even for a warbler, and usually stays high up in tall trees, especially sycamores. This inhabitant of bottomland forests can be located by its songs: one a long, buzzy, ascending trill, the other a less distinctive series of buzzes. Occasionally these parulas come down lower in the trees, and "spishing" will usually attract them. They occur not only along rivers but also, during migration, in upland woods, parks, and cemeteries. They are bluish with a green patch on the back and a yellow throat. Males have a dark bar across the lower throat. A breeding population north of Illinois probably accounts for most of the migrants in the northern part of the state.

Some spring migrants arrive very early: Cook County, March 29, 1986 (VB-AB40:480); southern Illinois, March 31 (George 1968); Charleston, April 3, 1981 (LBH-SR29:13). Average dates of arrival: Urbana, May 9 (15 years); Chicago, May 12 (14 years); Sangamon County, April 17 (19 years). High counts: 32, Crab Orchard National Wildlife Refuge, April 18, 1985 (JR-IB&B1:89); 13, Giant City State Park, May 11, 1985 (DR-IB&B1:89); 61, Cache River, Johnson County, April 24, 1973 (VK,HDB). Totals on spring bird counts ranged from 95 in 1973 to 283 in 1984. The highest count was 47 in Alexander County, May 4, 1985 (VK). Most migrants probably have passed through the state by late May. Dreuth listed May 22 (14 years) as a departure average. A singing male at Jackson Park, May 28, 1981 (RG,PC), was a late migrant.

Northern Parulas nest most commonly in southern Illinois, less so in central Illinois, and apparently very little in northern Illinois. Summering parulas were located recently in Henderson and Vermilion Counties. Robbins et al. (1986) noted an upsurge in the population in the eastern United States. The mean number of parulas on breeding bird survey routes in Illinois was only 0.1. In the Lake Shelbyville area 26 pairs were found in 1986 (SR-IB&B3:15). Of the very few nests found in Illinois, apparently not all have been in tall trees. Much more study is needed of this species in the state. Fall migrants have been detected as early as July. Average arrival dates: Chicago, September 13 (12 years); Sangamon County, August 16 (12 years). High counts for fall are very low: six, Mount Zion, August 31, 1985 (RP-IB&B2:54); eight killed at a television tower, Piatt County, September 27, 1972 (Seets). Average departure dates: Chicago, September 30 (12 years); Sangamon County, October 8 (18 years). Stragglers were detected fairly late at Springfield, November 7, 1985 (HDB). The one winter record for Illinois is of a male that survived on peanut butter at a feeder in Belleville from mid-December 1982 to early February 1983 (BR,RG). The Northern Parula winters from northern Mexico to Belize.

YELLOW WARBLER

Dendroica petechia

COMMON MIGRANT AND SUMMER RESIDENT

True to its name, this is the yellowest of the warblers, including yellow tail spots, wing bars, and eye ring. Males have rusty red streaks on the breast and occasionally a rusty patch on the crown that is usually concealed. The song is a short and rapid series of *seet*s. The Yellow Warbler has an extensive breeding range in North, Central, and even part of South America. In Illinois it is found mostly in riparian habitat, especially where willows are present, but also in woodlands, parks, and other woody habitats. At least two of the seven races have been recorded in Illinois: the breeding form, *D. p. aestiva*, and the northern form, *D. p. amnicola*, a migrant. This warbler eats Lepidoptera, Coleoptera, and spiders.

Occasionally Yellow Warblers arrive early: Mermet Lake, April 11, 1986 (DR-IB&B2:95). Average arrival dates are Urbana, May 2 (20 years); Chicago, May 3 (16 years); and Sangamon County, April 28 (19 years). High counts for spring: 19, Lake Calumet, May 10, 1987 (CM); 14, Knox County, May 10, 1986 (MB-IB&B2:95); 68, Mercer County, May 4, 1985 (PP-IB&B1:89). Totals on spring bird counts ranged from 330 in 1973 to 1723 in 1983; the high was 248 in Cook County, May 7, 1983. Most high counts are in northern Illinois, but 65 Yellow Warblers were recorded in Pope County on May 6, 1978 (VK). Migrants have been detected as late as June 13, 1984, on the Chicago lakefront (JL).

Yellow Warblers nest throughout Illinois. Their population apparently declined significantly very early, from around 1900 (see Graber et al. 1983). But Robbins et al. (1986), using 1965-79 breeding bird survey data, noted increases in Illinois, though the mean number of Yellow Warblers per survey route was only 0.4. As many as 33 pairs were at Lake Shelbyville in 1986 (SR-IB&B3:15); 178 were counted in Cook County on June 8, 1985 (IB&B2:16); and 50 pairs nested at Illinois Beach State Park in 1981 (SH,JN-SR30:14). Three to five eggs (usually four) are laid in a well-made cuplike nest. Most nests are placed fairly low in shrubby trees, such as willows, usually along watercourses but occasionally in residential areas. The eggs are whitish to greenish with brown markings. Illinois egg dates are May 20 to June 20. Cowbirds are heavily parasitic on Yellow Warblers' nests; when that happens, the warblers counter by covering over the old nest and eggs with a new nest. Thus several layers of nests are sometimes found. Young are prevalent in June and July.

These warblers begin their fall migration very early, but fewer are seen in fall than in spring. Early fall dates: two, Chicago, July 21, 1987 (JL); Chicago, July 31, 1983 (JL); Springfield, August 2, 1985 (HDB). The average arrival date in Sangamon County is August 11 (seven years). High counts for this season are scarce: 12, Chicago, September 16, 1983 (JL); 10, Chicago, September 7, 1987 (CM). Average departure dates: Chicago, September 12 (16 years); Sangamon County, September 15 (17 years). Late dates of departure: Springfield, November 7, 1979 (HDB); Decatur, October 13, 1985 (RP-IB&B2:54). The latest record is from Chicago, December 16–17, 1983 (RB,DJ-SR40:12).

CHESTNUT-SIDED WARBLER

Dendroica pensylvanica

COMMON MIGRANT; RARE SUMMER RESIDENT IN NORTHERN ILLINOIS

Because the Chestnut-sided Warbler breeds in brushy second-growth habitat, its numbers increased with the opening of the eastern deciduous forest. In Illinois it is found in woodlands of all types during migration. This bird's appearance changes considerably between spring and fall; only the adults retain some chestnut in the fall. The immatures are greenish with yellow wing bars. This warbler cocks its tail up, a habit that helps identify it even in silhouette. Its typical song is similar to the Yellow Warbler's, with a *whitch you* at the end. Its other songs are more rambling and difficult to identify. I have occasionally heard this warbler singing a subdued song in fall migration. Chestnut-sided Warblers forage from midheight to fairly high in the vegetation.

Early spring migrants arrive in late April: Crab Orchard National Wildlife Refuge, April 26, 1985 (JR-IB&B1:89); Olney, April 27, 1985 (LH-IB&B1:89). Average arrival dates: Urbana, May 4 (20 years); Chicago, May 8 (15 years); west-central, May 2 (13 years). High counts for spring: 21, Chicago, May 21, 1987 (CM); 20, Mercer County, May 4, 1985 (PP-IB&B1:89); 17, Lake Shelbyville, May 21, 1985 (SR-IB&B1:89); 35, Springfield, May 14, 1981 (HDB). Spring bird count totals ranged from 10 in 1978 to 766 in 1986; the highest count was 167 in Cook County, May 10, 1986 (VK). Average departure dates: Urbana, May 23 (20 years); Chicago, May 28 (15 years); Sangamon County, May 28 (18 years). Migration typically extends into June: Green

River Conservation Area, June 1, 1983 (JH-SR37:21); Lisle Arboretum, June 7, 1987 (EW); Jackson Park, June 28, 1986 (MSi-IB&B2:95); Giant City State Park, June 2, 1984 (BCho-SR41:24).

Some of the June records could be of breeding birds. Both Nelson and Kennicott listed this warbler as breeding in northern Illinois. It once nested as far south as St. Louis (Gault 1892). More recently, breeding or possible breeding records have occurred at Libertyville, 1977; Rockford, 1977; Vermilion County, 1984; Park Forest, 1983; Waukegan, 1981; Chain O'Lakes State Park, 1982; and Iroquois County Conservation Area, 1982. In their favored second-growth and forest edge habitat these warblers nest fairly low in the vegetation (one to four feet). Nests with eggs have been found in Illinois from May 24 to June 18 (Graber et al. 1983). The three to five eggs are whitish to pale greenish, marked with a wreath of brown and a few spots at the larger end.

The few July records are probably of wandering birds, perhaps from Illinois nestings: Chicago, July 26, 1987 (JL); Henderson County, July 20, 1985 (MB-IB&B2:54). Earliest arrival dates for fall are mid-August: Springfield, August 12, 1977 (HDB); Charleston, August 11, 1986 (LBH-AB41:98); Deerfield, August 18, 1987 (JL). Average arrival dates: Chicago, August 21 (16 years); Sangamon County, August 22 (18 years). High counts: 21, Henderson and Mercer Counties, September 22, 1984 (MB-IB&B1:21); 21, Springfield, September 21, 1985 (HDB). Average departure dates: Chicago, October 1 (16 years); Sangamon County, October 9 (18 years). Late departure dates: Springfield, October 25, 1977 (HDB); Crab Orchard refuge, October 15, 1983 (JR-SR39:22). Chestnut-sided Warblers winter from southern Mexico south to northern South America.

MAGNOLIA WARBLER

Dendroica magnolia

COMMON MIGRANT

All plumages of this warbler can be identified by a broad white band on the tail. Adult males in spring are gray crowned; have black on the wings, tail, and back; are yellow ventrally with black stripes; and have white wing bars and a yellow rump. Females and immatures look basically the same but duller. Magnolia Warblers forage from low to midheight in wooded areas and woodland edges. Their song is rather short, with full rich notes; it resembles the songs of such other warblers as the Chestnut-sided, Yellow, and Hooded. The call note, a distinctive squeak, can be identified with practice. These warblers breed in open coniferous woodlands in the northern United States and Canada.

Spring migrants usually arrive in late April. Early arrival dates: Chicago, April 10, 1966 (PD-IAB138:8); Urbana, April 14 (Smith 1930). Average spring arrival dates: Urbana, May 2 (20 years); Chicago, May 8 (16 years); west-central,

May 6 (10 years). High counts for spring: 55, Chicago, May 10, 1987 (CM); 20, Springfield, May 12, 1984 (HDB); 34, Lake Shelbyville, May 20, 1984 (SR-IB&B1:89). Spring bird count totals ranged from 43 in 1973 to 1187 in 1983; the highest count was 368 in Cook County, May 7, 1983 (VK). Average spring departure dates: Chicago, May 29 (16 years); Sangamon County, May 30 (16 years). Some late spring or early summer dates suggest breeding: Jackson Park, June 19, 1982 (HR-AB36:984); Giant City State Park, June 2, 1984 (BCho-SR41:24); Springfield, June 9, 1983 (HDB).

During fall migration, some Magnolia Warblers are seen in weedy patches, though most are still confined to woodlands. Numbers in fall are usually higher than in spring, primarily because of the presence of immature birds. Early fall arrival dates: Springfield, August 12, 1977 (HDB); Chicago, August 15, 1933 (Clark and Nice 1950). Average fall arrival dates: Chicago, August 21 (16 years); Sangamon County, August 25 (18 years). High counts for fall: 50, Chicago, September 2, 1980 (JL); 133 killed at a television tower, Piatt County, September 27, 1972, and 44 killed at a tower, Sangamon County, September 29, 1972 (Seets and Bohlen 1977); 20, Henderson County, September 21, 1985 (MB-IB&B2:54). Average fall departure dates: Chicago, October 10 (16 years); Sangamon County, October 13 (18 years). Occasionally a Magnolia lingers late: Jackson Park, November 3, 1980 (PC,RG-AB35:190); Joliet, December 17–19, 1981 (JM-AB36:301); Springfield, October 31, 1979 (CO). The Magnolia Warbler winters from central Mexico south to central Panama.

CAPE MAY WARBLER

Dendroica tigrina

UNCOMMON MIGRANT DECREASING
SOUTHWARD IN FALL

An adult male Cape May Warbler is one of the most intricate beauties of the warbler tribe, with tiger stripes, chestnut cheek patch, dark cap, and bright yellow color. Females are much duller, especially immatures, but they have enough of the coloration and markings to be identified. The Cape May's song is a weak series of squeaky *seet* notes resembling those of some other warblers, and this similarity, combined with treetop foraging habits, lets many Cape Mays go unnoticed. One afternoon I saw one sitting silently at midheight in a tree and not moving at all; no wonder many observers cannot find these warblers in the midday heat. As Sutton said, "The difference between warblers and no warblers is very slight." The Cape May's favorite habitat is conifers, especially spruce, but they also occur in deciduous trees such as oak, and I have seen them feeding around oak galls. Marvel (1948) observed one feeding on sap from holes drilled by a sapsucker. During spring migration in Chicago, Goetz noticed Cape Mays feeding on insects around flowering crabapple and cherry trees. Cape May Warbler populations fluctuate greatly from year to year

because of changes in food sources such as the spruce budworm. These warblers breed in coniferous areas in Canada and the northern United States.

Cape May Warblers have a clockwise elliptical migration route, which usually brings more birds to Illinois in spring than in fall, especially downstate. For the same reason the composition of fall warbler flocks in northeastern Illinois differs from that in central and southern Illinois. Those warblers that winter primarily in the southeastern states and the Caribbean islands head east or southeast in fall, not south. Early spring arrivals: male, Springfield, April 19, 1977 (HDB); Urbana, April 20 (Smith 1930). Average arrival dates: Urbana, May 5 (19 years); Chicago, May 9 (16 years); Sangamon County, May 2 (17 years). High counts: 45, Wilmette, May 9, 1961 (Mlodinow 1984); six, Mermet Lake, May 9, 1987 (DR); 16, Chicago, May 21, 1983 (DJ-SR37:21). Spring bird count totals ranged from two in 1973 to 333 in 1986. The high count was 86 in Cook County, May 10, 1980 (VK). Average spring departure dates: Urbana, May 20 (19 years); Chicago, May 25 (six years); Sangamon County, May 18 (17 years). Late departures: Urbana, June 6, 1982 (BCho-SR33:14); specimen, Glen Ellyn, June 3, 1917 (CAS#16858).

Fall arrivals may start in August: Jackson Park, August 15, 1986 (HR-IB&B3:46); Mount Zion, August 31, 1985 (RP-IB&B2:54). Average arrival dates: Chicago, August 23 (16 years); Sangamon County, September 5 (16 years). High counts for fall: 30, Chicago, September 1, 1980 (JL-AB35:190); 15, Chicago, August 28, 1982 (JL); 12, Illinois Beach State Park, September 2, 1985 (MB,KR-IB&B2:54). Average departure dates: Chicago, October 3 (16 years); Sangamon County, October 10 (17 years). They are often seen in mid- to late October and sometimes in November.

Though some of these warblers linger late, apparently feeding on scale insects and suet at feeders, very few overwinter. Winter records: one to three, Chicago, December 6, 1982–March 2, 1983 (RR,JG-AB37:308); one or two, Chicago, December 18–19, 1980 (RB,JL-AB35:306); one at feeder, Park Forest, December 10, 1986 (J.Koutsky-AB41:289); Makanda, December 7, 1983 (PH-SR40:12); Springfield, December 2, 1983 (HDB).

BLACK-THROATED BLUE WARBLER

Dendroica caerulescens

UNCOMMON MIGRANT DECREASING
SOUTHWESTERLY

This warbler is found in shaded undergrowth in forests. It feeds at midheights and has a slow buzzy song that helps locate it in spring. The male is a beautiful blue and black with white underparts. The female, quite different, is olive and could pass for an Orange-crowned Warbler except for a dark cheek patch and small white check in the wing.

The breeding range of the nominate form, *D. c. caerulescens*, is strictly northeastern North America. (Another subspecies, *D. c. cairnsi*, not found in Illinois, breeds in the Appalachians). Thus northeastern Illinois gets more migrants in spring than the rest of the state. Fall migrants are more evenly distributed but are still not common. Since this warbler winters in the Carribean area, Illinois lies chiefly to the west and south of its primary flight path. Graber et al. (1983) cited evidence for a decline in this warbler's numbers as early as 1912.

The earliest spring migrants arrive in late April: Decatur, April 28, 1975 (RS-AB29:861). Most arrive in May. Average arrival dates: Urbana, May 5 (20 years); Chicago, May 10 (15 years). High counts for spring are low and few: six males, Jackson Park, May 8, 1982 (PC,RG-SR33:14); nine, Chicago, May 16, 1981 (RB,JL-SR29:13). This warbler was missed the first three years of the spring bird count (1972–74), but totals after that ranged from one in 1978 to 38 in 1975, with the highest count 18 in Cook County, May 10, 1975 (VK). Average departure dates: Urbana, May 17 (20 years); Chicago, May 25 (15 years). The few June dates are evidently late departures: Lake Forest, June 8 (Bent 1953); Evanston, June 1, 1987 (EW); Woodstock, June 6, 1981 (DF-SR29:13).

While more Black-throated Blues are present in fall than in spring, they remain more numerous in eastern Illinois. The earliest fall migrants arrive in August: Jackson Park, August 13, 1986 (HR-IB&B3:46); Weldon Springs State Park, August 29, 1987 (RP). Average arrival dates: Chicago, September 8 (16 years); Sangamon County, September 10 (16 years). High counts: seven, Lake County, September 11, 1984 (SH-IB&B1:21); six, Waukegan, September 22, 1970 (LB-IAB156:22); 20 killed at television towers, central Illinois, September 26–27, 1972 (Seets and Bohlen 1977). Average departure dates: Chicago, October 10 (16 years); Sangamon County, October 4 (17 years). Late dates of departure: male, Champaign, November 14, 1987 (RCh); Jackson Park, November 4, 1979 (Mlodinow 1984); Springfield, October 24, 1983 (HDB).

YELLOW-RUMPED WARBLER

Dendroica coronata

ABUNDANT MIGRANT; UNCOMMON WINTER
RESIDENT IN SOUTHERN ILLINOIS
DECREASING NORTHWARD

Yellow-rumps are probably the most numerous warblers (Parulinae) in the world. In full migration these warblers with their characteristic *check* note seem to be everywhere. I have heard them even when I was standing in a cornfield miles away from any trees. They migrate both diurnally and nocturnally. Some show molt in spring, while others are brightly plumaged. Their song is difficult to learn because it is variable. Usually a somewhat juncolike trill, it sometimes has variations that sound like the warbles of other species. Yellow-rumped Warblers sometimes have a plumage that

looks frosted, with light feather edgings. There is also albinism; I have noted several albinistic Yellow-rumps while banding and in television tower kills. The name Yellow-rumped was given to these warblers when the "Myrtle" and "Audubon's" warblers were grouped together as one species. The "Myrtle" is the eastern *D. c. coronata*, which breeds mostly in the coniferous zone but as far west as Alaska. The western "Audubon's" reported in Illinois is presumably the subspecies *D. c. memorabilis*. There are several records for "Audubon's" in Illinois: Buffalo Prairie, date unknown (AOU 1957); Sanganois Conservation Area, December 19, 1970 (Bohlen 1971); female, Jackson Park, May 7 and 8, 1971 (CC,LB,RPu-AB25:753); Sand Ridge (Christmas bird count), December 29, 1979 (AB34:524); Riverton, December 31, 1982 (HDB); Springfield, November 11, 1985 (HDB). There are intergrades of the two subspecies that may be difficult to distinguish from "pure" birds. Moreover, some "Myrtles" show buffy throats in fall. Further information on differences between the races is found in the *Master Guide to Birding* (1983).

Although some Yellow-rumps winter in Illinois, returning spring migrants are usually easy to distinguish in most years except in southern Illinois. Early dates of arrival are in mid-to late March. Average spring arrival dates: Urbana, April 9 (20 years); Chicago, April 11 (16 years); Sangamon County, March 31 (18 years). High counts for spring: 100, Springfield, April 28, 1987 (HDB); 179, Vermilion County, April 28, 1985 (SB-IB&B1:89); 123, Massac County, May 4, 1985 (DR-IB&B1:89); 219, Lake County, May 7, 1983 (DJ-SR37:21). Spring bird count totals ranged from 1232 in 1973 to 8448 in 1983; the highest count was 1581 in Cook County, May 7, 1983 (VK). Average spring departure dates: Urbana, May 18 (20 years); Chicago, May 22 (16 years); west-central, May 16 (15 years). Some late dates: Charleston, June 19, 1979 (LBH-AB33:868); male, Chicago, June 16, 1985 (PWa-IB&B1:89); Jackson Park, June 14, 1983 (PC,HR-SR37:21); Urbana, June 1, 1983 (BCho-SR37:21).

Fall migration sometimes starts early. Some Yellow-rumps arrive even before their molt is finished. Early fall arrival dates: Jackson Park, August 24, 1983 (PC-SR39:23); Mokena, August 6,1985 (ADu-IB&B2:54). Average fall arrival dates: Chicago, September 15 (16 years); west-central, September 16 (11 years); Sangamon County, September 18 (18 years). These birds appear in loose flocks in woodlands, on woodland edges, and even in very open habitats. Fall high counts usually exceed spring counts: 5000, Chicago, October 9, 1983 (RB-AB38:210); 1800, Chicago, October 7, 1984 (JL); 150, Cumberland County, October 19, 1983 (RBr-SR39:23). "Myrtle" Warblers are frequently killed at television towers in fall, including 305 near Springfield in one night, October 14, 1985. Average fall departure dates: Chicago, October 31 (16 years); Sangamon County, November 25 (12 years).

"Myrtles" are the most hardy of the warblers, existing in winter on poison ivy berries and cedar berries. They roost in flocks, usually in conifers, coming into their roost areas in the evening. I once saw some returning to a roost at Villa Ridge Cemetery; I estimated up to 200 Yellow-rumps.

BLUE JAY
Cyanocitta cristata

Blue Jays eat a variety of foods and can frequently be seen foraging through the woods in pursuit of fruits, nuts, insects, and sometimes baby birds and eggs. In the fall their diet becomes almost exclusively fruits and nuts. Nothing is more striking than the brilliant plumage of this beautiful bird contrasted with the foliage of the persimmon (*Diospyros virginiana*), one of the trees that provide it with food.

Adult
(sexes similar)

EASTERN SCREECH-OWL
Otus asio

CAROLINA CHICKADEE
Parus carolinensis

TUFTED TITMOUSE
Parus bicolor

RED-BREASTED NUTHATCH
Sitta canadensis

WHITE-BREASTED NUTHATCH
Sitta carolinensis

The presence of the Eastern Screech-Owl is frequently only revealed at dusk by the nervous scolding of a band of woodland birds. Along with a wide variety of other prey, the Screech-Owl preys on small birds.

Tufted Titmouse
(sexes similar)

Carolina Chickadee
(sexes similar)   **Red-breasted Nuthatch**
(male; female duller)

Eastern Screech-Owl   **White-breasted Nuthatch**
(sexes similar)   *(male; female has gray on crown)*

BROWN CREEPER
Certhia americana

CAROLINA WREN
Thryothorus ludovicianus

Both of these small brown birds can be found in our winter woods. Carolina Wrens flit from branch to branch and along the ground, looking for insects hidden in rolled-up leaves, clusters of seeds, and other protected places. Brown Creepers most often forage by flying from the top of one tree to the base of another, then spiraling up the trunk searching for hidden food in the cracks and crevices of the bark.

Carolina Wren
(sexes similar)

Brown Creeper
(sexes similar)

GOLDEN-CROWNED KINGLET
Regulus satrapa

RUBY-CROWNED KINGLET
Regulus calendula

BLUE-GRAY GNATCATCHER
Polioptila caerulea

The paths of the three species of Old World warblers that occur in the state cross about the time the blooms of the Serviceberry (*Amelanchier arborea*) appear. Golden-crowned Kinglets are still lingering here on their wintering grounds. Ruby-crowned Kinglets are passing through en route from the south, and Blue-gray Gnatcatchers are just beginning to arrive and will stay to nest.

Blue-gray Gnatcatcher
(male; female lacks eyebrow)

Golden-crowned Kinglet

(male)

(female)

Ruby-crowned Kinglet
(male; female lacks red crown)

EASTERN BLUEBIRD
Sialia sialis

HERMIT THRUSH
Catharus guttatus

The ripening of the fruit of the Black Gum (*Nyssa sylvatica*) seems to coincide with the fall migration of thrushes. I have seen all seven species of thrushes that commonly occur in the state, including the Eastern Bluebird and the Hermit Thrush, feeding on the same heavily fruited gum tree during the same autumn.

Eastern Bluebird
(male)

(female)

Hermit Thrush
(sexes similar)

Christmas bird count totals for 1976–85 ranged from 121 in 1977 to 613 in 1982. Most high counts were in southern Illinois, including 301 in Union County in 1982 and 355 at Crab Orchard National Wildlife Refuge in 1963. But there were 126 at Chicago urban in 1983, attracted by insects at a warm area along a sewage canal. Other winter records: 100, Chicago, January 10, 1980 (SM-AB34:279); 50, Lawrence County, January 26, 1980 (LH-AB34:279); four, Rockford, December 20, 1983 (LJ-SR40:13). Large numbers either die or migrate in winter, for many Yellow-rumps disappear with severe weather.

BLACK-THROATED GRAY WARBLER

Dendroica nigrescens

VERY RARE VAGRANT

In all plumages this gray, black, and white warbler has a yellow spot on the lores. The Black-throated Gray is a western North American species that has wandered eastward fairly regularly. There are five Illinois records: male, Chicago, April 24, 1946 (H.Bennett); male, Winnetka, October 9, 1968 (T.K.Boyd); male, Springfield, May 3, 1975 (Bohlen 1976a); female, Urbana, September 6, 1975 (J.C.Franks); female photographed, Chicago, May 2–10, 1984 (RB,JL). Most of these warblers were seen in deciduous trees at close range. Nearby states that have reported this species are Minnesota, Wisconsin, Michigan, and Iowa. The Black-throated Gray winters from the southwestern United States to central Mexico.

TOWNSEND'S WARBLER

Dendroica townsendi

VERY RARE VAGRANT

This warbler somewhat resembles the Black-throated Green and the Blackburnian Warblers. A western montane species, it is usually found in conifers. There are two records for Illinois: female, Jackson Park, May 6, 1980 (PC-AB34:784); male photographed, Jacksonville, May 2, 1982 (J.Paris,S.Tavender,PW-SR33:14). The Townsend's Warbler has also been recorded in Minnesota, Iowa, and Tennessee. It winters from southern California south to Costa Rica.

HERMIT WARBLER

Dendroica occidentalis

HYPOTHETICAL

This western warbler has a limited breeding range along the Pacific Coast. It is found in conifers and oaks. The only report for Illinois is the sighting of a female at Schiller Woods, Chicago, April 24, 1988. Richard and Mary Biss watched this warbler for more than 30 minutes. The Hermit Warbler has been recorded in Minnesota and Missouri. It is known to hybridize with the Townsend's Warbler, and that may be the case with the Chicago bird. It winters from northern Mexico south to Nicaragua.

BLACK-THROATED GREEN WARBLER

Dendroica virens

COMMON MIGRANT

The buzzy *zee zee zee zoo zee* song of this yellow-faced warbler is easy to learn and remember. Its chip note is similar to the Yellow-rump's, but not as hard or loud. Black-throated Greens forage from midheight to fairly high in both deciduous and coniferous trees. Nelson (1876) thought a few remained in Illinois in summer to nest, but even though there have been some recent summer records, breeding has not been proved in Illinois. This species does breed as close as central Wisconsin. The nominate race is found in Illinois.

Early spring arrival dates: Alexander County, March 25, 1986 (ID-AB40:480), and March 31, 1984 (JR-AB38:919); Jackson Park, April 11, 1981 (T.McLarnan-SR29:13); Chautauqua National Wildlife Refuge, April 10, 1982 (JM-SR33:14). Average arrival dates: Chicago, May 7 (15 years); Urbana, April 27 (20 years); Sangamon County, April 21 (17 years). Totals on spring bird counts ranged from 120 in 1974 to 1206 in 1984. High counts: 184, Cook County, May 7, 1983; 154, Champaign County, May 5, 1984; 104, Will County, May 10, 1975 (VK). Average spring departure dates: Chicago, May 27 (15 years); Urbana, May 21 (20 years); Sangamon County, May 28 (17 years). This warbler lingers late in spring: Winnetka, June 21, 1977 (LY-AB31:1149); Trail of Tears State Forest, June 13, 1981 (MM-AB35:946); Joliet, June 21, 1984 (PWa,JO-AB38:1027); Mississippi Palisades State Park, June 12, 1985 (RGu-AB39:919). Some late birds may be attempting to set up breeding territories.

Some Black-throated Green Warblers either return very early or oversummer in Illinois: Springfield, July 26, 1980 (HDB); Woodstock, July 9–13, 1983 (A.Carroll-AB37:995). Normally they begin returning in August. Average arrival dates: Chicago, August 23 (15 years); west-central, September 4 (13 years). High counts for fall: 240 killed at television towers across central Illinois, September 27, 1972 (Seets and Bohlen 1977); 35, Knox County, September 13, 1982 (MB-SR35:14); 30, Giant City State Park, October 6, 1984 (JR-IB&B1:21); 20, Vermilion County, September 18, 1986 (SB-IB&B3:46). Average departure dates: Chicago, October 9 (15 years); west-central, October 9 (13 years). Late departure dates: Riverdale, November 21, 1982 (WM-AB37:188); Glen Ellyn, November 1, 1983 (RPi-SR39:23); Springfield, November 14, 1974 (HDB).

There is one winter record of a warbler at Grand Detour that stayed until January 14, 1983 (BSh-SR36:10). These warblers winter from southern Texas and Florida south to central Panama.

BLACKBURNIAN WARBLER

Dendroica fusca

COMMON MIGRANT

The throat of the adult male Blackburnian is such a bright reddish orange that this warbler is referred to as "little torch throat." The female's throat is duller, and some immature females have only a yellow wash on the throat. These dull females could be mistaken for Cerulean Warblers, but the observer should note the streaks on the backs of the Blackburnian Warblers. The song in spring has a few introductory notes and ends in a very high ascending squeak. Blackburnians usually forage so high in the tops of tall deciduous trees that they are known among birders as "pain in the neck" warblers. Occasionally, in cool, damp weather and when they come down to drink, they can be seen lower in the trees.

Males arrive earlier in spring than females. An early arrival date: Springfield, April 18, 1978 (HDB). Average arrival dates: Chicago, May 9 (15 years); Urbana, May 3 (20 years). High counts for spring: 20, Lake Shelbyville, May 14, 1985 (SR), and 12, Illinois Beach State Park, May 16, 1985 (KR-IB&B1:89); nine, Jackson Park, May 31, 1981 (RG,PC-SR29:13). Spring bird count totals ranged from 27 in 1974 to 609 in 1983, with high counts of 62 in Cook County, May 10, 1980; 59 in Champaign County, May 7, 1983; and 32 in Du Page County, May 8, 1982. Average spring departure dates: Chicago, May 26 (15 years); Urbana, May 22 (20 years). Late departure dates: female, Springfield, June 5, 1981 (HDB); male, Chicago, June 5, 1982 (AA-SR33:14); specimen collected by Gault (CAS#17160), Glen Ellyn, June 25, 1907.

Both in spring and in fall these warblers are more numerous on the eastern side of the state (Graber et al. 1983). In fall they travel with mixed foraging flocks and are seen in forests and on forest edges, sometimes fairly low. Early arrival dates: Springfield, August 7, 1972 (HDB); Charleston, August 11, 1986 (LBH-IB&B3:46). Average arrival dates: Chicago, August 19 (14 years); west-central, August 30 (10 years). High counts for fall: 20, Tazewell County, September 4, 1983 (MB-SR39:23); 10, Carlyle Lake, September 11, 1987 (RG); 15, Springfield, September 2, 1981 (HDB). Thirty-four were killed at central Illinois television towers on September 2, 1972 (Seets and Bohlen 1977). Average fall departure dates: Chicago, September 19 (14 years); west-central, September 24 (10 years). Late fall departure dates: Chicago, November 4, 1979 (Mlodinow 1984); Jackson Park, October 18, 1983 (HR-SR39:23); Springfield, October 17, 1987 (HDB).

Blackburnian Warblers winter from Costa Rica south to central Peru and Bolivia.

YELLOW-THROATED WARBLER

Dendroica dominica

COMMON MIGRANT AND SUMMER RESIDENT IN SOUTHERN ILLINOIS DECREASING NORTHWARD

This southern warbler is so closely associated with sycamore trees that the inland race, *D. d. albilora,* is often referred to as the Sycamore Warbler. In southern Illinois it is also found in cypress and pine trees. Yellow-throated Warblers inhabit bottomland forests and usually stay very high in tall trees. They would go unnoticed if it were not for their persistent and loud singing. Their song is similar to the Indigo Bunting's, but it is slower and ends differently, although Yellow-throated Warblers often do not finish their song, giving only the first few notes. As noted in Cooke (1888), when this warbler arrives in spring it sings constantly, stops or at least sings less frequently in midspring, and then about June once again sings constantly. Yellow-throated Warblers are so small and sycamore leaves so large that finding even a singing bird is a neck-straining job. These warblers feed by creeping on limbs like a Black-and-white Warbler; they also use other *Dendroica* methods of feeding.

The Yellow-throated Warbler arrives earlier in spring than most warblers: Pine Hills, April 2, 1966 (specimen SIU); Pike County, April 1, 1982 (RS-AB36:860); Union County, March 31, 1985 (JR-AB39:309); Charleston, April 8, 1986 (BJ-IB&B2:96); Chicago, April 12, 1986 (AS-IB&B2:96). The average arrival date for central Illinois is April 17 (17 years). Spring bird count totals ranged from 39 to 99, with a high count of 15 in Johnson County, May 7, 1977, and Vermilion County, May 5, 1984 (VK). Other high counts: 32, Crab Orchard National Wildlife Refuge, April 18, 1985 (JR-IB&B1:89); 18, Cache River, April 24, 1973 (VK,HDB). Some northern occurrences: Waukegan, April 30, 1972 (LC-AB26:768); Barrington, April 22, 1988 (CW); Winnebago County, May 21, 1982 (DW-SR33:14). Most Yellow-throated Warblers seen in northern Illinois must be overmigrants.

Not much is known about the nesting of Yellow-throated Warblers in Illinois. They generally nest high, and even if a nest is sighted the contents cannot be viewed. The four eggs are whitish with darker spots that are usually more numerous at the larger end of the egg. I saw two fledged young being fed by a female along the Sangamon River north of Springfield on July 15, 1987. The juveniles, which are grayish brown with streaks and yellowish on the sides of the breast, would have been difficult to identify had the parent not been there.

This warbler is even more difficult to see in fall than in spring. It quits singing, and any would-be observer has the added distractions of biting insects and heavy foliage to contend with. The best way to find Yellow-throated Warblers is to look among feeding flocks of warblers in bottomland forest in August and early September. On August 1, 1982, near Dawson I saw a bird land on a tall metal structure that supported power lines. This bird, which turned out to be a Yellow-throated Warbler, crept and flitted about on the structure feeding on insects, then flew southwest out of sight. Since the nearest forest was perhaps three miles away, this bird must have been a diurnal migrant. The average fall departure date for central Illinois is September 9 (11 years). Late departure dates: Giant City State Park, October 10, 1982 (JR-SR35:14); Shelby County, September 16, 1983 (KF-SR39:23); Carbondale, October 7, 1972 (VK-AB27:69). I found a Yellow-throated Warbler in a pine grove at Lake Springfield on the very late date of November 11, 1975; it appeared to have a long bill and definite yellow lores, suggesting the eastern subspecies. The latest Yellow-throated Warbler occurred along the North Shore channel in Chicago, December 11-16, 1982 (RR,JG-AB37:308).

The Yellow-throated Warbler winters from the Gulf states south to Costa Rica.

PINE WARBLER

Dendroica pinus

UNCOMMON MIGRANT; UNCOMMON
SUMMER RESIDENT IN SOUTHERN ILLINOIS;
VERY RARE WINTER RESIDENT

Pine Warblers are fairly nondescript. Although adult males may stand out if the observer gets a good look, females and immatures can appear very dull-colored. The song is much like that of the Chipping Sparrow, and the birds move so slowly that they can go undetected. Pine Warblers often creep along the larger limbs like nuthatches. Usually found in conifers, in migration they also occur in deciduous woods. Indications from earlier counts are that the Pine Warbler's migrant population has dropped in central and northern Illinois (see Graber et al. 1983). The race in Illinois is *D. p. pinus*.

Pine Warblers seen very early in spring may be wintering individuals rather than migrants: Giant City State Park, March 5, 1983 (JR-AB37:877); Pope County, March 5, 1985 (TF,JP-IB&B1:89); Springfield, March 13, 1986 (HDB). Average spring arrival dates: Urbana, April 23 (19 years); Chicago, April 26 (nine years); Sangamon County, April 9 (17 years). High counts for this uncommon bird are few. Spring bird count totals ranged from eight in 1973 to 74 in 1984, with high counts of 17 from Pope County on May 10, 1980, and Will County on May 5, 1984 (VK). Average spring departure dates: Urbana, May 10 (19 years); Chicago, May 8 (19 years); Sangamon County, May 1 (17 years). The latest migrants have occurred near the end of May: Chicago, May 28, 1937 (Clark and Nice 1950); one banded, Blue Island, May 28, 1985 (KB-IB&B1:89); Jackson Park, May 25, 1983 (PC,HR).

Although this warbler may have nested in northern Illinois at one time and there is a population that nests in the northern Great Lakes region, nesting in Illinois now seems confined to the south. The nests are in pines, usually in fairly mature stands. Twenty-four adults and four young were found in Pope County on May 27, 1986 (DR-

IB&B3:15), and nine Pine Warblers were at Crab Orchard National Wildlife Refuge, July 13-14, 1983 (JR-SR38:14). Records of nests containing eggs in Illinois are few. Graber et al. (1983) found a nest on April 9 at Pomona with four eggs that fledged young on April 24.

Fall migration starts as early as August. One migrant still showing molt was at Springfield on August 28, 1987 (HDB). Other early arrivals: Sand Ridge State Forest, August 19, 1987 (KR); Big River State Forest, August 31, 1986 (MB-IB&B3:46); Dundee, August 25, 1981 (SD-SR31:16). Average arrival dates: Chicago, September 28 (eight years); west-central, September 15 (five years); Sangamon County, September 21 (11 years). Pine Warblers are probably more common in eastern Illinois in fall. A few are killed at television towers, but there are no high counts for fall. Average departure dates: Chicago, October 11 (eight years); Sangamon County, October 12 (six years). Some Pine Warblers stay into November; one at Jackson Park, November 7, 1980 (RG,PC), was clearly a migrant.

Some Pine Warblers apparently winter, or attempt to, in Illinois, mostly in the south. They were recorded on Christmas bird counts only five times before 1983. Winter records: Urbana, December 5, 1982 (RCh-AB37:188); Crab Orchard refuge, January 11, 1986 (DR-AB40:288); Du Page County, December 24, 1971 (LB-AB26:612); Crab Orchard refuge, January 18-February 2, 1975 (BP-AB29:699). Most Pine Warblers winter in the southeastern United States.

KIRTLAND'S WARBLER

Dendroica kirtlandii

VERY RARE MIGRANT

This fairly large yellow and gray tail-wagging species is almost unknown away from its nesting grounds in central Michigan. Only about 200 pairs remain. The Kirtland's Warbler breeds in scrubby jack pines and winters in the Bahamas. It tends to stay low and has a loud song resembling that of the Northern Waterthrush. Apparently this species formerly had an expanded breeding range in Wisconsin, and a few have been found there recently. Of the 13 records for Illinois, not all are convincing. The most suspect record is of six Kirtland's seen in La Grange on May 12, 1947 (Ford 1956). Spring dates range from April 28 (1932, Blue Island) to June 3 (1910, Glen Ellyn). Three records are represented by specimens: male, Glen Ellyn, May 7, 1894 (Gault 1894); Winnebago County, May 25, 1894 (Jones 1895); male, Chicago, May 21-22, 1899 (Blackwelder 1899). The only recent spring record is of one Kirtland's at Chicago, May 10, 1979 (J.LaSalle-AB33:778). Two sight records are for fall: two Kirtland's in Winnebago County, September 2, 1948 (Smith and Parmalee 1955), and one at Chicago, September 26, 1978 (E.Abeles-AB33:778). The only downstate record is by Ridgway (1914) at Bird Haven, May 3, 1908. Future records should be well documented and the birds photographed if possible.

PRAIRIE WARBLER

Dendroica discolor

COMMON MIGRANT AND SUMMER RESIDENT
IN SOUTHERN ILLINOIS DECREASING
NORTHWARD AND BECOMING VERY LOCAL

This warbler favors upland old-field scrub habitats, but it is mostly confined to southern Illinois despite the presence of seemingly appropriate habitats in central and northern Illinois. The Prairie Warbler is also found at pine plantations, cedars, and woodland edges. There are some indications that it is also associated with sandy areas. Its distinctive song, a thin high buzz, ascends the scale. The Prairie Warbler bobs its tail, and the black markings on its face and the reddish streaks on its back are diagnostic. The race in Illinois in the nominate, *D. d. discolor*.

Early spring arrival dates: Giant City State Park, April 6, 1986 (DR-AB40:480); Pope County, April 13, 1984 (JP-SR41:24); Crab Orchard National Wildlife Refuge, April 15, 1985 (JR-IB&B1:89). Records from northern and central Illinois could represent either the very thin breeding population there or overmigrants: Westville, May 10, 1980 (MC-SR25:8); Springfield, April 21, 1974 (HDB); Iroquois County, April 28, 1984 (RPi-SR41:24); four, Cook County, May 11, 1983 (SR37:21). Spring bird count totals ranged from 11 in 1981 to 113 in 1979, with all high counts coming from the southern counties of Pope, Jackson, and Johnson. The highest count was 52 in Pope County, May 6, 1978 (VK).

Nolan (1978) listed 26 Illinois counties that contained breeding Prairie Warblers. These birds nest fairly low in saplings or small trees. The four to five eggs are whitish with reddish brown markings. Egg-laying season in Illinois is May 3 to June 11 (Graber et al. 1983). Areas outside southern Illinois that have records of breeding birds are Forest Glen, 1984; Sand Ridge State Forest, 1979; Peoria, 1982; Shelby County, 1985; McLean County, 1979.

Fall migration goes mostly undetected because few of these warblers go north of Illinois. The few that do nest farther north are probably deflected east. Some fall departure dates: Crab Orchard refuge, November 23, 1959 (Bush-AFN14:41); Vermilion County, September 21, 1986 (SB-IB&B3:46); Urbana, August 16, 1986 (RCh-IB&B3:46); Chicago, August 22–24, 1981 (JL); Crab Orchard refuge, September 17, 1982 (JR-SR35:14). Prairie Warblers winter from central Florida south to the West Indies and Central America.

PALM WARBLER

Dendroica palmarum

COMMON MIGRANT AND VERY RARE WINTER
RESIDENT

The Palm Warbler is a tail-wagging species with white in the corners of its tail. Its colors may be fairly bright in spring but are dull in fall. The Palm presents a greenish yellow rump, and so it can be mistaken for a Yellow-rumped Warbler, which has a call similar to the Palm's but more emphatic. The Palm Warbler's eyeline and the yellow coverts under its tail are useful field marks. It usually stays near or on the ground but is sometimes found higher up in trees, especially in spring. In fall it inhabits more open areas, weedy patches, even fields. It is sometimes seen along roadsides in the company of Eastern Bluebirds and Chipping Sparrows, and it even sits on fences. Its song is a buzzy trill that is easily confused with the songs of several other species. Palm Warblers breed in the coniferous zone in Canada. The race found in Illinois is the western *D. p. palmarum*. Sight records from Chicago, May 1, 1981, and Springfield, October 16, 1983, of the "Yellow Palm"—the eastern form, *D. p. hypochrysea*—are inadequately described, although there are records for the "Yellow Palm" from Missouri and Indiana (AOU 1957).

Palm Warblers seen on very early dates in spring may have wintered nearby, including one at Springfield, April 8, 1988 (HDB). Average spring arrival dates: Urbana, April 22 (20 years); Chicago, April 25 (16 years); west-central, April 23 (15 years). Maximum counts for spring: 190, Chicago, April 29, 1984 (JL); 75, Lake County, April 29, 1986 (DJ-IB&B2:96); 71, Jackson Park, May 4, 1982 (RG); 45, Springfield, May 5, 1982 (HDB). Spring bird counts come at about the right time to find this species in large numbers; totals have ranged from 521 in 1986 to 6842 in 1983. Most high counts were from Cook County, including 1462 on May 7, 1983 (VK). Average departure dates in spring: Urbana, May 18 (20 years); Chicago, May 23 (16 years); Sangamon County, May 16 (18 years). Some later dates: Springfield, May 26, 1976 (HDB); Jackson Park, May 22, 1983 (HR); three, Chicago, May 21, 1987 (JL). One injured bird was at Charleston June 7–22, 1984 (LBH-IB&B1:18).

Fall migration is fairly late. There is also a distinct eastward deflection, so that northeastern Illinois has good numbers in fall but the rest of the state does not, though that varies from year to year depending on such conditions as northeasterly winds and the strength of cold fronts. Early fall arrival dates: Normal, August 17, 1977 (DBi-IAB184:50); Jackson Park, August 18, 1980 (PC,RG); Evanston, August 23, 1977 (Mlodinow, 1984). Average fall arrival dates: Chicago, September 4 (16 years); Sangamon County, September 20 (18 years). High counts for fall: 380, Chicago, October 1, 1982 (JL); 150, Chicago, October 5, 1985 (AA-AB40:122); 190, Evanston, September 9, 1987 (EW). Palm Warblers are killed at television towers, especially on the eastern side of the state, but in small numbers: 14 in Sangamon County, September 29, 1972, and 20 in Vermilion County, September 27, 1972. Average fall departure dates: Chicago, October 21 (16 years); Sangamon County, October 23 (18 years). Most Palms are gone by the end of October, but a few linger into November and even later.

Winter records include up to 19 Palm Warblers seen on recent Christmas bird counts, mostly along the Chicago sanitary canal. Eight were there in December 1982. Other winter records: Forest Glen, January 14, 1980 (MC-SR24:4); three, Chicago, January 10, 1980 (SM-AB34:279); Urbana, December 1, 1985 (RCh); Lockport, December 16, 1984 (B.Rutter-IB&B1:70). Probably few if any survive in Illinois the whole winter. Palm Warblers winter in the Gulf states and south to Nicaragua and the Caribbean islands.

BAY-BREASTED WARBLER

Dendroica castanea

COMMON MIGRANT

Male Bay-breasted Warblers are unmistakable in breeding plumage. Females look much the same but are usually duller, though Stoddard (1921) collected a female at Chicago on May 21, 1915, that was as brightly plumaged as a male except for gray replacing black on the head. The song is weak, short, and high-pitched. It is similar to the songs of several other treetop warblers, especially the Cape May Warbler, and can be confused with the Black-and-white Warbler's song. In fall plumage, Bay-breasted Warblers look quite different; they usually show some bay on the flanks but are predominantly olive and gray. Some immature females show no bay at all. Bay-breasted Warblers usually forage high in oaks and other deciduous trees, but they also like spruce. In fall they can be seen much lower in the vegetation than in spring.

Probably because spring migration is late and rapid, these warblers seem less common in spring than in fall. Early spring arrival dates: Monroe County, April 26, 1984 (PS); Olney, April 23, 1985 (LH-AB39:309); Springfield, April 26, 1981 (HDB). Average arrival dates: Chicago, May 12 (15 years); Urbana, May 8 (20 years). High counts for spring: 36, Massac County, May 10, 1986 (DR-IB&B2:96); 50, Evanston, May 25, 1982 (Mlodinow 1984); 30, Lake Shelbyville, May 24, 1985 (SR-IB&B1:89). Wasson (1957) reported an estimated 100 at Chicago on May 14, 1956. Spring bird count totals ranged from three in 1978 to 428 in 1986. High count was 70 at Cook County, May 10, 1986 (VK). Average departure dates: Chicago, May 25 (15 years); Urbana, May 23 (20 years). Late departure dates: Elvaston, June 18, 1977 (ZW-AB31:1149); Springfield, June 30, 1980 (HDB); Giant City State Park, June 2, 1984 (BCho-SR41:24); Chicago, June 12, 1982 (AA-AB36:860).

Sometimes these warblers arrive early in fall. I saw an adult that still had not molted into basic plumage at Springfield on August 12, 1977. Another early record: two, Chicago, July 26, 1987 (JL). Average fall arrival dates: Chicago, August 27 (15 years); Sangamon County, August 25 (19 years). High counts for fall: 30, Carlyle Lake, September 11, 1987 (RG); 35, Vermilion County, September 15, 1985 (SB-IB&B2:54); 43, Springfield, September 12, 1982 (HDB). Average departure dates: Chicago, October 1 (16 years); Sangamon County, October 17 (18 years). Late departure dates: Kenilworth, November 8, 1986 (DJ-IB&B3:46); Springfield, November 13, 1987 (HDB). These

warblers are fairly frequent victims at television towers; 237 were killed across central Illinois on September 27, 1972 (Seets and Bohlen 1977). There are three early winter records: specimen (CAS#6439), Chicago, December 4, 1933; Charleston, December 11, 1981 (LBH-SR32:7); Chicago, December 17, 1983 (DJ,RB-SR40:13). The Bay-breasted Warbler winters from Panama east through Colombia and northwestern Venezuela.

BLACKPOLL WARBLER

Dendroica striata

COMMON MIGRANT IN NORTHERN ILLINOIS;
COMMON SPRING MIGRANT AND
UNCOMMON FALL MIGRANT ELSEWHERE IN
THE STATE

Although the Blackpoll and the Bay-breasted Warbler look distinctively different in spring plumage, they look very much alike in fall. The Blackpoll differs in having more streaks, whitish undertail coverts, and yellowish legs or feet. Its spring song is a high, thin series of notes like pebbles being tapped together. The song is penetrating and fairly easily heard. Blackpolls feed from midlevel to high in the trees, especially oaks. They nest in the spruce forests of northern Canada and Alaska.

Female migrants are olive streaked above and whitish below, but the observer should note the yellow legs. There is a differential migration of the sexes in which the females arrive later in spring than the males. Early spring arrival dates: Jackson Park, April 21, 1985 (HR-IB&B1:89); central Illinois, April 21, 1979 (Graber et al. 1983). Average arrival dates: Chicago, May 14 (15 years); Urbana, May 9 (20 years). High spring counts: 30, Lake Shelbyville, May 22, 1985 (SR-IB&B1:89); 53, Massac County, May 9, 1987 (DR); 55, Mahomet, May 8, 1982 (RCh-SR33:14). Totals on spring bird counts ranged from 43 in 1978 to 920 in 1982. The high count was 125 in Massac County, May 8, 1982 (VK). Average departure dates: Chicago, May 29 (15 years); Urbana, May 24 (20 years). Migration continues into June: Chicago, June 15, 1985 (JL); Springfield, June 4, 1983 (HDB); specimen (CAS#1205), Hyde Lake, June 9, 1907. A singing male was heard at Peoria June 24–25, 1922 (Graber et al. 1983).

In spring these warblers follow a migration route that takes them up the Mississippi Valley, but Nisbet (1970) has shown that in fall they complete an ellipse by going to the East Coast and making a long flight from the northeastern United States to northern South America, mostly over the Atlantic Ocean. As a consequence, the Chicago area has more Blackpolls in fall than in spring, while downstate Illinois has fewer. Even an active observer could miss these warblers in fall in central and southern Illinois. Early fall arrival dates: Chicago, August 21, 1987 (JL); Springfield, August 25, 1986 (HDB). Average arrival dates: Chicago, August 25 (16 years); Sangamon County, September 10 (17 years). High counts for fall: 55, Skokie Lagoons, September 22, 1974 (LB); 35, Jackson Park, September 15, 1980 (RG,PC); 35, Chicago, September 7, 1987 (CM). Given the correct winds or strong cold fronts, numbers can occur in central Illinois. On September 27, 1972, 59 Blackpolls were killed at television towers across central Illinois (Seets and Bohlen 1977). Average departure dates: Chicago, October 14 (16 years); Sangamon County, October 7 (15 years). Late departure dates: Lisle, November 22, 1956 (KB-AFN11:30); Springfield, November 22, 1976 (HDB); Chicago, November 4, 1983 (RB-AB38:210).

CERULEAN WARBLER

Dendroica cerulea

COMMON MIGRANT AND SUMMER RESIDENT BECOMING LESS NUMEROUS AND MORE LOCAL NORTHWARD

The pastel blue of the upperparts of the Cerulean Warbler makes it one of the most delicately beautiful of the wood warblers. It is rarely viewed so that the back can be seen, however, since it inhabits the treetops in bottomland forests. This warbler is almost always detected by its buzzy song; if it is seen, the necklace of the male, the *Dendroica* shape, and the white tail spots will identify it. The females may appear to be Tennessees or some other dull-colored warblers unless the two whitish wing bars are seen.

Cerulean Warblers generally arrive in late April, although there are earlier dates: Decatur, April 12, 1974 (RS); Pomona and Charleston, April 10, 1986 (KM,S.Steele-AB40:480); Glenwood, April 18, 1955 (Levy 1964). High numbers from spring bird counts include 30 on May 8, 1982, and 53 on May 10, 1986, in Carroll County (VK). Although Carroll is a northern county, it runs along the Mississippi River, and this warbler tends to inhabit the river areas of the state. The Cerulean Warbler may be more common in northern Illinois now than in the past, since Dreuth in his study of Lincoln Park, Chicago, saw only one, on May 25, 1942 (Clark and Nice 1950). Nelson (1876) listed it as a "regular but rare migrant." Yet on May 9, 1981, 14 were counted in Lake County, the highest number on the spring bird counts that year. In recent years two or more have been seen at Jackson Park each spring (RG). Another spring maximum was 58 along the Cache River, Johnson County, April 24, 1973 (VK,HDB).

Because this warbler breeds in bottomland forests, it is distributed along Illinois watercourses in the summer. There is a lesser amount of breeding in upland forests. Few nests have been found because the Cerulean nests high up in large trees, such as sycamores. Evidently three to five eggs are laid in an open nest resembling that of an Eastern Wood-Pewee. There are a few specific egg dates: May 29, Palos Park (Ford 1956); May 12–21, southern Illinois (Graber et al. 1983). There appears to be a fluctuation in the breeding populations in northern and possibly central Illinois. The summer of 1958 was reported to be a good year

for Cerulean Warblers near Rockford (LJ-AFN12:471), and they were detected at six locations in northern Illinois in summer 1983 (AB37:995). The mean number of Ceruleans per route (64 routes) in the 1965–79 breeding bird surveys was less than 0.1 (Robbins et al. 1986), but this species does not lend itself to roadside counting. I saw a Cerulean Warbler in heavy molt on July 26, 1980, along the Sangamon River near Riverton.

Most Cerulean Warblers leave Illinois early in fall, and the few that remain are difficult to detect because they have quit singing. In August they may be seen with early warbler flocks in bottomlands. I know of no maximum counts for fall. Some immatures have a yellowish wash on the throat and can easily be mistaken for other warblers, especially dull Blackburnians. Late dates of departure: September 14, southern Illinois (George 1968); one banded, Carbondale, September 16, 1970 (VK-AB 25:66); Springfield, September 13, 1981 (HDB). An Alexander County record for November 6 (Findley 1949), if accurate, is easily the latest for the state. This warbler winters in northern South America, mostly east of the Andes.

BLACK-AND-WHITE WARBLER

Mniotilta varia

COMMON MIGRANT AND RARE SUMMER RESIDENT

This warbler with the black and white stripes behaves much like a nuthatch as it creeps along the branches and trunks of trees. The males have a black throat patch that is lacking in females. The song, much like the songs of several other warblers, is a high thin series of *wee-see* notes. These warblers sometimes sing in fall; I heard them at Springfield, September 9 and 10, 1981. They forage from midheight to fairly low in trees. Their fairly long and slender bill allows them to exploit much the same food sources as creepers and nuthatches and to be rather early spring migrants.

Early spring arrivals: Springfield, March 29, 1981 (HDB); Pope County, April 6, 1986 (RP-IB&B2:96). Average arrival dates: Chicago, April 30 (16 years); Urbana, April 24 (20 years). High counts for spring: 18, Chicago, May 12, 1984 (JL); 14, Jackson Park, May 6, 1982 (PC,RG); 13, Lisle Arboretum, May 9, 1987 (EW). Totals on spring bird counts ranged from 117 in 1978 to 847 in 1983. High counts were 251, Cook County, May 7, 1983; 96, Champaign County, May 5, 1984; and 88, Lake County, May 7, 1977 (VK). Average departure dates: Chicago, May 25 (16 years); Urbana, May 21 (20 years). Migration continues into June. A Black-and-white Warbler at the Chicago lakefront on June 10, 1981, was a migrant (JL). The majority of these warblers go farther north to nest.

The thin Illinois breeding population is mostly in the south. Recent summer records: two, Mundelein, June 8, 1980 (JN-AB34:901); Jasper County, summer 1979 (AB33:868); two singing males, Joliet, June 6, 1984 (JM-

IB&B1:18); male, Lake Shelbyville, July 1 and 4, 1985 (SR-IB&B2:16); male, Warren County, June 22, 1986 (MB-IB&B3:15); female, Charleston, June 25, 1983 (LBH-SR38:14). Very little is known about the breeding cycle in Illinois.

Black-and-whites are among the first warblers to return in the fall: female, Springfield, July 16, 1986 (HDB); Champaign, August 8, 1985 (BCho-IB&B2:54). Average fall arrival dates: Chicago, August 18 (16 years); central Illinois, August 17 (19 years). High counts for fall: 10, Carlyle Lake, September 11, 1987 (RG); 10, Chautauqua National Wildlife Refuge, August 28, 1987 (KR); 14, Jackson Park, September 1, 1980 (RG,PC); 14, Springfield, September 5, 1985 (HDB). Average departure dates: Chicago, October 7 (16 years); central Illinois, October 6 (18 years). Most of these warblers have gone south by mid-October. Late departure dates: Chicago, November 28, 1984 (RB-AB39:62); female, Horseshoe Lake, Alexander County, December 30, 1974 (RS,HDB). The Black-and-white Warbler winters from the southern United States south to Colombia, Venezuela, and eastern Ecuador.

AMERICAN REDSTART

Setophaga ruticilla

COMMON MIGRANT AND LOCALLY COMMON SUMMER RESIDENT

Like an orange and black butterfly, the male American Redstart flits through leaves, flycatching. Both the male and the female droop their wings and fan their tails, showing off their bright colors. Immature males have a plumage like the female's but with orange at the bend of the wing instead of yellow. Some plumages of immature males and females are very much alike, however, and caution should be used in sexing and aging. A specimen of an adult female (ISM) shows orange patches rather than yellow, approaching the adult male coloration. The Redstart has several songs, the most common a short *zee* series with the last note higher. These warblers are mainly found in bottomland woods, but during migration they may be found wherever there are trees. The breeding subspecies in Illinois is the nominate form. The northern form, *S. r. tricolora*—if indeed it is truly distinct—is a migrant.

Males arrive first in spring. Early dates of arrival: two, Jackson County, April 21, 1985 (JR-IB&B1:89); male, Springfield, April 26, 1983 (HDB); two males, Jackson Park, April 28, 1981 (PC,RG). Average arrival dates: Chicago, May 6 (16 years); Urbana, May 2 (20 years). Maximum counts in spring: 180, Chicago, May 20, 1985 (CM-AB39:309); 200, Urbana, May 8, 1962 (Graber 1962). Spring bird count totals ranged from 68 in 1978 to 1794 in 1983, with the highest count 517 in Cook County, May 7, 1983. Another exceptional count was 141 in Carroll County, May 20, 1986 (VK). The average departure date for Chicago is May 30 (16 years). Landing saw five migrants that were still at the Chicago lakefront on June 10, 1984.

Graber et al. (1983) believed that the loss of riparian forest habitat in Illinois in recent years must have reduced the Redstart population. They showed that Redstart numbers are correlated with silver maples in bottomland forests. Redstarts use willows extensively for nest sites. The nest is much like the Yellow Warbler's and is placed in the crotch of a tree. There are three to five whitish eggs with reddish brown markings, mostly at the larger end. Illinois egg dates are May 4 to July 21.

Fall migration starts in late July and August, when only immature males and females are seen. It is usually September before adult males start passing through Illinois. Early arrival dates: Springfield, August 2, 1985 (HDB); Jackson Park, July 29, 1981 (PC-SR31:16). Average arrival dates: Chicago, August 14 (16 years); central Illinois, August 12 (16 years). High counts for fall: 100, Chicago area, September 7, 1968 (Mlodinow 1984); 59, Springfield, September 2, 1981 (HDB); 55, Chicago, August 29, 1985 (CM-IB&B2:54). Average departure dates: Chicago, October 8 (16 years); central Illinois, October 8 (18 years). Late departure dates: Chicago, December 10-17, 1983 (RB,JSa-SR40:13); female, Springfield, November 25, 1973 (KBo,HDB). The American Redstart winters from the southern United States south to South America.

PROTHONOTARY WARBLER

Protonotaria citrea

COMMON MIGRANT AND SUMMER RESIDENT IN SOUTHERN ILLINOIS DECREASING NORTHWARD

This golden yellow bird with bluish wings inhabits swampy places and bottomland forests. On rare occasions it is found in other wooded areas, even city parks, during migration. Its song, five or six *zweet* notes, all on one pitch, is easy to learn. But even when Prothonotary Warblers are singing, and even though they are very brightly colored, they can be difficult to see. The chip note is a fairly hard *chink*, but not as emphatic as the note of a waterthrush. Prothonotaries forage low, usually in trees such as willows that overhang water or on logs floating in the water. In southern Illinois the cypress swamps are their favored habitat.

Prothonotary Warblers may move up rivers during spring migration. Early arrival dates: Calhoun County, April 13, 1986 (RG); Crab Orchard National Wildlife Refuge, April 16, 1985 (JR-IB&B1:89); Jackson Park, April 20, 1982 (RG,PC-SR33:15); Springfield, April 16, 1977 (HDB). Average arrival dates: Urbana, May 2 (14 years); Sangamon County, April 26 (18 years). Spring bird count totals ranged from 84 in 1973 to 342 in 1986. All high counts were in southern Illinois except 25 in Marshall County, May 8, 1982. Other high counts: 40, Massac County, May 10, 1986; 44, Alexander County, May 7, 1977; 38, Pope County, May 10, 1980 (VK). Spring migration must continue at least until late May; late migrants, both females, were at Jackson Park on May 24, 1981, and May 26, 1982 (RG, JL).

The destruction of bottomland forests and the inundation of rivers for reservoirs have undoubtedly caused a reduction in the population of this warbler. It usually nests over water in tree cavities and is closely associated with willows. Other cavities will be accepted, such as tin cans, buckets, bridges, and nest boxes. Prothonotaries must now compete for nest sites with House Sparrows, Eurasian Tree Sparrows, and European Starlings as well as native species. The nest is usually made from tree moss. The three to eight eggs are creamy white marked heavily with reddish brown. Illinois egg dates are May 6 to June 21 (Bent 1953). Young look much duller than adults but are enough like them to be easily identified. A male in molt was at Riverton on August 18, 1983.

Fall migration usually goes unnoticed. A migrant was at Springfield as early as August 16, 1979, and Dreuth noted one at Chicago, August 13, 1934 (Clark and Nice 1950). The average departure date for central Illinois is August 29 (14 years). Late departure dates: Jackson Park, September 23, 1982 (HR, PC-SR35:15); Shelby County, September 12, 1987 (KF). Very late dates: one at a feeder at Table Grove, November 20–27, 1985 (KM-IB&B2:54), and a remarkable winter record of a male at Chicago, December 18, 1982–January 9, 1983 (IV-SR36:10). The Prothonotary Warbler winters from Yucatan south along the coast to northern South America.

WORM-EATING WARBLER

Helmitheros vermivorus

UNCOMMON MIGRANT AND SUMMER
RESIDENT IN SOUTHERN ILLINOIS
DECREASING NORTHWARD

This warbler, always uncommon, has probably suffered population losses because of the destruction of heavily wooded bottomlands. Its winter habitat in central America has also been severely reduced. This subtly beautiful buff and olive bird with four dark stripes on the head inhabits climax woods, especially ravines, in Illinois. In migration it can be found in almost any wooded situation. Its song is like the Chipping Sparrow's but thinner and more insect-like. It usually sings at midheight in the forest and forages on or near the ground.

Some Worm-eating Warblers that occur north of known breeding areas are overmigrants. Early spring arrival dates: Springfield, April 6, 1977 (HDB); Pere Marquette State Park, April 12, 1986 (RA-AB40:480). Average arrival dates: west-central, May 8 (six years); Sangamon County, April 26 (18 years). Spring bird count totals ranged from seven in 1981 to 40 in 1984. Highest count was 12 in Jersey County, May 7, 1983 (VK). Some migration occurs as late as June 1 (1978), when a male was in a city park in Springfield.

Not much is known about the density or the nesting of these warblers in Illinois, although the population in southern Illinois is substantial. They prefer north- and east-facing slopes on which to nest, and they place the nests on the ground. There are four to five white eggs, sometimes with reddish brown speckling. Illinois egg dates are May 7 to June 1 (Graber et al. 1983). Some of these warblers begin moving away from breeding areas as early as July. Whether they are migrants or nonbreeding wanderers is unknown. One at Springfield, July 22, 1981, was showing some molt.

Fall migration goes largely undetected but probably reaches its peak in early September. Late fall dates: Chicago, September 14, 1986 (WM-AB41:98); Henderson County, September 9, 1984 (LMc,MB-IB&B1:21); Kennekuk Cove Park, September 9, 1982 (MC-SR35:15); Peoria County, September 8, 1982 (VH-SR35:15). The latest date for the state by far was November 26, 1984, in Springfield (HDB).

SWAINSON'S WARBLER

Limnothlypis swainsonii

RARE MIGRANT AND SUMMER RESIDENT IN
SOUTHERN ILLINOIS; VERY RARE VAGRANT
ELSEWHERE IN THE STATE

Although the Swainson's Warbler is a nondescript brown and buff, it is so rare almost everywhere that its appearance causes excitement among birdwatchers. It is reclusive, inhabiting dark bottomland forests, especially muddy creeks and swamps where stands of giant cane (*Arundinaria*) are present. Even when its Louisiana Waterthrushlike song can be heard, seeing this warbler can be a real challenge. It stays from fairly close to the ground to midheight in the vegetation. It is at the northern limit of its range in southern Illinois. Swainson's Warblers that occur in north and central Illinois are overmigrants.

The first state record occurred at Mount Carmel in spring 1878, and this Swainson's was seen by Ridgway (1878) and Brewster. Few records were obtained between then and the early 1950s because of the scarcity of observers in southern Illinois. Gross (1908) reported a Swainson's north of Du Quoin on June 17, 1907, and Howell (1910) observed one at Olive Branch, May 15–20, and Reevesville, June 21, 1909. One of the few fall records is of a specimen collected just south of Cairo, September 1, 1938, by Ammann (1939). Brewer (1958) and Hardy (1955) found Swainson's Warblers at Pomona in the summers from 1951 to 1957 and suspected breeding, although they could not find a nest. Then George (1972) secured a female in breeding condition at Pomona on August 8, 1966, and found two nests in cane in 1971.

More recent summer records come from Pomona, Heron Pond, Union County, Alexander County, and Massac County. As many as 12 Swainson's Warblers were located on Cedar Creek, Jackson County, in June 1975 (MSw,MH). The northernmost territorial male was seen at the mouth of the Kaskaskia River in July 1972 (RA).

Recent overmigrant records: Evanston, May 9, 1979 (JW-AB33:778); Olney, May 9–11, 1981 (LH-AB35:831); Chicago, May 4, 1983 (JL-AB37:877); Palos, May 23, 1987 (KH); Fishhook, May 8, 1982 (D.Brown-SR33:15); Urbana, April 21, 1985 (RAp). Spring bird counts showed totals of one to eight in 13 of 15 years.

OVENBIRD

Seiurus aurocapillus

COMMON MIGRANT AND UNCOMMON SUMMER RESIDENT

The Ovenbird looks and acts more like a thrush than a warbler. It stays on or near the ground, walking around in leaf litter and at times cocking its tail up like a small grouse. It has the peculiar habit of walking along tree branches instead of hopping in the usual passerine manner. Its song, a series of *teacher*, is easy to recognize, but its chip note sounds very much like other woodland birds or a chipmunk. Ovenbirds inhabit forests of all kinds but are found much more often in upland forests than the water-thrushes. They are found in residential areas during migration, and these ground birds become prime targets for domestic cats that are allowed to roam. They are also among the birds most frequently killed at television towers while migrating. The American Ornithologists' Union lists all three subspecies of Ovenbirds in Illinois. The form found most regularly is the one that breeds in the state, *S. a. aurocapillus*. The northeastern breeding race, *S. a. furvior*, and the western form, *S. a. cinereus*, have been collected in Cook County (AOU 1957).

Early arrival dates for spring migrants: Long John Slough, April 4, 1969 (PD-IAB151:15); Springfield, April 14, 1986 (HDB). Average arrival dates: Chicago, May 3 (16 years); Urbana, May 2 (20 years). Spring bird count totals ranged from 65 in 1978 to 776 in 1983. The highest count was 312 in Cook County on May 7, 1983. Other counts: 56, Champaign County, May 5, 1984; 42, Lake County, May 7, 1977 (VK). An extraordinary count of 90 was made at Jackson Park, May 13, 1980 (RG,PC). Average spring departure dates: Chicago, May 26 (16 years); west-central, May 18 (10 years). Late departures: Braidwood, June 3, 1985 (JM-IB&B1:89); Jackson Park, June 10, 1982 (HR-SR33:15); Springfield, June 9, 1983 (HDB).

Though Ovenbirds apparently breed statewide, their distribution is spotty, and some areas with seemingly appropriate habitat have none. Northern Illinois has always had the highest summer population. Ovenbirds tend to nest on second-level ridges above the floodplains in bottomland forests (Graber et al. 1983). As their name suggests, they build domed nests that look like Dutch ovens, with a side entrance. The female lays four to six white eggs that are speckled with reddish brown, usually at the larger end. Illinois egg dates are May 16 to July 9. Some summer Ovenbird counts: 32, Pope County, 1986 (DR-AB40:1212); 31, Lake Shelbyville, 1985 (SR-IB&B2:16); 25, Cook County, June 8, 1985 (IB&B2:16); 15, Mississippi Palisades State Park, 1985 (RGu-IB&B2:16); 40 pairs, Starved Rock State Park, 1983 (RGu-SR38:14); 22, Thorn Creek, 1980 (MM-SR26:10).

Early fall arrival dates: Jackson Park, August 7, 1983 (PC-SR39:23); Springfield, August 3, 1986 (HDB). Average arrival dates: Chicago, August 30 (16 years); west-central, September 7 (nine years). High counts for fall: 72, television tower kills, Springfield, October 4, 1983 (ISM); 69, television tower kills, Springfield, September 2, 1981 (ISM). Ovenbirds are somewhat difficult to detect in fall, but they may be found by sitting quietly in a wooded area and giving screech-owl calls to attract them. Average fall departure dates: Chicago, October 3 (16 years); west-central, September 23 (nine years). Occasionally Ovenbirds linger late, and one tried to winter at Springfield, December 19–January 1, 1983 (HDB). Other late dates: Moline, December 16, 1982 (PP-SR36:10); Chicago, November 5, 1986 (JL); Springfield, December 5, 1984 (HDB). Ovenbirds winter from the southernmost portion of the United States south to northern Venezuela.

NORTHERN WATERTHRUSH

Seiurus noveboracensis

COMMON MIGRANT

Of the two waterthrush species, Northerns are the most widespread in Illinois and certainly the most numerous during migrations in central and northern Illinois. Although both Northern and Louisiana Waterthrushes occur early in spring, the Louisianas almost always arrive first. Waterthrush identification can be tricky; Balch (1978) gives details. One point often overlooked is leg color in spring birds; Louisianas have much brighter pinkish legs. Northern Waterthrushes are found around water: puddles in forests, lake edges, rivers, and thickets along streams. Their frequent hard chip note is usually the clue by which these waterthrushes are located as they teeter along the edge of a stream. Their song, given from a perch at midheight in the vegetation, is loud and clear, with a rapid ending. Two subspecies have been recorded in Illinois, the eastern form, *S. n. noveboracensis*, and the less common western form, *S. n. notabilis* (Ford 1956).

Early spring arrivals: Chicago, April 9, 1986 (HR-AB 40:480); Springfield, April 12, 1983 (HDB). Average arrival dates: Chicago, May 2 (16 years); west-central, April 26 (13 years); Urbana, April 30 (20 years). Totals on spring bird counts ranged from 109 in 1978 to 1121 in 1982. The highest count was 438 in Cook County, May 17, 1983. Other high counts: 50, Alexander County, May 7, 1977; 77, Piatt County, May 8, 1976 (VK). Average departure dates: Chicago, May 26 (16 years); Urbana, May 22 (20 years). Late dates of spring departure: Jackson Park, June 9, 1983 (PC-SR37:25); Chicago, June 6, 1982 (SP-SR33:15). Kennicott (1854) listed this waterthrush as known to nest in Cook County, but the closest breeding areas are in central Michigan.

Fewer Northern Waterthrushes are seen in fall, indicating that there may be a deflection eastward at this season. Migrants return early some years: Chicago, July 30, 1982 (PC-AB36:984); Springfield, July 29, 1985 (HDB). Average arrival dates: Chicago, August 12 (16 years); central Illinois, August 17 (18 years). High counts for fall: 28, television tower kills, Springfield, September 3, 1981 (ISM); 27, Jackson Park, September 7, 1983 (PC-SR39:23); 52, television tower kills, Sangamon County, September 2, 1972 (ISM). Average departure dates: Chicago, October 8 (16 years); central Illinois, September 29 (18 years). Ridgway (1889) remarked that "in the extreme southern portion a few pass the winter, especially if the season be mild." A few recent records are of very late Northerns, and perhaps some do attempt to winter: Chicago, January 30, 1977 (GN-AB31:338); Chicago, December 15, 1979 (SM-AB34:279); Snicarte, December 19, 1981 (VK-AB36:301); Chicago, December 28, 1975 (Bohlen 1978). Northern Waterthrushes winter from Mexico and southern Florida south to the Guianas and Peru.

LOUISIANA WATERTHRUSH

Seiurus motacilla

COMMON MIGRANT AND SUMMER RESIDENT IN SOUTHERN ILLINOIS DECREASING NORTHWARD

The Louisiana differs from the Northern Waterthrush in having a larger bill, a whiter and longer superciliary, and an unmarked throat. Its habitat is fast-running streams, creeks, ravines, and swamps. Stealth is often needed to obtain a good view of the Louisiana Waterthrush, since it is even more timid than the Northern. It flies up the creek ahead of the observer, giving its sharp chip note or pausing to sing its three clear whistles followed by twitting notes. It also bobs its tail and moves it from side to side.

Louisiana Waterthrushes are among the first warblers to arrive in spring, usually preceding even Yellow-rumped and Pine Warblers. Early arrival dates: Spring Lake, March 21, 1987 (LA); Sangchris State Park, March 25, 1986 (HDB); Pope County, March 23, 1975 (RGr-AB 29:699). Average arrival dates: west-central, April 30 (nine years); Sangamon County, April 6 (16 years). Totals on spring bird counts ranged from 37 in 1972 to 137 in 1976. High counts were 36, Vermilion County, May 8, 1976; 16, Jersey County, May 6, 1978; 12, Pike County, May 10, 1986; and 11, Jefferson County, May 5, 1979. Some migrate quite late, including a male at Springfield on May 28, 1978 (HDB).

The Louisiana Waterthrush's breeding stronghold is in southern Illinois, but these birds also breed in some areas in central and northern Illinois: 22 pairs, Starved Rock and Matthiessen State Parks, 1983 (RGu-AB37:995); 26 pairs, Lake Shelbyville, 1986 (SR-IB&B3:15); six pairs, Vermilion County, 1984 (SB-IB&B1:19). The nest is usually beside running water in tree roots or a crevice. The female lays four to six whitish eggs that are speckled and spotted with reddish brown. Illinois egg dates are May 9 to June 23 (Graber et al. 1983). Cowbirds have been known to parasitize waterthrush nests.

Fall migration goes almost undetected. These warblers usually leave very early, in July and August, and some reach the tropics by early August. In 18 years of record keeping in Sangamon County I have never seen this waterthrush in fall. Late departure dates: Chicago, October 7, 1984 (JL); Lawrence County, September 17, 1987 (TF); Jackson Park, September 10, 1983 (HR-SR39:23). The Louisiana Waterthrush winters as far south as northern South America.

KENTUCKY WARBLER

Oporornis formosus

FAIRLY COMMON MIGRANT AND SUMMER RESIDENT IN SOUTHERN AND CENTRAL ILLINOIS BUT RARE IN NORTH

This southern warbler is more frequently heard than seen. It inhabits upland or bottomland forests, especially well-shaded ravines. Its song is a series of gallopinglike *ca-che* notes, and it has a chip note that sounds like a chipmunk. Seeking it out in damp, dense woods is thus rather difficult despite its bright yellow plumage. Males and females have quite similar markings except females are duller black on the crown and face.

Spring migrants occasionally arrive early: Chicago, April 4, 1981 (LB-SR29:13); Springfield, April 12, 1974 (HDB); Anna, April 12 (Bent 1953). The average arrival date for central Illinois is April 28 (18 years); for Urbana, May 6 (nine years). The Kentucky Warbler is a good spring find in northern Illinois: Rockford, May 19, 1982 (DW); two, Waukegan, May 8, 1982 (JN-SR33:15). Two males were killed at a television tower east of Springfield on May 8, 1972, and May 14, 1974, attesting to this warbler's status as a night migrant. Only one was found dead at a television tower in fall. Spring bird count totals ranged from 54 in 1973 to 275 in 1986. Highest counts were in southern Illinois: 48, Alexander County, May 7, 1977, and 41, Pope County, May 6, 1978. Twenty-four were counted in Adams County in west central Illinois, May 5, 1979 (VK). Kentucky Warblers were still migrating at Springfield on June 3, 1983; May 27, 1986; and May 23, 1981—although they might have been overmigrants returning south.

The Kentucky Warbler has maintained or slightly increased its population recently. The mean number of these warblers per breeding bird survey route in Illinois for 1965–79 (64 routes) was 0.1 (Robbins et al. 1986). They reach the apex of their breeding range in northeastern Illinois, but on the west side of the state they range well into Wisconsin. Forty-three males were found in Vermilion County in summer 1985 (SB-IB&B2:16); 10 at Kinkaid Lake, June 19, 1983 (JR-SR38:15); and 31 males at Lake Shelbyville (645 acres) in summer 1985 (SR-IB&B2:16). This warbler nests on or near the ground. The female lays three to six whitish eggs with fine reddish brown marks, mostly at the larger end. Egg dates are early May to early July. Nests are fairly heavily parasitized by Brown-headed Cowbirds. In late June and July family groups can be seen. A specimen in juvenile plumage showing molt was taken at Lusk Creek, Pope County, July 28, 1971 (ISM).

Like other southern warblers the Kentucky disappears early in fall—or at least the cessation of song makes it seem to vanish. The average departure date for central Illinois is August 25 (12 years). I know of no maximum counts for fall, but I suspect that a late July or early August attempt in southern Illinois would produce a good count, especially since many fledged young would be present. Late dates of departure: Lincoln Park, September 16, 1947 (Ford 1956); north of Cobden, October 1-6, 1967 (W.George); near Decatur, October 4, 1974 (RP); television tower kill, Springfield, September 29, 1987 (ISM).

Kentucky Warblers spend the winter from central Mexico south to northern Colombia and Venezuela.

CONNECTICUT WARBLER

Oporornis agilis

UNCOMMON MIGRANT

When the foliage is getting thick, the temperature is warming up, and the last wave of spring warblers is passing through, the Connecticut Warbler finally arrives. It usually stays low to the ground in thickets and woodlands. Its song is loud and clear, resembling the song of an Ovenbird or a Common Yellowthroat. The call note is a rather hard chip but less emphatic than the Mourning Warbler's. Once I heard a Connecticut Warbler singing but was unable to locate it. Finally I saw it perched 20 feet overhead and noticed it only because it shook when it sang, especially the tail. The Connecticut is separated from Mourning Warblers by its heavier bill, complete eye ring, long wings, and heavy build. Very few female Connecticut Warblers are seen in spring. Most of these warblers breed in spruce and tamarack bogs in Canada.

April records of this late warbler are suspect, especially in northern and central Illinois. Early spring records: Chicago, May 5, 1986 (EW-IB&B2:96); Jackson Park, May 4, 1981 (RL-SR29:13). Average arrival dates: Chicago, May 21 (15 years); Urbana, May 17 (16 years). High counts for spring: seven, Chicago, May 19, 1987 (MS); four, McDonough County (spring bird count), May 7, 1983. Connecticuts were recorded on spring bird counts 11 of 15 years, with totals ranging from two to 14. Average

departure dates: Chicago, May 27 (15 years); Urbana, May 25 (16 years). Late departure dates: window casualty, Chain O'Lakes State Park, June 5, 1981 (F.Harty-SR29:13); Chicago, June 16, 1982 (IV-SR33:15); Belknap, June 5, 1984 (VK-SR41:25).

Only the Lake Michigan area seems to get any volume of these warblers in fall, since they deflect eastward. Downstate they are difficult to find, although television tower kills show that a few occur. Early fall arrival dates: Chicago, August 14, 1981 (JL); Urbana, August 25, 1985 (RCh-IB&B2:54). Average arrival dates: Chicago, September 1 (12 years); Sangamon County, September 6 (12 years). High counts for fall: 26, Chicago, August 25–September 17, 1980 (JL-AB35:191); 18, Chicago, August 14–September 20, 1981 (JL-AB36:185). Average departure dates: Chicago, September 16 (12 years); Sangamon County, September 20 (eight years). Late departure dates: Chicago, October 14, 1983 (RB-AB38:210); Chicago, November 1, 1967 (RR-IAB145:15); one banded, Springfield, October 6, 1980 (VK-SR27:11). Fall records in southern Illinois are rare; there are three September dates for 1946-47 (Bennett 1952), and Graber et al. (1983) give the dates October 4 and 29. The Connecticut Warbler winters in South America.

MOURNING WARBLER

Oporornis philadelphia

UNCOMMON MIGRANT; OCCASIONAL
SUMMER RESIDENT IN NORTHERN ILLINOIS

Like other *Oporornis* species, the Mourning Warbler stays near the ground in thickets and woodland undergrowth. It is usually located by its *chirry-chorry* song or its rather hard chip note, which is recognizable with practice. Whereas the undertail coverts of the Connecticut Warbler go almost to the end of the tail, they go only halfway in Mourning Warblers. Mourning Warblers have various amounts of eye ring, from none in adult males to complete in some females and immatures. Mournings can be distinguished from the similarly colored Nashville Warbler by their bigger size and larger bills. Mourning and MacGillivray's Warbler hybrids have been reported (Cox 1973; Patti and Myers 1976), but not in Illinois. The MacGillivray's Warbler has established vagrant records in Minnesota and Missouri.

Mourning Warblers arrive rather late in spring. Early dates: Jackson Park, April 29, 1987 (HR); six, Allerton Park, May 5, 1984 (RAp-SR41:25). Average arrival dates: Chicago, May 15 (16 years); Urbana, May 11 (18 years). Maximum counts for spring: 16, Chicago, May 26, 1985 (RB,MBi-IB&B1:89); 11, Lake Shelbyville, May 30, 1985 (SR-IB&B1:89); 16, Jackson Park, May 31, 1981 (RG-SR29:13). Spring bird count totals have varied considerably, probably because of the progression of the season, from one in 1973 to 46 in 1983. High counts: 21 (probably an error), Kane County, May 6, 1972; 13, Kankakee County, May 10, 1980 (VK). Average departure dates: Urbana, May 23 (18 years); Sangamon County, May 31 (16 years). Late spring departures: Union County, June 14, 1986 (DR-IB&B2:96); Jackson Park, June 15, 1983 (PC-SR37:25); Springfield, June 19, 1980 (HDB).

Northern Illinois has a small breeding population. Recent nesting evidence: five pairs nested, Chain O'Lakes State Park, 1982 (SH,JN-AB36:984); female with food, Des Plaines River, June 30, 1962 (CC-AFN16:480). There also are records of singing males: four, Libertyville, 1977 (JSu-AB31:1149); Waukegan, June 26, 1981 (JN-SR30:14). The only recorded nest contents were three eggs found May 31, 1985, near the Des Plaines River (Graber et al. 1983)

In fall most Mourning Warblers do not have the gray hood. They are observed in more open habitats, such as hedgerows and weed patches, as well as in bottomland forests. Fall migration begins in August: one banded, Chicago, August 12, 1983 (SP-SR39:24); Springfield, August 15, 1979 (HDB). Average arrival dates: Chicago, August 25 (10 years); Sangamon County, August 24 (18 years). High counts for fall: 28, Chicago, August 31, 1985 (CM-IB&B2:54); eight, Springfield, September 3, 1981 (HDB). Average departure dates: Chicago, September 11 (10 years); Sangamon County, September 28 (17 years). Late departure dates: Springfield, October 20, 1978 (HDB); one banded, Carbondale, October 10, 1980 (VK); one (possibly a MacGillivray's), Jackson Park, October 22, 1981 (PC,RG). The Mourning Warbler winters from southern Nicaragua south to northern South America.

COMMON YELLOWTHROAT

Geothlypis trichas

COMMON MIGRANT AND SUMMER
RESIDENT; RARE WINTER RESIDENT

Although the Common Yellowthroat is a warbler, its shape, song, and behavior are more wrenlike. It frequents marshy areas, old weedy fields, thickets, forest edges, and forest undergrowth. Like wrens it stays close to the ground and frequently sings its *witchity* song. Its call note is a distinctive *tcheck*, which can be learned and imitated with a little practice. It may give a flight song usually in the evening. Common Yellowthroats eat mostly insects of the orders Lepidoptera, Coleoptera, Diptera, and Hemiptera. The breeding population in Illinois belongs to the *G. t. brachidactylus* race. Other races may occur during migration, including *G. t. campicola*, which resides northwest of Illinois. Although adult males are easily identified by their black masks, in fall some immature females can be very dull, even the throat being more buff than yellow.

Common Yellowthroats seen in March may be wintering birds. Spring migrants usually arrive in late April. Early arrivals: Pomona, April 11, 1986 (KM-IB&B2:96). Average arrival dates: Chicago, May 3 (16 years); Urbana, April 29

(20 years); Sangamon County, April 23 (18 years). Spring bird count totals ranged from 960 in 1973 to 4560 in 1986, with the highest count 582 in Cook County on May 7, 1983 (VK). Other high counts: 47, Vermilion County, May 8, 1982 (SB-SR33:15); 52, Alexander County, May 5, 1984 (TF,KR-SR41:25); 61, Massac County, May 10, 1986 (DR-IB&B2:96); 93, Jackson Park, May 7, 1983 (PC,RL-SR37:25). Spring migration often continues into June. One Common Yellowthroat was reported at the Chicago lakefront, June 10, 1984 (JL), and an adult female hit a building in Springfield, June 2, 1970 (HDB).

Graber and Graber (1963) found that the estimated size of the Common Yellowthroat summer population had changed little between 1909 (414,000) and 1958 (427,000). Most of the population was in southern Illinois, and edge shrub was the favored habitat. These birds also inhabited drainage ditches, hedgerows, orchards, even clover fields. The Common Yellowthroat was found by the Grabers to be the most widespread of the Illinois warblers, both ecologically and geographically. Robbins et al. (1986) found a slight but significant upward trend in this species' numbers across the United States. The mean number per breeding bird survey route in Illinois for 1965–79 was 9.9. High counts for summer: 327, Cook County, June 8, 1985 (IB&B2:16); 49, Lake County, June 16, 1984 (SH-IB&B1:19); 127, Du Page County, June 14–25, 1985 (JM-IB&B2:16); 29, Alexander County, July 7, 1984 (TF,JR-IB&B1:19). Nests are placed fairly low in thick vegetation. A clutch of three to six whitish eggs marked with brown spots or blotches are laid between May 7 and July 9. The Common Yellowthroat's nests are frequently parasitized by Brown-headed Cowbirds. In late August yellowthroats are in molt; once that is completed they are ready to migrate.

Dreuth listed his earliest fall migrant at Chicago on August 21, 1941. A television tower kill occurred in Sangamon County on September 2, 1981. Maximum fall counts: 85 killed at a television tower, Sangamon County, October 4, 1983 (HDB); 16, Jackson Park, October 4, 1983 (PC,HR-SR39:24). Average departure dates: Chicago, October 9 (15 years); west-central, October 20 (six years); Sangamon County, October 30 (17 years). November stragglers are not rare: Jasper County, November 22, 1980 (RB-AB35:191); Danville, November 23, 1982 (ME-SR35:15); Carroll County, November 17, 1981 (PP-SR31:16).

Winter yellowthroats are usually found in cattail marshes and other sheltered areas. More are found in December than at winter's end. Some winter records: three, Chicago, January 7, 1980 (RB,SM-AB34:279); Crab Orchard National Wildlife Refuge, January 19, 1980 (MM-SR24:4); Mark Twain National Wildlife Refuge, January 1, 1983 (SHo-SR36:10). Mlodinow (1984) noted 11 December and January records from the Chicago area after 1970. I recorded a female that stayed all winter in a cattail marsh at Lake Springfield and was last seen March 16, 1983. The Common Yellowthroat winters mainly in the Gulf states south through Middle America to Panama.

HOODED WARBLER

Wilsonia citrina

UNCOMMON MIGRANT AND SUMMER
RESIDENT IN SOUTHERN ILLINOIS
DECREASING NORTHWARD

Occasionally a Hooded Warbler arrives in Illinois so early in spring that very few leaves are on the trees. Then this beautiful warbler is easily seen as it flycatches and flits near the ground, fanning its tail and revealing the white areas. Females are similar to males but usually lack the black hood, although some older females show traces of it. The Hooded Warbler's song is a loud and clear *weesy, weesy, weesy tu,* which sounds much like the Magnolia Warbler's song but louder and more distinct. The chip note is a fairly hard sound, somewhat like a chipmunk's call. Most of the time Hooded Warblers are found in low damp woods, but in migration they appear in almost any wooded area, including city parks.

Some spring Hooded Warblers, especially in northern and central Illinois, may be overmigrants. These warblers occur annually in several Chicago localities. There are a few March dates: Crab Orchard National Wildlife Refuge, March 30, 1950; Chicago, March 27, 1950 (Bent 1953). More recently the earliest dates have been in mid-April. The average arrival date for Sangamon County is April 26 (17 years). Spring bird count totals ranged from five in 1973 and 1974 to 44 in 1979. High counts came from southern and eastern Illinois, with 11 in Iroquois County, May 5, 1979, and 13 in Champaign County, May 5, 1985 (VK). Some recent northern records: Winnebago County, May 26, 1980 (LJ-AB34:784); McHenry County, May 14, 1986 (IB&B2:96); Glen Ellyn, April 28, 1984 (RPi-SR41:25). The average departure date for Sangamon County is May 14 (14 years). Wandering, especially of males, continues into June.

Most nesting occurs in bottomland forests with heavy undergrowth. Graber et al. (1983) also found nesting Hooded Warblers in mature mesic upland oak-hickory woods. The usual nest, placed in a small bush, resembles an Indigo Bunting's nest. The three to five eggs are whitish with reddish brown markings concentrated at the larger end. The few known Illinois egg dates are between May 6 and July 2. Recent areas where territorial males were present: Marshall County, 1982; Shelby County, 1981; Trail of Tears State Park, 1981; Starved Rock State Park, 1983; Charleston, 1983; Ryerson Conservation Area, 1987; Lusk Creek, 1985. Seventeen were counted in Pope County in summer 1986 (DR-AB40:1212).

Fall migration goes almost undetected. The earliest migrants arrive in early August. In Sangamon County I have seen Hooded Warblers in only three of 18 autumns; all appeared between August 6 and 24. Late dates of departure: Champaign, November 20, 1962 (AFN17:37); Chicago, October 14, 1983 (RB-AB38:210); Forest Glen Park, September 13, 1983 (G.Wilford-SR39:24). The Hooded Warbler winters from Mexico south to Panama.

WILSON'S WARBLER

Wilsonia pusilla

FAIRLY COMMON MIGRANT

The Wilson's Warbler is a rather small bright yellow and olive species with a black cap that is lacking in some females and immatures. It has a somewhat flattened bill adapted for flycatching. The song is a chattering trill. Most often this warbler is found at low to medium heights on forest edges in thickets and especially in willows. The race in Illinois is the eastern, *W. p. pusilla.* An apparent hybrid Wilson's X Canada Warbler was seen and heard at Chicago, June 1, 1982 (PC-AB36:860).

Early arrival dates for spring migrants: Urbana, April 14, 1977 (Graber et al. 1983); Union County, April 27, 1984 (TF,KR-SR41:26). Average arrival dates: Chicago, May 11 (15 years); Urbana, May 11 (19 years). High counts for spring: 30, Chicago, May 21, 1987 (CM); 20 (in one yard), Urbana, May 7, 1983 (BCho-SR37:26); 11, Springfield, May 14, 1983 (HDB). Spring bird count totals ranged from four in 1978 to 176 in 1983. The highest count was 34 in Champaign County, May 7, 1983 (VK). Average departure dates: Chicago, May 29 (15 years); Urbana, May 23 (19 years). Late departure dates: Jackson Park, June 21–22, 1981 (PC,HR-SR29:13); Springfield, June 15, 1985 (HDB); Green River Conservation Area, June 1, 1983 (JH-SR37:26).

The earliest fall arrival date is from Urbana, July 26, 1983 (BCho-SR39:24). Most Wilson's Warblers arrive in August: two, Henderson County, August 18, 1985 (MB-IB&B2:54); Springfield, August 11, 1981 (HDB). Average arrival dates: Chicago, August 24 (16 years); Sangamon County, August 24 (17 years). High counts for fall: 12, Chicago, August 28, 1982 (JL); nine, Jackson Park, September 1, 1983 (PC,HR-SR39:24). Average departure dates: Chicago, September 19 (16 years); Sangamon County, October 5 (18 years). Late departure dates: Springfield, October 23, 1987 (HDB); Chicago, October 30, 1976 (Mlodinow 1984); Kankakee River State Park, November 23, 1973 (C.Shaw-AB28:62).

There are three early winter records: Lisle Arboretum, December 1, 1963 (M.Lehmann-IAB129:6); Chicago, December 13–18, 1982 (RR,JG-AB37:308); Union County Conservation Area, December 22, 1982 (HDB). The Wilson's Warbler winters from the southern United States south to Panama.

CANADA WARBLER

Wilsonia canadensis

COMMON MIGRANT; RARE SUMMER
RESIDENT IN NORTHERN ILLINOIS

The Canada is the warbler with the black necklace. This feature is brightest in adult males but only vaguely present in immature females. Otherwise these warblers are gray dorsally and yellow ventrally. Their song suggests an Indigo Bunting trying to sing like a warbler. Canada Warblers stay from low to midheight in the vegetation, usually in bottomland forests. During migration they can be found wherever there are trees; in fall they can be found on forest edges.

Early spring arrival dates: Cook County, April 26, 1976 (Bohlen 1978); Urbana, April 26, 1979 (Graber et al. 1983). Average arrival dates: Chicago, May 14 (15 years); Urbana, May 7 (14 years). High counts for spring: 26, Lake Shelbyville, May 24, 1985 (SR-IB&B1:89); 16, Jackson Park, May 25, 1982 (PC,HR-SR33:15). These warblers arrive fairly late, and spring bird counts occur before their peak numbers. Totals on spring counts ranged from one in 1978 to 50 in 1986, with a high count of 13 in Edgar County, May 7, 1983 (VK). Average departure dates: Chicago, May 29 (15 years); Urbana, May 23 (14 years). Migration continues into June: Chicago, June 12, 1982 (AA-SR33:15); Lake Kinkaid, June 5, 1983 (JR-SR37:26); Urbana, June 19, 1984 (BCho-SR41:26).

The Canada Warbler was regarded by Nelson (1876) as a rare summer resident. Nevertheless, the first certain breeding evidence did not come until June 24, 1980, when a nest with five young was found on the ground in a city park at Joliet (Milosevich and Olson 1981). Other possible breeding evidence: a pair in Lake County, June 12–21, 1983 (SH-SR38:14). Other Canada Warblers have been seen in summer, but most records simply list them as singing males without further comment.

Fall migration begins early: Elmhurst, July 29, 1972 (LB-AB26:866); Urbana, August 4, 1976 (Graber et al. 1983). Average arrival dates: Chicago, August 19 (15 years); central Illinois, August 18 (19 years). High counts for fall: 27 killed at a television tower, Sangamon County, September 3, 1981 (ISM); nine, Jackson Park, August 18, 1980 (RG,PC); six, Chicago, August 27, 1983 (JL). Average departure dates: Chicago, September 11 (15 years); central Illinois, September 24 (18 years). Late departure dates: Springfield, October 15, 1982 (HDB); Forest Glen Park, October 5, 1983 (SB-SR39:24); Carbondale, October 4, 1986 (DR-IB&B3:46). The Canada Warbler winters in South America.

YELLOW-BREASTED CHAT

Icteria virens

COMMON MIGRANT AND SUMMER RESIDENT IN SOUTHERN ILLINOIS DECREASING NORTHWARD

The Yellow-breasted Chat, though a warbler, looks, behaves, and sings more like a thrasher. A skulker, it stays low in thickets and along forest edges and is heard more often than seen. The song, commonly sung at night, is made up of whistles, grunts, and cackles with pauses between phrases. Chats also have a flight song. Southern Illinois is the stronghold of this large warbler in the state. Near the northern edge of its range it becomes much less conspicuous, singing less often. The subspecies found in Illinois is the nominate race.

Early arrival dates for spring: Giant City State Park, April 6, 1986 (DR-AB40:480); Chicago, April 15, 1985 (RB,MBi-IB&B1:89). Average arrival dates: Urbana, May 4 (17 years); Sangamon County, May 5 (19 years). Spring bird count totals ranged from 68 in 1978 to 460 in 1986. All high counts were from southern or central Illinois, with highs of 111 in Vermilion County, May 7, 1983, and 75 in Alexander County, May 7, 1977 (VK). Some migration continues at least until late May; single chats were at Jackson Park on May 26, 1980 (PC), and May 26, 1982 (JL).

Graber et al. (1983) noted some evidence of a decline in this species' numbers. Robbins et al. (1986), using breeding bird survey data for 1965–79, also showed a decline, particularly in Illinois, where the mean number of chats per survey route was 1.9. Summer counts produced 25 at Lake Shelbyville in 1985 and 38 in Vermilion County in 1983. These chats nest in thickets and brushy areas, particularly those with briar patches. The nest is placed at ground level to a few feet above the ground. There are three to five whitish eggs with reddish brown markings. The nests are often parasitized by cowbirds. Illinois egg dates are May 20 to July 21. A female in molt was seen in Sangamon County, July 31, 1981.

Fall migration is difficult to detect; most chats seem to disappear when they quit singing. Fall departure dates: Chicago, September 30, 1983 (JL); Springfield, October 9, 1975 (HDB).

Three winter records are all from 1967–68: Shelbyville Reservoir (Christmas bird count), December 27 (AFN22:274); at a feeder in Urbana, late December (AFN22:275); one found dead at Chautauqua National Wildlife Refuge, January 21 (Graber et al. 1983). The Yellow-breasted Chat winters from the southern United States south to Panama.

HEPATIC TANAGER

Piranga flava

VERY RARE VAGRANT

This unlikely addition to the Illinois fauna occurred near Beverly in southeast Adams County on November 23, 1981. The Hepatic Tanager barely ranges to the southwestern United States in California, Arizona, New Mexico, and western Texas, let alone Illinois, so this record is unique east of the Mississippi River. The tanager was seen in farmyards and weed patches in the Beverly area until November 29. It was observed by 80 to 90 birders and photographed by several. It seemed moderately tame and allowed close approach, but that may have been because it was very actively feeding. It ate apples, frozen grasshoppers, and moths and caught various flying insects. Observers noted the tanager's large dark bill and a few red-orange feathers on its throat. It gave a *chuck* call note similar to the call of a Hermit Thrush. An interesting account of the occurrence is given by Funk (1982).

SUMMER TANAGER

Piranga rubra

COMMON MIGRANT AND SUMMER RESIDENT IN SOUTHERN ILLINOIS DECREASING NORTHWARD

The male Summer Tanager is the only all-red bird in Illinois. Females are greenish yellow, with less contrast between the wings and body than in Scarlet Tanager females. Both sexes of the Summer Tanager give the distinctive pebble note, *pit-a-chuck.* The song is somewhat like that of a robin or an oriole. Summer Tanagers are usually found in upland woods, especially in oaks. Often perched on a dead snag or a leafless branch hidden among the leaves, they are difficult to see until an observer finds the correct angle. These tanagers occasionally occur in pines, especially in the sand areas of Mason County. I have twice noted Summer and Scarlet Tanagers in competition, either in singing or giving chase; both occurrences were in bottomland forest.

When first-nuptial males arrive in spring, some are a combination red and yellow. Early spring arrival dates: Champaign, April 16, 1985 (RAp-AB39:309); Harrisburg, April 19, 1986 (KP-IB&B2:96). Average arrival dates: Urbana, May 1 (13 years); Sangamon County, April 30 (19 years). Spring bird count totals ranged from 40 in 1978 to 179 in 1986. Highest counts were 23, Edgar County, May 8, 1976; 19, Massac County, May 5, 1973; and 19, Alexander County, May 4, 1985. These tanagers may now be increasing northward; whereas Dreuth found only two in Chicago in 16 years (Clark and Nice 1950), more recently there were five birds in Jackson Park in four successive years, 1979–82 (PC,RG). Nelson (1876) knew of only a few records, and Coale (1912) did not list this tanager for Lake County. Many of the Summer Tanagers that have appeared annually in the north of late must be overmigrants. Recent spring records for northern Illinois: Ryerson Conservation Area, May 19, 1985 (DJ,SH-IB&B1:90); Naperville, May 11, 1984 (JWi-SR41:26); Skokie, May 6, 1984 (RE-SR41:26); Chicago, May 2, 1983 (RD-SR37:26).

Summer Tanagers nest in trees, usually on a horizontal limb. The nest is a loose shallow cap in which three to five eggs are laid. The eggs are bluish with brownish markings. Illinois egg dates are at least June 2 to June 21. Nesting occurred in Will County in northeast Illinois in 1985. Up to 22 pairs were found at Lake Shelbyville in 1986 (SR-IB&B3:16). I saw males in molt in Sangamon County on July 24, 1982, and August 6, 1980.

Fall migration is merely an evacuation from the breeding grounds, since very few Summer Tanagers go north of Illinois. They have not, for example, been found as victims of television towers. The high count for fall was 11 at Giant City State Park, September 18, 1982 (JR-SR35:15). The average departure date for central Illinois is September 16 (16 years). Late departure dates: Springfield, October 21, 1982 (HDB); Carbondale, October 11, 1982 (MM-SR35:15); two, Giant City State Park, October 8, 1983 (JR-SR39:24). Summer Tanagers winter from northern Mexico south through Middle America to South America.

SCARLET TANAGER

Piranga olivacea

COMMON MIGRANT AND UNCOMMON SUMMER RESIDENT

The bright red and glossy black plumage of the adult male makes the Scarlet Tanager one of the showiest birds in Illinois. Yet it is difficult to see because it usually stays in the canopy of dimly lit forests. Even when its hoarse robinlike song continues constantly, it can be difficult to locate, partly because the song is somewhat ventriloquial and partly because the tanager sits still. It also has a distinctive chip note, *chip-burr,* which when learned can save much time during census work. Scarlet Tanagers are found in both upland and bottomland forests and occur more often in the forest interiors than do Summer Tanagers. Scarlet Tanagers eat a fairly wide variety of insects, including Hymenoptera, Lepidoptera, and Coleoptera. At times they feed on the ground, taking grasshoppers and locusts. They also eat some fruit, such as mulberry, juneberry, and blackberry. This is the most northern of the 240 species of tanagers, most of which reside only in Central and South America.

Spring migrants usually arrive in late April, but unusually early birds sometimes occur: Joliet, April 16, 1985 (F.White-AB39:309); Urbana, April 13 (Smith 1930). Average spring arrival dates: Chicago, May 10 (16 years); west-central, May 3 (15 years); Sangamon County, April 25 (18 years). Spring bird count totals ranged from 99 in 1973 to 597 in 1980, with the highest count 81 in Cook County on May 10, 1980 (VK). Scarlet Tanagers are typically seen singly or in small loose groups. Spring migration continues into late May or early June.

Robbins et al. (1986) reported an overall increase in the number of Scarlet Tanagers in the eastern United States on breeding bird surveys for 1965–79. The mean number of tanagers per survey route in Illinois was 0.2. In the summer of 1985, 41 males were counted at the Lake Shelbyville (645 acres) study site (SR-IB&B2:16), and 47 pairs were counted at Starved Rock and Matthiessen State Parks in June 1983 (RGu-SR38:15). Other summer counts: 12, Pope County, June 2, 1986 (DR-IB&B3:16); 12, Will County, summer 1984 (JM-IB&B1:19); eight, McHenry County, July 7-8, 1986 (CMi-IB&B3:16); 10, Lake County, July 1,

1982 (SM-SR34:12). Scarlet Tanagers place their thinly woven nests on horizontal branches at fairly high levels, usually in oak or hickory trees. The female lays three to five greenish blue eggs marked with brown, usually more heavily marked at the larger end. Illinois egg dates are May 28 to August 2 (Bent 1958). Scarlet Tanagers nest most commonly in the northern two-thirds of the state. By late August, when winter plumage is acquired, all Scarlet Tanagers are greenish, with an occasional adult male showing a red feather here and there.

Fall migration may begin as early as mid-August, but it is usually obscured by summer residents. I saw a migrant as early as August 12, 1980, at Springfield. Average fall arrival dates: Chicago, September 18 (13 years); west-central, September 16 (seven years). Maximum fall counts: 13, Giant City State Park, September 18, 1982 (JR-SR35:15); six, Urbana, September 22, 1982 (BCho-SR35:15); six, Chicago, September 21, 1985 (AA-IB&B2:55). Scarlet Tanagers are frequently killed at television towers, but not in especially large numbers; 11 were killed in Sanagmon County on September 16–17, 1958 (Parmalee and Parmalee 1959). Average fall departure dates: Chicago, September 28 (13 years); Sangamon County, October 8 (17 years). These tanagers sometimes linger late: two, Decatur, November 5, 1974 (RS); Barrington, October 19, 1968 (RR-AFN23:65); Springfield, October 25, 1979 (HDB).

The Scarlet Tanager winters from Colombia south to eastern Ecuador and Peru to northwestern Bolivia.

WESTERN TANAGER

Piranga ludoviciana

RARE VAGRANT

This western species occurs only as a vagrant in Illinois. It breeds, at the closest point to Illinois, in South Dakota. Male Western Tanagers are unmistakable; females could be confused with female Orchard Orioles except for the bill. Identification may be complicated by the presence of wing bars on some Scarlet Tanagers. There are 11 reports of the Western Tanager from Illinois, some of which have little or no documentation: Rockford, May 5, 1916 (Nature Study Society of Rockford 1917–18); five miles northwest of Carbondale, May 14, 1948 (Smith and Parmalee 1955); perhaps a pair, Cook County, July 7, 1955 (Thompson 1955); male photographed, Crabtree Nature Center, May 8, 1964 (Westcott-photo on file ISM); male near Chesterfield, August 22, 1968 (L.Megginson-AFN23:65); Glenview, May 4, 1969 (Spitzer-IAB151:15); male, Belmont, May 11, 1980 (JL-AB34:785); male, Winnetka, May 2–9, 1981 (LB,JL-SR29:14); female with the preceding male, Winnetka, May 2, 1981 (LB-SR29:14); male, Chicago, May 14, 1981 (JL-AB35:831); Havana, September 9, 1987 (KR). The Western Tanager's habitat is woodlands and parks. It winters from northern Mexico south to Costa Rica.

NORTHERN CARDINAL

Cardinalis cardinalis

COMMON PERMANENT RESIDENT

As the state bird, the Northern Cardinal may well be the best-known species in Illinois. Baseball teams are even named after it. In winter a brilliant red male seen sitting in the sun will brighten any scene. The female's warm browns and dull reds are also pleasing. A few females show some albinism, especially whitish heads; I have seen four or five, and others have been reported. The songs of the cardinal are loud and rich and are especially welcome in January when few other birds are singing. Even the female cardinal sings. These birds are found in woodlands, especially on the edges, and in thickets, brushy and weedy areas, and residential areas and parks. Cardinals eat insects (Coleoptera, Hemiptera, Orthoptera, and Lepidoptera) and grains, wild fruits, and weed seeds. I have seen flocks of cardinals feeding in the tops of tulip trees, which is usually as high as they feed; most often they are in bushes or on the ground. The race found in Illinois and eastern North America is *C. c. cardinalis*. The other races are southern and western. Cardinals are resident as far south as Guatemala and Belize.

The cardinal is essentially a bird of southern affinities that has extended its range northward in Illinois since 1900. Although Kennicott (1854) marked it as known to nest in Cook County, Coale (1912) had heard of one specimen but had not seen it in Lake County. In 1934 the cardinal was considered a rare visitant in the Chicago area twenty-five years earlier but by then more common. Today it is found there in good numbers. The move northward was probably facilitated by bird feeders and urbanization. Graber and Graber (1963) estimated the statewide population in June 1958 at 1,300,000, with only 8 percent in northern Illinois. Even in southern Illinois the June population increased between 1909 (650,000) and 1958 (980,000). Breeding bird survey data for 1965–79 showed a slight decline in the cardinal population in the eastern United States. The mean number of cardinals per survey route in Illinois was 19.3. Kleen noted a 20–40 percent decline in 1979 from a nine-year average, but that was probably a result of winter kills (SR22:7). High summer counts: 557, Cook County, June 8, 1985; 144, Lake Shelbyville, summer 1985 (SR-IB&B2:16). Cardinals build their nests in bushes, usually four or five feet from the ground, sometimes higher. The female lays two to five whitish eggs with fairly heavy streaks and spotting. Cardinals are frequent victims of cowbird parasitism. Egg dates in Illinois are April 15 to August 12; cardinals have several broods each year. I found a dead young cardinal just out of the nest near Springfield as late as September 8, 1982.

Spring bird count totals ranged from 3619 in 1972 to 10,409 in 1984. Most high counts came from central and southern counties, but Cook County had the highest count with 714, May 10, 1986 (VK). Graber and Graber (1963) stated that southern Illinois has the highest number of cardinals, especially in winter—so much so that they thought some migration might take place. The statewide winter population was 2,000,000 in 1957, with 1,700,000 in southern Illinois. These birds utilize more open field habitats in winter. They also tend to gather in flocks; 92 were at one feeding station at Mode, February 12, 1986 (KF-IB&B2:78). Christmas bird counts for 1976–85 showed a definite decline during the late 1970s when severe winters killed many ground-feeding birds. Count totals ranged from 7049 in 1977 to 12,638 in 1983. The highest count was 1529 at Horseshoe Lake, Alexander County, in 1983.

ROSE-BREASTED GROSBEAK

Pheucticus ludovicianus

COMMON MIGRANT; COMMON SUMMER
RESIDENT EXCEPT IN SOUTHERN ILLINOIS

A black and white pattern with a red triangle on the breast makes the male Rose-breasted Grosbeak distinctive and easy to identify in spring. Females look like large, chunky sparrows. In fall, when there are both adults and immatures, several plumages can be recognized. Some may be buffy enough to look vaguely like Black-headed Grosbeaks. Male Rose-breasts have red underwings and females yellowish, but some older females have red under the wings (ISM specimen from Springfield, September 27, 1972). The Rose-breasted Grosbeak's song is similar to the robin's. The call note, a sharp *chink,* is well worth learning, since these grosbeaks sometimes stay high in trees and are difficult to detect unless heard. This woodland species can be found in residential areas and parks. In fall Rose-breasts are found in more open situations, especially giant ragweed patches, scrub, and hedgerows. Their diet includes both insects and fruits. They are noted for eating such pests as cucumber and potato beetles, tent caterpillars, and gypsy moths.

Early spring arrival dates are scanty: Mode, April 19, 1986 (KF-AB40:480). Average arrival dates: Urbana, April 30 (20 years); Chicago, May 7 (16 years); Sangamon County, April 25 (18 years). Spring bird count totals ranged from 416 in 1978 to 3401 in 1983. The highest count was 461 in Cook County, May 7, 1983. Other high counts: 227, Champaign County, May 5, 1984; 255, Will County, May 10, 1980 (VK). One-party high counts in spring are about 20 Rose-breasts. The average departure date for Chicago is May 24 (16 years). Summer residents prevent recognition of late migrants, but a female killed at a building in Springfield on June 3, 1981, was a migrant.

Rose-breasted Grosbeaks nest in central and northern Illinois, and recently began nesting in southern Illinois, apparently expanding their breeding range south. Recent records from the south: Carbondale, July 11, 1981, and Trail of Tears State Forest, June 2, 1981 (MM-SR30:16); Crab Orchard National Wildlife Refuge, June 1–8, 1984 (BCho-IB&B1:19); nest and young, Lawrence County, June

10, 1979 (LH-SR22:7); male, Richland County, June 5, 1979 (LH-SR22:7); pair with young, Clay County, June 26, 1983 (LH-SR38:15). Robbins et al. (1986), using breeding bird survey data for 1965–79, found a significant increase in the number of Rose-breasts in Illinois. The mean number per survey route was 1.2. Rose-breasted Grosbeaks' nests are loose cups usually placed in the fork of a branch in a tree or scrub. The greenish eggs, numbering three or four, are marked with brown, usually more densely toward the larger end. Illinois egg dates are May 17–July 10 (Austin 1968). Cowbirds parasitize this species' nests. Young Rose-breasts just out of the nest look rather comical, with white tufts of feathers sticking out on the head and sides.

Early fall migrants are difficult to distinguish from summer residents, but a male Rose-breasted was killed at a television tower at Springfield on September 3, 1981, and Dreuth noted a Rose-breasted Grosbeak at Chicago on August 6, 1937. Average fall arrival dates: Chicago, August 21 (15 years); west-central, September 10 (11 years). Maximum counts for fall: 70, Urbana, September 20, 1981 (RCh-AB36:185); 30, Chicago, September 21, 1985 (AA-IB&B2:55); 27, Springfield, October 4, 1983 (HDB). Average departure dates: Chicago, September 23 (15 years); Sangamon County, October 12 (18 years). Late departure dates: Palos, November 14, 1983 (PD-SR39:24); Carbondale, October 26, 1983 (B.Coleman-SR39:24).

The few recent winter records occurred mostly at bird feeders: Evanston, December 13–January 6, 1982 (AB36:301); Springfield, February 24–26, 1983 (C.Hanson); Champaign, December 7, 1983 (G.Swenson-AB38:324); Chicago, December 18, 1983 (PD-AB38:324); Rockford, January 1, 1979 (AB33:531). Normally these grosbeaks winter from Mexico south to central Peru.

BLACK-HEADED GROSBEAK

Pheucticus melanocephalus

RARE VAGRANT

This species is the western counterpart of the Rose-breasted Grosbeak. The two species are closely related and tend to hybridize where their ranges overlap on the Great Plains. In fall some Black-headed and Rose-breasted plumages are similar, but close views should separate most birds. Male Black-heads, with their distinctive plumage, are of course much easier to detect than the females. Illinois has nine records for this vagrant: male, Rockford, January 17, 1965 (WSh); male, Carbondale, mid-February–March 23, 1972 (Kleen 1972); male, Springfield, November 24, 1973 (HDB); male, Wilmette, May 21, 1974 (AB28:809); male, Salem, January 29–March 24, 1976 (BP); female, Des Plaines, January 4–8, 1978 (MCh,CC-AB32:360); female, Sterling, early February–April 13, 1980 (BSh-AB34:279); Champaign, May 4, 1982 (V.Loyd-AB36:860); male, Urbana, May 7, 1985 (RCh-AB39:309). Five of these records came in winter (usually Black-heads attending feeders), three in spring (all in May), and one in late fall. These vagrants presumably belonged to the nominate race, but there are no specimens from the state. Several photographs are on file. Black-headed Grosbeaks winter from southern California south to central Mexico.

BLUE GROSBEAK

Guiraca caerulea

UNCOMMON MIGRANT AND LOCAL SUMMER
RESIDENT DECREASING NORTHWARD

This larger-bodied and thicker-billed version of the Indigo Bunting is not common anywhere in Illinois. It seems to come and go at different localities, although it is most numerous in sandy areas in central Illinois and poor soil areas in southern Illinois. In bad light the silhouette of a Blue Grosbeak looks very much like a cowbird, and females are a nondescript brown. The song resembles that of a Purple Finch, and the call note is a sharp *chink*. Blue Grosbeaks inhabit mostly open areas with a few trees, scrubby areas, even cultivated situations. Several times I have seen them perched in cornfields like Indigo Buntings. They often seem to pick a dead portion of a tree from which to sing, but telephone wires and fence posts are also used. Blue Grosbeaks eat insects (grasshoppers, beetles, and caterpillars), grain, weed seeds, and some fruits. The subspecies found in Illinois is the eastern, *G. c. caerulea*.

Blue Grosbeaks arrive fairly late in spring, although there are some early dates: Fort Massac State Park, April 13, 1982 (RBr- SR33:16); an injured immature male, Chicago, April 15, 1969 (H.T.Dean-AFN23:597). The only computed average arrival dates are from central Illinois: May 12 (six years). Spring bird count totals are rather low, which is not surprising; they ranged from three in 1979 to 38 in 1985. The highest count was 18 in Massac County, May 6, 1972—so much higher than any other count as to be suspect, but a wave of these birds may have occurred on this date (VK). Other spring records: one banded, Rockford, May 27, 1984 (LJ-SR41:26); Oquawka, May 16, 1981 (LMc); two, Mercer County, May 16, 1981 (BB-SR29:14); Braidwood, April 28, 1985 (JM-AB39:309); Champaign County, May 7, 1983 (BCho-SR37:26).

Robbins et al. (1986) stated that there had been significant increases in the number of Blue Grosbeaks. The mean number per breeding bird survey route in Illinois for 1965–79 was 0.2. The Blue Grosbeak may be expanding its range northward, but it is still rare in northern Illinois and many parts of central Illinois. Few nests of this species have been discovered in Illinois. Recent nest records: one young, one egg, and two cowbird eggs, Knox County, June 29, 1986 (MB-IB&B3:16); female on nest near Hamilton, August 21, 1984 (ZW-IB&B1:19); nest with three young, Richland County, July 10, 1979 (LH-SR22:7). These grosbeaks nest in bushes, tall weeds, or low trees. There are usually four pale blue eggs.

Fall migration usually passes unnoticed. The average departure date for central Illinois is August 22 (five years). Departure dates for fall: female, Decatur, October 11, 1974 (RS); four, Crab Orchard National Wildlife Refuge, September 24, 1985 (TF-IB&B2:55); two, Giant City State Park, September 18, 1982 (JR-SR35:15). Oddly, there is a winter record of a male attending a feeder at Jacksonville, January 26–February 8, 1980 (S.Tavender,PW-SR24:5). The normal winter range of the Blue Grosbeak is from northern Mexico south to central Panama.

LAZULI BUNTING

Passerina amoena

VERY RARE VAGRANT

This western species breeds as close to Illinois as central North Dakota and northeastern South Dakota. The only substantiated Illinois record is of a male coming to a feeder at Elgin, December 17–21, 1973; it was photographed (RM,LB). Another Lazuli Bunting was reported near Pere Marquette State Park in 1950, but no date or description is available (AFN5:134). In its normal range this bird is found in brushy areas, thickets, chaparral, and open woodland. Its song is similar to an Indigo Bunting's, and hybrids of these two species exist where their ranges overlap. Lazuli Buntings winter in the extreme southwestern United States south to central Mexico.

INDIGO BUNTING

Passerina cyanea

ABUNDANT MIGRANT AND SUMMER
RESIDENT; VERY RARE WINTER RESIDENT

In open country in Illinois, Indigo Buntings are among the most conspicuous birds. On early summer mornings they sit in the roads, occasionally jumping up to give their flight song—which makes it difficult to miss them if they fly in front of a car. Later in the day they sit on wires and other exposed perches and sing. They sing incessantly, but their warbled song is varied and pleasant. They are among the few birds I find singing in the heat of the day in central Illinois as I travel down the corridors of corn. They can be found in extensively cultivated areas away from trees but are more numerous near wooded bottomlands.

The male Indigo Bunting seems to change colors from greenish blue to brilliant blue to black, depending on the light and the bird's feather wear. The first males arriving in spring are usually a mixture of brown and blue but quickly become all blue. When they arrive they are woodland birds, only later going into more open habitats. The brown females arrive later than the males (mid-May), making it seem that the more obvious the sexual dimorphism the greater the tendency for differential migration. On quiet nights Indigo Buntings can be heard migrating, giving a *zip* as they go over. Occasionally they migrate by day; this is especially noticeable along Lake Michigan. Spring migrants begin to arrive in late April, but there are a few earlier dates: Jackson County, April 3, 1986 (DR-AB40:480); Lawrence County, April 16, 1985 (DJo-IB&B1:90). The average spring arrival date for Urbana (Smith 1930) is May 3 (20 years); for Sangamon County, April 26 (18 years); and for Chicago (Dreuth, in Clark and Nice 1950), May 9 (15 years). Spring bird counts show that most maxima are in southern Illinois; totals ranged from 576 in 1978 to 7368 in 1986. The high county was Pope with 392 on May 10, 1980 (VK). Migration usually continues into June, but it is difficult to separate summer residents from migrants.

Graber and Graber (1963) noted that the summer population was densest in southern Illinois: 80 percent south, 15 percent central, and 5 percent north. They found a slight increase in this bunting's numbers in Illinois from 1909 to 1957, when the estimated population reached 1,700,000. This species has benefited from the opening of the forest to edge and shrub habitat. Robbins et al. (1986) found that the Indigo Bunting showed a slight but steady increase in numbers in eastern North America, with significant increases in Illinois. There were 24.4 Indigo Buntings per route in Illinois (64 routes) on breeding bird surveys for 1965–79. Nests are usually placed fairly low in dense vegetation. The three to four eggs are pale bluish and unmarked. Available egg dates are late May to at least mid-August, suggesting either two broods or renesting. The nests are commonly parasitized by Brown-headed Cowbirds. I have seen bobtailed young in Sangamon County as late as September 19 (1979).

Dreuth detected fall migrants at Chicago by August 29 (1942). In other parts of the state these buntings are so ubiquitous that arrivals from farther north go unnoticed. After molting, most Indigo Buntings are brown except the adult males, which retain some blue on the wings, tail, rump, and occasionally other areas. Fall maximum counts: 30, Henderson County, September 14, 1985 (MB); 25, Middlefork Fish and Wildlife Area, September 29, 1985 (SB-IB&B2:55). Indigo Buntings are frequently killed at television towers, including 23 near Springfield on October 14, 1985. Most of these buntings are gone by late October. Departure averages are October 8 (seven years) at Chicago and October 21 (17 years) in central Illinois.

In recent years the Indigo Bunting has been found in Illinois in winter in very small numbers, seemingly associated with milo fields or standing cornfields. There are several November records and these late records: near Pere Marquette State Park, December 30, 1950–January 1, 1951 (Bremser,Link-AFN5:134); banded, Union County Conservation Area, December 31, 1972–January 24, 1973 (Kleen 1973); two, Pike County, December 21, 1974 (RQR, HDB); Sangchris State Park, December 20, 1979 (HDB); Pulaski County, December 28, 1979 (HDB,VK); Springfield, until January 1, 1985 (HDB); Carbondale, through January 4–5, 1985 (M.Warren-AB39:174); four, Union County

Conservation Area, through January 7, 1986 (DR-AB40:288). The bulk of the Indigo Bunting population winters from Central America south as far as northwest Colombia.

PAINTED BUNTING

Passerina ciris

HYPOTHETICAL

Several Illinois reports of the Painted Bunting, a southern and south-central United States species, either are one-observer sightings or lack sufficient details. The first report, by Ridgway (1889), was of a female on the roadside in Wabash County, June 10, 1871. One was reported from Decatur, May 25, 1963 (IAB129:6). A male was seen at a feeder in Chicago, October 1, 1967 (IAB148:19), and a female was seen in Urbana, May 3, 1983 (R.Boehmer). All these reports are probably accurate, but not enough evidence is available to form state records. The Painted Bunting sings somewhat like an Indigo Bunting and prefers approximately the same habitat. In southwestern Missouri this habitat is old fields bordered by woodland. The Painted Bunting breeds as close to Illinois as southern Missouri and southwestern Tennessee, making overmigrants in spring a distinct possibility. Fall birds are more difficult to explain, but some southern birds appear in Illinois almost every fall. There is always the possibility of escaped cage birds, since Painted Buntings are sold on the street in Mexico. They winter from Florida and Mexico south to Panama.

DICKCISSEL

Spiza americana

COMMON MIGRANT AND SUMMER RESIDENT
DECREASING IN NORTHERN ILLINOIS

This finch is marked on the breast like a miniature meadowlark, and like the meadowlark it inhabits open areas. Its incessant song, which gives it the name Dickcissel, is heard all day, even during the hottest part of the summer. Dickcissels sing from telephone wires, fences, small trees, and weeds in rural areas and are numerous on roadsides. Females and immatures look much like female House Sparrows but can usually be distinguished by a bit of yellow on the breast or face, a malar stripe, or some rust color at the shoulder. In flight and when migrating, Dickcissels give a sharp *zrrat* as they go over. Farther south they sometimes migrate in large flocks, but these flocks are usually well dispersed by the time they reach Illinois.

Early arrival dates for spring migrants: one at feeder, Champaign, March 15, 1980 (H.Parker-AB34:785); two, Pere Marquette State Park, April 22, 1972 (HDB). Average arrival dates: Urbana, May 3 (20 years); west-central, May

2 (15 years). High counts: 92, Knox County, May 31, 1987 (MB); 37, Shelby County, May 9, 1987 (KF); 20, Sangamon County, May 19, 1984 (HDB). Spring bird count totals ranged from 228 in 1978 to 2248 in 1986, with all high counts occurring on the western side of the state and mostly in central Illinois: 322, Adams County, May 7, 1977; 296, St. Clair County, May 6, 1972; 169, McDonough County, May 9, 1981 (VK). Some Dickcissels are still migrating in June: Springfield, June 8, 1983 (HDB); Matthiessen State Park, late June 1983 (RGu-SR37:26).

Although Dickcissel numbers vary greatly from year to year, Graber and Graber (1963) showed that the statewide population had increased substantially from 1909 (1,700,000) to 1957 (3,350,000). More recently, however, Robbins et al. (1986) noted a decline. The mean number of Dickcissels on breeding bird survey routes in Illinois was 32.5. Prime summer habitat for Dickcissels is hayfields, grasslands, shrubs, and hedgerows. They build a substantial but bulky and crude nest on the ground or up to six feet high in weeds or small trees. The pale blue eggs number three to five. Illinois egg dates are May 17 to August 5. Counts of summer birds include 41 males, Union County Conservation Area, June 2, 1982 (PK-SR34:12); 44 males, De Witt County, July 4, 1980 (RCh-SR26:11); 115 males, Lawrence County, June 10, 1979 (LH-AB33:869); 100 in one field, Champaign County, 1986 (RCh-AB40:1212); and 62 males, Tazewell County, June 7-9, 1986 (JM-AB40:1212). Gross (1921) gives a detailed account of the Dickcissel in Illinois.

Fall migration seems to come early, but once Dickcissels stop singing they become inconspicuous. In late August and September some can usually be "spished" out of weed patches where they have been skulking. Gross learned that Dickcissels form roosts; he found a roost in a weedy drainage ditch and counted 485 Dickcissels there on August 10 (Austin 1968). The average departure date for Sangamon County is September 28 (18 years). Many stragglers have been recorded in October and some in November.

Dickcissels are rare in winter, but a few survive by attending feeders and staying around weedy feedlots with flocks of House Sparrows. Three Dickcissels were found on Christmas bird counts for 1976-85, one in Alexander County in 1976, one at Champaign in 1984, and one at Beverly in 1982. Other winter records: Macomb, December 11, 1982 (EFr-SR36:10); Harrisburg, January 18, 1986 (KF-IB&B2:78). Most Dickcissels winter from Mexico south to northern South America.

GREEN-TAILED TOWHEE

Pipilo chlorurus

VERY RARE VAGRANT

The Green-tailed Towhee is usually difficult to observe as it skulks in brushy, grassy areas with White-crowned Sparrows and other ground feeders. Of the seven records

of this western towhee in Illinois, four occurred in winter and three in spring. The winter records are of birds seen over a considerable length of time, whereas the spring records are one-day sightings: Bushnell, December 8, 1952–March 9, 1953 (Smith and Parmalee 1955); north of Murphysboro, April 17, 1953 (Brewer-AFN7:276); Lincoln Park, Chicago, June 1, 1954 (Eiseman and McQuate 1954); at feeder, Rockford, January 20–February 9, 1960 (Colehours-AFN 14:313); at feeder, Havana, December 1968 (Bellrose-AFN 23:296); one photographed (on file ISM), Sterling, April 25, 1979 (K.Mount-AB33:778); one mile north of Reynoldsville, January 3-10, 1987 (MD,RP).

The June 1 record shows a phenomenon that is missed by Illinois birders who hang up their binoculars before June: some vagrants arrive after the main migration is essentially over, probably due to the length of time it takes the birds to travel so far. Western birders for some time have taken advantage of this phenomenon to find eastern strays. The most likely place to look for late spring vagrants in Illinois, of course, is along Lake Michigan.

RUFOUS-SIDED TOWHEE

Pipilo erythrophthalmus

COMMON MIGRANT AND SUMMER RESIDENT; FAIRLY COMMON WINTER RESIDENT IN SOUTHERN ILLINOIS DECREASING NORTHWARD

The first warm days of spring, when not much else is happening and the trees are still bare, are a good time to find this bright bird with the rufous, white, and black plumage. Towhees appear on wood edges or in thickets, where they can be seen scratching in the leaves for food. They start singing as soon as they arrive if the weather permits. The song is a plaintive *drink-your-tea*. If "spished," the towhee gives a *chewink* call note or some similar version. The "Spotted" Towhee, *P. e. arcticus,* from the Northwest, occasionally occurs in Illinois: female specimen, Sangamon County, October 19, 1977 (ISM); one photographed, Decatur, May 8, 1983 (G.Doyle); one near Browning, December 15, 1973 (PW-AB28:380). The nominate race breeds in Illinois.

Rufous-sided Towhees do not usually appear in flocks in spring but can be seen with other early migrants, including White-throated Sparrows, Fox Sparrows, and juncos. Early migrants sometimes arrive in late February. Average arrival dates: Chicago, March 29 (16 years); Urbana, March 11 (20 years). Spring bird count totals ranged from 692 in 1972 to 2094 in 1984. High counts: 159, Will County, May 5, 1984; 107, Cook County, May 7, 1983; 97, Vermilion County, May 8, 1982 (VK). The severe winters of the late 1970s brought a slight downward trend in towhee numbers.

Robbins et al. (1986), using breeding bird survey data for 1965-79, found significant decreases in towhee numbers in Illinois. The mean number per survey route was 1.9. Towhees nest in brushy areas or undergrowth along wood edges. The nest, a well-made cup, is usually on the ground or occasionally a few feet off the ground. There are three or four eggs, whitish or bluish white with fine speckles of reddish brown. Illinois egg dates are May 1 to August 11. Cowbirds freqently lay their eggs in towhee nests. Young towhees have the same tail pattern as adults but are brown and streaked. High counts in summer: 109, Lake Shelbyville, 1985 (SR-IB&B2:16); 57, Cook County, June 8, 1985 (IB&B2:16).

It is difficult to tell, but towhees probably start their fall migration in mid-September. They may sometimes be found in goodly numbers in brush along railroad rights-of-way or similar linear habitats. They move with other sparrows, and occasionally the "Spotted" form can be seen. High counts for fall: 19, Chicago, October 9, 1982 (JL); 12, Big River State Forest, October 25, 1986 (MB-IB&B3:47); 18, Crab Orchard National Wildlife Refuge, October 30, 1982 (JR-SR35:15). Average departure dates: Chicago, October 24 (16 years); Sangamon County, November 11 (17 years).

Most of Illinois' winter population is in the south, where these birds are particularly found in giant cane areas. Some years they are very scarce in northern and central Illinois, occurring only at feeders or in very sheltered areas. Christmas bird count totals for 1976–85 ranged from 46 in 1978 to 185 in 1976. All high counts were in the south, with 87 in Alexander County in 1976 the highest. The lowest totals came during the severe winters of the late 1970s and in 1981. By 1985 towhee numbers were almost back to the pre-1977 level.

BACHMAN'S SPARROW

Aimophila aestivalis

VERY RARE MIGRANT AND SUMMER
RESIDENT IN SOUTHERN ILLINOIS;
FORMERLY MORE COMMON AND FOUND
MUCH FARTHER NORTH

This secretive species was first located in Illinois by Ridgway between Mount Carmel and Olney in June 1871. Ridgway, in fact, described a new subspecies from the specimens he and Nelson collected, and he named it *illinoensis*. He saw and heard several Bachman's Sparrows in weedy fields with scattered dead trees. They were singing in the heat of the day, when temperatures were ranging from 90 to 103 degrees in the shade. He also saw them that August. In July and August 1875 Nelson and Jencks collected several specimens near Mount Carmel and Fox Prairie, Richland County (Ridgway 1879). Nelson (1877) described the Bachman's near Mount Carmel:

Those obtained were found about the fences or brush piles in half-cleared fields. They were shy and quite difficult to secure from their habit of diving into the nearest shelter when alarmed, or skulking, wren-like, along the fences, dodging from rail to rail. One was observed singing from a fence stake, but seeing the intruder it stopped abruptly and darted into a patch of weeds.

Ridgway gave an earliest arrival date of April 3, 1910, at Mount Carmel and a late departure of October 28, 1882, near Mount Carmel. Otherwise, not much is found in the literature concerning this species in southern Illinois until the mid-1900s (Cooke 1914). Poling (1890) shot three Bachman's Sparrows and saw two others in an old apple orchard in Adams County in early May 1887. These records, apparently the first from central Illinois, represented a considerable northward expansion of the Bachman's range. In eastern Illinois, Hess (1910) collected a Bachman's Sparrow nest with four eggs on May 31, 1896, near Philo, Champaign County.

Musselman reported a Bachman's Sparrow in Adams County in 1914. Then there seemed to be a surge of records from northeastern Illinois. Eifrig (1915a) saw 10 to 15 in River Forest from May 9 to June 30, 1915, and collected a male with enlarged testes on June 30. A Bachman's Sparrow was seen at River Forest on April 24, 1920. Watson and Huesberg (1916) listed this species as breeding in summer 1916 at La Grange. Sanborn (1922a) collected a specimen in a pine grove at Waukegan, April 22, 1922 (now in the J. S. White collection, CAS). Lewis observed one in Jackson Park, Chicago, in June 1918. Dreuth's study of Lincoln Park, Chicago, produced three reports: April 7, 1932, and March 26 and 27, 1938 (Clark and Nice 1950). Apparently the last reports from the Chicago area were by Lewis: May 9, 1937; April 4, 1939; and April 18, 1941 (Ford 1956). *Birds of Rockford and Vicinity* listed the Bachman's as a summer resident but gave no records (Nature Study Society of Rockford 1917–18).

A male was collected by Quindry on April 2, 1932, near Champaign (Brodkorb 1934). The last record for central Illinois is Musselman's in Adams County in 1952 (no date given). In southern Illinois several pairs were observed near Murphysboro in spring 1948; they left in June and did not reappear (Hardy). A singing male was observed at Cave Hill Ridge in July 1952 (Bennett 1952). Then some Bachman's Sparrows appeared again near Murphysboro on June 7, 1953, and at Crab Orchard National Wildlife Refuge from April 16 through August 16 (Bush). Records since then have been few: Crab Orchard refuge, April 29, 1972 (VK,P.Biggers-AB26:768); Ferne Clyffe State Park, April 29 and June 3, 1972 (RR,JG-AB26:768); Pope County, summer 1974 (Grabers); two, Jackson County, September 7, 1975 (BP). Apparently none have been seen in southern Illinois or elsewhere in the state since 1975. Why is unknown. Their habitat seems to be still intact. Competition from Field Sparrows may be a cause.

The habitat of the Bachman's Sparrow is old fields, especially those on hillsides that have scattered dead trees, grasses (especially broom sedge), and blackberry brambles. It was in such a habitat that Russell and Rosenband showed me a Bachman's Sparrow at Ferne Clyffe State Park in 1972. When they played a tape of the Bachman's song, a bird flew up into the middle of a small tree. It sat there for a while, moving very little, then flew back into the brush. Finding this bird without the aid of a tape or knowledge of its habitat would have been extremely difficult. The Bachman's Sparrow is somewhat crepuscular, even though, as Ridgway indicated, it sometimes sings in the heat of the day. It is said to be one of the best singers. Its song is usually compared to the Field Sparrow's, but it is louder and more varied. It is also compared to the songs of the Hermit Thrush and towhee.

Female Bachman's Sparrows lay three to five white eggs in nests on the ground. Some nests are domed; some are open. Illinois egg dates are May 31 and June 1.

CASSIN'S SPARROW

Aimophila cassinii

VERY RARE VAGRANT

Cassin's Sparrow is a grassland species from the Southwest. It breeds as close to Illinois as western Kansas, and vagrant records have occurred in Nova Scotia, Ontario, New Jersey, Indiana, and Missouri. The only Illinois record was of a Cassin's Sparrow found up against Lake Michigan at Navy Pier, Chicago, May 27–June 6, 1983. This sparrow was banded and photographed; Landing and Patti (1986) give the details. It was probably an overmigrant. Identification in the genus *Aimophila* is difficult, especially separating Cassin's and Botteri's Sparrows. The Cassin's is grayer, and its song is diagnostic. It winters in the southern part of its breeding range.

AMERICAN TREE SPARROW

Spizella arborea

COMMON MIGRANT AND WINTER RESIDENT

One of the last regular passerines to arrive in fall, the American Tree Sparrow waits until most of the leaves have fallen and much of the earth is barren. Even then the majority of these sparrows linger farther north until wintry blasts push them into Illinois. They breed in the Arctic to the limits of tree growth. In Illinois they occur in open areas such as weedy fields, hedgerows, woodland edges, thickets, and grainfields. They tend to take the niche left vacant by Field Sparrows that have migrated farther south. Tree Sparrows travel in small to rather large flocks, sometimes numbering more than 100 individuals. Their call notes, variable jingling sounds, are sweet and pleasant when a large flock is calling. They are easily "spished" into view by an observer; whole flocks will sit up at once on the tops of weeds or the tips of branches. Tree Sparrows are hardy, enduring extreme cold and deep snow and sometimes being forced up to roads, where they feed on waste grain.

Hundreds may be counted as they fly from approaching automobiles—not always successfully. The subspecies occurring in Illinois is *S. a. arborea,* the eastern race. The western race, *S. a. ochracea,* could easily occur, as it has been taken in north-central Iowa.

Early arrivals in fall: Springfield, October 15, 1988 (HDB); Lansing, October 5, 1985 (MDa-IB&B2:55); Chicago, October 1, 1983 (SP-SR39:24). Average arrival dates: Chicago, October 10 (16 years); west-central, October 30 (eight years); Sangamon County, November 4 (18 years). High counts for fall: 125, Vermilion County, November 6, 1983 (SB-SR39:24); 350, Illinois Beach State Park, November 11, 1981 (AA-SR31:17); 60, Springfield, November 26, 1982 (HDB).

Graber and Graber (1963) found that American Tree Sparrow populations were highly variable from one winter to the next. They estimated the January population at 1,600,000 in 1907 and 6,900,000 in 1957. Winter is really the time for this sparrow, and it is one of the mainstays on Christmas bird counts. Totals for 1976–85 ranged from 7613 in 1979 (unusually low because of severe winters) to 42,824 in 1983. The highest count was 9455 at Shelbyville Reservoir in 1969. Other high counts: 601, Vermilion County, January 1, 1985 (IB&B1:70); 1100, Knox County, December 22, 1985 (MB-IB&B2:78); 1660, Lake County, January 1, 1984 (DJ,SM-SR40:13).

These sparrows start moving back north fairly early some years. Maximum counts for spring: 830, Springfield, February 6, 1985 (HDB); 200, Chicago, March 3, 1985 (JL); 105, Vermilion County, March 30, 1983 (SB-SR37:26). Spring bird counts come much past the peak date for these sparrows and always past their average departure dates. Nevertheless, they were recorded on every spring bird count up to 1986. They were reported in small numbers, however, and some may have been misidentified. Totals ranged from one in 1982 to 107 in 1973. All but one high count came from northern Illinois. The highest count was 41 in Bureau County, May 5, 1973 (VK). Average departure dates: Urbana, April 8 (19 years); Chicago, April 26 (16 years); Sangamon County, April 10 (18 years). The latest date is Joliet, May 21, 1985 (JM-AB39:309).

CHIPPING SPARROW

Spizella passerina

COMMON MIGRANT AND SUMMER RESIDENT; RARE WINTER RESIDENT

This sparrow lives close to people and is found in mowed grass, shrubbery, well-spaced trees, and manicured lawns. It is tame, allowing people to approach closely. It also occurs in coniferous areas, orchards, forest edges, thickets, and parks. The song of the Chipping Sparrow is a series of chips that may be confused with similar songs of other birds, including the Pine Warbler, Dark-eyed Junco, and Worm-eating Warbler. The similarity was brought to my attention once when I was in a wooded area and heard a bird giving a series of chipping notes. Based on the habitat, it should have been a Worm-eating Warbler. With diligent maneuvering I finally saw a bird—a Worm-eating Warbler, sure enough—but not 10 feet away, in uncharacteristically thick foliage, sat a Chipping Sparrow—and it was singing! The race found in Illinois is *S. p. passerina*.

Early spring arrival dates: Springfield, March 23, 1987 (HDB); Urbana, March 15, 1986 (P.Malmborg-IB&B2:96); Mason County, March 24, 1984 (LA-SR41:26). Average arrival dates: Chicago, April 20 (16 years); west-central, April 8 (15 years). Spring bird count totals ranged from 620 in 1972 to 2301 in 1986. The highest count was 216 in Cook County, May 7, 1983 (VK). Dreuth gave May 21 (16 years) as the average departure date for Chicago.

An inexplicable decline in the estimated Chipping Sparrow population occurred between 1909 (250,000) and 1958 (fewer than 50,000). Graber and Graber (1963) thought that habitat changes had little to do with this decline, even though Chipping Sparrows lost much of their orchard habitat during this period. Their distribution also changed, from mostly southern Illinois in 1909 to mostly northern Illinois in 1958. Robbins et al. (1986) noted more recent declines in the eastern United States but significant increases in the north-central states—perhaps an indication that at least a slight comeback is under way. The mean number of Chipping Sparrows on breeding bird survey routes in Illinois for 1965–79 was 1.4. Most of these sparrows nest around dwellings in evergreens or other trees from low to moderate heights. Their nests are cuplike, lined with hair, and contain three to four blue eggs with some dark marks at the larger end. Illinois egg dates are April 30 to July 17. Young Chipping Sparrows are streaked ventrally.

Dreuth noted fall migration as early as August 7, 1942. Larger flocks occur in fall than in spring, and these birds seem to have a multitude of plumages—some streaked, some unstreaked, some showing bold ear patches, some not, and some adults showing molt. Their particular gathering places are cemeteries and parks. The average arrival date for Chicago is September 20 (16 years). High counts for fall: 120, Big River State Forest, September 15, 1986 (MB-AB41:98); 34, Springfield, October 10, 1985 (HDB); 25, Chicago, September 18, 1982 (JL). Average departure dates: Chicago, October 22 (16 years); west-central, October 20 (11 years); Sangamon County, November 9 (18 years).

A few Chipping Sparrows are seen in winter, mostly in southern Illinois in mild years or at feeding stations in northern and central Illinois. Many records of supposed winter Chipping Sparrows are obvious misidentifications. Careful observation, detailed notes, and photographs are needed to clarify the status of these sparrows in winter. Some records, such as 20 at Sorento in 1910, are easily dismissed. Christmas bird counts for 1976–85 recorded Chipping Sparrows six years, but at least two are questionable. Winter records include Decatur, December 23, 1979 (HDB,RS); Carbondale, January 7, 1983 (DR-AB37:308);

Georgetown, January 1, 1984 (ME-SR40:13); three at feeders, Lake County, December 23, 1961 (RR-AFN16:211); Pere Marquette State Park, December 26, 1970 (AB25:358); Lisle Arboretum, December 26, 1966 (AFN21:255).

CLAY-COLORED SPARROW

Spizella pallida

OCCASIONAL MIGRANT; VERY RARE SUMMER RESIDENT IN NORTHERN ILLINOIS

Although the Clay-colored Sparrow is a regular migrant it is much sought after in Illinois because it usually passes through the state in a short span of time. Mostly a Great Plains species, it probably enters the state in the west-central section, since there are few spring records from southern Illinois and it is considered a very rare vagrant in Kentucky. In fall the records are more randomly scattered, probably because of the presence of immatures. The Clay-colored Sparrow's insectlike song comprises a weak series of buzzes. Sight identification is relatively simple in spring, but in fall confusion is possible with immature Chipping Sparrows (see Simon 1977). Clay-colored Sparrows occur in weedy and brushy areas, barrens, fencerows, and open coniferous areas. They stay fairly low to the ground and may associate with other *Spizella* species or White-crowned Sparrows.

Early arrival dates for spring: Monticello, April 14, 1977 (RP-AB31:1009); Lisle Arboretum, April 18, 1986 (EW-IB&B2:96); one banded, Harrisburg, April 29, 1984 (DR-SR41:26). Average arrival dates: Chicago, May 6 (14 years); west-central, May 7 (six years); Sangamon County, May 2 (11 years). Maximum counts for spring: four, Chicago, May 7, 1986 (RD-IB&B2:96); five, Chicago, May 16, 1981 (RB,JL-SR29:15). Spring bird count totals are low, from two to 15. The high count was six in Cook County, May 6, 1972. Average departure dates: Chicago, May 21 (14 years); west-central, May 8 (six years). Late departure dates: Jackson Park, May 21, 1980 (PC,RG); Chicago, May 18, 1985 (CM-IB&B1:90).

Nelson (1876) considered this sparrow "a rare summer resident about the borders of prairies" but listed no records. It was not until 1972 that two singing males were found in Lake County in July (GR,LB,CC-AB26:867). Then three territorial males were found at a Christmas tree farm near Rockton, June 27–mid-August 1979 (LJ-SR22:7). Two nests were found in the Rockton area in 1983, and singing males continued to be seen yearly. Up to seven males have been recorded there; Pucelik and Pucelik (1984) give the details. The nests were on the ground and contained three eggs (June 12) and four eggs (June 26). The eggs were blue-green with splotches of brown at the larger end. The outcome of the nestings was not determined. Other summer records: two, Illinois Beach State Park, June 7, 1981 (JN-SR30:17); singing male, southeast Cook County, late June 1980 (SR26:12).

Fewer records have come in fall than in spring, but that could be due to identification problems. Early fall arrival dates: Chicago, September 2, 1980 (PC,RG-AB35:191); Springfield, September 10, 1980 (HDB). Average arrival dates: Chicago, September 18 (six years); Sangamon County, October 2 (six years). Other fall records: three killed at a television tower, Springfield, October 14, 1985 (ISM); Carlyle Lake, October 14, 1986 (LH-AB41:98); four, Evanston, October 4, 1981 (JL). Mid-October appears to be the latest departure time for this sparrow. Dreuth gave October 4 (six years) as the average departure date for Chicago. Clay-colored Sparrows winter from central Texas to southern Mexico.

BREWER'S SPARROW

Spizella breweri

VERY RARE VAGRANT

This sparrow of the interior West breeds from southwestern Yukon south to southern California and east to southwestern Kansas. It winters in the southwestern United States and into Mexico. Accidental records come from Massachusetts, Minnesota, and Louisiana. The first of two Illinois records was of a male Brewer's Sparrow at Jackson Park, May 26, 1982. This bird was viewed as close as 10 feet and photographed. It was also heard singing—perhaps the crucial factor in its identification, since Brewer's and Clay-colored Sparrows look much alike. The song was described by Ron Goetz as a "highly variable series of trills at different speeds and different pitches within a given song." Several other knowledgeable birders also saw this sparrow, including Paul Clyne, Harriet Rylaarsdam, and James Landing. The second record was a male specimen, a building casualty at Chicago, May 29, 1986 (Willard). Brewer's Sparrows stay low to the ground in rather open areas of brush.

FIELD SPARROW

Spizella pusilla

COMMON MIGRANT AND SUMMER RESIDENT; COMMON WINTER RESIDENT DECREASING NORTHWARD

This is one of the plainest of sparrows, but what it does not have in dress it makes up for in song. It occasionally sings all day, even in the heat of the day, and at night or in midwinter on warmer days. Its plaintive trill is one of the most melancholy sounds in nature. Field Sparrows inhabit weedy and brushy areas, woodland edges, orchards, pastures, hedgerows, and roadside thickets. These birds are seen singly, in small flocks, or occasionally in winter in larger flocks. They stay close to the ground in fairly thick

cover except when singing and are fairly easily "spished up." The eastern race, *S. p. pusilla*, nests in Illinois, although *S. p. arenacea*, the western race, could occur in winter, as it has been recorded in Kentucky (Mengel 1965).

Spring migrants are sometimes found as early as late February, but most arrive in March. Average arrival dates: Chicago, March 27 (16 years); Urbana, March 22 (20 years); west-central, March 18 (14 years); Sangamon County, March 12 (17 years). Spring bird counts show low numbers for 1977–80, suggesting mortality due to severe winters. Count totals ranged from 1221 in 1972 to 3850 in 1983. The highest count was 761 in Jasper County in 1983. Other high counts: 225, Will County, May 4, 1974; 196, Perry County, May 10, 1986 (VK). Dreuth recorded the average of late migrants at Chicago to be May 23 (16 years).

In summer Field Sparrows are most numerous in southern Illinois. Graber and Graber (1963) estimated the statewide June population in 1909 at 2,100,000 (75 percent in southern Illinois); it was 1,400,000 in 1957 (62 percent in southern Illinois). Robbins et al. (1986), using breeding bird survey data for 1965–79, found highly significant decreases in numbers of Field Sparrows in eastern and central United States. They felt that even though there had been recent winter kills the main cause of the decline was intensive use of land, with less acreage reverting to fields suitable for these sparrows' habitat. The mean number of Field Sparrows per breeding bird survey route in Illinois was 11.4. On a nine-year average Field Sparrows showed an 80 percent decline in extreme southern Illinois (VK-SR22:7). These sparrows nest on or near the ground and make a cuplike nest. The female lays three to five whitish or pale bluish eggs finely speckled with reddish brown. More than one brood is produced each year. Illinois egg dates are April 20 to August 20. Two young were being fed by adults as late as September 11, 1949 (Ford 1956). The young, unlike adults, are streaked on the breast, although finely.

The commencement of fall migration is obscured by summer birds, but there is usually a noticeable buildup of numbers. Dreuth at Chicago noted migration as early as August 3, 1942, and found that the average arrival date was September 22 (16 years). High counts for fall: 50, Big River State Forest, September 29, 1985 (MB-IB&B2:55); 26, Springfield, October 20, 1985 (HDB); 60, Crab Orchard National Wildlife Refuge, October 24, 1982 (JR-SR35:16). Average departure dates: Chicago, October 28 (16 years); west-central, November 7 (10 years); Sangamon County, November 23 (18 years).

Graber and Graber (1963) noted that most of the winter population was in southern Illinois. The estimated January population was 85,000 in 1907 and 190,000 in 1957. They also found that the population in February 1958 was only 10,000, indicating that Field Sparrows drift farther south in late winter. Christmas bird counts for 1976–85 show the effects of severe winters. Totals ranged from 168 in 1979 to 721 in 1982. The highest count was 282 at Horseshoe Lake in 1983, and all high counts were from southern Illinois. Some northern winter records: Rockford, December

18, 1983 (LJ-SR39:24); two, Chicago, January 10, 1984 (SR40:13).

VESPER SPARROW

Pooecetes gramineus

COMMON MIGRANT, COMMON SUMMER RESIDENT DECREASING SOUTHWARD, AND RARE WINTER RESIDENT

Vesper Sparrows begin to return in March, but the usual arrival date is toward the end of the month, with larger numbers occurring in April. The fields are still barren at this time, so these sparrows stay near grassy ditch edges and fencerows, occasionally singing from a clod of dirt or a small tree. The song is similar to the Song Sparrow's, and as its name suggests, the Vesper sings late in the day. Early spring arrival dates: Chicago, April 1, 1941; two, Chicago, March 22, 1984 (JL); southern Illinois, March 14 (George 1968). The average arrival date for Chicago (14 years) was April 7 (Clark and Nice 1950) and for Sangamon County (15 years), March 28. Maximum counts are difficult to obtain for these sparrows. Spring bird counts show that the more northern counties have the highest counts: 41, De Kalb County, May 4, 1974; 28, Will County, May 9, 1981 (VK). Occasionally conditions are right to produce much larger counts. In Sangamon County on April 9, 1982, I counted 140 Vesper Sparrows in one day. A late snowstorm had brought these birds up near the roads, where they could be seen; there must also have been a downed wave and some probable reverse migration.

During the breeding season Vesper Sparrows are found at the edge of shrubs and in clover fields, pastures, and other open habitats. They reach the southern edge of their breeding range in southern Illinois. Graber and Graber (1963) stated that about 90 percent of the breeding population was in northern Illinois in 1957. They also showed that this species prefers red clover, the planting of which correlated with the birds' spread south between 1909 (none) and 1957 (about 10,000 birds). The breeding population, which should have increased if anything since these sparrows prefer open habitat, has remained fairly constant over the years; however, in the past few years even this habitat has begun to disappear. The mean number of Vesper Sparrows per breeding bird survey route in Illinois (64 routes) was 3.8 (Robbins et al. 1986). This species nests on the ground, lining a hollow with grasses. Four to five eggs are laid. Available egg dates in Illinois are May 9 to August 4. I have seen Vesper Sparrows in heavy molt in early September in Sangamon County.

Maximum counts and departure dates for fall are less obvious. These sparrows begin to return about the third week in September: September 18, 1936, at Chicago (Clark and Nice 1950) and September 21, 1979, in Sangamon County (HDB). They are usually seen in ones and twos, rarely in any sizable flocks. The maximum fall count was

10 in Sangamon County, September 28, 1984 (HDB). Departure dates are somewhat obscured by wintering birds, but October 28 (13 years) was the average departure date at Chicago and November 18, 1940, was the latest (Clark and Nice 1950). In Sangamon County the average departure date is November 3 (17 years), with November 22, 1977, the latest (HDB). George (1968) listed December 21 as the latest date for southern Illinois.

Vesper Sparrows usually migrate for the winter to the Gulf Coast and Mexico, but a few may stay, especially in southern Illinois. Christmas bird counts are the main source of Vesper Sparrow records in winter, and because these counts are conducted early in winter many of the Vesper Sparrows recorded on them may be very late fall migrants. Winter records: Winnebago County, January 29, 1972 (WSh-AB26:613); three wintered in Lawrence County, 1978–79 (LH-AB33:287); three, McLean County, February 3, 1980 (DBi-AB34:279); Plato Center, winter 1981–82 (JM-AB36:301).

LARK SPARROW

Chondestes grammacus

OCCASIONAL MIGRANT; LOCALLY COMMON SUMMER RESIDENT IN SAND AREAS; RARE SUMMER RESIDENT ELSEWHERE IN THE STATE

The bold head pattern, comparatively large size, and towheelike tail give the Lark Sparrow a distinctive appearance. These sparrows are tied to sand and poor soil areas in Illinois. They stay near the ground, perching on fences or in small trees. They are found higher only when singing. The song is usually given from telephone wires or from near the tops of trees, where they usually choose dead branches. It is a broken song with clear notes and trills punctuated by buzzes. The nominate form is found in Illinois.

Spring migration goes undetected in many areas. Early arrivals: Urbana, March 27 (Smith 1930); Springfield, April 11, 1974 (HDB); west-central, April 10 (Craig and Franks 1987). Average arrival dates: Urbana, April 22 (17 years); west-central, April 24 (14 years). High counts: 20, Henderson County, May 12, 1985 (MB-IB&B1:90); 17, Mercer County, May 4, 1985 (PP-IB&B1:90). Spring bird count totals ranged from 34 in 1975 to 158 in 1973. All high counts were in Mason County, with 107 on May 5, 1973, the highest (VK). A male was still wandering or migrating in Sangamon County on June 11, 1987.

Ridgway (1878) found the Lark Sparrow to be a common summer resident at Mount Carmel. This finding was backed up by the Grabers' study (1963), in which they showed that the distribution of the majority of the population had shifted from southern to central Illinois. The population also declined, from an estimated 500,000 in June 1909 (370,000 in southern Illinois) to 80,000 in 1957. This decline is difficult to explain, since soil type and not habitat is the indicator of the presence of this sparrow. More recently Robbins et al. (1986), using breeding bird survey data for 1965–79, noted decreases in Lark Sparrow populations in the United States and particularly in Illinois. The mean number of Lark Sparrows per survey route in Illinois was 0.5. These sparrows nest on the ground in open areas or areas of low brush or scattered trees. The three to five eggs are white with a few black or purplish markings. Illinois egg dates are May 5 to July 4 (Austin 1968). Young are seen by late May. Johnson (1968) recorded 12 pairs on 50 acres of sand prairie south of Havana. Nesting records from areas other than Mason and Henderson Counties: nest, Richland County, 1980; pair with young, Winnebago County, 1984; four, Williamson County, 1984; four young, Shelby County, 1984; adults and young, Charleston, 1987.

Fall migration goes largely undetected, even though some Lark Sparrows nest north of Illinois. High counts in fall: 15, Sand Ridge State Forest, August 12, 1984 (SB,RCh-IB&B1:21); 10, Havana, August 27, 1987 (KR). Late departure dates: Chicago, October 8, 1979 (RE-AB34:169); two, Horseshoe Lake, October 21, 1981 (BR-AB36:185); two, Cook County, October 11, 1985 (EL-IB&B2:55); Vermilion County, October 7, 1983 (JSm-SR39:24); Lawrence County, September 27, 1980 (LH-SR27:12). Some of the later birds should be checked for the western subspecies. The few winter records are inadequately documented. The Lark Sparrow winters from the southern United States south to southern Mexico.

BLACK-THROATED SPARROW

Amphispiza bilineata

VERY RARE VAGRANT

This distinctive little sparrow has a black throat and two white lines on the head in the superciliary and malar regions. As its other name, Desert Sparrow, indicates, it comes from the arid Southwest, where it inhabits desert scrub, thorn bush, mesquite, and juniper. There are six records from Illinois: immature, Lincoln Park, Chicago, September 11–13, 1948 (CC,T.Nork,A.Baldwin-AFN3:19); adult near Rockton, May 3–4, 1959 (Morse 1960); one with few details, Chicago, spring 1961 (Montague-AFN15:416); adult, Glencoe, January 6–early March 1980 (RB-AB34:279); one at Rockford, February 7–24, 1980 (KBr-AB34:279); one at Chicago, winter through April 16, 1980 (PS). Because these sparrows are partially migratory, some vagrants may arrive by overmigration. Some of the Illinois Black-throated Sparrows were at feeders, and one was with Field Sparrows. Several other eastern records come from Minnesota, Wisconsin, Ohio, and even the East Coast.

LARK BUNTING

Calamospiza melanocorys

RARE VAGRANT

This unique bird reaches its greatest abundance on the Great Plains. The black and white males are very distinctive. Females look like Vesper Sparrows but with a bolder pattern and much white in the wing. Lark Buntings are found in open country, sitting on the ground, on fences, and in low brush. They have been recorded casually in most eastern states. Illinois had at least 17 records up to 1987, more in spring (11) than any other season. The earliest spring record is March 17 (1974, Olympia Fields, AD), the latest May 17 (1988, Chicago, RB,JL); most are for May. Recent spring records: Lake County, May 8–9, 1981 (K.Langenburg-AB35:831); Urbana, May 4, 1982 (RCh-AB36:860). Fall records: Lake Calumet, September 4, 1949 (Smith and Parmalee 1955); Evanston, September 27, 1969 (IAB153:16). There are four winter records: Flora, February 27, 1971 (VK-AB25:587); Springfield, December 4, 1977 (HDB); Lawrence County, December 9, 1979 (LH,DJo-AB34:279); Shelby County, February 9–16, 1981 (KF-AB35:306). The December birds may be late fall migrants. Most Lark Buntings winter in the Southwest.

SAVANNAH SPARROW

Passerculus sandwichensis

COMMON MIGRANT; FAIRLY COMMON SUMMER RESIDENT IN NORTHERN ILLINOIS DECREASING SOUTHWARD; UNCOMMON WINTER RESIDENT IN SOUTHERN ILLINOIS DECREASING NORTHWARD

The Savannah Sparrow looks much like the Song Sparrow but is more slender, has a light median crown stripe, brighter colored legs, and usually a yellowish eyebrow. The Savannah Sparrow inhabits fairly open areas, including grasslands, agricultural fields of all types, marshy places, and weed patches. The song is a buzzing trill, the call note a *tsip*. These sparrows play hide and seek with an observer, often running from one grass clump to another. When they fly, they usually go farther and in a more direct flight than other grassland sparrows. They are also more inclined to perch at the top of a low bush or on a fence. The Savannah Sparrow has 17 races in North America. The breeding race in Illinois is *P. s. oblitus*. Two or three other races are present during migration, probably *P. s. nevadensis* and *P. s. savanna* and possibly *P. s. labradorius*. A thorough study of the available Illinois specimens needs to be done.

Early spring migrants probably arrive in late February or March, but the presence of winter birds makes it difficult to assess. Average arrival dates: Chicago, April 8 (16 years); Urbana, March 24 (13 years). High counts for spring: 117,

Sangamon County, April 9, 1982 (HDB); 25, Washington County, April 5, 1981 (M.Kemper-SR29:14); 23, Urbana, May 21, 1981 (RCh-SR29:14). Spring bird count totals ranged from 147 in 1973 to 737 in 1976, with high counts of 134 in Cook County, May 9, 1981, and 126 in St. Clair County, May 8, 1982 (VK). Average departure dates: Chicago, May 25 (16 years); Urbana, May 10 (13 years). Dreuth had a migrant still at Chicago on June 2, 1940 (Clark and Nice 1950).

Most of the breeding population in Illinois is in the north, although the central part of the state, especially in the east, has scattered populations. This species is one of the few to use highway cloverleaf medians as nesting areas. Graber and Graber (1963) thought that the Savannah Sparrow population had increased, from an estimated 160,000 in 1909 to 390,000 in 1957. Robbins et al. (1986) found that the Savannah Sparrow population in the United States was stable between 1965 and 1979, with a mean of 1.6 birds per breeding bird survey route in Illinois. These sparrows nest on the ground in a small hollow dug in the soil. The nest is built of grasses and concealed by overhanging vegetation. The female lays four to five heavily mottled brownish eggs. Illinois egg dates are May 6 to June 20 (Austin 1968). Summer records: small numbers, Wabash County, 1983; 241, Du Page County, 1985; 171, Cook County, 1980; three, Sangamon County, 1981; 40 pairs, Matthiessen State Park, 1983; 20 pairs, Champaign County, 1981.

Fall migrants have been detected by August: Wabash County, August 31, 1980 (LH-SR27:12); Springfield, August 5, 1978 (HDB). Average arrival dates: Chicago, September 7 (16 years); Sangamon County, September 1 (19 years). High counts for fall: 50, Vermilion County, September 13, 1986 (SB-IB&B3:47); 40, Monmouth, October 16, 1983 (MB-SR39:25). Average departure dates: Chicago, October 24 (16 years); Sangamon County, November 15 (18 years). Some Savannahs typically linger until early December.

Most of the state's winter population is in the south. Savannah Sparrows were recorded on all 10 Christmas bird counts from 1976 through 1985 but in low numbers most years. Totals ranged from six in 1977 to 118 in 1982. The highest counts were 67 in Alexander County in 1984 and 55 at Pere Marquette State Park in 1982. Other winter records: Waukegan, January 1, 1985 (RB-IB&B1:70); 22, Horseshoe Lake, January 9, 1983 (RG); Macomb, January 31–February 22, 1982 (EFr-SR32:8). Savannah Sparrows winter as far south as Guatemala, Belize, and northern Honduras.

BAIRD'S SPARROW

Ammodramus bairdii

HYPOTHETICAL

This rare sparrow of the Great Plains breeds in Canada and the northern United States and winters in the Southwest and northern Mexico. There are four sight reports of the Baird's Sparrow in Illinois: Evanston, April 4–12, 1968, and October 15, 1975; McHenry County, April 29, 1981; Whiteside County, November 5, 1983. Some of these birds are well described but by only one observer, and none of the reports meets the criteria for an acceptable state record. Confusion of Baird's Sparrows with immature Grasshopper Sparrows and other grassland species is easily possible. There are records for Wisconsin and Missouri. The Baird's Sparrow is found in weedy and grassy fields.

GRASSHOPPER SPARROW

Ammodramus savannarum

COMMON MIGRANT AND SUMMER RESIDENT

If an observer sees a flatheaded, short-tailed, buffy, plain-breasted sparrow sitting on a fence, wire, or weed in summer, it is surely a Grasshopper Sparrow. Closer views will show a yellow eyebrow and yellow at the bend of the wing. This sparrow's song is a long insectlike buzz. Grasshopper Sparrows inhabit open grasslands and have adapted to airports and open golf courses. In fall they may be seen in taller weedy fields and occasionally along hedgerows. Usually only singing males are easily seen, and in late summer and fall, especially when molting, these sparrows can be very difficult to see. They fly with a buzzing flight and appear grayer backed in fall than other grass sparrows. The breeding form in Illinois is *A. s. pratensis*, but *A. s. perpallidus*, the western form, may occur in migration.

Early arrival dates for spring: Sangchris State Park, April 1, 1977 (HDB); Vermilion County, April 4, 1986 (SB-AB40:481); Chicago, March 22, 1938 (Clark and Nice 1950). Average arrival dates: Chicago, April 13 (16 years); Urbana, April 14 (13 years). Spring bird count totals ranged from 159 in 1973 to 595 in 1986, with high counts of 96 in Mason County, May 10, 1986; 62 in Macon County, May 7, 1983; and 36 in Pope County, May 10, 1980 (VK). Dreuth's average departure date at Chicago was May 20 (16 years) and his latest date was May 31, 1938.

Graber and Graber (1963) found the highest numbers in summer in central Illinois and the lowest in the southern part of the state. They noted that the estimated statewide population was 500,000 in 1909 and 850,000 in 1958. More recently Robbins et al. (1986) noted significant declines throughout the species' range. In Illinois the mean number of Grasshopper Sparrows per breeding bird survey route was 4.4. These sparrows nest on the ground, making a domelike nest that is hidden from above. There are four to five white eggs with reddish brown blotches and spots. Illinois egg dates are May 18–July 10 (Austin 1968). Recent counts in summer: 41 pairs, Matthiessen State Park, 1983; 50, Vermilion County, 1985; 14 pairs, Goose Lake Prairie, 1982; 16 pairs, Des Plaines Conservation Area, 1982. Immature Grasshopper Sparrows have streaked breasts and can be confused with Henslow's Sparrows.

Fall migrants are difficult to find and there are no high counts. Average departure dates for fall are also difficult to determine, with dates scattered from late August to early November. The average for central Illinois is October 6 (18 years). Late dates of departure: Quincy, November 1, 1963 (TEM); three, Tazewell County, October 11, 1987 (KR,LA); three, Rochester, November 7, 1977 (HDB).

Winter records are very unusual: one banded, Carbondale, January 10, 1972 (VK,DH-AB26:613); male collected, Champaign, January 9, 1932 (Brodkorb 1934). Grasshopper Sparrows winter from the southern United States south to north central Costa Rica.

HENSLOW'S SPARROW

Ammodramus henslowii

OCCASIONAL MIGRANT AND VERY LOCAL SUMMER RESIDENT

Of all the grass sparrows, this one is the most elusive. It is difficult to flush, and it runs and hides when possible. When flushed, it flies with a wispy flight a short distance and drops back into the grass. I once flushed one and knew exactly where it landed; but only after a considerable search did I find it, hiding in a depression near a road. Once it saw me it came into the open and stood there, not moving, for about a minute. Sometimes, when flushed into hedgerows or fence lines, Henslow's Sparrows will perch for extended periods, allowing good views. The song is a hiccup, an insectlike *tsi-lick,* which is given from a weed just above the surrounding vegetation. There is some singing at night. The Henslow's Sparrow is unique in having an olive head and reddish brown body. It is flatheaded and short-tailed like other grass sparrows. Immatures are clear breasted; adults have streaks on the breast—just the opposite of the Grasshoppper Sparrow's plumages. The race in Illinois is the western, *A. h. henslowii.*

Early spring arrival dates: specimen, Du Page County, March 28, 1910 (Eifrig 1911); Evanston, April 2, 1967 (Mlodinow 1984). Average arrival dates: Chicago, April 18 (14 years); Urbana, April 14 (six years). In recent years most of these sparrows have been seen in April and May. The high count is 18 at Goose Lake Prairie State Park, May 11, 1985 (BGl-IB&B1:90). Henslow's Sparrows were recorded on 14 of 15 spring bird counts, with totals ranging from one in 1975 to 27 in 1978. Most high counts were in northern Illinois; the highest was 17 in Lake County, May 6, 1978. Dreuth's average departure date for Chicago was May 5 (14 years) and the latest date was May 21, 1943 (Clark and Nice 1950).

The nesting habitat for this sparrow was originally the prairie, which now exists only as a remnant. It has adapted to nesting in unmowed timothy-clover hayfields, although the population is probably much lower now than before the prairie was destroyed. It is such a local breeder that it is on the Illinois endangered species list. Henslow's Spar-

rows nest in loose colonies. The nest, a well-formed cup, is on or near the ground, usually at the base of a clump of grass. There are three to five light-colored eggs with fairly heavy reddish brown markings. Illinois egg dates are May 20 to July 4 (Austin 1968). Some recent breeding areas: 10-15 pairs, Adams County, 1983; 15 pairs, Goose Lake Prairie State Park, 1982; four, Johnson County, 1981; seven males, Kennekuk Cove Park, 1984. Some of these sparrows are still singing on territory in late August.

Fall migration probably starts in September, but most records are for October. These migrants are found in brushy areas and along hedgerows as well as in grassy places. Early arrivals: Chicago, September 5, 1985 (FS-IB&B2:55); Urbana, September 13, 1981 (RCh-SR31:17). Late departure dates: Horseshoe Lake, November 2, 1982 (RG-AB37:189); Clinton Lake, October 27, 1985 (RP,MD-AB40:123); Rend Lake, October 21, 1984 (LH-IB&B1:21); specimen (CAS#18299), Beach, November 12, 1927 (Stevenson); Montrose, November 21, 1976 (Mlodinow 1984).

Cooke (1888) and Ridgway considered this sparrow a winter resident in southern Illinois, but if it was there is little indication of it now. One was reported on the Christmas bird count in Mercer County, January 3, 1965 (AFN19:238). Most Henslow's Sparrows winter in the southern states.

LE CONTE'S SPARROW

Ammodramus leconteii

UNCOMMON MIGRANT AND RARE WINTER RESIDENT; FORMERLY A VERY RARE SUMMER RESIDENT

This secretive sparrow inhabits marshy grassland. Its numbers seem to fluctuate greatly from year to year. Buffy and short-tailed, the Le Conte's Sparrow is typically encountered when an observer is walking across a wet grassy field. A small bird flies up at the observer's feet, flies a short distance, and drops back into the grass, then begins running. The observer who wants a good view has to run to the spot to try to locate it. This can be very frustrating, and satisfactory looks at this sparrow are difficult to get. Once in a while Le Conte's Sparrows can be "spished up"; occasionally, after being pursued for some time and forced up against a fence or hedgerow, they will sit in the open. They can also be found in clover fields and tall-grass fields. Their song is a two-part buzz, their chip note a *tap,* given frequently.

Spring migrants usually arrive in March. Early spring arrival dates: Crab Orchard National Wildlife Refuge, March 15, 1986 (DR-IB&B2:96); television tower kill, Sangamon County, March 20, 1982 (ISM); Jasper County, March 17, 1985 (DJo-IB&B1:90). Average spring arrival dates: Chicago, April 18 (nine years); Sangamon County, March 22 (18 years). Spring bird counts are taken too late for peak counts, but other high counts are 24, Mark Twain

National Wildlife Refuge, March 19, 1983 (RG,JEa-AB37:878), and seven, New Athens, March 13, 1983 (TF-SR37:26). Most of these elusive sparrows have gone farther north by the end of April. Average spring departure dates: Chicago, April 24 (nine years); Sangamon County, April 20 (18 years). Late departure dates: Chicago, May 29, 1982 (JL-SR33:16); Peoria County, May 20, 1984 (LA-SR41:27); Jackson Park, May 22, 1983 (HR-SR37:27).

The few nesting records—mostly old ones—are from northeastern Illinois. The nearest nesting area is in northeastern Wisconsin. If nesting habitat for this species ever existed in Illinois, it is probably gone now. The first nests found were along the Calumet River in 1910; two eggs were collected on May 28 and eggs from the same birds were found several feet away on June 12 (Abbott 1911). A nest with three eggs was found at Evergreen Park, May 30, 1932 (Hammond 1943). The most recent nest and eggs were photographed at Lake Calumet in June 1960 (Mlodinow 1984). A singing male was at Lake Calumet all summer in 1968 (JG).

Fall migration begins as early as mid-September: Chicago, September 18, 1985 (MDa-IB&B2:55); two, Mark Twain refuge, September 28, 1982 (PS-SR35:16). Average fall arrival dates: Chicago, October 8 (three years); west-central, October 15 (five years); Sangamon County, October 13 (17 years). Maximum counts for fall: 11, Mason County, November 8, 1975 (RS,HDB); 10, Rock Island County, October 8, 1980 (PP-AB35:191); eight, Horseshoe Lake, October 22, 1982 (RG-SR35:16). Average departure dates: west-central, October 23 (five years); Sangamon County, November 5 (12 years).

Many years Le Conte's Sparrows stay for the winter. They were recorded on seven of the 10 Christmas bird counts from 1976 through 1985. In winter they tend to seek heavier cover—thicker and taller grassy areas—than in spring. Most wintering Le Conte's Sparrows are in central and southern Illinois. The highest count in winter was 66 at Rend Lake, January 2, 1977 (AB31:689). Other winter records: Dundee, January 5, 1975 (RM-AB29:699); 12, Carbondale, January 10, 1972 (VK,DH-AB26:613); seven, Horseshoe Lake, January 9, 1983 (RG-SR36:11); five, Beverly, through mid-February 1981 (JF-SR28:9). Le Conte's Sparrows winter regularly from southern Illinois to the Gulf Coast.

SHARP-TAILED SPARROW

Ammodramus caudacutus

OCCASIONAL MIGRANT

The first "Nelson's" Sharp-tailed Sparrow (*A. c. nelsoni*) was collected at Lake Calumet on September 17, 1874, by Nelson (1876). This inland form of the Sharp-tailed Sparrow was described by Allen (1875). Although Nelson thought these sparrows bred at Lake Calumet and so did Woodruff (1907), breeding in Illinois has never been sub-

stantiated. The closest breeding area is northwestern Minnesota. The beautiful Sharp-tailed Sparrow is reddish brown with an ocher face and breast. It looks much like a Le Conte's Sparrow but has a broad gray median stripe and nape. It arrives much later in spring and departs earlier in fall than other sparrows; in fact, its timing is more warbler-like than sparrowlike. Sharp-tailed Sparrows are found mostly in marshes, where they run around on mudflats at the edge of cattails, sedges, and grasses. They can also be found in weedy or brushy fields. They are somewhat difficult to flush, but they react to "spishing" more readily than other grass sparrows, sometimes sitting in the open for several minutes. Their song is a raspy buzz.

Early spring arrivals are in mid-May: Jackson Park, May 14, 1980 (RG,PC); Chicago, May 17, 1986 (RD-IB&B2:96); Sangchris State Park, May 13, 1971 (HDB). April dates are suspect unless substantiated by a photograph or specimen. There are no high counts for spring because these birds move through fairly fast and late in the season when fewer observers are in the field. Spring bird count data (Sharp-tails were seen in six of 15 years) are probably worthless because of identification problems. Late spring departure dates: Chicago, June 5, 1983 (JL); Goose Lake Prairie, June 6, 1971 (LB,CC-AB25:865). Most Sharp-tailed Sparrows are gone by late May.

These sparrows are more numerous in fall, but numbers seem to fluctuate greatly from year to year. Early fall arrivals: Havana, August 24, 1974 (RS,HDB); Chicago, September 7, 1987 (JL,CM); Chicago, September 3, 1976 (LB-AB31:186). High counts for fall: 14, Chicago, September 22-23, 1971 (LB,GR-AB26:73); 10, Evanston, September 20, 1975 (LB-IAB176:36). Most Sharp-tails are seen in late September and October. Late fall departures: Chicago, November 2, 1976 (CC-AB31:186); Savanna, October 29, 1983 (BSh-SR39:25); Rice Lake, October 28, 1987 (KR). Sharp-tailed Sparrows winter on the Gulf Coast.

FOX SPARROW

Passerella iliaca

COMMON MIGRANT; FAIRLY COMMON WINTER RESIDENT IN SOUTHERN ILLINOIS DECREASING NORTHWARD

This mostly reddish brown bird is one of the largest sparrows. Being thrush size, it is sometimes confused with the Hermit Thrush, since both have a reddish brown tail. The Fox Sparrow thrashes about in undergrowth kicking leaf litter in search of food. Its varied and musical song is often heard in Illinois before it leaves in the spring, and occasionally it even sings in winter. The chip note is a fairly distinctive, rather flat *nuch*. I have seen these birds going to roost in evergreens, sometimes in large numbers, while they are passing through on spring migration. The race of this variable species found in Illinois is *P. i. iliaca*, which breeds in eastern Canada. Other races may occur as vagrants. Fox Sparrows are found along woodland edges and in brush, weedy areas, hedgerows, and thickets. They usually occur singly or in small flocks.

The Fox Sparrow is one of the earliest woodland sparrows to return in spring. Early arrival dates: two, Thebes, February 14, 1984 (TF-SR41:27); Mode, February 17, 1984 (KF-SR41:27); two, Lisle Arboretum, February 21, 1987 (EW). Average arrival dates: Urbana, March 1 (20 years); Chicago, March 24 (16 years); west-central, March 6 (11 years). Maximum counts for spring: 132, Jackson Park, March 24, 1982 (RG,PC-AB36:860); 50, Springfield, April 6, 1982 (HDB); 80, Jackson Park, April 4, 1981 (RG,PC-SR29:15:). Spring bird count totals ranged from none in 1974 and 1976 to 30 in 1973. The highest count was 12 in Adams County on May 5, 1973 (VK); that seems very late for so many birds. Average departure dates: Chicago, April 22 (16 years); Urbana, April 15 (20 years); west-central, April 13 (11 years). Late departure dates: two, Peoria County, May 11, 1982 (LA-SR33:16); Chicago, May 25, 1930 (Clark and Nice 1950).

Fox Sparrows arrive fairly late in fall, although a few are found as early as September: Chicago, September 5, 1983 (HR-AB 38:211); Rockford, September 24, 1980 (LJ-SR27:12). Average arrival dates: Chicago, September 23 (16 years); west-central, October 8 (11 years). High counts for fall: 39, Chicago, October 21, 1982 (HR,PC-AB37:189); 25, Red Hills State Park, November 16, 1982 (LH-SR35:16); 23, Greene County, October 18, 1983 (HW-SR39:25). Very late dates are obscured by wintering birds.

In winter, brush piles and weedy areas within woods are good places to find Fox Sparrows. Totals on Christmas bird counts for 1976–85 ranged from 51 in 1978 to 196 in 1984. Numbers were low on Christmas counts in the late 1970s because of severe weather. The highest count was 72 in Alexander County in 1983. Numbers drop significantly in the northern part of the state; northern records include Pecatonica, January 17–26, 1986 (DW-IB&B2:78); Chicago, all winter 1981–82 (AA-SR32:8); Lake County, all winter 1983–84 (SR40:13).

SONG SPARROW

Melospiza melodia

COMMON MIGRANT; COMMON SUMMER RESIDENT DECREASING SOUTHWARD; COMMON WINTER RESIDENT DECREASING NORTHWARD

The Song Sparrow is often found singing in bushes around houses. It sings most of the year, the song starting with clear notes and ending with a trill. Its chip note is a distinguishable *chimp*. This sparrow has a streaked breast, the streaks forming a central spot on its breast. Besides its residential habitat, it is found in thickets, woodland edges, hedgerows, roadside areas, bushy pastures, parks, and many other places. When it flies it pumps its rather long tail.

Song Sparrows are mostly found in small groups or singly. At least two subspecies occur in Illinois. The breeding form is *M. m. euphonia;* some migrants may be the central western *M. m. juddi.*

Some Song Sparrows begin to arrive in February but wintering birds tend to obscure arrivals. Average arrival dates: Chicago, March 15 (16 years); west-central, March 13 (nine years). High counts: 200, Chicago, April 4, 1981 (JL); 118, Jackson Park, March 18, 1982 (PC,RG-SR33:16); 100, Springfield, March 20 1982 (HDB). Spring bird count totals ranged from 1732 in 1972 to 4405 in 1986, with the highest count 537 in Cook County, May 10, 1986. Most high counts were in northern Illinois (VK).

In 1907–9 the Song Sparrow was found in northern and central but not in southern Illinois in the breeding season. Evidently a range expansion occurred since then, because it now breeds in the south. The estimated June population statewide was 180,000 in 1909 and 290,000 in 1958 (Graber and Graber 1963). Robbins et al. (1986), using breeding bird survey data for 1965–79, found a significant decline in the population. The mean number of Song Sparrows per survey route in Illinois was 19.7. These sparrows build their cuplike nests fairly low in shrubs and thickets, lining them with grasses and hair. The three to five eggs are whitish or bluish white with reddish brown markings. Illinois egg dates are April 22 to August 7 (Austin 1968). Song Sparrow nests are frequently parasitized by cowbirds.

Dreuth recorded the earliest fall migrant at Chicago on August 4, 1941 (Clark and Nice 1950). One arrived at Jackson Park on August 5, 1981 (PC,HR-SR31:18). The average arrival date at Chicago is August 16 (16 years). Most migration occurs in October and November. High counts for fall: 80, Springfield, October 22, 1983 (HDB); 30, Warren County, October 11, 1986 (MB-IB&B3:47); 35, Chicago, October 16, 1983 (JL). The average departure date at Chicago is November 3 (16 years).

Most of the winter population is in southern Illinois. At this time grasslands, shrubs, marshes, and drainage ditches are favored habitat. Song Sparrows also like brush piles and logjams along creeks. Graber and Graber (1963) estimated the state's Song Sparrow population at 350,000 in January 1907 and 475,000 in January 1957. Christmas bird count totals for 1976–85 ranged from 1626 in 1979 to 3811 in 1976. The highest count was 610 in Alexander County in 1983. Winter kills were evident in 1977–79 and 1981. The population slowly recovered in the 1980s, but not to its original abundance.

LINCOLN'S SPARROW

Melospiza lincolnii

FAIRLY COMMON MIGRANT AND RARE WINTER RESIDENT

The Lincoln's Sparrow is a trim, streaked, woodland species that looks like a cross between the Swamp and Song Sparrows. It behaves like neither, however, since it migrates as late as the warblers and sings like a warbler. It is a skulker, staying low in brush and weeds, but it reacts readily to "spishing." The Lincoln's Sparrow nests in bogs and wet meadows from northern Wisconsin to Alaska. There is some evidence for breeding in Illinois: a nest found near the Waukegan Country Club in Lake County on May 17, 1936 (Smith and Parmalee 1955), and young of the year collected in Cook County on June 30 and July 16, 1896 (Woodruff 1907). Both locations are far south of the species' breeding range. The race in Illinois is the nominate form.

Lincoln's Sparrows seen early in spring may be local wintering birds. Most spring migrants arrive fairly late. Early arrivals: Chicago, February 25, 1985 (JL,CM); two, Jacksonville, April 13, 1981 (RQR-SR 29:15). Average arrival dates: Urbana, May 3 (19 years); Chicago, April 30 (16 years). High counts: 45, Chicago, May 14, 1982 (JL); 28, Jackson Park, May 13, 1981 (RG-SR 29:15). Spring bird count totals ranged from 32 in 1973 and 1978 to 318 in 1983. The highest count was 173 in Cook County, May 7, 1983 (VK). Average departure dates: Chicago, May 27 (16 years); Urbana, May 15 (19 years). Late departure dates: Urbana, June 3, 1982 (BCho-SR33:17); two, Chicago, June 5, 1983 (JL).

Early arrival dates for fall migration: two, Chautauqua National Wildlife Refuge, August 30, 1987 (KR); Chicago, September 1, 1986 (EW-IB&B3:47). Average arrival dates: Chicago, September 10 (16 years); central Illinois, September 18 (18 years). High counts for fall: 42 killed at a television tower, Springfield, October 14, 1985 (ISM); 35, Chicago, October 6, 1985 (JL); 16, Horseshoe Lake, October 5, 1983 (SRu-SR39:25). Average departure dates: Chicago, October 16 (16 years); central Illinois, November 3 (18 years).

Lincoln's Sparrows do not normally winter in Illinois except in mild years. On Christmas bird counts for 1976–85 they were found seven years in small numbers (one to 13). The highest count was six in Alexander County in 1982. Other winter records: two, Washington County Conservation Area, January 18, 1981 (M.Kemper,R.White-SR28:9); Crab Orchard National Wildlife Refuge, February 12 and 26, 1983 (JR-SR36:11); Batchtown, January 1, 1983 (SHo-SR36:11); Horseshoe Lake, January 9, 1983 (RG). Immature Swamp Sparrows are sometimes mistaken for Lincoln Sparrows in winter.

SWAMP SPARROW

Melospiza georgiana

COMMON MIGRANT; UNCOMMON SUMMER
RESIDENT IN NORTHERN ILLINOIS;
COMMON WINTER RESIDENT IN SOUTHERN
ILLINOIS DECREASING NORTHWARD

Swamp Sparrows, as their name suggests, are found in moist habitats—swamps, marshes, wet meadows. In migration they also occur in woodlands, weedy fields, and thickets. Rather shy, these reddish brown and gray sparrows are sometimes difficult to flush, but they are much easier to view than the grass sparrows. They sing during spring migration, a loud, metallic trill. More often heard is their call note, *chink*. Two races occur in Illinois: the more common and breeding form, *M. g. georgiana*, and *M. g. ericrypta*, which nests farther north.

Early arrival dates for spring migrants are difficult to determine because of the presence of wintering birds. Average arrival dates: Urbana, March 19 (20 years); Chicago, March 27 (16 years). High spring counts: 100, Crab Orchard National Wildlife Refuge, March 28, 1987 (DR); 80, Chicago, April 19, 1985 (CM-IB&B1:90); 50, Champaign, March 22, 1984 (RAp-SR41:27). Totals on spring bird counts ranged from 273 in 1972 to 1506 in 1984, with the highest count 494 in Lake County on May 6, 1978. All high counts were from the northern part of the state (VK). Average departure dates: Chicago, May 27 (16 years); central Illinois, May 14 (16 years). Late departure dates: Chicago, May 29, 1985 (CM-IB&B1:90); Springfield, May 23, 1971 (HDB).

Breeding Swamp Sparrows are now mostly confined to northern Illinois, though Hess (1910) noted nesting at Philo in central Illinois from May 17 (1906) to May 26 (1905) and a recent report of three young on June 12, 1979, comes from Pike County in west central Illinois (G.Miller-Periodic Report 18, p. 43). Most of the breeding population is in Lake, Cook, McHenry, and Du Page Counties. Other recent nesting sites: Goose Lake Prairie, two fledgings, July 3, 1971 (Birkenholz 1975); Kennekuk Cove Park, June 9, 1987 (ME). Swamp Sparrows usually nest in swamps or marshes and suspend the nest over the water in cattails or other marsh vegetation. The four to five eggs are pale bluish, spotted and blotched with purple and brown. Illinois egg dates are May 9 to June 29 (Austin 1968).

Early fall arrival dates: Buffalo, September 12, 1985 (HDB); Chicago, September 14, 1937 (Clark and Nice 1950). Average arrival dates: Chicago, September 22 (16 years); central Illinois, September 20 (17 years). High fall counts: 105, Havana, October 19, 1985 (RP-IB&B2:55); 100, Springfield, October 23, 1983 (HDB); 83, Vermilion County, October 6, 1985 (SB-IB&B2:55). Average departure dates: Chicago, October 31 (16 years); west-central, November 2 (nine years).

Some years a fair number of Swamp Sparrows winter in the state, depending on the availability of marshy habitat and the severity of the weather. Christmas bird count totals for 1976–85 ranged from 415 in 1981 to 1981 in 1976, suggesting that the numbers had not fully recovered after the severe winters of the late 1970s. The highest Christmas count was 430 in Alexander County in 1976. Recent northern winter records: 20, Joliet, December 15, 1984 (JM-IB&B1:70); 52, Lisle Arboretum, December 16, 1973 (AB28:383).

WHITE-THROATED SPARROW

Zonotrichia albicollis

COMMON MIGRANT; COMMON WINTER
RESIDENT IN SOUTHERN ILLINOIS
DECREASING NORTHWARD

When flocks of White-throated Sparrows give out their quavering whistled notes in Illinois woodlands, it means that spring migration is in full swing. These sparrows are also found along woodland edges and in thickets, hedgerows, weedy fields, and gardens. At times they are among the most numerous birds near woodlands. Although other species sometimes associate with them, they can be found in pure flocks. The White-throated Sparrow readily responds to "spishing" and an imitation of its song by flying up to perch in the open. These sparrows breed in the northern United States and Canada. Lowther (1961) discusses polymorphism among White-throats, in which adults of one type are brighter plumaged, with whiter head markings and less streaking, than adults of the other type, which look like immature birds.

Like the White-crowned Sparrow, the White-throated has a population that winters in Illinois and another that goes farther south. Average spring arrival dates: Urbana, March 19 (18 years); Chicago, April 15 (16 years); west-central, April 13 (15 years). These averages are probably muddied by wintering birds, however, and the true migrant flocks usually arrive about April 20. Spring bird count totals ranged from 1240 in 1986 to 7720 in 1984; the high count was 2032 in Cook County on May 7, 1983 (VK). Other high counts: 450, Chicago, April 26, 1984 (JL); 100, Joliet, April 22, 1985 (JM-IB&B1:90). Average spring departure dates: Urbana, May 19 (18 years); Chicago, May 26 (16 years); Sangamon County, May 19 (17 years). Some White-throats stay into June and a few have summered in Illinois: four, Evanston, summered, 1979 (RB-AB33:869); Chicago, July 9–24, 1986 (JL-IB&B3:16); subadult male singing, Lake Shelbyville, June 14, 1985 (SR-IB&B2:16); Jackson Park, June 18–19, 1982 (HR-SR33:17); Springfield, June 1, 1984 (HDB).

Most fall migrants arrive in September. Early arrivals: Chicago, August 30, 1933 (Clark and Nice 1950), and August 12, 1983 (SP-SR39:25); Jackson Park, August 19, 1983 (PC-SR39:25). Average arrival dates: Chicago, September 8 (16 years); west-central, September 19 (11 years). Maximum counts for fall: 200, Knox County, October 23, 1983 (MB-SR39:25); 240, Springfield, October 15, 1982 (HDB); 600, Urbana, October 13, 1981 (RCh-SR31:18); 398, Dundee, October 26, 1981 (SD-SR31:18). Average departure dates are somewhat unclear because of the presence of wintering birds: Chicago, November 4 (16 years); west-central, November 18 (11 years).

Christmas bird counts for 1976–85 showed a drop in the White-throated Sparrow's winter population coinciding with the severe winters of the late 1970s, when mortality was high for many ground feeding species. Totals ranged from 535 in 1977 to 4415 in 1984. The highest count was 1473

in Alexander County in 1984. Only moderate numbers are seen in central Illinois and even fewer in northern Illinois in winter. Many of these wintering White-throats are associated with feeders, and wintering in the north may be on the increase because of this practice. White-throated Sparrows winter south to northern Mexico.

GOLDEN-CROWNED SPARROW

Zonotrichia atricapilla

VERY RARE VAGRANT

This northwestern species is closely related to the White-crowned Sparrow. It has two records for Illinois. An immature male was collected at Waukegan on November 28, 1935, by Lyon and is in the collection at the Chicago Academy of Science. The other Golden-crowned Sparrow was observed at Lincoln Park on April 29, 1942, by Dreuth (Clark and Nice 1950). This sparrow breeds in Alaska and western Canada and winters mostly on the West Coast. It is a ground feeder found in brush, thickets, and landscaped areas. There are records for Minnesota, Wisconsin, and Iowa, among other eastern states. Immature birds show little yellow on the crown and could be mistaken for other *Zonotrichia*.

WHITE-CROWNED SPARROW

Zonotrichia leucophrys

COMMON MIGRANT; FAIRLY COMMON
WINTER RESIDENT IN SOUTHERN ILLINOIS
DECREASING NORTHWARD

Two races of the White-crowned Sparrow occur in Illinois: the eastern form, *Z. l. leucophrys*, which is most often seen, and *Z. l. gambelii* of the Northwest, of which there are a few records. The two races can be separated in the field only with great care by looking at the lores, which are white in *gambelii* and black in *leucophrys*. Most of the *gambelii* records are of specimens or banded birds in northern Illinois: specimens at Waukegan, May 14, 1922, and Beach, October 6, 1906 (Zimmer and Gregory 1929); one banded, Chicago, May 6, 1956 (KB-AFN10:338); two, Fulton County, October 11, 1971 (GR,LB-AB26:73); one, Beverly, December 21, 1974 (RQR,HDB). The White-crowned Sparrow is grayer than the White-throated Sparrow and in general prefers more open areas but often occurs in the same flocks as White-throats. It is found in hedgerows (especially multiflora rose), weedy fields, thickets, brush piles, and woodland edges. In spring White-crowns like to feed on dandelion heads and in winter they come to feeders. Their song, a plaintive whistle, is heard less often than the White-throats' song, but it is just as pleasing. Immature White-crowns have brown crown lines

BROWN THRASHER
Toxostoma rufum

Occasionally a Brown Thrasher will be found spending the winter in the state. The majority, however, winter a little to the south. Together with the first blooms of the violet (*Viola* sp.) and unfurling fronds of the Christmas fern (*Polystichum acrostichoides*), this thrasher's return is one of the earliest signs of spring. The vigorous tossing of leaf litter about with their bills is the activity for which the thrasher family is named.

Adults
(sexes similar)

BOHEMIAN WAXWING
Bombycilla garrulus

CEDAR WAXWING
Bombycilla cedrorum

During fall and winter, flocks of Cedar Waxwings wander the state in search of fruit-bearing trees and shrubs, which they frequently pick clean. Occasionally a few of their grayer and larger cousins, Bohemian Waxwings, have been sighted. Because of their social nature, the rare Bohemians when seen are often with flocks of Cedar Waxwings.

Bohemian Waxwing
(sexes similar)

Cedar Waxwing
Cedar Waxwing

Cedar Waxwing
(sexes similar)

LOGGERHEAD SHRIKE
Lanius ludovicianus

Because shrikes impale excess prey on the thorny branches of trees, the Loggerhead and other members of this family are frequently called butcher-birds. In some years grasshoppers and other insects such as the Seventeen-year Cicada (*Magicicada septendecim*) emerge in numbers so large that nothing could possibly consume them all. The shrike's unusual method of storing food can be handy when the supply is abundant. Since shrikes don't have sharp talons like most birds of prey, they also utilize the thorns of trees to hold their prey in place while they tear it apart.

Adult
(sexes similar)

SOLITARY VIREO
Vireo solitarius

YELLOW-THROATED VIREO
Vireo flavifrons

The Yellow-throated Vireo is a summer resident that spends much of its time in the upper two-thirds of our largest trees. Its cousin the Solitary Vireo seems to prefer the smaller trees and shrubs that make up the understory of our woods. Their paths occasionally cross where the preferred habitats of these two birds overlap.

Yellow-throated Vireo
(sexes similar)

Solitary Vireo
(sexes similar)

MAGNOLIA WARBLER
Dendroica magnolia

BLACK-THROATED GREEN WARBLER
Dendroica virens

BLACKBURNIAN WARBLER
Dendroica fusca

YELLOW-THROATED WARBLER
Dendroica dominica

BAY-BREASTED WARBLER
Dendroica castanea

BLACKPOLL WARBLER
Dendroica striata

In May, along with the warm balmy weather fronts pushing up from the south, come waves of migrating wood warblers. On a good day a lucky birder might find four or five species in a single tree, all flitting and chasing about in pursuit of caterpillars that are feeding on the newly emerging leaves.

Blackburnian Warbler *(male)*

Yellow-throated Warbler *(sexes similar)*

Blackburnian Warbler *(female)*   **Bay-breasted Warbler** *(female)*

Bay-breasted Warbler *(male)*

Blackpoll Warbler *(female)*

Black-throated Green Warbler
(male; female has less black on throat)   **Blackpoll Warbler** *(male)*

Magnolia Warbler
(male; female has less black on breast and white on wings)

SUMMER TANAGER
Piranga rubra

SCARLET TANAGER
Piranga olivacea

NORTHERN ORIOLE
Icterus galbula

In late June the fruit of the Wild Cherry (*Prunus serotina*) is one of the earliest to ripen in our woods. Scattered throughout the hardwood forest, Wild Cherry trees provide a welcome summer treat for a wide variety of birds, many of which, being territorial, are much less tolerant of intruders of their own kind than they are of the other species that come to feed. That may explain why several species can be found in the same tree feeding side by side.

Scarlet Tanager
(male)
(female)

Summer Tanager
(male)
(female)

Northern Oriole
(female)
(male)

NORTHERN CARDINAL
Cardinalis cardinalis

RUFOUS-SIDED TOWHEE
Pipilo erythrophthalmus

AMERICAN TREE SPARROW
Spizella arborea

FOX SPARROW
Passerella iliaca

SONG SPARROW
Melospiza melodia

SWAMP SPARROW
Melospiza georgiana

WHITE-THROATED SPARROW
Zonotrichia albicollis

DARK-EYED JUNCO
Junco hyemalis

EVENING GROSBEAK
Coccothraustes vespertinus

In late winter when the fields, fencerows, and woods are filled with drifts of snow, many species of seedeaters gather together in overgrown tangles of weeds where food and shelter can be found. On particularly stormy days, if food is plentiful and easy to obtain, the birds seem reluctant to stir from the spot where they spent the night.

Evening Grosbeak
(male)
    (female)

Song Sparrow
(sexes similar)

American Tree Sparrow
Northern Cardinal   *(sexes similar)*
    (female)
        (male)

White-throated Sparrow
(sexes similar)

Fox Sparrow
(sexes similar)

Dark-eyed Junco
    (male)   **Swamp Sparrow**
            (sexes similar)
        (female)

Rufous-sided Towhee
    (female)
(male)

RED-WINGED BLACKBIRD
Agelaius phoeniceus

RUSTY BLACKBIRD
Euphagus carolinus

COMMON GRACKLE
Quiscalus quiscula

Every fall, enormous mixed flocks of noisy blackbirds pass through the state. When they roost, their large concentrations can become quite a nuisance if they are located near buildings. Many towns and cities have resorted to drastic action when migrating blackbirds have chosen to roost in trees within their municipalities.

Red-winged Blackbird *(male)*

Rusty Blackbird *(male)*
Rusty Blackbird *(female)*

Red-winged Blackbird *(female)*

Common Grackle
(male; female smaller and duller)

rather than black. These are molted toward spring, so that all White-crowns have black and white striped crowns by May.

Some White-crowned Sparrows winter in Illinois, making it difficult to assess true spring arrival dates. The bulk of the population moves through in late April and early May. Average arrival dates: Urbana, April 30 (20 years); Chicago, April 29 (16 years); west-central, April 25 (15 years). Spring bird count totals ranged from 651 in 1979—which may be indicative of severe-winter mortality—to 4136 in 1983. The high count was 1423 in Cook County on May 10, 1986 (VK). Other high counts: 415, Will County, May 10, 1986 (IB&B2:97); 300, Chicago, May 10, 1987 (JL,CM). Average departure dates: Urbana, May 17 (20 years); Chicago, April 29 (16 years); west-central, April 25 (15 years). Whether the migrants from farther south or the wintering birds leave first is unknown. Late departure dates are all from the Chicago area: June 1, 1987 (JL); June 2, 1986 (CM-IB&B2:97); June 12, 1983 (JL); June 11, 1983 (SP-SR37:27). One adult summered at Meigs Field from May 28 to July 21, 1986 (K.Swagel-IB&B3:16)—which is very unusual, since these birds nest in the far north to the tree line.

An early fall arrival date is Chicago, September 11, 1985 (CM-IB&B2:55). Average arrival dates: Chicago, September 22 (16 years); central Illinois, October 1 (18 years). High counts for fall: 110, Decatur, October 22, 1985 (RP-IB&B2:55); 110, Springfield, October 25, 1980 (HDB). Most departure dates are obscured by wintering birds, but the average for Chicago is October 23 (16 years).

Wintering birds are most numerous in southern Illinois. Christmas bird count totals ranged from 357 in 1980 to 1010 in 1985. The highest count was 292 at Crab Orchard National Wildlife Refuge in 1974. High counts in the north: 52, Will County, 1978; 60, Lake Calumet, February 8, 1986 (JL). The White-crowned Sparrow winters as far south as northern Mexico.

HARRIS' SPARROW

Zonotrichia querula

UNCOMMON FALL AND RARE SPRING
MIGRANT; RARE WINTER RESIDENT

According to Ridgway (1889), the first Illinois specimen of these large, handsome sparrows was obtained at Bloomington in the spring of 1877 by W. H. Garman. They have always been uncommon to rare in Illinois, varying in numbers from none some years to locally numerous in other years. Harris' Sparrows are usually more numerous on the west side of Illinois, which is closer to the main population of the Great Plains. They breed in stunted spruce west of Hudson Bay, but the nest and eggs went unknown until 1930, when George Sutton found them. In Illinois the Harris' Sparrow is found in hedgerows, particularly multi-flora rose, just like the White-crowned Sparrow with which it flocks. It is also found in weedy areas, brush piles, and occasionally yards with conifer bushes or feeding stations. The Harris' Sparrow is shier than the other *Zonotrichia* and more difficult to "spish up" for a good view. Its song and call notes are similar to those of the White-crowned Sparrow but can be separated with practice. Harris' Sparrows have a pink bill in all plumages.

Harris' Sparrows are scarce in spring. Some seen in March may be locally wintering birds. Average spring arrival dates: Chicago, May 12 (eight years); west-central, April 28 (six years). Spring bird counts show Harris' Sparrows most years but in low numbers (one to eight); the high count was six in Lake County, May 6, 1978 (VK). There are no other high counts for spring. Average departure dates: Chicago, May 15 (eight years); west-central, May 4 (six years). Late dates for spring: Jackson County, May 8, 1971 (VK-AB25:753); Chicago, May 29, 1930 (Clark and Nice 1950).

In fall most of the Harris' Sparrows seen in Illinois are buffy-cheeked immatures with a black necklace. It is thought that winds and other weather factors determine whether Harris' Sparrows will be plentiful or not. Early fall arrivals: Chicago, September 20, 1981 (JL), and September 19, 1938 (Clark and Nice 1950); Monmouth, October 5, 1980 (LMc-SR27:12). Average arrival dates: Chicago, September 27 (14 years); central Illinois, October 13 (nine years). The highest fall count was 35–50 at Bushnell, November 5, 1956 (L.Hood-AFN11:30); otherwise, most reports in fall are of one to three birds. Average departure dates: Chicago, October 17 (14 years); central Illinois, November 11 (nine years).

A few Harris' Sparrows winter in Illinois, most of them probably in the south, although a lack of observers there makes it difficult to prove. There are some records for northern and central Illinois. Most of these sparrows occur at feeding stations. Christmas bird counts for 1976–85 listed Harris' Sparrows six years in low numbers (one to five). The highest Christmas count was six in Mercer County in 1964. Other winter records: Charleston, February 6, 1983 (RBr-SR36:11); Belvidere, December 9–February 1984 (RGa-SR40:14); Plato Center, wintered 1977–78 (LB-AB32:360); Beverly, January 25–31, 1979 (JF-AB33:287); Blue Island, January 5, 1986 (KB-IB&B2:78). Most Harris' Sparrows winter on the southern Great Plains.

DARK-EYED JUNCO

Junco hyemalis

ABUNDANT MIGRANT AND WINTER
RESIDENT

If a large flock of juncos is studied while they are feeding on the ground, the observer will realize that they exhibit widely varying plumages. All the juncos in North America were recently designated either Yellow-eyed or Dark-eyed species. Several Dark-eyed races occur in Illinois. The "Slate-colored" Junco, *J. h. hyemalis,* is the regular wintering bird. "Oregon" Junco types are many times reported, sometimes in numbers, especially on Christmas bird counts. Some of them are intergrades, some are the subspecies *J. h. cismontanus* (which was originally a subspecies of the "Slate-colored" Junco), and a few are probably "Oregon" Juncos. The race is casual in winter. The "Oregon" types are *J. h. montanus,* with several specimens listed in Ford (1956); *J. h. mearnsi,* with two good sight records (one banded, Blue Island, October 25, 1948, Ford 1956; Lake Shelbyville, June 11, 1985, SB); and *J. h. shufeldti,* with two specimens (Ford 1956; Praeger 1895). The "Gray-headed" Junco, *J. h. caniceps,* has five records (Blue Island, Springfield, Urbana, Decatur, and Mount Vernon on dates ranging from February 9 to May 20). The "White-winged" Junco, *J. h. aikeni,* has been reported but not documented. Miller (1941) has a good discussion of the genus. Juncos, called snowbirds by many people, are gray and brown with white outer tail feathers. Their song is a bubbling series of chip notes usually heard just before they leave in spring, when they become more woodland oriented. Their usual habitat in Illinois is edges, hedgerows, shrub and weedy areas, lawns, grasslands, and cornfields.

Early arrival dates for fall: Evanston, August 29, 1976 (LB-AB31:186); one still in juvenile plumage, Springfield, September 2, 1977 (VK-AB32:214); Naperville, September 5, 1985 (JWi-AB40:123). Average arrival dates: Chicago, September 16 (16 years); west-central, October 6 (15 years); Sangamon County, September 29 (18 years). Fall high counts: 1200, Chicago, November 7, 1981 (JL); 500, Clinton Lake, November 1, 1987 (RP); 545, Dundee, November 9, 1981 (SD-SR31:17).

Most of the winter population is in southern Illinois. January population estimates are 5,300,000 in 1907 and 6,400,000 in 1957. In February 1958 there were an estimated 10,000,000 juncos in Illinois, suggesting that spring migration was under way by that time (Graber and Graber 1963). Christmas bird count totals for 1976–85 ranged from 19,152 in 1978 to 41,018 in 1985. Highs were variable and came from all sections of the state. The highest Christmas count was 4044 at Shelbyville in 1969.

Spring migration can at times be detected by an increase in numbers of juncos. High counts are scarce for this season: 320, Jackson Park, March 30, 1982 (HR,RG-SR33:17); 150, Springfield, March 18, 1982 (HDB). Spring bird counts show juncos in low numbers (six to 112), but these counts come much past the peak for these birds. The highest spring bird count was 27 in Cook County, May 5, 1984 (VK). Average departure dates: Chicago, May 10 (16 years); west-central, April 28 (14 years); Sangamon County, April 26 (17 years). There are several very late dates: one collected near Elizabethtown, June 9, 1881 (Forbes 1881); Sangamon County, June 5, 1974 (VK-AB28:810); Streator, May 22, 1985 (JMc-IB&B1:90); Dundee, May 17, 1983 (RM-SR 37:27). Juncos breed in the boreal zone in the northern United States and Canada.

MCCOWN'S LONGSPUR
Calcarius mccownii
HYPOTHETICAL

This longspur breeds on the northern Great Plains in short-grass areas and winters on the southern Great Plains. The Illinois records have been sketchy at best. The McCown's Longspur was first recorded from specimens bought in a Chicago market. Coale (1877) purchased three males that supposedly came from Champaign. Under the circumstances the accuracy of the data on these specimens must be questioned. The Illinois State Museum has a mounted male specimen that has "Illinois" as the only datum; it may well be one of the specimens purchased by Coale. Other reports: 20 at Lisle Arboretum (Christmas bird count) in 1961 (AFN15:213); several seen at Rockford, October 15, January 7, and May 25 (no years given; Nature Study Society of Rockford 1917–18). These being the only records, it is difficult to see why the American Ornithologists' Union's *Check-List of North American Birds* (AOU 1983) gives this species' casual range as east to Illinois. The AOU must still be basing its information on Coale's specimens. Even Iowa lists this longspur as hypothetical. It has been recorded from Missouri (within 25 miles of Illinois), Michigan, and even Massachusetts and will probably be confirmed for Illinois eventually.

LAPLAND LONGSPUR
Calcarius lapponicus
COMMON MIGRANT AND UNCOMMON WINTER RESIDENT

This is a bird of open barren areas, corn and soybean stubble, short hayfields, and plowed fields. At times huge flocks of Lapland Longspurs occur; their clicking notes, their *tweuu* flight note, and their bullet shape identify them as they fly overhead. Numbers apparently vary from year to year but are difficult to track because observers tend to neglect open field habitats. These longspurs blend so well with their surroundings that a few sighted in a plowed corn stubble field might become a hundred or more when they fly up at the observer's approach, clicking as they gain altitude and becoming a compact flock, then flying to the other end of the field, where they swirl down, spread out, and suddenly alight on the ground—only to disappear. A few may not fly off but remain hidden and "freeze"; only a close approach in their direction sends them up and away also. Once in a great while some longspurs will sit on a telephone wire or fence. Lapland Longspurs eat mostly grass seed, waste grain, and available insects. Occasionally they migrate at night. An observer in Springfield once heard thousands flying over at night after a snowstorm had stilled the city noises. Lapland Longspurs will come to feeders, especially if grain is spread on the ground. They breed in the Arctic in both North America and Eurasia. The race found in Illinois is *C. l. lapponicus*, but *C. l. alascensis* of the western United States could also occur, since there are records for Tennessee and Ohio (AOU 1957).

In fall a few Lapland Longspurs show up as early as September along the Chicago lakefront, but most Illinois early arrival dates are in mid- to late October, with the majority of fall migrants coming in November. Early fall records: 12, Illinois Beach State Park, September 27, 1980 (JN-AB35:191); Chicago, September 21, 1984 (JL); Lake Clinton, October 6, 1984 (RCh-IB&B1:22). Average fall arrival dates: Chicago, October 4 (11 years); Sangamon County, October 30 (18 years). High counts in fall: 1000, Lawrenceville, November 30, 1982 (LH-AB37:189); 1850, Sangamon County, November 23, 1984 (HDB); 1210, Vermilion County, November 14, 1986 (SB-AB41:98); 1600, Stark County, November 9, 1984 (MBr-IB&B1:22).

Sometimes in winter Lapland Longspurs seem to be absent until there is enough snow to cover the ground; then they suddenly appear on the roadsides, at times in large numbers. Heavy mortality often occurs, though they quickly become wary of automobiles. Sensible driving and an awareness that birds come up to roads when snow covers the ground could prevent many casualties. Graber and Graber (1963) estimated Lapland Longspur populations for January 1907 at 700,000 (all in northern Illinois) and for January 1957 at 4,800,000 (86 percent in central Illinois). The Grabers noted that agricultural practices had favored these longspurs. They also discovered that the winter population sometimes shifts southward when the weather gets severe. High counts in winter: 1000, Sterling, January 15, 1981 (BSh-SR28:9); 6000, Carlyle Lake, January 13, 1985 (SR-IB&B1:70); 2000, Jasper County, February 3, 1985 (LH-IB&B1:70); 1000, Homer, December 18, 1983 (JSm-SR40:14). Totals on Christmas bird counts for 1976–85 ranged from 216 in 1979 to 4361 in 1983. The highest Christmas count was 3115 at Bloomington in 1968.

By late February and early March, the Lapland Longspurs that went south for the winter (to about the latitude of Tennessee and Texas) start returning. The males are in fairly high plumage at this time. In April, when flocks are encountered, the males—as many as 300 or 400 at once—sing as they perch on clods or bent-over cornstalks. Most longspurs then migrate farther north, though some are occasionally seen in May. Spring bird counts had Lapland Longspurs on 13 of 15 years, with the highest count 251 in 1977. Most high counts were from northern Illinois: 150, Kane County, May 4, 1974; 150, Lake County, May 7, 1977. The exception was one bird in McLean County in 1981 (VK). Other high counts in spring: 1000, Sangamon County, April 8, 1982 (HDB); 3000, Jasper County, March 10, 1984 (LH-SR41:27); 2200, Mason County, March 21, 1985 (KR-IB&B1:90). Late spring records: Jackson Park, May 27, 1981 (RG,PC-AB35:831); Stark County, May 16, 1984 (MBr-SR41:27).

SMITH'S LONGSPUR
Calcarius pictus

COMMON SPRING MIGRANT AND
OCCASIONAL FALL MIGRANT

This bird seems elusive, but only because it tends to stay in the middle of fallow fields and seldom comes up to roads. Thus any would-be observer is forced to walk the fields to find Smith's Longspurs. They seem to prefer clover and alfalfa fields, especially where water has stood and then mostly dried. But they also occur in corn and soybean stubble and grassy areas such as open golf courses and airfields. They occasionally sit on fences, and I once saw a flock land on a power line. They have the peculiar habit of waiting until the observer is 10 or 20 yards away before flying up and giving their dry rattling series of clicking notes. Their call notes can be distinguished from the Lapland Longspur's notes with some practice. These two species seldom flock together, although they may be found in the same field. Smith's Longspurs are much buffier than Lapland Longspurs, and the Smith's white shoulder patch and more extensive white in the tail are good field marks. Although most recent reports have come from central Illinois, Smith's Longspurs formerly occurred in northern Illinois, as shown by specimens in the Carpenter collection taken at Polo on April 3, 1905 (ISM), and a series of 19 specimens at the Chicago Academy of Science taken in Cook County from 1893 to 1910. Nelson (1876) noted a flock of about 75 at Lake Calumet on March 30, 1875, and there are other references. Southern Illinois, although not as level or as open as central Illinois, has areas where Smith's Longspurs occur. Specimens in the Steinhauer collection were obtained in Fayette County, April 16, 1909 (ISM). The gizzard contents from two specimens from Christian County collected April 9, 1974, contained *Setaria* and *Paspalum* seeds and beetles of the family Curculionidae. Smith's Longspurs nest on the tundra from east-central Alaska across northern Canada to Hudson Bay.

The migration route of these longspurs must be elliptical, since they are much more numerous in spring than in fall. Early spring arrival dates: six, Perry County, March 6, 1986 (TF-IB&B2:97); 20, Mason County, March 7, 1987 (TP,LA); two, Sangamon County, March 6, 1976 (HDB). Average arrival dates: west-central, March 21 (five years); Sangamon County, March 20 (18 years). High counts for spring: 300, Horseshoe Lake, April 15, 1980 (BR-SR25:15); 200, Argenta, April 16, 1983 (LA,TP-SR37:27); 80, Knox County, March 18, 1987 (MB); 215, Mason County, March 21, 1985 (KR-IB&B1:90); hundreds, Jasper County, April 7, 1985 (SB-IB&B1:90); 500, Sangamon County, April 4, 1980 (HDB). Most years these longspurs have departed by the end of April. The average departure date for Sangamon County is April 25 (17 years). Some years a few linger into May: two, Urbana, May 7, 1983 (BCho-SR37:27); eight, Sangamon County, May 6, 1978 (HDB).

Fall migration seems to be limited not only in numbers but also in the time these birds take to pass through. Most recent fall records have occurred around the first week of November: six, Lawrenceville, November 4, 1979 (LH-AB34:169); six, Sangamon County, November 4, 1979 (HDB); Clinton, November 11, 1979 (RCh-AB34:169); six, Carlyle Lake, November 7, 1987 (D.Jo,RG); Urbana, November 10, 1963 (PN-AFN18:43); Valmeyer, November 14, 1971 (Stricklings-AB26:73). These birds may arrive in northern Illinois somewhat earlier, probably in October, but records are scanty and not recent: 14, Joy, mid-October 1958 (Green and Trial-AFN13:37). In fall the Smith's Longspur is duller and identification is more difficult, but good views should prevent misidentifications.

If the Smith's Longspur winters in Illinois it does so only rarely. There are no acceptable records. Iowa is said to fall within this species' winter range (AOU 1983), but Dinsmore et al. (1984) list no winter records there either. The main wintering grounds are in the southern Great Plains.

CHESTNUT-COLLARED LONGSPUR

Calcarius ornatus

VERY RARE MIGRANT

Until recently this beautiful longspur was considered hypothetical in Illinois. Like the McCown's, the Chestnut-collared Longspur breeds on the northern Great Plains and winters on the southern Great Plains. But the Chestnut-collared seems to wander more, or perhaps it simply has a larger population. Three recent records from Illinois are properly documented: female photographed, west of Springfield, March 29, 1980 (Bohlen 1980); male, Tazewell County, May 12, 1981 (VH,LA-AB35:831); male, Sangchris State Park, April 10–11, 1982 (RCh-AB36:860). In my experience with two of these sightings, the Chestnut-collared Longspur did not give clicking or rattling notes in flight or on the ground, although some observers have stated that they do give clicking calls. The notes I heard were finchlike. The favored habitat is short grassy fields; bare spots or sparse vegetation may be important. In all three instances, these longspurs were essentially alone, even though other species of longspurs were nearby. There are a few older records, some of which are probably correct: 10–12 with Smith's Longspurs near Orland, April 24, 1910 (Coale 1910a); five, Du Page County, April 20, 1912 (Eifrig 1913); 100, Rantoul (Christmas bird count), 1914 (Bird-Lore 16:45); one, Washington Park, Chicago, April 18, 1923 (Smith and Parmalee 1955); two, Coles County, December 31, 1968 (AFN23:298); 20, Shelby County, December 30, 1968 (AFN23:301).

It will be noted that there are no fall records, and the winter records are dubious.

SNOW BUNTING

Plectrophenax nivalis

COMMON MIGRANT AND WINTER RESIDENT DECREASING SOUTHWARD

If one thinks of the coldest, most barren and windswept area imaginable, it would probably be a good place to find Snow Buntings. Like longspurs, Snow Buntings are found in fields, but they also occur at lake edges along the beach, at the wrack line, or among rocks. They are probably seen most often in Illinois along roadsides when snow covers the fields. They are also partial to feedlots in which manure is present and fields on which manure has been spread. At times they occur in large swirling masses of pure flocks and at other times with Lapland Longspurs and Horned Larks. They have call notes similar to those of longspurs, but when learned, these notes, along with the white in the Snow Buntings' wings and tail, make them recognizable on the wing even from a distance. On the ground some look quite brownish. Snow Buntings breed in the Arctic.

Early fall arrival dates: Chicago, September 27, 1984 (HR-AB39:62); Henderson County, October 29, 1983 (MB,LMc-SR39:25); Lake Springfield, October 25, 1987 (HDB); Carlyle Lake, October 30, 1986 (BR). Average arrival dates: Chicago, October 28 (14 years); west-central, November 3 (eight years); Sangamon County, November 18 (18 years). Apparently most of these birds fly on to the coasts for the winter. Others blend into the fields, only to reappear when it snows. The largest migration recorded in Illinois occurred at Glencoe on November 29, 1927; Grasett (1928) estimated that 25,000 passed by from 8:00 A.M. to 11:00 A.M. in flocks of 200 to 1000 birds. Other high counts: 2000, De Kalb, December 21, 1981 (MSw-AB36:301); 500, Illinois Beach State Park, November 7, 1981 (JL); 500, Rockford, January 10, 1987 (DW-AB41:289); 500, Lee County, February 26, 1986 (B.Grover-IB&B2:78); 1000, Macon County, January 13, 1982 (SS-SR32:8). Christmas bird count totals for 1976–85 ranged from 713 in 1984 to 4612 in 1981, with high counts all coming from northern Illinois. The highest count was 2133 at De Kalb in 1983. Southern Illinois gets only a few Snow Buntings, but they do occur there, and even in Kentucky (Mengel 1965): nine, Lawrenceville, November 19, 1983 (DJo-SR39:25); six, Rend Lake, November 8, 1975 (BP,R.Hayes); Union County, January 2, 1976 (PW,WO,BA); five, Carbondale, February 7, 1982 (MM-SR32:8).

Snow Buntings sometimes leave Illinois early, by late January or early February. Other years they linger quite late: two photographed, Lake Calumet, May 6, 1978 (RB-AB32:1017); Madison County, April 15, 1980 (BR-AB34:785); La Salle County, April 14, 1985 (JH-IB&B1:90). Several Snow Buntings were at Sangchris State Park on February 7, 1971; one landed in a small tree and sang its spring song.

BOBOLINK

Dolichonyx oryzivorus

FAIRLY COMMON MIGRANT; FAIRLY
COMMON SUMMER RESIDENT IN THE NORTH
DECREASING SOUTHWARD

The breeding male Bobolink is a very distinctive solid black below and buff and white above. The female is buff with dark stripes on the head. In fall most Bobolinks look like females, though some adult males show more black markings. The Bobolink's song, usually given in flight, has a bubbling quality. The flight note, a sharp *pink,* is often the only way to detect this species, especially in fall. The Bobolink is an open field bird, occurring along fence lines and in clover, alfalfa, and other hayfields and pastures. In fall it occurs more in marshy areas, making detection more difficult. Migrants usually form small flocks, with the males arriving first in spring and the females a short time later. Some migration is nocturnal, with television tower fatalities occurring in both spring and fall.

Early spring arrivals: Wabash County, April 19, 1981 (LH-AB35:831); Fulton County, April 16, 1983 (MB-AB37:877); Union County, April 12, 1987 (TF). Average arrival dates: Chicago, May 4 (16 years); west-central, May 1 (13 years); Sangamon County, April 30 (17 years). Maximum counts for spring: 120, Union County, April 12, 1987 (TF); 109, Monroe County, May 14, 1986 (RG,SRu); 100, Evanston, May 11, 1978 (Mlodinow 1984). Spring bird count totals ranged from 422 in 1973 to 3514 in 1976. No section of the state had consistently high counts. The highest count was 571 in Jersey County, May 6, 1972 (VK). Average dates of departure from areas where Bobolinks do not nest: Chicago, May 20 (16 years); Sangamon County, May 22 (15 years). Occasionally stragglers are seen in late May and even June. Some males seem to set up territories only to abandon them later.

Loucks (1893) summed up what was known about the Bobolink in Illinois from early observers: "The bobolink is transient throughout the state; summer resident in the northern half; abundant in the northern quarter." Graber and Graber (1963) estimated that the June Bobolink population had increased from 1,175,000 in 1909 to 1,860,000 in 1957. But when Robbins et al. (1986) analyzed the breeding bird survey data for 1965–79 they found decreases in the Illinois population. This finding fit in with the general downward trend in the populations of most Illinois grassland bird species. The mean number of Bobolinks per survey route was 4.5. Counts of summer birds: 380, Du Page County, June 1985 (JM-IB&B2:17); 203, Cook County, June 14, 1986 (IB&B3:16). One pair was noted as far south as Wabash County on June 14, 1983 (LH-SR38:17). Bobolinks nest on the ground, laying three to seven buffy eggs with dark spots or blotches. Illinois egg dates are May 25 to July 11. Cowbirds sometimes parasitize Bobolink nests.

Fall migration for this species, though partially diurnal, is little noted. Bobolinks make long flights, usually stopping at marshy areas, where they are fairly silent unless disturbed. The earliest fall arrival dates are early to mid-August. Average arrival dates: Chicago, August 14 (six years); Sangamon County, August 28 (18 years). High counts: 50, Winnebago County, August 22, 1984 (DW-IB&B1:22); 45, Piatt County, August 23, 1987 (RP); 35, Mark Twain National Wildlife Refuge, September 6, 1982 (BR-SR35:16). Average departure dates: Chicago, September 15 (six years); Sangamon County, September 29 (17 years). Some birds linger into early October. Bobolinks winter in southern South America east of the Andes. It is rather surprising to find three winter records in Illinois for this bird: Crab Orchard National Wildlife Refuge, December 6, 1953 (Smith and Parmalee 1955); Rockford, December 7, 1983 (DW-AB37:878); Carterville, January 26, 1983 (DR).

RED-WINGED BLACKBIRD

Agelaius phoeniceus

ABUNDANT MIGRANT AND SUMMER
RESIDENT; COMMON WINTER RESIDENT IN
SOUTHERN ILLINOIS DECREASING
NORTHWARD

One of the first birds many people learn to recognize is the male Red-winged Blackbird. Its bright red shoulder patches form a simple but pleasing pattern that makes it easy to see and identify. Its *konk-ka-reee* is one of the first spring migrant songs to be heard as males line up along roadsides and begin their fierce competition for territories. Female Red-wings often are misidentified, since they are smaller than the males and have the brown streaked pattern of a sparrow. Like other blackbirds, the Red-winged forms huge roosts in winter. One or several albinistic Red-wings can usually be observed in these large roosts. Although Red-wings cause some damage to crops, they also consume great quantities of insects and weed seeds. The breeding subspecies found in Illinois is *A. p. phoeniceus.* During migration and in winter the northern "Giant" Red-wing, *A. p. arctalegus,* may be seen and probably also *A. p. fortis,* the large, pale northwestern race. Specimens of winter Red-wings should be preserved and placed in appropriate collections.

The differential spring migration of the sexes in the Red-winged Blackbird is obvious. Males start arriving in Illinois as early as late January in mild springs. Average arrival dates: Chicago, March 13 (16 years); west-central, February 22 (15 years). Spring migration appears to be mostly diurnal; I have seen flock after flock moving north along the south fork of the Sangamon River. On March 7, 1982, a flock estimated at 10,000 individuals was at Springfield feeding in a corn stubble field. Most were males, and when they took flight they made a spectacular sight with their red shoulder patches showing in the sun. Spring bird count totals ranged from 29,859 in 1972 to 60,702 in 1984, with the highest count 3771 in Cook County, May 5, 1984 (VK). At roosts checked in late April and May, practically all Red-wings will be females; they are still moving north at that late time, while local birds are busy nesting.

Red-winged Blackbird populations in Illinois increased dramatically from 1909 (5,100,000) to 1958 (11,000,000), according to the estimates of Graber and Graber (1963). This blackbird was originally a marsh-dwelling species; in 1909, 60 percent of the Red-wings were in marsh habitats. But they switched to cultivated land—an adaptation that ensured their survival—and by 1958 only 3 percent of the Red-wings were in marshes. This change redistributed the population; it was formerly highest in the north, but now it is distributed evenly over the state. Robbins et al. (1986) found an increase for this blackbird in the central region of the United States in breeding bird surveys for 1965–79 but did not mention Illinois specifically. The mean number of birds per survey route was 191.7 in Illinois. Red-wings now nest in clover fields, drainage ditches, marshes, wood edges, fallow fields, and other cultivated fields. They nest rather low, sometimes on the ground, building substantial cuplike nests. Male Red-wings become very aggressive around their nests, even striking intruders, including humans. The female lays three to five (usually four) eggs, which vary from light brown to white to pale blue and have black squiggly marks. Available Illinois egg dates are May 12 to July 17. Cowbirds sometimes parasitize Red-wing nests. By mid-August most Red-wings are in molt, and they become harder to detect.

The start of fall migration is difficult to pinpoint, but average arrival dates are Chicago, October 6 (16 years), and west-central, November 10 (seven years). Hordes of these blackbirds pour into roosts in fall as in spring, but by mid- to late November numbers have dropped except in the largest roost sites, mostly in southern Illinois.

Graber and Graber (1963) estimated that fewer than 10,000 Red-wings winter in central and northern Illinois. In southern Illinois the distribution was spotty because of roost sites, but they estimated 5,200,000 in January 1957. Habitats in winter include cornfields, wood edges, and pastures. Christmas bird count totals for 1976–85 ranged from 7876 in 1979 (unusually low because of severe winters) to 1,585,916 in 1976. The highest single count was 1,000,000 at Crab Orchard National Wildlife Refuge in 1959.

EASTERN MEADOWLARK

Sturnella magna

COMMON MIGRANT AND SUMMER
RESIDENT; COMMON WINTER RESIDENT
DECREASING NORTHWARD

The plaintive whistled song of this open-country bird is one of the most melodious sounds in nature. The Eastern Meadowlark is the yellow-breasted bird with the black V that sits on fences and wires, or the chunky brown bird that pops from a grassy field and flies away with choppy flaps and a glide, with white outer tail feathers showing. In a sense meadowlarks symbolize rural America and its wide open spaces. Illinois has both the Eastern and Western Meadowlarks, including two forms of the Eastern: *S. m. magna*, the northeastern subspecies, and *S. m. argutula*, the southern subspecies. According to Ridgway (1902), *argutula* is smaller and darker than *magna* and occurs in Richland, Lawrence, and Wabash Counties. Between 1960 and 1967 in southern Illinois (no specific locations given), Hamilton and Klimstra (1985) collected 358 meadowlarks, of which 88 males and 87 females were *argutula*, 60 males and 8 females were intermediate between *magna* and *argutula*, and the remaining 115 were *magna*. The extent of the ranges of the subspecies in Illinois is not known.

Spring migration is mostly diurnal and occurs as short, low-altitude flights. I have seen these meadowlarks migrating over Lake Springfield in early spring. Average spring arrival dates: Chicago, March 10 (16 years); Urbana, February 26 (20 years); Sangamon County, February 20 (13 years). During warm springs these migrants may arrive as early as late January. Spring bird count totals ranged from 2652 in 1979 to 7360 in 1986. The 1979 count shows the effects of severe winters. Most high counts were from southern counties; the highest was 613 in St. Clair County on May 9, 1981 (VK).

Eastern Meadowlarks are found in pasturelands, hayfields, fallow fields, and row crops. Graber and Graber (1963) found that the June population in Illinois had decreased somewhat from 4,760,000 in 1909 to 3,800,000 in 1958 and that there had been a definite shift toward the north. The Grabers also thought that the meadowlark population of a field varied inversely with the Red-winged Blackbird population. On Illinois breeding bird survey routes (1965–79), the mean number of Eastern Meadowlarks was 41.3. Robbins et al. (1986) found that meadowlarks were declining in the eastern United States. Meadowlarks nest on the ground, laying two to six white eggs that are spotted to varying degrees with reddish brown. Illinois egg dates are April 6 to July 23. Roseberry and Klimstra (1970), in their study of the nesting ecology of meadowlarks, found that the number of eggs laid decreased as the season progressed but the percentage of successful nests increased. They found predation (51.2 percent) and mowing (12.2 percent) to be the primary reasons for loss of nests. Cowbirds parasitize meadowlarks' nests. Small flocks of meadowlarks, usually family groups, are encountered in late summer. Some of these individuals look rather ragged because of molt. At this season there is much less singing, and meadowlarks seem to drop out of sight for a while. Meadowlarks eat insects when available, especially cutworms, caterpillars, beetles, and grasshoppers. In the colder months they switch to seeds and waste grain.

Migration in fall is usually less noticeable than in spring, and wintering birds obscure departure dates. Gross (1958), however, stated that in southern Illinois during October immense flocks numbering in the hundreds of individuals concentrated in the lowland above Cairo. Average departure dates: Chicago, October 25 (11 years); Sangamon County, November 6 (nine years).

Most of the winter population is in southern Illinois. The favorite wintering habitat seems to be cornfields, but these meadowlarks also occur in fallow fields. During snows, when they are driven up to roads, they become much more noticeable. Graber and Graber (1963) estimated that the winter population in north and central Illinois was less than 10,000 in 1906-7 but had grown to 300,000 in 1957 because the meadowlarks were wintering farther north. The estimated January population in southern Illinois was 3,100,000 in 1907 and 3,400,000 in 1957. The Grabers noted that February populations are lower, suggesting either migration or die-off or both. Christmas bird counts showed a definite drop in the population due to the severe winters of the late 1970s. Unlike the spring figures, which show a complete recovery, winter counts do not, suggesting selection for migrant populations that survived. Christmas bird count totals ranged from 2225 in 1975 to 252 in 1979. The high count was 591 in Richland County in 1975.

WESTERN MEADOWLARK

Sturnella neglecta

UNCOMMON MIGRANT AND LOCAL SUMMER RESIDENT; UNCOMMON WINTER RESIDENT

The Western Meadowlark looks so much like the Eastern that its status in Illinois is somewhat uncertain. Most meadowlarks are presumed to be Easterns unless they are identified as Westerns by their song or call. But even the vocalizations sometimes seem to show a mingling of the two species. Sight identifications are difficult, and a look at the face is necessary. Zimmer (1984) discusses identification points. The best place to find Western Meadowlarks in Illinois is the sand prairie areas in Mason and Henderson Counties. They also inhabit large, rather dry pastures, airfields, and other treeless grassy areas. However, birds in these areas seem scarce and apparently come and go with various conditions. Most numerous in the northern and western sections of the state, they are known in southern Illinois only in winter. The Western Meadowlark extended its range eastward in the past 50 years, becoming more numerous in northern and central Illinois (Graber and Graber 1963; Lanyon 1956). But Westerns are still outnumbered by Easterns in most areas. When both species are present in the same area, the Eastern shows a preference for moist environments. The Western race found in Illinois is the nominate form.

Spring migrants are fairly easy to detect because of singing. Early arrivals are in February: seven, Jersey County, February 10, 1983 (HW-SR37:27); Danville, February 24, 1981 (MC- AB35:306); Knox County, February 17, 1987 (MB-AB41:289). Average arrival dates: west-central, March 23 (three years); Sangamon County, March 20 (11 years). Spring bird count totals ranged from 59 in 1985 to 355 in 1974. All high counts came from the northern or western sections of the state; the highest was 82 in Kendall County, May 6, 1972 (VK).

Western Meadowlarks undoubtedly have summered in Illinois for many years. Nelson (1876) listed a specimen collected on May 31, 1876, near Chicago. Robbins et al. (1986) noted declines in this species' numbers in Illinois using breeding bird survey data for 1965-79. The mean number of birds per survey route was 6.7. The nest and eggs are similar to those of the Eastern Meadowlark. Available Illinois egg dates are May 2 to June 15. Recent nesting areas away from northern and western Illinois are Champaign, 1982, and Springfield, 1986.

Fall migrants are difficult to detect, although some singing occurs and call notes of *kluk* are distinctive. Most departure dates are in October or November: Jasper County, November 14, 1985 (SS-IB&B2:55); five, Horseshoe Lake, November 4, 1982 (RG-SR35:16); Victoria, November 22, 1987 (MB).

Christmas bird count data show a few Western Meadowlarks in northwestern Illinois, including 80 at Rockford in 1970. Two were seen in Alexander County on December 21, 1982 (RG,JEa-SR36:11), and at Carlyle on February 13, 1983 (LH,DJo,SRu-SR36:11), both southern Illinois locations.

YELLOW-HEADED BLACKBIRD

Xanthocephalus xanthocephalus

LOCALLY UNCOMMON MIGRANT AND SUMMER RESIDENT IN NORTHERN ILLINOIS; RARE MIGRANT ELSEWHERE IN THE STATE; VERY RARE WINTER RESIDENT

Because of its bold coloration the male Yellow-headed Blackbird is unmistakable and should be easy to see. Yet, as a marsh-dwelling species this blackbird has the habit of sitting just low enough in the vegetation to be concealed most of the time. With patience an observer will be rewarded when one perches in the top of the cattails or rushes and sings its song, which sounds like a rusty hinge. Females are browner than males but have enough of a yellow splash to make them easily identifiable. Although this blackbird is mostly a western species, it has apparently been in Illinois for some time. Loucks (1893a) summarized the status of Yellow-headed Blackbirds. They were found breeding at that time in Lake, Cook, McHenry, Putnam, and Vermilion Counties. The Illinois State Museum has early specimens from Fayette County, 1891, and Winnebago County, June 14, 1905. Today Yellow-heads are considered to be an endangered species in Illinois because of localized breeding.

Early spring arrivals: three, Barrington, April 9, 1981 (TG-SR29:13); Stark County, April 8, 1986 (MBr-IB&B2:97); Bismark, March 20, 1987 (SB); Havana, March 29, 1987 (LA). Average arrival dates: west-central, May 1 (six years); Sangamon County, April 26 (six years). High counts are usually obtainable only on the breeding grounds. If these birds migrate in large flocks, few if any have been noted recently. Pearson stated that they arrived with Red-winged Blackbirds in parties of 30 to 100 individuals (Loucks 1893a). Spring bird count totals ranged from 22 in 1973 to 186 in 1986. The highest count was 102 in Lake County, May 10, 1980. Other counties with high counts were De Kalb, Cook, and McHenry (VK).

Recent breeding areas: Redwing Slough (61 adults, 1981), Lake Calumet (46 young, 1982), Illinois Beach State Park, Kane County marshes, Du Page County marshes, Moraine Hills State Park, Beardstown Marsh, Havana, Eggers Woods, Round Lake, Horseshoe Lake, and other areas, especially in northeastern Illinois. Breeding downstate seems fortuitous and intermittent, lasting only one to a few years. Yellow-heads nest in marshes, attaching their nests to cattails two or three feet above water. The female usually lays four, sometimes three or five, tan eggs with fine darker brown markings. Illinois egg dates are May 20 to June 28.

Fall migrants have been noted as early as July and August: Springfield, July 30, 1987 (HDB); Madison County, August 2, 1980 (MP-AB35:191); Manito, July 23, 1984 (KR-IB&B1:19). The average fall arrival date for Springfield is August 27 (six years). In fall and winter Yellow-heads feed with other blackbirds in cultivated fields and feedlots, sometimes at bird feeders. They roost at established blackbird roost sites. Six Yellow-heads were seen at a Springfield roost site on October 3, 1986 (HDB). Other fall records: a partial albino male, Lake Calumet, July 15, 1984 (JL); Lake Calumet, September 26, 1981 (JM-SR31:16); Lake Shelbyville, September 5, 1986 (KF-IB&B3:47); Horseshoe Lake, October 11, 1986 (RA-IB&B3:47). Most Yellow-heads leave the state by mid- to late October.

There are a few winter records even though the normal winter range is the southwestern United States south to southern Mexico: one each on three Christmas bird counts (Pere Marquette State Park in 1957, Crane Lake in 1978, and Calumet City in 1985); Fairbury, December 5, 1977 (P.Jeffries-AB32:360); Carterville, February 14, 1982 (DR-AB36:301); Chicago, January 26, 1986 (C.Hillegonds-AB40:288); Illinois Beach State Park, January 1-2, 1987 (T.Steele-AB41:289); Riverwoods, December 28, 1985 (IB&B2:78).

RUSTY BLACKBIRD

Euphagus carolinus

COMMON MIGRANT; UNCOMMON WINTER
RESIDENT USUALLY DECREASING
NORTHWARD

Rusty is a good name for this blackbird. It describes not only the color of its plumage in fall but also its song, which sounds like a rusty hinge. Both males and females have light eyes. These blackbirds are found in swamps, along woodland edges, and in cornfields. Rusty Blackbirds often feed by wading in shallow water. They are usually associated more with woodlands than are Brewer's Blackbirds, but they do occur in some open areas with other

blackbirds. Vernon Kleen and I discovered a site near Vienna on March 5, 1974, where Rusties and Red-wings were roosting on the ground in an open grassy field. In fact, we caught several of these birds with mist nets that night. Other roosts have been found in marshes and woodlands. Rusty Blackbirds breed primarily in conifers in Alaska, Canada, and the northern United States. The nominate form is found in Illinois.

Earliest fall arrival dates: Chicago, September 15, 1937 (Clark and Nice 1950); Wilmette, September 21, 1981 (JG-SR31:16); Horseshoe Lake, September 25, 1978 (RG). Most other early dates are in October. Average fall arrival dates: Chicago, September 26 (16 years); Sangamon County, October 24 (18 years). High counts for fall: 400, Lawrence County, November 22, 1981 (LH-SR31:16); 200, Lake Vermilion, November 21-22, 1983 (SB-SR39:26); 150, Moultrie County, November 17, 1986 (YM-IB&B3:47). Average fall departure dates: Chicago, November 2 (16 years); Sangamon County, December 7 (12 years). Rusty Blackbirds typically stay into December most years; some years they winter. Their winter movements usually depend on roosting sites, so distribution tends to be spotty. Christmas bird counts for 1976-85 showed a wide range of totals, from 72 in 1978 (a severe winter) to 7934 in 1976. The highest count was 6750 in Alexander County in 1985. Most high counts come from southern Illinois, but 1106 were counted at Morris-Wilmington in 1981 and 5000 at Springfield in 1975. Rusties attend bird feeders occasionally and are found in and around feedlots in winter.

Spring migration starts early, sometimes in early February. Average spring arrival dates: Chicago, April 2 (14 years); west-central, March 1 (11 years). Maximum counts in spring: 256, Waukegan, March 26, 1987 (JN); 100, Springfield, March 24, 1986 (HDB). Spring bird counts are done well past the peak period for this blackbird; totals ranged from one in 1985 to 403 in 1972, but I question the identification of so many in Fulton County (221) in 1972 (VK). Average spring departure dates: Chicago, April 26 (14 years); Sangamon County, April 19 (17 years). Late spring departure dates: two, Waukegan, May 4, 1983 (JN-SR37:28); a singing male, Jackson Park, May 4, 1980 (RG).

BREWER'S BLACKBIRD

Euphagus cyanocephalus

UNCOMMON AND ERRATIC MIGRANT; RARE
WINTER RESIDENT AND RARE SUMMER
RESIDENT IN NORTHERN ILLINOIS

Confusion between Brewer's and Rusty Blackbirds in Illinois has somewhat obscured the status of the Brewer's Blackbird. There is much less rust color in the winter plumage of the Brewer's than in Rusties, and Brewer's females have dark eyes. The major problem is with the adult males, since both species are glossy black with light eyes. Brewer's Blackbirds look somewhat like Common Grackles but with shorter tails. They are nearly always in open habitats, such as plowed fields, wet pastures, and marshy areas; in winter they are at feedlots and bird feeders. I have seen them at a roost with other blackbirds in a cattail marsh. Although Brewer's Blackbirds have been present for some time, as proved by a female collected at Mount Carmel in December 1866 (Ridgway 1889), they have increased in numbers in Illinois recently.

Spring migration begins as early as late February or early March: two, Horseshoe Lake, February 27, 1982 (RK-SR32:7); six, Springfield, February 28, 1981 (HDB); five, Winnebago County, March 8, 1985 (DW-IB&B1:90). Average spring arrival dates: west-central, April 9 (nine years); Sangamon County, March 26 (13 years). It is axiomatic that the more uncommon a bird species is the more likely it is to be missed by observers, thus presenting a more uneven picture of its migration in a given year. Winds and other migrational factors also play a role in whether Brewer's Blackbirds are common or rare in a given season. Maximum counts for spring: 60, Springfield, April 12, 1981 (HDB); 37, Lawrence County, April 8, 1980 (LH-SR25:8); 30, Henderson County, March 17, 1984 (LMc-SR41:28). Spring bird counts are of dubious value because of identification problems, but the totals ranged from two in 1974 and 1977 to 533 in 1972. High counts (if correct) were 425 in Boone County, May 6, 1972, and 236 in Adams County, May 5, 1973 (VK). Average departure dates: west-central, April 19 (nine years); Sangamon County, April 13 (11 years).

There has clearly been an expansion of the range of this western bird eastward, particularly since 1925 (Walkinshaw and Zimmerman 1961). As far as is known, it has nested in Illinois only in the north and principally the northeastern corner of the state. First nest records were by Lyon (1930) at Zion in June 1929. Brewer's Blackbirds still breed in that area. Other areas in which it has been found nesting are Northfield Township, Cook County; Lake Calumet; and Rockford. Recent breeding records: five pairs, Waukegan, 1978 (JN-AB32:1170); six pairs, Illinois Beach State Park, June 30, 1982 (AB36:984). They continue to be seen in these areas every summer. The few nests that have been located contained five eggs (June 7), four young and five young (May 30), four young and five young (June 26), five young and three young (June 28), and five young (June 30). They nest on or near the ground in clumps of vegetation.

Early fall arrival dates: Jackson Park, October 5–9, 1981 (RA, DP-SR31:16); female, Springfield, October 19, 1986 (HDB). Average arrival date for Sangamon County is November 4 (13 years). Maximum counts for fall: 50, Homer, December 2–4, 1983 (JSm-AB38:324); 12, Springfield, November 8, 1986 (HDB); nine, Chicago, November 29, 1983 (MS-SR39:26). The average fall departure date for Sangamon County is November 17 (five years). Two recent specimens are in the Illinois State Museum collection, both males from near Springfield, November 11, 1980, and November 14, 1983.

The winter status of this species is in disarray because of identification problems stemming from records that were not fully or accurately documented. Christmas bird count data are mostly worthless, although some records are surely

accurate. Rusty Blackbirds are much more prevalent in winter than Brewer's Blackbirds. Stepney (1975) reported that a Brewer's Blackbird banded in Illinois was recovered in winter in Louisiana. He also found that snow cover has a strong negative effect on wintering Brewer's Blackbirds. The wintering status of this species will have to be worked out by banding and collecting the birds and making reliable sight records. When large blackbird roosts are destroyed in winter, this species should be searched for among the dead.

GREAT-TAILED GRACKLE

Quiscalus mexicanus

VERY RARE VAGRANT

This southwestern species is expanding its range. It breeds locally as close to Illinois as southwestern Missouri. There has been only one record for the state, however—an adult female at Jacksonville, October 5–7, 1974 (Randall 1975). It was feeding at a sewage disposal plant on ragweed and grasshoppers. The specimen, in the Illinois State Museum collection, is of the *Q. m. prosopidicola* race (see Bohlen 1976). Identification problems arise with the Boat-tailed Grackle, from which the Great-tailed species was split; Pratt (1974) and Pruitt (1975) explain the differences. Reports of Boat-tailed Grackles being banded at Ohio, Illinois, are without any sort of documentation (*Wilson Bulletin* 35:169, 1923, and 36:42, 1924). Great-tailed Grackles are found in open and semiopen areas, usually near water, and in cultivated fields. They are distributed as far south as South America.

COMMON GRACKLE

Quiscalus quiscula

ABUNDANT MIGRANT AND SUMMER RESIDENT; COMMON WINTER RESIDENT IN SOUTHERN ILLINOIS DECREASING NORTHWARD

Even though this is a native species, it is widely thought of as disagreeable. After the cowbird it is the least liked by bird enthusiasts. Common Grackles gather in large flocks and are found in practically every habitat, intimidating other birds by their noise and gregariousness. In migration their large flocks undulating in the sky can sometimes take several minutes to pass. Their numbers can only be compared to those reported for Passenger Pigeons in the nineteenth century. Grackles thrive in manipulated environments, nesting abundantly in residential areas, feeding on crops, and roosting in towns and cities. Their roosting areas sometimes become health hazards and have to be broken up. Grackles are omnivorous, their diet changing with the seasons. They cause some damage to crops, especially corn. Grackles have even been seen catching small fish and killing other birds, especially House Sparrows. The subspecies found in Illinois is *Q. q. versicolor,* the Bronzed Grackle of the older literature.

Common Grackles usually arrive in late February, but these birds move somewhat with the weather. Average spring arrival dates: Chicago, March 14 (16 years); west-central, March 4 (15 years); Urbana, March 3 (12 years). The large flocks are usually seen in March; spring bird counts occur after most flocks have broken up and nesting has begun. Spring bird count totals ranged from 31,249 in 1972 to 59,264 in 1974. The highest count was 5495 in Will County, May 4, 1974 (VK).

Even though grackles seem ubiquitous, Graber and Graber (1963) found that there was a decline in the June populations between 1909 (4,100,000) and 1957 (3,600,000). They felt that the decline was caused by habitat changes, especially loss of orchards and marshes. The Common Grackle population is highest in northern Illinois and lowest in southern Illinois in summer. The Grabers found the most frequent habitat to be edge shrubs, hedgerows, marshes, and residential areas. Breeding bird surveys (1965-79) also showed a decrease in Illinois of this high-density species, although Illinois was one of the states with the greatest abundance. There were 131.5 birds per route (Robbins et al. 1986). Common Grackles usually nest at about medium height in conifers and other trees. They build bulky loose nests with a mud cup lining. There are usually four or five, sometimes six or seven, pale blue eggs with blackish markings. Illinois egg dates are April 21 to June 5. Flocks of Common Grackles can be seen as early as July, the young duller in color than the adults. Young grackles have dark eyes and have been mistaken for Brewer's Blackbirds.

Fall migration is a reverse of spring migration, but at times it is difficult to distinguish between daily movements to and from roosts and diurnal migration. Numbers begin dropping off when cold winter weather starts, usually in mid- to late November. There may be no noticeable drop if a large winter roost is nearby; these roosts are mostly in southern Illinois.

In winter the distribution of Common Grackles is spotty, with most of these birds dependent on roosting sites. Christmas bird count totals for 1976-85 ranged from 5434 in 1979 (unusually low because of severe winters) to 1,716,512 in 1976. Highest count was 1,350,000 at East St. Louis in 1973.

BROWN-HEADED COWBIRD

Molothrus ater

COMMON MIGRANT AND SUMMER RESIDENT; COMMON WINTER RESIDENT IN SOUTHERN ILLINOIS DECREASING NORTHWARD

In spring the liquid notes of the Brown-headed Cowbird are frequently heard in the woodlands where pairing and

mating take place. Although cowbirds feed mostly in open areas around cattle and in short grassy fields, it is in the woodlands that they look for nests in which to lay their eggs. Cowbirds do not build their own nests but are brood parasites of other birds. This adaption has been very successful for the cowbirds, allowing the adults to roam with feeding flocks while foster parents raise their young. Cowbirds usually choose smaller birds on which to inflict their brood parasitism, since the young cowbirds hatch earlier, mature faster, and thus have the advantage over their foster siblings. Cowbirds seem to pick on Neotropical migrants that are plagued by other population-limiting factors such as habitat losses in North, Central, and South America.

Spring migrants, hard to distinguish from wintering birds, arrive as early as February. Average arrival dates: Urbana, March 11 (19 years); Chicago, March 27 (16 years); west-central, March 9 (15 years). Cowbirds, among the most numerous birds on Illinois spring bird counts, were seen in all 102 counties in 1986. Totals ranged from 2896 in 1972 to 8096 in 1984. The highest count was 708 in Rock Island County, May 6, 1978 (VK).

Cowbirds are found statewide in summer but are most dense in northern Illinois. They are found in practically all habitats, but forest edges, hedgerows, and shrubs are the most densely populated. Graber and Graber (1963) noted that the estimated June cowbird population declined from 1,800,000 in 1909 to 1,130,000 in 1957, probably owing to the loss of pastures. Breeding bird surveys for 1965-79 showed significant increases in cowbird numbers in the central states. There were 10.2 cowbirds per route on Illinois surveys (Robbins et al. 1986). A single female cowbird can lay up to 30 eggs in one season. The eggs are whitish, speckled or spotted with brown. Illinois egg dates are April 26 to July 11 (Bent 1958). Once the young cowbirds are raised by the foster parents they join flocks of other cowbirds. In late summer these flocks contain mottled birds, which are juveniles molting into adultlike plumage.

Cowbirds form huge roosts with other blackbirds and starlings in fall and winter. Some roosts form as early as July; 500 cowbirds were at Channahon, July 21, 1962 (CC). Average fall departure dates: west-central, December 22 (six years); Sangamon County, November 22 (seven years). Many cowbirds typically stay into December or until they are forced out by severe weather. Christmas bird count totals for 1976-85 varied greatly, from 629 in 1979 to 193,330 in 1977. This difference may be real some years, but it also depends on whether a roost is in the count circle and whether it is checked by observers. High counts: 115,000, Sangamon County, 1977; 200,000, Crab Orchard National Wildlife Refuge, 1960; 20,000, Alexander County, 1982. Graber and Graber (1963) indicate that wintering in Illinois is a relatively recent phenomenon for cowbirds. None were recorded in winter 1906-7, whereas 350,000 were estimated in southern Illinois in January 1957. In some severe winters most or all of the population may be deflected farther south. In northern and central Illinois cowbirds are casual in winter, some going to bird feeders and others to cattle feedlots. Brown-headed Cowbirds winter south as far as Oaxaca and central Vera Cruz.

Following is a list of 61 host species from Illinois known to be parasitized by Brown-headed Cowbirds: Yellow-billed Cuckoo, Eastern Wood-Pewee, Acadian Flycatcher, "Traill's" Flycatcher, Eastern Phoebe, Great Crested Flycatcher, Eastern Kingbird, Horned Lark, Bank Swallow, Cliff Swallow, Blue Jay, Black-capped Chickadee, Tufted Titmouse, White-breasted Nuthatch, Blue-gray Gnatcatcher, Eastern Bluebird, Veery, Wood Thrush, American Robin, Gray Catbird, Brown Thrasher, European Starling, White-eyed Vireo, Bell's Vireo, Solitary Vireo, Yellow-throated Vireo, Warbling Vireo, Red-eyed Vireo, Blue-winged Warbler, Yellow Warbler, Chestnut-sided Warbler, Prairie Warbler, Black and White Warbler, American Redstart, Prothonotary Warbler, Worm-eating Warbler, Ovenbird, Louisiana Waterthrush, Kentucky Warbler, Mourning Warbler, Common Yellowthroat, Hooded Warbler, Yellow-breasted Chat, Summer Tanager, Scarlet Tanager, Northern Cardinal, Rose-breasted Grosbeak, Indigo Bunting, Dickcissel, Rufous-sided Towhee, Chipping Sparrow, Field Sparrow, Vesper Sparrow, Henslow's Sparrow, Song Sparrow, Red-winged Blackbird, Eastern Meadowlark, Yellow-headed Blackbird, Common Grackle, Orchard Oriole, and American Goldfinch.

ORCHARD ORIOLE

Icterus spurius

COMMON MIGRANT AND SUMMER RESIDENT
DECREASING NORTHWARD

In spring Orchard Orioles appear with the bursting forth of flowering trees and the first rush of insectivorous birds. They are usually announced by their song, which is rich and varied but characteristically has down-slurred notes at the end. Adult males appear in chestnut and black. First-year males share the female's olive green and yellow with two whitish wing bars but also have a black throat. Orchard Orioles prefer open wooded situations, especially orchards, willow-lined streams, brushy pastures, and hedgerows. They eat a mixture of insects and fruits, especially mulberries and wild cherries. In Tazewell County they were seen eating canker worms from an orchard. They spend much of the year in the tropics and only about three months in Illinois.

Dreuth's average for their arrival in Chicago is May 10 (six years); Smith's for Urbana is May 5 (19 years); and the average for Sangamon County is April 29 (17 years). Early arrival dates: two, Pomona, April 19, 1986 (DR-IB&B2:97); Jackson Park, April 26, 1984 (HR-SR41:28); Danville, April 27, 1884 (Cooke 1888). Spring bird count totals ranged from 70 in 1978 to 667 in 1986. High counts: 46, Pike County, May 4, 1985; 85, Moultrie County, May 10, 1986 (VK).

Graber and Graber (1963) found that the estimated Orchard Oriole population in Illinois dropped from 465,000 in 1909 to 90,000 in 1957. Not only has orchard

habitat declined but the number of orioles per acre of orchards has also declined drastically. Southern Illinois has four times more Orchard Orioles than central Illinois. More recently, Robbins et al. (1986) noted no change in Orchard Oriole populations in the eastern United States but found a decline in the central region on breeding bird survey data for 1965–79. The mean number of Orchard Orioles per survey route in Illinois (64 routes) was 0.7. This oriole's nest is cuplike and pensile or semipensile, usually placed at the tips of branches in apple or willow trees. The eggs are very light bluish with dark markings, especially near the larger end. Most Illinois clutches are four or five eggs, usually completed in early to mid-June. Some must be earlier, however, since young were reported as early as June 5, 1979, at Olney and June 6, 1980, at Georgetown. Orchard Orioles are frequent victims of cowbird parasitism. Some nesting is reported virtually every year in northern Illinois, though much less than elsewhere in the state. Family groups are seen in July, usually on the move. Some arrive in Central America in late July. In late summer and early fall Orchard Orioles are found in more open areas, along roadsides and in weedy and brushy areas. Some years these orioles just disappear in late July. My latest departure date for Sangamon County was September 20, 1984, with an average of August 17 (14 years). Other late dates: Shelby County, September 20, 1986 (KF-AB41:98); Middle Fork, September 11, 1985 (SB-IB&B2:55); Forest Glen Preserve, September 14, 1983 (MC-SR39;26). Very few if any maximum counts for fall are available. Oddly for a bird that leaves so early, there are two December occurrences. Merriman photographed an adult male near Cobden, Union County, on December 16, 1975, and one was seen at Carlyle Lake on December 15, 1982 (RG,PS-SR36:11). These late birds may have been vagrants from other populations or very late stragglers. Orchard Orioles winter as far south as northern Colombia and northern Venezuela, where they form large roosts.

NORTHERN ORIOLE

Icterus galbula

COMMON MIGRANT AND SUMMER RESIDENT

Northern Orioles seen in Illinois are represented by the "Baltimore" form, but a very few of the more western "Bullock's" Orioles have been recorded: two males, Horseshoe Lake, Alexander County, May 8, 1965 (WS); female, Fort Kaskaskia State Park, May 3, 1986 (RG-AB40:481). These two forms hybridize on the Great Plains (see Sutton 1938 and Rising 1970), and there is controversy over their taxonomy. Male Northern Orioles are a bold bright orange and black, females a variable orangish yellow and olive. Northern Orioles are found in woodlands, especially along watercourses and around lakes. They have a rich, full-whistled song and a chattering call note. Though bright, they are often somewhat difficult to see because they tend to stay high in heavily leaved trees. Early spring arrival dates: Saline County, April 10, 1987 (KP); Jackson County, April 13, 1986 (DR-IB&B2:97). Average arrival dates: Chicago, May 5 (16 years); west-central, April 27 (15 years); Sangamon County, April 27 (17 years). Spring bird count totals ranged from 705 in 1973 to 5532 in 1986, with a high of 345 in Cook County, May 10, 1986. Other high counts: 208, Adams County, May 4, 1985; 100, Madison County, May 5, 1979 (VK). Dreuth still had migrants at Chicago on May 31, 1929 (Clark and Nice 1950).

Robbins et al. (1986) noted recent increases in the number of "Baltimore" Orioles in Illinois, using breeding bird survey data for 1965–79. The mean number of orioles per survey route was 2.4. Orioles use elm trees to a great extent for nesting sites, but many elms have been killed by disease and these birds also use cottonwood and maple trees. The nest is a woven, hanging pouch in which three to five eggs are laid. A nest found near Beardstown was made of strips of cellophane and looked artificial. The eggs are whitish to pale blue with dark scrawls and markings. Illinois egg dates are May 25 to June 20. When the young are begging in the nest they sound somewhat like tree frogs.

Fall migration starts early; groups of orioles are seen in late July and August. High fall counts: 22, Olney, July 31, 1978 (LH-AB33:184); 15, Darien, August 14, 1982 (RPi-SR35:17); 15, Springfield, August 28, 1983 (HDB). Average departure dates: Chicago, August 30 (12 years); west-central, September 3 (nine years); Sangamon County, September 14 (18 years). Though some fall migration is diurnal, most is nocturnal. Television tower kills are sometimes fairly large: 35 at Springfield, September 3, 1981.

There are several very late fall dates and even wintering birds, usually attending bird feeders. These late birds should be examined closely to distinguish "Bullock's" or other western strays. Recent winter records: Effingham, January 2–February 13, 1980 (W.Sargent-AB34:279); Jacksonville, December 15–19, 1984 (AB:39:174); Plainfield, December 18–January 1, 1983 (JM-SR36:11). "Baltimore" Orioles winter from central Mexico south to northern South America.

PINE GROSBEAK
Pinicola enucleator

RARE AND IRREGULAR WINTER RESIDENT DECREASING SOUTHWARD

These large finches erupt out of the coniferous zone into Illinois at irregular intervals, most coming from the north and some from the west. In Illinois they are found mostly in coniferous areas. They feed in hemlock, ash, crabapple, and high bush cranberry. Occasionally they come to feeders, where they prefer sunflower seeds. Males are bright pinkish red, while females can be quite dull colored, mostly gray. Pine Grosbeaks are almost robin-sized, with stubby bills and two white wing bars. Of several subspecies, the

one recorded in Illinois is *P. e. leucura*, but others could occur, especially *P. e. eschatosus*. Pine Grosbeaks have invaded Illinois three times recently: 1968–69, 1971–72, and 1977–78. They have been recorded from late October to early April. They are usually confined to northern Illinois, but a few records come from southern Illinois: three, Pere Marquette State Park, December 20, 1969 (AFN24:313); two, Crab Orchard National Wildlife Refuge, December 30, 1972 (AB27:369). Sometimes in nonflight years single birds appear: Chicago, October 30, 1986 (WM-IB&B3:47); male, Springfield, February 7–24, 1985 (HDB); Jackson Park, January 6 and 18, 1981 (PC-SR28:8). Some maximum counts: 80, Lisle Arboretum, December 18, 1977 (AB32:693); 25, Rockford, March 19, 1972 (WSh-AB26:613); 30, Chicago, January 30–March 4, 1972 (AB26:613).

PURPLE FINCH
Carpodacus purpureus

COMMON MIGRANT AND UNCOMMON WINTER RESIDENT

Purple Finches are usually encountered in small groups in woodlands. They are especially fond of ash and sycamore seeds. Their rich song is loud, warbled, and bubbly, and they also have a distinctive *tic* flight note. They are found on forest edges and in hedgerows, giant ragweed patches, and city parks as well as in bottomland and upland forests. These finches are mainstays at feeding trays; sometimes they are absent from woods and can be found only at feeders. Adult males are bright raspberry, while females and immature males are brown with streaked underparts and a distinct face pattern. Purple Finches in Illinois belong to the nominate race, *C. p. purpureus*.

While precise detection of the arrival of spring migrants is sometimes difficult because of the presence of wintering birds, there is a definite increase in numbers. Sometimes dozens, many of them in song, will be seen in the tops of trees that are just leafing out. Average spring arrival dates: Chicago, April 5 (15 years); Urbana, April 1 (18 years); Sangamon County, April 14 (eight years). Totals on spring bird counts have ranged widely, from 35 in 1980 to 663 in 1984, with no trend apparent. The highest count was 68 in Will County, May 5, 1984 (VK). Average spring departure dates: Chicago, May 10 (15 years); Urbana, May 8 (18 years); Sangamon County, May 7 (17 years). Some of these finches linger late in spring: one banded, Springfield, May 21, 1980 (VK-AB34:785); Jackson Park, June 2, 1983 (HR,PC-SR37:28); Urbana, May 28, 1981 (JWh-SR29:14).

Although no recent nesting has been found, there are some old nesting records. Nelson (1876) stated that "a few breed"; Cooke (1888) recorded a set of eggs at Polo; and Cory (1909) listed an egg collected at Waukegan on May 13, 1875.

Some years fall migrants start returning as early as

August: Chicago, August 28, 1981 (JL); Winnebago County, August 31, 1981 (LJ-SR31:17); Chicago, August 18, 1983 (SP-SR39:26). Average arrival dates: Chicago, September 11 (16 years); Sangamon County, September 21 (18 years). High counts for fall: 96, Vermilion County, November 13, 1985 (MC-IB&B2:55); 30, Mendota, September 24, 1982 (JH-SR35:17); 18, Knox County, September 26, 1982 (MB-SR35:17). Departure dates are usually difficult to determine because of wintering birds, but the majority typically go farther south.

In winter the best counts of Purple Finches usually come from along wooded rivers. Christmas bird count totals for 1976-85 ranged from 50 in 1979 to 231 in 1976. The highest count was 276 at Rockford in 1959.

HOUSE FINCH
Carpodacus mexicanus

UNCOMMON PERMANENT RESIDENT AND INCREASING

House Finches are native to western North America, but they spread to Illinois from the East. These Hollywood Finches, as they were known in the pet trade, were released in the New York City area in 1940 after it was learned that they were illegal as pets. At first their population increase was gradual because they were adversely affected by extremely cold winters. But they now inhabit most of eastern North America (see Bohlen 1986). They reached Illinois in mid-November 1971, at Mount Vernon. The first nest record for the state was at Robinson in June 1982. By 1984 or 1985 House Finches had probably occurred in all Illinois counties, but they had been recorded in only 26. In 1987 they still remained most common on the eastern side of the state but were steadily increasing. They nest in gutters, awnings, and conifer trees. House Finches behave much like House Sparrows and in some instances compete with them. There is evidence that House Sparrow populations decline as House Finch populations increase.

The House Finch has a nice warbled song, and the brightly colored male makes this species much more attractive than the House Sparrow. House Finches, like the Purple Finches that they resemble, readily come to bird feeders. The House Finch males are reddish while the Purple Finches are pinkish rose; the House Finch also has a more rounded head and more streaked appearance. Immature males and females are brownish in both species, but House Finches lack the definite face pattern and whisker mark. The eastern House Finch population most closely resembles *C. m. frontalis,* the western California race. This newly established bird migrates, but to what extent is unknown.

House Finches were first noted on Illinois Christmas bird counts in 1980, when two were at Springfield. By 1985, 50 were recorded. None were seen on spring bird counts until 1982, when two were found. By 1986, 140 were recorded, with Vermilion County having the highest count: 33 on May 10, 1986. Other high counts: 100, Danville, winter 1986-87 (ME-AB41:289); 40, Springfield, December 22, 1986 (HDB); 12, Elmhurst, June 25, 1987 (JH); 25, Evanston, October 18, 1986 (RD-IB&B3:47). Nesting has occurred in all sections of the state, and many young have been seen.

RED CROSSBILL
Loxia curvirostra

UNCOMMON AND IRREGULAR WINTER RESIDENT; VERY RARE SUMMER RESIDENT

These plump birds with crossed bills remind one of little parrots as they hang upside down in conifers feeding on cones. They can be very quiet, with only the crunching of cones giving their presence away. They can also be very noisy, with their loud *jip* call notes audible at long distances. Some are very tame and approachable within arm's length. They have actually been caught by hand, for when they feed on pine cones they close their eyes. At other times they are unapproachable, flying away in a loose flock with an undulating flight. When the flock is feeding, one bird usually sits higher than the others and acts as sentinel. Red Crossbills feed on hemlock, pine, larch, birch, alder, and apple. They also eat insects. Occasionally a flock sits in the road ingesting grit and salt. Red Crossbill taxonomy is in a state of confusion, but apparently three of the eight subspecies that occur in North America have been collected in Illinois: *L. c. neogaea,* the northeastern population; *L. c. percna,* the Newfoundland population; and *L. c. bendirei,* the California population (see Dickerman 1987). More specimens are needed to determine the origins of these highly irruptive birds. Any road kills or window-killed Red Crossbills should be presented to museums for further study. Also, singing birds should be recorded, as vocalizations may provide clues to the subspecies.

Red Crossbills arrive in Illinois from August to December. The average date for central Illinois is October 20 (nine years). They occur during most years in varying numbers, but there are a few years when none are recorded. Fall arrival dates: 10, Springfield, August 9, 1972 (HDB); 10, Decatur, September 6, 1985 (RP-AB40:123); Peoria, October 7, 1981 (MSw-SR31:17); Carbondale, October 24, 1981 (MM-SR31:17). High counts for fall: 200, November 4, 1984 (AS-IB&B1:22), and 120, July 30–August 20, 1961 (Mlodinow 1984), at Illinois Beach State Park. Apparently in some years these crossbills pass through but do not stay for the winter, perhaps depending on the local cone crop.

Red Crossbills occurred on eight of the Christmas bird counts for 1976-85, with totals ranging from three in 1985 to 113 in 1979. The highest count was 66 at Lisle Arboretum in 1961 and Barrington in 1973. Other winter records: 30, Green River Conservation Area, January 11, 1981 (BSh-

AB35:306); 82, Sand Ridge State Forest, January 11, 1987 (LA-AB41:289); 12, Crab Orchard National Wildlife Refuge, December 16–January 1, 1985 (JR-IB&B1:70).

The average departure date in spring for central Illinois is May 6 (five years). Other spring records: 60, Big River State Forest, with some present through May 16, 1987 (MB); Urbana, May 27, 1981 (JWh-SR29:14); Sterling, May 30–June 1, 1982 (BSh-SR33:17). Spring bird count totals ranged from one to 38. The highest count was 24 in Mason County, May 10, 1980 (VK).

The nearest stable breeding population is in northern Wisconsin. Illinois nest records: nest destroyed by House Sparrows, Normal, April 1973 (Forsythe 1973); two nests, both unsuccessful, Springfield, March and April 1976 (HDB); female with three young, Illinois Beach State Park, June 10, 1973 (Mlodinow 1984). These nests were in larch, juniper, and Australian pine trees. There may be a permanent population in Sand Ridge forest; several are seen there nearly every summer. Summer records: 24, Sand Ridge forest, 1980 (RBj-AB34:902); Urbana, June 13, 1981 (JWh-AB35:946); female, Crawford County, June 3–11, 1986 (D.Schuur-IB&B3:16); male and female collected, Beach, June 1, 1923 (CAS).

WHITE-WINGED CROSSBILL

Loxia leucoptera

UNCOMMON AND IRREGULAR WINTER
RESIDENT DECREASING SOUTHWARD

This crossbill looks and acts much like the Red Crossbill. The males are colored somewhat differently, being pinkish red. The females and young are grayish olive. Both sexes and all ages have white wing bars. The calls of the two crossbills are much the same but can be distinguished with practice. The White-winged Crossbill's flight note is *chief.* White-wings feed in hemlocks, spruce, fir, and other conifers and in some deciduous trees, such as sweet gum (see George 1968a). The White-winged attends feeding trays more often than the Red Crossbill, though neither does so to any great extent. Sometimes the two crossbills feed in mixed flocks. The only White-winged Crossbill race in North America is *L. l. leucoptera.*

Dreuth recorded this species at Chicago as early as September 9, 1935, and one was seen at Illinois Beach State Park on September 29, 1973 (CC-AB28:62), but most arrival dates are in November. The average date for central Illinois is November 16 (five years). Other fall records: 32, Dundee, November 2, 1981 (SD-SR31:17); 26, Rockford, November 30, 1981 (LJ-SR31:17); Charleston, November 12, 1980 (LHB-SR27:12); 40, Springfield, November 25, 1977 (HDB). One of the largest invasions occurred November 9–20, 1904, when enormous flocks passed along the Lake Michigan shore and many White-winged Crossbills were shot by boys with slingshots (Woodruff 1907).

Christmas bird counts for 1976–85 recorded White-winged Crossbills only four years, with totals ranging from 16 in 1976 to 67 in 1980. The highest count was 47 at Lisle Arboretum in 1966. Other winter records: 36, Sterling, January 25–February 7, 1981 (BSh-AB35:306); 12, Urbana, winter 1980–81 (RB-SR28:9); 50, Lisle Arboretum, February 13, 1982 (PH-SR32:8); five, Union County, February 7, 1966 (George 1968); six, Union County, January 2, 1976 (M.Biggers).

This species tends to leave earlier in spring than the Red Crossbill. The average departure date for central Illinois is March 24 (six years). Late dates for spring departure: 15, Cook County, May 4, 1974 (spring bird count); two, Springfield, May 7, 1981 (HDB); Barrington, May 30, 1973 (LB-AB27:781); Winnetka, May 15, 1974 (RR-AB28:810). There is one summer record for the White-winged Crossbill, at Chicago in 1869 (Butler 1897).

COMMON REDPOLL

Carduelis flammea

UNCOMMON AND IRREGULAR MIGRANT AND
WINTER RESIDENT DECREASING
SOUTHWARD

These streaked, red-capped, black-chinned, and light-colored finches are closely related to American Goldfinches and Pine Siskins. They are more northerly in distribution, however, and much more erratic in occurrence. They breed circumboreal in forests and shrub areas and on the tundra in dwarf trees. In Illinois they are found in weedy areas and in alder, hemlock, sweet gum and especially birch trees, where they feed on the catkins. They sometimes flock with Pine Siskins. Common Redpolls have a chattering call note, which in Illinois is similar to the call of the Eurasian Tree Sparrow. When feeding, these redpolls can be very quiet; occasionally an observer can approach them very closely. Males are especially splendid, with a rosy blush on the breast. Of the three races found in North America, two have occurred in Illinois. The widespread form, *C. f. flammea,* is the one usually found in Illinois, but *C. f. rostrata,* the northwestern form, was taken in Cook County in 1878 and again at Beach in 1919 (Ford 1956). The third race, *C. f. holboellii,* could also occur, since it has been taken in Iowa and Wisconsin.

Dreuth's average arrival date in fall for Chicago is October 29 (11 years). Arrival is much later in central Illinois, with December 27 (four years) the average. Early arrival dates: Chicago, October 17, 1977 (Mlodinow 1984); Evanston, October 19, 1985 (AS-AB40:123). Sometimes redpolls do not arrive until January. They are recorded practically every year in northern Illinois, though some years their numbers are very small. In central Illinois several years may pass without a record. Although George (1968) and Bennett (1952) did not record any in southern Illinois, a few reach there in big flight years. They have been reported several times in Kentucky, with one specimen taken (Mengel 1965). Southern Illinois records: six, Olney, December 27, 1969 (AFN24:306); Beall Woods, February 5, 1972 (R.Dolphin); Carbondale, winter 1981–82 (DR-AB36:301) and end of February 1981 (HD-SR28:8); male specimen near Nutwood, February 26, 1972 (ISM collection). High counts for fall: 1000, Evanston, late October-November 3, 1968 (CC,JG,RR-AFN23:65); 145, Lisle Arboretum, December 21, 1969 (AFN24:311); 250, Rockford, January 25, 1972 (Shaws); 300, Willow Springs, mid-February 1982 (PD-SR32:7); 100, Wilmette, February 28, 1982 (DJ-SR32:7); 604 banded, Blue Island, February 6-March 31, 1982 (KB-SR32:8). Christmas bird counts for 1976–85 showed Common Redpolls every year except 1984. Totals ranged from one in 1979 to 377 in 1977. Highest count was 204 in Morris-Wilmington in 1970. In south and central Illinois, most of these redpolls leave early. Even in the north most are gone by the end of March. Late records: female collected near Glenwood, May 10, 1956 (Levy 1963); seven, Kane County (spring bird count), May 6, 1972 (VK); Winnetka, April 23, 1978 (DJ-AB32:1016); Peoria, April 12, 1966 (AFN20:515). The most recent large influxes of Common Redpolls were in 1971–72, 1977–78, and 1981–82.

HOARY REDPOLL

Carduelis hornemanni

VERY RARE WINTER RESIDENT

If indeed this is a "good" species, the Hoary Redpoll is difficult to distinguish from the Common Redpoll. Balch (1978b) used unstreaked rump, under-tail coverts, bill size and shape, and other characteristics for separating the two redpolls. Of the two Hoary Redpoll subspecies, *C. h. exilipes* breeds in Alaska and northern Canada and is the one most likely to appear in Illinois. The larger, paler *C. h. hornemanni* breeds mainly in Greenland. Although Mlodinow (1984) suggests there are records of *hornemanni* for Illinois (the Chicago area), I was unable to find any specific records. This rare form has been recorded from northern Michigan.

The first records of the Hoary Redpoll were reported by Ridgway (1889). They include a specimen of an adult female taken by Nelson in Cook County in March 1845 (USNM) and two specimens taken by Shimer in Mount Carroll and apparently lost or destroyed (USNM). Thirteen other reports are all from northern Illinois except one redpoll attending a feeder at Jacksonville in February 1978 (AB32:360). All records fall between late October (Evanston, 1968) and April 8 (Blue Island, 1982) and are apparently of single birds. Hoary Redpolls occur in flocks of Common Redpolls and behave much the same. The two redpolls are suspected of hybridizing. Milosevich obtained excellent photographs of a Hoary Redpoll that stayed at Joliet from January 30 to early February 1982 (on file ISM). Other recent records: Calumet, January 15, 1978 (DJ-

AB32:360); Daysville, February 5, 1982 (MSw-SR32:7); Sterling, January 15, 1982 (BSh-SR32:7).

PINE SISKIN

Carduelis pinus

COMMON BUT SOMEWHAT ERRATIC MIGRANT AND WINTER RESIDENT; RARE SUMMER RESIDENT

This little streaked finch has become better known in recent years because it faithfully attends bird feeders, especially the relatively new Niger seed feeders. Pine Siskins also frequent conifers and weed patches with American Goldfinches and can be seen in sunflower fields and sweet gum, alder, birch, and hemlock trees. They visit parklands and residential areas to a large extent but can also be seen in woodlands. They occur in small to medium-sized flocks and occasionally in larger flocks in sunflower fields or other places with a good food source. The Pine Siskin's flight call is a distinct buzzy *zzzhrreee*, which birders should learn, since many siskins are encountered as flybys. The race occurring in Illinois and most of the United States is *C. p. pinus*.

Fall migration usually starts in October, although there are some September dates: Illinois Beach State Park, September 19, 1985 (SP-IB&B2:55); Forest Glen Park, September 14, 1983 (SR39:26); 16, Sand Ridge State Forest, September 23, 1972 (HDB). Average fall arrival dates: Chicago, October 19 (seven years); west-central, October 13 (eight years). Siskins sometimes migrate diurnally in waves, flying just above the treetops. Among the vantage points where these flocks may be seen is the Lake Michigan shore. High counts: 1000, Illinois Beach State Park, October 15, 1977 (JN-AB32:214); 50, De Witt County, November 13, 1983 (RCh-SR39:26); 200, Dundee, November 2, 1981 (JWi-SR31:17). Many siskins undoubtedly move farther south to winter, since they are found to the Gulf Coast, but departure dates are obscured by the presence of wintering birds.

The number of wintering Pine Siskins varies greatly from year to year. Recent Christmas bird count totals ranged from 15 in 1979 to 2522 in 1980. The highest count was 598 at Lisle Arboretum in 1972. Other winter maxima: 400, Clinton Lake, January 31, 1987 (MD-AB41:290); hundreds, Carbondale, winter 1985–86 (TF-IB&B2:79); 200, Lisle Arboretum, December 6, 1980 (SR28:9).

Spring migration, too, is obscured by wintering birds but probably starts in March or April. Maximum counts for spring are few: 150, Harrisburg, April 10, 1987 (KP); 40, Champaign County, May 8, 1988 (RCh). Spring bird count totals ranged from seven in 1980 and to 379 in 1984. The highest count was 57 in Lake County, May 5, 1984 (VK). Average departure dates: west-central, May 7 (10 years); Sangamon County, May 15 (13 years). Stragglers linger into May or even June, but many of them may be breeding birds.

Siskins regularly breed south to northern Minnesota, Wisconsin, and Michigan, but only recently have they stayed to breed in Illinois. Though many attempts fail, young have been fledged several times. The first Illinois breeding record was in 1973 at Normal. Chapel (1983-84) listed 16 breeding records from 1973 to 1982, and there have been at least two since then, in 1985 and 1986. Most of Chapel's records came from residential areas, cemeteries, city parks, and school campuses. The nest is usually placed in a conifer. The only egg date recorded is May 4. Most young have been seen from mid-April to mid-June.

AMERICAN GOLDFINCH

Carduelis tristis

COMMON MIGRANT; SUMMER AND WINTER RESIDENT

Although American Goldfinches are common at all seasons, they also migrate and wander about. Those seen in one season are not necessarily the same birds occurring in another season. These bright yellow and black birds are often referred to as wild canaries. Males are in their bright plumages only from April, when the colors are acquired by partial prenuptial molt, to mid-September, when basic plumage is acquired after complete postnuptial molt. Goldfinches have an undulating flight in which they give call notes with each dip. The song is canarylike but jumbled. In spring many often sing together in fully leaved trees, making it difficult to determine the number present. They are found in many habitats, including forests, forest edges, weedy fields, shrub areas, pasturelands, and suburban areas. They have become mainstays at thistle feeders (a bird with expensive taste). They are mostly seed eaters, and goldfinches feeding on dandelions are a common sight. They feed on birch, thistle, hemlock, sweet gum, sunflower, and ragweed. Goldfinches also take insects, especially to feed to their young. The subspecies in Illinois is *C. t. tristis*.

Even though the wintering population most years is fairly large, an increase in numbers becomes evident about mid- to late April. Numerous goldfinches are recorded nearly every year on spring bird counts, but totals have ranged from 3287 in 1978 (low because of severe winters) to 11,067 in 1986. The highest count was 1211 in Calhoun County on May 8, 1982 (VK). Other high counts for spring: 80, Jackson Park, May 4, 1981 (HR-SR29:14); 120, Chicago, May 14, 1982 (JL); 60, Palos, April 4, 1981 (JL).

Graber and Graber (1963) found little change in the estimated goldfinch population in Illinois between 1907 and 1958, but there is some year-to-year fluctuation: 880,000 in June 1957 and 1,000,000 in 1958. Robbins et al. (1986) found the population declining in eastern and central North America, except in Illinois and Indiana. The mean number of goldfinches per breeding bird survey route for 1965-79 in Illinois was 9.7. Goldfinches nest rather late; Illinois egg dates are June 14 to August 27. They nest in weedy,

shrubby areas, usually in small trees. The lining of the nests is normally thistledown. These well-made nests last many seasons, and some are so well built they can hold water. The full clutch is five to six eggs, which are pale bluish. Young have been noted in the nest as late as September 27 in Whiteside County (IAB108:11).

The beginning and end of fall migration goes undetected, but concentrations have been recorded: 270, Vermilion County, September 15, 1985 (SB-IB&B2:55); 175, Chicago, September 6, 1985 (JL); 172 banded, Blue Island, November 10, 1982 (KB-SR35:17); 400, Springfield, October 24, 1981 (HDB); 115, Quincy, November 6, 1983 (AD-SR39:26).

Winter numbers are fairly high, probably because these birds are easy to detect in winter. Graber and Graber (1963) estimated the winter population at 1,600,000 in 1906-7 and 900,000 in 1957. Christmas bird count totals for 1976-85 ranged from 4898 in 1978 (a severe winter) to 8650 in 1985. The highest count was 769 in Union County in 1985. Eight hundred were counted at Sand Ridge State Forest on January 26, 1986 (LA-IB&B2:79).

EUROPEAN GOLDFINCH

Carduelis carduelis

HYPOTHETICAL—PROBABLE ESCAPES

These Old World finches were released in the United States as early as 1846 at Brooklyn, New York. Several other releases followed from Cincinnati; Cambridge, Massachusetts; and San Francisco (Long 1981). These populations eventually died out, however, and European Goldfinches seen recently are probably escaped cage birds. Recent records for Illinois: one with a flock of American Goldfinches, Barrington, November 13-23, 1981 (RM-SR31:18); male, Wilmette, January 31, 1971 (RR-AB25:585); one with American Goldfinches, Quincy, October 26, 1957 (TEM-AFN12:36).

EVENING GROSBEAK

Coccothraustes vespertinus

UNCOMMON AND IRREGULAR MIGRANT AND WINTER RESIDENT

These large, plump finches show white patches in the wings during their undulating flight, and they give a rasping call note that is easily recognized with practice. They also have a loud House Sparrowlike call. Male Evening Grosbeaks are yellowish. Females are grayish, but they resemble the males enough to be easily identified. The large greenish bill should especially be noted. Evening Grosbeaks are most often seen at bird feeders, where they may stay a few minutes or all winter. They are also found in bottomland woods in box elder and maple trees and in coniferous areas. They usually occur in small to medium-sized flocks. In the afternoons they sit quietly and are seldom seen. In spring they sit in the tops of leafy trees and are difficult to locate without knowledge of their call notes. The race in Illinois is the eastern, *C. v. vespertinus*.

Evening Grosbeaks are erratic. Some years they occur in large numbers; other years few if any are seen. Earliest fall occurrences: Chicago, August 22, 1981 (JL-AB36:185); Jackson Park, September 4, 1981 (PC-SR31:17). Most fall arrival dates are in late October or early November. Some years most of these finches pass through Illinois to winter elsewhere.

High counts for winter: 200, Saline County, winter 1986–87 (KP-AB41:290); 100, Golconda, January and February 1984 (RGr-SR40:15); 50, Oregon, winter 1983–84 (BSh-SR40:15); 70, Cowden, February 25, 1987 (KF-IB&B3:69). On Christmas bird counts for 1976–85 they were encountered nine years, with totals ranging from three in 1976 and 1984 to 532 in 1977. Ogle County had the highest count: 142 in 1977. Other years of high influx appear to be 1980, 1983, and 1985.

A few migrants usually come through in spring. High counts for spring: 90, Shelby County, March 20–May 1, 1987 (KF); 77, Saline County, April 25, 1986 (KP-IB&B2:97); 60, Mode, April 15, 1986 (KF-IB&B2:97). Evening Grosbeaks were missed on four of the 15 spring bird counts (1974, 1977, 1982, and 1985). Totals ranged from one in 1975 and 1979 to 226 in 1984. The highest count was 47 in Schuyler County on May 8, 1976 (VK). Late spring departure dates: Chicago, June 1, 1986 (RB-IB&B2:97); two, Chicago, May 20, 1984 (JL); two, Carbondale, May 12, 1984 (TF- SR41:29); Springfield, May 22, 1978 (HDB).

HOUSE SPARROW

Passer domesticus

INTRODUCED; NOW AN ABUNDANT PERMANENT RESIDENT

Although this pest species was initially introduced at New York in 1852, there were many other introductions. Most of the birds came from Great Britain, but some were from Germany. At least four introductions occurred in Illinois in 1868–76 (Barrows 1889). By 1886 all of Illinois was occupied by to House Sparrows except the heavily forested areas. They are excluded from this habitat and gain access only when these areas are fragmented, which is important to know if woodland is to be managed for native species.

This is the "sparrow" known to every person with a pellet gun, except that many native sparrows suffer the same fate because they look somewhat similar. Native sparrows are not closely related to House Sparrows. Nor are American sparrows pests; indeed, many are extremely beneficial. While farmers and municipalities are concerned about the

House Sparrow for economic and health reasons, biologists are concerned because of its competition with native birds. The biologists' concern may ultimately be the more important one. The House Sparrow population may have declined somewhat about 1920 as automobiles replaced horses and cleaner farming practices left less grain for House Sparrows to feed on. Graber and Graber (1963) estimated that the House Sparrow population had changed little from 1909 (5,300,000) to 1958 (5,500,000). Breeding bird survey data for 1965–79 showed that Illinois, Indiana, and Ohio have the dubious distinction of being the leading states for this species. The mean number of House Sparrows per survey route in Illinois was 235.7 (Robbins et al. 1986). In the late 1970s severe winters killed many House Sparrows in Illinois; they froze to death in roost sites.

A study by Will (1973) showed an average House Sparrow population of 275 adults and 130 nests in a 100-acre area of McLeansboro. House Sparrows nest in a variety of places, usually near human habitation. Aggravatingly, they tend to take over bluebird boxes and Purple Martin houses. The eggs usually total four or five; they are light in color but heavily streaked with a darker color. Nesting probably occurs every month of the year, but the principal time is from May to July. There is more than one clutch per season. Will also found that each nest averaging two clutches produced 3.14 fledged young.

Mlodinow (1984) reported 3000–4000 House Sparrows migrating along Lake Michigan on September 25, 1977, but that may have been a local daily movement to or from roost sites. Such local movements are not uncommon at Springfield. Spring bird count totals ranged from 20,672 in 1972 to 34,704 in 1983. The highest count was 4577 in St. Clair County, May 7, 1983 (VK). Christmas bird count totals for 1976–85 ranged from 133,548 in 1982 to 190,126 in 1976. Chicago urban had all the high counts, from 85,000 in 1982 to 225,000 in 1974. More House Sparrows turn up on Christmas than on spring bird counts due to flocking and roosting behavior in winter versus the scattering of pairs in the breeding season.

EURASIAN TREE SPARROW

Passer montanus

INTRODUCED; NOW A COMMON PERMANENT RESIDENT IN WEST-CENTRAL ILLINOIS

This close relative of the House Sparrow was introduced to North America at Lafayette Park in St. Louis on April 20, 1870. The birds (20 to 32) came from Germany (Flieg 1971). Populations were established in Illinois at Alton, Grafton, East St. Louis, and Belleville at least by 1906 (Widmann 1907). Apparently Eurasian Tree Sparrows build up a local colony for several years; then the colony's numbers drop and they build up in another area. This movement may be a result of competition with House Sparrows or a change in the Tree Sparrows' habitat from rural to urban caused by people.

The present distribution of the Eurasian Tree Sparrow covers 8500 square miles in eastern Missouri and west-central Illinois. The estimated population is 25,000 (Barlow 1973). In Illinois they have been recorded east to Springfield and Sharpsburg, Christian County. They go north at least to Macomb, with outlying records in Galesburg and Princeton. The population has not spread very far south; Belleville is near the edge, and a bird recorded farther south in Modoc was a vagrant. There are several "vagrant" Illinois records (as well as records from Wisconsin and Kentucky): Urbana, April 18, 1983 (RCh-SR37:28); Winnetka, December 26, 1983 (RB-SR40:16); Hampton, winter 1980–81 (EF-SR28:8); Evanston, March 28, 1976 (Mlodinow 1984). These sparrows tend to gather in winter to form flocks, some fairly large (100–300 birds), and then scatter widely in pairs in spring to breed. Eurasian Tree Sparrows are usually found in flat farming areas. They prefer hedgerows, farmyards, and willow areas. I have seen them in summer in marsh areas that have willow trees. They use the cavities in willows for nest sites. In winter they are found around livestock and at bird feeders. These "weaver finches" also nest in cavities in fence posts, trees, and especially bluebird boxes. The females lay four to six eggs, which are variable in color with heavy streaking. They have more than one brood per season, and nesting is from early April to late July. The young show a spot on the face as soon as enough feathers appear.

Spring bird count totals ranged from 54 in 1972 to 583 in 1982, with a maximum of 20 counties reporting these sparrows. Morgan County had the highest count: 345 on May 8, 1982. Christmas bird counts have shown higher totals in recent years, ranging from 250 in 1978 to 2332 in 1984. The highest count was 1490 in 1985 at Meredosia—which may indicate the center of abundance for this species in Illinois.

Literature Cited

Abbott, G. A. 1911. Le Conte's Sparrow at home near Chicago. Wilson Bulletin 23:53–54.

Aldrich, J. W. 1944. Geographic variation of Bewick's Wrens in the eastern United States. Occasional Papers of the Museum of Zoology, Louisiana State University 18:305–9.

———, and A. J. Duvall. 1958. Distribution and migration of races of the Mourning Dove. Condor 60:108–28.

Allen, J. A. 1875. Description of Nelson's Sharp-tailed Sparrow. Proceedings of the Boston Society of Natural History 17:292–93.

American Ornithologists' Union. 1957. Check-list of North American birds. 5th ed. Baltimore: Lord Baltimore Press. 691 pp.

———. 1983. Check-list of North American birds. 6th ed. Lawrence, Kansas: Allen Press. 877 pp.

Ammann, G. A. 1939. Swainson's Warbler in Illinois. Wilson Bulletin 51:185–86.

Anderson, H. G. 1959. Food habits of migratory ducks in Illinois. Illinois Natural History Survey Bulletin 27:289–344.

Anderson, R. A. 1964. Observations from southern Illinois. Audubon Bulletin 129:18.

———. 1968. Spring report for St. Louis. Audubon Bulletin 147:27–28.

Anderson, W. L. 1975. Lead poisoning in waterfowl at Rice Lake, Illinois. Journal of Wildlife Management 39:264–70.

Appleby, R. H., S. C. Madge, and K. Mullarny. 1986. Identification of divers in immature and winter plumages. British Birds 76:365–91.

Armstrong, E. E. 1920. Remarkable migration of robins. Auk 37:466.

Audubon, J. J. 1831. Ornithological biography. Vol. 1. Edinburgh: Adam and Charles Black. 512 pp.

———. 1835. Ornithological biography. Vol. 3. Edinburgh: Adam and Charles Black. 638 pp.

———. 1929. Journal of John James Audubon, edited by Howard Carming. Boston: Club of Odd Volumes. 234 pp.

———, 1942. Audubon's "Journal up the Mississippi," edited by J. F. McDermott. Journal Illinois State Historical Society 35:148–73.

Austin, O. L. 1968. Life histories of North American cardinals, grosbeaks, buntings, towhees, finches, sparrows, and allies. Parts 1–3. U.S. National Museum Bulletin 237. 1889 pp.

Baird, S. F., J. Cassin, and G. N. Lawrence. 1858. Birds. Pacific R. R. Reports 9. Washington: A. O. P. Nicholson. 1005 pp.

Baker, F. C. 1937. An Illinois record for the Little Brown Crane. Auk 54:388.

Balch, L. G. 1977. Identifying scaup. Illinois Audubon Bulletin 182:27–29.

———. 1977–78. Shrike identification. Illinois Audubon Bulletin 183:25–27.

———. 1978. Waterthrush identification. Illinois Audubon Bulletin 184:21–24.

———. 1978a. Eared owls in flight. Illinois Audubon Bulletin 186:25–26.

———. 1978b. Redpoll identification. Illinois Audubon Bulletin 186:39–44.

———. 1979. Identification of Groove-billed and Smooth-billed Anis. Birding 11:295–97.

———, H. D. Bohlen, and G. B. Rosenband. 1979. The Illinois Ross' Gull. American Birds 33:140–42.

Balding, T. 1964. Ancient Murrelet taken in Illinois. Auk 81:443.

Barlow, J. C. 1973. Status of the North American population of the European Tree Sparrow. In A Symposium on the House Sparrow and European Tree Sparrow in North America. AOU Ornithological Monographs 14:10–23.

Barrows, W. B. 1889. The English Sparrow in North America, especially in its relations to agriculture. U.S. Department of Agriculture Division of Economic Ornithology and Mammalogy Bulletin 1. 405 pp.

Bartel, K. E. 1932. A rare specimen. Oologist 49:91.

———. 1978. A Yellow-Rail at Gensburg-Markham Prairie. Illinois Audubon Bulletin 186:23–26.

———, and F. A. Pitelka. 1939. Western Sandpiper in Illinois. Auk 56:334–35.

———, and A. Reuss. 1932. Birds of Blue Island, Cook Co., Illinois. Oologist 49:112–13.

Bartsch, P. 1922. Some tern notes. Auk 39:101.

———. 1922a. An inland record for the Man-O'-War Bird. Auk 39:249–50.

Baum, M. J. 1987. Illinois' Black-shouldered Kite. Illinois Birds and Birding 3:60–61.

Beal, F. E. L. 1900. Food of the bobolink, blackbirds, and grackles. U.S. Department of Agriculture Biological Survey Bulletin 13.

Beecher, W. J. 1942. Nesting birds and the vegetation substrate. Chicago: Chicago Ornithological Society. 69 pp.

Bellrose, F. C. 1938. Glaucous Gull in Illinois. Auk 55:277.

———. 1939. American Egret nesting along the Illinois River. Auk 56:73-74.

———. 1944. Bald Eagles nesting in Illinois. Auk 61:467-468.

———. 1976. Ducks, geese and swans of North America. Stackpole Books. 544 pp.

Bennett, E. 1952. Checklist of birds of southern Illinois. Southern Illinois University, Carbondale. Mimeographed. 19 pp.

———. 1957. Nesting birds of the shoreline and islands of Crab Orchard Lake, Illinois. Transactions of the Illinois State Academy of Science 50:259-64.

Bent, A. C. 1926. Life histories of North American marsh birds. U.S. National Museum Bulletin 135. 490 pp.

———. 1929. Life histories of North American shore birds. Part 2. U.S. National Museum Bulletin 146. 412 pp.

———. 1932. Life histories of North American gallinaceous birds. U.S. National Museum Bulletin 162. 490 pp.

———. 1938. Life histories of North American birds of prey. Part 2. U.S. National Museum Bulletin 170. 482 pp.

———. 1939. Life histories of North American woodpeckers. U.S. National Museum Bulletin 174. 334 pp.

———. 1940. Life histories of North American cuckoos, goatsuckers, hummingbirds and their allies. U.S. National Museum Bulletin 176. 506 pp.

———. 1942. Life histories of North American flycatchers, larks, swallows, and their allies. U.S. National Museum Bulletin 179. 538 pp.

———. 1948. Life histories of North American nuthatches, wrens, thrashers, and their allies. U.S. National Museum Bulletin 195. 475 pp.

———. 1949. Life histories of North American thrushes, kinglets, and their allies. U.S. National Museum Bulletin 196. 454 pp.

———. 1950. Life histories of North American wagtails, shrikes, vireos, and their allies. U.S. National Museum Bulletin 197. 411 pp.

———. 1953. Life histories of North American wood warblers. U.S. National Museum Bulletin 203. 734 pp.

———. 1958. Life histories of North American blackbirds, orioles, tanagers, and allies. U.S. National Museum Bulletin 211. 549 pp.

Birkenholz, D. E. 1958. Notes on a wintering flock of Long-eared Owls. Transactions of the Illinois State Academy of Science 51:83-86.

———. 1973. Pintails, Green-winged Teal nest at Goose Lake. Audubon Bulletin 166:32.

———. 1975. The summer birds of Goose Lake Prairie Nature Preserve, 1970-1973. Chicago Academy of Sciences, Natural History Miscellanea 193. 11 pp.

———, and R. D. Weigel. 1972. First Illinois specimen of the Rock Wren. Transactions of the Illinois State Academy of Science 65:77.

Bjorklund, R. G. 1979-80. Nesting Solitary Vireo in central Illinois. Illinois Audubon Bulletin 191:21-23.

———. 1980-81. Observational evidence for homing in birds. Illinois Audubon Bulletin 195:27-28.

———, and E. R. Bjorklund. 1983. Abundance of Whip-poor-wills, *Caprimulgus vociferous*, in the Sand Ridge State Forest. Transactions of the Illinois State Academy of Science 76:271-76.

Black, C. T. 1937. Additional Illinois Golden Eagle records. Auk 54:385-88.

Blackwelder, E. 1899. A note on Kirtland's Warbler. Auk 16:359-60.

Blake, E. R., and E. T. Smith. 1941. Chicago region. Audubon Magazine 43:570-72.

Bohlen, H. D. 1971. First record in Illinois of Audubon Warbler. Audubon Bulletin 158:26.

———. 1974. An apparent differential migration of Cedar Waxwings in west-central Illinois. Audubon Bulletin 170:13.

———. 1975. Ash-throated Flycatcher in Illinois: summary of records east of the Mississippi River. Auk 92:165-66.

———. 1976. A Great-tailed Grackle from Illinois. American Birds 30:917.

———. 1976a. Black-throated Gray Warbler in Illinois. Illinois Audubon Bulletin 176:27.

———. 1977. Western Grebes display on Lake Springfield. Illinois Audubon Bulletin 182:36-37.

———. 1978. An annotated check-list of the birds of Illinois. Illinois State Museum Popular Science Series, Vol. IX. 156 pp.

———. 1980. Chestnut-collared Longspur in Sangamon County, Illinois. Illinois Audubon Bulletin 194:20-21.

———. 1982. Mountain Bluebird in Illinois. Illinois Audubon Bulletin 202: 24-25.

———. 1983. Western Wood-Pewee in Sangamon County, Illinois. Illinois Audubon Bulletin 205:39.

———. 1986. House Finches in Illinois. Living Museum 48:4-7.

———. 1986a. Snowy Plover in Illinois. Illinois Birds and Birding 2:39.

———. 1986b. The status of the Ferruginous Hawk in Illinois. Illinois Birds and Birding 2:40-41.

———, and J. Funk. 1974. A winter record of the Least Flycatcher in central Illinois. Audubon Bulletin 169:14.

———, and V. M. Kleen. 1973-74. The first Black-headed Gull for Illinois. Audubon Bulletin 167:18-20.

———, and ———. 1976. A method for aging Orange-crowned Warblers in fall. Bird Banding 47:365.

———, and R. Sandburg. 1975. Sight record of the Sharp-tailed Sandpiper in Illinois. Illinois Audubon Bulletin 172:4-5.

Bossu, N. 1768. Nouveaux voyages aux Indes Occidentales. Part l. Paris.

Boulton, R., and W. J. Beecher. 1940. The season: Chicago region. Bird-Lore 42:218-19.

———, and F. A. Pitelka. 1938. The season: Chicago region. Bird-Lore 40:290-91.

———, and ———. 1938a. The season: Chicago region. Bird-Lore 40:372-73.

Bowles, M. L. 1981. Endangered and threatened vertebrate animals and vascular plants of Illinois. Illinois Department of Conservation. 189 pp.

Brewer, R. 1958. Some corrections to "A distributional check-list of the birds of Illinois." Audubon Bulletin 106:9.

———. 1963. Ecological and reproductive relationships of Black-capped and Carolina Chickadees. Auk 80:9-47.

Brewster, W. 1906. The birds of the Cambridge region of Massachusetts. Mem. Nuttall Ornithological Club No. 4.

Brodkorb, P. 1926. Chicago region. Bird-Lore 28:407-8.

———. 1928. Notes on the food of some hawks and owls. Auk 45:212-13.

———. 1934. Notes from central Illinois. Auk 51:41.

———, and J. Stevenson. 1934. Additional northeastern Illinois notes. Auk 51:100-101.

Brooks, W. S. 1967. Food and feeding habits of autumn migrant shorebirds at a small midwestern pond. Wilson Bulletin 79:307-15.

Bujak, B. J. 1935. A recent record of the Hudsonian Curlew in the Chicago, Illinois, region. Wilson Bulletin 47:294.

Burnside, F. L. 1987. Long-distance movements by Loggerhead Shrikes. Journal of Field Ornithology 58:62–65.

Burr, B. M., and D. M. Current. 1974. The 1972–1973 Goshawk invasion in Illinois. Transactions of the Illinois State Academy of Science 67:175–79.

———, and ———. 1975. Status of the Gyrfalcon in Illinois. Wilson Bulletin 87:280–81.

Butler, A. W. 1897. The birds of Indiana. 22d Annual Report of the Department of Geology and Natural Resources of Indiana, pp. 515–1187.

Cahn, A. R. 1930. Additions to the Easter birds of Little Egypt. Wilson Bulletin 42:214–15.

Calhoun, J. C., and J. K. Garver. 1974. The Wild Turkey in Illinois. Illinois Department of Conservation. 7 pp.

Carpenter, C. K. 1948. An early Illinois record of "Cory's Least Bittern." Auk 65:80–85.

Carson, M. P. 1926. The Wood Ibis in Jefferson County, Illinois. Bird-Lore 28:195–96.

Chapel, R. 1983–84. Illinois breeding Pine Siskins. Illinois Audubon Bulletin 207:46–48.

———, and R. Applegate. 1987. First central Illinois nesting record of the Ruddy Duck. Illinois Birds and Birding 3:83.

———, and E. Chato. 1986. Illinois' first Scrub Jay. Illinois Birds and Birding 2:7.

Chartier, B., and F. Cooke. 1980. Ross' Gulls (*Rhodostethia rosea*) nesting at Churchill, Manitoba, Canada. American Birds 34:839–41.

Clark, C. T. 1985. Caribbean Coot? Birding 17:84–88.

———, and M. M. Nice. 1950. William Dreuth's study of bird migration in Lincoln Park, Chicago. Chicago Academy of Science Special Publications 8. 43 pp.

Clark, W. S., and B. K. Wheeler. 1987. A field guide to Hawks North America. Boston: Houghton Mifflin. 198 pp.

Clemans, A., and G. Kulesza. 1973–74. Swallow-tailed Kite. Champaign County Audubon Society Newsletter 9:4.

Coale, H. K. 1877. McCown's Longspur in Illinois. Bulletin of the Nuttall Ornithological Club 2:52.

———. 1877a. Notes on *Nyctale acadica*. Bulletin of the Nuttall Ornithological Club 2:83–84.

———. 1910. A new bird for Illinois. Auk 27:75.

———. 1910a. The Chestnut-collared Longspur in Illinois. Auk 27:341–42.

———. 1911. Clark's Nutcracker in Illinois. Auk 28:266.

———. 1912. Birds of Lake County. In A history of Lake County, Illinois, pp. 353–70.

———. 1914. Richardson's Owl in northeastern Illinois. Auk 31:536.

———. 1915. The present status of the Trumpeter Swan. Auk 32:82–90.

———. 1916. Bicknell's Thrush in northeastern Illinois. Auk 33:203.

———. 1920. Bohemian Waxwing in Illinois. Auk 37:301–2.

———. 1924. *Tyrannus verticolis*, a new bird for Illinois. Auk 41:603.

———. 1925. Violet-green Swallow in Illinois. Auk 42:137–38.

———. 1925a. Barn Owls at Chicago. Auk 42:444.

Comfort, J. E. 1941. Webster Groves notes. Bluebird 16.

———. 1961. The St. Louis area. Bluebird 28:17.

Conley, C. L. 1926. Purple Martin in winter. Audubon Bulletin 17:26.

Connors, P. G. 1983. Taxonomy, distribution, and evolution of Golden Plovers (*Pluvialis dominica* and *Pluvialis fulva*). Auk 100:607–20.

Conover, H. B. 1941. A study of the dowitcher. Auk 58:376–80.

———. 1944. The races of the Solitary Sandpiper. Auk 61:537–44.

Cooke, W. W. 1888. Report on bird migration in the Mississippi Valley in the years 1884 and 1885. U.S. Department of Agriculture, Division of Economic Ornithology Bulletin 2. Washington, D.C. 313 pp.

———. 1914. The migration of North American sparrows. Bird-Lore 16:176–78.

Cory, C. B. 1909. The birds of Illinois and Wisconsin. Field Museum of Natural History Publication 131, Zoological Series, vol. 9. 764 pp.

Coues, E. 1876. Eastward range of the Ferruginous Buzzard. Bulletin of the Nuttall Ornithological Club 2:26.

Coursen, C. B. 1947. Birds of the Orland Wildlife Refuge. Turtox News supplement. 30 pp.

Cox, G. W. 1973. Hybridization between Mourning and MacGillivray's Warblers. Auk 90:190–91.

Craig, D. R., and E. C. Franks. 1987. Bird migration phenology in west central Illinois. Transactions of the Illinois State Academy of Science 80:129–56.

Craigmile, E. A. 1934–35. Three rare records. Audubon Bulletin 24 and 25:45–46.

Davis, D. E. 1949. Recent emigrations of Northern Shrikes. Auk 66:293.

Davis, G. J. 1970. Seasonal changes in flocking behavior of starlings as correlated with gonadal development. Wilson Bulletin 82:391–99.

Deane, R. 1895. Additional records of the Passenger Pigeon in Illinois and Indiana. Auk 12:298–300.

———. 1903. Richardson's Owl in Illinois. Auk 20:305.

———. 1903a. Richardson's Owl in Illinois. Auk 20:433–34.

———. 1905. Hybridism between the Shoveller and Blue-winged Teal. Auk 22:321.

———. 1908. Curious fatality among Chimney Swifts. Auk 25:317–18.

DeVine, J. L. 1909. Capture of an American eider at Chicago. Auk 26:426.

Dickerman, R. W. 1987. The "Old Northeastern" subspecies of Red Crossbill. American Birds 41:189–94.

Dickinson, J. E. 1885. [No title]. Ornithologist and Oologist 10:47.

Dillon, S. T. 1968. A bird census on a restricted site in northeastern Illinois. Audubon Bulletin 146:16–19.

Dinsmore, J. J., T. H. Kent, D. Koenig, P. C. Petersen, and D. M. Roosa. 1984. Iowa birds. Ames, Iowa: Iowa State University Press. 356 pp.

DuMont, P. A. 1935. An old record of the Brown-headed Nuthatch in Iowa and Illinois. Wilson Bulletin 47:240.

———. 1947. Middle-western region. Audubon Field Notes 1:154–56.

Dunn, J. O. 1895. Notes on some birds of northeastern Illinois. Auk 12:393–95.

Dwight, J. 1925. The gulls (Laridae) of the world: their plumages, moults, variations, relationships and distribution. Bulletin of the American Museum of Natural History 52:63–401.

Eaton, S. H. 1926. Wood Ibis in Illinois. Auk 43:90.

Eckert, K. R. 1982. Field identification of the Ferruginous Hawk. Loon 54:161–64.

Eddy, S. 1927. Notes on the occurrence of shorebirds and waterfowl on a new artificial lake. Wilson Bulletin 39:223–28.

Ehrlich, P., and A. Ehrlich. 1981. Extinction. New York: Random House. 305 pp.

Eifrig, C. W. G. 1911. A paradise for longspurs. Wilson Bulletin 23:49–52.

———. 1913. Notes on some of the rarer birds of the prairie part of the Chicago area. Auk 30:236–40.

———. 1915. Cory's Least Bittern in Illinois. Auk 32:98–99.

———. 1915a. Bachman's Sparrow near Chicago, Illinois. Auk 32:496–97.

———. 1919. Notes on birds of the Chicago area and its immediate vicinity. Auk 36:513–24.

———. 1921. Unusual winter occurrences at Chicago. Auk 38:609–10.

———. 1927. Notes from the Chicago area. Auk 44:431–32.

———. 1944. The Passenger Pigeon's last stand. Audubon Bulletin 50:6–7.

Eiseman, R. M., and N. McQuate. 1954. Green-tailed Towhee in Illinois. Audubon Bulletin 92:4.

Ekblaw, G. E. 1917. Rantoul, and Rantoul winter record. Audubon Bulletin, Spring 1917, pp. 52 and 54.

Ellis, J. A., and B. R. Mahan. 1987. Illinois hunter harvest survey, 1986. Illinois Department of Conservation, Job Completion Report Study 15: Wildlife Harvests Job No. 1.

Enderson, J. H. 1960. A population study of the Sparrow Hawk in east-central Illinois. Wilson Bulletin 72:222–31.

Ernst, L. R. 1934. Some interesting bird observations. Journal of the Webster Groves Nature Study Society, January, p. 63.

Erskine, A. J. 1972. Buffleheads. Canadian Wildlife Service Monograph Series 4. 240 pp.

Evans, D. L. 1982. Status reports on twelve raptors. U.S. Fish and Wildlife Service Special Scientific Report, Wildlife 238. Washington, D.C. 68 pp.

Everman, B. W. 1889. The Wood Ibis in Indiana. Auk 6:186–87.

Farrand, J., Jr. 1983. The Audubon Society master guide to birding 3. Warblers to sparrows. New York: Alfred A. Knopf. 399 pp.

Farris, A. L. 1970. Distribution and abundance of the Gray Partridge in Illinois. Transactions of the Illinois State Academy of Science 63:240–45.

Fawks, E. 1936. Warblers of Rock Island County in 1935. Audubon Bulletin 26:40–41.

Felger, A. H. 1909. Wild Turkeys in Illinois. Auk 26:78.

Ferry, J. F. 1907. Ornithological conditions in northeastern Illinois, with notes on some winter birds. Auk 24:121–29.

———. 1907a. Further notes from extreme southern Illinois. Auk 24:430–35.

Findley, C. H. 1949. Trip to Horseshoe Lake. Bluebird 16.

Fiske, K. 1968. Migration fluctuations: one flooded acre in McHenry County, Ill. Audubon Bulletin 147:20–21.

Fleming, J. H. 1912. Sabine's Gull on the Mississippi River. Auk 29:388–89.

Flieg, G. M. 1971. The European Tree Sparrow in the Western Hemisphere—its range, distribution, life history. Audubon Bulletin 157:2–10.

———. 1971a. The Illinois American Bottom: summer birding area of Illinois. Audubon Bulletin 157:31–32.

Forbes, S. A. 1880 (or 1903). The food of birds. Illinois State Laboratory of Natural History Bulletin 1:80–148.

———. 1881. The snowbird in southern Illinois in June. Bulletin of the Nuttall Ornithological Club 6:180.

———. 1883. The regulative action of birds upon insect oscillations. Illinois Natural History Survey Bulletin 1:1–32.

Ford, E. R. 1932. The season: Chicago region. Bird-Lore 34:344–45.

———. 1936. The western pigeon hawk in Louisiana, Florida, and Illinois. Auk 53:210.

———. 1956. Birds of the Chicago region. Chicago Academy of Sciences Special Publication 12. 117 pp.

———, C. C. Sanborn, and C. B. Coursen. 1934. Birds of the Chicago region. Chicago Academy of Sciences Program of Activities 5:17–80.

Forsythe, C. J. 1973. Red Crossbill on a very busy campus. Audubon Bulletin 166:31–32.

Funk, J. L. 1982. Illinois' first Hepatic Tanager. Illinois Audubon Bulletin 200:36–37.

Gantlett, S. J. M., and A. Harris. 1987. Identification of large terns. British Birds 80:257–76.

Gault, B. T. 1892. The Chestnut-sided Warbler nesting in Missouri. Auk 9:396.

———. 1894. Kirtland's Warbler in northeastern Illinois. Auk 11:258.

———. 1901. April and May bird-life at Glen Ellyn (near Chicago), Illinois. Bird-Lore 3:65–67.

———. 1910. The Brown Pelican in Illinois. Auk 27:75.

———. 1922. Checklist of the birds of Illinois. Chicago: Illinois Audubon Society. 80 pp.

Geis, A. D., R. I. Smith, and J. P. Rogers. 1971. Black Duck distribution, harvest characteristics, and survival. U.S. Fish and Wildlife Service Special Science Report: Wildlife 139. 241 pp.

George, W. G. 1968. Check-list of birds of southern Illinois. Southern Illinois University, Carbondale. Mimeographed. 28 pp.

———. 1968a. The association of invading White-winged Crossbills with a southern tree. Wilson Bulletin 80:496–97.

———. 1971. Vanished and endangered birds of Illinois: a new "black list" and "red list." Audubon Bulletin 158:2–11.

———. 1971a. Foliage-gleaning by Chimney Swifts (*Chaetura pelagica*). Auk 88:177.

———. 1972. Breeding status of the Purple Gallinule, Brown Creeper, and Swainson's Warbler in Illinois. Wilson Bulletin 84:208–10.

Goetz, R. E. 1983. Spring identification of Laughing Gulls and Franklin's Gulls. Illinois Audubon Bulletin 204:33–36.

———. 1987. Illinois' first *Selasphorus* hummingbird: an identification problem. Illinois Birds and Birding 3:56–59.

———, W. M. Rudden, and P. B. Snetsinger. 1985–86. Slaty-backed Gull winters on the Mississippi River. American Birds 40:207–16.

Gosselin, M., and N. David. 1975. Field identification of Thayer's Gull (*Larus thayeri*) in eastern North America. American Birds 29:1059–66.

Graber, J. W., and R. R. Graber. 1973. Nesting distribution of the Veery in Illinois. Illinois Audubon Bulletin 164:50–52.

———, ———, and E. L. Kirk. 1977. Illinois birds: Picidae. Illinois Natural History Survey Biological Notes 102. 73 pp.

———, ———, and ———. 1978. Illinois birds: Ciconiiformes. Illinois Natural History Survey Biological Notes 109. 80 pp.

———, ———, and ———. 1979. Illinois birds: Sylviidae. Illinois Natural History Survey Biological Notes 110. 22 pp.

———, ———, and ———. 1983. Illinois birds: wood warblers. Illinois Natural History Survey Biological Notes 118. 144 pp.

———, ———, and ———. 1985. Illinois birds: vireos. Illinois Natural History Survey Biological Notes 124. 38 pp.

———, ———, and ———. 1987. Illinois birds: Corvidae. Illinois Natural History Survey Biological Notes 126. 42 pp.

Graber, R. R. 1957. Sprague's Pipit and Le Conte's Sparrow in Illinois. Audubon Bulletin 102:5–7.

———. 1962. Middlewestern prairie region. Audubon Field Notes 16:413.

————. 1962a. Food and oxygen consumption in three species of owls (Strigidae). Condor 64:473-87.

————, and J. S. Golden. 1960. Hawks and owls: population trends from Illinois Christmas counts. Illinois Natural History Survey Biological Notes 41. 24 pp.

————, and J. W. Graber. 1963. A comparative study of bird populations in Illinois, 1906-1909 and 1956-1958. Illinois Natural History Survey Bulletin 28(3):383-528.

————, and ————. 1980-81. Sharp-shinned Hawk (*Accipter striatus*) nest in southern Illinois. Illinois Audubon Bulletin 195:28-31.

————, ————, and E. L. Kirk. 1970. Illinois birds: Mimidae. Illinois Natural History Survey Biological Notes 68. 38 pp.

————, ————, and ————. 1971. Illinois birds: Turdidae. Illinois Natural History Survey Biological Notes 75. 44 pp.

————, ————, and ————. 1972. Illinois birds: Hirundinidae. Illinois Natural History Survey Biological Notes 80. 36 pp.

————, ————, and ————. 1973. Illinois birds: Laniidae. Illinois Natural History Survey Biological Notes 83. 18 pp.

————, ————, and ————. 1974. Illinois birds: Tyrannidae. Illinois Natural History Survey Biological Notes 86. 56 pp.

Grant, P. J. 1984. Identification of stints and peeps. British Birds 77:293-315.

————. 1986. Gulls: a guide to identification. Vermillion, South Dakota: Buteo Books. 352 pp.

————, and R. E. Scott. 1969. Field identification of juvenile Common, Arctic, and Roseate Terns. British Birds 62:297-99.

Grasett, F. G. 1926. Notes on some rare birds of northeastern Illinois. Auk 43:556.

————. 1928. A flight of Snow Buntings at Glencoe, Illinois. Auk 45:221-22.

Green, J. C., and R. B. Janssen. 1975. Minnesota birds. Minneapolis: University of Minnesota Press. 217 pp.

Greenberg, J. 1980. Sandhill Cranes nesting in Illinois. Wilson Bulletin 92:527.

Greer, R. M. 1966. The Brown Creeper in Illinois. Audubon Bulletin 140:24-25.

Gregory, S. S. 1923. Western Grebe in Illinois. Auk 40:526.

————. 1948. Ferruginous Roughleg in Cook County, Illinois. Auk 65:317.

Grier, J. W., J. B. Elder, F. J. Gramlich, N. F. Green, J. V. Kussman, J. E. Mathisen, and J. P. Mattsson. 1983. Northern states Bald Eagle recovery plan. U.S. Fish and Wildlife Service, Denver. 71 pp.

Gross, A. O. 1908. Swainson's Warbler (*Helinaia swainsoni*). Auk 25:225.

————. 1921. The Dickcissel (*Spiza americana*) of the Illinois prairies. Auk 38:(pt. 1)1-26, (pt.2)163-84.

————. 1958. Eastern Meadowlark. U.S. National Museum Bulletin 211:53-80.

Groth, B. 1964. Whooping Crane sighted in Illinois. Illinois Audubon Bulletin 130:24.

Guth, R. W. 1986. Nesting Yellow-bellied Sapsucker in Carroll County. Illinois Birds and Birding 2:37.

Hahn, P. 1963. Where is that vanished bird? Toronto: University of Toronto Press. 347 pp.

Hamilton, J. D., and W. D. Klimstra. 1985. Taxonomy of southern Illinois meadowlarks. Transactions of the Illinois State Academy of Science 78:223-40.

Hammond, E. K. 1943. Unusual breeding records from the Chicago region. Auk 60: 599-600.

Hanson, H. C., and C. W. Kossack. 1963. The Mourning Dove in Illinois. Department of Conservation Technical Bulletin 2. 133 pp.

Hardin, M. E., J. W. Hardin, and W. D. Klimstra. 1977. Observations of nesting Mississippi Kites in southern Illinois. Transactions of the Illinois State Academy of Science 70:341- 48.

Hardy, J. W. 1955. Records of Swainson's Warbler in southern Illinois. Wilson Bulletin 67:60.

————. 1957. The Least Tern in the Mississippi Valley. Publications of the Museum, Michigan State University, Biological Series 1:1-60.

Harrison, P. 1983. Seabirds: an identification guide. Boston: Houghton Mifflin. 448 pp.

Hayman, P., J. Marchant, and T. Prater. 1986. Shorebirds: an identification guide to the waders of the world. Boston: Houghton Mifflin. 412 pp.

Hess, I. 1910. One hundred breeding birds of an Illinois ten- mile radius. Auk 27:19-32.

Hine, A. 1924. Lewis's Woodpecker visits Chicago. Auk 41:156-57.

Hodge, C. F. 1912. A last word on the Passenger Pigeon. Auk 29:169-75.

Howell, A. H. 1910. Breeding records from southern Illinois. Auk 27:216.

Hull, E. D. 1913. The Swallow-tailed Kite in De Witt County, Illinois. Auk 30:112.

————. 1915. The Old Squaw in Jackson Park, Chicago. Bird-Lore 17:450.

Hunt, L. B. 1978. Extreme nesting dates for the Mourning Dove in central Illinois. Wilson Bulletin 90:458-60.

Hurter, J. 1881. The Harlequin Duck and Glossy and Wood Ibis in southern Illinois. Bulletin of the Nuttall Ornithological Club 6:124.

Hussell, D. J. T. 1980. The timing of fall migration and molt in Least Flycatchers. Journal of Field Ornithology 51:65-71.

Hyde, A. S. 1927. Rock Wren in Illinois. Auk 44:111-12.

Illinois Audubon Society. 1916-72. Audubon Bulletin 1- 163.

————. 1973-84. Illinois Audubon Bulletin 164-177.

Illinois State Water Survey. 1964. Local climatological data 1901-1962.

Irwin, F. 1964. A note on Short-eared Owls. Illinois Audubon Bulletin 130:14.

Jehl, J. R., Jr. 1963. An investigation of fall-migrating dowitchers in New Jersey. Wilson Bulletin 75:250-61.

————. 1973. Breeding biology and systematic relationships of the Stilt Sandpiper. Wilson Bulletin 85:115-47.

————. 1987. Geographic variation and evolution in the California Gull (*Larus californicus*). Auk 104:421-27.

Johnsgard, P. A. 1983. Cranes of the world. Bloomington: Indiana University Press. 258 pp.

Johnson, W. W. 1968. On the Lark Sparrow in Illinois. Audubon Bulletin 148:7.

Jones, K. P. 1985. A Long-billed Curlew in Morgan County. Illinois Birds and Birding 1:61.

Jones, L. 1895. Record of the work of the Wilson chapter for 1893 and 1894 on the Mniotiltidae. Wilson Bulletin 7:1-20.

Jones, L. R. 1987. Yellow-billed Loon. Illinois Birds and Birding 3:3-4.

Judd, S. D. 1905. The bobwhite and other quails of the United States in their economic relations. U.S. Department of Agriculture Biological Survey Bulletin 21. 66 pp.

Kaiser, E. T., W. L. Reichel, L. N. Locke, E. Cromartie, A. J. Krynitsky, T. G. Lamont, B. M. Mulhern, R. M. Prouty, C. J. Stafford, and D. M. Swineford. 1980. Organochlorine pesticide, PCB, and PBB residues and necropsy data for Bald Eagles from 29 states—1975-1977. Pesticides Monitoring Journal 13:145-49.

Keir, J. R., and D. D. L. R. Wilde. 1976. Observations of Swainson's Hawk nesting in northeastern Illinois. Wilson Bulletin 88:658–59.

Kellogg, J. 1903. Trading trip to Illinois in 1710. In T. Hopkins, The Kelloggs of the Old World and the New. San Francisco: Sunset Press. 826 pp.

Kennicott, R. 1854. Catalogue of animals observed in Cook County. Illinois State Agriculture Society Transactions 1:577–95.

Kleen, V. M. 1972. Black-headed Grosbeak in Illinois. Audubon Bulletin 163:20–21.

———. 1972–86. Report of the statewide spring bird count. In Illinois Department of Conservation Periodic Reports 1, 3, 5, 8, 11, 14, 16, 19, 21, 22, and 24; Illinois Birds and Birding 1:51–54 and 2:59–64; and two mimeographed reports (1972 and 1973).

———. 1979–84. Seasonal Reports 22–41. Illinois Department of Conservation.

———. 1983. 1983 survey of Illinois heron colonies. Illinois Department of Conservation Periodic Report 23. 9 pp.

———. 1985–87. Field notes. Illinois Birds and Birding 1- 3.

Knox, A. 1987. Taxonomic status of Lesser Golden Plovers. British Birds 80:482–87.

Lambert, E. L. 1930. A Burrowing Owl record for Hancock County, Illinois. Wilson Bulletin 42:213.

Landing, J. E. 1984. Western Wood-Pewee at Chicago. Illinois Audubon Bulletin 208:51–52.

———. 1985. Thayer's Gull in the Chicago area. Indiana Audubon Quarterly 63:58–63.

———. 1987. On Yellow-bellied Sapsuckers with red napes. Illinois Birds and Birding 3:62–63.

———, and S. Patti. 1986. Cassin's Sparrow in Chicago, Illinois, 1983, Indiana, 1984, and notes on field identification of Cassin's, Botteri's, and Bachman's Sparrows. Indiana Audubon Quarterly 64:122–26.

Lanyon, W. E. 1956. Ecological aspects of the sympatric distribution of meadowlarks in the north-central states. Ecology 37:98–107.

Larson, G. E. 1973. The Monk Parakeet in Illinois: new views of alarm. Audubon Bulletin 166:29–30.

Lauro, A. J., and B. J. Spencer. 1980. A method for separating juvenile and first-winter Ring-billed Gulls and Common Gulls. American Birds 34:111–17.

Lehman, P. 1980. The identification of Thayer's Gull in the field. Birding 12:198–210.

———. 1983. Point: some thoughts on Thayer's Gull and Sterna Terns. Birding 15:107–8.

Levy, S. H. 1963. Late spring record of the Common Redpoll in northern Illinois. Wilson Bulletin 75:205.

———. 1964. Unusual records for Illinois migrants. Audubon Bulletin 129:17.

Lewis, G. P. 1921. Occurrence of the Buff-breasted Sandpiper (Tryngites subruficollis) in Chicago parks. Auk 38:600.

Liette, P. 1947. The memoir of Pierre Liette. In M. M. Quaife, The western country in the 17th century. Chicago: Lakeside Press. 181 pp.

Lish, J. W., and W. G. Voelker. 1986. Field identification aspects of some Red-tailed Hawk subspecies. American Birds 40:197–202.

Lockart, J. [No date]. The last chance. Illinois Department of Conservation. [No page numbers].

Long, J. L. 1981. Introduced birds of the world. New York: Universe Books. 528 pp.

Loucks, W. E. 1892. Birds of Peoria and Tazewell Counties, Illinois. Mimeographed. 23 pp.

———. 1893. Distribution of the Bobolink in Illinois. Ornithologist and Oologist 18:52–56.

———. 1893a. Distribution of the Yellow-headed Blackbird in Illinois. Ornithologist and Oologist 18:109–12.

Lowther, J. K. 1961. Polymorphism in the White-throated Sparrow, Zonotrichia albicollis (Gmelin). Canadian Journal of Zoology 39:281–92.

Lyon, W. I. 1930. Brewer's Blackbird nesting in Illinois. Wilson Bulletin 42:214.

———. 1937. First record of Common Terns nesting in Illinois. Audubon Bulletin 27:29.

Marquette, J. 1903. Recit des voyages et des decouvertes. In J. G. Shea, Discovery and exploration of the Mississippi Valley, 2d ed. Albany: Joseph McDonough. 268 pp.

Marvel, C. S. 1948. Unusual feeding behavior of a Cape May Warbler. Auk 65:599.

Massey, B. W. 1976. Vocal differences between American Least Terns and the European Little Tern. Auk 93:760–73.

Matthews, P. 1969. An Anhinga in Marion County. Audubon Bulletin 149:16.

Maxwell, H. A. 1921. Records, regular and periodic. Audubon Bulletin, Fall, p. 6.

McKinley, D. 1978. The Carolina Parakeet in Illinois: a recapitulation. Indiana Audubon Quarterly 56:53–68.

McLaughlin, V. P. 1979. Occurrence of Large-billed Tern (Phaetusa simplex) in Ohio. American Birds 33:727.

Mengel, Robert M. 1965. The birds of Kentucky. AOU Ornithological Monograph 3. 581 pp.

Miller, A. H. 1941. Speciation in the avian genus Junco. University of California Publication in Zoology 44:173–434.

Mills, H. B., and F. C. Bellrose. 1959. Whooping Crane in the mid-west. Auk 76:234–35.

———, W. C. Starrett, and F. C. Bellrose. 1966. Man's effect on the fish and wildlife of the Illinois River. Illinois Natural History Survey Biological Notes 57. 24 pp.

Milosevich, J., and J. Olson. 1981. Nesting Canada Warblers in Joliet, Illinois. Audubon Bulletin 197:23–26.

Mindell, D. P. 1985. Plumage variation and winter range of Harlan's Hawk. American Birds 39:127–33.

Mlodinow, S. 1984. Chicago area birds. Chicago: Chicago Review Press. 220 pp.

Mohlenbrock, R. H. 1986. Guide to the vascular flora of Illinois. Carbondale: Southern Illinois University Press. 507 pp.

Morse, R. 1960. Unusual bird in northern Illinois. Passenger Pigeon 22:26–27.

Moyer, J. W. 1931. Black-bellied and Fulvous Tree Duck in Illinois. Auk 48:258.

Mueller, H. C., D. D. Berger, and G. Alley. 1981. Age, sex, and seasonal differences in size of Cooper's Hawks. Journal of Field Ornithology 52:112–26.

Mumford, R. E., and C. E. Keller. 1984. The birds of Indiana. Bloomington: Indiana University Press. 376 pp.

Munyer, E. A. 1965. Inland wanderings of the Ancient Murrelet. Wilson Bulletin 77:235–42.

———. 1966. Winter food of the Short-eared Owl Asio flammeus in Illinois. Transactions of the Illinois State Academy of Science 59:174–80.

Murchison, A. C. 1893. Distribution of Cooper's Hawk in Illinois. Ornithologist and Oologist 18:49–51.

Musselman, T. E. 1916–17. Unusual birds along the Mississippi River near Quincy. Audubon Bulletin, Winter, pp. 39–40.

———. 1921. A history of the birds of Illinois. Journal of the Illinois State Historical Society 14:1-73.

———. 1930. Starlings in western Illinois in quantity. Auk 47:255-56.

———. 1932. Egrets at Quincy, Illinois. Auk 49:78-79.

———. 1937. Young Black Rail banded in Illinois. Auk 54:204.

———. 1938. Mockingbirds in central western Illinois. Auk 55:537.

———. 1945. Bald Eagles and Woodcocks in central western Illinois. Auk 62:458-59.

———. 1948. Hawk Owl in Illinois. Auk 65:456.

———. 1950. Three Brown Pelicans in Illinois. Auk 67:233.

———. 1950a. Two calamities to roosting Chimney Swifts. Auk 67:238-39.

———. 1951. Saw Whet Owl, *Aegolius a. acadicus*, nesting in Illinois. Auk 68:378-79.

Myers, N. 1979. The sinking ark. Pergamon Press. 307 pp.

National Audubon Society. 1947-70. Middlewestern prairie region. Audubon Field Notes 1-24.

———. 1971-87. Middlewestern prairie region and Illinois Christmas bird counts. American Birds 25-41.

Nature Study Society of Rockford. 1917-18. Birds of Rockford and vicinity. From Audubon Bulletin 1917-18.

Nelson, E. W. 1876. Birds of north-eastern Illinois. Essex Institute Bulletin 8(9-12):90-155.

———. 1877. Notes upon birds observed in southern Illinois between July 17 and September 4, 1875. Essex Institute Bulletin 9:32-65.

Nisbet, I. C. 1970. Autumn migration of the Blackpoll Warbler: evidence for long flight provided by regional survey. Bird Banding 41:207-40.

Nolan, V., Jr. 1978. The ecology and behavior of the Prairie Warbler *Dendroica discolor*. AOU Ornithological Monographs 26. Washington, D.C. 595 pp.

Oberholser, H. C. 1914. A monograph of the genus *Chordeiles* Swainson, type of a new family of goatsuckers. U.S. National Museum Bulletin 86. 123 pp.

Odom, R. R. 1977. Sora. In G. C. Sanderson, Management of migratory shore and upland game birds in North America. International Association of Fish and Wildlife Agencies, Washington, D.C. 358 pp.

Olsen, K. M., and S. Christensen. 1984. Field identification of juvenile skuas. British Birds 77:448-50.

Packard, G. C. 1958. Yellow Rail at Champaign. Audubon Bulletin 107:8.

Palmer, R. S. 1962. Handbook of North American birds. Vol. 1. New Haven: Yale University Press. 567 pp.

Parkes, K. C. 1988. A brown-eyed adult Red-eyed Vireo specimen. Journal of Field Ornithology 59:60-62.

Parmalee, P. W. 1957. Vertebrate remains from the Cahokia site, Illinois. Transactions of the Illinois State Academy of Science 50:235-42.

———. 1958. Remains of rare and extinct birds from Illinois Indian sites. Auk 75:169-76.

———. 1967. Additional noteworthy records of birds from archaeological sites. Wilson Bulletin 79:155-62.

———, and A. E. Bogan. 1980. A summary of the animal remains from the Noble-Wieting site (11ML28), McLean County, Illinois. Transactions of the Illinois State Academy of Science 73:1-6.

———, and B. G. Parmalee. 1959. Mortality of birds at a television tower in central Illinois. Audubon Bulletin 111:1-4.

———, and G. Perino. 1970. A prehistoric archaeological record of the Roseate Spoonbill in Illinois. Transactions of the Illinois State Academy of Science 63:254-58.

———, and J. M. Speth. 1981. A prehistoric archaeological record of the Pomarine Jaeger, *Stercorarius pomarinus* (Temminck) from central Illinois. Transactions of the Illinois State Academy of Science 74:29-32.

Patti, S. T., and M. L. Myers. 1976. A probable Mourning x MacGillivray's Warbler hybrid. Wilson Bulletin 88:490-91.

Peale, T. R. 1946-47. The journal of Titian Ramsey Peale, pioneer naturalist. Missouri Historical Review 41:147-63, 266-84.

Perry, L. G. 1987. Illinois component of the National Wetlands Inventory. Natural History Survey Report 264.

Peterjohn, B. G., and M. D. Morrison. 1977. Sight record of a Curlew Sandpiper in southern Illinois. Illinois Audubon Bulletin 180:29-30.

Petersen, P. C. 1959. TV tower mortality in western Illinois. Audubon Bulletin 112:14-15.

———. 1972. Brown Pelican in Muscatine County. Iowa Bird Life 42:51.

Phillips, A. R., M. A. Howe, and W. E. Lanyon. 1966. Identification of the flycatchers of eastern North America, with special emphasis on the genus *Empidonax*. Bird Banding 37:153-71.

Pitelka, F. A. 1935. Sight records of the Horned Grebe and Mourning Warbler. Chicago Academy of Science Program of Activities 6:85-87.

———. 1938. Melanism in the Black-crowned Night Heron. Auk 55:518-19.

———. 1938a. Red Phalarope in northeastern Illinois. Wilson Bulletin 50:287-88.

———. 1940. Nashville Warbler breeding in northeastern Illinois. Auk 57:115-16.

Poling, O. C. 1890. Notes on the Fringillidae of western Illinois. Auk 7:238-43.

Polk, J. 1979-80. Breeding Red-breasted Nuthatches and Pine Siskins in Champaign County. Illinois Audubon Bulletin 191:23-24.

Praeger, W. E. 1895. Two records from Keokuk, Iowa. Auk 12:85-86.

———. 1925. Birds of the Des Moines Rapids. Auk 42:565-77.

Prater, T., and J. Marchant. 1977. Guide to the identification and aging of Holarctic waders. British Trust for Ornithology. Tring, Herts: Maund and Irvine. 168 pp.

Pratt, H. D. 1974. Field identification of Great-tailed and Boat-tailed Grackles in their zones of overlap. Birding 6:217-23.

———. 1976. Field identification of White-faced and Glossy Ibises. Birding 8:1-5.

Preno, W. L., and R. F. Labisky. 1971. Abundance and harvest of doves, pheasants, bobwhites, squirrels and cottontails in Illinois, 1956-69. Illinois Department of Conservation Technical Bulletin 4. 76 pp.

Prentice, D. S. 1949. Nesting of a Swainson's Hawk in Illinois. Auk 66:83.

Princen, L. H. 1969. Unusual bird sightings in central Illinois during 1968. Proceedings of the Peoria Academy of Science 2:20-23.

———. 1970. Unusual bird sightings in central Illinois during 1969. Proceedings of the Peoria Academy of Science 3:24-27.

———. 1975. Unusual bird sightings in central Illinois during 1974. Proceedings of the Peoria Academy of Science 8:35-40.

Pruitt, J. 1975. The return of the Great-tailed Grackle. American Birds 29:985-92.

Pucelik, T. M. 1983-84. A northern Gannet in central Illinois. Illinois Audubon Bulletin 207:34-36.

————, and P. Pucelik. 1984. The discovery of Illinois' first nesting Clay-colored Sparrows. Illinois Audubon Bulletin 208:27-28.

Pym, A. 1982. Identification of Lesser Golden Plover and status in Britain and Ireland. British Birds 75:112-24.

Quaife, M. M., ed. 1947. The western country in the 17th century: the memoirs of Lamothe Cadillac and Pierre Liette. Chicago: Donnelly.

Randall, R. Q. 1975. First state record—Great-tailed Grackle. Illinois Audubon Bulletin 172:3.

Ribeau, W. 1891. Brief notes. Ornithologist and Oologist 16:47.

Ridgway, R. 1873. The prairie birds of southern Illinois. American Naturalist 7:197-203.

————. 1874. The times of migrating and nesting of the birds of the lower Wabash Valley. Proceedings of the Boston Society of Natural History 16:318-19.

————. 1878. Notes on birds observed at Mount Carmel, southern Illinois, in the spring of 1878. Bulletin of the Nuttall Ornithological Club 3:162-66.

————. 1879. On a new species of *Peucaea* from southern Illinois and central Texas. Bulletin of the Nuttall Ornithological Club 4:218-22.

————. 1880. On six species of birds new to the fauna of Illinois, with notes on other rare Illinois birds. Bulletin of the Nuttall Ornithological Club 5:30-32.

————. 1881. A revised catalogue of the birds ascertained to occur in Illinois. Illinois State Laboratory of Natural History Bulletin 4:163-208.

————. 1889. The ornithology of Illinois. Pt. 1, vol. 1. State Laboratory of Natural History. Springfield. 520 pp.

————. 1895. The ornithology of Illinois. Pt. 1, vol. 2. State Laboratory of Natural History. Springfield. 282 pp.

————. 1902. The birds of North and Middle America. U.S. National Museum Bulletin 50, pt. 2. 834 pp.

————. 1907. The birds of North and Middle America. U.S. National Museum Bulletin 50, pt. 4. 973 pp.

————. 1914. Bird life in southern Illinois: I. Bird Haven. Bird-Lore 16:409-20.

————. 1915. Bird life in southern Illinois: IV. Changes which have taken place in half a century. Bird-Lore 17:191-98.

Rising, J. D. 1970. Morphological variation and evolution in some North American orioles. Systematic Zoology 19:315-51.

Robbins, C. S., D. Bystrak, and P. H. Geissler. 1986. The Breeding Bird Survey: its first fifteen years, 1965-1979. U.S. Department of the Interior Fish and Wildlife Service Resource Publication 157. Washington, D.C. 196 pp.

Robinson, J. C. 1985. Recent nesting attempts of Bald Eagles in Illinois. Illinois Birds and Birding 1:4-7.

Robinson, S. K. 1987. Woodland birds of Illinois. Field Museum of Natural History Bulletin 58:15-21.

Roseberry, J. L., and W. D. Klimstra. 1970. The nesting ecololgy and reproductive performance of the Eastern Meadowlark. Wilson Bulletin 82:243-67.

Rosenband, G. 1983. Ancient Murrelet on Lake Michigan. Illinois Audubon Bulletin 20:42-44.

Roth, R. 1967. An analysis of avian succession on upland sites in Illinois. Master's thesis. University of Illinois.

Rowan, W. 1932. The status of the dowitchers with a description of a new subspecies from Alberta and Manitoba. Auk 49:14-29.

Russell, R. P., S. Hedeen, and C. Easterberg. 1962. Grosse Pointe check-list. Evanston, Illinois, Bird Club.

Russell, R. P., Jr. 1970. The Harlequin Duck in Illinois. Audubon Bulletin 156:23-24.

————. 1983. The Piping Plover in the Great Lakes region. American Birds 37:951-55.

————. 1983-84. A possible Three-toed Woodpecker sight record for Illinois. Illinois Audubon Bulletin 207:32-33.

Sabine, N., and W. D. Klimstra. 1985. Ecology of Bald Eagles wintering in southern Illinois. Transactions of the Illinois State Academy of Science 78:13-24.

Sanborn, C. C. 1922. The season: Chicago region. Bird-Lore 24:45-46.

————. 1922a. Bachman's Sparrow (*Peucaea aestivalis bachmani*) in N. E. Illinois. Auk 39:420.

————. 1930. Recent notes from the Chicago area. Auk 47:268-69.

Schnell, G. D. 1967. Frequency distribution of Rough-legged Hawks. Audubon Bulletin 143:13-14.

Schorger, A. W. 1954. Color phases of the Screech Owl between Madison, Wisconsin, and Freeport, Illinois. Auk 71:205.

————. 1955. The Passenger Pigeon: its natural history and extinction. Madison: University of Wisconsin Press. 424 pp.

————. 1964. The Trumpeter Swan as a breeding bird in Minnesota, Wisconsin, Illinois, and Indiana. Wilson Bulletin 76:331-38.

————. 1973. The Passenger Pigeon: its natural history and extinction. Norman: University of Oklahoma Press. 424 pp.

Schuberth, C. J. 1986. A view of the past: an introduction to Illinois geology. Springfield: Illinois State Museum. 181 pp.

Seets, J. W., and H. D. Bohlen. 1977. Comparative mortality of birds at television towers in central Illinois. Wilson Bulletin 89:422-33.

Shirreff, P. 1835. A tour through North America. Edinburgh: Olvie & Boyd.

Simon, D. 1977. Identification of Clay-colored, Brewer's, and Chipping Sparrows in fall plumage. Birding 9:189-90.

Smart, G. 1960. Ross' Goose taken at Horseshoe Lake, Illinois. Wilson Bulletin 72:288-89.

Smith, E. T. 1941. The seasons. Audubon Magazine, July-August, p. 393.

Smith, F. 1930. Records of spring migration of birds at Urbana, Illinois, 1903-1922. Illinois Natural History Survey Bulletin 19:105-17.

Smith, H. R., and P. W. Paramalee. 1955. A distribution checklist of the birds of Illinois. Illinois State Museum Popular Science Series, vol. 4. 62 pp.

Smith, P. W. 1888. Nesting of the Nashville Warbler in Fulton County, Illinois. Bay State Oologist 1:44.

Spiers, J. M. 1940. Mortality of Barn Owls at Champaign, Illinois. Auk 57:571.

Springer, P. F. 1949. Recent records of the Ring-necked Duck. Auk 66:200.

Starrett, W. C. 1936. Some birds notes from central Illinois. Wilson Bulletin 48:53.

Stepney, P. H. R. 1975. Wintering distribution of Brewer's Blackbird: historical aspect, recent changes, and fluctuations. Bird Banding 46:106-25.

Stevenson, J. 1929. Some shorebird records for northern Illinois. Auk 46:538.

Stoddard, H. L. 1917. The Roseate Tern (*Sterna daugalli*) on Lake Michigan. Auk 34:86.

————. 1921. Female Bay-breasted Warbler in male plumage. Auk 38:117.————. 1921a. Some old shorebird records for the Chicago area. Auk 38:110.

Strode, W. S. 1890. The American Long-eared Owl. Ornithologist and Oologist 2:26-28.

Sutherland, D. E. 1971. A 1965 waterfowl population model. Bureau of Sport Fish and Wildlife, Flyway Habitat Management Limit Project 4. 11 pp.

Sutton, G. M. 1938. Oddly plumaged orioles from western Oklahoma. Auk 55:1-6.

Swengel, A. B. 1987. Detecting Northern Saw-whet Owls (*Aegolius acadicus*). Passenger Pigeon 49:121-26.

Swink, F. [No date]. Birds of the Morton Aboretum. Lisle, Illinois. Morton Arboretum. 33 pp.

Taber, W. B., Jr. 1930. The fall migration of Mourning Doves. Wilson Bulletin 42:17-28.

Thayer, G. H. 1904. A Massachusetts Duck Hawk aery. Bird-Lore 6:47-53.

Thomas, G. 1987. New beginnings for Ruffed Grouse. Outdoor Highlights 15:3-9.

Thompson, D. 1973. Feeding ecology of diving ducks on Keokuk pool, Mississippi River. Journal of Wildlife Management 37:367-81.

Thompson, M. 1955. Notes on unusual birds. Audubon Bulletin 95:15.

Thwaites, R. G., ed. 1896-1901. The Jesuit relations and allied documents. Cleveland: Burrows Bros. 73 vols.

Tobish, T. 1986. Separation of Barrow's and Common Goldeneyes in all plumages. Birding 18:17-27.

Tranaer, E. J., and L. W. Campbell. 1986. Laughing Gull nesting attempt on Lake Erie. Wilson Bulletin 98:170-71.

Tuttle, H. E. 1918. Notes on the nesting of the Nashville Warbler. Bird-Lore 20:269-72.

Veit, R. R., and L. Jonsson. 1984. Field identification of smaller sandpipers within the genus *Calidris*. American Birds 38:853-76.

Verner, J. 1975. Pintails nest again at Goose Lake Prairie. Illinois Audubon Bulletin 173:15.

Waldbauer, G. P., and J. Hays. 1964. Breeding of the Purple Gallinule in Illinois. Auk 81:227.

Walkinshaw, L. H. 1960. Migration of the Sandhill Crane east of the Mississippi River. Wilson Bulletin 72:358-84.

————, and D. A. Zimmerman. 1961. Range expansion of the Brewer's Blackbird in eastern North America. Condor 63:163-77.

Wallace, D. I. M., and M. A. Ogilvie. 1977. Distinguishing Blue-winged and Cinnamon Teals. British Birds 70:290-94.

Warner, R. E. 1981. Illinois pheasants: population, ecology, distribution, and abundance, 1900-1978. Illinois Natural History Survey Biological Notes 115. 22 pp.

————. 1985. Demography and movements of free-ranging domestic cats in rural Illinois. Journal of Wildlife Management 49:340-46.

Wasson, I. B. 1956. Close view of Black Swift. Audubon Bulletin 99:5.

————. 1957. Effects of cold spring of 1956 in Chicago area. Audubon Magazine 59:4.

Watson, J. D., and E. Huesberg. 1916. Notes on the fall migrations of 1916 in Chicago area. Wilson Bulletin 28:199-200.

Wetmore, A. 1935. A record of the Trumpeter Swan from the late Pleistocene of Illinois. Wilson Bulletin 47:237.

————. 1940. The western Golden-crowned Kinglet in Indiana. Wilson Bulletin 52:35.

Wheeler, L. 1937. King Eider taken on Illinois River. Auk 54:203.

Whitney, B., and K. Kaufman. 1986. The *Empidonax* challenge III. "Traill's" Flycatcher: the Alder/Willow problem. Birding 18:153-59.

————, and ————. 1986a. The *Empidonax* challenge IV. Acadian, Yellow-bellied, and Western Flycatchers. Birding 18:315-27.

Widmann, O. 1880. Notes on the birds of St. Louis, Mo. Bulletin of the Nuttall Ornithological Club 5:191-92.

————. 1898. The great roosts on Gabberet Island, opposite north St. Louis, Mo. Auk 15:22-27.

————. 1907. A preliminary catalog of the birds of Missouri. Transactions of the Academy of Science of St. Louis 17:1-288.

————. 1909. A second record for the Fulvous Tree Duck taken in Missouri. Auk 26:304.

————. 1928. Chimney Swifts in November 1925. Wilson Bulletin 40:151-54.

Wilds, C. 1982. Separating the yellowlegs. Birding 14:172-78.

————, and M. Newlon. 1983. The identification of dowitchers. Birding 15:151-66.

Will, R. L. 1973. Breeding success, numbers, and movement of House Sparrows at McLeansboro, Illinois. AOU Ornithological Monographs 14:60-78.

Woodruff, F. M. 1907. The birds of the Chicago area. Chicago Academy of Science Natural History Survey Bulletin 6. 221 pp.

————. 1912. Two interesting captures in Lincoln Park, Chicago. Auk 29:109.

Wright, A. H. 1915. Early records of the Wild Turkey. Auk 32:348-66.

Wright, E. G., and E. Komarek. 1928. The Western Gull (*Larus occidentalis wymani*) in the Chicago area. Auk 45:200.

Wyman, L. E. 1915. Richard's Owl in Illinois. Auk 32:101.

Zimmer, J. T., and S. S. Gregory. 1929. Gambel's Sparrow in Illinois and Michigan. Auk 46:244-45.

Zimmer, K. J. 1984. I.D. point: Eastern vs. Western Meadowlarks. Birding 16:155-56.

Zimmermann, J. H. 1949. Rare birds visit Chicago area. Audubon Bulletin 71:4-5.

Initials and Corresponding Names of Observers

A
AA = Alan Anderson
BA = Bob Adams
JA = Jack Armstrong
KA = Kathryn Arhos
LA = Louise Augustine
RA = Richard Anderson
RAd = Roger Adair
RAp = Roger Applegate

B
ABa = Al Balliett
BB = Bill Bertrand
CB = Carl Becker
DB = David Becher
DBi = Dale Birkenholz
EB = Eilene Bunker
FB = Fred Brecklin
GB = Gary Bowman
HB = Howard Blume
HDB = H. David Bohlen
IB = Irene Benjamin
KB = Karl Bartel
KBo = Ken Bohlen
KBr = Kay Brickey
LB = Lawrence Balch
LBi = Laurence Binford
MB = Mike Baum
MBi = Mary Biss
MBr = Maury Brucker
PB = Paul Bauer
RB = Richard Biss
RBj = Richard Bjorklund
RBo = Rose Bodman
RBr = Ron Bradley
SB = Steve Bailey
TB = Tim Barksdale
VB = Vicki Byre
ViB = Viola Bucholz
YB = Yvonne Balsiger
Bush = Lee Bush

C
AC = Al Campbell
BCho = Beth Chato
CC = Charlie Clark
DC = Dick Collins
DCa = David Carey
GC = Glen Cooper
HC = Hal Cohen
JC = John Cebula
JEC = J. Earl Comfort
KC = Kristin Cronin
LC = Lew Cooper
MC = Marilyn Campbell
MCh = Michael Chaneske
PC = Paul Clyne
RC = Robert Crompton
RCe = Robert Cecil
RCh = Robert Chapel
RCo = Robert Collins
RCot = Robert Cottingham
TC = Ted Cable

D
AD = Al Dierkes
ADu = Aura Duke
DD = Diane Doig
HD = Henry Detwiler
ID = Ida Domazlicky
JD = Jon Dunn
MD = Myrna Deaton
MDa = Michael Dani
PD = Pete Dring
RD = Richard DeCoster
SD = S. Ted Dillon

E
DE = Dave Easterla
HE = Homer Esbaugh
IE = Ivan Easton
JEa = Joe Eades
ME = Mary Easterday

RE = Ralph Eiseman

F
DF = Darlene Fiske
DFi = David Fischer
DFr = Darlene Friedman
EF = Elton Fawks
EFr = Ed Franks
HF = Harold Fetter
JF = James Funk
JFr = Jim Frank
KF = Karen Forcum
TF = Todd Fink

G
BG = Brad Grover
BGl = Bill Glass
JG = Joel Greenberg
JGa = Jared Garver
MG = Maryann Gossmann
RG = Ron Goetz
RGa = Roger Gustafson
RGr = Richard Graber
RGu = Robert Guth
TG = T. Gates
WG = Wally George

H
BHu = Bob Hues
DH = David Hayward
HAW = James Haw
JH = Jim Hampson
JHe = Jim Herbert
KH = Kay Hanson
LH = Leroy Harrison
LBH = L. Barrie Hunt
MH = Mark Harris
MHm = Mike Homoya
PH = Phil Hughes
RHe = Randy Heidorn
RHu = Robert Hughes

SH = Scott Hickman
SHo = Steve Hossler
VH = Virginia Humphreys
VHa = Vic Hamer

I
WI = William Iko

J
BJ = Bill James
DJ = David Johnson
DJaq = Deborah Jaques
DJo = Denny Jones
DaJ = Dave Jones
KJ = Kent Jones
LJ = Lee Johnson

K
AK = Al Kostyniak
DK = Daniel Klem
JK = Jack Keegan
PK = Paul Kittle
RK = Randy Korotev
RKn = Roy Knisley
VK = Vernon Kleen
WK = Walter Krawiec

L
BL = Brian Lane
EL = Eugenia Larson
Elo = Earl Long
HL = Helen Lane
JL = James Landing
RL = Robert Lewis

M
CM = Catherine Monday
CMa = Charley Marbet
CMi = Craig Miller
CMq = Catherine McQuarrie
DM = Dan Martin

IM = Inez McLure
JM = Joe Milosevich
JMc = John McKee
KM = Keith McMullen
LMc = Lynn McKeown
MM = Mike Mlodinow
MMd = Mike Madsen
MMo = Michael Morrison
RM = Robert Montgomery
SM = Steve Mlodinow
TM = Tom McLean
TEM = T. E. Musselman
WM = Walter Marcisz
YM = Yvonne Maynard

N
GN = Greg Neise
JN = Jim Neal
KDN = K. Duane Normam
PN = Phil Norton
RN = Randy Nyboer
RNi = Ron Niewiarowski
TN = Turner Nearing

O
CO = Clark Olson
DO = Dennis Oehmke
JO = Jerrold Olson
SO = Steve Olson
WO = William O'Brien

P
BP = Bruce Peterjohn
BPr = Bert Princen
CP = Carmen Patterson

DP = Dale Pontius
DPr = Don Prentice
JP = Jeffrey Priest
JPo = Janine Polk
JPr = J. Probst
KP = Kathy Phelps
KPi = Ken Pierson
MP = Mark Peters
PP = Pete Petersen
PeP = Penny Pucelik
RP = Richard Palmer
RPi = Richard Peiser
RPu = Ron Pulliam
SP = Sebastian Patti
TP = Tom Pucelik

R
AR = Arlo Raim
BR = Bill Rudden
DR = Doug Robinson
GR = Gerald Rosenband
HR = Harriet Rylaarsdam
HRi = H. Riegel
JR = John Robinson
JRu = Jim Ruschill
KR = Kevin Richmond
KRe = Kevin Renick
LR = Larry Rice
RR = Robert Russell
RQR = Robert Randall
SR = Scott Robinson
SRu = Skip Russell

S
AS = Andy Sigler
BSh = Betty Shaw

(or Shaws = Harry and Betty)
CS = Clark Scott
CSp = Claudia Spener
FS = Fred Stoop
JSa = Jeffrey Sanders
JSm = James Smith
JSu = Joe Suchecki
JSt = J. Stafferahn
J&CS = Jim and Carol Surman
LS = Larry Stritch
MS = Muriel Smith
MSc = M. Schaeffer
MSi = Mary Sidney
MSt = Mike Sweet
MSw = Mark Swan
MSy = Mark Swayne
PS = Phoebe Snetsinger
RS = Richard Sandburg
SS = Sue Stroyls
SSi = Scott Simpson
WS = William Southern
WSc = William Schennum
WSh = William Shepherd

T
A&JT = Arnold and Janet
   Tebussek
BT = Bill Tweit
DT = Dennis Thornburg
MT = Michael Tove
TT = Tedd Teeter

V
IV = Isodore Venetos
JVB = J. VanBenthuysen

JVS = Jeff VerSteeg
SV = Sally Vasse

W
BW = B. Willcutts
CW = Charles Westcott
DW = Dan Williams
DWa = David Watson
DWe = Doris Westfall
EW = Eric Walters
HW = Helen Wuestenfeld
JW = James Ware
JWa = Joe Walsh
JWar = John Warnock
JWh = John White
JWi = John Wier
KW = Kurt Wesseling Jr.
   and Kurt Wesseling III
KWa = Keith Walker
LW = Lucas Wrischnik
PW = Patrick Ward
PWa = Peg Walsh
PaW = Pat Ware
RW = Rich Wagner
TW = Tony Ward
ZW = Zelma Williams

Y
DY = Dick Young
LY = Lynne Yaskot

Z
JZ = Jim Ziebol
RZ = Ray Zoanetti

Index

THE BIRDS OF ILLINOIS

Editor: Kenneth Goodall
Designer: Matt Williamson
Managing Editor: Roberta L. Diehl
Production Coordinator: Harriet Curry
Typeface: Sabon with Janson display
Compositor: Impressions, Inc.
Printer & Binder: Toppan